MEDIA LAW

Sallie Spilsbury
Solicitor, Senior Lecturer in Law
Manchester Metropolitan University

Cavendish
Publishing
Limited

London • Sydney

First published in Great Britain 2000 by Cavendish Publishing Limited, The Glass House, Wharton Street, London WC1X 9PX, United Kingdom
Telephone: +44 (0)20 7278 8000   Facsimile: +44 (0)20 7278 8080
Email: info@cavendishpublishing.com
Website: www.cavendishpublishing.com

British Library Cataloguing in Publication Data

Spilsbury, Sallie
Media law in theory and practice
1 Mass media – law and legislation – Great Britain
I Title
343.4'1'099

ISBN 1 85941 530 X

Printed and bound in Great Britain

CONTENTS

PART 3

TABLE OF CASES

TABLE OF STATUTES

TABLE OF STATUTORY INSTRUMENTS

TABLE OF INTERNATIONAL INSTRUMENTS

PART 1

CHAPTER 1

THE HUMAN RIGHTS ACT 1998 AND THE MEDIA

> Freedom of expression constitutes one of the essential foundations of a
> democratic society, one of the basic conditions for its progress, and for the
> development of every man.[1]

The Human Rights Act 1998 ('the Act') has now come fully into force
throughout the UK on 2 October 2000.[2] It is likely to have far-reaching
implications for most, if not all, areas of civil and criminal law, including the
law affecting the media.

The objective of the Act is stated to be 'to give further effect'[3] in UK law to
the majority of the rights provided for in the European Convention of Human
Rights ('the Convention'). The Act does not create new substantive rights
under domestic law, but it makes existing Convention rights more immediate
and relevant.

THE CONVENTION

The Convention is a statement of rights and freedoms drawn up in 1950 in the
aftermath of the Second World War. Its full title is 'the Convention for the
Protection of Human Rights and Fundamental Freedoms'. The objectives of
the Convention are set out in the Convention's preamble. They include the
maintenance and further realisation of human rights and fundamental
freedoms, and the maintenance of effective political democracy. Section 1 of
the Convention is headed 'Rights and Freedoms' and provides for a number
of rights for citizens of Convention countries. Some of the rights and freedoms
established by the Convention are absolute and others are subject to specific
limitations. Where they apply, the limitations are designed to ensure respect
for competing rights and freedoms or for other legitimate public purposes.

The Convention rights are as follows:

Art 2 – right to life;

Art 3 – prohibition of torture;

Art 4 – prohibition of slavery and forced labour;

---

1   *Handyside v UK* (1976) 1 EHRR 737, ECHR.
2   The Act is already in force in Scotland at the time of writing.
3   As stated in the long title to the Act.

Art 5 – right to liberty and security;

Art 6 – right to a fair trial;

Art 7 – no punishment without law;

*Art 8 – right to respect for private and family life;

*Art 9 – freedom of thought, conscience and religion;

*Art 10 – freedom of expression;

Art 11 – freedom of assembly and association;

Art 12 – right to marry;

*Art 13 – right to an effective remedy (for the violation of rights and freedoms provided for in the Convention);[4]

Art 14 – prohibition of discrimination on any ground (in relation to the rights and freedoms provided for in the Convention);

Art 15 – derogation in times of emergency;

Art 16 – restrictions on political activity of aliens;

Art 17 – prohibition on abuse of rights;

Art 18 – limitation on use of restrictions of rights.

The rights marked * are of particular relevance to media law and will be considered in further detail in this chapter and throughout this book.

There have been a number of protocols to the Convention since the early 1950s which have provided for additional rights and freedoms. The first protocol, which has been ratified by the UK, provides for the following additional rights:

Art 1 – right to peaceful enjoyment of possessions/property;

Art 2 – right to education;

Art 3 – right to free elections.

The sixth protocol provides, *inter alia*, for the abolition of the death penalty.

Section II of the Convention provides for the establishment of a European Court of Human Rights to function on a permanent basis.[5] The Court was established at Strasbourg in 1959 to hear petitions against *States* who are

---

4   The right to an effective remedy is not amongst the 'Convention rights' provided for in the Act. The view of the Government is that the operation of the Act will by implication provide for an effective remedy (in particular, s 8 of the Act) and that an express inclusion of Art 13 would be unnecessary and would involve duplication. The decisions of the European Court of Justice under Art 13 will, however, be relevant under domestic law (an assurance given by the Lord Chancellor during the report stage of the Bill; *Hansard*, 19.1.1998, col 1266).

5   HRA 1998, Art 19.

signatories to the Convention. Complaints to Strasbourg may only be brought against Contracting *States*, rather than against private individuals or organisations who are domiciled or resident in those States. Since 1966, individual claimants in the UK have had the right to complain directly to the European Court in Strasbourg about alleged breaches of the Convention. Where a country is found to have violated a Convention right, the court's judgment does not have the automatic effect of changing the national law of the Contracting State, but the State is obliged to change its law in line with the Convention.

THE POSITION UNDER ENGLISH LAW
BEFORE THE ACT CAME INTO FORCE

The Convention was ratified by Britain in 1951, but has never been directly incorporated into UK law. The lack of incorporation into UK law has meant that, whilst private litigants could, in some circumstances, complain to the European Court in Strasbourg that their Convention rights had been violated, they could not make any such complaint to the British courts. There was no domestic cause of action for breach of a Convention right.

Litigants who took their cases to Strasbourg faced a lengthy and expensive journey. On average, it took five to six years to get judgment from the European Court from the time of the petition being lodged, and all national avenues for complaint and appeal must previously have been exhausted.

The Convention, whilst not part of national law, has had a role to play prior to October 2000. By way of example, where the terms of legislation were ambiguous, the Convention might be used as an aid to construction.[6] In addition, increasingly in the field of media law, the judiciary have had regard to the Convention in their decision making (although, in some instances, 'have regard to' has amounted to little more than paying lip service to). But there has been no *obligation* on the courts to apply the Convention or to follow Strasbourg jurisprudence in reaching their decisions.

---

6   For an example, see *AG v Secretary of State for the Home Department ex p Brind* [1991] 1 AC 696, p 760.

THE SCHEME OF THE ACT

The Act does *not* incorporate the Convention itself into UK law. It does, however, elevate the Convention and the jurisprudence of the Strasbourg Court from the sidelines to a central place in domestic law.

The focal point of the Act is the so called 'Convention rights'. These are defined in s 1 of the Act as meaning the rights set out in Arts 2–12 and 14 of the Convention, the rights provided for in the first protocol and the abolition of the death penalty contained in the sixth protocol. There is also provision for new rights to be added if further protocols to the Convention are ratified by the UK in the future.

The key effects of the Human Rights Bill were summarised by the Lord Chancellor in the following terms:

> The Bill is based on a number of important principles. Legislation should be construed compatibly with the Convention as far as possible. Where the courts cannot reconcile legislation with Convention rights, Parliament should be able to do so – and more quickly, if thought appropriate, than by enacting primary legislation. Public authorities should comply with Convention rights or face the prospect of legal challenge. Remedies should be available for breach of Convention rights by a public authority.[7]

THE MAIN PROVISIONS OF THE ACT

Interpretation

Duty to have regard to Strasbourg jurisprudence

- *Section 2* of the Act provides that a court or tribunal determining a question which has arisen in connection with a Convention right must *take into account* any relevant jurisprudence of the European Court of Human Rights, whether judgment, decision, declaration or advisory opinion and whether or not it relates to a decision involving the UK. The national court or tribunal must also take into account any opinions or decisions of the European Commission of Human Rights and decisions of the Council of Ministers (although the Commission and Council ceased to have a judicial function in 1998). Significantly, the obligation is to 'take into account', rather than 'to follow'. Strasbourg jurisprudence will not be binding on

---

7   *Hansard*, HL, 5.2.1998.

domestic courts in the same way as we think of precedents under English law.

Example

The *Daily Tabloid* is sued for defamation by the pop star Sharon Sparkle. The *Daily Tabloid* might claim in its defence that the defamation action interferes with the Convention right to freedom of expression. Under s 2 of the Act, the court must take into account the jurisprudence of the European Court of Human Rights on the question whether the defamation action is a legitimate restriction on the right to freedom of expression. The court does not have to follow that jurisprudence, but it is under an obligation to take it into account.

The Lord Chancellor explicitly rejected the idea of including a statutory formula in the Act providing that Convention jurisprudence should bind the national courts. He observed that 'our courts must be free to develop human rights jurisprudence by taking into account European judgments and decisions, but they must also be free to distinguish them and to move out in new directions to the whole area of human rights law'.[8]

This move away from binding precedent is also in line with the approach of the Strasbourg Court itself, which tends not to regard its own decisions as binding on itself. For example:

(a) the Convention has often been described by the Strasbourg Court as a *'living instrument'*,[9] to be interpreted afresh in the light of prevailing conditions of the day, rather than by reference to earlier precedent;

(b) the doctrine of the *margin of appreciation* is a further reason for rejecting the idea of a binding system of precedent under Strasbourg case law. The margin essentially allows each Contracting State leeway in determining what is compatible with the Convention, provided always that the actions of the State conform to the objectives of the Convention. The margin of appreciation is considered further below.

Statutory interpretation

- *Section 3* of the Act provides that, *so far as it is possible to do so*, primary legislation (such as Acts of Parliament) and subordinate legislation (for example, statutory instruments and Orders in Council) must be read and given effect to in a way which is compatible with Convention rights. This will apply whether or not the legislation was enacted before the Act came into force. The obligation to construe legislation in line with the

---

8   *Hansard*, HL, 24.11.1997, col 835.
9   *Tyrer v UK* (1978) 2 EHRR 1.

Convention is not limited to courts and tribunals. Everyone should construe legislation in this way.

Where primary legislation cannot be given effect to in a way which is compatible with Convention rights the legislation is *not* invalid. However, under s 4, certain courts[10] have discretion to make a *declaration of incompatibility*[11] where a provision of *primary* legislation is incompatible with a Convention right. The Crown has a right to notification and an opportunity to intervene in any proceedings where the court is considering whether to make a declaration of incompatibility.[12]

A declaration of incompatibility will not affect the validity of the legislation,[13] which will continue to apply unless and until the legislation in question is amended. Nor is the declaration binding on the parties to any legal proceedings in which it is made.

During the second reading of the Bill in the House of Commons, the Home Secretary, Jack Straw, observed that 'a declaration of incompatibility will not affect the continuing validity of the legislation in question. That would be contrary to the principle of the Bill. However, it would be a clear signal to the Government and Parliament that, in the court's view, a provision of legislation does not conform to the standards of the Convention ... it is likely that Government and Parliament would wish to respond to such a situation and would do so rapidly'.[14]

In relation to *subordinate* legislation, where it is not possible to construe such legislation in a way which is compatible with the Convention, the court should treat the subordinate legislation as invalid, unless the primary legislation under which the subordinate legislation was made prevents the removal of the incompatibility (when considering whether the primary legislation prevents the removal of the incompatibility, any possibility of revocation of the subordinate legislation should be disregarded).[15] Where the primary legislation *does* prevent the removal of the incompatibility, the court has no discretion to find the subordinate legislation invalid and must give effect to it.

The obligation to construe legislation in line with the Convention is likely to have far-reaching effects on the way that the courts interpret legislation.

---

10 In England and Wales, the courts which may make a declaration of incompatibility are the House of Lords, the Court of Appeal, the Judicial Committee of the Privy Council and the High Court (s 4(5)).

11 HRA 1998, s 4(2) for primary legislation and s 4(3) for subordinate legislation.

12 *Ibid*, s 5.

13 *Ibid*, s 4(6).

14 *Hansard*, 16.2.1998, col 778.

15 HRA 1998, s 3(2).

Interpretations of legislation which were made before the Act came into effect may no longer apply. The courts are likely to move away from a technical way of construing legislation which focuses on the detailed meaning of particular words. Instead, it is probable that the courts will adopt a broader, more purposive construction dependent on the overall objective of the statute and the relevant Convention right.[16] Lord Cooke described the change in approach in the following terms:

> The clause will require a very different approach to interpretation from that to which UK courts are accustomed. Traditionally, the search has been for the true meaning; now it will be for a possible meaning that would prevent the making of a declaration of incompatibility[17] ... in effect, the courts are being asked [to apply] a rebuttable presumption in favour of the Convention rights ...

Jack Straw, the Home Secretary, assured Parliament that it was not the Government's intention that the courts should contort the meaning of words to produce implausible or incredible meanings.[18]

• Where a provision of legislation is declared incompatible, the Act makes provision for amendment of the legislation by statutory instrument where a minister of the Crown considers there are *compelling reasons* for doing so, but only to the extent necessary to remove the incompatibility.[19] This introduces a new fast track procedure. Even primary legislation which has been declared to be incompatible with the Convention may be amended by way of this fast track procedure. It will no longer be necessary for the government of the day to wait for an opportunity to introduce the appropriate amendments to primary legislation into a crowded parliamentary timetable. The procedure will also be available if legislation appears to a minister to be incompatible with the Convention because of a finding of the European Court of Human Rights. The Act provides for two different procedures for amending legislation, which has been declared incompatible by domestic higher courts or by the European Court: a standard procedure under which prior parliamentary approval is required to the amendment and an emergency procedure,[20] under which no prior approval is necessary.

There is no *obligation* on the government to amend offending legislation. If a piece of legislation were not to be amended, a disgruntled victim of a breach of a Convention right would have to pursue its remedies to the

---

16 Wadham, J and Mountfield, H, *Blackstone's Guide to the Human Rights Act*, 1999, London: Blackstone, has a useful commentary in this regard.

17 *Hansard*, HL, 3.11.1997, col 1272.

18 *Hansard*, 3.6.1998, col 422.

19 Section 10.

20 Both are contained in Sched 2 to the Act.

European Court of Human Rights. The domestic courts have no power to disapply or strike down the offending provision.

- Under s 19 (which has been in force since November 1998), a minister of the Crown in charge of a Bill in Parliament must, before the second reading of the Bill, make a statement to the effect that, in his view, the provisions of the Bill are compatible with the Convention rights (a statement of compatibility) or make a statement that, although he is unable to make a statement of compatibility, the Government nevertheless wishes the House to proceed with the Bill. In either case, the statement must be in writing and published in such a manner as the minister considers appropriate.[21] The Lord Chancellor has indicated that a statement of compatibility will provide a 'strong spur' to the interpretation of legislation so as to render it compatible with the Convention.[22]

Public authorities

Section 6 of the Act provides that it is unlawful for a *public authority* to act in a way which is incompatible with a Convention right except where, as the result of provisions of primary legislation, the authority could not have acted differently[23] or where the authority was acting to give effect to provisions of primary legislation which cannot be read or given effect in a way which is compatible with the Convention rights.[24] Section 6 (and the complementary s 7) apply to public authorities only. Private individuals or businesses are under no direct obligation to behave compatibly with Convention rights.

For the purposes of s 6, an act includes a failure to act[25] where the failure is incompatible with a Convention right. It would appear that this would cover both deliberate and unintentional omissions.[26]

The meaning of 'public authority'

The Act defines 'public authority' as 'any person whose functions are functions of a public nature'.[27] This definition is wide ranging and focuses on the nature of the acts performed by the authority, rather than the make up or

---

21 HRA 1998, s 19.
22 Tom Sargant Memorial Lecture, 16 December 1997: available on the LCD website.
23 HRA 1998, s 6(2)(a).
24 *Ibid*, s 6(2)(b).
25 *Ibid*, s 6(6).
26 Mike O'Brien, *Hansard*, 24.6.1998, col 1097.
27 HRA 1998, s 6(3), although note that it does not include either House of Parliament (unless the House of Lords is acting in a judicial capacity, in which case, it is a public authority for those purposes (s 6(4))).

substance of the body itself. This approach is intended to be in line with Strasbourg jurisprudence where national States have been held to be responsible for the actions of authorities which carry out functions of a public nature. The question whether a particular body is a public authority will be for the courts. It is the sort of question which the courts are accustomed to considering in the context of judicial review proceedings. In deciding whether a party is a public authority for the purposes of the Act, the Government envisages that the court should consider the jurisprudence already developed in respect of judicial review applications.[28] The reader is referred to Chapter 2, where the application for judicial review is considered in more detail.

During the passage of the Bill, the Home Secretary explained that there are three categories of person for the purposes of the Act:

- *obvious public authorities*, for example, government departments and the police, all of whose functions will be public and so who will be caught by the Act in respect of everything that they do;

- *organisations which have a mix of private and public functions*, for example, private security firms which run prisons as well as providing security services for private organisations. These bodies will be public authorities in relation to their public role (and so will be subject to the Act in relation to those functions), but they will not be public authorities in relation to acts which they carry out which are private in nature.[29, 30]

- *organisations or individuals with no public functions* against whom the Act will not be directly applicable.[31]

The Government gave the following indications during the passage of the Bill about organisations in the media industry which might be classified as public authorities (although it was stressed that the decision would ultimately be for the courts):

- the BBC would probably be regarded as a public authority, as it is 'plainly performing a public function'.[32] Channel 4 might also be a public authority;

- the Press Complaints Commission is a body exercising public functions and, therefore, a public authority, but the press as a whole or as individual publications are not;[33]

---

28 *Hansard*, 17.6.1998, col 410.

29 HRA 1998, s 6(5).

30 During the passage of the Bill, the Lord Chancellor also gave the example of Railtrack, which as a public utility has public functions and so would qualify as a public authority in relation to those functions. On the other hand, if Railtrack was acting in its capacity of private property developer, that would probably be construed by the courts as being a private activity outside the scope of s 6 of the Act. *Hansard*, 24.11.1997, col 796.

31 *Hansard*, 17.6.1998, col 409.

32 *Hansard*, HL, 16.2.1998, col 776.

33 *Ibid*, col 777.

- the Independent Television Commission exercises public functions and is therefore a public authority, but independent private television companies are unlikely to be.[34]

Significantly, a court or tribunal is a public authority under the Act. This is an important point. It means that courts and tribunals must decide cases before them in a way which is compatible with the Convention. A failure to do so will be an unlawful breach of s 6.

Redress for unlawful acts of public authorities

Under s 7, a person who claims that a public authority has acted or proposes to act in a way which is unlawful under s 6 may take action against the authority, provided that he is a victim of the unlawful act.[35] There is *no* corresponding right of action for breach of a Convention right against a private person or against a body with a mixture of private and public functions where the conduct complained of relates to the private functions only. It follows that the Act does not provide for rights of action for breach of Convention rights as between private entities; only as against public authorities (the so called *'vertical effect'*).

The right to take action is limited to the victim of the unlawful act. Under Strasbourg jurisprudence, a victim is someone who has been, or will potentially be, directly affected by the unlawful act in question. Pressure groups are unlikely to fall within this definition.

The right of action against the public authority for its failure to act compatibly with the Convention may take one of two main forms as follows:

- the Convention right(s) may be relied on in any legal proceedings taken against or brought by a public authority, for example, as a defence to any proceedings or as a counterclaim or during the course of an appeal;[36] or
- the victim may bring specific proceedings against the public authority under the Act. This is a new type of action introduced by the Act based solely on a breach of the Convention rights. Remember that it will *not* be available for claims against non-public authorities.

The Act provides that proceedings against public authorities under s 7 must be commenced in the 'appropriate court or tribunal'.[37] A claim that a judicial decision is incompatible with the Convention may only be brought in the High Court or by the usual method of appeal. Any other claim under s 7 may

---

34   *Hansard*, 16.2.1998, col 776.
35   HRA 1998, s 7(1).
36   *Ibid*, s 7(2).
37   *Ibid*, s 7(1)(b) and (2).

be brought in any court. It is likely that the s 7 action may take the form of an application for *judicial review* or a new tort for breach of statutory duty.[38] In view of the fact that the action can only lie against public authorities and that the test to determine whether a body is a public authority will draw heavily on the law relating to judicial review, it is probable that an application for judicial review will be the most common method of obtaining s 7 redress.

Where it is alleged that a court or tribunal is in breach of s 6, the Act says that the claim for redress must take the form of an appeal using the conventional appeal procedure or, alternatively, an application for judicial review.[39]

Time limit for bringing an action

Any proceedings for breach of a Convention right must be brought before the end of the period of one year beginning with the date on which the act complained of took place (or such longer period as the court or tribunal considers equitable, having regard to all the circumstances).[40] *Note that where the procedures under which proceedings are brought provide for a shorter time limit, that shorter time limit will apply.* In relation to judicial review an application must be made as promptly as possible and, in any event, within three months of the action complained of.

Remedies

A court which holds that a public authority has committed an unlawful breach of a Convention right may grant 'such relief or remedy or make such order within its powers as it considers just and appropriate'.[41] The remedies include damages where the court is satisfied that an award is necessary to afford just satisfaction to the person in whose favour it is made.[42] The decision whether to award damages and the amount of an award must be made in accordance with the principles of the European Court of Human Rights,[43] under which a successful applicant has no automatic entitlement to a damages

---

38 Note that, in deciding whether a body has acted unlawfully, the courts cannot act as legislators.
39 HRA 1998, s 9.
40 *Ibid*, s 7(5).
41 *Ibid*, s 8.
42 *Ibid*, s 8(3).
43 *Ibid*, s 8(4).

award. On some occasions, the court has found that the finding of violation of a Convention right is itself is sufficient to provide redress.[44]

A person who relies on his Convention rights under s 7 does so without prejudice to any other right or freedom he has under any law having effect in the UK[45] or his right to bring proceedings on any other ground. The right to petition the European Court of Human Rights is thus preserved.

Impact of the Act

It is probable that the Act will have repercussions beyond claims against public authorities.

First, the obligation to have regard to Convention jurisprudence under s 2 of the Act and to construe legislation in a way which is compatible with the Convention under s 3 will apply whatever type of claim is before the court or tribunal, whether against a public authority or not. Although a claim which is not brought against a public authority cannot be based solely on breach of a Convention right, the court will have a duty to consider the Convention rights and Convention jurisprudence where the claim concerns Convention rights.

Secondly, there is an argument that, because courts and tribunals are themselves public authorities, any decision by the court which is incompatible with a Convention right will give rise to a claim against the court under s 7 – notwithstanding that the claim arose during the course of litigation between private entities. In this way, so it is argued, Convention rights will become relevant to all types of dispute (an indirect 'horizontal effect'). This approach is in line with government thinking. The Lord Chancellor has observed that 'we believe that it is right as a matter of principle for the courts to have the duty of acting compatibly with the Convention not only in cases involving public authorities, but also in developing the common law in deciding cases between individuals'.[46]

THE CONVENTION RIGHTS

The two Convention rights which are of particular relevance to the media are the right to freedom of expression (Art 10) and the right to respect for private

---

44 In *Soering v UK* (1989) 11 EHRR 439, the European Court held that the domestic remedy of judicial review was, in principle, an effective remedy for breaches of the Convention rights.

45 HRA 1998, s 11.

46 *Hansard*, 24.11.1997, col 783.

and family life (Art 8). Neither of these rights is absolute. The permitted limitations to each right are similar, but not identical.

The articles read as follows:

Article 10

1   Everyone has the right to freedom of expression. This right shall include freedom to hold opinions and to receive and impart information and ideas without interference by public authority and regardless of frontiers. This Article shall not prevent States from requiring the licensing of broadcasting, television or cinema enterprises.

2   The exercise of these freedoms, since it carries with it duties and responsibilities, may be subject to such formalities, conditions, restrictions or penalties as are prescribed by law and are necessary in a democratic society, in the interests of national security, territorial integrity or public safety, for the prevention of disorder or crime, for the protection of health or morals, for the protection of reputation or rights of others, for preventing the disclosure of information received in confidence or for maintaining the authority and impartiality of the judiciary.

Article 8

1   Everyone has the right to respect for his private and family life, his home and his correspondence.

2   There shall be no interference by a public authority with the exercise of this right except such as is in accordance with the law and is necessary in a democratic society in the interests of national security, public safety or the economic well being of the country, for the prevention of disorder or crime, for the protection of health or morals, or for the protection of the rights and freedoms of others.

The Strasbourg Court has indicated that Art 8 'does not merely compel the State to abstain from interference [with private and family life]: in addition to this primary negative undertaking, there may be positive obligations inherent in an effective respect for private and family life. These obligations may involve the adoption of measures designed to secure respect for private life even in the sphere of the relations of individuals between themselves'.[47]

---

47   *X v Netherlands* (1985) 8 EHRR 235.

The Approach of the European Court of Human Rights to Art 8 and Art 10

When considering whether an interference with Convention rights is reconcilable with the Convention, the European Court of Human Rights adopts the following sequence of reasoning:

- Does the complaint in question actually concern a Convention right? The Court tends to take a wide approach to the scope of the Convention rights and so will readily find that the complaint concerns a Convention right.
- If so, can the interference about which complaint is made be justified as being compatible with the Convention? This involves consideration of the following matters:
  (a) the interference must be prescribed by law;
  (b) it must serve a legitimate purpose;
  (c) it must be necessary in a democratic society; and
  (d) it must not be discriminatory.

Looking at each of these criteria in turn.

Was the interference prescribed by law?

To be lawful, an interference with a Convention right must have a basis in law (common law or statute).

However, it will not be sufficient to show that the interference is based in law. The law itself has to be of sufficient quality. In order to be lawful, any interference with the Convention rights must be both *ascertainable* and *sufficiently precise*. If it is not, it will be an unlawful interference, no matter how laudable the purpose of the interference.

In *Sunday Times v UK*,[48] the Court made the following observation:

> The law must be adequately accessible: the citizen must be able to have an indication that is adequate in the circumstances of the legal rules applicable to a given case. Secondly, a norm cannot be regarded as 'law' unless it is formulated with sufficient precision to enable the citizen to regulate his conduct: he must be able – if need be with appropriate advice – to foresee, to a degree that is reasonable in the circumstances, the consequence which a given action may entail.

> These consequences need not be foreseeable with absolute certainty; experience shows this to be unattainable. Again, whilst certainty is highly desirable, it may bring in its train excessive rigidity and the law must be able to keep pace with changing circumstances.

---

48   *Sunday Times v UK* (1979) 2 EHRR 245, para 49.

The test whether a measure is prescribed by law tends to be applied generously by the European Court. Absolute certainty about the scope of the law is not necessarily required. A law which confers a discretion on the part of the decision maker can be prescribed by law, provided that the scope of the discretion and the manner of its exercise are indicated with sufficient clarity to give adequate protection against arbitrary interference.[49] The English law of blasphemy has been found to be sufficiently precise for the purposes of the Convention, notwithstanding the fact that a finding of blasphemy involves an element of subjectivity on the part of the court and the fact that the law had been criticised by the Law Commission as being unreasonably vague.[50]

In cases involving violations of the right to respect for private and family life, the European Court has twice found that the UK has permitted interception with telephone conversations by public authorities in circumstances where the interference was not prescribed by law.[51] In neither case was the law sufficiently clear in its terms to give citizens an adequate indication about the circumstances in and conditions on which public authorities were empowered to resort to surveillance measures.

Was the aim pursued by the interference with the right legitimate?

The legitimate purposes which may justify an interference with freedom of expression or the right to respect for home and family life are set out in Arts 10(2) and 8(2) of the Convention. The purposes are drawn widely in the Convention and tend to be interpreted widely by the Court. For example, the phrase 'authority of the judiciary' in Art 10(2) has been interpreted to cover the machinery of justice as well as the members of the judiciary and, in particular, the notion that the courts are the proper forum for hearing disputes.[52]

But an interference with a Convention right will not necessarily be compatible with the Convention simply by virtue of the fact that it falls within the limitations contained in the relevant Article. The Court has to be satisfied that the interference was necessary having regard to the circumstances of each particular case.

---

49 *Wingrove v UK* (1996) 24 EHRR 1.
50 Law Commission, *Offences Against Religion and Public Worship,* Working Paper No 79, 1981.
51 *Malone v UK* (1984) 7 EHRR 14 and *Halford v UK* (1997) 24 EHRR 523.
52 *Sunday Times v UK* (1979) 2 EHRR 245.

Was the interference necessary in a democratic society?

The requirement that the restriction should be necessary involves three considerations as follows:

- the interference must correspond to a pressing social need; and
- it must be proportionate to the legitimate aim pursued; and
- the State must give relevant and sufficient justifications for the interference.

The margin of appreciation

In assessing whether an interference with a Convention right is necessary, the European Court permits Contracting States to exercise a margin of appreciation. The margin is essentially a device adopted by the Strasbourg Court to facilitate its functioning as an international court. As a court for all signatories to the Convention, the Strasbourg Court must give rulings which are acceptable to a variety of States which may have radical different cultures and outlooks (within the general parameters of a democratic society). What offends against the morals of the majority of citizens in one State may be perfectly acceptable to citizens of another and the margin recognises that, in many respects, the individual State is in a better position to make judgments as to what is necessary and proportionate than the international court.

The margin enables the State to use its discretion in deciding whether there is a pressing social need for a particular limitation of a Convention right and, if there is, in deciding the nature of the measure which should be invoked to meet the need. The width of the margin will vary according to the nature of the interference in question. Where no common standard exists throughout Contracting States, the margin will be relatively wide. This will particularly be the case where the interference is for the protection of morals or religion, where Contracting States are likely to have different opinions as to the standard which should prevail.[53] This point was expressly recognised by the Strasbourg Court in relation to laws which seek to uphold moral values:

> By reason of their direct and continuous contact with the vital forces of their countries, State authorities are in principle in a better position than the international judge to give an opinion on the exact content of those requirements [of morals] as well as on the 'necessity' of a 'restriction' or 'penalty' intended to meet them.[54]

However, the margin of appreciation must be exercised subject to the supervisory jurisdiction of the Strasbourg Court. The task of the Court is not

---

53 *Wingrove v UK* (1996) 24 EHRR 1.
54 *Handyside v UK* (1976) 1 EHRR 737, paras 48–49.

to take the place of the national authority by substituting its own judgment, but rather to review the decision of the national State in the light of the case as a whole, to ensure that the interference is proportionate to the legitimate aim pursued and in line with the objectives of the Convention. Where a wide margin is appropriate, the international court should only intervene if the national decision cannot reasonably be justified.[55] On the other hand, where the issue involves a commonly recognised standard, such as the importance of enabling freedom of political discussion in a democratic society, the margin (or each State's room for the exercise of discretion in putting in place limitations on political discussion) will be much more restricted.

When the Human Rights Bill was going through Parliament, the Home Secretary observed that 'we are giving a profound margin of appreciation to the British courts to interpret the Convention in accordance with British jurisprudence as well as European jurisprudence'.[56]

In other words, the margin of appreciation provides a rationale for rejecting the idea of a binding system of precedent in respect of the decisions of the Strasbourg Court, particularly those decisions to which the UK is not a party. Whether this will lead to our national courts watering down the impact of the Convention rights by finding a way to distinguish Strasbourg judgments remains to be seen.

Non-discrimination

Under Art 14, any interference with a Convention right must not discriminate in a way which has no objective or reasonable justification.

It is probable that the English criminal law of blasphemy, which is considered in further detail in Chapter 12, offends against Art 14 of the Convention. The law of blasphemy operates in a discriminatory fashion in that it offers redress only against material which offends against the established Anglican Church. In recent times, a cause of action has been denied to Muslims who sought to prosecute Salman Rushdie for blasphemy in respect of his novel *The Satanic Verses*. The prosecution was struck out on the ground that the blasphemy laws do not offer protection to Muslims.[57]

---

55 *Wingrove v UK* (1996) 24 EHRR 1.
56 *Hansard*, 3.6.1998, col 424.
57 *R v Chief Metropolitan Stipendiary Magistrate ex p Choudhury* [1991] 1 All ER 306.

The right to freedom of expression (Art 10)

The Strasbourg Court has interpreted freedom of expression as extending to a wide variety of material, such as:

- works of art;[58]

- the freedom of commercial expression, for example, the freedom to advertise;[59]

- information or ideas which offend, shock or disturb as well as to those which are favourably received or regarded as inoffensive or as a matter of indifference;[60]

- importantly, the right includes not only the right to impart information and ideas, but equally the right to receive them.

The Court has consistently reiterated that freedom of expression constitutes one of the essential foundations of a democratic society. Nevertheless, it recognises that it is not an absolute right. As we have seen, the right to freedom of expression is subject to the exceptions set out in Art 10(2) of the Convention. The Strasbourg Court has stressed that the exceptions in Art 10(2) must be narrowly interpreted in every case.[61] It is not simply a question of balancing the right to freedom of expression against the exception in any particular case. In the *Sunday Times* case, the Court observed that:

> The Court is faced not with a choice between two conflicting principles, but with a principle of freedom of expression that is subject to a number of exceptions which must be narrowly interpreted.[62]

The interpretation of any limitation focuses on whether the limitation is necessary and proportionate, and on the justification for exercising it.

The Court has imposed varying degrees of necessity and proportionality, which it has applied to limitations on the expression of different types of material.

Material in the public interest

When considering whether an interference with freedom of expression is necessary, regard must be had to whether the material in question involves questions of public interest.[63] Whilst it is not the case that the right to freedom of expression only protects material which is in the public interest, material of

---

58 *Muller v Switzerland* (1991) 13 EHRR 212.

59 *Ibid.*

60 *Observer v UK* (1991) 14 EHRR 153.

61 *Ibid.*

62 *Sunday Times v UK* (1979) 2 EHRR 245.

63 *Bladet Tromso-Stensaas v Norway* (1999) 28 EHRR 534.

that quality is afforded special protection. The Court has often observed that the most careful scrutiny on the part of the Court is called for when the interference in question is capable of discouraging the participation of the media in debate over matters of legitimate public concern.[64]

The Court has explicitly recognised that it is incumbent on the press to impart information and ideas on matters of public interest. Not only does the press have the task of imparting such information and ideas, but the public also has a right to receive them. Were it otherwise, the Court has observed, the press would be unable to play its vital role of 'public watchdog'.[65]

Public authorities, the Government and politicians

The Strasbourg Court has imposed particularly strict limits on the interference with the publication of facts and opinions which refer to the activities of *public authorities*.[66] This is on the basis that it is essential to put the public in a position where it can keep a critical control on the exercise of public power. The limits of permissible criticism of the *Government* are wide: '... in a democratic system, the actions or omissions of government must be subject to the close scrutiny of legislative and judicial authorities and public opinion'.[67] Similarly, the limits of acceptable criticism are wider as regards a *politician* than as regards a private individual. A politician is deemed to have knowingly laid himself open to close scrutiny of his every word and deed by journalists and by the public at large, and he must display a greater degree of tolerance: '... the requirements of the protection of reputation has to be weighed in relation to the interests of open discussion of political issues.'[68] English law has also acknowledged this distinction between private and public, at least in relation to breach of confidence and defamation cases.[69]

The Court has found that the exercise of freedom of expression is particularly important for elected representatives of the people[70] and for political parties and their active members.[71]

---

64 *Jersild v Denmark* (1995) 19 EHRR 407.
65 *Observer v UK* (1991) 14 EHRR 153.
66 *Thorgeirson v Iceland* (1992) 14 EHRR 843.
67 *Incal v Turkey* (2000) 29 EHRR 449.
68 *Lingens v Austria* (1986) 8 EHRR.
69 Breach of confidence: *AG v Jonathan Cape* [1976] QB 752; defamation: *Reynolds v Times Newspapers Ltd* [1999] 4 All ER 609, HL.
70 *Castells v Spain* (1992) 14 EHRR 445.
71 *Incal v Turkey* (2000) 29 EHRR 449.

Other types of information

As regard other categories of information/ideas, States are granted a wider margin of appreciation when deciding whether restrictions on freedom of expression are necessary and proportionate to meet a pressing social need. There is relatively wide scope for a State to interfere with right to freedom of expression where the limitation is not capable of discouraging the participation of the media in matters of legitimate public concern; nor does it stifle criticism of public authorities, etc. This is considered further in the chapters relating to breach of confidence, privacy, defamation and copyright laws.

Journalists' sources

Another area in which freedom of expression plays an important role is the enforced disclosure by journalists of the identity of their sources. The European Court has held that, if journalists are forced to disclose their sources, the role of the media as public watchdog could be seriously undermined, because of the effect such disclosure would have upon the free flow of information. An order for the disclosure of sources cannot, according to the Court, be compatible with Art 10, unless there is an overriding public interest in identifying the source.[72] We shall see in Chapter 11 that it is at least arguable that English law concerning the disclosure of sources has been applied in a way which cannot be reconciled with the Convention.

Duties and responsibilities

In every case involving freedom of expression, the media must not overstep the boundaries set out in Art 10(2). Their duty is to impart information and ideas on all matters of the public interest in a manner which is compatible with their obligations under the Convention.

Article 10(2) points out that freedom of expression carries duties and responsibilities. The safeguards afforded by Art 10 to journalists in reporting matters of public interest is accordingly subject to the proviso that the media must act in good faith in order to provide accurate and reliable information in accordance with the ethics of journalism.[73] The judgment as to whether these standards have been met depends on the facts of the particular case. In the *Bladet-Tromso* case, a newspaper reported on alleged violations of seal hunting regulations. The article was, in large part, based on, and quoted from, an

---

72 *Goodwin v UK* (1996) 22 EHRR 123.
73 *Bladet Tromso-Stensaas v Norway* (1999) 28 EHRR 534.

official report. The newspaper had not carried out independent research in order to verify the findings of the official report and was sued for defamation. The question arose as to whether Norwegian libel law was compatible with the right to freedom of expression. The European Court noted that no independent research had been carried out by the newspaper to verify the official report. It observed that, where assertions of fact are made, the ordinary obligation on the media is to verify statements which were defamatory of individuals, unless there were any special grounds for dispensing with this requirement. However, the media were normally entitled, when contributing to a public debate on matters of legitimate concern, to rely on the contents of official reports without having to undertake independent research. Otherwise, their vital watchdog role would be undermined. This line of reasoning which emphasises the importance of ensuring that information is accurate and reliable was also displayed by the House of Lords in *Reynolds v Times Newspapers Ltd*[74] (considered in further detail in Chapter 3).

In construing whether the media had acted in good faith, the Court in the *Bladet-Tromso* case cited with approval an earlier judgment on a similar question, where it was stated that journalistic freedom also covers possible recourse to a degree of exaggeration or even provocation[75] – although the permissible limits of this type of reporting will depend on the facts of each case.

Freedom of expression, privacy and the Human Rights Act 1998

The media initially feared that the implementation of the Act would give fresh impetus to the development of a legally enforceable right to privacy in English national law, which would have the effect of limiting the media's freedom of expression. As a result of strenuous lobbying by the media, a new clause was added to the Human Rights Bill relating specifically to the right to freedom of expression. That clause is now s 12 of the Act. It is in the following terms:

(1) This section applies if a court is considering whether to grant any relief which, if granted, might affect the exercise of the Convention right to freedom of expression.

(2) If the person against whom the application for relief is made ('the respondent') is neither present nor represented, no such relief is to be granted unless the court is satisfied:

(a) that the applicant has taken all practicable steps to notify the respondent; or

(b) that there are compelling reasons why the respondent should not be notified.

---

74 *Reynolds v Times Newspapers Ltd* [1999] 4 All ER 609, HL.
75 *Prager and Oberschlick v Austria* (1996) 21 EHRR 1.

(3) No such relief is to be granted so as to restrain publication before trial, unless the court is satisfied that the applicant is likely to establish that publication should not be allowed.

(4) The court must have particular regard to the importance of the Convention right to freedom of expression and, where the proceedings relate to material which the respondent claims, or which appears to the court, to be journalistic, literary or artistic material (or to conduct connected with such material), to:

    (a) the extent to which:

        (i) the material has, or is about to, become available to the public; or

        (ii) it is, or would be, in the public interest for the material to be published;

    (b) any relevant privacy code.

(5) In this section:

'court' includes a tribunal; and

'relief' includes any remedy or order (other than in criminal proceedings).

Points to note about s 12

Section 12 will apply in any case where a court or tribunal is considering granting relief which might affect the right to freedom of expression, not just to cases involving freedom of expression and questions involving privacy. The section is not limited to cases to which a public authority is a party.[76] It applies to any person whose right to freedom of expression might be affected, including the media.

The Home Secretary explained[77] that under sub-s 2, interim injunctions applied for without notice (*ex parte* injunctions) will be granted only in 'exceptional circumstances', where all practicable steps have been taken to notify the respondent or where there are compelling reasons why the respondent should not be notified. In relation to what might amount to 'compelling reasons', the Home Secretary thought that it might arise in a case raising issues of national security where the mere knowledge that an injunction was being sought might cause the respondent to publish the material immediately. He said that the Government did not anticipate that the limb would be used often.[78]

Sub-section 3 deals with interim injunctions generally where they might affect the right to freedom of expression, whether applied for with or without notice. An interim injunction is a prior restraint measure. Before an interim

---

76 The Home Secretary, *Hansard* 2.7.1998, col 536.
77 *Ibid.*
78 *Ibid.*

injunction is granted, *the court must be satisfied that the applicant is likely to establish at trial that publication should not be allowed*. The onus of establishing a likelihood of success on the merits is on the applicant for the injunction.[79] The Home Secretary explained that the courts must consider the merits of the application. Interim injunctions should not be granted simply to preserve the status quo between the parties (the reader is referred to Chapter 2, where the significance of the status quo test and interim injunctions is explained).

In relation to all forms of relief which might affect freedom of expression (whether interim or not and whether an injunction or other type of relief), sub-s 4 provides that the court must have particular regard to certain matters.

First, it must have regard to the importance of the Convention right to freedom of expression. As we have seen, the European Court regards freedom of expression as an essential foundation of democracy and considers that permitted limitations of the right must be narrowly interpreted.

In addition, where the proceedings relate to material which the respondent claims, or which appears to the court, to be journalistic, literary or artistic material, the court should have regard to certain extra factors. 'Journalistic, literary or artistic material' is not defined in the Act. Will the mere fact that the media publishes the material mean that it will be deemed to be published for journalistic purposes or will the media have to establish also that the material is newsworthy or is to be used for reporting current events? This point has to be clarified. It is likely that, over time, a body of case law will emerge to define the meaning with greater precision. The European Court of Human Rights has emphasised the media's role as public watchdogs. Media activities which fall within this watchdog role will almost certainly fall within the definition of journalism.

The phrase 'journalistic, literary or artistic purposes' also appears in the Data Protection Act 1998.[80] Case law under that Act might help to clarify the definition.

The extra factors which the court must have regard to when the proceedings relate to journalistic, literary or artistic material are:

(a) the extent to which the material is or is about to become available to the public. This factor is aimed at avoiding the type of situation which arose in the *Spycatcher* litigation, where the publication of a book was restrained in the UK as being in breach of confidence at the same time as it was freely available elsewhere in the world. The Home Secretary has explained that, under s 12, where the material at issue will shortly be available anyway in another country or on the internet, it must affect the decision whether it is appropriate to restrain publication in this country.[81]

---

79 Home Secretary, *Hansard*, 2.7.1998, col 356.
80 Considered in Chapter 9.
81 Home Secretary, *Hansard*, 2.7.1998, col 538.

The Home Secretary observed that 'there is no direct qualification to the word "public" in the new clause. Ultimately, it would be a matter for the courts to decide, based on common sense and proportionality. The fact that the information was available across the globe in very narrow circumstances would be weighed in the balance … [the courts] would also take into account the extent to which the information was available in another country or on the internet, but in each case, the courts would have to apply balance and proportionality';[82]

(b) in relation to journalistic, literary or artistic material, the court must also have regard to the extent to which it is, or would be, in the public interest for the material to be published. The scheme of the Act suggests that public interest is a factor to take into account in the *context* of the relative importance of the right to freedom of expression in a particular case, rather than as *a prerequisite to the right to freedom of expression being invoked at all.* The Parliamentary Under Secretary of State at the Home Office indicated that the basic question is whether the public should have particular information. Examples of information which the public should have were put forward as information which might have an effect on proper political discourse or a matter of public policy or that might affect individual behaviour. These areas, according to the Under Secretary of State, were matters in which there is a proper public interest in revealing information. He gave the example of information about BSE which, he said, might have affected a person's decision about whether or not to eat beef if it had been made available. He observed that a judge would have to ask 'is a matter only of interest to the public, or is it a matter of public interest? *There should be some good reason why the public should know';*[83]

Domestic case law interpreting the phrase 'the public interest' is discussed in Chapter 5.

(c) the court must, in relation to journalistic, literary and artistic material, also have regard to any relevant privacy code (such as the Press Complaints Commission Code of Practice, the Independent Television Commission Code, the Advertising Standards Authority Code of Practice and the BBC Producers' Guidelines). The fact that the media has complied with the relevant Code of Practice, or conversely if it is in breach of the Code, is one of the factors which the court should take into account in deciding whether or not to grant relief. Note that it will not be determinative. It is open for the courts to grant relief in circumstances where the privacy provisions of the Codes have been complied with, for example, where the court is of the view that the Codes do not create sufficiently stringent requirements. The Home Secretary indicated that 'the higher the conduct

---

82 *Hansard*, 2.7.1998, col 540.
83 *Ibid*, col 562.

required [by the Code], the better for the public and – this is why the provision created a virtuous circle – the better the defence available under the new clause to a newspaper [or other media entity], should it be subject to an application for relief'.[84] It is therefore possible that a sufficiently stringent privacy code could be elevated into the *de facto* legal standard for the protection of privacy in the context of the media. It would be enforced not through the courts, but through the regulatory authorities such as the PCC or the ITC. This view was echoed by the Lord Chancellor when he said 'it is strong and effective self-regulation if it – and I emphasis the "if" – provides adequate remedies which will keep these cases away from the courts'.[85] The privacy provisions of the various codes are considered further in the chapter on privacy.

Section 12 as a whole is intended to regulate the relationship between freedom of expression and other competing rights, including rights of privacy. The Government rejected an amendment to the Bill which would automatically favour Art 10 (freedom of expression) over Art 8 (respect for private and family life). As the Home Secretary explained:

> The difficulty with that is that it goes further than the terms of the Convention and Strasbourg case law. Nothing in the Convention suggests that any one right is normally to be given precedence over any other right ... so far as we are able, in a manner consistent with the Convention and its jurisprudence, we are saying to the courts that whenever there is a clash between Art 8 and Art 10 rights, they must pay particular attention to the Art 10 rights.[86]

Sub-section 4 does not simply relate to journalistic, literary or artistic material, but also conduct connected with such material. It is intended to apply where inquiries or research is ongoing, although the actual material in question is yet to be produced.[87]

The section does not apply to freedom of expression issues which arise in criminal proceedings. However, the Home Secretary stressed that criminal courts, like other courts, are required to act in a way that is not incompatible with the Convention right.[88]

The development of a right to privacy in the wake of the Human Rights Act 1998

English law does not presently recognise a right to privacy as such. Will it be obliged to do so in order to give effect to Art 8 of the European Convention?

---

84 *Hansard*, 2.7.1998, col 539.
85 *Hansard*, 3.11.1997, col 1229.
86 *Hansard*, 2.7.1999, col 542–43.
87 *Hansard*, 2.7.1998, col 540.
88 *Ibid*.

The Lord Chancellor has made it clear that the Act does not represent the introduction of a privacy statute.[89]

This question may be academic. The courts had already begun to enforce rights to privacy indirectly, notably through the law relating to breach of confidence, and this trend looks set to continue. In addition, as we have seen, the scheme of s 12 of the Act places emphasis on the provisions of the media industry codes when a court is called upon to adjudicate on issues of privacy. Over time, the codes may be transformed into a *de facto* legal right to privacy, at least in so far as the media are concerned.[90]

The Lord Chancellor has made it clear that the courts will not be permitted to act as legislators in the creation of a right of privacy where there is no existing statutory or common law right to do so:

> In my opinion, the court is not obliged to remedy the failure by legislating via the common law either where a Convention right is infringed by incompatible legislation or where – because of the absence of legislation – say, privacy legislation – a Convention right is left unprotected. In my view, the courts may not act as legislators and grant new remedies for infringement of Convention rights unless the common law itself enables then to develop new rights or remedies.[91] I believe that the true view is that the courts will be able to adapt and develop the common law by relying on existing domestic principles in the laws of trespass, nuisance, copyright, confidentiality and the like, to fashion a common law right to privacy.

A disgruntled person unable to obtain redress under domestic law for an alleged infringement of privacy could pursue a claim to the European Court of Human Rights. However, there would be no guarantee of success. In *Winer v UK*,[92] the European Commission of Human Rights did not consider that the absence of an actionable right to privacy to show a lack of respect for the applicant's private life.[93]

An overview of the likely impact of the Human Rights Act on media law

The English courts have increasingly had an eye to the Convention when considering matters involving freedom of expression, despite there being no obligation to do so. The House of Lords have felt able to pronounce on at least two occasions[94] that English common law in the field of freedom of expression issues is consistent with the requirements of the Convention.

---

89 *Hansard*, 3.11.1997, col 1229.

90 This is discussed further in Chapter 8.

91 *Hansard*, 24.11.1997, col 783.

92 *Winer v UK* (1986) 48 DR 154.

93 The possibility of a claim in breach of confidence rather than privacy may also lead to an application to the Strasbourg Court being dismissed: *Spencer v UK*. This is considered further in Chapter 5.

94 Lord Keith [1993] AC 534, p 658; Lord Templeman and Lord Goff [1987] 1 WLR 1248.

So, what changes is the Act likely to bring? Specific areas of the law are considered in the relevant chapters in Part 1 of this book. But, on an overview basis, it is suggested that the Act is likely to herald a change of approach in decision making in at least the following ways:

(a) prior to the Act, freedom of expression was not recognised by the English courts as an enforceable right. It was one of the many residual freedoms which permeated English law. As Lord Donaldson explained, 'the starting point of our domestic law is that every citizen has a right to do what he likes, unless restrained by common law or by statute'.[95] In other words, 'you have the right to say that which you are not otherwise restrained from saying'. This approach leaves the nature and extent of our 'freedoms' at the whim of the legislature and the judiciary. There is no obligation to preserve rights. Erosions of the extent of the rights can take place gradually and virtually unnoticed.

Under the Act, English law must give further effect to the *right* of freedom of expression. The existence of the right is presupposed and will be the starting point for any consideration of the question whether a particular restraint on the right is justifiable. This is likely to have a profound effect on the focus of arguments before a court. A submission seeking to give effect to a recognised right will have a stronger focus than an application which is seeking to demonstrate a negative such as an absence of any restriction on a residual freedom. This change in focus ought to put the media in an overall stronger position;

(b) the change in focus is not merely cosmetic. Traditionally, the English courts have viewed freedom of expression not as a stand alone right or freedom, but as a consideration to be weighed in the balance in any particular case against competing factors (for example, the need in that case to protect of the rights of others or the administration of justice).

This demotion of freedom of expression from an absolute value to an issue whose importance will vary depending on the other factors present in a particular case has given rise to numerous examples where freedom of expression has been overridden. As Lord Hoffman has observed:

> There are in the law reports many impressive and emphatic statements about the importance of freedom of speech and the press. But they are often followed by a paragraph which begins with the word 'nevertheless';[96]

---

95 *AG v Guardian Newspapers* (No 2) [1990] AC 109.
96 *R v Central Television* [1994] 3 All ER 641, p 650.

(c) this failure to protect freedom of expression is not just because freedom of expression is reduced to just one of the competing factors in the decision making process. It also stems from the fact that the courts have tended to see freedom of expression narrowly, in terms of the particular publication at issue. But freedom of expression also involves a wider and subtler aspect. There is a wider public interest in freedom of expression, which may be damaged if a limitation of freedom of expression is allowed in a particular case.[97] Organisations such as the media might be deterred from reporting on comparable matters if they face the prospect of large damages awards and court costs (the so called chilling effect). Sources may be deterred from coming forward if they face the prospect of identification and legal action. So notwithstanding that a particular outcome may be justified in a particular case, the courts should bear in mind the wider effect which the judgment might have on freedom of speech generally. We shall examine the failure of the courts to pay adequate regard to the wider public interest in the context of disclosure of sources, where the failure has been most easily apparent, in Chapter 11, but it is a failure which has permeated throughout media law.

In *R v Central Television*,[98] Lord Hoffman went on to say, with words which illustrate the new approach which the Act ought to herald:

> The motives which impel judges to assume a power to balance freedom of speech against other interests are almost always understandable and humane on the facts of the particular case before them ... But a freedom which is restricted to what judges think to be responsible or in the public interest is no freedom. Freedom means the right to publish things which government and judges, however well motivated, think should not be published. It means the right to say things which 'right thinking people' regard as dangerous or irresponsible. This freedom is subject only to clearly defined exceptions laid down by common law or statute ... It cannot be too strongly emphasised that outside the established exceptions, there is no question of balancing freedom of speech against other interests. It is a trump card which always wins.

Or, in the words of the European Court:

> The Court is faced not with a choice between two conflicting principles, but with a principle of freedom of expression that is subject to a number of exceptions which must be narrowly interpreted;[99]

(d) the fourth main change in approach is likely to be a move away from decisions based on technical points of detail towards broader, more

---

97   It is interesting to note that the Data Protection Act 1998 (considered in Chapter 9) refers to the need to have regard to the *public interest* in freedom of expression. This implies a recognition on the part of the legislature that public interest extends beyond the particular material concerned.

98   *R v Central Television* [1994] 3 All ER 641, p 650.

99   *Sunday Times v UK* (1979) 2 EHRR 245.

purposive decisions. The spirit of the Convention must be kept in mind by the judiciary. There are a number of cases considered in Part 1 of this book which reflect a technical analysis of the law on the part of the courts.[100] It remains to be seen whether the change in approach which the Act promises will lead to a greater emphasis on the broad effect which a particular decision would have on the ability of citizens to exercise their Convention rights, rather than an introverted examination of technical legal principle.

---

100 Eg, *Hyde Park Residences v Yelland* [2000] RPC 249; and *Telnikoff v Matusevitch* [1991] 4 All ER 817.

CHAPTER 2

REMEDIES

This chapter is intended to give an overview of the remedies which may be awarded by the courts for infringement of the substantive private and public law rights considered in Part 1 of this book. An appreciation of the nature of the remedies will help to increase understanding of the impact that the law can have on the media's activities. The detailed law relating to the specific causes of action, and remedies in defamation cases, are considered separately in the relevant subject chapters.

PRIVATE LAW

(a) Monetary compensation

The claimant will invariably claim financial recompense for loss suffered as a result of the defendant's wrongdoing. This can take the form of a claim for damages or, in cases involving the infringement of intellectual property, an account of profit.

Damages

Damages are awarded to compensate a successful claimant for loss or injury caused by the defendant's wrongdoing. Generally, the measure of damages is the sum required to put the claimant in the position it would have been in if the wrongdoing had not occurred. The claimant may recover damages which are:

(a) a foreseeable consequence of the defendant's wrongdoing;

(b) caused by the defendant's wrongdoing; and

(c) not otherwise excluded by statute or common law.

Aggravated damages

Aggravated damages are awarded as a form of compensation. They are intended to reflect the disapproval of the court for the manner in which a wrong has been committed. They recognise the fact that the motives and conduct of the defendant in relation to wrongdoing may serve to aggravate the injury done to the claimant. Their aim is primarily compensatory. The claimant must specifically plead them[1] in its claim form and statement of case.[2]

Exemplary damages

Exemplary damages are awarded to the claimant in order to *punish* the defendant and to *deter* further infringement. They are usually awarded in addition to compensatory damages. They can only be awarded in a limited number of situations which were enumerated by Lord Devlin in *Rookes v Barnard*[3] as follows:

- oppressive, arbitrary or unconstitutional action by servants of the Government;

- cases where the defendant's conduct is calculated by him to make a profit which may well exceed the compensation payable to the claimant or, in other words, where 'it is necessary to teach a wrongdoer that tort does not pay'; or

- cases where exemplary damages are authorised by statute.

The second of these circumstances is the most relevant for the media. Lord Devlin went on to explain that, in order to recover exemplary damages in relation to his second category (conduct calculated to make a profit which may exceed the amount of compensation payable), the following should be borne in mind:

- the claimant must be the victim of the defendant's conduct;

- exemplary damages should be awarded with restraint;

- the means of the parties are relevant to the decision to award exemplary damages and to the amount of exemplary damages awarded;

- also relevant is anything which aggravates or mitigates the defendant's conduct;

- in cases tried by a jury (principally, defamation cases), the jury should be directed that if, *but only if*, the sum that they have in mind as compensation (including aggravated damages) is inadequate to punish the defendant, to mark the jury's disapproval of such conduct and to deter him from repeating it, then it can award a larger sum as exemplary damages.[4]

In the case of *Cassell v Broome*,[5] the House of Lords emphasised that the mere fact that the wrongdoing was committed by the defendant during the course

---

1   *Khodaporast v Shad* [2000] 1 All ER 545 and CPR 16.4.
2   CPR Pt 16.4.
3   *Rookes v Barnard* [1964] AC 1129, pp 1226–27.
4   Exemplary damages and defamation cases are considered in Chapter 3.
5   *Cassell v Broome* [1972] 1 AC 1027.

of business was not in itself sufficient to bring a case within Lord Devlin's second category. A claimant had to show that:

- the defendant knew that what he proposed to do was against the law or had a reckless disregard whether it was legal or illegal; and

- a decision to carry on doing it was made, because the prospects of material advantage as a result of the conduct outweighed the prospects of material loss. In other words, *a cynical disregard for the claimant's rights*. The claimant does not have to establish that the defendant tried to calculate in the arithmetical sense whether his profits would outweigh any likely damages. It is sufficient to show that he appreciated that 'the chances of economic advantage outweighed the chances of economic penalty'.

The economic advantage is not limited to moneymaking. It can also include the gain of any other type of property.[6] A claimant who seeks exemplary damages should plead them in its claim form and statement of case.[7]

Damages as compensation for hurt and distress

Sometimes, the real harm caused by a defendant's wrongdoing does not present itself in money terms. This particularly so in cases involving violations of privacy,[8] where the hurt and distress caused by the violation is generally the essence of a claim.

It is a moot point whether a claimant can recover damages for distress and injury to feelings caused by the defendant's wrongdoing. Although defamation law provides a precedent for such awards, the courts have traditionally been reluctant to award compensation for distress in other types of case. Compensation for distress is sometimes recoverable as aggravated damages[9] (especially likely where the defendant's behaviour has been particularly reprehensible), but not usually as a head of damages in its own right.

Damages in intellectual property cases

In a case of intellectual property right infringement (copyright/design infringement, patent infringement, passing off, trade mark infringement or breach of confidence), the starting point for an assessment of compensatory damages will usually be the licence fee or royalties, which would have been agreed between the parties if the claimant had licensed the defendant's

---

6   *Rookes v Barnard* [1964] AC 1129.

7   CPR Pt 16.4.

8   Generally brought under the guise of a different cause of action because, as explained in Chapter 8, English law does not currently recognise a right of privacy as such.

9   Support for this view can be found in the malicious falsehood cases of *Joyce v Senagupta* (*obiter*) and *Khodaporast v Shad* [2000] 1 All ER 545.

infringing use of its intellectual property. Where the claimant would never have licensed the right in the first place, this will be something of an artificial exercise; it is difficult for the court to assess the reasonable royalty rate in respect of a right which would never have been licensed. Nevertheless, the court will generally seek to do so.

In addition to the notional licence fee, the claimant may claim for lost profits on sales he would otherwise have made if there had been no infringement and lost profits on his own sales to the extent that he was forced to reduce his own price as a result of the infringement.[10]

In patent infringement cases, the Court of Appeal has held that 'secondary loss' may also be compensated for, provided that the claimant can establish the loss as being a foreseeable consequence of and caused by the wrongdoing.[11] Secondary loss might include matters such as loss of sales of articles, which are not the subject of the infringement action, but which were sold by the claimant alongside the article in respect of which its rights have been infringed. It is likely that secondary loss would also be recoverable where other types of intellectual property rights have been infringed, although the courts have not confirmed that this would be the case.

In relation to passing off actions, damages seek to compensate the claimant for the damage to its goodwill as a result of the defendant's misrepresentation.[12] This can include compensation for lost sales, devaluation of business reputation, lost opportunities to expand and, controversially, for dilution of goodwill.[13]

Damages are *not* recoverable against a defendant who is an innocent infringer of copyright.[14]

Additional damages

The Copyright Designs and Patents Act 1988 provides for awards of additional damages in copyright infringement cases.[15] Additional damages are *only* available in claims for copyright infringement.[16] As a precondition to receiving additional damages, the claimant must claim them in its claim form and statement of case.

---

10 *Gerber v Lectra* [1995] RPC 383, approved by the Court of Appeal [1997] RPC 443. This was a patent infringement case, but the same principles would seem to apply to other intellectual property rights.

11 *Ibid.*

12 The elements of the passing off action are considered in Chapter 14.

13 See Carty, H, 'Heads of damages in passing off' [1996] EIPR 487 for more detail.

14 CDPA 1988, s 97(1).

15 *Ibid*, s 97(2).

16 *Ibid.*

The decision whether to award additional damages and, if so, the amount to award are at the discretion of the court, taking into account all the circumstances of the case. Relevant factors include the flagrancy of the infringement and any profit which accrued to the defendant as a result of its infringing activities. Additional damages are *not* available where the claimant elects for an account of profits. They are also not available against innocent copyright infringers.[17] The House of Lords have declined to give a view whether additional damages are compensatory in nature or punitive.[18] It therefore remains unclear whether they are intended to be alternatives to aggravated or exemplary damages or both.

Example of an additional damages award

In *Springsteen v Flute*,[19] a case involving infringing CDs, Ferris J awarded additional damages against the defendant. In doing so, he had regard to the fact that the defendant appeared to have calculated the amount of profit which his infringing activities would generate and to have taken few precautions against being found in breach of copyright. These factors come close to factors which would be relevant to an award of exemplary damages. The judge provisionally awarded additional of damages of £1 per infringing CD manufactured by the defendant and £5 for CDs manufactured and sold (there being at least 54,000 CDs in total).

Additional damages might be awarded to reflect any hurt or distress caused to the claimant by the defendant's activities, although the author is not aware of a case where additional damages have been awarded on this basis.

Account of profit

In litigation involving infringement of intellectual property, the claimant can elect for an account of profit as an alternative to damages. The defendant is required to account to the claimant for the profit which it has made as a result of its infringing activities. It cannot claim an account and damages for the same wrongdoing. The purpose of the remedy was outlined by Slade J in *My Kinda Town v Soll*[20] as:

> To prevent an unjust enrichment of the defendant by compelling him to surrender those profits or those parts of the profits actually made by him which were made improperly.

The objective of the account is not to punish the defendant, but to ensure that he does not unjustly enrich himself at the expense of the claimant. The account

---

17   *Redrow Homes v Betts* [1998] FSR 345.
18   *Ibid.*
19   *Springsteen v Flute* (1998) unreported.
20   *My Kinda Town v Soll* [1982] FSR 147.

is an equitable remedy and therefore discretionary. The court could refuse to order an account even where the claimant expresses a preference for the remedy.[21]

The claimant will not normally elect whether it wants damages or an account until after liability has been determined at trial. It is important that a claimant makes it clear in its claim form and statement of case that it will seek damages or at its election an account of profit in order to keep its options open until liability has been determined.

There is surprisingly little case law on accounts of profits. The remedy is generally regarded as technical and complex. Following determination of liability, most parties agree the amount of damages or profits, which must be paid to the claimant rather than incur the further cost of an inquiry into damages or an account of profit.

The basic mechanism behind the account can be clearly stated, at least in relation to the manufacture and sale of infringing goods. It involves subtracting the amount which the defendant expended in making the infringing goods from the price he received on sale of the goods. The difference between the two amounts, so the reasoning goes, is the profit to be paid over to the claimant.[22] A case in which this approach was used concerned a breach of confidence. The defendant had misused the claimant's confidential information to develop and market a new design of bra. It was not disputed that the infringing bras derived solely from the breach of the intellectual property right and, therefore, it was ordered that all of the defendant's profit calculated in accordance with the above principles should be paid over to the claimant.

Unfortunately, most cases are not so clear cut. Often, one cannot say that the whole of the defendant's profits were generated solely as a result of the infringement. The profit must be apportioned so that only the part of the profit which was actually generated by the infringement is paid over.

Some cases of infringement do not involve the manufacture of infringing articles. For example, take a newspaper which publishes a photograph in breach of copyright. If an account of profit is the chosen remedy, the account will involve calculating the proportion of the defendant's profit which is attributable to the infringing use of the photograph.

In a recent case involving patent infringement, Laddie J set out a number of guiding principles in relation to the taking of an account of profit:[23]

---

21 *Unic SA v Lyndeau Products* (1964) 81 RPC 37, where the judge indicated that damages would be a more appropriate remedy. He gave no reason for his decision, which was *obiter*, the claimant subsequently deciding to elect damages in any event.

22 *Peter Pan v Corsets Silhouette* [1963] 3 All ER 402.

23 *Celanese International Corpn v BP Chemicals* [1999] RPC 203.

- the question to be answered on an account is 'what profits were in fact made by the defendant by the wrongful activity?'. The profits were not reduced if all or most of them might instead have been made in a non-infringing way if, in fact, they were generated by the wrongful activity;
- the claimant must take the defendant as he found him. He cannot complain that the defendant should have generated greater profits by taking an alternative course. The court is finding out what profits were made in fact by the defendant, not what profits he could have made;
- the maximum payment was the total profit made by the defendant. There is therefore an ascertainable upper limit on the amount which the defendant can pay to a claimant on an account;
- if different claimants sought accounts in respect of different infringing activities carried out by a defendant within a single business, the totality of the profits ordered to be paid could not exceed the total profits made by the defendants in that business. There is only one 'profits pot';
- the defendant is allowed to deduct from revenues all allowable costs. The claimant is entitled not to the stream of income received by the defendant, but his profits net of all proper deductions. These may include tax payable by the defendant on the profits and the costs of advertising and marketing the product;[24]
- where the defendant carried on multiple businesses or sold different products and only one infringed, he only had to account for the profits made by the infringement. The claimant cannot recover profits not earned by the infringement;
- where only part of a product or process infringed, profits attributable to the non-infringing parts were not caused by or attributable to the infringement *even if the infringement was the occasion for the generation of those profits*. The profits must be apportioned between the different parts of the product;
- a logical basis for the apportionment must be found. The 'whole picture' must be considered, that is, the defendant's business and the market as a whole. The court must not back a hunch. Nor must it pull a figure out of the air which bears no resemblance to the relevant facts. The question of apportionment is a matter of fact in any particular case. Form must not triumph over substance. Where there is insufficient information available to the court to make a fair adjudication, it will be necessary to adjourn the account to allow more information to be produced;
- a useful guide to apportionment was likely to be provided by ordinary accounting principles where profits of a project were attributed to different parts of the project in the same proportion as the costs and expenses were

---

24 *Potton v Yorkclose* [1990] FSR 11.

attributed to them. This method involves dividing the whole product or project 'cake' into slices which are determined by the slice's costs and expenses. It is only the profit icing on the infringing slice (the relative size of which is measured by reference to its relative costs and expenses) for which the defendant has to account;

- where credible evidence existed that the infringement had made a particularly significant contribution to the profits, the profits attributable to the infringement could be weighted to take account of its added merit, which might not be apparent on the simple apportionment referred to above;

- once the court had decided what a fair apportionment was, it must not round up the figure to a substantial extent. The account is not a camouflaged method of making the defendant pay punitive compensation;

- there are *dicta* in case law to the effect that, generally, the profits ought not to be apportioned by reference to evidence of or speculation about the motives of real or hypothetical purchasers or the relative attractions to such purchasers of different aspects of the work;[25]

- the court can only hope to achieve a reasonable approximation – there is no such thing as a perfectly right figure on an account.

An example of a case where an account was taken in passing off proceedings is the *My Kinda Town* case.[26] The defendant did not have to pay over all the profits generated by the use of the offending name which was the subject of the action, but only those resulting from confusion on the part of the public.

Financial compensation and the Human Rights Act 1998

The chilling effect

Large awards of damages, or the threat of such awards, can generate a climate where the media are reluctant to run the risk of wrongdoing. This effect is often referred to as 'the chilling effect'. The chilling effect can have an inhibiting effect on the media's willingness to risk legal action. As a result, they may be deterred from publishing matters of public concern because of the threat of legal action against them. Yet, the European Court of Human Rights has repeatedly highlighted the media's function of reporting matters of

---

25 An *obiter* comment of Millet J in *Potton v Yorkclose*, a case involving copyright in architect's drawings, in which he stressed that he did not intend to bind other courts in expressing this view. The decision was cited with approval by Laddie J in the *Celanese* case.

26 *My Kinda Town v Soll* [1982] FSR 147.

public concern as being necessary in a democratic society.[27] If the media are deterred from performing this function, large awards of damages may be incompatible with the European Convention of Human Rights.

Section 12 of the Human Rights Act 1998 (which came into force on 2 October 2000) intends to ensure that courts in the UK have regard to the right to freedom of expression whenever they are considering the grant of any relief which might affect the exercise of that right. 'Any relief' includes an award of damages or an account of profits. Under s 12(4), the court must have particular regard to the importance of the Convention right to freedom of expression and, in relation to a journalistic, artistic or literary material, it must also have regard to the extent to which the material is or is about to become available to the public, whether it is or would be in the public interest for the material to be published and any relevant privacy code.[28]

It will be interesting to see whether s 12 will deter courts from making large damages awards. Historically, the English judges have had a tendency to give precedence to more immediate factors in their decision making, such as the defendant's conduct in any particular case or the need to protect the claimant's specific rights, rather than considering the wider chilling effect which an award may have. For that reason, the impact of s 12 is unlikely to have the effect of reducing damages awards against media defendants across the board,[29] but it may deter awards of aggravated and exemplary damages in borderline cases where it is not clear that such awards are justified.

Proportionality

The European Court of Human Rights has considered the fairness of an award of damages against the media in *Tolstoy v UK*,[30] a case involving an award of damages in a defamation case. The European Court found that an award of £1,500,000 could not be reconciled with the Convention because it was out of proportion to the legitimate aim pursued by the damages award, namely, the protection of the claimant's reputation.

Damages awards ought therefore to be limited to what is proportionate to protect the rights or interests of the claimant. If an award goes further, it is unlikely to be necessary in a democratic society and may therefore be incompatible with the Convention.

---

27 Eg, *Observer v UK* (1991) 14 EHRR 843.

28 Section 12 was considered in more detail in Chapter 1.

29 Although the section might lead to a general reduction in defamation awards. This is considered further in Chapter 3.

30 *Tolstoy v UK* (1995) 20 EHRR 442.

(b) Delivery up

Delivery up is the sanction whereby the defendant is ordered to deliver up and forfeit all infringing material or to destroy the infringing material on oath. An order for delivery up is generally made in intellectual property cases.

(c) Injunctions

An injunction is a court order. It can be *prohibitory*, which means that it will restrain the defendant from carrying out the act(s) complained of, or *mandatory*, which means that it will require the defendant to take a positive step, usually to put right its wrongdoing.

Injunctions are equitable remedies. This means that there is never an automatic right to an injunction. The grant is *always* at the discretion of the court, even if the claimant is successful at trial.

The following matters will generally defeat an application for injunctive relief.

The claimant does not have 'clean hands'

The claimant's conduct in relation to the dispute must not have been so improper that it does not deserve to be helped by the grant of an injunction.

The claimant must be prepared to do what is right and fair in relation to the defendant (he who seeks equity must do equity)

The claimant must be willing to perform its own obligations towards the defendant.

The claimant must not have acquiesced in the defendant's wrongdoing

The claimant must not actively or passively have encouraged the defendant to believe that he has no objection to the defendant's wrongdoing in a way which has led the defendant to act to his detriment in reliance on that encouragement.

The terms of the injunction

In recent times, the court has stressed that injunctions must be directed only to the wrong or threatened wrong at issue and they should only be granted where necessary. In *Coflexip SA v Stolt Comex Seaway Ltd*,[31] the court laid down the following guidelines for the grant of injunctive relief:

- the grant of an injunction is in the discretion of the court, which must tailor it to match the wrong which had been committed and/or is threatened;

- the injunction should protect the claimant from a continuation of the perceived threat of infringement, but it must also be fair to the defendant;

- if no future threat of wrongdoing exists, injunctive relief should be refused;

- a defendant who is the subject of an injunction must know what he can and cannot do. Where the injunction asked for by the claimant is obscure in extent, the court should either not grant it at all or, where possible, it should express it in terms which meet the precise needs of the claimant;

- in intellectual property cases, the claimant normally alleges that the defendant had committed a specific type of infringement, for example, in a copyright case, the allegation may be that the defendant has infringed copyright by reproducing a copyright work without permission. In almost all cases, the defendant's wrongdoing occupies only a small part of the monopoly secured by the intellectual property right. It is generally only the current wrongdoing activities which the defendant might threaten to continue. An injunction in general terms, restraining the defendant from infringing the copyright generally, goes further than is necessary – it covers more than the defendant has threatened, more than it might even think or be capable of doing and more than the court had considered when granting the injunction;

- where a narrow injunction is granted, it is appropriate for the injunction to include an express liberty to apply to the court if new wrongdoing of a similar nature occurs. The possible new infringements could then be determined in the same proceedings, without the claimant having to commence infringement proceedings afresh.

The above principles were laid down in relation to intellectual property cases, but they apply in spirit to other type of cases, for example, injunctions preventing repetition of libels or malicious falsehoods. The approach is in line with the case law of the European Court of Human Rights,[32] which has held that an injunction which restrained a repetition of a libel was reconcilable with the European Convention of Human Rights where it was confined to the allegations made by the claimant. Had the injunction gone further, it might have not been reconcilable.

---

31 *Coflexip SA v Stolt Comex Seaway Ltd* [1999] FSR 473, approved by the Court of Appeal in *Microsoft Corpn v Plato Technology* (1999) unreported.
32 *Tolstoy v UK* (1995) 20 EHRR 442.

Final and interim injunctions

Injunctions can be final or interim. A final injunction is generally awarded to a successful claimant after the trial of an action when judgment has been granted. Such an injunction will remain in force, unless and until it is lifted or varied by the court.

Interim injunctions

An interim injunction is a temporary order which is granted prior to trial and is intended to last until the trial at the latest.

Interim injunctions may be granted to prevent an apprehended wrong occurring. Injunctions of this type are known as *quia timet* injunctions. The claimant must show that the wrong is highly probable to occur imminently before a *quia timet* injunction will be granted.[33]

The advantage of interim relief is that it can be obtained *quickly*. The whole *raison d'être* of legal proceedings may disappear if the claimant has to wait until trial to get relief.

Example

An employee leaves her job, taking confidential lists of customers with her. There would be a breach of confidence if she disclosed the information to a third party, such as a journalist. If the old employer brings proceedings against her for breach of confidence, it would get an award of damages (or an account of profits) maybe 12 months later, once the trial has taken place. But in the period leading to trial, she could make use of the customer lists causing damage to the old employer. Damages or an account might compensate for this damage, but how accurately? Could she afford to pay such damages? The claimant's key objective is likely to be preventing use of the customer lists. The interim injunction offers a way for it to do that.

An interim injunction is therefore designed to protect the claimant's alleged rights during the delay before trial. The fact that interim injunctions are obtained before trial means that the court is usually not in a position to form an accurate view of the merits of the dispute. At an interim stage of the proceedings, the court will not have all of the relevant information available to it. Witnesses will not have given their evidence; matters calling for complex legal argument will not have been fully addressed. The lawyers may not even have been fully instructed! Instead of deciding the case on the merits, the court will look to hold what is called 'the balance of convenience' when deciding whether an interim injunction is appropriate. It will ask itself who will suffer most if an interim injunction is granted or if it is not granted. In doing so, the court often

---

33   *Redland Bricks v Morris* [1970] AC 652.

applies the test first formulated in *American Cyanamid v Ethicon*,[34] which is considered below.

Interim injunctions can be obtained very quickly and in cases of sufficient urgency without notice to the other side. Injunctions obtained without notice are often referred to as *ex parte* injunctions. The defendant to an *ex parte* injunction will have no opportunity to put its case at the initial hearing of the application. The first that the defendant will know about the grant of such an injunction will be at the time when the injunction is served on the defendant. The defendant will have an opportunity to come before the court with the claimant in order to argue that the *ex parte* injunction should be varied or discharged.

Interim injunctions and the cross-undertaking in damages

Because the hearing for an interim injunction is not determinative of the merits of a dispute, it is possible that an interim injunction may be discharged at trial where the court is in a better position to decide the issue. The courts have developed the device of the cross-undertaking in damages in order to ensure that that the defendant receives compensation for loss which it suffers as a result of an interim injunction being in place where the injunction is subsequently discharged. At the time of the grant of the interim injunction, the applicant for the injunction must give an undertaking to the court to compensate the defendant for any such loss. It will also have to demonstrate to the court that it has the means to pay such compensation. In some cases, the court will require security to be given under the cross-undertaking, for example, a bank guarantee or a payment into court. The obligation to compensate is an undertaking given to the court and, if not satisfied, could amount to a contempt of court which may be punishable by fines or imprisonment.

Liability under the cross-undertaking can be large. For example, where an interim injunction results in a publication having to be pulped and reprinted without the offending material, the cross-undertaking will cover the costs of the wasted copies of the publication and the cost of the reprints. An applicant who obtains an interim injunction in such circumstances faces a very heavy liability if the interim injunction is subsequently discharged at trial.

The American Cyanamid *test*

Because the court is not usually in a position to decide the case on its merits at the hearing of the interim injunction, alternative criteria are applied to

---

34   *American Cyanamid v Ethicon* (1975) AC 396, HL.

determine whether an interim injunction should be awarded. These were formulated by the House of Lords in *American Cyanamid v Ethicon*.[35]

In the *American Cyanamid* case, the claimants were seeking an interim injunction to prevent the defendant from infringing their patent. The House of Lords laid down the following procedure, which must generally be followed by the court when considering an application for an interim injunction:

(a) the claimant must establish that there is a serious question to be tried. In other words, it must show that its claim is not frivolous or vexatious;

(b) assuming that it can do so, the claimant must show that the balance of convenience favours the granting of an interim injunction. In assessing this the following sequence of questions should be considered:

- will damages adequately compensate the claimant for its loss up to trial and, if so, can the defendant pay them? If yes, the interim injunction should *not* be granted;

- if the answer is no, will damages payable under the claimant's cross-undertaking adequately compensate the defendant for its loss up to trial and can the claimant pay the damages? If yes, there is a strong case for the interim injunction;

- if there is doubt as to the adequacy of the damages above, the question turns on the balance of convenience generally. Would it cause greater hardship to make or to refuse the injunction?;

- where the issue is evenly balanced the court can take into account two further factors:

  o the desirability of preserving the status quo (generally the situation as it stands immediately before the issue of the claim form or where there is delay from issue of the claim form and making the application the time when the application for an injunction is made);[36]

  o the relative strengths of each party's case.

Damages are unlikely to be an adequate remedy where the harm is irreparable, outside the scope of pecuniary compensation or would be difficult to assess, for example, damage to goodwill.

On the facts of *American Cyanamid*, the interim injunction was granted, because it was a *serious issue* whether the defendants were infringing the claimant's patent and because the balance of convenience favoured the grant of the interim injunction. This was particularly because the claimant's monopoly of the market would be effectively destroyed forever if the interim injunction was refused – a loss that could not be adequately compensated in monetary terms.

---

35 *American Cyanamid v Ethicon* (1975) AC 396, HL.

36 *Garden Cottage Foods v Milk Marketing Board* [1984] AC 130.

Rationale behind the American Cyanamid decision

The *American Cyanamid* decision established that an application for an interim injunction should not serve as a mini trial, in which the court tries to form a view on the merits of the claim. The claimant has to show only that there is a serious question to be tried. The strength of the parties' cases is only relevant as a last resort on the balance of convenience. In his judgment in the case, Lord Diplock observed that:

> It is no part of the court's function at this stage of the litigation to try to resolve conflicts of evidence on affidavits as to facts on which the claim of either party may ultimately depend nor to decide difficult questions of law which call for detailed argument and mature consideration. These are matters to be dealt with at trial.[37]

Exceptions to American Cyanamid

The courts have recognised a number of exceptions to the *American Cyanamid* approach. The main exceptions, from the media's point of view, have been the following.

Where the application for a final injunction will not reach trial

Where the grant or refusal of an interim injunction will dispose of the case it will not be appropriate to apply *American Cyanamid*. This is because, where an injunction is granted on *American Cyanamid* principles, it would effectively be an end to the matter without the defendant being able to challenge the claimant's substantive case and dispute the matter at trial. The court is therefore likely to require the claimant to show more than just a serious issue to be tried. In essence, the claimant would have to show that on the merits it is likely to succeed at trial.

Example – Athletes Foot Marketing Inc v Cobra Sports[38]

This was a passing off case. The interim injunction would have required the defendant to change the name of its mail order operation. It would be unrealistic to expect it to do so and to continue the case to trial having expended time, money and effort in promoting and trading under the new name. In practice, if ordered to change the name at an interim stage, that was likely to be the end of the litigation. *American Cyanamid* was not therefore the appropriate approach.

---

37   (1975) AC 396, HL , p 407.

38   *Athletes Foot Marketing Inc v Cobra Sports* (1980) RPC 343.

Where it is apparent from the material before the court at the hearing of the interim injunction that a party's case is stronger than the other, that should not be ignored on the balance of convenience[39]

Whilst the court should not attempt to resolve difficult questions of law and fact at the interim hearing, any clear view the court may reach as to the relative strength of the parties' case will be relevant to the balancing stage of the *American Cyanamid* approach.

Cases involving freedom of expression issues – the position before the Human Rights Act 1998

American Cyanamid *often works against the media*

As we have seen, the focus of the *American Cyanamid* test revolves around the balance of convenience. The balance of convenience test and, in particular, the presumption in favour of preserving the status quo, often operates in favour of a grant of an interim injunction restraining publication by the media.

This is most often the case in breach of confidence cases and, by analogy, cases involving issues of privacy. It is invariably open to the claimant to allege that, if an interim injunction is not awarded, the confidence or privacy at issue will be forever destroyed. The claimant will be left to his monetary remedies, but these may well be difficult to obtain and, in any event, may prove to be inadequate, especially where the disclosure of the confidential information does not involve loss which can be measured in money terms.

In relation to the law of breach of confidence, Sir John Donaldson MR observed in *AG v Newspaper Publishing plc*:[40]

> Confidential information whatever its nature ... has one essential common character. It is *irremediably* damaged in its confidential character by every publication and the more widespread the publication, the greater the damage. If a *prima facie* claim to confidence can be established, but this is opposed by a claim of a right to publish, whether on the grounds of public interest or otherwise, opposing and inconsistent claims must be evaluated and balanced against the other ... Pending trial, the balance will normally come down in favour of preserving confidentiality for the very obvious reason that, if this is not done and publication is permitted, there will be nothing left to have a trial about ...

Similarly, in relation to privacy, as long ago as the 1840s, Lord Cottenham LC observed that 'where privacy is the right invaded, the postponing of the

---

39 *Series 5 Software v Clarke* [1996] 1 All ER 853.

40 *AG v Newspaper Publishing plc* [1987] 3 All ER 276.

injunction would be equivalent to denying it altogether ... to be effectual, it must be immediate'.[41]

Interim injunctions and third parties

An injunction restraining the publication of confidential and private information will bind third parties who were not parties to the injunction if they know of the injunction.[42] The objective of such an injunction is the protection of the subject matter of the action pending trial. A third party who contravenes the injunction and so destroys or causes serious damage to the subject matter is in contempt of court if he intended to impede or prejudice the course of justice. This intention is likely to be presumed where the third party had knowledge of the injunction at the time that he breached its terms. If third parties wish to vary the terms of the injunction, they may apply to the court to do so. Similarly, they may apply to the courts to seek guidance about whether what they intend to do will be in breach of the injunction or undertakings.

This principle was established during the course of the *Spycatcher* litigation (considered in more detail below). The Crown had obtained interim injunctions against *The Guardian* and *The Observer*, restraining the publication of confidential information. Subsequent to that injunction being granted, *The Independent*, which was not a party to the interim injunction, published a description of the confidential information. The Attorney General moved for contempt against *The Independent* for breach of the provisions of the interim injunction granted against *The Guardian* and *The Observer*. The application was based on the fact that *The Independent*'s publication was bound to frustrate the purpose of the interim injunctions and to render them worthless. Notwithstanding that *The Independent* was not a party enjoined by the interim injunction on its face, the Court of Appeal held that the article was a contempt of court. In effect, the interim injunction was then extended to all media outlets within the jurisdiction of the English court.

Freedom of expression and the rule against prior restraint

Interim injunctions are an example of what is known as *prior restraint*. Prior restraint is a form of censorship. It operates to prevent publication. For this reason, interim injunctions against the media are often referred to as gagging orders.

Where the defendant is a member of the media, the grant of an interim injunction may be used to stifle the discussion of matters which are of legitimate public concern. This raises the question of whether interim

---

41 *Prince Albert v Strange* (1849) 2 De G & Sm 652.

42 *AG v Newspaper Publishing plc* [1987] 3 All ER 276.

injunctions should ever be awarded in matters involving freedom of expression and if they should, whether the guidelines laid down in *American Cyanamid* are the appropriate criteria to apply. This is particularly relevant because, as we have seen, an injunction against one media entity will be binding on other media entities.

There is a principle against prior restraint in English law. It was first formally set out in *Blackstone's Commentaries*, published in 1830. It provides that the media should not be restrained in advance from publishing whatever it thinks right to publish. But it publishes at its own risk. As Lord Denning observed, in *Schering v Falkman*:[43]

> Afterwards – after the publication – if the press has done anything unlawful – it can be dealt with by the courts. If it should offend – by interfering with the course of justice – it can be punished in proceedings for contempt of court. If it should damage the reputation of innocent people by telling untruths or making unfair comment, it may be made liable in damages. But always afterwards. Never beforehand. Never by previous restraint.

American Cyanamid *v the rule against prior restraint*

The *American Cyanamid* test and the rule against prior restraint are at odds. As we have seen, the balance of convenience test and presumption in favour of the status quo often come down in favour of the grant of an interim injunction. On the other hand, the rule against prior restraint provides that interim injunctions should only be awarded in exceptional circumstances. Which prevails?

An example where the English courts gave precedence to the claimant's rights rather than the rule against prior restraint occurred in the convoluted *Spycatcher* litigation. This involved a number of separate sets of proceedings against various parties. The central facts of each set of proceedings were as follows.

Peter Wright was a former member of the British security services with access to highly classified information. At the time of the litigation, he had retired and was living abroad. He proposed to publish his memoirs describing his experiences in the security services. In 1985, the Attorney General, acting on behalf of the UK Government, commenced proceedings for breach of confidence in the courts of New South Wales to restrain publication of the memoirs in Australia.

Meanwhile, back in Britain, a number of national newspapers (notably *The Observer* and *The Guardian*) published accounts of the Australian litigation commenced by the Attorney General, including an outline of some of Mr Wright's allegations as contained in his (then) unpublished manuscript. In

---

43 *Schering Chemicals v Falkman* [1982] QB 1; [1981] 2 WLR 848; [1981] 2 All ER 321, CA.

1986, the Attorney General commenced proceedings for breach of confidence against *The Observer* and *The Guardian,* seeking interim injunctions to restrain further publication of the revelations. In support of the application, the government contended that Mr Wright owed a duty to the Crown not to disclose information obtained by him while a member of the security service and that the writing of his memoirs and the taking of steps to publish them was a breach of that duty of confidentiality. Interim injunctions were awarded at first instance by Millet J. The injunctions granted against *The Observer* and *The Guardian* restrained the newspapers from publishing or disclosing any information obtained by Mr Wright in his capacity as a member of MI5 (subject to a number of limited exceptions relating to certain incidents which were already in the public domain). At this stage, *Spycatcher* was still unpublished. The contents of the book as a whole were not in the public domain.

The *Spycatcher* book itself was first published in the US on 13 July 1987, at a time when the interim injunctions awarded by Millet J were still in force. The UK Government was unable to restrain publication in the US because of the rule against prior restraint which exists there. Copies of the book were imported from the US into the UK. No attempts were made by the British Government to stop the imports.

Upon publication of the book in the US, *The Observer* and *The Guardian* applied to discharge the injunctions against them on the principal ground that the injunction had been granted in order to preserve, pending trial, the confidentiality of the information contained in Mr Wright's manuscript and that, by reason of the US publication, the information was no longer confidential and, therefore, the object of the injunctions could no longer be achieved.

At first instance, Sir Nicolas Browne-Wilkinson VC discharged the Millet injunctions. He stated:

> Once news is out by publication in the US and the importation of the book into this country, the law could, I think, be justifiably accused of being an ass and brought into disrepute if it closed its eyes to that reality and sought by injunction to prevent the press or anyone else from repeating information which is now freely available to all.

The first instance decision was reversed by the Court of Appeal, who found that, on the *American Cyanamid* balance of convenience, the Attorney General had an arguable case that any further publication of the book in the UK would cause further damage to British national security in various ways. Although the original purpose of the Millet injunctions could no longer be achieved (the maintenance of confidentiality), the secondary objective (the avoidance of further damage) could be.

The majority of the House of Lords concurred.

The decision to continue the interim injunctions was subsequently held by the European Court of Human Rights to be incompatible with the right to freedom of expression enshrined in Art 10 of the European Convention.[44] The Court held that the interest in maintaining the confidentiality of the memoirs had, for the purposes of the Convention, ceased to exist by the time that the book was in the public domain. Yet the decision of the Court of Appeal and the House of Lords, although making little sense on the basis that the information in the manuscript was freely available, makes more sense within the narrow and theoretical context of the *American Cyanamid* approach. Rather than concentrating on the overall picture and the merits of the claim, the courts were drawn by the application of the balance of convenience into balancing potential damage caused to the media by virtue of the interim injunctions remaining in place, against potential damage to national security interests if further publication were allowed during the period up to trial. The result of the balance was wholly unsatisfactory and was roundly criticised on all sides.

Prior restraint and the European Convention of Human Rights

The European Court of Human Rights has held that measures of prior restraint are not automatically prohibited under Art 10 of the Convention.[45] But the Court has observed that the dangers inherent in such measures are such that they called for the most careful scrutiny. This, the court observed, was especially so as far as the news media are concerned, because news is a perishable commodity and to delay its publication, even for a short period, may well deprive it of all its value and interest. The interim injunction which was in force during the *Spycatcher* litigation before the book was published in the US was judged by the court to be reconcilable with the Convention in the interests of national security and for maintaining the authority of the judiciary. However, once the book had been published, it could no longer be reconciled and should have been lifted.

The European Court declined to rule that the *American Cyanamid* test should never apply to cases involving breach of confidence and freedom of expression. It expressed the view that it was not part of its function to comment on provisions of national law in the abstract.

In the wake of the *Spycatcher* litigation, the English courts have gone some way to excluding cases involving freedom of expression from the *American Cyanamid* guidelines.

---

44 *Sunday Times v UK* (1979) 2 EHRR 245.
45 *Observer v UK* (1991) 14 EHRR 153 and *Wingrove v UK* (1996) 24 EHRR 1.

Topical information

In *Cambridge Nutrition Ltd v BBC*,[46] the Court of Appeal held that where the subject matter of the application for the interim injunction was the transmission of a broadcast or the publication of an article the impact and value of which depended on its timing, the court should not grant an interim injunction restraining broadcast or publication merely because the claimant was able to show a serious issue to be tried and that the balance of convenience lay in granting an injunction. Instead, the court should assess the relative strength of the parties' cases before deciding whether the injunction should be granted. No injunction should be granted unless the claimant could show a likelihood of success at trial. Kerr LJ said:[47]

> It seems to me that cases in which the subject matter concerns the right to publish an article, or to transmit a broadcast, whose importance may be transitory but whose impact depends on timing, news value and topicality, do not lend themselves easily to the application of the *American Cyanamid* guidelines. Longer term publications, such as films or books, may not be in the same category ... one must be careful not to lose sight of the real demands of justice in any given case by attaching too much importance to the *Cyanamid* guidelines.

Relative strengths unclear

The *Cambridge Nutrition* decision was cited with approval by the Court of Appeal in *Secretary of State for the Home Department v Central Broadcasting*.[48] The case concerned an application by the Home Secretary for an interim injunction to restrain the broadcast of an interview between the convicted murderer Denis Nilsen and a Home Office psychologist. The Court of Appeal declined to grant an interim injunction. Sir Thomas Bingham MR indicated that, where the relative strengths of the parties' cases on the merits was unclear, the court should not interfere with the defendant's freedom to publish by way of an interim injunction. A similar approach was applied in *Macmillan Magazines v RCN Publishing*[49] (a comparative advertising case), where Neuberger J held that, where, on an application for interim relief the balance of justice favoured neither party, the fact that the granting of relief would effectively interfere with the defendant's right of free speech meant the injunction should be refused.

---

46 *Cambridge Nutrition Ltd v BBC* [1990] 3 All ER 523.
47 *Ibid*, p 535.
48 *Secretary of State for the Home Department v Central Broadcasting* [1993] EMLR 253.
49 *Macmillan Magazines v RCN Publishing* [1998] FSR 9.

The effect of the Human Rights Act on injunctions restricting freedom of expression

The coming into force of the Human Rights Act 1998 in October 2000 is likely to have significant effects on the grant of interim injunctions against the media.

Section 12 of the Act is intended to provide a safeguard against injunctions (and other forms of relief) being granted without proper regard being had to the right to freedom of expression. The provisions of s 12 were considered in detail in Chapter 1. In summary, the Act underlines that *ex parte* interim injunctions should only be sought in exceptional circumstances where all practicable steps have been taken to notify the respondent or where there are compelling reasons why notice should not be given. The section also makes clear that the *American Cyanamid* test is inappropriate for injunctions which would limit the respondent's freedom of expression. The applicant for the injunction must establish more than just a serious issue to be tried. Instead, it must establish that it is likely to establish at trial that publication should not be allowed. The courts will accordingly have to consider the merits of any cause of action when deciding whether to grant interim relief.

Other considerations (which will apply in relation to the decision to grant final or interim injunctions) are the importance of the right to freedom of expression under the European Convention of Human Rights and, in relation to journalistic, literary or artistic material, the extent to which the material is or is about to become available to the public and the extent to which the publication of the material would be in the public interest. Where the action involves privacy issues, the extent to which any industry code of practice has been complied with will also be a material factor.

The extent to which s 12 is likely to have implications for particular causes of action is considered in the specific subject chapters.

PUBLIC LAW

Judicial review

The legality of actions taken by public authorities may be challenged by way of an application to the courts for judicial review. The use of judicial review is likely to increase in the wake of the incorporation of the Human Rights Act 1998. It is envisaged that the most common means of obtaining redress against public authorities who act in breach of the Convention rights will be by way of application for judicial review.[50] The Government has indicated that it

---

50   HRA 1998, s 7.

expects the number of applications for judicial review to double to 600 per annum once the Act comes into force.[51] This section provides a general overview of the nature of the application. Readers should note that this area of law is complex and specialist texts should be consulted for further analysis.

The meaning of public authority

The application for judicial review lies against public authorities. It is not available against private persons or bodies. The courts have had to consider what constitutes a public authority on a number of occasions. The case law will also be an important consideration for the courts to have regard to when they are considering whether a person is a public authority under ss 6 and 7 of the Human Rights Act 1998.

Under the case law, the functions of the body tend to be determinative rather than the source from which it derives its functions.[52]

Applications for judicial review will generally be based on one or more of the following grounds:

- the public authority has exceeded its jurisdiction or has taken a step which it is not authorised to do;

- the public authority is in breach of the rules of natural justice. The application for judicial review may be made on the ground that the authority in question has not acted fairly when reaching a decision. The applicant might claim that it was denied a fair hearing, for example, because it was not fully informed of the case that it had to meet or that it was not given a proper opportunity to correct or contradict that case;

- the authority has not exercised its discretion in a reasonable manner. Public authorities are under a duty to act reasonably when reaching their decisions. Where the authority reaches a decision which no reasonable authority, properly instructed, would have come to, for example, because it did not consider certain pieces of evidence or it acted on irrelevant grounds, an application can be made to the courts for the decision to be quashed. An application may also be made where the authority's decision is based on a point of law and the authority has misdirected itself on the law;

- the public authority has acted in a way which is incompatible with the Convention rights provided for in the Human Rights Act 1998. This is a new ground for review introduced by s 7 of the Human Rights Act, which will come into force on 2 October 2000.

---

51 (2000) *The Times*, 18 April.
52 *R v Panel of Takeovers and Mergers ex p Datafin* [1987] 1 QB 815.

The procedure for making an application for judicial review is set out in Ord 53 of the former Rules of the Supreme Court, now contained in Sched 1 to the Civil Procedure Rules. Note that this was revoked as from 2 October 2000 and replaced with a new Pt 5 of the CPR. No application for judicial review may be made, unless permission of the court for the commencement of the application is first obtained. An application for permission must be made promptly and, in any event, within three months from the date when grounds for the application first arose, unless there is good reason for extending the period within which the application shall be made.[53] This time period will apply even where the ground for judicial review is that a public authority has acted in breach of the Convention rights provided for by the Human Rights Act 1998.

The application may be made by a person with 'sufficient interest' in the matter to which the application relates.[54] This has been interpreted by the domestic courts to include pressure and public interest groups. However, where an application for judicial review is made on the ground that the public authority has acted unlawfully in breach of the Convention rights provided for under the Human Rights Act 1998, the test is narrower. In relation to such an application, the applicant will only have sufficient interest where it is, or would be, a victim of the Act.[55] The Human Rights Act provides that the definition of 'victim' should be interpreted in line with the jurisprudence of the European Court of Human Rights. Under the current case law of the Strasbourg Courts, an application by pressure or public interest groups on this ground will not be permitted. It would seem that different standards would apply to different types of judicial review application.

Remedies available for judicial review

Under the judicial review procedure, remedies are always discretionary. The following types of relief will generally be available where appropriate:

- mandamus – an order for the performance of a public duty;
- certiorari – an order to quash a decision;
- prohibition – an order to prevent a decision;
- injunction (mandatory or prohibitory);
- declaration;
- damages – on an application for judicial review, the court may award damages to the applicant if he has included in his application for

---

53   RSC Ord 53, r 4(1) (contained in Sched 1 to the CPR). This was revoked as from 2 October 2000 and replaced by a new Pt 5 of the CPR.
54   Supreme Court Act 1981, s 3.
55   HRA 1998, s 7(3).

permission to bring the proceedings a claim for damages arising from the matter to which the application relates and the court is satisfied that, if the claim had been made in proceedings for damages begun by the applicant at the time of making his application for judicial review, he could have been awarded damages.[56]

The Advertising Standards Authority, the Broadcasting Standards Commission, the Independent Television Commission and the Radio Authority are all subject to judicial review by the High Court. It is probable that the Press Complaints Commission is also amenable to review. In practice, judicial review is the only mechanism for disgruntled media entities wishing to apply to the courts for redress against adverse decisions under the relevant Codes of Practice.

Judicial review is *not* a right of appeal against a decision of a public authority. Where an application is successful, it will not result in the court substituting its decision in place of the public authorities' decision. Instead, the decision will be remitted back to the authority for fresh consideration in the light of the court's findings. The decision of the authority may be the same at the end of the day. The effect of the judicial review application may only be to change the way in which the decision is reached.

Interim injunctions and judicial review

It is possible for applicants to obtain interim injunctions to restrain the publication of an adverse decision in the authority's reports whilst an application for judicial review is pending. Direct Line Financial Services Ltd obtained such an injunction against the ASA, which resulted in the pulping of the relevant monthly report and its republication in an amended form, without reference to the Direct Line Financial Services decision.[57] Advertisers and media entities who are tempted to try a similar tactic should bear in mind that they will be asked to give a cross-undertaking in damages to compensate the authority for its losses if the application for judicial review turns out to be unsuccessful. The losses in question may be considerable.

---

56 RSC Ord 53, r 7(1) (contained in Sched 1 to the CPR). This will be revoked as from 2 October 2000 and replaced by a new Pt 5 of the CPR.

57 *R v ASA ex p Direct Line* (1997) unreported.

CHAPTER 3

DEFAMATION

The law of defamation has attained a degree of refinement and sophistication besides which the equitable doctrine of the constructive trust is a model of clarity and simplicity.[1]

THE CIVIL LAW

The law of defamation is primarily concerned with the protection of the *reputation* of individuals and corporations. If I were to make an unjustifiable statement about X, X may be able to bring a claim against me in defamation, provided that the statement is damaging to his standing amongst reasonable members of society. The relief available to X would include damages to compensate him for the damage to his reputation and an injunction to restrain further publication of the allegation.

The procedure relating to defamation claims has evolved into one of the most technical areas of civil litigation. It remains to be seen to what extent the Civil Procedure Rules (CPR) will succeed in practice in their objective of simplifying the legal process. The Defamation Act 1996 has introduced a number of procedures which are also designed to simplify defamation litigation, most of which have very recently been implemented. Again, it is too early to assess the impact of these measures at the time of writing. Before the introduction of the CPR, a defendant to a libel claim could generally expect to be embroiled in protracted and expensive litigation which often came to have little relevance to the original publication which ostensibly formed the subject matter of the action.

In recent times, the damages awarded to successful claimants spiralled out of control. Take, for example, the following typical awards:

- £200,000 awarded to the pop star Jason Donovan over an article in *The Face,* suggesting that he was a liar and a hypocrite by denying that he was gay;

- £45,000 awarded to the well known businessman Victor Kiam over an allegation in a national newspaper that Mr Kiam was financially ruined. The award was made even though the newspaper immediately retracted the statement and published an apology;

---

1   Millet LJ in *Gillick v BBC* [1996] EMLR 267, p 274.

- £750,000 awarded to the footballer Graeme Souness over a statement made by his former wife that he was a tight fisted 'dirty rat'.

The size of awards such as these operate to deter many members of the media from making contentious allegations. We shall see in this chapter how the balance which, in the past, has been overwhelmingly favourable to the claimant in a defamation claim, is beginning to operate more fairly. Defamation does, however, remain one of the most significant restraints on media freedom. The chilling effect which the threat of a defamation claim might have on freedom of expression have been recognised at the highest level.[2]

What is defamation?

Damage to reputation

A defamatory statement is a statement which has a tendency to damage a party's reputation. The tendency to cause damage is a prerequisite to the cause of action. It is not defamatory to make a critical statement which does not have a tendency to cause damage, even if the statement turns out to be untrue.

To make the statement that company X's product (say, an electric fan) is dangerous, because the company neglects to take vital health and safety precautions during the manufacturing process, might be defamatory. The statement would cause damage to X's reputation as a responsible manufacturer (as well as reducing its profits). The statement may also damage the personal reputation of each of X's directors with responsibility for ensuring that the product is manufactured safely. The statement could be understood to portray them as having a cavalier attitude towards health and safety issues. The directors (and, for that matter, any other employees with responsibilities for complying with health and safety regulations) might be able to sue for the damage to their respective reputations if they can show that reasonable readers would have understood the statement to refer to them.

On the other hand, if I were to say that company X's electric fan is not as efficient as the fan produced by a trade rival, my statement is unlikely to be defamatory. Although it may result in lost sales, it cannot really be said that it has damaged X's reputation or that of its directors or employees. It is a statement about X's product, rather than about X or its employees or directors. Even if my statement about the fans was incorrect, X would not have a claim

---

2   Eg, by Lord Keith in *Derbyshire CC v Times Newspapers Ltd* [1993] 1 All ER 1011, p 1017.

against me in *defamation*. X might have a claim for malicious falsehood. Malicious falsehood is considered in Chapter 4.

What type of material can be defamatory?

Throughout this chapter, reference is made to defamatory 'statements'. However, a cause of action in defamation is not limited to the publication of words. Pictures, cartoons and caricatures can be defamatory, as can other non-verbal statements. In *Monson v Tussaud*,[3] the claimant alleged that he had been defamed by the exhibition of a waxwork effigy of him in close proximity to a number of more infamous figures. The court held that the positioning of the waxwork was capable of being defamatory.

The technical meaning of defamatory

In order to assess the prospects of success of any defamation claim, it is first necessary to determine whether the statement in question is defamatory or, in other words, whether it has a tendency to damage the subject's reputation.

There is no entirely satisfactory definition of 'defamatory', nor for 'reputation'. Those definitions that have evolved through case law are generally illustrations of the ways in which damage might manifest itself. What has been termed 'the classic definition'[4] of the meaning of defamatory was laid down in the case of *Parmiter v Coupland*[5] in the following terms:

> A publication, without justification or lawful excuse, which is calculated to injure the reputation of another, by exposing him to *hatred, contempt or ridicule* ... (calculated here bears the meaning of 'likely to').

The *Parmiter* definition was extended in the case of *Youssoupoff v Metro-Goldwyn-Mayer Pictures Ltd*,[6] where it was established that, in addition to exposing the claimant to hatred, contempt or ridicule, a publication would be defamatory if it tends to make the claimant *shunned and avoided*. This was so even where there was no moral discredit on the claimant's part. If a person were incorrectly said to have a seriously infectious disease, he might be able to bring an action for defamation even though no moral responsibility could possibly be placed on him for his condition, the reasoning being that the suggestion of the disease would lower the subject's standing, causing him to be shunned and avoided by society generally.

The above formulae can be too narrow to fit all cases. For example, in *Tournier v Provincial Union Bank of England Ltd*,[7] Atkin LJ observed:

3 *Monson v Tussaud* [1894] 1 QB 671.
4 *Berkoff v Burchill* [1996] 4 All ER 1010.
5 *Parmiter v Coupland* (1840) 6 M & W 105, p 108.
6 *Youssoupoff v Metro-Goldwyn-Mayer Pictures Ltd* (1934) 50 TLR 581.
7 *Tournier v Provincial Union Bank of England* [1924] 1 KB 461, p 561.

It is obvious that suggestions might be made very injurious to a man's character in business which would not, in the ordinary sense, excite either hate, ridicule or contempt – for example, an imputation of a clever fraud which, however much to be condemned morally and legally, might yet not excite what a member of a jury might understand as hatred or contempt.

In *Sim v Stretch*,[8] Lord Atkin sought to widen the definition. Concentrating on the essential focus of the defamation action, he applied the following test:

Would the words tend to lower the plaintiff in the estimation of right thinking members of society generally?

Lord Atkin's more all-encompassing approach was also adopted by the Faulks Committee on Defamation,[9] which suggested in its 1975 Report that a statutory definition for defamation should be adopted in the following terms: 'Defamation shall consist of the publication to a third party of matter which in all the circumstances would be likely to affect a person adversely in the estimation of reasonable people generally.'[10] This definition has never been formally adopted.

Reputation

So far as the meaning of 'reputation' goes, the meaning to be drawn from case law is that reputation is to be equated with the estimation of right thinking members of society/reasonable people generally.

Particular types of reputation

Professional reputation

The law of defamation operates to protect professional reputations from disparagement. Where a person's job performance is criticised, the criticism is capable of being defamatory, even though it may not impute any blame or defect of personal character. The imputation of a lack of qualification, knowledge, skill, judgment or of inefficiency in carrying out professional duties is capable of being defamatory.[11]

Creditworthy reputation

It can be defamatory to say of a person that he is insolvent or bankrupt or a poor payer of debts, notwithstanding that a person's insolvency may not be

---

8   *Sim v Stretch* [1936] 2 All ER 1237, p 1240.

9   *Report of the Committee on Defamation*, Cmnd 5909, 1975.

10 Para 65.

11 See, eg, *Drummond-Jackson v British Medical Association* [1970] 1 All ER 1094 and *Irving v Penguin Books Ltd* (2000) unreported, 11 April, which concerned defamatory allegations about the claimant's abilities as a professional historian.

attributable to any fault on his part. The law takes the view that a person is entitled to a reputation for creditworthiness.[12]

Determining whether the meaning is defamatory: applying the tests

The borderline between what is defamatory and what is not can be difficult to define. *Berkoff v Burchill* is an illustration of the potential difficulties in applying the test.[13] The case concerned comments made by a journalist about the physical appearance of the actor Stephen Berkoff. The journalist described Mr Berkoff as being 'hideously ugly' and compared his appearance unfavourably with that of the monster Frankenstein. Mr Berkoff commenced proceedings for defamation. The Court of Appeal was called upon to decide whether the allegation that someone is hideously ugly was capable of being defamatory of the claimant (that is, capable of having a tendency to damage Mr Berkoff's reputation).

The majority of the Court of Appeal was of the view that the description was *not* capable of being defamatory. Millett LJ was of the view that the words were an attack on Mr Berkoff's physical *appearance*, rather than his reputation. The words did not make Mr Berkoff look ridiculous or lower his standing in the eyes of ordinary people. The journalist had ridiculed Mr Berkoff but, by doing so, she had not *exposed* him to ridicule. He observed that to hold such comments as defamatory would be an unwarranted restriction on freedom of speech. People must be allowed to poke fun at another without fear of litigation.

In a powerful dissenting judgment, Neill LJ drew on earlier authorities to show that to describe someone as being hideously ugly was capable of being defamatory. He observed that the concept of 'reputation' should be interpreted in a broad sense to comprehend all aspects of the claimant's standing in the community. The words had to be judged in all the circumstances of publication, including the particular circumstances of the claimant. Mr Berkoff is an actor and a figure in the public eye. To describe him as hideously ugly was, in such circumstances, capable of lowering his standing in the estimation of the public and of making him an object of ridicule. That would not necessarily be the case if Mr Berkoff were less well known or if he worked in a different profession.

---

12 See, eg, *Aspro Travel Ltd v Owners Abroad Group plc* [1996] 1 WLR 132.
13 *Berkoff v Burchill* [1996] 4 All ER 1010.

The meaning of the statement

In order to decide whether a statement is defamatory, one first has to determine what the statement actually means. This exercise is not as straightforward as it might at first seem. Often, different people interpret the same statement in different ways. It is quite usual in a defamation action for the claimant to assert that a statement would be understood by the ordinary reader to mean one thing and for the defendant to assert a different meaning, often equally credible. For example, consider the following statement: *'X has today been charged with an offence under the Food Act 1984.'*

This statement could be interpreted in a number of different ways. For example:

- X has been charged with an offence – the mere fact of charge; or
- X has committed an offence; or
- X is suspected of committing an offence.

Unusually for civil cases, defamation trials are usually heard by a judge and jury. In cases tried by jury, the meaning to be attributed to a defamatory item is a question for the jury. A judge can be asked to rule whether the item in question is *capable of* bearing a meaning which either the claimant or defendant alleges that it bears. If the judge decides that it is so capable, the actual decision on meaning is for the jury. The jury does not have to accept the meaning(s) put forward by the parties.

The test to determine the meaning of the statement is *'what would the reasonable reader or viewer consider the natural and ordinary meaning of the words to be?'*

When applying this test, the following issues should be borne in mind:

- the meaning of the statement is determined by the reaction of the ordinary, reasonable and fair minded reader or viewer and not by what the publisher intended the statement to mean. It is how words are understood by the notional audience that counts and not how they were meant. This often surprises unwary journalists. The fact that a particular meaning was not intended will not therefore generally provide a defence to a defamation claim. The media should check material to assess all possible meanings that material might reasonably be understood to mean. The temptation to rely on your own subjective interpretation of the material should be avoided. In *Henty's Case*,[14] Cotton LJ observed:

  > One must consider, not what the words are, but what conclusion could reasonably be drawn from it, as a man who issues such a document is answerable not only for the terms of it, but also for the conclusion and

---

14   *Henty's Case* 5 CPD 514, p 536.

meaning which persons will reasonably draw from and put upon the document;

- although a combination of words may convey different meanings to the minds of different readers, the court is required to determine the single meaning which the publication would convey to the hypothetical reasonable reader and to base any award of damages on the assumption that this is the one sense in which all readers would have understood the statement. This single meaning is known as *'the natural and ordinary meaning'* of the publication. The reasons behind this 'one meaning' rule derive from the entitlement to a jury trial in most defamation cases. It is for the jury to determine meaning, rather than the public at large. This, coupled with the fact that, unless one settles on a particular meaning, one cannot judge the extent of the damage suffered by the claimant in a reliable way, has led to the establishment of the 'one meaning' rule;[15]

- words should be interpreted in their ordinary and natural sense.[16] Meanings which emerge only after a strained or forced interpretation of the statement should accordingly be rejected;[17]

- the natural and ordinary meaning of words will include implications or inferences which a reasonable reader, guided by his general knowledge and unfettered by the strict legal rules of construction, would draw from the words on reading between the lines. One should therefore avoid too literal an interpretation of the words used;[18]

- It is the broad impression conveyed that has to be considered. The reasonable reader or viewer would not engage in an over-elaborate analysis of the words used. The case of *Skuse v Granada Television*[19] concerned a television documentary broadcast as part of the 'World in Action' series. The natural and ordinary meaning of the documentary was at issue. Sir Thomas Bingham observed:[20]

  > In the present case, we must remind ourselves that this was a factual programme likely to appeal primarily to a serious minded section of television viewers, but it was a programme which, even if watched continuously, would have been seen only once by viewers, many of which would have switched on for entertainment. Its audience would not have given it the analytical attention of a lawyer to the meaning of a document, an auditor to the interpretation of accounts or an academic to the content of a learned article;

---

15 *Per* Jacob J in *Vodafone v Orange* [1997] FSR 34, p 38. See, also, Diplock LJ in *Slim v Daily Telegraph* [1968] 2 QB 171 for an explanation of the 'one meaning' rule.

16 *Lewis v Daily Telegraph* [1964] AC 234.

17 *Jones v Skelton* [1963] 1 WLR 1362; [1963] 3 All ER 952.

18 *Lewis v Daily Telegraph* [1964] AC 234.

19 *Skuse v Granada Television* [1996] EMLR 278.

20 *Ibid*, p 285.

- in assessing what a reasonable person would think, it should be borne in mind that 'ordinary men and women have different temperaments and outlooks. Some are unusually suspicious and some are unusually naïve. One must try to envisage people between these two extremes and see what is the most damaging meaning they would put on the words in question'.[21] On that basis, a statement of suspicion ought not to be interpreted as a statement of guilt. The ordinary reader would not be 'avid for scandal'. In *Capital and Counties Bank Ltd v Henty,*[22] Lord Blackburn indicated 'it is unreasonable that when there are a number of good interpretations, the only bad one should be seized upon to give a defamatory sense to the document'.

Taking our example about the Food Act, the reasonable reader would not infer guilt from the mere fact of charge. He might, however, infer more than that basic fact, perhaps concluding that there must have been something worth investigating about X's activities, that is, reasonable suspicion, rather than actual guilt.

Examples of this principle

Mapp v News Group Newspapers[23]

The case concerned an article in the *News of the World,* headed 'Drug quiz cop kills himself'.

The article consisted of the following text:

Police Sergeant Gerry Carroll killed himself after being ordered to provide information about ex-colleagues accused of peddling drugs. Sergeant Carroll, 46, shot himself through the head in a cell. He was custody officer with the drugs squad in Stoke Newington, north London, when eight fellow officers were alleged to have been involved in drug dealing and bribery. The accused officers have been transferred to other police stations while an investigation is carried out.

The claimants were amongst the officers transferred to other police stations during a major police investigation into police corruption in Stoke Newington. The claimants pleaded that the article had the following defamatory meaning:

That the claimants were guilty of involvement in drug dealing and bribery, that Sergeant Carroll had been in a position to know this because he had been working with the claimants at the time and he had killed himself because he would otherwise have to confirm the claimants' involvement.

---

21 Lord Reid in *Lewis v Daily Telegraph* [1964] AC 234, pp 258–60.
22 *Capital and Counties Bank Ltd v Henty* (1882) 7 App Cas 741, p 786.
23 [1997] NLJR 562.

The court was asked to rule as a preliminary issue whether the article was capable of bearing that meaning. The Court of Appeal took the view that it was not. Hirst LJ indicated that it would be virtually impossible to suggest that the words complained of impugned actual guilt of drug dealing and bribery on the part of the claimants, unless the meaning of the article was transformed by the reference to Sergeant Carroll's suicide. But, the court held, the meaning was not transformed by the reference to suicide. The reasonable reader could interpret the reference to suicide in a number of more plausible ways; for example, that Sergeant Carroll was overwhelmed by stress or depression for reasons unconnected with the investigations. The words were not capable of imputing actual guilt on the part of the officers.

On the other hand, the words were capable of suggesting that there were reasonable suspicions that the officers were guilty of the offences under investigation. It may still be defamatory to say of someone that they are under suspicion of malpractice. In the *Mapp* case, the claimants were allowed to amend their pleadings to refer to this lesser allegation.

Goldsmith v Bhoyrul[24]

The claimant was a founder member of a political party, the Referendum Party, which was officially fielding 550 candidates for the 1997 general election. In the run up to the election, an article appeared under the headline 'Goldsmith looks for "dignified exit" from election race'.

The article contained the following comments: 'Sir James Goldsmith has begun to pave the way for pulling his Referendum Party completely out of the general election … Goldsmith is understood to be disenchanted by the lack of popular support for the party and preparing the way for a 'dignified exit' before the deadline to declare candidates …' There was also a photograph of the claimant, under which appeared the following caption 'Goldsmith: ready to pull out of May's general election'.

The claimant alleged that the natural and ordinary meaning of the article taken as a whole included the meaning that he had lied to the electorate and/or misled them about the true intentions of the party by campaigning on the basis that the party would participate fully in the general election when in truth, they had begun to prepare themselves to withdraw from the election.

The court held that, whilst the article attributed a change of attitude on the part of the claimant, it gave reasons for the change, for example, the lack of popular support for the party. Accordingly, the reasonable reader, not being avid for scandal, would not understand the article as a charge of lying or deceit. The words were capable of less serious meanings, such as that the

---

24   *Goldsmith v Bhoyrul* [1998] QB 459.

party was not prepared to risk electoral humiliation, but these were not the meanings which had been put forward by the claimant.

More guidance on determining meaning

The item in question should be assessed *as a whole*. When assessing the meaning of an article or a programme, a claimant cannot select part to support the meanings which he alleges that the publication bears and ignore other parts which qualify or negate the defamatory meaning.

In the case of *Charleston v News Group Newspapers*,[25] the claimants were actors who played the characters 'Harold' and 'Madge' in the television series *Neighbours*. The *News of the World* published an article about a pornographic computer game in which the actors' faces had been superimposed on pornographic pictures. The article featured two photographs of the visual displays produced by the computer game under the main headline 'Strewth! What's Harold up to with our Madge?'. The text of the article, and one of the captions under the photographs, explained that the claimants were unwitting victims of the publishers of the game.

The claimants brought an action against the publishers of the *News of the World*, alleging that the photographs published by the newspaper together with the headlines and some of the captions bore the meaning that the claimants had posed for pornographic pictures. The claimants conceded that a reader who read the whole article would realise they had not posed for the pictures, but argued that a substantial number of the readers would look at the photographs and the headline without reading the text of the article.

The defendants denied that the photographs and words complained of taken in their proper context as part of the whole article were capable of bearing any meaning defamatory of the claimants.

The House of Lords held that the photographs and headline, taken in the context of the entire article, were not capable of bearing the meaning that the claimants had posed for pornographic pictures. *A prominent headline and photograph could not found a claim in defamation in isolation from the related text of the accompanying article.*

It follows that if something disreputable to a claimant is stated in one part of the item in question, but this stain is removed in another part of the same publication, the disreputable comment must be taken together with the more favourable part. In defamation law, this is known as the '*bane and antidote*'. In cases involving a 'bane and antidote', the antidote must be sufficient to counteract the bane if a defamation claim is to be avoided. Factors which might be relevant to this decision are the nature of the defamatory comment, the language of the accompanying text and the way in which the whole of the

25 *Charleston v News Group Newspapers* [1995] 2 All ER 313.

material is set out and presented. The antidote may not counteract the bane where the reasonable reader might not see the explanation. This could occur where the defamatory words appear on a prominent front page splash of a newspaper and the main article, containing the clarification or explanation is printed elsewhere in the publication.

An example of the bane and antidote in operation is the case of *Norman v Future Publishing Ltd*,[26] which concerned a profile of the opera singer, Jessye Norman, which appeared in *Classic CD* magazine. In the course of the profile, the journalist referred to Ms Norman's 'statuesque physique' and made the following observation: 'This is the woman who got trapped in swing doors on her way to a concert and, when advised to release herself by turning sideways replied: "Honey, I ain't got no sideways".'

Ms Norman brought proceedings for defamation against the magazine over the way that it had portrayed her use of language. She alleged that the natural and ordinary meaning of the article was that she had a mode of speech which was vulgar and undignified and/or conformed to a degrading racist stereotype or that she was guilty of patronising mockery of the modes of speech stereotypically associated with certain groups or classes of black Americans.

The Court of Appeal was called on to state whether the statement was capable of bearing that meaning. It held that it was not in the context of the article as a whole. The article was held to be extremely complimentary of Ms Norman, portraying her as a person of high standing and impeccable dignity (in the words of Hirst LJ, 'the very reverse of vulgar'). In the context of the article as a whole, Ms Norman's pleaded meaning was held to be too far fetched.

- The context of the publication of the defamatory words will have a bearing on the conceivable meanings that words bear. For example, where words are spoken in the course of a public meeting, their meaning might be affected by the general course of a speech of which the words formed part.[27]

- The publication should be judged through the eyes of the reasonable viewer or reader who would be likely to read/see the publication in question. For example, where the defamatory statement is made in the context of advertising or marketing, the meaning should be construed as if seen through the eyes of the reasonable reader or viewer to which the claim is addressed.[28] The construction of meaning in an advertising context is considered further in Chapter 4.

---

26 *Norman v Future Publishing Ltd* [1999] EMLR 325, CA.

27 *Bookbinder v Tebbit* [1989] 1 All ER 1169, CA.

28 *Emaco Ltd v Dyson Appliances* (1999) *The Times*, 8 February.

- The single ordinary and natural meaning is to be determined from the *item*. It is not permissible for a party to a defamation action to adduce evidence about what members of the public actually understood the publication to mean. In *Charleston v News Group Newspapers*,[29] the claimants were not allowed to produce evidence about how many *News of the World* readers had confined their attention to the photographs which purported to show Harold and Madge. The Faulks Committee Report[30] rejected a change in the law which would allow such evidence, observing that to decide otherwise would add heavily to the length and expense of trial and would only cause confusion.

When assessing the item, the expectations and reactions of reasonable fair minded readers should be kept in mind. Material will not be actionable if no one would take it seriously. For example, in the context of advertising, the reasonable reader will be presumed to be accustomed to the ways of advertisers and will generally expect a certain amount of hyperbole which they would not take seriously.[31] Similarly, 'chaff and banter'[32] are unlikely to be taken seriously; nor are items which would reasonably be understood to be humorous.

Is the natural and ordinary meaning defamatory?

Once the natural and ordinary meaning of a statement has been determined, the jury must decide whether the meaning is defamatory (a judge can rule whether a meaning is *capable of* being defamatory, but assuming that the meaning is so capable, the decision is then for the jury).

When considering whether a statement is defamatory, the statement should be considered in the context of its subject. In the *Berkoff* case, it was sufficient that the allegation that the claimant was 'hideously ugly' was defamatory of Mr Berkoff in particular because, he happened to be an actor and someone in the public eye. There was no need for the claimant to go on to show that the allegation would have been defamatory of members of the general public. Similarly, it has been held defamatory to call a beauty therapist a 'boot' (meaning, according to the claimant, an ugly harridan) because, in the claimant's case, it might affect her professional standing, because customers would not want to be attended by an ugly beautician. If the comment had been made about your average solicitor, the defamation claim would perhaps have been less likely to succeed![33]

---

29 *Charleston v News Group Newspapers* [1995] 2 All ER 313.
30 *Report of the Committee on Defamation*, Cmnd 5909, 1975, para 103.
31 *Vodafone v Orange* [1997] FSR 34 and *De Beers Abrasive Products Ltd v International General Electric Co of New York Ltd* [1975] 2 All ER 599. This point is discussed further in Chapter 4 in relation to comparative advertising.
32 Millett LJ in *Berkoff v Burchill* [1996] 4 All ER 1010, p 1018.
33 *Winyard v Tatler Publishing Co Ltd* (1991) *The Independent*, 16 August.

It is dangerous to rely on case law as a reliable precedent to determine whether a meaning is defamatory. The views of reasonable people will vary from generation to generation. In 1934, it was thought defamatory to suggest that a woman had been raped. In the case of *Youssoupoff v Metro-Goldwyn-Mayer Pictures Ltd*,[34] Slesser LJ stated: 'One may, I think, take judicial notice of the fact that a lady of whom it has been said that she has been ravished, albeit against her will, has suffered in social reputation and in opportunities of receiving respectable consideration from the world.' One would hope that such attitudes would no longer prevail in the 21st century. Reasonable members of society would hopefully not take the view that a woman's standing had been diminished because of a sexual assault.

It is the views of reasonable members of society generally which determine whether a statement is defamatory. In *Byrne v Dean*,[35] it was held that to say that a member of a golf club had informed the police about an illegal fruit machine operating in the club was not defamatory, notwithstanding that the statement lowered him in the estimation of his fellow club members. Respectable members of society would not have thought less of the claimant for bringing the matter to the attention of the police.

Hidden meanings

An item can sometimes mean something which is not apparent from a straightforward reading of the text or a viewing of the programme. This secondary meaning is known as an *innuendo*. The innuendo is dependent on knowledge of special circumstances which convey a secondary meaning which would not be conveyed to persons who do not possess the knowledge of the facts. The special facts relied on to support the innuendo must be known to at least some of the audience *at the time of publication*. A claim will not be actionable if the defamatory meaning arises from facts which became known after publication has taken place.[36]

An example of an innuendo occurred in the case of *Cassidy v Daily Mirror Newspapers Ltd*.[37] The defendants published in their newspaper a photograph of a gentleman called MC (who was a race horse owner) with a young woman. The photograph, which appeared under the headline 'Today's Gossip', was accompanied by a caption which stated 'Mr MC, the race horse owner and Miss X, whose engagement has just been announced'. There was nothing objectionable about the picture or the words. So far as the newspaper

---

34 *Youssoupoff v Metro-Goldwyn-Mayer Pictures Ltd* (1934) 50 TLR 581.
35 *Byrne v Dean* [1937] 2 All ER 204.
36 *Grappelli v Derek Block (Holdings) Ltd* [1981] 2 All ER 272.
37 *Cassidy v Daily Mirror Newspapers Ltd* [1929] 2 KB 331.

was aware, the statement about the engagement was true – MC himself had told the reporter that the newspaper could print details of the engagement.

The claimant was the wife of MC. She claimed that her reputation had been damaged by the item as several people who knew her as MC's wife understood from the article that she was not in fact his wife, but that she had been living with him in 'immoral cohabitation'.

The meaning which the claimant alleged that the article bore was not apparent from the face of the item which did not even refer to the claimant. It would only have been apparent to people with the knowledge that the claimant had been representing herself as MC's wife. The defendants were not aware that MC had a wife when they published the picture and caption. The Court of Appeal held that the item was capable of being defamatory of the claimant notwithstanding: (a) that the defendants had not known the true facts; and (b) that the defamatory meaning was only apparent to the relatively few people who knew the claimant to be MC's wife.

Pleading an innuendo

A claimant who wishes to rely on an innuendo must set out all of the facts and matters he relies on to support the innuendo meaning. The claimant may also be required to identify those members of the audience whom he alleges knew the special facts. He does not need to show that those people understood the words to bear the alleged defamatory meaning, simply to prove that they had knowledge of the facts which might have led them to have understood the words in the sense that is alleged to be defamatory.[38] It is then a question for the jury whether the words would in fact have been understood by reasonable people with the requisite knowledge to bear the meaning alleged and whether that meaning is defamatory.

Often, innuendo meanings are unintended. As in the *Cassidy* case, the defendant may not have the special knowledge which would enable it to appreciate the defamatory meaning. This can lead to injustice for the media. However, the introduction of the new unintentional defamation defence (discussed below) will, hopefully, go some way to ameliorating the position. The Court of Appeal in the *Cassidy* case felt that their judgment was just because it was the defendant's failure to check their information that had led to the error. Scrutton LJ observed: '... to publish statements first and inquire into their truth afterwards may seem attractive and up to date. Only to publish after inquiry may be slow, but at any rate, it would lead to accuracy and reliability.'[39]

---

38   *Hough v London Express Newspapers Ltd* [1940] 2 KB 507.
39   *Cassidy v Daily Mirror Newspapers Ltd* (1929) 2 KB 331, p 342.

Another form of innuendo can arise where words could be understood to bear a meaning other than their literal meaning. This issue often arises from the use of slang which has not yet entered everyday language. Where a statement would be understood in a defamatory sense by those with an appreciation of the meaning of the slang, this secondary meaning should be pleaded as an innuendo. It would then be a question for the jury whether a reasonable person with knowledge of the slang would understand the words to bear the meaning alleged and, if so, whether that meaning is defamatory.

The claimant's burden of proof in defamation actions

One of the reasons why the threat of defamation claims weighs so heavily on media defendants is that the burden of proof in a defamation action is very much weighted in the claimant's favour. The claimant has only to prove the following:

- the matter complained of is defamatory (essentially, a tendency to cause damage to the claimant's reputation must be shown); and
- the matter would be understood to refer to the claimant; and
- the matter has been published to a third person.

Where the action is for slander, the claimant will also have to prove that the allegation has actually caused damage (subject to certain exceptions). In other types of defamation cases, a claimant need only show a tendency to cause damage. Damage will be presumed without the need for the claimant to adduce evidence. The distinction between libel and slander is considered below.

The law presumes in the claimant's favour that the words are untrue unless and until the defendant proves to the contrary. We shall see below that if the defendant attempts unsuccessfully to prove that the words are true, it is likely to increase the amount of damages payable to the claimant.

We have considered the law relating to the defamatory meaning above. The second and third factors which the claimant must prove to establish both libel and slander will now be discussed.

Identification

The claimant must show that the material which is the subject of the defamation claim would have been understood to refer to him. Where the claimant is identified, this will be a straightforward matter. But material is capable of being understood to refer to the claimant, even where the claimant is not named or even referred to expressly. As with meaning, the intention of the publisher is irrelevant.[40] The test is *whether reasonable members of the audience would understand the item to refer to the claimant*. Merely refraining from identifying the subject matter of a statement by name is not, therefore, an effective safeguard against defamation claims.

Identification may be dependent on special knowledge about the claimant which may only be known to a few people. It will be for the claimant to show that at least some of the audience had that special knowledge which would enable them to appreciate that the article refers to the claimant. It is then a question for the jury to decide whether a reasonable reader or viewer with the requisite knowledge would have understood the article to refer to the claimant. It is immaterial to the issue of liability that only a small number of readers or viewers have the knowledge which enables them to identify the claimant.[41]

Identification and groups of people

Where a defamatory statement is made about a class or group of persons without naming a particular individual, the test to determine whether a member of the class or group can bring proceedings for defamation was laid down by the House of lords in *Knupffer v London Express Newspaper Ltd*.[42] The test is '*are the words such as would reasonably lead persons acquainted with the claimant to believe that he was the person referred to?*'.

There is nothing to stop a statement about a group or class of people being actionable, provided that the words would reasonably be understood to refer to each member of the group. In practice, a statement about a large group of people is generally not actionable, because of the difficulties of establishing that the claimant was, in fact, included in the defamatory statement. To say that all lawyers are thieves is unlikely to be actionable by any particular lawyer, unless there is something to point to him particularly.[43] But to say that all of the lawyers in the media department of a particular firm are incompetent might well be actionable. It is more likely that the statement would be understood by the reasonable reader or viewer to refer to a particular individual. Factors which may be relevant are the size of the class, the generality of the charge and the extravagance of the accusation.

The *Knupffer* case concerned an article about a pro-Hitler movement of Russian *émigrés* which was allegedly trying to infiltrate the USSR in the early 1940s. The group was described in the article in sketchy terms as being 'established in France and the US' with secret agents able to enter and leave

---

40   *Hulton v Jones* [1910] AC 20.

41   Although the extent of knowledge may be relevant to the amount of damages which the defendant is ordered to pay.

42   *Knupffer v London Express Newspaper Ltd* [1944] AC 116.

43   *Eastwood v Holmes* (1858) 1 F&F 347, p 349.

the USSR at will. The claimant was a Russian resident in London. He brought an action in defamation, alleging that the article would reasonably be understood to refer to him. The House of Lords unanimously held that it would not. The size of the class of Russian émigrés was too broad.

Unintended identification

Sometimes, a person can be mistakenly identified as the subject of a defamatory statement. The fact that the defendant did not intend to refer to the particular claimant will not prevent a claim being brought. The test is whether reasonable people would believe that the statement referred to the claimant. In the case of *Hulton v Jones*,[44] the defendants published defamatory statements in an article about a fictitious person, which it called 'Artemus Jones'. The name chosen by the defendants happened to be the name of the claimant. The claimant brought proceedings for defamation, alleging that certain of his acquaintances believed that the article referred to him. The House of Lords held that the correct approach was to decide whether sensible and reasonable people reading the article would think that it concerned a real or an imaginary person. If they would think that the character was imaginary, the words were not actionable. If the reasonable and sensible readers who knew the claimant would suppose the article to concern a real person who was the claimant, the action would be maintainable.

On the basis of the court's approach in the *Hulton v Jones* case, most cases where the name of a real person is used in a fictional work would not be actionable in defamation. The reasonable and sensible reader or viewer would appreciate that the work is fictional and that the material did not concern a real person. To underline this belief, publishers and programme and film makers often include a statement that all characters are fictional and that any references to individuals is unintentional.

Identification by association

Where someone is identified in an article or programme, the identification could also infer a reference to some other person by association. The *Cassidy* case is an example of this.[45] The claimant could be identified by association with her husband. In that case, Scrutton LJ stated 'I think it is clear that words published about A may indirectly be defamatory of B. For instance "A is illegitimate". To persons who know A's parents those words may be defamatory of A's parents'.[46] This would be the case even though A's parents were not named.

---

44 *Hulton v Jones* [1910] AC 20.
45 *Cassidy v Daily Mirror Newspapers Ltd* (1929) 2 KB 331.
46 *Ibid*, p 338.

Publication

The claimant also has to prove that the defamatory material has been communicated to a third party. Publication is not actionable if the material is only communicated to the claimant. There must be publication to at least one other person. The concept of publication is not confined to a publication to the general public. A private letter which A writes to B, containing a defamatory statement about C, would be an actionable publication. Nor does the publication have to be in a permanent form. A could tell B about C, and A's oral remarks could be an actionable publication. In most cases involving the media, the publication will generally be a communication to or accessible by the general public. An actionable publication can also take place on the internet either by transmission by e-mail, publication on a website or the posting of defamatory material on a bulletin board or a usenet newsgroup. Publication on the internet is discussed further below.

Each publication of the defamatory material gives rise to a separate cause of action. Every copy of a newspaper or book or every broadcast of an item is a separate publication giving rise to its own cause of action.

Libel and slander

The law draws a distinction between a publication in a permanent form (a libel) and publication in a non-permanent form (a slander). Spoken words will generally be slander, whilst written words will be libel. Section 166 of the Broadcasting Act 1990 provides that publication of words during a broadcast programme on television or radio, whether to the general public or not, is to be classed as libel. Similarly, the Theatres Act 1968 provides that words spoken during the performance of a play should also be treated as libel.

The distinction between libel and slander is important in the context of what a claimant must prove to succeed in its claim. Libels are actionable *per se* without the need to prove that damage has actually been caused by the publication. The law presumes that a libel has caused damage to its subject.

Slander generally requires the claimant to prove that damage has been suffered. There are exceptions to this rule where the slander concerns one of four types of subject matter, namely:

- the imputation of a crime punishable by imprisonment;
- the imputation of certain types of diseases which are likely to deter persons from associating with the claimant (for example, venereal diseases);
- disparagement of the claimant in his profession, trade or business;
- an imputation of unchastity in a woman.

In each of the above cases, the slander will be actionable without proof of actual damage.

Who may sue for defamation?

Any living person may bring proceedings for defamation.

Dead people

Under civil law, the estates of dead people cannot commence proceedings, no matter how untrue or defamatory a statement may be.[47] The reputation of a dead person is deemed to die with him. The Faulks Committee was of the opinion that the law does not adequately take into account the interests of the public and near relatives of the deceased in protecting a deceased's reputation from unjustified damage. It recommended that a new cause of action should be introduced, exercisable by the estate of the deceased. The remedies available for this cause of action would include a declaration that the statement was defamatory and an injunction to restrain further publication. It would not include damages. The proposed cause of action would have a limitation period of five years of death. The recommendation was never adopted.

Trading corporations

A trading corporation has a reputation separate from that of its members, directors or employees. It is entitled to sue in the same way as individual claimants. However, care should be taken to ensure that it is the *corporation's* reputation which is actually affected. The defamatory comment must reflect on the corporation itself[48] before the corporation can properly bring proceedings. A corporation cannot sue over what is in reality an attack on its officers or employees.

Although corporations can bring proceedings for defamation, the heads under which they can recover damages are narrower than for individuals. Corporations cannot recover damages for distress or hurt feelings. These can make up a substantial part of an individual claimant's damages. On the other hand, a company may be able to obtain compensation for damage to its goodwill in appropriate circumstances.[49]

---

47 It would seem that a prosecution for criminal libel might be brought in respect of allegations about a dead person. Criminal libel is considered at the end of this chapter.

48 *Derbyshire CC v Times Newspapers Ltd* [1993] AC 534; [1993] 1 All ER 1011.

49 *Per* Lord Reid in *Lewis v Daily Telegraph* [1964] AC 234, p 262.

Non-trading corporations

Non-trading corporations may also bring proceedings for defamation, at least over allegations which damage its 'business' activities or standing. A trade union may successfully bring proceedings over statements which adversely affect its ability to keep members.[50] Similarly, a charity may sue where the effect of the statement is to impede its ability to carry out its charitable objects.[51]

Organisations which may not bring proceedings for defamation

There are certain types of organisation which *cannot* bring proceedings for defamation. Currently these are as follows:

- government bodies;[52]
- local authorities;[53]
- political parties;[54]
- nationalised industries.[55]

The categories of organisation which are not permitted to bring a claim in defamation are not closed.

The reasoning behind these prohibitions from bringing actions is the public interest which the court has found to exist in the uninhibited public criticism of bodies which put themselves forward for office or who are democratically elected to govern or responsible for public administration. As Lord Bridge has observed:

> In a free democratic society, it is almost too obvious to need stating that those who hold office in Government and who are responsible for public administration must always be open to criticism. Any attempt to stifle or fetter such criticism amounts to political censorship of the most insidious and objectionable kind.[56]

As we saw in Chapter 1, the same sentiments have been articulated by the European Court of Human Rights in relation to Art 10 (freedom of expression).

An unsuccessful attempt to widen the categories of prohibited claimants occurred in the well known litigation which McDonald's Restaurants

---

50 *National Union of General and Municipal Workers v Gillan* [1945] 2 All ER 593.
51 Lord Keith in *Derbyshire CC v Times Newspapers Ltd* [1993] AC 534.
52 *Derbyshire CC v Times Newspapers Ltd* [1993] AC 534.
53 *Ibid.*
54 *Goldsmith v Bhoyrul* [1998] QB 459.
55 *British Coal Corpn v National Union of Mineworkers* (1996) unreported.
56 *Hector v AG of Antigua and Barbuda* [1990] 2 All ER 103, p 106.

commenced against London Greenpeace activists Helen Steele and Dave Morris. Steele and Morris argued that multinational commercial corporations such as McDonald's should not be permitted to sue for defamation. Their argument was that multinational corporations have such an effect on the lives of people around the world that the public interest strongly favours the ability for people to make unfettered criticism of their actions.[57] The Court of Appeal lost no time in rejecting their argument.[58] It pointed out that the basis on which it was decided that a local authority could not maintain an action for libel did not apply to commercial corporations, however large, which were constitutionally in a different position. It was not open to the court, as opposed to Parliament, to invent a category of commercial corporation which should not be able to maintain an action for defamation.

The courts have stressed that organisations which are prohibited from suing in the civil courts retain the right to bring a private prosecution for criminal libel (considered below). They can also bring proceedings for malicious falsehood, provided that they can prove the necessary elements of that cause of action.[59] Although the decision that public bodies retain these rights may be open to challenge under the Human Rights Act 1998 on the ground that they are limitations on freedom of expression which are unnecessary in a democratic society. For the time being at least, it is not the case that the media have complete freedom to criticise public bodies, especially where the criticism is made without positive belief in the truth of what is stated.

The prohibition is on organisations, rather than individuals

Significantly, where a defamatory comment about a prohibited organisation such as a local authority identifies an individual member of the above organisations, it *remains open* for the individual to bring a civil claim in defamation.

In *Derbyshire CC v Times Newspapers Ltd*, the Court of Appeal declined to extend the prohibition on defamation claims to individual members of the claimant county council – a conclusion confirmed by the House of Lords. Butler-Sloss LJ referred to the retention of the right for the individual to sue in defamation as 'a valuable, although indirect, additional protection for the local authority'.[60]

---

57 See John Vidal's book on the *McDonald's* case, *McLibel*, 1997, Macmillan, for a more eloquent version of the argument.

58 *McDonald's v Steel and Morris* (1999) unreported.

59 *Derbyshire CC v Times Newspapers Ltd* [1993] AC 534.

60 [1992] 3 All ER 65, p 96.

The efficacy of the objective of facilitating unfettered public criticism of government and local authority activities must be open to doubt where the individual members of government retain the right to sue in defamation.[61] Although a local authority has a reputation distinct from that of its councillors and officials, a slur on the local authority is invariably capable of being understood as a slur on the officials concerned. The *Derbyshire* case concerned articles in *The Times*, questioning the propriety of certain investments which the council had made for its superannuation fund. Defamation proceedings were brought by the local authority and by the councillor responsible for the investment. Whilst the local authority could not maintain its action, the councillor could.

The public interest in unfettered public discussion of governmental activities would have been better served if the individual members of the bodies in question were also prohibited from bringing civil claims for defamation in respect of defamatory comments made about their performance in office. The individuals would still be able to bring civil proceedings for defamation in respect of allegations made about their personal life which could not have a bearing their professional role.[62]

Another alternative open to the courts would be to allow officials to bring civil defamation proceedings for comments made about their official roles and duties only in cases where the individual claimant can show that the claim would be in the public interest. This approach is akin to breach of confidence cases which are brought by the Crown.[63] The Crown has to demonstrate as part of its positive case that it is in the public interest that the confidentiality of the material in question be preserved. On this approach, a would-be defamation claimant would have to show that it is in the public interest that it sues in defamation about disparaging comments about his performance in office. In the light of the comments in the *Derbyshire* case about the public interest in uninhibited criticism, he would face an uphill struggle in doing so.

The recent House of Lords decision in *Reynolds v Sunday Times*[64] has confirmed that the defence of qualified privilege may extend to publication of defamatory allegations which are in the public interest. Allegations about an official's performance in office may very well be in the public interest. Although a public official is not debarred from bringing a claim in defamation for such allegations, the media will have the benefit of the qualified privilege defence, provided that it acted responsibly when publishing the allegations.[65]

61 For further detail, see Barendt, E, 'Libel and freedom of speech in English law' [1993] PL 449.

62 This is in line with the jurisprudence at the European Court of Human Rights as discussed in Chapter 1.

63 *AG v Jonathan Cape* [1976] QB 752.

64 *Reynolds v Sunday Times* [1999] 4 All ER 609.

65 Qualified privilege is discussed below.

Who may be sued?

The claimant has a cause of action against anyone who is involved in the publication of the defamatory material, even if they had no direct responsibility for or editorial control over the contents of the publication. At common law, liability is strict. There is an actionable publication even where the publisher was not aware that a publication contained defamatory material. In the case of a newspaper or periodical, proceedings can therefore be brought against the following parties:

- the person who made the defamatory comments in the article, say in an interview;
- the journalist who wrote the item containing the comments (even though he did not originate them);
- the editor of the publication;
- the publishers of the publication;
- the printers who printed the publication;
- the distributors of the publication;
- the retailers who sell the publication.

The commencement of or the threat of proceedings against parties with no direct control over content, such as retailers or distributors, has often been the most effective option available to a claimant for getting a publication containing defamatory material off the shelves. Retailers are unlikely to want the nuisance value of a defamation claim against them. They are unlikely to have involvement in the content of the allegations or any personal motives for defending the claim. From their commercial viewpoint, it will often be more efficient to accede to a claimant's request that the publication be withdrawn from sale than to defend the case on its merits. They are also more likely to have deeper pockets than the publication in question and so more likely to be able to pay substantial damages and costs. This was particularly the case before the introduction of the innocent dissemination defence contained in the Defamation Act 1996 (discussed below), which now provides a defence for parties with no editorial responsibility where they can show that they took reasonable care in relation to the publication.

The position of internet service providers

In the case of *Godfrey v Demon Internet Ltd*,[66] the court had to consider the position of the defendant internet service provider (ISP) which provided usenet facilities to its customers. The defendant carried a usenet newsgroup.

---

66 *Godfrey v Demon Internet Ltd* [1999] EMLR 542.

This is a system by which postings (or articles) are sent by internet users to particular forums. Such a posting is readable anywhere in the world by an internet user whose ISP offers access to the newsgroup in question. As part of its service, the defendant stored postings within the newsgroup which were then available to be accessed by its customers. Someone unknown made a posting to the defendants' news server. The posting purported to come from the claimant, but it was actually a forgery. The posting was described by the court as 'squalid, obscene and defamatory' of the claimant.

The court held that an ISP such as the defendant was in the same position as a bookseller who sells a book defamatory of the claimant. Whenever there is transmitted from the storage of their news server a defamatory posting, they publish that posting to any of their subscribers who accesses the newsgroup containing that posting. Demon subsequently settled the action, reportedly agreeing to pay £15,000 damages and £230,000 costs.[67]

The defence of innocent publication

The Defamation Act 1996 introduced a statutory defence to a defamation claim for parties who, although they are technically publishers, do not have primary responsibility for the content of what they publish. Section 1 of the Defamation Act 1996 provides the defence for such parties provided that the party can prove that it: (a) took reasonable care in relation to the publication; *and* (b) did not know or had no reason to believe that it caused or contributed to the publication of a defamatory statement. Note that these criteria are not alternatives. They must both be proved. The defendant must take reasonable care and have no reason to believe. The onus is on the defendant to prove that it meets these conditions. We will look at the provisions of the section in more detail.

Primary responsibility

The defence is *not* available to the author, editor or commercial publisher of the statement complained of or their employees or agents to the extent that the employees or agents are responsible for the content of the statement or the decision to publish it. Authors, editors and commercial publishers are assumed to have primary responsibility for content (s 1(1)(a)).

For the purposes of the defence:

- *author* means the originator of the statement, but does not include a person who did not intend the statement to be published at all. If there were no

67 (2000) Law Soc Gazette, 20 April.

intention for the statement to be published, it would seem that an author could still rely on this defence (s 1(2));

- *editor* means a person having editorial or equivalent responsibility for the content of a statement or the decision to publish it (s 1(2));

- *publisher* means a commercial publisher whose business is issuing material to the public or a section of the public, who issues material containing the statement in the course of that business (s 1(2)).

The defence *will* be available to parties whose involvement is restricted to the following activities, or activities which are analogous to them in relation to the defamatory material:[68]

- printing;
- producing;
- distributing; or
- selling,

the material containing the defamatory statement.

Where the defamatory material is a film or sound recording, the defence will be available to those involved in:

- processing;
- making copies of;
- distributing;
- exhibiting; or
- selling,

the film or sound recording containing the statement.

A person involved in processing, making copies of, distributing or selling any electronic medium in or on which a statement is recorded, or in operating any equipment or system or service by means of which the statement is retrieved, copied, distributed or made available in electronic form, will not be considered the author, editor or publisher if that is the only extent of his involvement.

The broadcaster of a live programme will not be liable in respect of the broadcast of a defamatory statement in circumstances in which it has no effective control over the maker of the statement.

An ISP, or other provider or operator of a communications system by means of which the defamatory statement is transmitted or made available, will not be liable for the statement, provided it is made by a person over which it has no effective control.

---

68   Defamation Act 1996, s 1(3).

The court can extend the above situations by analogy in a case which does not fall within the above provisions. The crux is essentially whether the defendant has responsibility for content or the decision to publish.

Reasonable care and reason to believe (s 1(5))

In determining whether a person without primary responsibility took reasonable care or had no reason to believe that what he did caused or contributed to the publication of a defamatory statement, regard should be had to the following:

- the extent of that person's responsibility for the content of the statement or the decision to publish it;
- the nature or circumstances of the publication; and
- the previous conduct or character of the author, editor or publisher (if the publication in question is notorious for its involvement in defamation actions, presumably the defendant will be expected to be more vigilant in checking for defamatory material than in the case of more innocuous publications).

There has been little case law interpreting this section. In *Godfrey v Demon Internet Ltd*[69] the defendant ISP relied on the s 1 defence in relation to its provision of a usenet newsgroup on which a defamatory statement had been posted. The court held that, because the claimant had given the defendant notice that he considered the posting to be defamatory and had requested its removal from the usenet news server, the innocent dissemination defence had not been made out in relation to the period after notice had been given.

The court adopted the following approach:

- was the defendant an author, editor or commercial publisher for the purposes of s 1(2)? On the facts, the defendant was not an author, editor or commercial publisher for the purposes of the Act;
- the court should then consider whether the defendant had taken reasonable care in relation to the publication *and* whether it did not know, and had no reason to believe that what it did caused or contributed to the publication of the defamatory statement. On the facts, the judge thought that the defendants were 'in an insuperable difficulty' in meeting these criteria once they knew of the defamatory posting, having been put on notice by the claimant, and yet neglected to move it from their news server. So great was this difficulty that the judge felt able to strike out the innocent dissemination defence on the ground that it disclosed no sustainable defence. He described it as 'hopeless'.

---

69 *Godfrey v Demon Internet Ltd* [1999] EMLR 542.

The *Godfrey* case concerned a statement which was obviously defamatory. The judge was clearly of the view that having been put on notice by the claimant, the statement should have been removed. The case leaves open what the position would be where it is not so clear that a statement is defamatory. Should the service provider or other defendant remove such a statement simply because the claimant has asked it to, or is it entitled to form its own view about whether the statement is defamatory? Does the claimant have to provide a full complaint about the statement or is an unsupported complaint sufficient to give the defendant reason to believe that it has caused or contributed to a defamatory statement? These issues are still to be clarified.

Another area requiring clarification in relation to reasonable care is the extent to which a party with no direct editorial control is required to monitor the material with which it is involved for defamatory content. There is a draft EC directive concerning electronic commerce which provides that ISPs are not obliged to monitor their services for unlawful content.[70] Once in force, the directive will help to clarify the position in so far as service providers on the internet are concerned. The Defamation Act 1996 tells us that one of the factors which is relevant to the availability of the innocent publication defence is the nature or circumstances of the publication. Presumably, a busy printing company or large retailer which handles a large quantity of material would not be expected to monitor each publication. The position might be different for bodies such as ISPs which store postings sent in by others. Are they expected to monitor the postings for defamatory material? If they do provide a monitoring service, are they more or less likely to be found to lack reasonable care if that service misses a defamatory posting? We will need further cases before these matters are clarified.

A further example of the operation of the innocent publications defence occurred recently in litigation commenced by the opinion poll organisation MORI against the BBC. The action concerned allegations which Sir James Goldsmith made about MORI during a live radio broadcast. The BBC relied on a defence under s 1 of the Defamation Act. MORI sought to show that the BBC had not taken reasonable care in relation to the broadcast. It should have realised that Sir James Goldsmith was prone to making controversial remarks and should not have interviewed him without a delay device, which would enable the deletion of controversial material before it was transmitted. The action settled whilst the trial was taking place. It is accordingly unclear whether the BBC could have escaped liability by relying on the s 1 defence.

---

70   COM (1998) 586 2000/C 128/02, Art 15.

Defamation and limitation

The limitation period for defamation actions is one year from the date of publication. If proceedings are not commenced within this period, limitation may be raised by the defendant as a defence to the proceedings. Section 5(4) of the Defamation Act 1996 allows the court discretion to extend the period where equitable to do so, having regard to the degree to which the claimant will be prejudiced by not being able to bring an action and the degree to which the defendant will be prejudiced if the claimant is allowed to bring the action.[71]

OTHER DEFENCES TO DEFAMATION CLAIMS

The Faulks Committee identified defamation law as having two basic purposes. The first is protection of reputation. The second is the preservation of the right to free speech. It observed that the two purposes necessarily conflict, but that the law was sound if it preserves a proper balance between them.[72] That balance arises from the existence of a number of defences to defamation claims which are intended to protect in appropriate circumstances a defendant's right to express what he wishes at the expense of a claimant's reputation. The question whether the balance comes down fairly in the interests of freedom of expression is an issue which will considered in this chapter. The defences at issue are examined below.

Defences involving proof of truth: justification and fair comment

It has to be remembered that the defences of justification and fair comment form part of the framework by which free speech is protected. It is therefore important that no unnecessary barriers to the use of these defences are erected.[73]

Justification: statements of fact

Where a statement of fact is defamatory, there will be a complete defence to the claim if the defendant can prove on the balance of probabilities that the natural and ordinary meaning of the statement, or the gist of it, is true. The defence is known as *justification*. Note that the onus of proof is on the

---

71 The court has considered the operation of s 5(4) in *Hinks v Hinks* (2000) and *Smith v Probyn* (2000) unreported.

72 Faulks Committee, *Report of the Committee on Defamation*, Cmnd 5909, 1975, para 19.

73 Neill LJ in *McDonald's v Steel and Morris* (1999) unreported.

defendant. *The law will presume that the statement is false, unless the defendant can prove otherwise.* The defendant does not have to prove the truth of every last detail of its statement, but the substance of it must be proved.

The defendant must prove the truth of the statement using admissible evidence. Often, defendants struggle to do so, even if their statement was thoroughly researched and verified before it was made. For example, interviewees who were quite happy to help a journalist with his investigations may get cold feet about appearing in court to give evidence. It is not unusual for defences to collapse in these circumstances. A defendant who pleads justification invariably faces an uphill struggle. As Lord Keith recognised in *Derbyshire CC v Times Newspapers Ltd*:[74]

> Quite often the facts which would justify a defamatory publication are known to be true, but admissible evidence capable of proving those facts is not available. This may prevent the publication of matters which it is very desirable to make public.

Defamation trials are not public inquiries. They are rarely the most appropriate for arriving at 'the truth'. They are civil trials to be played by the rules of litigation. The defendant bears the burden of proving that a statement is true. The claimant will seek to undermine its opponents' position by use of the means available to it. These will include rigorous cross-examination, objection to the admissibility of evidence and the taking of procedural and technical points of procedure and pleading.

The general rule is that, before making a plea of justification, the defendant should believe his words to be true and to intend to prove them at trial. There should also be reasonable evidence to support a plea of justification or reasonable grounds for supposing that sufficient evidence to prove the allegations will be available at the trial.

The defendant is entitled to make use of all sources of material available to him in order to support a plea of justification. This will include not only the sources available at the time that the statement is made, but also sources which may become available as part of the litigation process, including evidence which the claimant may give during cross-examination or documents which are obtained from the claimant during the disclosure and inspection process.[75]

The standard of proof

The defendant generally has to prove the truth of the substance of its allegations on the balance of probabilities. In *Irving v Penguin Books*,[76] Gray J

---

74 *Derbyshire CC v Times Newspapers Ltd* [1993] AC 534; [1993] 1 All ER 1011.
75 *McDonald's v Steel and Morris* (1999) unreported. The judgment in this case applies equally towards facts which are relied on in support of a plea of fair comment.
76 *Irving v Penguin Books* (2000) unreported, 11 April.

accepted that, where the defendant's allegations are of a serious nature (such as, on the facts of the *Irving* case, the assertion that the claimant, Mr Irving, had deliberately falsified historical evidence), the standard of proof should be commensurately higher to reflect that seriousness.

What must be justified?

The meaning which has to be justified is the natural and ordinary meaning which the jury attributes to the statement. As we have seen, this meaning may not be what the maker of the statement intended the statement to mean. There may also be innuendo meanings and inferences arising from the statement which the defendant did not appreciate, but which will have to be justified if the action is to be defended successfully by a plea of justification. As part of this process, the defendant may seek to justify the meaning which he thinks that the words have,[77] which may be different to the meaning which the claimant seeks to place on the words. As we have seen, the final decision about what the words mean will be for the jury, who will then determine whether the defendant has justified that meaning.

Rumours and hearsay

Where the statement in question purports to repeat a statement made by a third party or to report on rumours and gossip, there is a well established rule that it is not sufficient to prove that the rumour is in circulation or that the third party did in fact make the statement in question. This rule is known as 'the repetition rule'.[78]

Example 1

If you publish a statement that Y said that X is guilty of a criminal offence, it is not a defence to an action to establish that literal proof. By making the statement, the writer is taken to repeat and endorse what Y said, as Lord Reid has observed: '... repeating someone else's libellous statement is just as bad as making the statement directly.'[79] Your defence of justification must address the substance of what Y said and not just the fact that he said it.[80]

Example 2

X makes a television documentary concerning rumours in common circulation that Mr Grey, a well known politician, is having an affair with his cook. X is

---

77 See, eg, *Lucas Box v News Group Newspapers* [1986] 1 All ER 177; [1986] 1 WLR 147.
78 See *Stern v Piper* [1997] QB 123; [1996] 3 All ER 385; [1996] 3 WLR 715, for a consideration of the history and merits of the rule.
79 *Lewis v Daily Telegraph* [1964] AC 234, p 260.
80 *Per* May LJ in *Shah v Standard Chartered Bank* [1998] EMLR 597, p 623.

careful to make clear that he is reporting on rumours and that he is not purporting to allege that the rumours are true. Mr Grey brings proceedings for libel, alleging that the natural and ordinary meaning of the programme was that he was having an affair. X will have to prove that the rumours are true in order to succeed in his defence. It will not be sufficient for him to show that the rumours are in fact circulating.

Proving the defamatory 'sting'

It is not necessary to prove that every single factual allegation is true, provided that the overall defamatory impact can be proved to be true. This overall impact is known as the defamatory 'sting'.

Section 5 of the Defamation Act 1952 provides that, where an action for defamation concerns two or more distinct charges against the claimant, a defence for justification will not fail by reason only that the truth of every charge is not proved if the words which are not proved to be true do not materially injure the claimant's reputation, having regard to the truth of the remaining charges.

Adducing evidence of the same type of conduct to support a claim in justification

It will sometimes suit the defendant's purpose to allege that an item which makes specific allegations bears a natural and ordinary meaning which goes beyond the specific allegation. The wider the meaning, the greater the scope for particulars of justification. Take, for example, the case of *Williams v Reason*.[81] The claimant was an international amateur rugby player who sued for defamation over allegations in a newspaper that he was a 'shamateur', that is, that he was abusing his amateur status by writing a book for money whilst he was still playing amateur rugby. The claimant alleged that the words bore the specific defamatory meaning concerning his book.

The defendants contended that the natural and ordinary meaning of the article was wider. It was making a general charge of 'shamateurism' against the rugby player, of which the book was one instance. It suited its purpose to do so because, if the meaning was the general charge, it could adduce evidence to support its plea in justification which went beyond the book. In fact, the defendants wanted to adduce evidence relating to payments which the defendants alleged that the claimant had accepted from a sports equipment manufacturer for wearing their rugby boots. The acceptance of boot money had not been mentioned in the article. This evidence was relevant

---

81   *Williams v Reason* [1988] 1 All ER 262, CA.

on an overall charge of shamateurism, but not to the specific allegation in the article.

The court held that a defendant was not entitled to rely on a general charge of wrongdoing, unless a wider meaning or a more general charge could fairly be gathered from the words used in the article. A defendant who has made a specific claim ought not to be allowed to justify that claim by reference to other alleged examples of conduct of the same type merely because they relate to the same kind of wrongdoing of which a specific charge has been made. However, where the words could reasonably be understood in the wider sense as making a general charge, the defendant could adduce the evidence. On the facts of the *Williams* case, the court held that the article was reasonably capable of being understood as making a general charge of shamateurism and the defendants were permitted to call evidence about the boot money to justify that general charge.[82]

Separate allegations and evidence of justification

Subject to the above point, where a defendant has published two distinct libels about a claimant, the law permits the claimant to decide which of the libels it wishes to sue over. The claimant can complain about one of the libels and, if it does so, the defendant is not then permitted to justify the libel about which complaint is made by proving the truth of the other libel. For this rule to apply, the libels must be distinctly severable into separate parts. If they are not, the claimant cannot pick and choose between them.[83] This will be a question of fact and degree in every case. Where the separate and distinct libels have a common sting, they ought not to be regarded as separate and distinct allegations. The defendant is entitled to justify the overall sting.[84]

Special rules about references to previous convictions

The fact that a person has been convicted of a criminal offence is deemed to be conclusive proof that he committed the offence and the conviction can be admitted in evidence as proof of that fact.[85]

The Rehabilitation of Offenders Act 1974 provides that certain criminal convictions become spent after a specified period of time. Once a conviction is 'spent', it is treated for most purposes as if it never occurred, the rationale being that a person ought not to be haunted by his past where the conviction was an isolated incident for a relatively minor offence. The Act applies to convictions which have resulted in custodial sentences not exceeding

---

82 See, also, *Bookbinder v Tebbit* [1989] 1 All ER 1169, CA.

83 *Polly Peck (Holdings) v Trelford* [1986] 2 All ER 84.

84 *Cruise v Express Newspapers plc* [1999] QB 931, CA.

85 Civil Evidence Act 1968, s 13(1).

30 months. The applicable rehabilitation period will vary according to the nature of the offence in question.

Where the media make a statement imputing that the claimant has committed or been charged with or prosecuted for or convicted of an offence which is the subject of a spent conviction, the media may make a plea of justification, referring to the spent conviction, and to adduce evidence of the spent conviction in court.[86] This is subject to the exception set out below.

Exception

Where the claimant can prove that the defendant was actuated by malice when it made the statement, the defendant will *not* be able to rely on the spent conviction.[87] The legal meaning of malice is considered below.

Fair comment: statements of opinion – 'the critic's most valuable defence'

Distinguishing comment from fact

The defence of justification applies to the assertion of facts. Where the defamatory statement is a comment or an expression of opinion, the defence of fair comment may be relevant.

It is sometimes difficult to draw the distinction between an expression of opinion on the one hand (for which the defence of fair comment will be relevant) and an assertion of fact on the other (for which the defence of justification will be relevant). The test as to what is opinion and what is fact is objective – what would ordinary readers or viewers think? The intention of the publisher is irrelevant. The onus is on the originator of the comment to ensure that it is identifiable as comment. The writer or broadcaster must make clear that he is expressing opinion and not making factual statements about the subject matter on which he is commenting. The use of phrases such as 'it seems to me' or 'in our view' will help to establish this, although they will not be conclusive. The decision will depend on a consideration of the words used, taken in their context and the circumstances of publication. It must be clear from the *face of the item* that the comment or opinion *is* comment or opinion, rather than an assertion of fact.

Where it is not possible to make the distinction, the statement will be presumed to be factual.

---

86 Rehabilitation of Offenders Act 1974, s 8(3).
87 *Ibid*, s 8(5).

Context

The context in which a statement is made is often important in determining whether it is comment or a factual assertion. But consideration of the context in which the statement is made must be confined to the consideration of the document or item in which the comment was actually made.[88] For example, where a statement is contained in a letter, the court is entitled to look at the letter as a whole to determine whether it is comment or fact. *However, the context cannot be considered beyond the document in which the statement is made.* Where a letter was written in response to an earlier article, the court was not permitted to determine the status of the contents by reference to the earlier article.[89] The court observed that the editor responsible should have insisted that the letter in response set out the matters on which it was commenting, to make it clear that it contained comment and not factual assertion.

The facts on which comment is based

In order for a statement to be recognised as comment, it is often necessary to set out or at least to refer to the facts, or some of them, on which the comment is based.

Example

The statement that 'solicitor A is incompetent' is a statement of fact.

However, if the statement is recast to read 'Solicitor A has been found liable for professional negligence on four occasions in the last three years and he must therefore be judged to be incompetent', the allegation of incompetence would be understood as a comment based on the facts of the solicitor's liability in negligence.

In the former case, if I were to defend my statement I would have to prove that my factual assertion of incompetence is true (justification). In the second case, I could rely on the less onerous defence of fair comment.

The facts must be set out in sufficient detail that my assertion of incompetence is capable of being understood as comment by the reasonable reader or viewer. But it is not always necessary to set out all the facts on which the publisher relies in relation to his comment. This will be a question of fact in every case. Where the subject of the comment is already before the public, for example, a book or a play, it may not be necessary to set out any of the facts on which the comment is made provided that the subject matter of the comment is plainly identified in the article. In the case of *Kemsley v Foot*,[90] the

---

88   *Telnikoff v Matusevitch* [1991] 4 All ER 817, HL.
89   *Ibid.*
90   *Kemsley v Foot* [1951] 2 KB 34, CA; [1951] 1 All ER 331.

comment concerned a criticism of the defendant's newspapers. The criticism did not set out any of the facts on which it was based, although the subject of the comment (that is, the newspapers) was identified. The court held that, given that the defendant's newspapers were before the public, there was no need to set out any supporting facts in order for the statement to be understood as comment.

The requirements of the fair comment defence

Fair comment has been defined as 'the right of the citizen honestly to express his genuine opinion on a matter of public interest, however wrong or exaggerated or prejudiced that opinion may be'.[91] The requirements of the defence of fair comment are less onerous than the defence of justification. The reason for this is the recognition by the courts that freedom to hold an opinion is important in a democratic society. As Diplock J observed in *Silkin v Beaverbrook Newspapers Ltd*:[92]

> Freedom of speech ... is freedom under the law and, over the years, the law has maintained a balance between the right of the individual ... to his unsullied reputation if he deserves it. This is on the one hand. On the other hand, but equally important, is the right of the public which means you and me, and the newspaper editor and the man who, but for the bus strike, would be on the Clapham omnibus, to express his views honestly and fearlessly on matters of public interest, even though this involves strong criticism of the conduct of public people.

This distinction between facts and comments can also be seen in the jurisprudence of the European Court of Human Rights. In the case of *Lingens v UK*,[93] the court emphasised the difference between facts and value judgments. The essence of facts can be demonstrated, but the truth of value judgments is not so susceptible to proof.

The law therefore permits criticism and comment on matters in the public interest provided that the comment is fair. The limits of the defence are wide.

In order to establish the fair comment defence, it must be shown that:

(a) the comment or opinion was:

- based on facts; and
- those facts are true (essentially, the same criteria in relation to those facts as we have seen in relation to justification); and

(b) that the opinion or comment is honest; and

(c) on a matter of public interest.

---

91 *Per* Lord Ackner in *Telnikoff v Matusevitch* [1991] 4 All ER 817, p 862.
92 *Silkin v Beaverbrook Newspapers Ltd* [1958] 2 All ER 516, p 517.
93 *Lingens v UK* (1986) 8 EHRR 103.

The supporting facts

The defendant must show that the facts supporting his opinion or comment are true. To falsify or distort facts and then to comment on them as if they were true would not be fair. If the facts upon which the comment purports to be based do not exist, the defence fails, even if the maker of the comment believes the facts to be true and honestly holds the views stated.

The facts which support the comment should not confused with the comment itself. To take our earlier example about the incompetent solicitor: my comment is that he is incompetent. The supporting facts are the previous convictions. To succeed in my defence of fair comment, I would have to prove the truth of the supporting facts (the convictions). I would not have to prove that my allegation of incompetence was true.

The comment is honest

The issue of whether comment is honest involves the following sequence of questions:

- taken objectively, is the comment one that an honest minded person *could* have made on the facts which can be proved to be true? This is for the defendant to prove. The defendant does not have to show that the comment is an honest expression of his *own* views, but merely that the comment is objectively fair;

- if so, is the comment the defendant's honest opinion? It is for the claimant to prove that it is not. The comment will be presumed to be an honest expression of the defendant's views, unless the claimant proves otherwise.

Even if the comment taken objectively satisfies the first question, that is, it is an opinion which a reasonable person could have held on the facts, the claimant will succeed in his claim if he/she can show that the comment was not honestly held by the defendant on a subjective level. If the comment was not made honestly, it will be considered to have been actuated *by malice*.

'Malice' is a technical term that will arise again in relation to other defences considered in this chapter. It is considered in detail in the context of the defence of qualified privilege.

We will look at the above questions in more detail.

Step 1: the objective test

The question for the jury is 'would any fair man, however prejudiced he may be, however exaggerated or obstinate his views, have said that which this criticism has said?'.[94] This can be rephrased as 'could a fair man, holding a

---

94 *Merivale v Carson* (1880) 20 QB 275, p 280, *per* Lord Esher.

strong view, holding perhaps an obstinate view, holding perhaps a prejudiced view – could a fair man have been capable of writing this?'.[95] This question has to be decided *without reference to the personal motivation of the defendant*.

The jury should put aside their own opinions. The test is not whether they agree with the comment. If that were the case, the right to express an opinion would be severely curtailed. As Diplock J explained: 'The basis of our public life is that the crank, the enthusiast, may say what he honestly thinks just as much as the reasonable man or woman who sits on a jury and it would be a sad day for freedom of speech in this country if a jury were to apply the test of whether it agrees with the comment instead of applying the true test.'[96]

A comment might be unfair on an objective basis where it amounts to little more than abuse or invective against the claimant. However, countless cases caution against drawing the limits of fair comment too narrowly. The issue is objective honesty. So, for example, if comments would appear to be exaggerated, it will not follow that they are not honest comments. Similarly, if comments appear to be overly prejudiced, it will not follow that they are not honest. The limits of the right to comment are wide.

Step 2: the subjective test

It is for the claimant to show that, whilst the comment or opinion is capable of being honestly held on an objective basis, it was not held honestly by the defendant. This is a subjective test which will depend on the defendant's motivations in making the comment. Motive will generally have to be inferred from what the defendant said or did or knew.

The comment is in the public interest

The concept of public interest in fair comment defences is much wider than we will encounter in relation to copyright infringement and breach of confidence. In *London Artists v Littler*,[97] Lord Denning observed 'whenever a matter is such as to affect people at large, so that they may be legitimately *interested in* or *concerned at*, what is going on or what may happen to them or others, then it is a matter of public interest on which everyone is entitled to make fair comment' (italics for emphasis). This stretches beyond the public actions of public officials. In the *London Artists* case, a threat to the running of a play in London's West End because of the withdrawal of three of the actors was considered to be in the public interest, because of the public's interest in the theatre.

---

95 *Per* Diplock J in *Silkin v Beaverbrook* [1958] 2 All ER 516, p 520.

96 *Per* Diplock J in *ibid*, p 518.

97 *London Artists v Littler* [1968] 1 All ER 1075; [1968] 1 WLR 607.

Fair comment and the critic: an example

Journalist A reviews a play which has just opened in the West End. His review is very short and consists of the following remarks.

> The play is obscene. It concerns promiscuity and drug taking amongst homosexuals. The playwright is the most debauched and sordid writer of his generation.

The playwright, B, brings proceedings for defamation against A, alleging that the natural and ordinary meaning of the review is that he is a sordid and debauched person. A denies that meaning. He pleads that the review was an expression of his opinion and means that B writes about sordid and debauched subjects, rather than a personal attack on B's character.

A will first have to convince the jury that the words are an expression of his opinion, rather than an assertion of fact. A might have made this clearer by prefacing his final sentence with an expression like 'in my view' or 'the nature of B's work suggests that …'. If the jury decide that the statement is an assertion of fact, A will have to rely on the defence of justification, which will entail him proving that B is the most debauched and sordid writer of his generation according to the jury's interpretation of the meaning of that sentence. If the jury decides that it is comment, A can rely on the defence of fair comment. He must show:

- the facts which support his comment are true. A is not restricted to the supporting facts which he refers to in the article. However, assume that A's supporting facts are the content of the play which is the subject of the review. A must prove that what he says about the play's content (promiscuity, drug taking and homosexuality) is correct. If it turns out that A has never seen the play and has misrepresented its contents, A's defence will fail at the first hurdle;

- assuming that A can satisfy the above, A must then show that his comment about B is one which a reasonable man (although prejudiced) could have held. A's own state of mind will be irrelevant to this question, as will the personal views of the jury. A's comment may be interpreted to be a personal attack on B's private character, rather than his work. If so, a jury may find that, taken objectively, the comment goes beyond the limit of an opinion that a reasonable reader (albeit a prejudiced one) could hold on the basis that a reasonable person would not cast aspersions about a man's private character because of what he chooses to write about.[98] If the jury think that, the defence must fail;

- if A succeeds in convincing the jury that his comment was objectively fair, the onus switches to B to prove that A does not honestly hold the opinion that he expressed. If, for example, there is a past history of animosity

---

98 See, eg, *Merivale v Carson* (1880) 20 QB 275.

between A and B, the jury may be prepared to infer that A published his comment to get even with B, rather than as an honest expression of his sincerely held view;

- A must also show that his comment was made on a matter of public interest. This is a matter for the judge. Case law suggests that matters to do with the theatre are of legitimate concern or interest to the public. A may however find it more difficult to show that an attack on B's private character is in the public interest.

Privilege

The defence of privilege, unlike the defences of justification and fair comment, is not dependent on proving the truth of what is asserted or commented on. It applies in circumstances where the law recognises that the public interest requires freedom of expression, even where that expression consists of defamatory and untrue statements. There are two types of privilege – absolute privilege and qualified privilege.

Absolute privilege

Absolute statement is a *complete defence* to a claim of defamation and so acts as a bar to an action in defamation – even where the defamatory allegation is untrue. The defence of absolute privilege differs from the defence of qualified privilege in that it will not be defeated by malice. Absolute privilege is the most powerful defence and the type of statements to which it applies is strictly defined. The categories of most relevance to the media are as follows:

- statements made in the course of parliamentary proceedings in either House of Parliament or in parliamentary committees. Note that this does not apply to media reports of parliamentary proceedings which are the subject of *qualified* privilege;

- statements made in the course of court proceedings. This extends to civil and criminal cases and covers all participants in such cases: the judge, the barristers, the witnesses and the parties to the action. There is no statutory definition of the meaning of 'court proceedings'. However, the Defamation Act 1996 extended absolute privilege to *reports* of court proceedings and defines what is meant by 'proceedings' in that context.[99] It would make sense if the same definition also applied to statements made *in* proceedings, although there is no authority on this point at the time of writing. There is a body of case law pre-dating the 1996 Act on the

---

99 Defamation Act 1996, s 14.

question of what constitutes 'court proceedings'. This is beyond the scope of a book on media law, where the onus will generally be on what can be reported rather than what can actually be said. The statutory definition of 'court proceedings' is considered immediately below;

- reports of court proceedings provided that the report is fair and accurate and published contemporaneously with the proceedings. The defence extends to any court in the UK, the European Court of Justice or any court attached to that Court, the European Court of Human Rights and any international criminal tribunal established by the security council of the United Nations or by an international agreement to which the UK is a party (such as a War Crimes Tribunal).[100] 'Court' is also defined to include any tribunal or body exercising the judicial power of the State. The privilege will not attach to non-State tribunals, such as professional disciplinary bodies. It would also seem that it would not apply to arbitrations to which the parties to a dispute voluntarily submit themselves. Arbitrations usually take place in private in any event;

- official reports of parliamentary proceedings. This category does not extend to the media. It is restricted to reports made by or under the authority of either House of Parliament.[101] For example, the content of *Hansard* is protected by absolute privilege.

Qualified privilege

Qualified privilege attaches to specific types of statement which are considered below. Unlike absolute privilege, qualified privilege will always be destroyed if the maker of the statement was actuated by *malice* when he made the statement. The burden of proof in relation to malice rests on the claimant who must show that the defendant was motivated by malice and, as a result, the defence of qualified privilege is not available. As Slade J has observed, 'malice has nothing to do with the creation of privilege, but only with its destruction'.[102]

The meaning of malice

The authoritative consideration of malice is contained in the decision of the House of Lords in *Horrocks v Lowe*.[103] The legal concept of malice is broader than the dictionary definition of wickedness or evil intent. For a defamation

---

100 Defamation Act 1996, s 14. This is the statutory definition referred to above.
101 Parliamentary Papers Act 1840, s 1.
102 Slade J in *Longdon-Griffiths v Smith* [1951] 1 KB 295, p 304.
103 *Horrocks v Lowe* [1975] AC 135.

lawyer, a statement is made maliciously for one of two reasons. The first is where the publisher does not have a positive belief in the truth of what he publishes. This is a *subjective test*. Where the maker is reckless as to the truth or falsity of his statement, he will be deemed to have made the statement without positive belief. Recklessness means an indifference to the statement's truth or falsity. The onus is always on the claimant to prove a lack of honest belief and the burden is inevitably a heavy one.

This test for malice is not to be equated with negligence, impulsiveness or irrationality. As Lord Diplock observed:[104]

> The freedom of speech protected by the law of qualified privilege may be availed by all sorts and conditions of men. In affording to them immunity from suit if they have acted in good faith in compliance with a legal or moral duty or in protection of a legitimate interest, the law must take them as it finds them. In ordinary life, it is rare indeed for people to form their beliefs by a process of logical deduction from facts ascertained by a rigorous search for all available evidence and a judicious assessment of its probative value. In greater or in less degree according to their temperaments, their training, their intelligence, they are swayed by prejudice, rely on intuition instead of reasoning, leap to conclusions on inadequate evidence and fail to recognise the cogency of material which might cast doubt on the validity of the conclusions they reach. But despite the imperfections of the mental process by which the belief is arrived at, it may still be 'honest', that is, a positive belief that the conclusions they have reached are true. The law demands no more.

The second way in which a statement can be made maliciously is where the defendant, although having an honest belief in his statement, misused the publication for a purpose other than for that which privilege is granted. The commonest case is where the *dominant* purpose for which the statement was published was not, for example, the performance of a duty or the protection of an interest, but instead to give vent to ill feeling towards the person who is the subject of the statement. The claimant must show what the defendant's dominant motive was when they made the statement to establish malice on this ground. If it was an improper motive, that will be sufficient to establish malice, even though the defendant believed his statement to be true.

The existence of malice is a question of fact for the jury.

The claimant will rarely be in a position to give evidence about the defendant's state of mind or motivation. Malice will generally have to be inferred from what the defendant said or did or knew. The words used and the circumstances of the publication will be relevant. According to Lord Diplock, 'juries should be instructed and judges should remind themselves that this burden of affirmative proof is not one which is lightly satisfied'.[105]

104 Lord Diplock in *Horrocks v Lowe* [1975] AC 135.
105 *Ibid.*

Malice and unintended meanings

The natural and ordinary meaning conveyed by a statement is an objective test. The meaning actually intended by the maker of the statement is irrelevant. But the question whether a statement was made maliciously is a subjective test. So what if the natural and ordinary meaning of the defendant's words is found to be A, but he actually intended the words to mean B and positively believed in the truth of meaning B? Is he malicious vis à vis meaning A? Case law suggests that in such circumstances a claimant's case on malice will fail.[106]

Malice and co-defendants

Qualified privilege is a defence for each of the defendants. If malice is proved against one defendant, it will not automatically be found in relation to the other defendants.[107] So, if two journalists are co-defendants in a libel action over a story appearing under both of their by-lines, but in respect of which they each wrote distinct parts, if malice is alleged and proved against one journalist, it would not automatically prevent the second journalist from relying on the defence of qualified privilege.

Qualified privilege: specific classes of report

The Defamation Act 1996 lists a number of types of statements in Sched 1 which enjoy qualified privilege either alone or 'subject to explanation or contradiction', provided always that the subject matter is of public concern and the publication is for the public benefit. The most relevant to the media are:

Part 1

STATEMENTS HAVING QUALIFIED PRIVILEGE WITHOUT
EXPLANATION OR CONTRADICTION

1   A fair and accurate report of proceedings in public of a legislature anywhere in the world.

2   A fair and accurate report of proceedings in public before a court anywhere in the world.

3   A fair and accurate report of proceedings in public of a person appointed to hold a public inquiry by a government or legislature anywhere in the world.

---

106 See *Loveless v Earl* [1999] EMLR 530 and *Heath v Humphreys* (1990) unreported.
107 *Egger v Chelmsford* [1964] 3 All ER 406.

4   A fair and accurate report of proceedings in public anywhere in the world of an international organisation or an international conference.

5   A fair and accurate copy of or extract from any register or other document required by law to be open to public inspection.

6   A notice or advertisement published by or on the authority of a court, or of a judge or officer of a court, anywhere in the world.

7   A fair and accurate copy of or extract from matter published by or on the authority of a government or legislature anywhere in the world.

8   A fair and accurate copy of or extract from matter published anywhere in the world by an international organisation or an international conference.

Part 2

STATEMENTS PRIVILEGED SUBJECT TO EXPLANATION OR CONTRADICTION

9(1)A fair and accurate copy of or extract from a notice or other matter issued for the information of the public by or on behalf of–

(a) a legislature in any Member State or the European Parliament;

(b) the government of any Member State, or any authority performing governmental functions in any Member State or part of a Member State, or the European Commission;

(c) an international organisation or international conference.

(2)In this paragraph, 'governmental functions' includes police functions.

10   A fair and accurate copy of or extract from a document made available by a court in any Member State or the European Court of Justice (or any court attached to that court) or by a judge or officer of any such court.

11(1)A fair and accurate report of proceedings at any public meeting or sitting in the UK of:

(a) a local authority or local authority committee;

(b) a justice or justices of the peace acting otherwise than as a court exercising judicial authority;

(c) a commission, tribunal, committee or person appointed for the purposes of any inquiry by any statutory provision, by Her Majesty or by a Minister of the Crown or a Northern Ireland Department;

(d) a person appointed by a local authority to hold a local inquiry in pursuance of any statutory provision;

(e) any other tribunal, board, committee or body constituted by or under, and exercising functions under, any statutory provision.

(2) …

(3)A fair and accurate report of any corresponding proceedings in any of the Channel Islands or the Isle of Man or in another Member State.

12(1)A fair and accurate report of proceedings at any public meeting held in a Member State

(2)In this paragraph, a 'public meeting' means a meeting *bona fide* and lawfully held for a lawful purpose and for the furtherance or discussion of a matter of public concern, whether admission to the meeting is general or restricted.

13(1)A fair and accurate report of proceedings at a general meeting of a UK public company.

(2)A fair and accurate copy of or extract from any document circulated to members of a UK public company–

   (a) by or with the authority of the board of directors of the company,

   (b) by the auditors of the company, or

   (c) by any member of the company in pursuance of a right conferred by any statutory provision.

(3)A fair and accurate copy of or extract from any document circulated to members of a UK public company which relates to the appointment, resignation, retirement or dismissal of directors of the company.

(4)...

(5)A fair and accurate report of proceedings at any corresponding meeting of, or copy of or any extract from any corresponding document circulated to members of, a public company formed under the law of any of the Channel Islands or the Isle of Man or of another Member State.

14 A fair and accurate report of any finding or decision of any of the following descriptions of association, formed in the UK or another Member State, or of any committee or governing body of such an association–

   (a) an association formed for the purpose of promoting or encouraging the exercise of or interest in any art, science, religion or learning, and empowered by its constitution to exercise control over or adjudicate on matters of interest or concern to the association, or the actions or conduct of any person subject to such control or adjudication;

   (b) an association formed for the purpose of promoting or safeguarding the interests of any trade, business, industry or profession, or of the persons carrying on or engaged in any trade, business, industry or profession, and empowered by its constitution to exercise control over or adjudicate upon matters connected with that trade, business, industry or profession;

   (c) an association formed for the purpose of promoting or safeguarding the interests of a game, sport or pastime to the playing or exercise of which members of the public are invited or admitted, and empowered by its constitution to exercise control over or adjudicate upon persons connected with or taking part in the game, sport or pastime;

(d) an association formed for the purpose of promoting charitable objects or other objects beneficial to the community and empowered by its constitution to exercise control over or to adjudicate on matters of interest or concern to the association, or the actions or conduct of any person subject to such control or adjudication.

15(1)A fair and accurate report of, or copy of or extract from, any adjudication, report, statement or notice issued by a body, officer or other person designated for the purposes of this paragraph–

(a) for England and Wales or Northern Ireland, by order of the Lord Chancellor; and

(b) for Scotland, by order of the Secretary of State.

(2)An order under this paragraph shall be made by statutory instrument which shall be subject to annulment in pursuance of a resolution of either House of Parliament.

'Court' bears the same meaning and extends to the same bodies as in relation to absolute privilege attaching to reports of court proceedings as set out in s 14 of the 1996 Act.

The reference to 'explanation or contradiction' in Part 2 is to the right of a complainant to publication of a reasonable letter or statement by way of explanation or contradiction of the report. The explanation or contradiction must be published in 'a suitable manner' which must be in the same manner as the publication complained of or in a manner which is adequate and reasonable in the circumstances. Qualified privilege is lost if the defendant refuses or neglects to allow a statement of explanation or contradiction where it is requested.

The list of statements extends to all publications of the above classes of report howsoever published and whether the report is published to the public as a whole or to a section of the public.[108]

Where the material which is published is protected or prohibited by law other than defamation law, for example, by copyright or breach of confidence law or by obscenity laws, the fact that it is included in the above schedule will not protect the publisher from liability under the other law.

---

108 The 1952 Act only applied to newspapers and the relevant provisions are now repealed.

Fair and accurate reports

It will be seen from Sched 1 above that, in some instances, media reports will attract qualified privilege where they are 'fair and accurate'. The term 'fair and accurate' has been interpreted by the courts.[109] It does not mean that reports must be verbatim accounts of the matters reported on. They must, however, be balanced, presenting all sides of the matter reported on so as to give readers or viewers an overall picture.

The facts reported on should also be correct. Care should be taken to ensure that they are not presented in such a way as to create a misleading impression.

The case of *Cook v Alexander*[110] concerned a media report of parliamentary proceedings. Lord Denning observed as follows:

> When a debate covers a particular subject matter, there are often some aspects of greater public interest than others. If the reporter is to give the public any impression at all of the proceedings, he must be allowed to be selective and to cover those matters only which appear to be of particular public interest. Even then, he need not report it verbatim, word for word or letter by letter. It is sufficient if it is a fair presentation of what took place so far as to convey to the reader the impression which the debate itself would have made on the hearer of it.

Fair and accurate reports of parliamentary proceedings by the media also attract qualified privilege at common law. This extends to proceedings in both Houses of Parliament and in select committee.

Right to reply

Qualified privilege will attach to a statement which is made in rebuttal of, or defence of oneself from, a defamatory attack. As Lord Oaksey observed, '... there is an analogy between the criminal law of self-defence and a man's right to defend himself against written or verbal attacks. In both cases, he is entitled, if he can, to defend himself effectively, and he only loses the protection of the law if he goes beyond defence and proceeds to offence'.[111]

Where the reply is made in the media, qualified privilege will also protect the media entity which publishes the reply. The privilege will apply to a right to reply, provided that the publicity given to the reply is commensurate with the publicity given to the original defamatory comment and insofar as the response is restricted to the defamatory allegations. In *Adam v Ward*,[112] the claimant, an MP, falsely attacked X, a Major General in the army, in a speech

---

109 *Cook v Alexander* [1974] 1 QB 280.
110 *Ibid*.
111 *Turner v MGM Pictures* [1950] 1 All ER 449, pp 470–71.
112 *Adam v Ward* [1917] AC 309.

in the House of Commons (the speech was protected by absolute privilege, as we have seen). The Army Council investigated the charge, rejected it and directed their secretary to write a letter to X, vindicating him. The letter contained defamatory statements about the claimant. The letter was released to the press. It was held to be protected by qualified privilege.

The publication by an agent (such as a solicitor) of a reply to a defamatory allegation attracts the same qualified privilege as it would if the publication had been made by the agent's principal.[113]

Qualified privilege at common law – general categories

In addition to the above specific occasions of privilege, there are a number of general occasions which have been recognised as being protected by qualified privilege at common law. The rationale behind these more general occasions is the public interest in permitting free and frank communications about matters in respect of which the law recognises that there is a duty to perform or an interest to protect. In *Horrocks v Lowe*,[114] Lord Diplock observed:

> In all cases of qualified privilege, there is some special reason of public policy why the law accords immunity from suit – the existence of some public or private duty, whether legal or moral, on the part of the maker of the defamatory statement which justifies his communicating it or of some interest of his own which he is entitled to protect by doing so.

In such cases, reputation has to give way to the wider public interest.

The categories of qualified privilege are not closed.[115] The categories considered below are applications of the underlying principle of public policy. But it has been said that any extension of the categories must fall within established principles,[116] and that 'the principles themselves are not unduly elastic'.

The established categories are as follows:

(a) Statements made where there is a *duty* to communicate information believed to be true to a person who has a *material interest* in receiving the information ('the reciprocity is essential').[117] The duty is not restricted to a legal duty. A moral or social duty to communicate information will suffice.

Example

An MP wrote a letter to the Law Society and the Lord Chancellor, saying that he had been specifically requested by a constituent to refer the claimant's firm of solicitors to the Law Society for investigation and setting

---

113 *Regan v Taylor* [2000] 1 All ER 307.
114 *Horrocks v Lowe* [1975] AC 135.
115 *Watts v Times Newspapers* [1996] 1 All ER 152; [1996] 2 WLR 427, *per* Hirst LJ, p 158.
116 *Reynolds v Times Newspapers* [1998] 3 All ER 961, CA, *per* Lord Bingham CJ, p 994.
117 *Adam v Ward* [1917] AC 309.

out the constituent's complaints. The communication was privileged. In general, an MP had both an interest and a duty to communicate to the appropriate body at the request of a constituent any substantial complaint from the constituent.[118]

In order for privilege under this head to be made out, the following questions have to be answered in the affirmative:

- was the publisher under a legal, social or moral duty to those to whom the material was published to publish the material in question (the duty test)?

- did those to whom the material is published have an interest to receive that material (the interest test)?

- regard must be had to the position of both communicator and recipient when deciding whether an occasion is privileged under this head.

(b) Where the maker of the statement has an *interest to be protected* by communicating true information which is relevant to that interest, to a person honestly believed to have *a duty to protect that interest*.

Example

A complaint made to the police or other appropriate authority about suspected crimes.

(c) Where the maker of the statement and the recipient of the information have *a common interest and a reciprocal duty* in respect of the subject matter of the communication.

Example

An invigilator who believed that an exam candidate was cheating had a common interest with the examinees to ensure the fair conduct of the examination and by virtue of that common interest had the moral duty to inform the examinees if he felt one examinee was taking unfair advantage.[119]

---

118 *Beach v Freeson* [1972] 1 QB 14.
119 *Bridgman v Stockdale* [1953] 1 All ER 1166.

DUTY AND INTEREST: A DEFENCE FOR PUBLICATIONS IN THE PUBLIC INTEREST?

One of the most topical issues in defamation law is the extent to which qualified privilege provides a defence for publication by the media of material which, by virtue of its subject matter, can be said to be in the public interest. If the defence were available, the media could rely on qualified privilege instead of having to rely on the defences of justification or fair comment. Until very recently, the prevailing view was that public interest defence would tip the balance too far in favour of defendants who would no longer be required to prove the truth of what they publish in order to successfully defend an action. This was articulated by Canter J in *London Artists Ltd v Littler*:[120]

> It would indeed be a charter to persons, including those whom counsel for the first plaintiffs classified as the obstinate, the stupid and the unreasonable, to disseminate untrue defamatory information of apparently legitimate public interest provided only that they honestly believed it and honestly thought that it was information which the public ought to have. If that were the law, few defendants would ever again need to plead the defence of fair comment or take on themselves the burden of proving that their comment was founded on facts and that the facts were true.

The Neill Committee agreed. It thought that 'the media are adequately protected by the defences of justification and fair comment at the moment, and it is salutary that these defences are available to them only if they have got their facts substantially correct'.[121]

In the face of such reluctance to introduce a new legal defence for publication of material in the public interest, media defendants have sought to establish a *de facto* public interest defence by reference to the duty and interest qualified privilege criteria. The question for media defendants who seek to rely on this ground of qualified privilege is whether they can meet the duty and interest tests by virtue of the fact that the material which they publish is in the public interest.

The availability of the qualified privilege defence has recently been considered by both the Court of Appeal[122] and the House of Lords[123] in *Reynolds v Times Newspapers Ltd*. This was an action brought by Albert Reynolds, the former Prime Minister of Ireland, against *The Sunday Times* over an article which alleged malpractice whilst carrying out his governmental duties.

---

120 [1968] 1 All ER 1075, p 1081 (approved by the Court of Appeal in *Blackshaw v Lord*).

121 *The Report of the Supreme Court Procedure Committee on Practice and Procedure in Defamation*, July 1991.

122 *Reynolds v Times Newspapers Ltd* [1998] 3 All ER 961, CA.

123 *Reynolds v Times Newspapers Ltd* [1999] 4 All ER 609, HL.

The majority of the House of Lords held that the duty-interest test was capable of covering the publication by the media of stories in the public interest, provided that the information published was of sufficient quality to render the occasion of publication privileged.

An analysis of the Court of Appeal and House of Lords' judgments

Court of Appeal

The Court of Appeal's judgment, which was delivered by Lord Bingham CJ, simultaneously widened and narrowed the scope of the qualified privilege as it relates to the publication of material in the public interest. The Court of Appeal expanded the duty-interest test into a three stage test. It reiterated the conventional duty and interest test and added a new third element as follows:

- was the publisher under a legal, social or moral duty to those to whom the material was published to publish the material in question (the *duty test*)?;

- did those to whom the material is published have an interest to receive that material (the *interest test*)?;

- were the nature, status and source of the material and the circumstances of the publication such that the publication should in the public interest be protected in the absence of proof of express malice (the *circumstantial test*)?

The circumstantial test was not put forward before the Court of Appeal by either side, nor was it raised in argument. It had its origins in an earlier Court of Appeal decision,[124] which had emphasised the need to consider the status of a publication in order to decide whether the publication was made on an occasion attracting privilege. The Court of Appeal took hold of this baton and raced much further with it, using it to establish a new circumstantial test of general application to duty-interest qualified privilege. We shall see below that the House of Lords rejected the circumstantial test as an independent third limb of duty-interest privilege, but the spirit of the circumstantial test lives on in the speeches of the Law Lords.

Widening the scope of qualified privilege

The court recognised that it is the *duty* of the news media to inform the public and to engage in discussion of matters of public interest. By public interest, Lord Bingham CJ explained that the court meant matters relating to the public life of the community and those who take part in it, including such activities as the conduct of government and political life, elections and public

---

124 *Blackshaw v Lord* [1983] 2 All ER 311.

administration and also extending to matters such as (for instance) the governance of public bodies, institutions and companies. Public interest therefore extends beyond the political. He did, however, exclude from the ambit of public interest the disclosure of matters which are personal and private, disclosure of which, he said, could not be said to be in the public interest.

The Court of Appeal also recognised that the public generally has an interest in receiving information published by the media. In modern conditions, the court held, the duty and interest tests should readily be satisfied where the subject matter of the report is in the public interest.

Narrowing the scope of qualified privilege

The sting in the tail of the *Reynolds* judgment was in the application of the Court of Appeal's circumstantial test. This test was described by the court as an essential 'safeguard for truth'.[125] As Lord Bingham stated in the Court of Appeal:

> It is one thing to publish a statement taken from a Government press release, or the report of a public company chairman, or the speech of a university vice chancellor, and quite another to publish a statement of a political opponent, or a business competitor or a disgruntled ex-employee; it is one thing to publish a statement which the person defamed has been given the opportunity to rebut, and quite another to publish a statement without any recourse to the person defamed where such recourse was possible; it is one thing to publish a statement which has been so far as possible checked, and quite another to publish it without such verification as was possible and as the significance of the statement called for. Whilst those who engage in public life must expect and accept that their public conduct will be the subject of close scrutiny and robust criticism, they should not in our view be taken to expect or accept that their conduct should be the subject of false and defamatory statements of fact, unless the circumstances of the publication are such as to make it proper, in the public interest, to afford the publisher immunity from liability in the absence of malice.[126]

The circumstantial test involves scrutiny by the court of the steps taken to verify the truth of a story, the reliability of the source of the information and whether the subject of an allegation was given an opportunity to rebut the allegation. The Court of Appeal professed that the primary purpose of the circumstantial test was to maintain the proper balance between the claimant and defendant in defamation cases and not to regulate the practice of journalism. However, it is difficult to see how the practical effect of the decision would be anything other than indirect regulation.

125 [1993] 3 All ER 961.
126 *Ibid*, p 1005.

The circumstantial test and the media

From the media's point of view, the Court of Appeal's judgment would undoubtedly lead to delay in publication of stories in many cases. Stories would have to be carefully verified, with an eye to satisfying the court that the story is of sufficient 'status' to justify publication in the public interest. This would be likely to involve more exhaustive checks than might otherwise be made or thought necessary. The requirement that subjects be given the opportunity to rebut allegations has the potential to cause enormous problems in practice. Sometimes, the story will disappear if the subject is alerted beforehand. The subject, having been placed on notice, may seek an interim injunction. These are rarely granted in defamation cases, but a court can be persuaded to grant interim relief where the claimant can assert that other rights are being infringed, such as copyright or breach of confidence. Subjects on prior notice may also destroy vital supporting evidence or fabricate their version of the story.

The circumstantial test has the potential to be incompatible with s 10 of the Contempt of Court Act 1981, which allows journalists to keep their sources confidential (subject to certain limited exceptions). The circumstantial test presupposes that the identity of the source of a story should be made available so that its reliability may be verified. This issue arose in the case of *Saif Al Islam Gaddafi v Telegraph Group Ltd*,[127] which was considered by the Court of Appeal some months after the Court of Appeal judgment in the *Reynolds* case. The defendants in that case sought leave to amend their defence to plead qualified privilege in the light of the *Reynolds* decision. Strict compliance with the circumstantial test would have meant that the defendant would have to identify its source for the story (which concerned the son of the Libyan leader, Colonel Gaddafi). The defendant was unwilling to name its source, fearing that the safety of the source could be endangered if their identity was known. Hirst LJ expressed himself to have experienced considerable anxiety about the compatibility of the *Reynolds* test with the law relating to confidentiality of journalistic sources.

The Court of Appeal's conclusion in the Reynolds *case*

On the facts of the *Reynolds* case, the Court of Appeal held that:

(a) the circumstances in which Mr Reynolds' Government fell from power were matters of undoubted public interest to the people of the UK;

(b) it was clear that the defendants had a duty to inform the public of the matters in question and that the public had a corresponding interest to

---

127 *Saif Al Islam Gaddafi v Telegraph Group Ltd* (1998) unreported.

receive that information. The duty and interest tests were therefore satisfied;

(c) the circumstantial test was not satisfied. The defendants failed to record Mr Reynolds's own account of his conduct, nor did they alert him before publication to their highly damaging conclusions set out in the article;

(d) given the nature, status and source of the defendants' information and all the circumstances of publication, this was not a publication which should, in the public interest, be protected by privilege.

The House of Lords

When the *Reynolds* case came before the House of Lords, all the Law Lords upheld the finding of the Court of Appeal that a qualified privilege defence might, in appropriate circumstances, be available for publication of material in the public interest. The Law Lords described the Court of Appeal judgment as 'a valuable and forward looking analysis of the common law' and 'an admirable, forward looking and imaginative judgment'. However, each of the Law Lords felt that the Court of Appeal had erred in introducing the circumstantial test as a separate criterion to be established before the duty-interest qualified privilege could be made out.

The majority of the Law Lords were of the view that, notwithstanding that the circumstantial test was no longer a separate requirement, the factors set out in the circumstantial test, or some of them, should, where appropriate, be taken into account in determining whether the duty-interest tests were satisfied.

The duty and interest tests would not automatically be satisfied by virtue only of the fact that the subject matter of the publication happened to be in the public interest. Qualified privilege will not apply by virtue of the subject matter of the publication alone. The value to the public of information (and their interest in receiving it) depends not just on any particular subject matter of a publication, but also on the *quality of the information* which is published. Lord Hobhouse stressed that there is no duty to publish what is not true, nor any interest in being misinformed. The defendant must demonstrate that it acted responsibly in ensuring that the material it published was of a high quality before it could avail itself of a qualified privilege defence. When assessing the quality of a report, Lord Nicholls stressed that the court is not seeking to set a higher standard than that of responsible journalism.

An illustrative list of matters to be taken into account in determining whether a publication is privileged was set out by Lord Nicholls. It consisted of the following factors:

- the seriousness of the allegation. The more serious the charge, the more the public is misinformed and the individual harmed if the allegation is not true;

- the nature of the information and the extent to which the subject matter is a matter of public concern;
- the source of the information. Some informants have no direct knowledge of the events. Some have their own axes to grind, or are being paid for their stories (presumably, if sources are being paid, this will increase the risk that the information is not accurate, although this point was not elaborated);
- the steps taken to verify the information;
- the status of the information. The allegation may already have been the subject of an investigation which commands respect;
- the urgency of the matter. News is often a perishable commodity;
- whether comment was sought from the defendant. He may have information others did not possess or have not disclosed. An approach to the defendant will not always be necessary. The requirement that a comment is sought was not to be elevated into a rigid rule of law;
- whether the article contained the gist of the claimant's side of the story;
- the tone of the article. A newspaper can raise queries or call for an investigation. It need not adopt allegations as statements of fact;
- the circumstances of publication, including the timing.

Lord Nicholls went on to say: 'This list is not exhaustive. The weight to be given to these and any other relevant factors will vary from case to case.' Lord Cooke thought the above has 'the advantage of underlining media responsibility'. Lord Hobhouse thought that the mere repetition of overheard gossip, whether attributed or not, would not meet the requirements, nor would speculation, 'however intelligent'.

In considering the standard of journalism that would be required, Lord Nicholls considered and endorsed the jurisprudence of the European Court of Human Rights on the reporting of matters of public concern. He stated that a statement of fact raises different considerations than a statement of opinion or comment on a matter of public interest which has an accurate factual basis. Article 10 of the Convention protects the right of journalists to divulge information on matters of general interest, provided they are acting in good faith and on an accurate factual basis. Journalists are not required to guarantee the truth of their facts, but they must act in accordance with the ethics of journalism.[128]

The majority of the Law Lords emphasised the elasticity of their decisions, indicating that it would enable the court to give appropriate weight to the importance of freedom of expression by the media on all matters of public

---

128 *Bladet Tromso and Stensaas v Norway* (1999) 28 EHRR 534; and *Thorgeirson v Iceland* (1992) 14 EHRR 843.

concern. An encouraging note was sounded by Lord Nicholls, who indicated that 'the press discharges vital functions as a bloodhound as well as a watchdog. The court should be slow to conclude that a publication was not in the public interest and, therefore, the public had no right to know, especially when the information is in the field of political discussion. Any lingering doubts should be resolved in favour of publication'.

Whilst the return to the conventional two stage duty and interest tests gives the court more flexibility than the Court of Appeal decision, it remains to be seen whether the application of the Law Lords' decision will be different in practice to the three stage test. By way of example, consider the statement which the Law Lords made in relation to two of Lord Nicholls' categories – the disclosure of sources and the requirement that the subject of the stories be given a right to comment before publication.

Disclosure of sources

Whilst acknowledging that s 10 of the Contempt of Court Act 1981 gives the media immunity from disclosure of sources, subject to limited exceptions, Lord Steyn observed that: 'If a newspaper stands on the rule protecting its sources, it may run the risk of what the judge and jury will make of the gap in the evidence.' Reliance on the immunity granted by the statute can make it more difficult for a media defendant to rely on a qualified privilege defence to a defamation claim. The inconsistency identified by the Court of Appeal in the *Gaddafi* case has not been remedied.

Lord Nicholls, on the other hand, indicated that a newspaper's unwillingness to disclose the identity of its source should not weigh against it. This would seem to be the better view.

Consultation before publication

Lord Nicholls observed that:

> ... it goes without saying that a journalist is entitled and bound to reach his own conclusions and to express them honestly and fearlessly. He is entitled to disbelieve and refute explanations given. But that cannot be a good reason for omitting, from a hard hitting article making serious allegations against a named individual, all mention of that person's own explanation ... Further, it is elementary fairness that, in the normal course, a serious charge should be accompanied by the gist of any explanation already given. An article which fails to do so faces an uphill task in claiming privilege if the allegation proves to be false and the unreported allegation proves to be true.

Lord Steyn indicated that 'a failure to report the other side will often be evidence tending to show that the occasion ought not to be protected by qualified privilege. But it would not necessarily always be so, for example, when the victim's explanation is unintelligible or plain nonsense'.

Clearly, the requirement that reports should be balanced and should include at least the gist of the subject's own account or explanation is to be viewed as the norm. Any departure from this practice would have to be convincingly explained if it is not to scupper qualified privilege. One ground for explanation might be the urgency surrounding publication. The inclusion in Lord Nicholls' list of this as a factor to be taken into account is to be welcomed. It represents an endorsement of the decision of the European Court of Human Rights in *Oberschlick v Austria*[129] that 'news is a perishable commodity and to delay its publication, even for a short period, may well deprive it of all its value and interest'.

Does the House of Lords' decision extend beyond political speech?

Lord Nicholls spoke about the duty of the media and the interest of the audience in reporting and receiving information in the public interest. He drew no real distinction between political information and other kinds of material which could be said to be in the public interest. Indeed, he thought to do so would be unsound in principle: '... the common law should not develop "political information" as a new "subject matter" category of qualified privilege.' Lord Cooke agreed. Lord Steyn also spoke of the 'public interest' as being potentially wider than political information, describing it 'as a corner of the law which could do with the minimum of legal rules'.

Lord Hope thought that where political information is at issue, the duty and interest tests are likely in principle to be satisfied without too much difficulty. He did not consider other types of information, nor did Lord Cooke or Lord Hobhouse.

Lord Steyn also echoed the views of the Court of Appeal that speech about political matters has a higher value than speech about the private lives of politicians, the publication of the latter information being less likely to be in the public interest.

The relationship between malice and qualified privilege

The decision of the majority of the House of Lords and the Court of Appeal blurs the distinction between the defence of qualified privilege and malice. As we have seen, the existence of malice is for the claimant to prove in order to defeat a defence of qualified privilege. But, in effect, many of the factors included in Lord Nicholls' list of factors to be taken into account when assessing the quality of what is published are matters which a claimant might rely on to establish that the defendant was actuated by malice. If a defendant

---

129 *Oberschlick v Austria* (1991) 19 EHRR 389, p 422, para 59.

has to prove that it has acted responsibly in order to satisfy the duty and interest tests, what function will malice now perform? Does the House of Lords' decision simply shift the burden of proof on malice from the claimant to the defendant, who must now, in effect, show that it was not actuated by malice when it made the publication? These issues will no doubt be clarified as more 'public interest' cases come before the courts.

The danger of blurring the boundaries between qualified privilege and malice was recognised by Lord Hope in the *Reynolds* case. He was concerned to consider to what extent the availability of the defence of qualified privilege should be dependent on the circumstances surrounding publication. In Lord Hope's view, the Court of Appeal's circumstantial test and (although he did not actually express it), by analogy, the criteria identified by the majority of the Law Lords go too wide for establishing whether the defence exists at all. 'It has had the effect in this case of introducing, at the stage of examining the question of law whether the occasion was privileged, assumptions which I think are relevant only to the question of fact as to the motive of the publisher.'

Amongst the questions which, in the opinion of Lord Hope, go to malice, rather than the existence of qualified privilege (that is, to the loss of privilege, rather than its existence), were:

- questions about sources;
- the failure to publish Mr Reynolds' own account;
- the failure to alert Mr Reynolds to the newspaper's conclusions that he had lied to the Irish parliament.

No generic right to qualified privilege

All the Law Lords rejected the introduction of a generic defence of qualified privilege which would apply, in the absence of malice, to all political statements simply by virtue of the nature of the subject under discussion.

Counsel for the defence had invited the House of Lords to develop English law along similar lines to the 'public figure' defence first enunciated by the US Supreme Court in the case of *New York Times v Sullivan*.[130] It was held in the *Sullivan* case that public officials should not succeed in an action for defamation, unless the claimant could show that the defendant was actuated by malice. The defence was extended in subsequent US cases to cover publications about all public figures. Counsel for the defendants in the *Reynolds* case argued for a similar generic type privilege to cover the publication of speech concerning political figures. Lord Steyn set out two reasons for declining to endorse the availability of a generic defence which

---

130 *New York Times v Sullivan* (1964) 376 US 254.

would apply across the board to particular categories of case, regardless of individual circumstance. His views were endorsed by the other Law Lords. The reasons he gave for his views were:

- English law generally will not compel a journalist to reveal his sources. By contrast, a claimant in the US is entitled to a pre-trial inquiry into the sources of a story about him and the editorial decision making. Without such an inquiry, a claimant in England would be at a substantial disadvantage in showing malice, making it 'unacceptably difficult for a victim of defamation and false allegations to prove reckless disregard of the truth';

- a generic right to qualified privilege is contrary to the jurisdiction of the European Court of Human Rights which, in cases of competing rights and interest (freedom of expression versus the right to an untarnished reputation), requires that they be balanced against each other, as opposed to one automatically wiping out the other.

Evaluation of the Reynolds decision

Overall, the majority decision of the House of Lords is probably something to be welcomed. We have a decision establishing that the media have a duty to report on matters of public interest and the public has an interest in receiving such stories. That is something which, in itself, is of significant value. The rejection of the circumstantial test as a separate limb in its own right to a factor to be taken into account in determining duty and interest is also to be welcomed. Similarly, the general tenor of the speeches of the Law Lords leaves room for hope that the media's role as watchdog and bloodhound will be recognised as legitimate and protected. But, as is often the case, the devil is in the detail. How will the judiciary assess the quality of material? Will the problems identified in relation to the Court of Appeal's circumstantial test still occur? They certainly have the potential to do so.

The majority test carries with it an element of uncertainty. The Law Lords spoke of the elasticity of their decisions as a desirable feature. Editors can, on one level, take comfort from Lord Nicholls' view that all that is required is responsible journalism but do we, at the time of writing, have any consensus on what that might involve? This may become clear as a body of case law emerges over time to act as guidance but, in the meantime, the uncertainty is likely to be another aspect of the chill factor which the potential for defamation actions continues to exert over the media generally.

The question also arises as to whether the courts are the most suitable bodies to determine the scope of responsible journalistic practices in the first place. In the Reynolds case, counsel for the defendant argued that such an approach would place the courts in the position of censor or of a licensing body. Lord Nicholls countered this argument by highlighting that the court has the advantage of being impartial, independent of government and accustomed to deciding disputed issues of fact. In a sideswipe at the press, he indicated that 'the sad reality is that the overall handling of these matters by the national press, with its own commercial interests to serve, does not always command general confidence'. The broadcast media may have a degree of righteous indignation that they are, by implication, tarred by the same brush. The decision of the Law Lords does not give any indication that different categories of media defendant should be treated differently.[131]

Offer of amends defence

The offer of amends defence to a defamation claim was introduced by ss 2–4 of the Defamation Act 1996.[132] It provides that a defendant may be able to offer the claimant a public correction, apology and damages in order to bring an action for defamation to an end. Where the offer is rejected, the fact that the offer was made can be used as a defence in the proceedings.

At the time of the passage of the Act through the House of Lords, Lord Kilbracken described the defence as 'an important new provision – a fast track procedure – which should have the effect of reducing the immense cost of litigation to all parties and saving the time of the courts'.

The procedure

In order to benefit from the defence, an offer of amends has to be in writing and expressed to be an offer made pursuant to the Act. The offer can relate to the statement generally, or it can be limited to a specific defamatory meaning which the person making the offer accepts that the statement conveys. In the latter case, it will be known as a *qualified offer*. If it is a qualified offer, the offer must state that fact. The offer must be made before the defendant serves its defence.

The offer to make amends must offer:

- to make a suitable *correction* of the statement concerned and a sufficient *apology* to the aggrieved party;
- to *publish* the correction and apology in a manner that is reasonable and practicable in the circumstances; and
- to pay the aggrieved party such *compensation* (if any) and such costs as may be agreed or determined to be payable.

---

131 For an early example of the application of the *Reynolds* approach, see *Saad Al-Fagih v HM Saudi Research and Marketing (UK) Ltd* (2000) unreported.

132 It did not come into force until 28 February 2000.

The offer has to deal with each of the above elements. It need not, however, set out the precise steps to be followed or the wording of the apology/correction. Once the defendant agrees to the offer in principle, the Act provides for enforcement mechanisms where the detail cannot be agreed.

Once made, an offer can be withdrawn at any time before it has been accepted. The renewal of an offer which has been withdrawn is to be treated as a new offer.

Where the offer to make amends is accepted by the aggrieved party, he may not bring or continue with defamation proceedings against the person who has made the offer (but he can continue against other persons involved in the publication).

He may take steps to enforce the offer of amends in the following ways:

- where the parties agree on the steps to be taken in fulfilment of the offer, the aggrieved party may apply for a court order to give effect to the agreement. The agreement will then be embodied in the court order and non-compliance with it will potentially be punishable as a contempt of court;

- if the parties do not agree on the steps to be taken by way of correction, apology and publication (despite there being an agreement in principle), the party who made the offer may take such steps as he thinks appropriate and may, in particular:

  o make the correction and apology by a statement in open court in terms approved by the court; and

  o give an undertaking to the court as to the manner of their publication.

There is no reference in the Act to the court having the power to determine the terms of the apology or the method of publication (other than via a statement in open court). In this regard, the Act reflects the concern expressed by the media during the passage of the Bill at the prospect of the court deciding the prominence and wording of apologies and corrections. Newspapers feared that they would be ordered to print apologies on their front page whilst broadcasters, who are generally reluctant to concede broadcast apologies at all, because of their restricted airtime, were resistant at the idea of having to devote valuable airtime to publication of apologies pursuant to orders of the court.

As an alternative to leaving this issue to be determined by the court, the Act now provides that the defendant is free to do as it wishes vis à vis the apology and correction, but the adequacy of the defendant's decision can be reflected in any damages which the court orders under the offer of amends procedure, either to *increase* or decrease the amount of damages payable:

- if the parties do not agree on the amount of compensation, the court will determine it on the same principles as damages in defamation proceedings, taking into account any steps taken in fulfilment of the offer and (so far as not agreed between the parties) of the suitability of the correction, the sufficiency of the apology and whether the manner of their publication was reasonable in the circumstances and may reduce *or increase* the amount of compensation accordingly;

- if the parties do not agree on the amount to be paid by way of costs, it should be determined by the court on the same principles as costs awarded in defamation proceedings;

- proceedings under the above are to be determined by a judge without a jury.

Where the offer of amends is not accepted, the fact that the offer was made is a defence to defamation proceedings by the person who made the offer. Where the offer was a qualified offer, it can be a defence only in relation to the meaning to which the offer related. The defendant can choose not to rely on the offer as a defence, but where it does so he may not rely on any other defence (where the offer was qualified this applies only to the meaning to which the offer related). Where the offer is not relied on as a defence, it can still be used in mitigation of damages.

If relied on as a defence, the defence will succeed, unless the *claimant* can show that the party making the offer knew or had reason to believe that the statement complained of:

- referred to the claimant or was likely to be understood as referring to him; *and*

- was both false and defamatory of that party.

But it shall be presumed until the contrary is shown (by the claimant) that the defendant did not know and had no reason to believe that was the case. It is not clear whether 'reason to believe' is to be equated with negligence or recklessness. For example, is it sufficient that a claimant can show that, had the defendant taken reasonable care in its research, it would have realised that its allegation was false or defamatory? This question must await clarification by the courts.

Unlike the defences of justification and fair comment, where the offer is relied on as a defence, the burden of proof shifts from the defendant to the claimant to prove that the defendant did not know and had no reason to believe that the statement was false. If the claimant cannot discharge this burden, his claim will fail. It remains to be seen the extent to which the availability of this defence will deter claimants from commencing proceedings or seeing them through once an offer of amends has been made. In theory, this defence may prove to be the most effective weapon in the defendant's armoury and its introduction was long overdue.

The offer of amends defence will be of enormous assistance in those cases where the libel or slander arose from an honest mistake – for example, mistaken identification or unintended innuendo meanings. Although the offer must consist of an apology and correction which must be published, and usually also a payment of damages and costs, that is likely to involve much less inconvenience, anxiety and expense than a case which is litigated all the way to trial.

Does the offer of amends defence discriminate against broadcast media?

As mentioned above, the broadcast media are traditionally hostile to publishing apologies and/or corrections. Unlike newspapers which contain numerous items and photographs, any of which can be read at any one time, broadcasters are restricted to broadcasting one thing at a time (at least before the onset of digital services). If valuable airtime is taken up by an apology which will be of no interest to the vast majority of viewers, broadcasters will tend to lose viewers.

But an offer of amends under the above procedure *must* include an offer to publish a correction and apology, howsoever publication is effected. For that reason, broadcasters are less likely to be in a position to make use of the offer of amends procedure and defence than the print media. The Act provides that a defendant can choose to publish the correction and apology in whatever medium it considers to be reasonable and practicable if the manner of publication is not agreed. If there are deficiencies in their publication, it will be reflected in an increased damages award. Nothing in the Act provides that the apology has to be in the same media as the original comment. However, one can easily picture an application by an aggrieved claimant that an offer to publish on, say, a website, does not amount to an offer to publish at all for the purposes of an offer of amends. The chances of such an application succeeding will be lessened if the broadcaster combines such a publication with a statement in open court. The difficulties for broadcast defendants are greater than for the press. They do not appear to be insurmountable, but they may lead to broadcast defendants paying higher damages under the offer of amends procedure than their print counterparts.

An alternative offer of amends procedure was laid down in the Defamation Act 1952 and remains in force. It has proved to be overly technical and is very little relied on in practice. For that reason it is not considered in this book.

Consent

Where a claimant has expressly or impliedly consented to publication of defamatory material, the consent will provide a complete defence for the defendant. However, the consent must be specific and given for the purposes in question if the defence is to succeed. A person who agrees to appear on a television programme, for example, will not be taken to have consented to the publication of defamatory material about him during the course of the programme unless he knew of the subject matter of the programme. Similarly, if a person discloses information about themselves in a private context which is then published by the media to the world at large, the limited disclosure is unlikely to be taken to be consent to the wider publication.[133]

Summary procedure

For the first time ever, the Defamation Act 1996 introduced a new summary procedure for the disposal of defamation claims (ss 8–11). Summary judgment had not previously been available for such claims.

The objective behind the new procedure is the introduction of a fast track procedure for appropriate cases so that they can be disposed of without the need for an expensive trial. It is envisaged that the suitability of every claim for summary disposal will be assessed at an interim stage of the proceedings by a judge sitting without a jury. The court may consider the procedure of its own initiative. At that hearing, the judge will decide whether, and how, the claim should be summarily disposed of.

It may dismiss the claimant's claim if it appears that it has no realistic prospect of success *and* there is no reason why the claim should be tried. If either or both of these criteria are not met, the claim ought not to be dismissed.

On the other hand, the court may grant summary judgment to the claimant if it appears that there is no defence to the claim which has a realistic prospect of success *and* there is no other reason why the claim should be tried. Where the claimant does not ask for summary relief, the court will not grant it unless it is satisfied that summary relief will adequately compensate him for the wrong he has suffered. The objectives behind compensatory damages are considered below.

In considering whether a claim should be disposed of summarily or proceed to trial, the Act says that the court shall have regard to the following:

- whether all the persons who are or might be defendants in respect of the publication complained of are before the court at the hearing. If an order

---

133 See, eg, *Cook v Ward* (1830) 6 Bing 409.

for summary relief is made without all the defendants being able to make representations, the order granting relief may be set aside;

- whether summary disposal of the claim against another defendant would be inappropriate. It is possible that summary relief may be granted against one defendant but not against his co-defendants, who may have stronger defences;

- the extent to which there is a conflict of evidence;

- the seriousness of the alleged wrong (as regards the content of the statement and the extent of publication). Subject to the overriding objective (see below), a court is less likely to be inclined to dispose summarily of a case where the defamation is of a very serious nature and/or publication is widespread;

- whether it is justifiable in the circumstances to proceed to a full trial. An example of a case which might fall under this heading would be a particularly complex case which is unlikely to be capable of determination on a summary process but which will require a full investigation of all relevant facts and matters.

In reaching its decision, the court will also have to have regard to the overriding objective and its duty to manage cases, which are both set out at Pt 1 of the Civil Procedure Rules, which provides as follows.

THE OVERRIDING OBJECTIVE

1(1) These Rules are a new procedural code with the overriding objective of enabling the court to deal with cases justly.

(2) Dealing with a case justly includes, so far as is practicable–

(a) *ensuring that the parties are on an equal footing;*

(b) *saving expense;*

(c) *dealing with the case in ways which are proportionate–*

(i) *to the amount of money involved;*

(ii) to the importance of the case;

(iii) to the complexity of the issues; and

(iv) *to the financial position of each party;*

(d) *ensuring that it is dealt with expeditiously and fairly;* and

(e) *allotting to it an appropriate share of the court's resources, while taking into account the need to allot resources to other cases.*

APPLICATION BY THE COURT OF THE OVERRIDING OBJECTIVE

2   The court must seek to give effect to the overriding objective when it–

(a) exercises any power given to it by the Rules; or

(b) interprets any rule.

COURT'S DUTY TO MANAGE CASES

3(1)The court must further the overriding objective by actively managing cases.

(2)Active case management includes:

(a) encouraging the parties to co-operate with each other in the conduct of the proceedings;

(b) *identifying the issues at an early stage;*

(c) *deciding promptly which issues need full investigation and trial and accordingly disposing summarily of the others;*

(d) deciding the order in which issues are to be resolved;

(e) encouraging the parties to use an alternative dispute resolution procedure if the court considers that appropriate and facilitating the use of such procedure;

(f) helping the parties to settle the whole or part of the case;

(g) fixing timetables or otherwise controlling the progress of the case;

(h) *considering whether the likely benefits of taking a particular step justify the cost of taking it;*

(i) dealing with as many aspects of the case as it can on the same occasion;

(j) dealing with the case without the parties needing to attend at court;

(k) making use of technology; and

(l) *giving directions to ensure that the trial of a case proceeds quickly and efficiently.*

(Italics for emphasis.)

The application of the overriding objective and duty to manage cases, particularly those parts underlined above, is likely to lead to judges being strongly disposed towards the summary disposal of claims, unless there is a reason why summary disposal is not appropriate.

Summary relief

If the court grants summary relief to the claimant, the remedies available to it are set out at s 9 of the Act. It provides that the court may grant such of the following as may be appropriate:

- a declaration that the statement was false and defamatory of the claimant;
- an order that the defendant publish or cause to be published a suitable correction or apology (the content, time, manner, form and place of publication will be for the parties to agree. If they cannot, the court may direct the defendant to publish or cause to be published a summary of the court's judgment agreed by the parties or settled by the court in accordance with rules of the court. As to time, place, form and manner of publication the court may order the defendant to take such reasonable and practicable steps as the court considers appropriate);
- damages not exceeding £10,000 or such other amount as may be prescribed by order of the Lord Chancellor;
- an order restraining the defendant from publishing or further publishing the matter complained of.

From a claimant's point of view, the summary procedure will be a particularly useful weapon against defendants who do not have a defence to the claim, especially where the main objective of the claimant is to vindicate its good name by the publication of an apology or correction rather than by a large award of damages. The procedure will also offer impecunious claimants (who do not qualify for legal aid for defamation claims) an opportunity for speedy redress against what may be very wealthy defendants.

The potential downside for media defendants is the need for it to have its house in order at a relatively early stage in the proceedings, either to demonstrate that a claimant has no realistic prospect of success at trial or to show that its defence does have a realistic prospect of success.

A defendant is entitled to rely on all the sources of information available to it to justify a statement of fact, including sources which may only become available as the litigation progresses (even information which may only become available during cross-examination at trial), provided that it believes that its words are true and there are reasonable grounds for supposing that sufficient evidence to prove the allegations will be available at trial.[134] If care is not taken, defendants may be denied the opportunity to make use of these later sources of evidence because the court may order summary relief on the basis that on the evidence available at the summary procedure hearing, the defence has no realistic prospect of success. In *McDonald's v Steel and Morris*, the Court of Appeal stressed that the defences of justification and fair

---

134 *McDonald's v Steel and Morris* (1999) unreported.

comment form part of the framework by which free speech is protected and it is important that no unnecessary barriers to the use of these defences are erected. The application of the procedure for summary disposal is capable of constituting such an unnecessary barrier unless the spirit of the *McDonald's* judgment is kept in mind.

Parliamentary privilege

Article 9 of the Bill of Rights 1689 precludes any court from impeaching or questioning proceedings in Parliament. Prior to the Defamation Act 1996, it was well established that Art 9 prevented the court from entertaining an action *against* an MP or a Member of the House of Lords which sought to make him liable in criminal or civil law for acts done or things said by him in Parliament. This doctrine is known as *parliamentary privilege*. It should not be confused with absolute or qualified privilege.

The Privy Council decision in *Prebble v Television New Zealand*[135] confirmed that this preclusion extended to any party to litigation. It would therefore extend not just to proceedings against MPs, but also to proceedings commenced by MPs where the allegations concerned their parliamentary conduct. It is an infringement of parliamentary privilege for any party or witness in a legal action to call into question words spoken or actions done in Parliament whether by direct evidence, cross-examination, inference or submission.

The practical effect of the above was to preclude MPs from bringing defamation proceedings against defendants who alleged some professional impropriety about the MP. Perhaps the most notorious recent case where this situation arose concerned an article in *The Guardian* in 1994 about the MP Neil Hamilton. The story alleged that Mohamed Al Fayed had paid Tory MPs (including Mr Hamilton) thousands of pounds and other benefits in kind in return for the MPs asking questions in Parliament on Mr Al Fayed's behalf. Neil Hamilton sued the newspaper for libel. In its defence, the newspaper pleaded justification, alleging that, during the period 1987–89, Mr Hamilton had sought and received from Mr Al Fayed money in return for Mr Hamilton's parliamentary services. Mr Hamilton denied receiving payment from Mr Al Fayed.

Under the rules of parliamentary privilege, the parties could not adduce evidence or make submissions about Mr Hamilton's actions in Parliament. *The Guardian* was effectively precluded from linking the alleged payments with the parliamentary services which it claimed that Mr Hamilton had provided. In 1995, Mr Hamilton's action was stayed by the court on the ground that the

---

135 *Prebble v Television New Zealand* [1995] 1 AC 321.

claims and defences would infringe parliamentary privilege to such an extent that they could not fairly be tried.

But that was not the end of the matter. With the backing of a number of Tory MPs (including Mr Hamilton), an amendment was made to the Defamation Bill which was then going through Parliament to give individual MPs the right to waive their parliamentary privilege. Until the 1996 Act, parliamentary privilege was thought to belong to Parliament as a whole, rather than to any single individual, and so it was thought that no one individual MP could waive the privilege. The Act changed that position. The provision was enacted in part so that Mr Hamilton could pursue his action against *The Guardian*, which he then did (although the case settled before trial).

The provision can be found at s 13 of the Defamation Act 1996, sub-s 1 of which provides as follows:

13(1) Where the conduct of a person in or in relation to proceedings in Parliament is in issue in defamation proceedings, he may waive for the purposes of those proceedings, so far as concerns him, the protection of any enactment or rule of law which prevents proceedings in Parliament being impeached or questioned in any court or place out of Parliament.

It can be seen that s 13 is very much a 'claimant friendly' measure. An MP (or former MP) can choose whether or not to waive privilege as it suits. There is no corresponding right given to defendants to force the waiver of privilege.

Where an MP waives privilege, he does so on his own behalf only. His waiver does not affect the operation of privilege in relation to another person who has not waived it.[136] Once Mr Hamilton's case resumed against *The Guardian*, the newspaper sought to adduce evidence relating to a fellow Tory MP, Tim Smith, who had also featured in their article and who had admitted receiving payments from Mr Al Fayed in return for parliamentary services. The court held that *The Guardian* could not adduce such evidence, as it would be protected by parliamentary privilege. Mr Hamilton's waiver of privilege did not operate to waive Mr Smith's privilege. If the action had not settled, the defendants' ability to conduct its defence would have been severely restricted. In effect, the defendants could only put forward half of their case. There must be serious doubts that s 13 is compatible with Art 6 of the European Convention of Human Rights (the right to a fair trial).

Further consideration on the scope of parliamentary privilege occurred recently in another case arising from the Al Fayed-Hamilton saga. The case arose from a Channel 4 documentary about the issues first raised in *The Guardian* article. In the course of an interview which formed part of the programme, Mr Al Fayed stated that he had personally handed cash over to Mr Hamilton on a number of occasions. Mr Hamilton sued Mr Al Fayed for libel. In the meantime, Mr Hamilton's alleged activities had been investigated

---

136 Defamation Act 1996, s 13(3).

by the internal parliamentary Committee on Standards and Privileges, which made an adverse finding on Mr Hamilton's activities (subsequently upheld by the Parliamentary Commissioner for Standards).

In the light of those adverse findings, the defendants sought to strike out Mr Hamilton's claim on the ground that his case (denying that he had behaved improperly) was, in effect, a 'collateral attack' on the internal parliamentary findings and so infringed the parliamentary privilege which existed in relation to those internal proceedings. The defendants argued that the court might come to a different result from the internal inquiries. The Court of Appeal declined to strike out the proceedings, holding that it would only infringe parliamentary privilege if the claim were clearly a threat to undermine the authority of Parliament. The mere possibility that the court might come to an inconsistent result was not in itself a threat.[137] The House of Lords disagreed with the appeal court's reasoning.[138] Lord Browne-Wilkinson (with whom the other Law Lords agreed) indicated that the consequences of Mr Hamilton's waiver of his protection by way of parliamentary privilege were that any privilege of parliament as a whole would not be regarded as being infringed. The waiver of individual privilege operates to override any privilege belonging to Parliament as a whole. The findings of the internal parliamentary proceedings could therefore be considered by the courts in so far as they related to Mr Hamilton. But if Mr Hamilton had not waived his privilege, it would not be permissible for the courts to consider the proceedings of the parliamentary inquiry.

It is a moot point whether the House of Lords' decision has reversed the earlier finding that waiver by Mr Hamilton did not operate as a waiver by Mr Smith in relation to conduct concerning Mr Hamilton. The House of Lords' case concerned the effect of waiver on parliamentary proceedings, rather than the effect of waiver vis à vis another MP.

REMEDIES

Damages

Compensatory damages

General damages

An award of compensatory damages is usually the primary remedy in a defamation claim. A successful claimant is entitled to receive such sum as will compensate him for the damage to his reputation, vindicate his good name and, in the case of an individual claimant, take account of the distress, hurt

---

137 *Hamilton v Al Fayed* [1999] 3 All ER 317, CA.
138 *Hamilton v Al Fayed* [2000] 2 All ER 224, HL.

and humiliation. There is no arithmetical formula to govern the assessment of such damages. Factors relevant to an award include the gravity of the libel or slander, the extent of publication and the defendant's conduct after publication. If the defendant tries unsuccessfully to prove that the words are true, it is likely to lead to higher damages. A corporate claimant cannot recover damages for distress, hurt or humiliation, its claim being restricted to loss of income (which is likely to be a special damages claim) and damage to its goodwill.[139]

Over the last 20 years or so, claimants have been awarded a series of awards which were clearly disproportionate to any damage conceivably suffered by the claimant. The awards culminated in an award of £1.5 million in the case of *Tolstoy Miloslavsky v UK*.[140] This award was criticised by the European Court of Human Rights as being excessive and a violation of the defendant's rights of freedom of expression under Art 10 of the European Convention on Human Rights. The European Court indicated that if an award went beyond the proper bounds of protecting the reputation or rights of others, it should be regarded as incompatible with the Convention.

The main reason for the disproportionately large damages awards has arisen from the fact that, unless the case is heard by judge alone, the level of damages is left to be determined by the jury. Judicial reluctance to interfere into the jury's province tended to result in judges confining their directions on quantum to a statement of general principles, rather than giving specific guidance on the appropriate level to award. In the leading case of *John v Mirror Group Newspapers*,[141] Sir Thomas Bingham MR likened the jury's position to 'sheep loosed on an unfenced common without a shepherd' (p 49), lacking an instinctive sense of where to pitch their award.

The succession of disproportionate awards has led to widespread criticism of defamation law amongst the public generally. It was a major contributor to the 'chilling factor' discussed elsewhere in this chapter, operating as an invidious and serious restriction of the media's freedom to report freely on matters of public interest. Defendants know that they are usually at the mercy of juries who are likely to award vast sums of money to claimants. The jury is something of a 'wild card'. It is difficult for media defendants (and, in some cases, their insurers) to organise their business effectively, with appropriate reserves to cover any claims made against them when no one can predict with certainty what the likely band of damages will be.

From the early 1990s onwards, steps were taken to improve the position. The Courts and Legal Services Act 1990 empowered the Court of Appeal to substitute an award of damages for the sum awarded by a jury in cases where

---

139 *Lewis v Daily Telegraph* [1964] AC 234.

140 *Tolstoy Miloslavsky v UK* (1995) EHRR 442.

141 *John v Mirror Group Newspapers* [1996] 2 All ER 35; [1996] 3 WLR 593, CA.

the jury's award was either excessive or inadequate.[142] Since the Act came into force in 1991, the court has exercised this power on a number of occasions where the claimant has appealed against the level of award. Its decisions have begun to provide a corpus of guidance which can assist both the parties to an action to assess with some level of confidence what a claim might ultimately be worth, as well as being available to jurors who have to decide how much to award a claimant in any particular case.

The Court of Appeal guidance

In the case of *Gorman v Mudd*,[143] an award by a jury of £150,000 was reduced to £50,000. The claimant, a Tory MP, sued one of her constituents for a libel contained in a mock press release. The document had a limited circulation – it was published to only 91 people – but these were prominent and influential members of her local constituency party. The defendant had advanced and persisted in pleas of justification and qualified privilege. During the trial, the claimant had been subjected to insulting and distressing questioning by the defendant's counsel.

In *Rantzen v Mirror Group Newspapers*,[144] an award to the claimant, the well known television personality and founder of the Childline charity, of £250,000 was reduced to £110,000. The claimant's action was against a national newspaper in respect of articles which alleged that, knowing a teacher to be guilty of sexually abusing children, she had nevertheless protected him, because of his previous assistance in the preparation of a television programme. The Court of Appeal held that, in exercising its power to substitute an award, it should ask itself '*could a reasonable jury have thought that this award was necessary to compensate the claimant and to re-establish her reputation?*'. The jury was entitled to conclude that the publication of the article and its aftermath were a terrible ordeal for the claimant. But the claimant still had an extremely successful career as a TV presenter and was a distinguished and highly respected figure in the world of broadcasting. Her work in combating child abuse had received much acclaim. Judging by objective standards of reasonable compensation or necessity or proportionality, the £250,000 award was excessive.

In *Houston v Smith*,[145] an award of £150,000 was reduced to £50,000. The parties were GPs. The claimant sought damages for slander against the defendant, who had accused him of sexually harassing her and members of her staff. The allegation was made in the practice waiting room in front of a small audience, but it was also subsequently repeated and a defence of

---

142 Courts and Legal Services Act 1990, s 8(2).
143 *Gorman v Mudd* [1992] CA Transcript 1076.
144 *Rantzen v Mirror Group Newspapers* [1993] 4 All ER 975.
145 *Houston v Smith* [1993] CA Transcript 1544.

justification was advanced and persisted in. Hirst LJ observed that he regarded the substitute award of £50,000 to be 'at the very top of the range for a slander of this kind ... Had the slander remained within the confines of the waiting room and, still more, if the defendant had promptly apologised, the appropriate sum would have been a very small fraction of £50,000'.

In *John v Mirror Group Newspapers*,[146] a jury award of compensatory damages of £75,000 was reduced to £25,000 and an award of exemplary damages (see below) was reduced from £275,000 to £50,000. The *John* case concerned an article about the pop star, Elton John, alleging that he was hooked on a bizarre new diet involving him eating food and then spitting it out without swallowing. In relation to the jury's compensatory damages award, the court took into account the prominence of the article and the distress and hurt which the claimant had described in his evidence and the fact that, although the defendant had offered an apology, no apology had ever in fact been printed. It observed that it was not a trivial libel and, given Elton John's international reputation, probably every reader of the newspaper would have known to whom the story referred. Nevertheless, although the article was false, offensive and distressing, it did not attack the claimant's integrity or damage his reputation as an artist. The decision in relation to exemplary damages is considered below.

In *Kiam v Neil (No 2)*,[147] a jury award of £45,000 was left unchanged. The claimant was a successful businessman known for his business flair and success as an entrepreneur. *The Sunday Times* published an article incorrectly alleging that the claimant was being sued by Natwest bank after defaulting on a loan and that he had filed for bankruptcy protection. Three weeks later, the newspaper, having received a complaint from the claimant, published an apology in agreed terms. Notwithstanding publication of the apology, the claimant commenced proceedings for defamation. The judgment of the Court of Appeal highlights the limitations of s 8(2) as a mechanism for the review of defamation awards. First, the court made clear that a defendant must appeal to the court before the court will consider the level of award. The court will not substitute an award of its own initiative. Secondly, the defendant must establish that the award is out of proportion to the damage suffered. The court will not act as an automatic arbiter of awards.

The court highlighted the test propounded by the Court of Appeal in *Rantzen*, namely, 'could a reasonable jury have thought that this award was necessary to compensate the claimant and to re-establish her reputation?'. It emphasised that the jury should be allowed flexibility in reaching the decision. The Court of Appeal must not substitute its own assessment of the appropriate level of award if the above question can be answered

---

146 *John v Mirror Group Newspapers* [1996] 2 All ER 35; [1996] 3 WLR 593, CA.
147 *Kiam v Neil (No 2)* [1996] EMLR 493, CA.

affirmatively – to do so would usurp the traditional and statutory function of the jury. This is in line with the case law of the European Court of Human Rights, which stated in the *Tolstoy* case that 'a considerable degree of flexibility may be called for to enable juries to assess damages tailored to the facts of the particular case'.[148] On the facts, judged by the criteria of reasonableness and proportionality, the award was not excessive. The libel was widespread, grave and irresponsible. It alleged insolvency against a prominent entrepreneur striking to the core of his life's achievement. The jury was entitled to take account of Mr Kiam's prominence when deciding what figure was required to vindicate his reputation. *The Sunday Times* had made no effort to check the accuracy of its statement and, according to Mr Kiam's evidence (which was not challenged) the libel had had a prolonged and significant effect on him personally.

In *Jones v Pollard*,[149] an award of £100,000 was reduced to £40,000. The case concerned two articles published in the *Sunday Mirror*, alleging that the claimant was a pimp in Moscow and that he was also a party to blackmail of foreign businessmen by the KGB.

The Court of Appeal observed that it was difficult, save in possibly the most exceptional cases, to imagine any defamation action where even the most severe damage to reputation, accompanied by maximum aggravating factors, would be comparable to physical injuries such as quadriplegia, total blindness and deafness, where the top of the range for such awards for general damages is £130,000. The court did, however, stress that £130,000 was not a 'ceiling' on compensatory awards.

Guidance for juries?

One of the most important factors in the 'telephone number' awards of damages over the last 20 years has been the lack of guidance given to juries as to the appropriate level of damages to award. The Court of Appeal has reviewed the extent to which guidance can legitimately be given without usurpation of the jury's role on a number of occasions, most recently in *John v Mirror Group Newspapers*.[150] Under the present law, juries can now be referred to the following material:

- previous decisions of the Court of Appeal using its power to substitute its own award in place of the jury award where the jury award is excessive. It is anticipated that over the course of time these awards will establish standards as to what level of award is 'proper' in certain cases so as to

---

148 *Tolstoy Miloslavsky v UK* (1995) EHRR 442, para 41.
149 *Jones v Pollard* (1996) unreported, 12 December, CA.
150 *John v Mirror Group Newspapers* [1996] 2 All ER 35; [1996] 3 WLR 593, CA.

guide juries in their awards (although they will not operate as binding precedents);

- the jury should be asked to ensure that their award is proportionate to the damage which the claimant has suffered and is a sum which is necessary to provide adequate compensation and to re-establish reputation;[151]

- judges should ask jurors to consider the purchasing power of any award that they make and of the income it would produce. Juries are often reminded of the cost of buying a car, a holiday or a house;[152]

- the *John* decision established for the first time that juries can now be referred to personal injury awards for pain and suffering and loss of amenity, not in an attempt to equate such awards with defamation awards, but instead as a check on the reasonableness of their proposed award. Sir Thomas Bingham MR observed 'it is in our view offensive to public opinion, and rightly so, that a defamation plaintiff should recover damages for injury to reputation greater, perhaps by a significant factor, than if that same plaintiff had been rendered a helpless cripple or an insensate vegetable';

- again following the *John* decision, figures (or suitable brackets for awards) may now be mentioned by counsel for each party and by the judge to the jury 'to induce a mood of realism'. In every case, the jury should be directed that it is for them to make up their own minds and that the figures or financial brackets suggested to them are not binding.

The jury *cannot* properly be directed by reference to previous awards of juries. These will have been made in the absence of any specific guidance and so may be unreliable markers. The Court of Appeal envisaged that this position might change over time as a coherent body of jury awards emerges once the post-*John* guidance rules have established themselves.

It is not permissible for the jury to allow the question of the amount of legal costs which an unsuccessful claimant will have to pay to influence the size of their award.[153]

In *John*, the court expressed the hope that the additional guidance which can now be given to juries would make defamation proceedings more rational and so more acceptable to the general public.

It is debatable whether the *John* guidelines are having the desired effect. Large awards continue to be made by juries. For example, the following amounts have been awarded over the last few months:

---

151 *Rantzen v Mirror Group Newspapers* [1993] 4 All ER 975.
152 *Sutcliffe v Pressdram* [1990] 1 All ER 269.
153 *Pamplin v Express Newspapers* [1988] 1 WLR 116.

- £400,000 to a man wrongly accused of rape;[154]
- £105,000 to Victor Kiam over allegations about his business practices;
- £375,000 to ITN and two journalists over allegations that footage of Muslims in concentration camps in Bosnia had been exaggerated by the use of misleading camera angles and editing;
- £85,000 to the footballer Bruce Grobelaar over claims that he accepted bribes in return for fixing the results of football matches.

Under s 12 of the Human Rights Act 1998, courts (including juries) must have regard to the importance of the right to freedom of expression (amongst other things) when considering relief which might affect that right. Once the Act is in force in October 2000, juries will presumably be directed that their awards must both be proportionate to the damage to the claimant's reputation and yet must not stifle the exercise of the right. The potential effect which the Act will have on the size of damages awards was considered in Chapter 2. The Act itself was considered in Chapter 1.

Special damages

Special damages are a type of compensatory damages for loss which is capable of quantification. A typical example is where a claimant claims general compensatory damages for damage to reputation and special damages for loss of business as a result of the libel or slander. The loss of business is generally capable of quantification. The actual loss must be proved by the claimant: (a) to have occurred; and (b) to have been caused by the libel or slander. Special damages do not generally involve the same complexities of quantification as general damages, as the court will usually have the claimant's figures to work from as a base for the award. Unless the case is heard by judge alone, special damages are assessed by the jury.

Exemplary damages[155]

Exemplary damages are additional to compensatory damages. The two types of damages are not alternatives. The function of exemplary damages is to punish the defendant and to act as a deterrent both to the defendant and to society generally. If a claimant is seeking exemplary damages, it must state so in its pleadings and give the facts on which it relies in support. The decision whether to award exemplary damages and, if so, how much, is a matter for the jury. An award of exemplary damages should only be made in exceptional circumstances where *both* of the following factors are present:

---

154 (2000) *The Guardian*, 8 February.
155 Exemplary damages were also described in Chapter 2.

- the jury is satisfied that the publisher did not have a genuine belief in the truth of what he published. This might be inferred where the publisher suspected that the words were untrue and deliberately refrained from taking obvious steps which would have turned suspicion into certainty. As with malice, where the publisher was reckless as to the truth of what he published, that will equate to publication without positive belief in the truth of the publication. Carelessness alone will not be sufficient to justify an inference that the publisher had no honest belief in the truth of what he published;

- the jury is satisfied that the defendant acted in the hope or expectation of material gain. There must be a belief that he would be better off financially if he violated the claimant's rights than if he did not. Mere publication of a newspaper for profit will not be enough – the claimant must show that mercenary considerations in respect of that particular libel or slander motivated the defendant.

The jury should be directed that the proof of the above factors must be clear. An inference of reprehensible conduct and cynical calculation of advantage should not be lightly drawn.

No award of exemplary damages should be made where the sum awarded as compensatory damages (whether special or general) is sufficient in itself to satisfy the objectives of exemplary damages (punishment and deterrence).

The amount of exemplary damages

The following factors may be relevant in deciding how much should be awarded as exemplary damages:

- the means of the defendant;
- his degree of fault;
- the amount of profit resulting from the publication of the libel or slander.

The damages should not exceed *the minimum sum necessary* to meet the objectives of punishment and deterrence: '... freedom of speech should not be restricted by awards of exemplary damages save to the extent shown necessary for the protection of reputation.'[156] Any award of exemplary damages which exceeds this sum is likely to be an unlawful violation of Art 10 of the European Convention on Human Rights.

---

156 *John v Mirror Group Newspapers* [1996] 2 All ER 35, p 58.

On the facts of the *John* case, the court held that the jury's award of £275,000 exemplary damages was 'manifestly excessive' against Mirror Group Newspapers, going well beyond the minimum necessary to meet the objectives of such damages, and replaced it with an award of £50,000, so 'ensuring justice is done to both sides and securing the public interest involved'.

Evidence in mitigation of damages

The defendant is entitled to adduce evidence in mitigation of the amount of damages which should be awarded which the jury can take into account when calculating its award.

Evidence in mitigation typically consists of one or more of the following:

- *Evidence of other damages recovered by the claimant or proceedings commenced by the claimant*

  Section 12 of the Defamation Act 1952 provides that where the claimant has already recovered or has brought actions for damages for libel or slander in respect of the publication of words to the same effect as the words on which the action is founded or has agreed to receive compensation in respect of any such publication, the defendant may give evidence in mitigation of damages about such matters.

- *Offer of an apology*

  Section 1 of the Libel Act 1843 provides that the defendant may adduce evidence in mitigation of damages that he made or offered an apology to the claimant in respect of the publication complained of before the commencement of the action, or as soon afterwards as he had an opportunity of doing so, in case the action shall have been commenced before there was an opportunity of making or offering such apology. The defendant must give notice in writing of his intention to rely on such evidence at the time of serving his defence.

- *Offer of amends*

  Where the offer of amends under the Defamation Act 1996 is made and rejected, and the defendant chooses not to rely on it in defence, the offer can operate to mitigate the amount of damages if the defendant is subsequently found liable.

  The extent that the defendants succeed in partially justifying the defamatory imputations complained of may serve to reduce the amount of damages payable.[157]

---

157 *Irving v Penguin Books* (2000) unreported, 11 April.

- *The claimant's reputation*

  The defendant can adduce evidence to show that the claimant has a general bad reputation at the time of publication. However, the defendant may not rely on particular acts of misconduct of the claimant[158] to support a claim of bad reputation. In the words of the Faulks Committee, 'it is open to the defendant to prove that the plaintiff *did* in fact have a general bad reputation, but not that he *ought* to have had such a reputation'.[159] When the recent Defamation Bill was passing through Parliament, it was generally thought that it would abolish this rule. However, at the 11th hour, the provision was omitted from the 1996 Act. It was feared that the abolition of the rule would result in defendants seeking to uncover misconduct by the claimant which may have no connection with the subject matter of the defamation action, in the hope of reducing the size of any damages award, leading to prolongation of defamation trials and a disproportionate increase in costs. The rule prohibiting evidence about specific misconduct is therefore unaltered. A defendant must confine itself to evidence about general bad character.

Injunctions

A successful claimant will generally be awarded an injunction against the defendant restraining repetition of the defamatory statement. Often, the defendant will give an undertaking instead. Breach of the injunction or of an undertaking to the court will generally be punishable as contempt of court. Media organisations should therefore take care to keep an accessible record of all undertakings they have given or injunctions awarded against them to ensure against unintentional breach. Defendants should take care that the injunction or undertaking is not broader than the defamatory meaning(s) for which judgment has been given. A loosely worded injunction or undertaking could prevent the defendant from publishing any story against the claimant even if it is on a different topic to the alleged libel or slander. A broad undertaking of that type may well be a breach of Art 10 of the European Convention on Human Rights as being disproportionate to the legitimate aim of protecting reputation.[160]

---

158 *Scott v Sampson* (1882) 8 QBD 491.
159 *Report of the Committee on Defamation*, Cmnd 5909, 1975, para 363.
160 *Tolstoy Miloslavsky v UK* (1995) EHRR 442.

Interim injunctions: prior restraint

It has long been established that, in defamation cases, interim injunctions ought not to be granted except in the clearest of cases where the material is so obviously defamatory of the claimant that no reasonable jury could think otherwise.

Additionally, where the defendant indicates that he will be able to justify the libel or slander if the case goes to trial, no interim injunction should be granted unless the court is satisfied that he may not be able to do so.[161] As long ago as 1891, the judges recognised that 'the importance of leaving free speech unfettered is a strong reason in cases of libel for dealing most cautiously and warily with the granting of [interim] injunctions'.[162] The burden of proving that the defendant will not be in a position to justify his allegations rests with the claimant on the hearing for interim relief. The mere assertion that the statement is made maliciously will not in itself be sufficient to justify the grant of an interim injunction.[163]

Where a defendant faces an application for an interim injunction, it should carefully consider whether it will actually be able to justify the contentious allegations in court. If the defendant indicates that it will be able to do so in its evidence, and therefore prevents the grant of an interim injunction, if it cannot then justify the allegations at trial his conduct during the interim injunction application will inevitably increase the amount of damages payable.

Apology

The remedies available in defamation cases do not include the right to an apology or correction. The award of damages and the jury verdict or judgment is considered to be sufficient to vindicate the claimant's reputation. Claimants whose main motivation in commencing proceedings is to obtain an apology should be advised that litigation might not be the appropriate way of achieving that aim. On the other hand, both the offer of amends procedure and the summary disposal procedure, when implemented, do provide for the publication of an apology.

International defamation

Often, publication of defamatory material is not confined to the territory of one State and/or the claimant and defendant may be based in different States.

---

161 *Bonnard v Perryman* [1891] 2 Ch 269.
162 *Ibid*, p 284.
163 *Boscobell Paints v Bigg* [1975] FSR 42.

Publications on the internet can, of course, be downloaded around the world. The English courts are often a very attractive forum from a claimant's point of view in which to bring proceedings. At least until the impact of the reforms in the Defamation Act 1996 begin to be felt, the burden of proof on claimants is low and the chances of an award of substantial damages are good. So, in what circumstances will the English courts assume jurisdiction in proceedings concerning a defamatory statement which is published in more than one State? The answer to this question will depend on whether the States in question are parties to the Brussels Convention on Jurisdiction and the Enforcement of Judgments in Civil and Commercial Matters 1968 or the parallel Lugano Convention ('the Conventions') or not.

The Conventions

The Conventions govern jurisdiction as between the Convention States. The provisions which are relevant to defamation claims are Art 2 and Art 5(3). These two Articles are alternatives. Art 2 provides that the general rule on jurisdiction is that a party is to be sued in the country of his domicile. In deciding where a defendant is domiciled, a country will apply the national law of the State in question. If, for example, the English court must decide whether a defendant is domiciled in Germany, it will apply German law to reach its decision (Art 52(2)).

Art 5(3) offers an alternative way in which the courts of a country can assume jurisdiction. It provides that a defendant may be sued in the courts for the place where the harmful act occurred.

A claimant therefore has a choice whether to sue in the country where the defendant is domiciled or where the harmful act occurred. The relationship between the two articles was considered by the European Court of Justice in *Shevill v Presse Alliance*.[164] The case was an action commenced in the English courts by an English claimant against the French publishers of the newspaper *France-Soir*. The newspaper mainly circulated in France. It had a relatively tiny circulation in England. The defendants argued that, under the Brussels Convention, the action should have been commenced in France, as that was where they were domiciled and the place where the harmful event occurred (publication). The English court referred this issue to the ECJ, which ruled that a claimant in defamation proceedings in respect of a publication distributed in several Convention countries could either sue in the country where the publishers of the newspaper were domiciled, where they could claim damages for *all* the harm to their reputation in each of the Convention States (Art 2), or, alternatively, they could commence separate actions in the courts of each Convention State where the newspaper was distributed for the harm

---

164 *Shevill v Press Alliance* [1995] 2 AC 18.

done to the claimant's reputation in that State (Art 5(3)). The latter option might involve the claimant in a multiplicity of proceedings, but that is a choice for the claimant.

On the facts of the *Shevill* case, the claimant could have sued in France for the harm done to her reputation in all the Convention States where the libel had been distributed or in England for the damage to her reputation in England, as well as, if she chose, the other Convention States where the newspaper had been distributed.

Where an English newspaper or broadcast circulates in Convention States, it can therefore be sued in England for all its publications or in one or more of the States where it is circulated.

Non-Convention States

Where the Conventions do not apply, the question as to whether the English courts have jurisdiction is determined by the English common law. The general principle is that the court must identify the jurisdiction in which the case may be tried most suitably for the interests of all the parties and for the ends of justice. The burden of proof is on the claimant to establish that the English courts meet these criteria.[165]

In defamation claims, it is a prerequisite that the publication or broadcast in question has a degree of circulation within the jurisdiction of the English court. The claimant must also have some kind of connection with, or reputation in, the jurisdiction. It is then a question of degree as to whether England is the most appropriate forum for the action to be tried, bearing in mind all the relevant factors in the case at issue.

Where the English circulation of a foreign publication gave rise to a substantial complaint that a tort had been committed in England, having regard to the scale of the publication in England and the extent to which the claimant had connections with and a reputation to protect in England, England was *prima facie* the natural forum for resolution of the dispute.[166] On the other hand, where there is no complaint of substance that a tort had been committed in England, either because the publication had only an insignificant English circulation or because the claimant had no connection with or reputation to protect in England, the claimant will fail to establish that England was the appropriate forum.[167]

---

165 *Spiliada Maritime Corpn v Consulex Ltd, The Spiliada* [1987] AC 460.
166 *Distillers Co v Thompson* [1971] AC 458, PC.
167 *Kroch v Rossell* [1937] 1 All ER 725.

Further guidance

Schapira v Ahronson[168]

The claimant was an Israeli citizen resident in London and also a UK citizen. He sued in the English courts for defamation over two articles which appeared in an Israeli newspaper written in Hebrew and printed in Israel. The newspaper had a limited circulation in England. Evidence was produced that the first article had been circulated to 141 readers in England and the second article to 19 readers. The newspaper had a circulation of 60,000 in Israel. The Court of Appeal ruled that the English court did have jurisdiction to hear the case in relation to the alleged damage to the claimant's reputation in England arising from the English circulation of the newspaper. Peter Gibson LJ said:[169]

> Where the tort of libel is allegedly committed in England against a person resident and carrying on business in England by foreigners who were aware that their publication would be sent to subscribers in England, that English resident is entitled to bring proceedings here against those foreigners and to limit his claim to publication in England, even where the circulation of that article alleged to be defamatory was extremely limited in England and there was a much larger publication elsewhere.

Berezovsky v Forbes Inc[170]

The claimant was a businessman resident in Russia and a former member of the Russian Government. He commenced proceedings for defamation over an article in *Forbes* (an internationally published business magazine whose publishers were based in the US). The proceedings were commenced in the English courts and were confined to publication of the magazine within the jurisdiction of the English courts. The magazine had an English circulation of some 2,000 with approximately 6,000 readers. It was also published worldwide on the internet. The court heard evidence that 98.9% of the issue in question was sold in the US or in Canada or to US forces.

The case therefore concerned a Russian claimant suing an American defendant over a magazine with a relatively small circulation in England. Was the claimant able to demonstrate that the English courts were the most appropriate forum for proceedings concerning damage to the claimant's reputation in England?

The Court of Appeal thought he was.[171] and the House of Lords agreed.[172] The claimant's evidence showed that he had a substantial

---

168 *Schapira v Ahronson* [1999] EMLR 735, CA.
169 *Ibid*, p 19.
170 *Berezovsky v Forbes Inc* [2000] 2 All ER 986, HL.
171 [1999] EMLR 278, CA.
172 *Berezovsky v Forbes Inc* [2000] 2 All ER 986, HL.

connection with England and an important business reputation in this jurisdiction. Whilst the claimant had the closest connection to Russia (where he lived and where the alleged events referred to in the article had taken place), Russia was ill suited to hear the case. The magazine had only a minute circulation in Russia and Russia was also ill equipped to assess the impact of the article in England and the appropriate level of damages, having regard to the extent of the damage caused in England. The defendants, on the other hand, had the closest connection with the US. However, the claimant's connections with the US were far less strong than their connections in England. As with the Russian court, the US court would also be ill equipped to assess the impact of the article in England and the appropriate level of damages, having regard to the extent of damage to the claimant's reputation in England. The Court of Appeal stressed that the countries where the respective parties had the closest connections respectively were important factors to take into account, but they were not determinative. On the facts, they were overridden by the matters set out above.

The fact that the case would involve an understanding of the intricacies and subtleties of Russian political and business life was not considered to be an objection of any weight or significance. The court observed that English juries were capable of grappling with cases concerned with complex events in a foreign country.

In *Chada v Dow Jones and Co Inc*,[173] the Court of Appeal stressed that the *Berezovsky* case did not mean that whenever there has been a publication of an alleged libel in the jurisdiction there was a presumption that England was the most appropriate forum for the claim in respect of the harm suffered in the jurisdiction. The extent of publication in the country and the question of whether the claimant has sufficient connections with and a reputation to protect in England had to be considered. The court stressed that, in considering jurisdiction, the court must give consideration to the reality of the question, and if the reality was one which belonged to a foreign country and, above all, where it was a question which probably would be better tried in the foreign country for any particular reason which appeared in the circumstances of the case, permission ought not to be granted.

---

173 *Chada v Dow Jones and Co Inc* [1999] EMLR 724, CA.

A global cause of action?

In the *Berezovsky* case, counsel for the defendants argued that the correct approach in multi-jurisdiction cases was to treat them as giving rise to one single global cause of action and then to ascertain where that one cause of action arose. Such an approach would stop a defendant facing a multiplicity of actions by a claimant seeking damages in each State where his reputation has been damaged. It would also make life difficult for those claimants who commence proceedings in England with a view to obtaining a large award of damages from a jury in circumstances where the real damage to their reputation occurred elsewhere. However, the Court of Appeal rejected the approach out of hand, pointing out that it was inconsistent with the basic principle that each publication gives rise to a separate cause of action. The House of Lords has indicated that it is in agreement with the Court of Appeal on this point.[174]

There seems little scope for the development of an international cause of action at least for the foreseeable future. In the meantime, the new regime for guidance for juries, the ability of the Court of Appeal to reduce excessive damages awards, the offer of amends defence and the availability of summary judgment may make England a less attractive forum for those claimants who are motivated more by mercenary considerations than by a desire to re-establish their good name.

A right to a jury trial?

So far in this chapter, we have assumed that a trial in an action for defamation will be heard by a judge and jury. Most defamation trials are tried this way. The mode of trial is governed by s 69 of The Supreme Court Act 1981, which provides as follows:

(1) Where, on the application of any party to an action to be tried in the Queen's Bench Division, the court is satisfied that there is in issue–

(a) a charge of fraud against that party; or

(b) a claim in respect of *libel, slander,* malicious prosecution or false imprisonment; or

(c) any question or issue of a kind prescribed for the purposes of this paragraph, the action shall be tried with a jury, *unless the court is of the opinion that the trial requires any prolonged examination of documents or accounts or any scientific or local investigation which cannot conveniently be made with a jury.*

(The words in italics in this sub-section are known as 'the proviso'.)

---

174 *Berezovsky v Forbes Inc* [2000] 2 All ER 986, HL.

(2) ...

(3) An action to be tried in the Queen's Bench Division which does not by virtue of sub-s (1) fall to be tried with a jury shall be tried without a jury unless the court in its discretion orders it to be tried with a jury.

(4) ...

Actions for libel and slander are accordingly tried with a jury unless the proviso applies or the parties to the action elect trial by judge alone. The proviso will apply where the court is of the opinion that the trial involves any prolonged examination of documents or accounts or any scientific or local investigation which cannot conveniently be made by a jury.

Where the proviso applies, the court will order trial by judge alone unless it exercises its discretion under s 69(3) of the Supreme Court Act and orders that, notwithstanding the provisions of the proviso, the trial should be heard by judge and jury. However, it will be seen from the cases considered below that, once the proviso to s 69 has been invoked, the court is unlikely to exercise its discretion in favour of trial by jury.

The proviso

The courts have interpreted the proviso strictly, in recognition of the fact that by enacting s 69, Parliament's intention is that, in the ordinary way, defamation actions should be tried with a jury.[175] Unless the court is of the opinion that the criteria in the proviso are satisfied, it must order trial by jury (if one of the parties has requested it), however wide ranging and difficult the issues may be and whatever the judge's personal doubts as to the appropriateness of a jury for the trial of a particular case.

The cases involving the proviso which have been considered by the courts have involved prolonged examination of documents or accounts. 'Examination' has been construed to mean 'careful reading'.[176] In *Goldsmith v Pressdram*,[177] the Court of Appeal held that a jury trial would be inappropriate because resolution of the issues raised would have involved frequent references to statutory provisions and complex documents involving the claimant's share dealings. This exercise would be more conveniently conducted by a judge alone than by judge and jury. In contrast, in *Viscount de L'Isle v Times Newspapers*,[178] whilst the trial would involve a reference to accounts, it would only be necessary to take a 'broad brush' or general overview of the financial situation in question. This would not involve a prolonged examination of the accounts, nor constant references to them. A jury trial was therefore appropriate.

175 Lawton LJ in *Goldsmith v Pressdram* [1987] 3 All ER 485.
176 Slade LJ in *ibid*, p 496.
177 *Goldsmith v Pressdram* [1987] 3 All ER 485.
178 *Viscount de L'Isle v Times Newspapers* [1987] 3 All ER 499.

The number of documents which will need to be looked at is not conclusive. There may be cases where a substantial number of documents have to be looked at, but no substantial practical difficulties are likely to arise in the examination being made by a jury. On the other hand, there may be relatively few documents, but where a long and minute examination of them is required, a satisfactory examination of them by a jury may present practical difficulties.[179]

The meaning of 'conveniently'

The word 'conveniently' is to be read in the context of the efficient administration of justice rather than in the context of the probable difficulty or otherwise of the issues involved.[180] The question for the court to consider is whether the trial is likely to involve any of the matters referred to in the proviso in such a way as it is likely that the administration of justice will suffer if the trial is with a jury rather than by judge alone. In the *Goldsmith* case, Kerr LJ indicated that 'conveniently' means without substantial difficulty in comparison with carrying out the same process with a judge alone.

In *Beta Construction v Channel Four Television*,[181] Stuart Smith LJ highlighted four main areas in which the efficient administration of justice might be rendered less convenient if the trial takes place with a jury:

- the physical problem of handling large bundles of documents (perhaps where there is a need to cross-refer to different bundles) or documents which are so bulky that they cannot conveniently be looked at;

- the issue of prolongation of the trial. A jury trial inevitably takes longer than a trial by judge alone. Stuart Smith indicated that this is generally an acceptable price to pay for the advantage of having juries decide the issues raised in cases referred to in s 69(1). However, where the prolongation is likely to become substantial because of the number and complexity of documents or scientific or local inquiries, the administration of justice is affected. Substantial prolongation of the trial uses up resources in court and judge time so that they are not available to other litigants (echoed in the CPR overriding objective) but also adds significantly to the cost burden;

- the costs of copying large numbers of documents for the jury members can add significantly to the costs of trial;

- there is the risk that the jury may not sufficiently understand the issues on the documents or accounts (or scientific or local inquiry) to resolve them correctly. A judge may not understand the documents, but he has to give a

---

179 Slade LJ in *Goldsmith v Pressdram* [1987] 3 All ER 485.
180 *Ibid.*
181 *Beta Construction v Channel Four Television* [1990] 2 All ER 1012.

reasoned judgment and any error in it can be corrected in court. No one can know the grounds on which the jury reaches its verdict. Where the documents requiring prolonged examination are such that the average juryman cannot be expected to be familiar with them, this risk is enhanced.

This last ground comes perilously close to upholding the notion that trials raising complex and difficult issues ought to be heard by judge alone, at least where the complexity arises from documents, accounts, or scientific or local inquiries, because of the risk of the jury getting it wrong; a notion expressly rejected by the Court of Appeal in the *Goldsmith* case. In the *Beta Construction* case, whilst agreeing with Slade LJ's four grounds in principle, Neill LJ pointed out that the fourth ground was 'a subsidiary point' because juries often have to grapple with complex issues with which they do not deal in their daily lives. Neill LJ did, however, recognise the importance of obtaining a reasoned judgment in some cases.

Discretion

If a defamation case satisfies the criteria in the proviso, the case is *prima facie* unsuitable for trial by jury. The court may still exercise its discretion in favour of jury trial pursuant to s 69(3), but in doing so the emphasis is at this stage *against* trial with juries.[182] Only in rare cases of public importance should the judge exercise its discretion under s 69(3) to order trial by jury notwithstanding the fact that the proviso applies. In *Goldsmith v Pressdram*,[183] the claimant, Sir James Goldsmith, argued that the libels against him attacked his honour and integrity and, given his status as a public figure of some importance, the court should exercise its discretion to order jury trial. The Court of Appeal declined to do so. The mere fact that the allegations were serious and attacked his honour and integrity would not in itself cause the court to exercise its discretion.

A more recent defamation case involving the former MP Jonathan Aitken followed much the same lines as the *Goldsmith* case. It was held that the trial of the action would involve a prolonged examination of documents and that the convenient administration of justice required trial by judge alone. The defendants argued that the court should exercise its discretion under s 69(3) and order a jury trial. The case concerned the claimant's fitness to hold public

---

182 Neill LJ in *Beta Construction v Channel Four Television* [1990] 2 All ER 1012.
183 *Goldsmith v Pressdram* [1987] 3 All ER 485.

office and the claimant argued that the public interest in allowing a jury trial in such circumstances should be a weighty factor in the court's decision.

The Court of Appeal declined to exercise its discretion in favour of a jury trial. It held that the fact that the proceedings concerned a prominent public figure and raised issues of national interest were factors in favour of jury trial, as was the fact that the case concerned issues of credibility and an attack on A's honour and integrity. But these factors were not overriding considerations in support of a jury trial. The need to obtain a reasoned judgment was also relevant. It was for the court to decide what mode of trial would best serve the interests of justice with regard to both the parties and the public and in view of the complex and controversial nature of the instant case, a trial before a judge alone would be more appropriate.[184]

The *Aitken* decision echoes Stuart Smith LJ's fourth criteria in the *Beta* case – the desirability of being able to see and correct any errors in understanding factual matters which are relevant to the court's findings at trial. Judges give reasoned judgments. Juries do not.

THE CRIMINAL LAW

'A monstrous offence' – JR Spencer.[185]

In addition to being a tort, libel (but not slander) can also be a criminal offence carrying a maximum of one year's imprisonment and an unlimited fine[186] or two years' imprisonment and an unlimited fine if the libel is published in the knowledge that it is known to be false.[187] Prosecutions for libel are rare, but the offence remains in existence. The possibility of a private prosecution should never be disregarded. A claimant may, if it chooses, pursue its civil remedies at the same time as launching a private prosecution in respect of the same publication. There is no requirement that the prosecutor has to be the person who is the subject of the libel. In theory, any disgruntled citizen could launch a prosecution over material that he believes to be defamatory of a third party.

The essentials of the criminal offence and the available defences are similar to that of the tort, with the following important differences:

---

184 *Aitken v Preston* [1997] EMLR 415.
185 Spencer, JR [1977] Crim LR 465.
186 Libel Act 1843, s 5.
187 *Ibid*.

- publication to a third party does not appear to be essential for the criminal offence. An action for criminal libel could theoretically be brought in respect of a publication to the claimant alone;[188]

- there is some authority to suggest that a prosecution for criminal libel can be brought by the estates or families of dead people[189] and members of large groups (even if the particular claimant cannot be identified);[190]

- most significantly, justification is not in itself a complete defence *unless the defendant can also show that the publication was for the public benefit*.[191] The onus is on the defendant to show this public benefit and the burden in doing so will inevitably be a heavy one. The defences of fair comment and privilege will apply (there is no requirement for the defendant to show publication for the public benefit in relation to the latter defences);

- there is no equivalent to s 5 of the Defamation Act 1952. If a defendant wishes to rely on justification (showing also publication for the public benefit), he must therefore prove the truth of every charge that he has published.

It is a basic foundation of criminal law that the prosecution is required to prove its case against the defendant beyond reasonable doubt in order to secure a conviction. The offence of criminal libel is an exception to this rule. The onus on the prosecutor is to show that the words are defamatory and that they refer to him. The burden then switches, as with the tort, to the defendant to prove that his words were true (and that his publication was for the public benefit) or that the facts on which his comment was based were true.

There have been no prosecutions by the State in recent times, but there have been a handful of private prosecutions or attempted private prosecutions. Before an individual can bring proceedings for criminal libel against a *newspaper or periodical* (as defined in the Newspaper Libel and Registration Act 1881) or anyone responsible for such a publication, the consent of a High Court judge must be given.[192] This is intended to act as a check on the commencement of vexatious or malicious prosecutions, but it only applies where the defendant is a newspaper or periodical. If the safeguard is to be truly effective, the need for consent should be extended to a prosecution against any kind of defendant. The House of Lords has also recommended that consent should be required, not from a judge, but from the

---

188 *R v Adams* (1888) 22 QBD 66.
189 *Libellis Famosis* 5 Co Rep 125a; and *Hilliard v Penfield Enterprises* [1990] IR 38.
190 Osborne (1732) 2 Barnard KB.
191 Libel Act 1843, s 6.
192 Law of Libel Amendment Act 1888, s 3.

Attorney General, but this recommendation has not been implemented by Parliament.

In the past, the criminal law of libel was intended to be used to prevent disorder and, in particular, duelling. Claimants who felt that they had been defamed were encouraged to launch a prosecution against the publisher, rather than to resort to violence. The offence could accordingly be classified as a public order offence. However, the case of *R v Wicks*[193] confirmed that in more modern times it is no longer *necessary* for the claimant to show that the libel is likely to provoke a breach of the peace as a prerequisite to establishing criminal liability. It might still be a relevant factor for a judge to bear in mind when considering whether to allow a prosecution against a newspaper to go ahead, but it is not determination. The *Wicks* decision was confirmed by the House of Lords in *Gleaves v Deakin*.[194]

Leave to prosecute

So, in what circumstances will leave to prosecute against a newspaper be granted?

The leading case is *Goldsmith v Pressdram*,[195] a first instance decision of Wien J which was subsequently approved by the House of Lords in *Gleaves v Deakin*.[196] Wien J laid down the following guidelines:

- the applicant must show a clear *prima facie* case so that is 'beyond argument' that there is a case to answer;
- the libel must be serious – 'so serious that it is proper for the criminal law to be invoked'. The fact that the libel may provoke a breach of the peace will be a relevant factor here;
- the judge must ask himself 'does the public interest *require* the institution of criminal proceedings?' (judge's emphasis);
- it may be relevant that the libel forms part of a campaign of vilification against the applicant;
- the status of the applicant may be relevant. If he holds a position whereby an attack on him raises issues in the public interest, that may make a criminal prosecution more appropriate.

---

193 *R v Wicks* [1936] 1 All ER 338.
194 *Gleaves v Deakin* [1980] AC 477.
195 *Goldsmith v Pressdram* [1977] QB 83.
196 *Gleaves v Deakin* [1980] AC 477.

Factors which are not relevant

The *Goldsmith* case established that the following factors will *not* be relevant in the decision whether to grant leave:

- the fact that there is no likelihood of any repetition of the libel;
- the question whether an award of damages would provide an appropriate remedy for the applicant;
- the question whether an award of damages is or is not likely to be satisfied by the defendant.

The *Goldsmith* case concerned an application by Sir James Goldsmith, the chairman of a number of large and well known companies, for leave to commence a private prosecution against the publishers of *Private Eye* (which is classed as a newspaper). The application was in respect of articles alleging that Sir James was the ringleader of a conspiracy to obstruct the course of justice over police inquiries into the disappearance of Lord Lucan and reporting that the Bank of England was alleged to have become worried about the applicant. The applicant alleged that the articles formed part of a campaign of vilification against him. *Private Eye* had admitted that its original article (making the conspiracy allegation) was untrue, but had continued their campaign against him with the second article complained of. The court granted leave for the applicant to prosecute. It held that there was a clear *prima facie* case to answer, the libels were serious and that the public interest required the institution of criminal proceedings – particularly relevant here was the evidence of the campaign of vilification and the applicant's professional position, which was such as to make his integrity a matter of general public interest. Sir James Goldsmith was subsequently given leave to withdraw his prosecution after a private settlement was reached with *Private Eye*.

The *Goldsmith* guidelines were also applied in *Desmond v Thorne*,[197] a case which concerned a newspaper article alleging that the applicant had constantly beaten up his girlfriend during what was described as 'a stormy love affair'. The article described him as 'a boastful bully' and as a drunkard. In addition to the *Goldsmith* guidelines, the judge added that, in considering whether to grant leave, he was required to consider all the circumstances surrounding publication and not just the evidence adduced by the applicant in support of his application for leave. The judge was therefore entitled to consider a proposed plea of justification by the defendant and to take into account the likelihood of the defence succeeding by weighing evidence adduced in support of the proposed plea against the applicant's evidence on the leave application.

---

197 *Desmond v Thorne* [1982] 3 All ER 268.

On the facts, the judge expressed himself to be 'far from satisfied' that there was a clear *prima facie* case. The facts which the applicant admitted took too much of the sting out of the article and the affidavit evidence (which included evidence from independent witnesses) tended to undermine the reliability of the applicant. Further, the position of the applicant was not such as to make his integrity a matter for the public interest. It was accordingly not a case where the public interest required the institution of criminal proceedings.

Should the criminal offence be abolished?

Most of this chapter is devoted to civil defamation law. We have seen that, although recent reforms have begun to even the balance, the tort is by and large a 'claimant friendly' cause of action. Given that claimants have such an effective tool to vindicate their reputations in the civil law, what possible use is the criminal law of libel in modern society? Its original role of keeper of the peace has long gone. The Law Commission has recommended the abolition of the criminal offence.[198] Conversely, the Faulks Committee recommended that the criminal offence remain in being.[199] It drew attention to the fact that the criminal offence fills a lacuna in a number of cases, principally in relation to libels on impecunious people. Legal aid is not available in civil defamation cases. This means that only litigants who can afford to fund litigation have effective redress to the civil courts. The criminal offence offers an alternative method of obtaining redress to those people who are left without any other redress. However it must be queried whether the retention of such a draconian offence is really the best way of filling this gap.

If the offence is not abolished, what changes should be made to it?

Where the proposed defendant is not a newspaper, there are no effective safeguards to ensure that a criminal prosecution in a particular case is justified in the public interest. Consent should accordingly be required before a prosecution for criminal libel may be brought against any kind of defendant.

Even where the defendant is a newspaper and judicial consent is required before a prosecution can be commenced, the test for consent should be made more stringent. Less emphasis should attach to the status of the applicant for leave *per se*. At present, the law makes it easier for public figures to obtain leave on the relatively glib ground that their integrity is a matter of public interest. The concept of public interest should be clarified so that it applies in a

---

198 Law Commission, *Criminal Libel*, Working Paper No 84.
199 Faulks Committee, *Report of the Committee on Defamation*, Cmnd 5909, 1975, para 444.

non-discriminatory way but, at the same time, ensuring that consent to the prosecution will only be forthcoming in the most serious of cases.

If a criminal offence is to be preserved, permission for the commencement of the prosecution should be granted by the Attorney General in every case. The applicant should have to demonstrate that the alleged defamatory material is of a kind which it is *necessary* in a democratic society to suppress or penalise in order to protect the public interest.[200] If it cannot do so, the prosecution should fail or leave should not be granted. The onus should not be on the defendant to show that its publication was for the public benefit.

The onus should also be on the prosecution to show that the material is false and that the defendant knew it to be so (or was reckless as to whether it was true). The burden of proof would therefore be the opposite to civil cases, but in view of the fact that the defendant's liberty is at stake, the prosecution ought fairly to be in a position to prove its case that the words are untrue rather than rely on a presumption of falsity. The rules on publication and identification should also be brought into line with civil law.

These reforms are the minimum necessary to modernise the offence from the days of the Star Chamber to 21st century society. They are also the minimum required to square with the UK's obligations under the European Convention on Human Rights to safeguard freedom of expression, save where limitation of the right is necessary in a democratic society.

---

200 Lord Diplock in *Gleaves v Deakin* [1980] AC 477, p 482.

CHAPTER 4

MALICIOUS FALSEHOOD

Malicious falsehood is primarily concerned with damage to profits or earnings caused by the publication of untrue statements of fact. For the purposes of this cause of action, it is immaterial whether the untrue statement causes damage to the claimant's reputation. A statement may be actionable as a falsehood even though it is not defamatory. On the other hand, the fact that the untrue words are also defamatory will not exclude a claim being made in malicious falsehood, although the courts will not allow the claimant to recover damages for both defamation and malicious falsehood for the same loss.[1]

ESTABLISHING MALICIOUS FALSEHOOD

To succeed in a malicious falsehood claim the claimant must show all of the following.

The defendant has published an untrue statement of fact about the claimant

In malicious falsehood cases, the law does not presume that the words are false. The onus is on the claimant to prove that they are.

The court must first determine the meaning of the words in the same way as it would in defamation cases. The meaning that the maker of the statement *intended* will be irrelevant to meaning. Having determined the natural and ordinary meaning, the court will go on to consider whether the claimant has proved that that meaning is not true. Note that the statement has to be an untrue statement of *fact*. An expression of opinion is unlikely to give rise to a claim in malicious falsehood, provided that it is clear from the statement that it is an expression of opinion and not a statement of fact.[2]

The defendant published the words maliciously

Malice bears the same meaning as it does in defamation law. The concept of malice is broader than wickedness or evil intent. The claimant must show either:

---

1   *Joyce v Senagupta* [1993] 1 All ER 897.
2   *Emaco v Dyson Appliances* (1999) *The Times*, 8 February.

(a) that the defendant did not have a positive belief in the truth of his statement (where he is reckless as to whether a statement is true or false he will be treated as if he knew that it was false); or

(b) that the defendant's *dominant* motive in making the statement was dishonest or improper. If a statement is made maliciously, it must be made with the *dominant* object of injuring the claimant's business. The mere fact that the statement has damaged the claimant's business will not in itself be sufficient to prove malice.[3] Similarly, a statement is not made maliciously simply because the maker of the statement wanted to improve his own business. As in defamation cases, the claimant will rarely be in a position to give evidence about the claimant's state of mind. Malice will generally have to be inferred from what he said or did or knew. The difficulties involved in establishing malice are described below, p 158.

The words have caused the claimant pecuniary loss as a natural and direct result of the publication

The claimant must prove: (a) that pecuniary loss has been suffered; and (b) that the loss is attributable to the defendant's statement. The second limb of this test is often difficult to satisfy. It is usually difficult to find witnesses who will say that they stopped doing business with the claimant as a result of the untrue statement. It will not usually be sufficient to show a downturn in sales for about the time that the statement was made, unless the claimant can also show that the downturn could not be attributable to other factors such as a seasonal downturn or the economic climate generally.[4]

It is vital that loss or the likelihood of it is established. As Lord Robertson cautioned in *Royal Baking Powder v Wright Crossley and Co*:[5]

> Unless the plaintiff has in fact suffered loss which can be and is specified, he has no cause of action. The fact that the defendant has acted maliciously cannot supply the want of special damage, nor can a superfluity of malice eke out a case wanting in special damage.

Where the words are published in writing or other permanent form, the claimant does not have to show *actual* loss. It is sufficient to prove that the untrue words were likely to cause pecuniary loss.[6] The likelihood of pecuniary loss should be judged objectively.

---

3   *Dunlop Pneumatic Tyre Company v Maison Talbot* (1904) 20 TLR 579.
4   In relation to comparisons see *Emaco v Dyson Appliances* (1999) *The Times*, 8 February.
5   *Royal Baking Powder v Wright Crossley and Co* (1900) 18 RPC 103.
6   Defamation Act 1952, s 3(1)(a).

Similarly, where the untrue words are likely to cause pecuniary damage to the claimant in respect of any office, profession, calling, trade or business held by or carried on by him at the time of publication, it will not be necessary for the claimant to prove actual damage.[7]

The loss or likelihood of loss must be a natural and probable consequence of the falsehood. In *Stewart Brady v Express Newspapers*,[8] the convicted murderer, Ian Brady, brought proceedings for malicious falsehood against the *Express* over an allegation that he had assaulted a female prison visitor. The court held that Mr Brady did not have a reasonable cause of action, as he could not show that the publication was likely to cause him financial loss. Mr Brady tried to rely on the possibility that the prison authorities would remove his discretionary weekly allowance as a result of the report. The court ruled that the natural and probable consequence of the publication was that there would be an internal prison inquiry into the allegation, at which the claimant would have an opportunity to put his case. If the inquiry decided to withdraw his allowance, that would be as a result of their findings, rather than as a natural and probable result of the newspaper report.

The limitation period in relation to malicious falsehoods is one year from the date that the cause of action arose, although the court has discretion to extend the period in appropriate cases.[9] The same position applies in defamation cases.

The burden of proof in relation to all three of the above requirements is on the claimant. A claim in malicious falsehood tends to be a difficult claim for a claimant to bring successfully. Where a claimant has a choice of a claim for defamation or malicious falsehood, his burden of proof in the defamation claim will be lighter.

Differences in the burden of proof in defamation cases and malicious falsehood cases

- In defamation cases, a factual statement is presumed to be false, unless the defendant can show that it is true. In malicious falsehood, the burden of showing that the statement is untrue rests on the claimant.

- In defamation cases, a defamatory statement is presumed to cause damage to the claimant without the need to produce evidence to establish damage.[10] In malicious falsehood cases, the claimant must prove actual damage or the likelihood of such damage.

---

7   Defamation Act 1952, s 3(1)(a).

8   *Stewart Brady v Express Newspapers* (1994) unreported.

9   Defamation Act 1996, ss 5–6.

10 The position is different in relation to some forms of slander where loss must be proved – see Chapter 3 for further detail.

- In defamation cases, the claimant does not have to establish malice, unless the defendant is able to rely on the defences of fair comment or qualified privilege. In malicious falsehood cases, the claimant must show that the defendant made the statement maliciously.

- Unlike defamation claims, there is no right to trial by jury in malicious falsehood cases. Most malicious falsehood claims are heard by, and damages are assessed by, a judge sitting alone.

Potential advantages of bringing a claim in malicious falsehood rather than in defamation are:

- an interim injunction to restrain publication of the falsehood for the period up to trial may be easier to obtain for a malicious falsehood than it would be in proceedings for defamation;[11]

- legal aid is not available to claimants who wish to bring defamation claims. It is available in theory to claimants in malicious falsehood cases. In *Joyce v Senagupta*,[12] the claimant obtained legal aid for, and brought proceedings in, malicious falsehood. Her claim could equally have been brought for defamation. An attempt to strike out the malicious falsehood claim on the ground that it was in reality a defamation claim was unsuccessful. The Court of Appeal found that the claimant had an arguable case in malicious falsehood which she could choose to pursue at her option;

- a cause of action in defamation cases cannot be commenced or continued on behalf of a dead claimant. A cause of action in malicious falsehood may be commenced or continued by the estate of a deceased person.

MALICIOUS FALSEHOOD – SOME TERMINOLOGY

The cause of action known as malicious falsehood is also referred to as injurious falsehood. The terms are interchangeable. There are also particular types of malicious/injurious falsehood, known as slander of title and trade libel (the terms 'slander' and 'libel' in this context are misleading. They do not bear the same meaning as for defamation law. A trade libel can be made orally and a statement which amounts to slander of title can be made in writing or other permanent form). Whatever terminology is used in each case, the claim is essentially one for redress for loss caused as a result of false statements.

---

11 The award of interim injunctions in malicious falsehood cases is considered at the end of this chapter.

12 *Joyce v Senagupta* [1993] 1 All ER 897.

Trade libel (also known as slander of goods)

A trade libel arises from an untrue statement which is critical of the claimant's *goods* or *services*. At the beginning of Chapter 3, an example was given concerning disparaging comments made in relation to a company's goods (in the example, the goods were electric fans). Where the disparaging comment could be understood to be an attack on the manufacturer's reputation (for example, by inferring that it is cavalier about health and safety issues), a claim in defamation might lie. However, where the criticism is in reality a criticism of the manufacturer's *product*, defamation will not be an appropriate cause of action, because the statement will not have caused damage to the claimant's reputation (despite the fact that it has damaged the claimant's profits). The manufacturer can bring a claim in malicious falsehood, provided that it can satisfy the criteria set out above. This type of malicious falsehood is often referred to as trade libel, because the untrue statement is critical of the claimant's goods or services, rather than of the claimant itself.

Slander of title

A false statement in relation to the claimant's title to property is known as slander of title.

Other types of malicious falsehood

The cause of action is not confined to trade libel cases or slander of title cases. It extends to all types of untrue statements which cause or are likely to cause pecuniary loss.

Examples

(a) Kaye v Robertson[13]

The claimant was an actor. He was in hospital recovering from extensive surgery to his head and brain following an injury sustained in a severe storm. The defendant was the editor of the *Sunday Sport* newspaper. Journalists from the newspaper gained access to Mr Kaye's private hospital room, ignoring notices which prohibited such entry, and interviewed Mr Kaye at length and took photographs of him, despite the fact that he was only in partial command of his facilities – as the journalists were well aware. Eventually, the hospital staff realised what was going on and the journalists were ejected from the

---

13   *Kaye v Robertson* [1991] FSR 62.

room. Shortly after the 'interview' had taken place, Mr Kaye had no recollection of it. The newspaper threatened to publish the interview in such a way as to create the impression that Mr Kaye had consented to it. Mr Kaye sought an interim injunction to restrain publication. He claimed that he had not given his consent to the interview and, indeed, he had been in no fit state to give his consent in any event, as the defendant would have appreciated.

The Court of Appeal held that the publication of the defendant's story as an 'interview' would be a falsehood, in that it would represent that the claimant had willingly consented to the process. The falsehood was made maliciously, because the defendant was well aware that Mr Kaye had not consented to the story. The story was also likely to cause Mr Kaye pecuniary loss, as he has a potentially valuable right to sell the story of his accident to the media. If the defendant published its story, the value of Mr Kaye's rights would be seriously reduced.

(b) Comparisons

One of the main areas in which malicious falsehood claims are brought is manufacturers' comparison of their goods with the goods of a trade rival. These types of comparison are often referred to as 'knocking copy' and they usually involve trade libels in the form of disparaging comments about the competitor's products.

There have been a number of important cases involving claims of malicious falsehood in the field of comparisons, especially in relation to comparative advertising. The cases have involved allegations that the comparative advertisements in question contain untrue statements about the defendant's goods and services.[14]

The construction of natural and ordinary meanings in relation to advertising and marketing material

When construing the claims made in comparative advertisements, the court is concerned to determine what the reasonable man would find the claim to mean taken in the context in which the words were intended to be read or viewed.[15] The courts are aware that the public tends to take most kinds of advertising with a pinch of salt. They therefore consider whether the reasonable man would take the claims made in the advertising seriously. If not, the claim is unlikely to succeed. In the *Dyson* case,[16] which involved the

---

14 Note that in *Cable and Wireless plc v BT plc* [1998] FSR 383, Jacob J observed that, where a claimant also had a cause of action for trade mark infringement in addition to malicious falsehood, the claim in malicious falsehood added little to the trade mark claim; the implication being that the malicious falsehood claim would be superfluous in such circumstances.

15 *Emaco v Dyson Appliances* (1999) *The Times*, 8 February.

16 *Ibid.*

construction of the meaning of certain promotional literature produced by Electrolux and Dyson making comparisons between their respective vacuum cleaners, the court held that the material must be read and viewed through the eyes of a potential customer interested in purchasing a vacuum cleaner who is being subjected to sales patter designed to persuade him or her to purchase one machine rather than the other. In the same case, comments made to a trade journalist were to be interpreted in the sense that they would have been reasonably understood by someone in the journalist's position. When interpreting statements made in advertisements the following will apply:

- the court will not make a minute word for word analysis of the content of an advertisement. The court will take a more broad brush approach in recognition of the way that the majority of people would consider an advertisement;[17]

- the court will make an allowance for puffery (exaggerated claims which are not intended to be taken seriously). It will ask would the reasonable man take the claim seriously? If the answer is yes, the claim may be a trade libel if it is unsupported by evidence;

- it follows that the use of puffery will not in itself make an advertisement dishonest or the claims made false.[18] In *Timothy White v Gustav Mellin*,[19] Lord Herschell LC observed that, to hold puffing actionable, 'the courts of law would be turned into a machinery for advertising rival productions by obtaining a judicial determination which of the two was better;

- the advertisement should be considered as a whole so that, for example, constituent parts of a mail shot should be read together;[20]

- each advertisement should be considered on its own merits. What would be understood as mere puffery by a reasonable man in an advertisement for, say, soap powder, might be taken seriously in an advertisement for a pharmaceutical product.

This point was illustrated in the case of *Ciba-Geigy plc v Parke Davis and Co Ltd*.[21] The case concerned comparative advertising of competing drugs. The judge observed:

I have no doubt that statements such as A's flour is as good as B's or A's flour can be substituted in all recipes for B's flour are puffs and are not actionable. However, that does not mean that a similar statement would be a puff and not actionable if made in relation to a pharmaceutical product. Parliament has thought it necessary to regulate the sale of pharmaceutical products in ways

---

17 *Barclays Bank plc v RBS Advanta* [1996] RPC 307; and *McDonald's v Burger King* [1986] FSR 45.
18 *Vodafone v Orange* [1997] FSR 34.
19 *Timothy White v Gustav Mellin* [1895] AC 154.
20 *Barclays Bank plc v RBS Advanta* [1996] RPC 307.
21 *Ciba-Geigy plc v Parke Davis and Co Ltd* [1994] FSR 8.

which have not been applied to flour and therefore the common law could apply different standards to statements about pharmaceuticals to those made about flour.

The more specific or precise a statement is, the more likely that it will be taken to mean what it literally says as opposed to be conveying a more general message. The case of *De Beers Abrasive Products Ltd v International General Electric Co of New York Ltd*[22] concerned a pamphlet which was presented to be a scientific comparison of the claimant and the defendant's products. The court held that, because the defendant's pamphlet gave the impression that it was a scientific test, it would be likely to be taken seriously be the reasonable reader or viewer.

Some examples

Vodafone v Orange[23]

The case concerned an advertising campaign mounted by Orange, which compared its operating tariff with those of certain of its competitors, including Vodafone. The advertising included the phrase: 'On average, Orange users save £20 every month.' The saving was expressed to be in comparison with Vodafone and Cellnet's equivalent tariffs. Vodafone sued Orange over the use of the comparison, alleging malicious falsehood. Jacob J observed as follows:

> This is a case about advertising. The public are used to the ways of advertisers and expect a certain amount of hyperbole. In particular, the public are used to advertisers claiming the good points of a product and ignoring the others ... and the public are reasonably used to comparisons – knocking copy, as it is called in the advertising world. This is important in considering what the ordinary meaning may be. The test is whether the ordinary man would take the claim being made as one made seriously. The more precise the claim, the more it is likely to be so taken – the more general or fuzzy, the less so.

In interpreting the advertisement, the judge took its natural meaning to be that it was a statement about an average rate. The public would understand it to mean that if Orange users had been on Vodafone or Cellnet making the same use as they did on Orange they would, as a mathematical average, have had to pay £20 more a month. He held that it did not mean that if Vodafone users transferred to Orange, £20 per month would automatically be saved.

Taken objectively, the phrase was not dishonest. The cause of action failed.

---

22 *De Beers Abrasive Products Ltd v International General Electric Co of New York Ltd* [1975] 2 All ER 599.

23 *Vodafone v Orange* [1997] FSR 34.

McDonald's v Burger King[24]

The claimant objected to an advertisement placed by Burger King which featured a photograph of their whopper burger with a strapline 'It's Not Just Big, Mac' and in smaller writing the words 'Unlike some burgers, it's 100% pure beef, flame grilled, never fried, with a unique choice of toppings'.

McDonald's sought an interim injunction to restrain the use of the advertisement alleging that it was a passing off and a malicious falsehood. In relation to the malicious falsehood claim, they alleged that the natural and ordinary meaning of the advertisement was that McDonald's hamburgers were not 100% pure beef, a statement which was untrue.

The judge refused to grant the injunction on the basis of the malicious falsehood claim. He did not agree that reasonable readers of the advertisement would find that it bore McDonald's pleaded meaning. Most people would not read the words in smaller print and would not even realise that it was an advertisement for Burger King. He cautioned against a close analysis of the wording, saying: 'Advertisements are not to be read as if they were some testamentary provision in a will or a clause in some agreement, with every clause being carefully considered and the words as a whole being compared.'

Malice and comparisons

A claimant in a comparative advertising claim will generally find it difficult to show malice. As we have seen, the mere fact that the comparison has damaged the claimant's sales will not in itself be sufficient. The claimant must either prove that the defendant had no positive belief in the truth of what he published or that his dominant motive in making the statement was to harm the claimant's business or was otherwise improper. The claimant often tries to show that the claimant was reckless in making the comparison. However, recklessness is difficult to establish. It cannot be equated with carelessness or negligence. The difficulties associated with proving recklessness are illustrated by the *Dyson* case,[25] where Electrolux complained about a graph produced by Dyson, which sought to show that the Dyson cleaner had greater suction power than Electrolux's equivalent machine. The graph referred to the results shown as being 'independent test results'; at the time that the graph was published, no independent tests had actually been carried out. The reference to the tests had not appeared in the draft version of the graph, but had been inserted into the final version. The Dyson employee who was responsible for making the change had not realised that no independent tests

---

24 *McDonald's v Burger King* [1986] FSR 45.
25 *Emaco v Dyson Appliances* (1999) *The Times*, 8 February.

had been carried out. The court held that the employee was manifestly guilty of gross negligence in not checking the reference to independent tests. After the graph had been put into circulation amongst the public, the error came to light. Dyson did not withdraw the graph. They felt confident that independent tests would verify the results shown in the graph and they subsequently commissioned the tests. In the meantime, Dyson had taken no steps to correct the inaccurate reference to independent tests.

The court held that Dyson had not acted maliciously. They had been careless, but this did not equate to recklessness.

The *Dyson* case illustrates the real difficulties that claimants can face when they seek to establish malice.

Remedies for malicious falsehood

Damages

The usual remedy in a claim for malicious falsehood is compensation for financial loss in the form of damages for losses which the claimant must prove were caused by publication of the falsehood.

It used to be a moot point whether the claimant could also recover damages for distress and injury to feelings caused by the falsehood. In the 1967 case of *Fielding v Variety Inc*,[26] Lord Denning MR expressed the view that claimants could only recover for their probable money loss and not their injured feelings.

However, in the more recent case of *Khodaporast v Shad*,[27] the Court of Appeal awarded damages for distress as aggravated damages.[28] It was stressed that, in order to recover such damages, the claimant must as a precondition be able to show that it has suffered pecuniary loss as a natural and direct result of the publication.[29] In other words, a claimant may not recover aggravated damages, unless it can satisfy all three elements of the cause of action described above. If the claimant seeks aggravated damages, it must plead them in its claim form and statement of case.

Injunction

A final injunction will normally be awarded at trial to restrain further publication of the falsehood. Sometimes, the defendant will give an undertaking in lieu of the undertaking. Breach of the injunction or of an

---

26 *Fielding v Variety Inc* [1967] 2 All ER 497.
27 *Khodaporast v Shad* [2000] All ER (D) 21 (provided that the claimant pleads them).
28 For more detail on aggravated damages, see Chapter 2.
29 Or a likelihood of such loss under the Defamation Act 1952, s 3.

undertaking to the court is likely to be a contempt of court potentially punishable by a fine or imprisonment.

Interim injunctions: prior restraint

Often, claimants in malicious falsehood cases are anxious to restrain repetition of the alleged falsehood as a matter of urgency and will seek an interim injunction to restrain repetition during the period to trial. In what circumstances will the claimant be able to obtain such relief?

The cases on this point are not altogether clear and they pre-date the coming into force of the Human Rights Act 1998. The following guidance can be extracted:

- in most instances, an interim injunction to restrain publication of the falsehood will be an interference with the defendant's freedom of expression. Where the statement in question is not obviously untrue or where the defendant indicates on oath that it is intending to prove the truth of the statement at trial, the rule in *Bonnard v Perryman*[30] will apply. This means that no injunction ought to be granted unless the court is satisfied that the defendant will not be able to prove the truth of the statement;[31]

- in the case of *Microdata v Rivendale*,[32] the Court of Appeal indicated that the rule in *Bonnard v Perryman* ought not to be extended any further than is necessary to preserve 'the fundamental right' of free speech. The mere fact that a claim brought under one cause of action could also have been framed in defamation will not mean that the rule in *Bonnard v Perryman* should automatically apply if, in reality, the case is not a defamation case. The claim in the *Microdata* case was for interference with contractual relations. The court held that the rule in *Bonnard v Perryman* ought not to apply simply because the claimant could have reframed the claim in defamation if it had wanted to. Griffiths LJ observed:

  > Although the claimant might have framed his cause of action in defamation he has in fact a different, and separate, cause of action on which he chooses to rely. In those circumstances the court weighs in the balance the right of free speech against the right asserted by the claimant in the alternative cause of action. If the court were to conclude that though the claimant had framed his claim in a cause of action other than defamation, but nevertheless his principal purpose was to seek damages for defamation, the court will refuse interim relief. If, on the other hand, the court is satisfied that there is some other serious interest to be

---

30 *Bonnard v Perryman* [1891] 2 Ch 269.
31 *Boscobell Paints v Bigg* [1975] FSR 42.
32 *Microdata v Rivendale* (1984) unreported, 11 September.

protected, such as confidentiality, and that outweighs considerations of free speech, the court will grant an injunction.

In *Consorzio del Prosciutto di Parma v Marks and Spencer*,[33] Morritt J followed *Microdata*, holding that a claim brought in passing off was not subject to the rule in *Bonnard v Perryman* simply because the grant of an interim injunction might interfere with the defendant's freedom of speech. In the malicious falsehood case, *Compaq v Dell*,[34] Aldous J followed *Microdata* and the *Parma Ham* case. He held the rule in *Bonnard v Perryman* was not applicable in circumstances where the defendant's case was a denial that they had made the alleged representations and there had been no attempt to prove the truth of the alleged falsehoods.

If the rule in Bonnard v Perryman is not applicable, what test should be applied?

Both Morritt J in the *Parma Ham* case and Aldous J in *Compaq v Dell* applied the *American Cyanamid v Ethicon* test to decide whether an interim injunction ought to be granted.[35] When applying the test, the fact that an interim injunction would interfere with the defendant's freedom of expression was a factor to be taken into account in the balance of convenience.[36] In *Macmillan Magazines v RCN Publishing*,[37] Neuberger J held that, where on an application for interim relief the balance of justice favoured neither party, the fact that the granting of relief would effectively interfere with the defendant's right of free speech meant the injunction should be refused. In both the *Compaq* and *Parma Ham* cases an interim injunction was granted, leading one to conclude that although interference with freedom of speech is acknowledged to be a factor to take into account in deciding whether or not to grant an interim injunction, it will not necessarily be the determining factor. This is also implicit in the extract from Griffiths LJ's judgment (cited above) where he refers to interests which might outweigh considerations of free speech in a particular case.

Following the coming into force of the Human Rights Act 1998, the *American Cyanamid* test will no longer be appropriate in deciding whether to grant an interim injunction in cases involving freedom of expression issues.[38] Under the Act, the claimant must demonstrate a likelihood of obtaining relief at trial and consideration must also be given to the importance of the right to freedom of expression (which includes the right to receive as well as to impart information).

---

33 *Consorzio del Prosciutto di Parma v Marks and Spencer* [1991] RPC 351.
34 *Compaq v Dell* [1992] FSR 93.
35 *American Cyanamid v Ethicon* (1975) AC 396, analysed in Chapter 2.
36 Discussed in Chapter 2.
37 *Macmillan Magazines v RCN Publishing* [1998] FSR 9.
38 Human Rights Act 1998, s 12 – see Chapter 1 for more detail.

But the Act may not usher in a brave new world in relation to the commercial information which is typically at issue in malicious falsehood cases. The European Court of Human Rights allows Contracting States a wide margin of appreciation in relation to commercial information,[39] especially where the information involves no public health or safety issues. It is therefore possible that, given the fundamental preference of the courts for safeguarding the commercial interests of the claimant, rather than the broader public interest in freedom of expression, the position may not be greatly changed by the Act where commercial information is concerned.

39   See, eg, *Muller v Switzerland* (1991) 13 EHRR 212.

CHAPTER 5

BREACH OF CONFIDENCE

The emergence of the law of breach of confidence is one of the most significant developments for media law. The cause of action is relatively flexible and has been adapted to suit a variety of circumstances. In some instances, the action for breach of confidence has given claimants a legal tool to restrain unethical media activity. The action also provides an indirect means for the protection of privacy – a development that has the blessing of the Lord Chancellor.[1]

Yet the very flexibility which makes the action for breach of confidence such a useful tool for claimants also diminishes the action. As we shall see, there are uncertainties about the fundamental elements of the action, including the very principles on which it is based. In such a sea of uncertainty it is often difficult to predict with accuracy how the law of confidence will be applied. As Knox J noted in the case of *De Maudsley v Palumbo*,[2] 'so far as the law on the subject is concerned, although the broad general principles have been established at the highest level, there are still important issues which remain to be definitively settled'. One might even dispute whether the broad general principles are firmly established, at least outside the context of commercially valuable trade secrets. This makes it difficult for the media to regulate their own activities when the legal background against which those activities are judged is regularly shifting. On the plus side, the inherent flexibility means that the action can be adapted by the judiciary to provide relief where there is none available from any other source.

In this chapter, we shall examine how the action for breach of confidence has been developed with particular reference to media activity. As we shall see, this has largely been a piecemeal development on a case by case basis which has led to inconsistencies. It has also fostered an atmosphere where deficiencies in English law, such as the current lack of the right to privacy, can go uncorrected. The action for breach of confidence creates the impression that the law offers redress for such grievances, when in fact it goes only part of the way to doing so.

The law of confidence affects the media in two key areas. The first, and most significant for the long term interests of the media, is that the courts have tended to be easily persuaded to grant interim injunctions to restrain publication of allegedly confidential material, at least before the coming into

---

1   *Hansard*, HL, 24.11.1997, col 783.
2   *De Maudsley v Palumbo* [1996] FSR 447.

force of the Human Rights Act 1998. The action for breach of confidence is one of the main ways in which prior restraint has been applied to the media.[3]

The second area in which the cause of action can have relevance for the media relates to the protection of ideas which are submitted on a confidential basis, for example, ideas for scripts or television show formats.

The basis of the action for breach of confidence

In its 1984 Report,[4] the Law Commission noted that there was 'uncertainty as to the nature and scope of the remedy [for breach of confidence] owing to its somewhat obscure basis'.

One of the earliest cases which might properly be described as an action for breach of confidence dates back to 1849. The case concerned royalty in the shape of Prince Albert, consort to Queen Victoria.[5] The facts were as follows.

Prince Albert and Queen Victoria created a series of etchings. A number of impressions of their drawings were made from the etchings by a printer at the request of the royal couple. It seems that one of the employees of the printer retained a number of the copy drawings and sold them to the defendant, who planned to exhibit the copy drawings in public. The Prince Consort commenced proceedings against the defendants, claiming an injunction to restrain publication of any of the etchings and of the prints made from them. In his evidence, the prince deposed to the fact that the etchings in question were kept securely at Windsor Castle and were not made available to the general public.[6]

The court granted the injunction at first instance. The decision was confirmed on appeal.

In his judgment, the Vice Chancellor referred with approval to *obiter* remarks made by Yates J in the 1769 case of *Miller v Taylor*,[7] concerning a confidential manuscript:

> Every man has a right to keep his own sentiments, if he pleases. He has certainly a right to judge whether he will make them public or commit them only to the sight of his friends. In that state, the manuscript is, in every sense, his personal property; and no man may take it from him, or make any use of it which he has not authorised, without being guilty of a violation of his property.

---

3   Prior restraint and breach of confidence was considered in Chapter 2.

4   Law Commission, *Report on Breach of Confidence*, Law Com No 110, 1984.

5   *Prince Albert v Strange* (1849) 2 De G & Sm 652.

6   Original drawings would qualify for copyright protection in modern times, but not at the time of this case. The prince's counsel conceded at the hearing that prints made from etchings did not qualify for copyright protection. The prince therefore had to find other causes of action in order to obtain relief.

7   *Miller v Taylor* (1769) 4 Burr 2303.

By analogy to the above, the court held that the Prince Consort had a right of personal property in the etchings and in prints or impressions taken from the etchings. The unauthorised reproduction of the etchings would be a violation of that right.

The Vice Chancellor also placed weight on the *means* by which the defendant had obtained the etchings. He found that the defendant must have come into possession of the etchings by 'a breach of trust, confidence or contract'.

He noted that 'this case by no means depends solely on the question of property, for a breach of trust, confidence or contract, would *of itself* entitle the plaintiff to an injunction' [emphasis added].

The breach of trust, confidence or contract rationale for awarding relief recurred in the 1851 case, *Morrison v Moat*.[8]

The claimant brought proceedings in respect of the unauthorised disclosure of a secret recipe for medicine which he has disclosed to his business partner, the defendant. The disclosure had been on the express undertaking given by the defendant that he would not disclose the recipe to anyone else. In breach of that obligation the defendant disclosed the recipe to his son.

The court granted relief to the claimant. Turner VC stated that 'it was clearly a breach of faith and of contract ... to communicate that secret'.

As with the *Prince Albert* case, the court in *Morrison v Moat* focused on the relationship between the parties and, in particular, on the obligation of trust and confidence that had been found to exist. Neither decision was dependent on the breach of a *contractual* duty of good faith or confidentiality. The obligations were deemed to arise independently of any contract. In more recent times, Lord Denning made the same point when he stated that 'the law on this subject [breach of confidence] does not depend on any implied contract. It depends on the broad principle of equity that he who has received information in confidence shall not take unfair advantage of it'.[9]

Defining the action

An attempt to define the constituent elements of the emerging cause of action was not made until the 1969 case of *Coco v AN Clark (Engineers) Ltd*.[10] In that case, Megarry J identified the essentials of the cause of action, drawing on what was then the case law to date, as follows:

8   *Morrison v Moat* (1851) 9 Hare 241.
9   *Fraser v Evans* [1969] 1 All ER 8.
10   *Coco v AN Clark (Engineers) Ltd* (1969) 86 RPC 41, p 47.

- the information for which protection is sought must have 'the necessary quality of confidence' about it; and
- the information must have been imparted in circumstances importing an obligation of confidence; and
- there must have been unauthorised use of the information (to the detriment of the party communicating it?).

These elements offer a useful starting point for examining the ambit of the cause of action as it exists today. The elements have been refined over time and continue to exist as a focus for debate. They form the basis for much of the present day uncertainty about the ambit of the action.

Identifying the confidence

It is essential that a claimant in an action for breach of confidence is able to identify with precision what the material is for which confidentiality is alleged. A defendant must know what it is he is accused of misusing. Actions for breach of confidence can fail because the material on which a claim is based is not clearly identified or identifiable. In the case of *CMI-Centers for Medical Innovation GmbH v Phytopharm plc*,[11] the parties entered into an agreement for the development of a drug. During the lifetime of the agreement, the claimant alleged that it had made certain oral disclosures about the drug to the defendant. The negotiations between the parties then broke down. The claimant later learnt that the defendant was working independently on its own drug derived from the same plant. It alleged breach of confidence against the defendant. The claim failed, partly on the ground that the claimant was unable to identify with any precision what information of a confidential nature it had disclosed to the defendant. The court held that an injunction based on the oral explanations that the claimants said they had provided to the defendant would be too uncertain.

It is therefore a good idea for a party who is disclosing information to a third party on the basis that it is to be kept confidential (for example, an idea for a show format or a play synopsis) to ensure that the confidential information can be readily and precisely identified. To this end, the disclosure ought ideally to be made in writing so that there can be no argument as to what has been disclosed, with the date and the circumstances of disclosure also recorded.

---

11 *CMI-Centers for Medical Innovation GmbH v Phytopharm plc* [1999] FSR 235.

The 'necessary quality' of confidence

The first of the criteria identified by Megarry J in the *Coco* case was that the material which the claimant seeks to protect must be confidential. As Megarry J observed in *Coco*, 'there can be no breach of confidence in revealing to others something which is already common knowledge'.

Megarry J based his views on the earlier judgment of Lord Greene MR in *Saltman Engineering v Campbell Engineering*.[12] In that case, Lord Greene noted that information, in order to be confidential, must 'have the necessary quality of confidence about it, namely it must not be something which is public property and public knowledge'.

In the case of *Woodward v Hutchins*,[13] when the claimant pop singer, Tom Jones, sought to restrain disclosure of confidential information by a former employee about the singer's lifestyle, the Court of Appeal declined to award an injunction. One of the grounds for the refusal was the lack of confidence in the material which the claimant sought to restrain. Lord Denning observed that:

> [The injunction] speaks of 'confidential information'. But what is confidential? … The incident [concerning allegedly drunken behaviour on an aircraft] … was in the public domain. It was known to all the passengers on the flight. Likewise with several other incidents in the series.

He also observed:

> Any incident which took place at [a public dance] would be known to all present. The information would be in the public domain. There could be no objection to the incidents being made known generally. It would not be confidential information.

The meaning of the 'public domain'

In the case of *Barrymore v News Group Newspapers*,[14] (the facts of which are considered below), Jacob J felt that information ceased to be confidential, and therefore entered the public domain, when known to 'a substantial number of people'. He noted that 'the mere fact that two people know a secret does not mean that it is not confidential. If, in fact, the information is secret, in my judgment it is capable of being kept secret by the imposition of a duty of confidence on any person to whom it is communicated'.

---

12 *Saltman Engineering v Campbell Engineering* [1963] 3 All ER 413.

13 *Woodward v Hutchins* [1977] 2 All ER 751.

14 *Barrymore v News Group Newspapers* [1997] FSR 600.

In the *Spycatcher* litigation, Lord Goff expressed the view that information entered the public domain when it is so generally accessible that, in all the circumstances, it cannot be regarded as confidential.[15]

The question whether information is confidential for the purposes of an action for breach of confidence is therefore a question of degree. It involves asking such questions as 'who had access to the information?' and 'was it generally available or was it restricted to certain people?'. The fewer people who have access to it, the more likely it is to be confidential.

It is clear that the test is dependent on the accessibility of the information. This is a question of substance rather than form. Simply labelling material 'confidential' will not of itself give the information confidential status if it is in fact generally available.

Breach of confidence and particular types of confidential information

Information of a trivial nature may not be protected

In the *Coco* case,[16] Megarry J observed in *obiter* remarks that it was doubtful whether equity would intervene to protect information by way of breach of confidence unless the circumstances in question were of sufficient gravity. He said that equity ought not to be invoked merely to protect trivial tittle-tattle, however confidential. Lord Goff supported this view in the *Spycatcher* litigation, although he observed that it would only apply to prevent the protection of trivia 'of the most humdrum kind'.[17] In *Stephens v Avery*,[18] it was held that it was doubtful whether gossip about a person's sex life could properly be construed as 'trivial' and thus unprotectable under the law of confidence.

Personal information

The protection which the law of confidence provides for confidential personal information has given rise to a situation where the law of confidence is akin to a law for the protection of privacy. Lord Keith has observed, of the law of confidence: 'the right to personal privacy is clearly one which the law in this field should seek to protect'.[19] The Court of Appeal has also explicitly

---

15   *AG v Guardian (No 2)* [1988] 3 All ER 545; [1990] 1 AC 109.

16   *Coco v AN Clark (Engineers) Ltd* (1969) 86 RPC 41.

17   *AG v Guardian (No 2)* [1988] 3 All ER 545; [1990] 1 AC 109.

18   *Stephens v Avery* [1988] Ch 449; [1988] 2 All ER 477.

19   *AG v Guardian* (No 2) [1988] 3 All ER 545, p 638.

recognised that, in relation to confidential information, 'the concern of the law here is to protect the confider's personal privacy'.[20]

Communications between husband and wife and disclosure of details of intimate relationships by a party to the relationship

In the case of *Argyll v Argyll*,[21] the court held that the publication of confidential information relating to the claimant's private life, personal affairs or private conduct by the claimant's husband would be restrained on the ground that communications between husband and wife were capable of being confidential information, the disclosure of which by one party to the marriage could be restrained by injunction. Ungoed Thomas J was of the view that:

> There could hardly be anything more intimate or confidential than is involved ... in the mutual trust and confidences which are shared between husband and wife. The confidential nature of the relationship is of its very essence ...

The decision has been extended in other cases to cover disclosure of details of a relationship outside marriage by one of the parties to the relationship. For example, in the case of *Barrymore v News Group Newspapers*,[22] Jacob J considered disclosures to the media by one partner in a sexual relationship of details of that relationship to be in breach of confidence. He observed that common sense dictated that, when people entered into a personal relationship of that nature, it was not done for the purpose of publication in the newspapers; the information about the relationship was for the relationship, not for a wider purpose.

He went on to say that:

> When people kiss and later one of them tells, the second person is almost certainly breaking a confidential relationship, although this might not be the case if they merely indicate that there had been a relationship and do not go into detail. In this case the article went into detail about the relationship and crossed the line into arguable breach of confidence.

This judgment, like the *Argyll* judgment before it, is an important milestone in the development of the law of breach of confidence in its role as protector of privacy. It paves the way for a party who is the subject of a 'kiss and tell' exposé in the media to restrain the disclosure of confidential and private information about the relationship (subject to any defences which might be raised by the defendant. These are considered below).

---

20 *R v Department of Health ex p Informatics* [2000] 1 All ER 786.
21 *Argyll v Argyll* [1965] 1 All ER 611.
22 *Barrymore v News Group Newspapers* [1997] FSR 600.

Information of a sexual nature

The court has considered whether information relating to sexual conduct can have the necessary quality of confidence on a number of occasions.

In *Stephens v Avery*,[23] the claimant and the first defendant were close friends who discussed matters of a private nature on the basis that what the claimant told the defendant was secret and disclosed in confidence. The first defendant passed on to the second and third defendants (who were the editor and publisher of a national newspaper) details of the claimant's sexual conduct, including details of the claimant's lesbian relationship. The claimant sought to restrain publication on the ground that it was in breach of confidence. The defendants applied to strike out the claim on the ground that it disclosed no reasonable cause of action. They contended that information about a person's sexual behaviour outside marriage was not protected by the law relating to confidential information because such behaviour was immoral. The defendant's application was unsuccessful. The court declined to grant the injunction. Whilst Browne-Wilkinson VC fully accepted that a court of equity would not enforce a duty of confidence relating to matters with a grossly immoral tendency, he found it hard to identify what sexual conduct would fall into that category in the present day when there is no generally accepted code of sexual morality. He noted that 'the court's function is to apply the law, not personal prejudice. Only in a case where there is still a generally accepted moral code can the court refuse to enforce rights ...'. He also rejected as misconceived an argument that information relating to mutual sexual conduct could not be confidential because both parties to it must be aware of the conduct (see above in relation to the point at which information ceases to be confidential).

Jacob J followed *Stephens v Avery* in the more recent case of *Barrymore v News Group Newspapers* (which also concerned the disclosure of details of a homosexual relationship). He observed that 'to most people, the details of their sexual lives are high on their list of those matters which they regard as confidential'.

Photographs as confidential material

A person's appearance would not normally be thought of as confidential. The appearance is there for the entire world to see. But the courts have shown themselves willing in certain circumstances to treat the publication of photographs of an individual without consent as a breach of confidence.[24]

---

23 *Stephens v Avery* [1988] Ch 449; [1988] 2 All ER 477.

24 The courts have not yet found a breach of confidence where a photograph has simply been taken with no threat to publish.

This application of the law of confidence has important repercussions for the protection of privacy.

Photographs taken for a particular purpose

The earliest instance of the unauthorised use of a photograph giving rise to a breach of confidence occurred in 1889 in the case of *Pollard v Photographic Co.*[25] Mrs Pollard had her photograph taken at the defendant's photographic shop for her own private use. The defendant used the photograph without her consent by displaying it in the shop window in the form of a Christmas card. North J held that the unauthorised use of the photograph was a breach of confidence and observed that:

> The customer who sits for the negative ... puts the power of reproducing the object in the hands of the photographer: and, in my opinion, the photographer who uses the negative to produce other copies for his own use, without authority, is abusing the power confidentially placed in his hands merely for the purpose of supplying the customer.

A similar decision was reached in *Hellewell v Chief Constable of Derbyshire.*[26] The facts of the case were as follows. In 1989 the claimant, who had a number of previous convictions, was arrested and taken to a police station where he was charged with theft. At the station, he was photographed pursuant to the provisions of the Police and Criminal Evidence Act 1984. The photograph took the form of a 'mug shot'. The judge found that it was in such a form that it would convey to anyone looking at it that its subject was known to the police.

In 1992, an organisation of shopkeepers in the vicinity, who were concerned about the local level of shoplifting, asked the police to supply them with photographs of known local troublemakers with the idea that it would help the shopkeepers and their staff to recognise them. The police supplied the shopkeepers with a number of photographs – including the 1989 mug shot of the claimant. The police gave the shopkeepers guidelines for the use of the photographs – namely, that they should not be publicly displayed, and that only the shopkeepers and their staff should see them.

When the claimant learned of this use of his mug shot, he commenced proceedings for breach of confidence against the police seeking an injunction to restrain the police force from disclosing the photograph. The judge, Laws J, found that a duty of confidence could arise when the police took a photograph of a suspect.

The judge analysed what the confidential material consisted of. He noted that the photograph would convey the fact that the claimant was known to the

---

25 *Pollard v Photographic Co* (1889) 40 Ch D 345.
26 *Hellewell v Chief Constable of Derbyshire* [1995] 1 WLR 804; [1995] 4 All ER 473.

police. That, he said, was not a public fact. It was capable of being a piece of confidential information. Citing *Pollard*, he stated that:

> I entertain no doubt that disclosure of a photograph may, in some circumstances, be actionable as a breach of confidence. If a photographer is hired to take a photograph to be used only for certain purposes but uses it for an unauthorised purpose of his own, a claim may lie against him.

But what of the situation where rather than the photograph being taken for a particular purpose, the photograph is taken without the subject being aware that it has been taken at all? In *Hellewell*, Laws J considered this scenario. He observed that if someone with a telephoto lens were to take from a distance and with no authority a picture of another engaged in some private act, his subsequent disclosure of the photograph of the private act would surely amount to a breach of confidence as if he had found or stolen a letter or diary in which the act was recounted and proceeded to publish it. He noted that:

> In such a case, the law would protect what might reasonably be called a right of privacy, although the name accorded to the cause of action would be breach of confidence.

Whether this is a determinative statement of the law is far from conclusive. The remarks were *obiter*. There was no consideration of what might amount to a 'private act'. Nor did the judge consider whether there was a need for an obligation of confidence (the second of the elements of the action identified by Megarry J in *Coco*) between the unknown photographer and the subject of the photograph. The need for an obligation of confidence is considered below.

The contents of conversations

The courts have had to consider on two occasions whether the contents of a telephone conversation which was being surreptitiously tapped could be said to be confidential. Different conclusions were reached in both cases. In *Malone v Metropolitan Police Commissioner*[27] (the facts of which are considered below in relation to the duty of confidence), Megarry VC held that, in an instance of 'authorised' tapping by the Metropolitan Police, the conversation could not be said to be confidential information. He said: 'It seems to me that a person who utters confidential information must accept the risk of any unknown overhearing, that is inherent in the circumstances of communication ... when this is applied to telephone conversations, it appears to me that the speaker is taking such risks of being overheard as are inherent in the system.'

The second case is *Francome v Mirror Group*,[28] which concerned unlawful tapping by a private individual. The Court of Appeal distinguished *Malone*

---

27 *Malone v Metropolitan Police Commissioner* [1979] 1 Ch 344.
28 *Francome v Mirror Group* [1984] 2 All ER 408.

from the *Francome* case on the ground that *Malone* concerned the authorised tapping by the police. *Francome* concerned unsanctioned, and therefore illegal, tapping by a private individual. The court said that it must be questionable whether the user of a telephone could be regarded as accepting the risk of illegal tapping in the same way as he accepts the risk that his conversation may be overheard in consequence of the risks inherent in the telephone system. The Court of Appeal held that there was a serious issue to be tried on the matter of confidentiality. The case did not proceed further.

It is difficult to reconcile the approach which the court took in the *Malone* case with Jacob J's decision in the *Barrymore* case as to the meaning of the 'public domain'. Jacob J emphasised the degree to which the confidential information is generally available as the determining factor in deciding whether information is confidential. The *Malone* decision, and to a lesser extent the decision in *Francome*, focuses on the reasonable expectations of the parties to the conversation – should a reasonable person expect to be overheard? If someone accidentally overhears a face to face conversation concerning something confidential, would the parties to the conversation lose the right to restrain disclosure of the conversation by the eavesdropper because they ought to have appreciated that they might be overheard (as the *Malone* case suggests) or ought the confidential nature of the information be dependent on the extent to which it is generally known (the *Jacob* decision)?

It is suggested that Jacob J's approach is to be preferred. Once material becomes known to a substantial number of people, it should cease to be confidential. This test should not be dependent on whether the subject has knowledge of the risk that the confidential material might be seen or overheard.

The disclosure of ideas[29]

In the media industries, literary, creative or entertainment ideas are often disclosed to broadcasters or to the press as proposals for development. For example, television programme formats, film treatments and plot synopses are sent to film and television companies on a regular basis. To what extent are they capable of protection as confidential information? The leading case in this area is *Fraser v Thames Television*.[30] ✓

The claimants conceived the idea for a television series about the formation of a female rock group. Much of their idea was based on the lives of the claimants themselves. They disclosed their ideas to the defendant television company. The television company decided to make the series

---

29 Where an idea is sufficiently developed and recorded in a permanent form, eg, in writing, it may also qualify for copyright protection. See Chapters 6 and 7 for further detail.

30 *Fraser v Thames Television* [1983] 2 All ER 101 (the 'Rock Follies' case).

without the involvement of the claimants. The claimants alleged that the use of their ideas without permission was in breach of confidence.

Counsel for the defendant accepted that, as a matter of principle, the law of confidence was capable of protecting the confidential communication of an idea. However, he argued that a literary or dramatic idea cannot be protected unless it is fully developed in the form of a synopsis or treatment and embodied in a permanent form.

Hirst J did not accept the defendants' arguments. He held that for a literary, dramatic or entertainment idea to have the status of confidential information it must:

- contain some significant element of originality not already in the realm of public knowledge. The originality could take the form of a significant twist or slant to a well known concept;
- be clearly identifiable as the idea of the confider;
- be of potential commercial attractiveness;
- be sufficiently well developed to be capable of actual realisation and attractiveness. This would not necessitate a full synopsis in every case. It would depend on the facts.

The idea need not be expressed in writing:

> Neither the originality nor the quality of the idea is in any way affected by the form in which it is expressed. No doubt both the communication and the content of an oral idea may be more difficult to prove than in the case of a written idea, but difficulties of proof should not affect the principle ...

The judge concluded on the facts that there had been a breach of confidence.

Similar facts arose in the case of *De Maudsley v Palumbo*.[31] The case concerned disclosure of an idea for a night club. The claimant alleged that the defendants had used his idea without his consent and that the use was a breach of confidence. The claimants' idea had five features which, in combination, were said to be original. They were:

- the club would open all night long (at the time of the disclosure of the idea, this was highly unusual in the UK);
- the club would be large and decorated in 'high tech industrial' style;
- the club would incorporate separate areas for dancing, resting and socialising and a VIP lounge;
- the club would have a separate enclosed dance area having an acoustic design to ensure high sound quality, light and atmosphere with no leakage outside the dance area;
- top UK and international DJs would appear.

---

31 *De Maudsley v Palumbo* [1996] FSR 447.

Considering the criteria for a protectable idea identified by Hirst J in the *Rock Follies* case, Knox J held that the features which formed the claimant's idea were too vague, they were not sufficiently elaborated, nor were they sufficiently novel either individually or in combination to enjoy the status of confidential information. To enjoy protection as a confidential idea, he held that the idea must go beyond identifying a desirable goal. A 'considerable degree of particularity in a definite product needs to be shown'. He said that this did not exclude simplicity, but that vagueness and simplicity were not the same thing.

Information which is embargoed for a limited time

What is the position where information is confidential in the short term only, but will shortly be made available in the public domain?

Limited exclusivity

The media sometimes purchase the exclusive rights to publish extracts from books in advance of the publication date. Where a rival media entity publishes a 'spoiler' in order to diminish the value of the exclusivity, to what extent can the owner of the exclusive rights claim that the rival has breached its confidence in the material? The material has not yet been published and is therefore not freely available to the general public. But it will be published at a future date. Can it therefore be considered to be confidential?

This point was considered in the case of *Times Newspapers v Mirror Group Newspapers*.[32] *The Sunday Times* had obtained exclusive serialisation rights to publish extracts from Lady Thatcher's memoirs in advance of their publication date. Prior to the serialisation by *The Sunday Times*, the *Daily Mirror* published a series of articles based on, and containing quotations from, the book. The claimant, which publishes *The Sunday Times*, sought an interim injunction to restrain the publication of any further articles in breach of confidence. The Court of Appeal declined to award an interim injunction. It noted that the information contained in the memoirs was not confidential in the sense that the public were never supposed to know about it. The confidentiality arose from the fact that the material was not intended to be made public until publication by *The Sunday Times*. Sir Thomas Bingham MR stated that to class such information as having the necessary quality of confidence appeared to him 'to be transferring from the area of commercial interest in exclusivity to the realm of confidence, a right which has not hitherto been recognised in law'. The court did not feel that it was appropriate to restrain publication by the defendant on an interim basis in such

---

32   *Times Newspapers v Mirror Group Newspapers* [1993] EMLR 443.

circumstances. The question whether such information could properly be regarded as confidential has therefore been left open. As far as the author understands it, *The Sunday Times* has not pursued the application.

Injunctions to restrain the publication of information which is or will shortly be in the public domain

Under s 2 of the Human Rights Act 1998 (discussed in detail in Chapter 1), the fact that information is or will shortly be in the public domain is a factor which the court must consider when deciding whether to grant an injunction (or other relief, including damages) where the relief may affect freedom of expression in relation to journalistic, literary or artistic material.[33] The Home Secretary has indicated that, where the material at issue will shortly be available anyway, for example, in another country or on the internet, it must affect the decision whether it is appropriate to restrain publication.[34] Note that the impending publication will not be determinative as to whether relief should or should not be granted. In *AG v Guardian Newspapers (No 2)*,[35] Lord Keith indicated that even where information was in the public domain abroad, it might still be appropriate to restrain publication in this country, for example, where publication in England would bring the information to the attention of people who would otherwise be unlikely to learn of it and/or where English audiences would be more likely to be interested in the information than foreign audiences would be.

Often, claimants argue that, although the information has been published in the public domain, further publication should still be restrained by injunction on the basis that it will exacerbate the damage already caused. Before the Human Rights Act comes into force, the courts lent a sympathetic ear to such arguments. It remains to be seen how the Human Rights Act will affect the position in practice. Pre-Human Rights Act case law on this issue is likely to remain relevant once the Human Rights Act comes into force, at least as a pointer of the type of issues and argument which may come before the courts.

Where information has become public, a claimant will also have difficulties in establishing that the obligation of confidence (the second requirement identified in *Coco v Clark*) remains in force. This is discussed in relation to the existence of the obligation of confidence, below.

---

33 HRA 1998, s 12. See Chapter 1 for further detail.
34 *Hansard*, 2.7.1998, col 538.
35 *AG v Guardian Newspapers (No 2)* [1988] 3 All ER 545, p 642; [1990] 1 AC 109.

Information already in the public domain – pre-Human Rights Act case law

There have been cases where the courts have restrained publication of information as a breach of confidence, although the information is already generally available.

In the case of *Schering Chemicals v Falkman*,[36] the Court of Appeal found that information which had already been publicised to the general public could still be the subject of an injunction to restrain breach of confidence.

The first and second defendants undertook to organise a training course for the claimant's management. The impetus for the course was the need to counter bad publicity surrounding one of the claimant's products, the drug Primodos. The first defendant contracted with the claimant that it would keep information imparted to it by the claimant for the purposes of the course confidential. The first defendant engaged the second defendant as an independent contractor to provide tuition to the claimant's management. There was no contract between the claimant and the second defendant. The second defendant was not under an express obligation not to disclose the information provided to him by the claimant for the course. The claimants alleged that the information which it disclosed to the first and second defendants for the purposes of the course was confidential. In fact, the court found that the information had previously been published in a number of press articles and television programmes. The third defendant, Thames Television, made a television documentary about Primodos based on some of the information given to the second defendant by the claimant. The claimant alleged that the defendants were in breach of confidence.

Of the three defendants, only the first defendant had a contract with the claimant. The action against the second and third defendant was based solely on the equitable principle of breach of confidence.

The majority of the Court of Appeal held that all three defendants were in breach of confidence. The decision was reached notwithstanding that the information disclosed by the second defendant to Thames Television had already been published. Templeman LJ stated:

> The information supplied by Schering to the second defendant had already been published, but it included information which was damaging to Schering when it was first published and which could not be republished without the risk of causing further damage to Schering. The second defendant must have realised that Schering would not supply [him] with any information at all if they thought for one moment that there was any possibility that he might make use of that information for his own purposes and in a manner which Schering might find unwelcome or harmful.

---

36 *Schering Chemicals v Falkman* [1981] 2 All ER 321.

He went on to say:

> There is nothing to prevent any journalist or television company ... from
> making a film about Primodos provided that they do not employ the services
> of [the first and second defendants] who can only give those services by
> making use of information which they received from Schering.

The majority of the Court of Appeal appeared to be outraged at the notion
that someone who had obtained information for a specific purpose should be
able to make use of it to the detriment of the communicator. In their view,
such a situation was unconscionable. When the second defendant agreed for
reward to take part in the training course and received information from the
claimant, the court held that he came under a duty not to use that information
for the very purpose which the claimant sought to avoid, namely, bad
publicity in the future. The court's focus was on the breach of trust that had
occurred between the claimant and the first and second defendants
notwithstanding that the material disclosed to the second defendant was not
confidential at the time of disclosure. That focus appears to have weighed
more heavily in the judges' minds than the need for the information actually
to be confidential.

The dissenting judgment came from Lord Denning, who took the more
orthodox view that, whilst the defendants owed a duty to the claimant not to
disclose confidential information, there was no breach of the duty (at least by
the defendants who had no contractual relationship with the claimant) where
the information in question had entered into the public domain. It is
submitted that Lord Denning's judgment is to be preferred. The majority
decision was criticised by the Law Commission in its 1984 Report[37] and by the
House of Lords in *AG v Guardian Newspapers (No 2)*.[38]

A similar issue fell to be considered during the course of the *Spycatcher*
litigation.[39] Unlike the *Schering* case, the information in the *Spycatcher* case *was*
originally confidential when disclosure was first threatened. The issue was not
prior publication, but publication during the course of the litigation – could
the further disclosure by the defendants who were already subject to interim
injunctions continue to be restrained as a breach of confidence once the
information had become public? Whilst it was eventually held that permanent
injunctions should not be granted in respect of information in the public
domain, interim injunctions were continued despite the fact that the
allegations were freely available around the world, the damage which could
accrue to national interest if the injunctions were lifted being held to outweigh
the fact that the information was in the public domain.[40]

---

37 Law Commission, *Report on Breach of Confidence*, Law Com No 110, 1984.

38 *AG v Guardian Newspapers (No 2)* [1988] 3 All ER 545; [1990] 1 AC 109.

39 The facts of the litigation were described in Chapter 2.

40 This reasoning was subsequently rejected by the European Court of Human Rights:
Observer v UK (1991) 14 EHRR 153.

Despite the fact that both the *Schering* case and the *Spycatcher* decision have been comprehensibly discredited, the spectre of the injunction to restrain what is in the public domain continues to live on. This was graphically illustrated in a recent high profile case (decided before the Human Rights Act came into force).

The case[41] related to the family life of the Prime Minister Tony Blair. The family's former nanny provided information to *The Mail on Sunday* about the Blair family life. An article appeared in the first edition of the newspaper, which is available on late Saturday evening both for purchase and for transportation around the country. In the very early hours of Sunday morning, the Prime Minister's wife obtained an injunction restraining publication of the information about the family. The cause of action was breach of confidence (although it was, essentially, the family's privacy for which protection was being sought). The nanny had signed a confidentiality agreement with the Blairs, which placed her under an obligation to keep information about the Blairs secret.

By the time that the application for the injunction was made, the newspaper was already on the streets and in the process of being transported around the country (the injunction does not appear to have been brought to the attention of the transport company). The information contained in the first edition had accordingly already entered the public domain. There was no confidence left to protect. Yet an interim injunction was granted – resulting in the production of a later edition of the newspaper without the offending article.

It is inappropriate that an injunction should have been granted to restrain further publication of information already in the public domain. It is not clear whether this point was brought to the attention of the judge (the application having been heard over the telephone) but it would appear that the spectre of *Schering* lives on.

This is perhaps unsurprising, at least where the protection of personal information is concerned. Where the line between privacy and confidentiality becomes blurred, it is only to be expected that the focus of an application will be less on whether the information is, as a matter of fact, confidential (something that ought to be a prerequisite for an action for breach of confidence) and more on the violation and damage that the publication might cause (the very essence of an action for infringement of privacy).

In an almost simultaneous application to the Blairs', Mohamed Al Fayed sought an interim injunction to restrain the further serialisation by *The Daily Telegraph* of the memoirs of a former Al Fayed employee who had survived

---

41 Media coverage of the application included 'Nannygate' (2000) *The Guardian*, 7 March and 'Too much intrusion' (2000) *The Guardian*, 7 March. This case is not reported in the law reports.

the crash which killed Dodi Al Fayed and Diana, Princess of Wales. The injunction was refused, one of the grounds being that the application should have been made earlier, extracts from the memoirs having already been serialised in previous editions of the newspaper.[42] This decision would seem to be more in line with the nature of the action for breach of confidence, uncontorted to become a substitute for a privacy law.

The changes which s 12 of the Human Rights Act may bring to remedies which may affect freedom of expression were considered in detail in Chapter 1.

Where information is partly public and partly confidential

Where material is part public and part private, the courts have not been shy to restrain breach of confidence in the part of the material having confidential status. The practical difficulty arises in trying to separate the confidential material from the material in the public domain.

Lord Denning MR has offered the following advice to recipients of information which is partly public and partly confidential:

> When the information is mixed being partly public and partly private, then the recipient must take special care to use only the material which is in the public domain. He should go to the public source and get it: or, at any rate, not be in a better position than if he had gone to the public source. He should not get a start over others by using the information which he received in confidence.[43]

This was supported by Megarry J in the *Coco* case,[44] who noted that where information is a mixture of confidential and public material, the recipient must take care to segregate the two and, although free to use the public material, he must take no advantage of the communication of the confidential material.

The information must have been imparted in circumstances importing an obligation of confidence

This is the second element identified by Megarry J in *Coco*. He observed that 'however secret and confidential the information, there can be no binding obligation of confidence if that information is blurted out in public or is communicated in other circumstances which negative any duty of holding it confidential'.

---

42 (2000) *The Daily Telegraph*, 7 March.

43 *Seager v Copydex* [1967] 2 All ER 414, p 417.

44 *Coco v AN Clark (Engineers) Ltd* (1969) 86 RPC 41.

The obligation of confidence

The obligation of confidence can be imposed *contractually*. It is commonplace for commercial development agreements to contain a clause that information made available by one party to the other which is not in the public domain should not be disclosed by the other party. If that clause is breached, the owner of the confidential information would potentially have a remedy in breach of contract as well as for breach of confidence.[45]

But the obligation of confidence is not dependent on the existence of a contract. The law may imply an obligation of confidence in a wide variety of circumstances. This is one of the most crucial areas for the media. The implied duty might arise from the circumstances of the disclosure of the information or, more significantly, from the nature of the information itself. So, for example, if you were to find an obviously confidential document in the street, a duty of confidence might arise to restrain your use of the document even though there is no relationship whatsoever between the owner of the confidential information and you. This point is discussed further below.

The basis of the obligation of confidence

Contemporary case law has not tended to go down the route of seeking to define precise situations in which a duty of confidence might be found to exist. In the same way as it is not dependent on the existence of a contract, the duty is not confined to the existence of specified types of relationship.[46] Instead, the cases have tended to establish overreaching principles which apply in an infinite variety of situations.

The obligation of confidence has been expressed to depend 'on the broad principle of equity that he who has received information in confidence shall not take unfair advantage of it'[47] being based 'not so much on property or on contract, but rather on the duty to be of good faith'.[48] In the Australian case of *Moorgate Tobacco v Philip Morris*[49] (cited with approval by both the English Court of Appeal and the House of Lords in *AG v Guardian Newspapers (No 2)*),[50] the court observed that 'like most heads of equitable jurisdiction, its

---

45 Note that, where the obligation of confidence is imposed by an express or implied contract, any inducement by the media for one party to breach his contractual obligations could give rise to tortious liability for inducing breach of contract. The defendant (eg, the media) must know of the existence of the contract and must have intended to procure the breach before liability can arise. Film buffs may recognise this as the cause of action which caused problems in the film, *The Insider*, which concerned disclosures in the American tobacco industry.

46 *Stephens v Avery* [1988] Ch 449; [1988] 2 All ER 477.

47 *Seager v Copydex* [1967] 2 All ER 414, p 417.

48 *Fraser v Evans* [1969] 1 All ER 8, p 11.

49 *Moorgate Tobacco v Philip Morris* (1984) 56 ALR 193, p 208.

50 *AG v Guardian (No 2)* [1988] 3 All ER 545; [1990] 1 AC 109

rational basis does not lie in proprietary right. It lies in the notion of an obligation of conscience arising from the circumstances in or through which the information was communicated or obtained'.

In *R v Department of Health ex p Informatics*,[51] Simon Brown LJ reviewed existing case law and indicated that:

> To my mind, the one clear and consistent theme emerging from all these authorities is this; the confidant is placed under a duty of good faith to the confider and the touchstone by which to judge the scope of his duty and whether or not it has been fulfilled or breached is his own conscience, no more or less.

A key issue in establishing that a duty of confidence exists in any particular case is whether the existence of the obligation of confidence is a subjective test (which depends on the recipient's actual understanding of the position) or an objective test (dependent on whether a reasonable person in the position of the recipient would have understood there to be an obligation of confidence). This question has been the subject of a number of contradictory judgments, respectively favouring a subjective test, an objective test, or a combination of the two. The reference in Simon Brown LJ's decision to the recipient's 'own conscience' seems to suggest that a subjective test would be appropriate. However, a purely subjective test would be inappropriate. An unscrupulous defendant is unlikely to suffer any pangs of conscience over the misuse of information. In any event it must be open to doubt whether a law which equates lawfulness with a defendant's conscience is a law at all. It could not set any meaningful standard against which to regulate one's conduct and may therefore be incompatible with the European Convention on Human Rights, which requires that restrictions on Convention rights must be prescribed by law.[52]

In the *Coco* case,[53] Megarry J proceeded on the basis that the test was probably an objective test. He said:

> I have not been able to derive any very precise idea of what test is to be applied in determining whether the circumstances import an obligation of confidence ... It may be that that hard-worked creature, the reasonable man, may be pressed into service once more ... It seems to me that if the circumstances are such that the reasonable man standing in the shoes of the recipient of the information would have realised that upon reasonable grounds the information was being given to him in confidence, then this should suffice to impose upon him the equitable obligation of confidence.

Megarry J's comments were *obiter*. On the facts of *Coco*, he was able to reach his decision without the need for application of the reasonable man test.

---

51   *R v Department of Health ex p Informatics* [2000] 1 All ER 786.

52   Refer to Chapter 1 for further detail of this requirement.

53   *Coco v AN Clark (Engineers) Ltd* (1969) 86 RPC 41.

In its 1984 Report on the law of confidence,[54] the Law Commission noted the uncertainty of the basis for establishing the existence of the obligation of confidence. The Commission referred to comments it had received about the reasonable man test which pointed out the potential hardships that the application of the test could cause to those recipients of unsolicited information.

For example: a commissioning editor of a television company receives unsolicited proposals for a new game show from a member of the public. He returns the proposal with a letter, politely thanking the sender and indicating a lack of interest in the idea. Two years later, the company makes and broadcasts a game show in a similar format to the sender's idea. The sender alleges breach of confidence by the company in his idea. He alleges that a reasonable person in the position of the commissioning editor would have understood that he was under an obligation of confidence in relation to the proposal. The question of reasonableness would therefore have to be considered.

Having considered these comments, the Law Commission was not in favour of an objective test in that form. It suggested that an obligation of confidence should come into being where the recipient has either expressly given an undertaking to the giver of the information that he will keep it confidential or where such an obligation can be inferred from the relationship between the giver and the recipient or from the recipient's conduct (unless there is any indication to the contrary).

In our example, the commissioning editor would be less likely to be under an obligation of confidence under the Commission's proposal. There is no express undertaking. It may be an uphill struggle for the sender to show that an obligation is to be inferred from his relationship with the commissioning editor or from the editor's conduct (although where the disclosure involves information which has a commercial value an obligation of confidence is more likely to be inferred from the relationship).[55]

The Law Commission's proposals have not been incorporated into English law. The test to establish the existence of a duty of confidence remains unclear. In the case of *Carflow Products (UK) Ltd v Linwood Securities (Birmingham) Ltd*,[56] Jacob J considered the subjective and objective approach to establishing a duty of confidence. His decision was in the context of a registered design right dispute rather than breach of confidence, but his observations are equally relevant to breach of confidence.

---

54 Law Commission, *Report on Breach of Confidence*, Law Com No 110.

55 *Fairie v Reed* (1994) unreported.

56 *Carflow Products (UK) Ltd v Linwood Securities (Birmingham) Ltd* [1998] FSR 424.

Jacob J defined the subjective and objective approaches as follows:

- *subjective* – what did the parties themselves think they were doing by way of imposing or accepting obligations?;
- *objective* – what would a reasonable person have thought they were doing?

Jacob J indicated that he preferred the subjective approach.

The case of *De Maudsley v Palumbo*[57] contains a further consideration of the meaning of 'circumstances importing an obligation of confidence' as set out by Megarry J in the *Coco* case. The case concerned a dispute over an idea for a night club. The claimant claimed that he disclosed a novel idea for a night club to the defendants at a supper party. He alleged that the defendants had made use of the idea without his consent and so were in breach of confidence. The defendants argued (amongst other things) that the claimant had not disclosed his idea in circumstances importing an obligation of confidence. Knox J held that the test to apply to determine whether an obligation existed was an objective test. However, a factor to consider in applying the objective test (and, he said, it might be an important factor) was whether the parties regarded themselves as under an obligation to preserve confidence. But he did not accept that the test is entirely subjective. Another relevant factor to the decision would be any usual industry practice. We therefore see both subjective and objective elements emerging in Knox's test.

On the facts, Knox J held that the disclosure had taken place on a social occasion. There had been no mention of confidentiality. There was no evidence of trade or professional practice that such a disclosure would be regarded as confidential. On the facts, the defendants had not breached the claimant's confidence.

The position of employees and former employees and employers

The media may obtain confidential information about an employer from an employee or a former employee. Special rules apply to determine the obligation of confidence owed by an employee/former employee to an employer.

Employment contracts generally contain confidentiality provisions restricting the ability of the employee to disclose or make use of confidential information both whilst in the employ of the employer *and* after leaving that employment. Contractual provisions restricting a former employee from using confidential information must be reasonable in terms of subject matter, geographical area and duration. If the provisions are unreasonable, they may be void under the law relating to restraint of trade.

---

57 *De Maudsley v Palumbo* [1996] FSR 447.

Even where there is no express provision in an employment contact, duties of confidentiality will be implied by law.

The implied duties

An employee owes an implied duty of good faith and fidelity to his employer, whether or not the duty is expressly provided by a contract of employment. The extent of that duty will vary according to the seniority of the employee in question[58] and the nature of the employment. As a general rule, the more senior the employee, the more extensive the duty. In principle, the disclosure by an employee of his employer's confidential information would be a breach of the implied duty. The breach of duty will also extend to the employee who makes or copies his employer's property (for example, customer lists) for his own use after his employment comes to an end.

Former employees

The implied duty of confidentiality which applies *after* an employee has left his employer's employ is much more limited in scope. The extent of the duty was laid down in *Faccenda Chicken v Fowler*.[59] In that case, the Court of Appeal confirmed that in the first instance the obligations of the employee are determined by the contract of employment. Where there is no express term, the obligation of confidence will be implied as follows:

- the former employee must not use or disclose information of a sufficiently high degree of confidentiality to amount to a trade secret (for example, information about secret processes of manufacture);
- the implied duty does *not* extend to all information given to or acquired by the employee in the course of his employment unless it is a 'trade secret' as defined above;
- whether or not something is a trade secret is to judged on the circumstances of every case. Factors which may be relevant are: (a) the nature of the employment; (b) the nature of the information itself; (c) whether the employer expressed on the employee the confidentiality of the information; and (d) whether the relevant information can easily be isolated from other information which the employee is free to use or disclose.

Even where there is a restrictive covenant in the contract of employment, it will only be valid if there is some subject matter which the employer has a legitimate interest to protect. A court will not uphold a restrictive covenant

---

58   *Hivac v Park Royal Scientific Instruments Ltd* [1946] Ch 169; [1946] 1 All ER 350.
59   *Faccenda Chicken v Fowler* [1986] FSR 291.

taken by an employer merely to protect himself from competition from a former employee. The employer must be able to point to identifiable objective knowledge constituting the employer's trade secrets which have come into the employee's knowledge as a result of the employment. Protection cannot legitimately be claimed in respect of the skill, experience, know how and general knowledge gained from the employment. The employee can legitimately regard such matters as his own property.[60]

The Public Interest Disclosure Act 1998 and whistleblowers at work

The Public Interest Disclosure Act 1998 came into force on 2 July 1999. The Act makes it unlawful for an employer to subject any worker who makes a 'qualifying disclosure' to detrimental treatment (such as dismissal). In other words, the Act is intended to offer protection to employees who make disclosures in good faith. It does not, therefore, directly affect the position of the media, although it may affect their informants.

The Act is a response to a number of reports into public scandals or disasters which identified that employees of certain organisations were aware of the risk of harm occurring as a result of their employer's practices, but they did not dare to voice their opinions because of, for example, the 'autocratic environment' which existed. However, the definition of 'qualifying disclosure' in the Act is drawn in such a way that the worker is encouraged to disclose information to his employer in the first instance (or to a person appointed by his employer) rather than to the media or to the world at large. It is therefore to be queried how effective the Act will be in practice in encouraging effective disclosure of malpractice or dangerous practices.

The Act protects workers who make qualifying disclosures from unfair treatment. 'Workers' includes independent contractors, home workers, trainees on work experience programmes and employees.

Qualifying disclosure

A 'qualifying disclosure' means any disclosure of information which, in the reasonable belief of the worker making the disclosure, tends to show one or more of six categories of information, which are as follows:

- that a criminal offence has been committed, is being committed or is likely to be committed;
- that a person has failed, is failing or is likely to fail to comply with any legal obligation to which he is subject;

---

60 *FSS Travel and Leisure Systems v Johnson* [1999] FSR 505, CA.

- that a miscarriage of justice has occurred, is occurring or is likely to occur;
- that the health or safety of any individual has been, is being or is likely to be endangered;
- that the environment has been, is being or is likely to be damaged; or
- that information tending to show any of the above matters has been, is being or is likely to be deliberately concealed.

The Act does not provide that the malpractice falling within the above categories has to be those of the employer in order to be a qualifying disclosure.

Information protected by legal professional privilege cannot be a qualifying disclosure, nor can the disclosure of information involving commission of a criminal offence (such as a breach of the Official Secrets legislation.

The Act sets out five ways in which a worker can make a 'qualifying disclosure'. The protection under the Act will only apply if a disclosure of information is made in accordance with one of the five methods. These methods are as follows:

- disclosure to the employer or to another person in pursuance of a procedure authorised by the employer;
- disclosure to a legal adviser;
- disclosure to a minister of the Crown (where the workers' employer is an individual or body appointed by a minister of the Crown);
- disclosure to a prescribed person (this term has not been defined at the time of writing);
- wider disclosure in other cases, for example, disclosure to the media. Such disclosure is permitted, provided that the following criteria are all met;
- the worker must reasonably believe that the information disclosed and any allegation is substantially true;
- he must not make the disclosure for personal gain (note that the Act does not refer to financial gain. It seems that any kind of personal gain would be covered);
- in all the circumstances it is reasonable for the worker to make the disclosure; and
- at least one of the following conditions must be met:
  - the worker reasonably believes that he would be subjected to a detriment by the employer if the disclosure was made to the employer or the prescribed person; or
  - if there is no prescribed person, the worker reasonably believes that it is likely that the evidence relating to the relevant failure would be concealed or destroyed if there was a disclosure to the employer; or

    ○   that the worker had previously made a disclosure of substantially the same information to the employer or to a prescribed person.

The Act gives some guidance as to what factors should be borne in mind when considering the reasonableness of a worker's actions, for example, where disclosures are made to the media. The factors include:

• the identity of the person to whom the disclosure is made. Disclosure of an offence to the police, for example, would be more likely to be reasonable (and therefore protected) than disclosure to the media;

• the seriousness of the matter disclosed;

• whether the problem is continuing or most likely to occur in the future;

• the actions of the employer following any previous disclosure made to the employer on the same matter. Disclosure is more likely to be reasonable if the employer did not address the worker's concerns when first raised (although even in such circumstances, disclosure would not automatically be reasonable);

• the fact that a disclosure was made in breach of confidence will not in itself necessarily make the disclosure unreasonable.

A disclosure to the media may be true, but if the above criteria are not met, the worker will not enjoy the protection envisaged by the Act. A public disclosure is viewed as very much the last resort under the Act's provisions.

Example

Bill is an employee of Bloggs Biscuit Makers. He obtains a copy of his employer's confidential new recipe for a prototype biscuit. On reading it, he quickly sees that the recipe is in fact unfit for human consumption and would be dangerous to public health. He raises this with his employers, who do nothing about Bill's concerns. In desperation, Bill gets in touch with his local paper and informs it about the potential danger. The newspaper publishes the story, generating bad publicity for Bloggs Biscuits. Bloggs wish to dismiss Bill for what it sees as his act of treachery against the company and for breach of the implied duty of good faith in his employment contract and for breach of confidence.

Bill can rely on the Act to protect him from dismissal provided that he has made a qualifying disclosure. The information about the biscuits falls within one of the six categories identified above (namely, danger to the health or safety of any individual). However, Bill has made a disclosure of the information to the media. In order to gain protection, he must meet the requirements for a protected disclosure set out above. One of those factors is that it was reasonable in all the circumstances for him to make the disclosure. The fact that he has apparently breached his employer's confidence will be a material factor going against Bill, but will not in itself be determinative. Other facts which tend to show that the disclosure was reasonable in the circumstances are the seriousness of the problem and the fact that Bill had already tried to get his employers to address his concerns.

This short example is an illustration of how difficult it will be to advise and make disclosures to the media with any certainty under the Act's regime.

So far as the newspaper is concerned, the Act only affects the worker's position. If Bloggs bring proceedings for breach of confidence against the newspaper it would either have to show that there was no breach of confidence on the facts or that the defence of public interest is available to justify the disclosure.

Where information disclosed concerns 'an exceptionally serious breach', the procedures set out above can be bypassed provided the worker can show:

- a reasonable belief that the information disclosed and any allegations are substantially true;
- that the disclosure is not made for personal gain; and
- in all the circumstances it must be reasonable for the individual to make the disclosure.

The Act provides no guidance as to what might be classed as 'exceptionally serious'.

Non-employees and the duty of confidence

Will the courts imply a duty of confidence in circumstances where information has been improperly obtained?

We have seen that the basis of the action for breach of confidence is generally accepted to be the enforcement of the duty of good faith.

The basis of the test to determine whether a duty of good faith exists has never been authoritatively determined. As we have seen, the test may be objective or subjective.

A number of cases have involved situations where the confidential material has been obtained by unlawful or improper means. To what extent will the courts find that a duty of confidence exists to restrain the publication of confidential material which is obtained by subterfuge? The application of the *objective test* to establish a duty of confidence has enabled the courts to infer an obligation of confidence in such circumstances. In essence, the courts apply themselves to the question whether, in such cases, the circumstances were such that it would be right to impose or imply an obligation of confidence.

The situation can be distinguished from what might be termed a 'straightforward' breach of confidence case involving breach of an express or implied *undertaking* to keep material confidential. In cases where information is improperly obtained, the complaint is often about disclosure of information to which the recipient had no right at all. The duty of confidence arises in such cases because the defendant must have realised or ought to have realised that he was not entitled to the information. The case of *Prince Albert v Strange*[61] is an early example of an obligation of confidence arising from the manner in which confidential material was obtained.

When the Law Commission reported on the law of confidence in 1984, one of its terms of reference was whether information acquired not with an obligation to keep it confidential, but without the authority of the owner of the information, could be the subject of an action for breach of confidence. The origins of this term of reference is to be found in the Younger Report on privacy (published in 1972),[62] in which, concern had been expressed that a person who had obtained information without consent ought not to be in a better position than someone whom the holder of the information had entrusted in confidence.

The Law Commission recommended that the law of confidence be amended to provide that a person should owe an obligation of confidence in respect of confidential information acquired in circumstances which included the following:

- the unauthorised taking, handling or interfering with anything containing the information;
- by violence, menace or deception;
- while the user is in a place where he has no authority to be;
- by a device made or adapted solely or primarily for the purpose of surreptitious surveillance where the user would not have obtained the information without the device;
- the obligation ought not to arise where the information was obtained by any of the above methods by a person in the exercise of an official function (for example, a police officer).

This revision and codification of the law was never adopted. Instead, the flexibility of the equitable jurisdiction of the courts has been allowed to fill in the gap. Where material has been obtained surreptitiously in circumstances where it is evident that the material was to be kept confidential, the courts have been willing to restrain publication – at least on an interim basis. But a lack of defined principles has led to a position of uncertainty, making it difficult to predict the outcome of any particular case with certainty. It means that it is this area of the law of confidence which poses one of the greatest threats to the media's ability to act as public watchdog.

---

61 *Prince Albert v Strange* (1849) 2 De G & Sm 652.
62 *Report of the Committee on Privacy*, Cmnd 5012, 1972.

The traditional emphasis on the need for a duty of confidence to be positively asserted by the claimant is illustrated by the 1979 case of *Malone v Metropolitan Police Commissioner*,[63] in which Megarry VC held that, for an action in confidence to lie, the information must have been imparted in circumstances importing an obligation of confidence. The judge observed that 'No doubt a person who uses a telephone to give confidential information to another may do so in such a way as to impose an obligation of confidence on that other; but I do not see how it could be said that any such obligation is imposed on those who overhear the conversation, whether by means of tapping or otherwise'.

On Megarry VC's analysis, even where the eavesdropper would have appreciated that the information was confidential, an obligation would not be implied. This decision has been distinguished on the basis that it concerned authorised telephone tapping by the police. We shall see below that in more recent times, the courts have been more willing to imply obligations of confidence.

Meanwhile, in the case of *Franklin v Giddens*,[64] the Australian courts considered whether an obligation of confidence would be implied in circumstances where the confidential matter had been obtained unlawfully.

The claimant bred a new strain of nectarine. The defendant stole cuttings from the claimant's orchard and, taking the genetic information from the cutting, he developed his own competing strain of nectarine. The court dealt with the defendant's argument that there was no breach of confidence on the facts because no duty of confidence had ever been imposed in relation to the plants as follows:

> I find myself unable to accept that a thief who steals a trade secret, knowing it to be a trade secret with the intention of using it in commercial competition with the owner, to the detriment of the latter, and so uses it, is less unconscionable than a traitorous servant. The thief is unconscionable because he plans to use and does use his own wrong conduct to better his position in competition with the owner, and also to place himself in a better position than that of a person who deals consensually with the owner.[65]

The court held that there was a breach of confidence. The confidential information had become impressed with the obligation of confidence *by reason of the reprehensible means by which it was acquired*.

The English courts have applied the same principles in two recent cases. The first of these was *Shelley Films Ltd v Rex Features*.[66] The case concerned the film *Mary Shelley's Frankenstein*. The claimant gave evidence to the effect that it

---

63   *Malone v Metropolitan Police Commissioner* [1979] 1 Ch 344.
64   *Franklin v Giddens* [1978] Qd R 72.
65   Dunn J in *ibid*, p 80.
66   *Shelley Films Ltd v Rex Features* [1994] EMLR 134.

was to be an essential part of the marketing of the film that the appearance of the actor who played the Frankenstein character should be kept secret prior to the film's release. To this end, steps were taken to ensure that there was no unauthorised access to the film set. There were, for instance, security guards and signs at the main gate of the studios, which stated that entry was by permission only and that photography was prohibited. Similar signs appeared around the actual set. Notwithstanding these precautions, a photograph of a scene which featured the Frankenstein character was published in *The People* prior to the release of the film. The claimant alleged that the publication of the film was a breach of confidence and sought an interim injunction restraining any further breach.

The court held that there was a serious question to be tried as to whether the photograph was subject to an equitable obligation of confidence imposed on the defendants unilaterally because of the defendant's knowledge of the circumstances in which the photograph was taken.

The decision in the *Shelley Films* case was cited in the case of *Creation Records Ltd v News Group Newspapers Ltd*.[67]

The case concerned an album cover for the group Oasis. The cover consists of photographs of the group in a setting devised by the group. The setting consists of a number of carefully arranged props, such as a Rolls-Royce positioned in a swimming pool. The court heard evidence that it was essential for the group's plans that the photography and the appearance of the cover be kept secret. The defendant, who publishes *The Sun*, learnt of the photo shoot for the album and commissioned a freelance photographer to stay at the hotel where it was taking place and to take photographs of the shoot itself. Some of these photographs were included in *The Sun* before the album was released. One of the photographs taken and printed by *The Sun* was very similar to an 'official photograph' considered suitable for the album cover itself. *The Sun* subsequently invited readers to purchase that photograph in the form of a poster.

The claimants sought an interim injunction to restrain what they alleged was a breach of confidence, namely any further photographs taken by the photographer or the poster. They relied on evidence to the effect that efforts had been made to prevent unauthorised persons from photographing the scene, for example, security guards were patrolling the site and the area of the shoot was cordoned off. The claimants contended that the photographer must have been aware of these efforts to prevent people from taking photographs of the shoot and that he had only succeeded in doing so by being surreptitious and, if so, there was a clear inference that he did so because he realised that he was not permitted to take photographs of the scene. The photographer

---

67 *Creation Records Ltd v News Group Newspapers Ltd* [1997] EMLR 444.

disputed the claimant's evidence, alleging that he had quite openly taken the photographs and that no attempt was made to stop him.

The court held that there was an arguable case that the nature of the operation plus the imposition of the security measures made it an occasion of confidentiality. It was also arguable that, in order to get his photographs, the photographer must have been less than open. If he did so, it was an easy inference that he did so because he knew that photography was not permitted. A reasonable man in the position of the photographer would have realised on reasonable grounds that he was obtaining the view of the posed set in confidence, that is, he was obliged by that confidentiality not to photograph the scene.

Counsel for the defendant argued that merely because a well known person tries to stop people taking photographs of him, it does not follow that any picture taken in evasion or defiance of those attempts is in breach of confidence. Lloyd J accepted the submission, but noted that the scenario which counsel had described was 'very far from this case' given the extensive security precautions which the claimants had taken. The injunction was granted.

Support for the view that an obligation of confidence will be imposed where confidential information is obtained by surreptitious means is also to be found in the *obiter* comments of Laws J in *Hellewell v Chief Constable of Derbyshire* (referred to above).[68]

The obligation of confidence and obviously confidential information

Will a duty of confidence be imposed simply by virtue of the fact that the information is obviously confidential, for example, against someone who finds confidential material in the street? The focus of the complaint in such circumstances would be on the nature of the information. The argument would run that the material is so obviously private that by virtue of that status it becomes automatically imbued with an obligation of confidence rendering any unauthorised disclosure a breach of confidence.

Obiter comments from case law suggest that an obligation would be inferred in such circumstances.

In *AG v Guardian (No 2)*,[69] Lord Goff suggested that the nature of the information and the fact that it was not intended that the defendant should acquire it, could lead to the imposition of the duty.

Simon Brown LJ in *R v Department of Health ex p Informatics*[70] equated the law of confidence with the conscience of the recipient of the information. If a

---

68   *Hellewell v Chief Constable of Derbyshire* [1995] 1 WLR 804; [1995] 4 All ER 473.
69   *AG v Guardian (No 2)* [1988] 3 All ER 545; [1990] 1 AC 109.
70   *R v Department of Health ex p Informatics* [2000] 1 All ER 786.

document or information depicts something which is obviously private or confidential, the conscience of the 'confidant' is likely to feel troubled by public disclosure. But, once again, this leaves open the question whether should this be judged on a subjective basis or an objective basis. The issue has yet to be determined.

The position of third parties

In many cases, the media are not the direct recipients of information which was originally disclosed in confidence. Take, for example, the *Stephens v Avery* case.[71] The claimant disclosed certain information to her friend in confidence. The friend then disclosed it to a newspaper. The claimant sought an injunction to restrain breach of confidence by the *newspaper*. This raises the question, in what circumstances will third parties such as the media be placed under an obligation of confidence to the original confider?

The general position is that the third party will be placed under an obligation of confidence to the original confider in circumstances where it is on notice that the information is confidential. The notice can be actual or constructive (that is, would a reasonable party in the defendant's position have known that the information was confidential?).

This is the general rule, but it will vary from case to case. In *AG v Guardian (No 2)*,[72] the House of Lords stressed that there is no absolute rule that a third party who receives confidential information will be restrained from using it, even when placed on notice.[73] For example, there may be a public interest justification for disclosure by the third party which does not exist in relation to disclosure by the original confidant. This was the case in *AG v Guardian (No 2)* itself, where the majority of the House of Lords were of the view that the media were free to publish details about Peter Wright's book once the contents were in the public domain, but Wright (the original confidee) could not. Each party must, therefore, be considered separately when assessing whether an obligation of confidence exists.

A third party will not necessarily be placed on notice that information is confidential by a bare assertion to that effect. The third party should be given sufficient information as enables it to have a reasonable belief that the information is confidential.[74]

---

71 *Stephens v Avery* [1988] Ch 449; [1988] 2 All ER 477.
72 *AG v Guardian (No 2)* [1988] 3 All ER 545; [1990] 1 AC 109.
73 See, eg, Lord Griffiths in *ibid*, p 272.
74 *Fraser v Thames Television* [1983] 2 All ER 101.

When does the obligation of confidence come to an end?

Where a party is under an express or implied obligation of confidence, will the duty come to an end when the information enters the public domain? This point was considered during the course of the *Spycatcher* litigation, where the majority of the House of Lords held that Peter Wright did continue to be under an obligation of confidence despite the information in question no longer being confidential. The rationale behind this decision appears to be the fact that the original breach of confidentiality by Mr Wright was of such a flagrant nature that he could not be said to have relieved himself of the duty in circumstances where the information had lost its private character as a direct result of his own wrongdoing. He must not be allowed to profit from his wrongdoing.

Lords Goff and Brightman dissented on this point. Lord Brightman observed that it was meaningless to talk of a continuing duty of confidence owed by Wright or anyone else in relation to material already disclosed worldwide. Once information is no longer confidential, the duty not to disclose can no longer apply. It was, however, a different question whether Peter Wright could *profit* from his disclosures. The dissenting Law Lords were of the view that any profit which he made as a result of his disclosures should be held on trust for the owners of the confidential information – the Crown in the *Spycatcher* case.

In *AG v Blake*,[75] a case which was heard some time after the *Spycatcher* litigation, the Court of Appeal adopted the same reasoning as the minority speeches in the House of Lords. The appeal judges observed that the duty to protect confidential information lasts only so long as the information is confidential.

If *AG v Blake* were to be followed in subsequent cases, it would seem that a duty to keep information confidential is not to be equated with a duty of loyalty or fidelity.[76] It ought therefore not to be possible to maintain a cause of action for breach of confidence based on an obligation to maintain the confidentiality of information which has ceased to be either confidential or secret.

Unauthorised disclosure of the confidential information

In order for there to be an action in breach of confidence, there must have been actual or threatened disclosure of the confidential information in breach of the express or implied duty of confidence.

---

75 *AG v Blake* [1998] 1 All ER 833 and see, also, the decision of the House of Lords [2000] 3 WLR 625.
76 This is more support for the view that *Schering v Falkman* was wrongly decided.

There has been some debate in case law as to whether it is necessary for the owner of the information to establish that the unauthorised disclosure was to his detriment. In *Coco v Clark*,[77] Megarry J left the question open.

As the law currently stands, it would appear that some form of threatened or actual detriment must be shown.[78] But detriment is a broad concept. It can take the form of financial loss (as in a case involving confidential trade secrets) or it could take a broader form, such as personal distress caused by the disclosure. The latter type of detriment is often the only damage which can be established where the claimant's claim is essentially a claim for breach of privacy, albeit in the guise of an action for confidence. In such cases, the claimant is complaining about the disclosure of private information rather than the disclosure of a piece of confidential business information whose value may be assessed in monetary terms.

During the course of the *Spycatcher* litigation, Lord Keith observed:

> As a general rule, it is in the public interest that confidences should be respected, and the encouragement of such respect may in itself constitute a sufficient ground for recognising and enforcing the obligation of confidence even where the confider can point to no specific detriment to himself. Information about a person's private and personal affairs may be of a nature which shows him in a favourable light and would by no means expose him to criticism. The anonymous donor of a very large sum of money to a very worthy cause has his own reasons for wishing to remain anonymous, which are unlikely to be discreditable. He should surely be in a position to restrain disclosure in breach of confidence of his identity in connection with the donation. *So, I think it a sufficient detriment to the confider that information given in confidence is to be disclosed to persons whom he would prefer not to know of it*, even though the disclosure would not be harmful to him in any positive way. (Italics for emphasis.)[79]

Lord Keith's views make sense in the context of the origins of the action for breach of confidence. If the basis of the action in equity is to uphold obligations of confidence, then it ought not to be fatal to the success of the action if the breach of the duty does not cause detriment sounding money terms. The obligation of conscience is to protect the confidence, not merely to refrain from causing financial detriment to the claimant.

Who can sue for breach of confidence?

On an orthodox analysis, the cause of action for breach of confidence belongs to the person to whom the obligation of good faith is owed. If A tells B something in confidence about C, then if B discloses that information to D, the

---

77   *Coco v AN Clark (Engineers) Ltd* (1969) 86 RPC 41.
78   *R v Department of Health ex p Informatics* [2000] 1 All ER 786.
79   *AG v Guardian (No 2)* [1988] 3 All ER 545, p 639.

claim for breach of confidence belongs to A (the discloser of the information), and not to C (the subject of the information). This is the case even though B's unauthorised disclosure might be to C's detriment.

This principle is illustrated by the case of *Fraser v Evans*.[80] The claimant was a public relations expert employed to write a report by the Greek Government. The claimant agreed to keep information obtained for the purposes of the report confidential. There was no corresponding undertaking by the Greek Government. A copy of the report was obtained by the defendant newspaper, which threatened to publish it. The claimant, fearing that the defendant's article would be damaging to him, sought an injunction to prevent the publication of the report, which he claimed the newspaper had obtained in breach of confidence. The Court of Appeal held that the defendant's obligation to be of good faith was owed to the government and it was for the government to say whether or not it could be published. Accordingly, the claimant had no standing to bring a claim in breach of confidence.

This principle is an important reason why the action for confidence cannot operate as a substitute for a law of privacy. It is generally the subject of personal information who will suffer a violation of privacy if the information is published to the world at large. The subject will not always be the person to whom the obligation of confidence is owed.

The disclosure of confidential information in the public interest

It is well established that where the *public interest* in the disclosure of confidential information outweighs the desirability of enforcing the obligation to protect confidence, the disclosure of the confidential information will be permitted. Outside the field of government affairs (see below), the public interest in the disclosure of confidential information is generally seen to be a defence to an action for breach of confidence or as a weighty factor militating against the grant of an interim injunction. 'I have no doubt ... that in the case of a private claim to confidence, if the three elements of quality of confidence, obligation of confidence and detriment or potential detriment are established, the burden will lie upon the defendant to establish that some other overriding public interest should displace the plaintiff's right to have his confidential information protected' observed Lord Griffiths in *AG v Guardian (No 2)*.[81]

The public interest defence will arise where there is just cause or excuse for the publication of the confidential information. Or, in other words, as Megaw LJ observed in *Hubbard v Vosper*,[82] 'there are some things which may be

---

80   *Fraser v Evans* [1969] 1 All ER 8.

81   *AG v Guardian (No 2)* [1988] 3 All ER 545, p 649.

82   *Hubbard v Vosper* [1972] 2 QB 84.

required to be disclosed in the public interest, in which event no confidence can be prayed in aid to keep them secret'.

Under s 12 of the Human Rights Act 1998, the question whether the publication of journalistic, literary or artistic works is in the public interest is a consideration which the courts must have regard to when considering whether to grant any relief which might affect freedom of expression.

The meaning of public interest

It is easier to define what is not in the public interest than to attempt to provide a definitive definition of the concept. Going back as far as the Report of the Younger Committee,[83] a distinction was drawn between information which is actually *in* the public interest and information which is *of* public interest. This was recognised by the House of Lords in *British Steel Corpn v Granada Television Ltd*,[84] where Lord Wilberforce stated that 'there is a wide difference between what is interesting to the public and what it is in the public interest to make known'. In order for the public interest defence to arise, the publication of the confidential information must genuinely be in the public interest. In the words of the Under Secretary of State, the courts must consider whether there is a good reason why the public should be told the confidential information.[85]

Each individual case should be judged on its own merits. It is in the interest of the media that the concept of disclosure in the public interest should be kept flexible to meet particular cases. In the case of *Lion Laboratories v Evans*,[86] the Court of Appeal declined to restrict the scope of the defence to any particular categories of information. The court pointed out that the public interest defence was best categorised in broad terms of whether there was *just cause or excuse* for publication of the information in question rather than on focusing on the narrow question whether it was information which can be described as of a particular type.

It is well recognised that there will generally be a just cause or excuse for publication where the disclosure of the confidence is made in order to disclose iniquity. For example, the case of *Gartside v Outram*[87] concerned a disclosure of information relating to the claimant's alleged habits of defrauding customers. In the case of *Initial Services v Putterill*,[88] Lord Denning MR held that the public interest in the disclosure of iniquities goes wider than

---

83 *Report of the Committee on Privacy*, Cmnd 5012, 1972.

84 *British Steel Corpn v Granada Television Ltd* [1981] AC 1096.

85 *Hansard*, 2.7.1998, col 562, in the context of debate about the HRA 1998, s 12.

86 *Lion Laboratories v Evans* [1984] 2 All ER 417.

87 *Gartside v Outram* (1856) 26 LJ Ch 113.

88 *Initial Services v Putterill* [1967] 3 All ER 145.

information relating to a proposed crime or the contemplated commission of a crime or civil wrong. He said that the defence extended to any type of misconduct of such a nature that it ought in the public interest to be disclosed to others. In *Lion Laboratories v Evans*, the Court of Appeal extended the scope of the public interest defence by making it clear that there could be a public interest in the disclosure of information which does not relate to misconduct. The information in question in the *Lion Laboratories* case concerned defects in a type of intoximeter approved by the Home Office for use by police forces. The Court of Appeal took the view that the public interest in the disclosure of the information about the defects in the intoximeter (which could lead to wrongful convictions if not corrected) outweighed the obligation to keep the information confidential.

The decision was cited with approval by Lord Griffiths, in *AG v Guardian (No 2)*,[89] who observed as follows:

> I can see no sensible reason why the defence should be limited to cases in which there has been wrongdoing on the part of the plaintiffs. I believe that the so called iniquity rule evolved because in most cases where the facts justified a publication in breach of confidence, it was because the plaintiff had behaved so disgracefully or criminally that it was judged in the public interest that his behaviour should be exposed. No doubt it is in such circumstances that the defence will usually arise, but it is not difficult to think of instances where, although there has been no wrongdoing on the part of the plaintiff, it may be vital in the public interest to publish a part of his confidential information.

The allegations must have substance

Where a party published allegations using confidential information, the allegations themselves will not give rise to a claim of public interest unless the publisher had grounds to believe that they are true. This point was made by Lord Keith in *AG v Guardian (No 2)*,[90] where he said 'it is not sufficient to set up the defence merely to show that allegations of wrongdoing have been made. There must be at least a *prima facie* case that the allegations have substance.'

So, if I use confidential information to support an allegation that solicitor X is defrauding his clients, I would not be able to rely on the public interest defence if in fact I had no real evidence to support my claim. I could not argue that the making of unfounded allegations *per se* would be in the public interest.

---

89   *AG v Guardian (No 2)* [1988] 3 All ER 545.
90   *Ibid*, p 643.

The commercial interests of the media and the motives of the defendant in disclosing the information

Certain sections of the media will have their own commercial interests in mind when disclosing alleged confidences: for example, increasing circulation or viewing figures. This is a factor which the court should bear that in mind when deciding whether there is just cause or excuse for the disclosure in question.

Where confidential information is sold to the media for gain, who then defend their publication as being in the public interest, the question has arisen whether the fact that the information has been sold in breach of confidence could negative any public interest defence. In *Initial Services v Putterill*,[91] Lord Denning implied that the sale of information could prevent the public interest defence from arising. He said: 'I say nothing as to what the position would be if [an employee] disclosed [information] out of malice or spite or sold it for reward. That indeed would be a different matter. It is a great evil when people purvey scandalous information for reward.'

The Court of Appeal in the *Lion Laboratories* case refused to take into account the motives of the defendants in making the material about the intoximeter to the *Express*. There was no evidence whether the defendants had been paid for the material they had disclosed, but that issue did not concern the court. Stephenson LJ observed:

> There is confidential information which the public may have a right to receive and other which, in particular the press, now extended to the media, may have a right and even a duty to publish, even if the information has been unlawfully obtained in flagrant breach of confidence and irrespective of the motive of the informer.

More recently, Jacob J was of the view that the public interest defence was available in respect of the publication of certain video camera stills by *The Sun* even though the newspaper had paid for the pictures. He observed:

> I do not think that the fact that ... was paid and that *The Sun* expected to make money derogates in any way from the fair dealing (or any public interest) justification.[92]

It is submitted that the approach in the *Lion Laboratories* and *Hyde Park Residence* cases is to be preferred. If there is a public interest in the disclosure of information, the fact that it was sold to the media for money or out of an ulterior motive ought not to negative the existence of the defence.

---

91   *Initial Services v Putterill* [1967] 3 All ER 145.

92   *Hyde Park Residence v Yelland* [1999] RPC 655. This was a copyright case. The first instance decision on public interest and copyright was overturned by the Court of Appeal in relation to copyright infringement, but the first instance judgment will probably continue to apply in relation to public interest and other areas of law, such as breach of confidence.

Public interest v obligation of confidence: a balancing exercise

In *Lion Laboratories v Evans*,[93] the *Daily Express* published details of a confidential report alleging that an intoximeter used by a number of police forces was liable to serious error. The newspaper argued that the disclosure of the report's findings was in the public interest. The Court of Appeal held that there was a serious defence of public interest which may succeed at trial. The approach that the court adopted was to look at the evidence in order to decide whether a defence of public interest existed. Having found that there was such a defence, it sought to balance: (a) the need to enforce obligations of confidence, based on the moral principle of loyalty; against (b) the public interest in disclosure of the information of the type at issue on the facts. The court observed that it may be that whilst there is a public interest in disclosing the information in question, it does not outweigh the public interest in the maintenance of confidences on the facts of any particular case. On the facts of *Lion Laboratories*, the court found that the issues raised about the intoximeter were serious questions concerning a matter which affects the life and the liberty of members of the public. On that basis, it observed that 'we must not restrain the defendants from putting before the public this further information … although the information is confidential and was unlawfully taken in breach of confidence'.

Example of the balancing exercise

In the case of *Hellewell v Chief Constable of Derbyshire*,[94] the court held that the circulation of a police 'mug shot' for purposes unconnected with the offence for which it was taken was justified in the public interest. Whilst the photograph itself was confidential, the publication of the image was excused on the facts of the case because it was for the purposes of the prevention and detection of crime and the distribution was restricted to those persons with a need to make use of it. The defendant has a public interest defence to the claim for breach of confidence. The breach of confidence was therefore outweighed by the public interest in preventing crime.

An interesting example of the operation of the balancing exercise occurred in the case of *Robert Bunn v BBC*,[95] which involved a number of conflicting elements of public interest, all of which had to be balanced against each other. The case concerned an alleged breach of confidence in a statement given to the police under caution. The claimant was a former employee of Robert Maxwell Group plc. In a statement under caution, he had admitted to conspiring to defraud certain banks. His prosecution never went to trial despite the

---

93   *Lion Laboratories v Evans* [1984] 2 All ER 417.
94   *Hellewell v Chief Constable of Derbyshire* [1995] 1 WLR 804; [1995] 4 All ER 473.
95   *Robert Bunn v BBC* [1998] 3 All ER 552.

confession and, as a result, the Serious Fraud Office was heavily criticised over its handling of the prosecution. The BBC intended to refer to the case, including the admission as part of a series on the SFO called *The Fraudbusters*. It informed the claimant of its intention to do so. The claimant brought proceedings for breach of confidence to restrain the references to his admission. He contended that the police statement was the subject of a confidential obligation owed to him by the police which precluded its use save for the purposes for which it was provided (the aborted criminal trial).

The defendants argued that, even if the admission was confidential, the public interest in its disclosure in the context of a critique of the SFO outweighed the obligation of confidence. Lightman J rejected the defendant's argument. He observed:

> The fact that the statement discloses wrongdoing by Mr Bunn cannot as such destroy its confidentiality. The public interest may on occasion require the disclosure of confidential information disclosing iniquity, but this is not invariably so ... The fact that the public debate about the SFO will be better informed by disclosure is insufficient in itself to justify overriding confidentiality.

He took the view that there was a substantial public interest in an accused person being able to make full disclosure to the police without fear of their statement being used for extraneous purposes; that public interest outweighed the public interest in publicising Mr Bunn's confession or in exposing the shortcomings of the SFO.

The balancing test and the Human Rights Act 1998

Once the Human Rights Act comes into force, the nature of the 'balancing test' ought to change to bring it into line with the jurisprudence of the European Court of Human Rights. It may no longer be appropriate to balance the public interest in maintaining confidence against the public interest in disclosure of the information in any particular case. Instead, a free standing right to freedom of expression must be recognised subject to specific limitations (for example, the protection of the rights of others) which must be narrowly interpreted and necessary to meet a pressing social need, especially where publication of the confidential material is in the public interest. The courts must also have regard to the broader public interest in freedom of expression on matters of public interest as it applies generally rather than in relation to a specific case. This change in approach is considered in Chapter 1.

Disclosure must be proportionate to the public interest

Even where disclosure of confidential information may *prima facie* be in the public interest; the public interest defence will only protect such disclosures as are proportionate to the public interest. It does not, therefore, follow that publication should be to the world through the media. In some cases, the public interest may be adequately served by a limited form of publication, such as to the police or some other responsible authority.

In *Initial Services v Putterill*,[96] Lord Denning MR said that the disclosure must be to someone who has a proper interest to receive the information. Thus, it would be proper to disclose a crime to the police rather than to the public at large. He did, however, note that there might be cases where the misdeed was of such a character that the public might demand publication on a broader field 'even to the press'.

To illustrate this point, consider the two cases set out below.

In *Francome v Mirror Group*,[97] the claimant was a successful horseracing jockey whose telephone was tapped without his knowledge. During the course of a number of recorded telephone conversations, he allegedly admitted to a number of breaches by him of Jockey Club Rules. On an application to restrain publication by the defendant of the recorded conversations in the form of an 'exposé', the defendant alleged that publication of the allegations would be in the public interest. The Court of Appeal held that there was no public interest in the disclosure of the information in question by the press to the public at large. On the facts, disclosure to the police or to the Jockey Club would satisfy the public interest in disclosure. The court would not allow disclosure by the press prior to the full trial of the claimant's action.

Contrast this with the case of *Cork v McVicar*,[98] in which the claimant, a former detective sergeant in the Metropolitan Police, agreed to supply information about corruption in that police force to the defendant, who was a journalist. They agreed a contract under which the defendant agreed that the conversations were to be tape recorded, but that the claimant would supply certain confidential information on an 'off the record, non-attributable' basis. The defendant agreed not to record those parts of the conversation which related to the confidential information and not to use such information in his writing.

In breach of the agreement the defendant did in fact record the off the record information by use of a hidden tape recorder. He used the information to compile a manuscript to be serialised in the *Daily Express*. The claimant sought an injunction to restrain the publication of the information which he had given on an off the record basis. He claimed that the publication was in breach of confidence. In its defence, the defendant argued that publication of the confidential parts of the material disclosed by the claimant was in the public interest. The judge refused to grant the injunction. He observed that the

---

96   *Initial Services v Putterill* [1967] 3 All ER 145.
97   *Francome v Mirror Group* [1984] 2 All ER 408.
98   *Cork v McVicar* (1984) *The Times*, 31 October.

court would not protect confidential information which disclosed an iniquity or which the public interest required to be disclosed. The information in question related to alleged iniquities in the Metropolitan Police Force. Publication was in the public interest.

The *Cork* case can be distinguished from *Francome* on the ground that *Cork* concerned allegations of corruption in the police force itself. It could be said that, in such circumstances, a referral of the matter to the police was inappropriate. The same could perhaps be said of the *Lion Laboratories* decision, which concerned intoximeters used by the police. In that case, the Court of Appeal observed that the Home Office was 'an interested and committed party'. It was therefore no answer to say that the defendants should have taken the report about the intoximeter to the Home Office (and therefore presumably also to the police) instead of going to the press.

In *Hyde Park Residence v Yelland*,[99] one of the factors which Jacob J had regard to when considering whether the public interest defence was made out arose from the fact that the material published by the defendant was intended to correct a misleading story which had been put forward by a third party. That misleading story had enjoyed a wide circulation in the media. It was therefore appropriate and proportionate for the defendant to publish the confidential information in the same forum (that is, the media) in order to correct the misleading impression.

The public interest in correcting misimpressions

One of the areas where the courts have found there to be a public interest in disclosure relates to the use of confidential information to correct a false impression promulgated by the claimant or by a third party, particularly where they have sought publicity for that false impression. Most recently, in *Hyde Park Residence v Yelland*, Jacob J held there to be a public interest in the use of material to correct a version of events concerning Diana, Princess of Wales and Dodi Al Fayed. The case concerned copyright law, but the decision on the public interest defence will apply to breach of confidence cases. The facts of the case were as follows.

The claimant provided security services to Mohamed Al Fayed in relation to a house he owned in Paris. The security services included the use of a video security system. On 30 August, Diana, Princess of Wales and Dodi Al Fayed visited the house. Still pictures taken from the footage showed the arrival and departure of the couple. They show that the couple spent less than half an hour in the house and that they were unaccompanied by anyone except a member of the security staff. The car accident which killed the couple occurred the next day.

---

99   *Hyde Park Residence v Yelland* [1999] RPC 655.

Following their deaths, Mohamed Al Fayed led the media (and therefore the public) to believe that the couple had visited the house in Paris in preparation for their new life together, consistent with their intention to get married and to live in the house. He represented that the couple had spent a number of hours at the house, accompanied by an interior designer. In fact, as the video stills show, the couple was unaccompanied and spent a very short time at the villa. *The Sun* newspaper obtained copies of the video stills and published them in order to correct the misimpression which Mr Al Fayed had allowed to take place. Jacob J held that the publication of the stills was in the public interest (that is, there was just cause or excuse for their publication), because there was a genuine public interest in the information disclosed and the correction of the false image which the public had been given to date.

Similar issues arose in *Woodward v Hutchins*,[100] which concerned an exposé of certain scandalous behaviour on the part of Tom Jones. The Court of Appeal declined to restrain publication of the stories. One of their grounds for doing so was the desirability of correcting the false images which the claimant had portrayed of himself to the world. Lord Denning noted as follows:

> If a group of this kind seek publicity which is to their advantage, it seems to me that they cannot complain if a servant or employee of theirs afterwards discloses the truth about them. If the image which they fostered was not a true image, it is in the public interest that it should be corrected.

And then:

> As there is truth in advertising so there should be truth in publicity. The public should not be misled.

Similar views were also expressed by Bridge LJ:

> It seems to me that those who seek and welcome publicity of every kind bearing upon their private lives so long as it shows them in a favourable light are in no position to complain of an invasion of privacy by publicity which shows them in an unfavourable light.

The *Hyde Park Residence* and the *Woodward* cases are restricted to those areas where the party who has fostered the misleading impression has sought publicity for that false image. So, a celebrity who has publicised his seemingly happy marriage may not be able to restrain the publication of confidential information about an extra-marital affair. The defendant could rely on the defence of publication in the public interest; the public interest being that of correcting the false image which the celebrity has created for himself. On the other hand, if the celebrity has never actively sought any publicity about his marriage, there would be no misimpression to correct and therefore there is unlikely to be any public interest defence in relation to publication of details about his affair.

---

100 *Woodward v Hutchins* [1977] 2 All ER 751.

It is yet to be determined whether disclosures about the private life of a public official, such as an MP, could be said to be in the public interest. The speeches of the Law Lords in the defamation case of *Reynolds v Times Newspapers*[101] indicate that they would not be, unless the disclosures impinged in some way on the public duties carried out by the official.

The Crown and the public interest

There are rights available to private citizens which institutions of ... government are not in a position to exercise unless they can show that it is in the public interest to do so.[102]

The courts have held that where it is the Crown that seeks to prevent the disclosure of allegedly confidential information, significant differences apply when considering the burden of proof in relation to public interest.

In the case of *AG v Jonathan Cape*,[103] it was held that the Crown must show as a positive part of its case that the disclosure of the confidential information which it seeks to restrain has damaged or is likely to damage the public interest. Public interest does not operate as a defence in such cases. The claimant (that is, the Crown) must positively show detriment to the public interest in order to succeed in its claim. The House of Lords confirmed this special position of the crown in *AG v Guardian (No 2)*.[104] Lord Goff explained that the reason for this additional requirement in cases concerned with government secrets was that it was in the public interest that the workings of government should be the subject of scrutiny and criticism and the Crown therefore had to demonstrate that that public interest was overridden by the requirements of confidentiality in any particular case.

In the *Jonathan Cape* case, the crown sought to restrain publication of the diaries of the former cabinet minister Richard Crossman as a breach of confidence. The diaries contained details of cabinet discussions and differences of opinion amongst the members of the cabinet as well as of matters relating to the civil service. Lord Widgery CJ emphasised that the publication of the diaries could only be restrained when it was clearly necessary to do so in the public interest. He noted that in order to succeed in his claim the Attorney General had to show that:

(a) the publication would be a breach of confidence;

(b) that the public interest requires that the publication be restrained; and

(c) there are no other facets of the public interest contradictory or more compelling than that relied upon by the Crown, for example, the public

---

101 *Reynolds v Times Newspapers Ltd* [1999] 4 All ER 609.

102 Lord Keith in *Derbyshire CC v Times Newspapers Ltd* [1993] 2 WLR 449, p 451.

103 *AG v Jonathan Cape* [1976] QB 752; [1975] 3 All ER 484.

104 *AG v Guardian (No 2)* [1988] 3 All ER 545; [1990] 1 AC 109.

interest that the workings of government should be open to scrutiny and criticism.

In relation to (b) above, Lord Widgery was of the view that the Crown could not restrain publication of all types of confidential information without regard to the passage of time. The time limit after which the confidential character of the information would lapse might vary according to the nature of the information involved. However, the information at issue in the case was at the time of the proposed publication over 10 years old. He dismissed the argument that the disclosure would inhibit frank discussion in Cabinet or damage the doctrine of joint Cabinet responsibility. He also dismissed the argument that it would inhibit the frankness of the advice given to ministers by civil servants. The Crown had not demonstrated that publication of the diaries after that passage of time would do any harm to the public interest. In order to show public interest, it would seem that the Crown must be able to pinpoint a specific danger to the public interest to justify the grant of an injunction. Assertions of damage in the abstract will not do.

All levels of court cited the *Jonathan Cape* decision with approval in *AG v Guardian (No 2)*,[105] along with the Australian decision of Mason J in the case of *Commonwealth of Australia v John Fairfax and Sons Ltd*,[106] which concerned the publication by the defendants of a book on Australian defence and foreign policy by reference to a series of confidential governmental documents. In the *Fairfax* decision, Mason J had observed:

> It is unacceptable in our democratic society that there should be a restraint on the publication of information relating to government when the only vice of that information is that it enables the public to discuss, review and criticise government action. Accordingly, the court will determine the government's claim to confidence by reference to the public interest. Unless disclosure is likely to injure the public interest, it will not be protected.[107]

Applying this approach to *Spycatcher*, the Crown's inability to show that an injunction to restrain the media from further publication of allegations contained in *Spycatcher* was necessary in the public interest was instrumental in its failure to secure permanent injunctions in *AG v Guardian (No 2)*,[108] although interim injunctions remained in force. As Lord Keith indicated, 'the general publication in this country would not bring about any significant damage beyond what has already been done'.[109]

---

105 *AG v Guardian (No 2)* [1988] 3 All ER 545; [1990] 1 AC 109.
106 *Commonwealth of Australia v John Fairfax and Sons Ltd* (1980) 32 ALR 485, p 493.
107 Cited with approval by Lord Keith in *AG v Guardian (No 2)* [1988] 3 All ER 545, p 641.
108 *Ibid*.
109 *Ibid*.

Breach of confidence and privacy

This chapter has highlighted three principal reasons why the law of confidence cannot be equated with a law of privacy. In summary, they are as follows:

- not all personal information is confidential. As the Tony Blair/nanny case illustrates, the desire to protect privacy can easily lead to a contortion of the action for confidence to restrain publication of material which has passed into the public domain. This cannot be squared with a law of confidence on any analysis;

- at present, only the person to whom the obligation of confidence is owed may bring proceedings for breach of confidence. This may not be the party (or the only party) whose privacy has been violated. The law could overcome this difficulty by imposing a wider obligation of confidence to cover the subject of the confidential material, but that may lead to the law becoming unacceptably wide;

- the efficacy of the action for confidence as a way of protecting privacy is largely dependent on the courts giving recognition to the distress and feelings of violation which invariably accompanies an infringement of privacy. But the need to provide for this type of 'detriment' graphically illustrates the differences between the traditional action for breach of confidence and a violation of privacy. This was recognised by Lord Mustill in *R v BSC ex p BBC*,[110] where he observed:

    > Privacy and confidentiality are not the same. For example, the reading and copying of personal diaries, letters to relatives or lovers, poems and so on could ground not only an allegation of tortious conduct, but also an *additional complaint* that the privacy of the writer and perhaps also of the recipient have been intruded upon. Such conduct is specially objectionable, not because legal rights have been infringed but because of the insult done to the person as a person [emphasis added].

The most explicit consideration of detriment in the context of privacy occurred in the recent case of *R v Department of Health ex p Informatics*,[111] which concerned the unauthorised disclosure by pharmacists of confidential information concerning patients. The information which had been disclosed was anonymised, so that the identity of the patients could not be discovered. The Court of Appeal held there was no breach of confidence because the identity of the patients was protected. It did not matter that the details which were disclosed happened to be confidential. Detriment had not been established on the facts. The law of confidence in the context of personal

---

110 *R v BSC ex p BBC* (2000) unreported.

111 *R v Department of Health ex p Informatics* [2000] 1 All ER 786.

information was only concerned to protect privacy. If privacy was already safeguarded, there could be no breach of confidence.

But, as we have seen in Chapter 2, under the present law one cannot be sure that the courts will recognise distress and hurt feelings as a separate head of damages. Lord Mustill thought that these feelings are an additional claim to any claim in confidence.[112] The law must be clarified to allow for recovery of such loss as a head of compensatory damages in its own right if adequate compensation is to be guaranteed.

---

112 *R v BSC ex p BBC* (2000) unreported.

CHAPTER 6

PROPERTY RIGHTS AND FREEDOM OF EXPRESSION

COPYRIGHT, DESIGN RIGHT, MORAL RIGHTS AND PERFORMERS' RIGHTS

(a) Copyright

The civil law

Copyright confers the right to control the exploitation of certain sorts of material. It defines what can and cannot be done to the material without the copyright owner's consent. Under English law, copyright is generally viewed as an economic right because it confers the right to control the exploitation of something of value – such as a work of art or a piece of music. Copyright also acts as an incentive to creativity. By conferring the right to control the exploitation of the work, copyright goes some way to ensuring that the creator of the work is rewarded for his creativity. As the flip side to this economic function, copyright has important repercussions for freedom of expression. The owner of copyright in a newsworthy document or piece of film footage may be able to exercise its copyright to prevent the use of the material by the media – either at all or on terms requiring payment of a fee. Rival media entities often seek to enforce the copyright in their material against their rivals.[1]

UK copyright law is largely contained in an Act of Parliament, the Copyright, Designs and Patents Act 1988 (CDPA) as amended.[2] The CDPA came into force on 1 August 1989.

What is copyright?

Copyright is a property right which protects the skill and labour which goes into the creation of a work from unauthorised appropriation. Copyright exists in certain types of material (classified by the CDPA into nine types of 'work'). Ownership of copyright in a work enables the copyright owner to restrain or license a number of activities specified in the Act in relation to that work.

The law rests on two basic principles. The first is that unauthorised appropriation of the product of an author's skill and labour is wrong and

---

1   By way of example, see *BBC v British Satellite Broadcasting Ltd* [1991] 3 WLR 174.
2   Amended by the Duration of Copyright and Rights in Performances Regulations 1995, the Copyright and Related Rights Regulations 1996 and the Copyright and Rights in Databases Regulations 1997.

ought to be restrained. The second principle is that works which have been generated by the exercise of skill and labour should be capable of exploitation for commercial reward without undue hindrance, the rationale being that creativity should be encouraged by allowing creative works to be profitably exploited. In recent times it is this second principle which has become paramount. In the media industries many copyrights are owned and exploited by large businesses rather than by the individuals who created the works. The emphasis is on ever greater protection for copyright owners, ensuring that copyright owners can keep lucrative markets for themselves or demand large fees in return for permission to use their material. But at what price for freedom of expression and freedom of innovation?[3]

International protection

Copyright is a national right. A work qualifies for copyright protection in the UK if the creator of the work (known, for copyright purposes, as the 'author') is a 'qualifying person' as defined in s 154 of the CDPA. The definition includes an individual domiciled or resident in the UK. As an alternative to the individual residence criterion, copyright will subsist under the laws of the UK if the work was first published in the UK.[4]

If the owner of UK copyright wishes to enforce his UK copyright outside the UK, he must confirm that it has the right to do so under the laws of the country in which he wants to enforce. This will involve looking at relevant international treaties, principally the Berne Convention 1886 for the Protection of Literary and Artistic Works and the Universal Copyright Convention 1952 (UCC), which respectively lay down minimum standards for the national copyright law of the Contracting States. Under the provisions of these treaties, Contracting States are obliged to give the foreign copyright owner the same protection as is afforded to their own nationals. The UK has ratified both the Berne Convention and the UCC.

---

3   At the time of writing, this emphasis can be seen in relation to the record industry's lobbying for greater protection for digital works. This is considered towards the end of this chapter.

4   CDPA 1988, Chapter 9, ss 153–162.

Copyright works

Under the CDPA, copyright subsists in works of the following types.

Original literary works[5]

These are defined as any work, other than a dramatic or musical work, which is written, spoken or sung. It does not matter whether the work has been published. The term encompasses more than just works of prose. The words 'literary work' covers 'work which is expressed in print or writing, irrespective of the question whether the quality or style is high'.[6] Literary works can take the form of computer programs, tables, compilations or databases.[7] Copyright has been successfully claimed in material as diverse as examination papers,[8] football coupons[9] and a label containing instructions placed on the side of a barrel of herbicide.[10] The Court of Appeal has laid down a threshold which a literary work must meet before it can qualify for copyright protection.[11] The work must convey information, provide instruction or give pleasure (in the form of literary enjoyment). Single words, titles and commonplace slogans and phrases are unlikely to satisfy any of these criteria.[12]

Original scripts, screenplays and lyrics are literary works in their own right as well as being part of a play, film or song.

The meaning of 'original' is considered below.

Original dramatic works[13]

These are defined in the CDPA as including a work of dance and mime. This is not a comprehensive definition.[14] The Court of Appeal has held that the term 'dramatic work' should bear its natural and ordinary meaning, namely a work of action, with or without words or music, which is capable of being performed before an audience.[15] A film may, therefore, be a dramatic work,

---

5   CDPA 1988, s 3(1).

6   *University of London Press v University Tutorial Press* [1916] 2 Ch 601.

7   Defined by the CDPA as a collection of independent works, data or other materials which are arranged in a systematic or methodical way and are individually accessible by electronic or other means. Databases are considered further below.

8   *University of London Press v University Tutorial Press* [1916] 2 Ch 601.

9   *Ladbroke (Football) v William Hill (Football)* [1964] 1 All ER 465.

10   *Elanco v Mandops* [1979] FSR 46.

11   *Exxon v Exxon Insurance Consultants International Ltd* [1982] Ch 119; [1981] 3 All ER 241.

12   See below, p 227 for more detail.

13   CDPA 1988, s 3(1).

14   *Norowzian v Arks (No 2)* [2000] EMLR 1.

15   *Ibid.*

provided that it meets the originality requirements. The requisite performance in public could, according to the Court of Appeal, take the form of showing the film. We shall see below that 'film' is also one of the types of work which is recognised in the CDPA. Films may therefore enjoy dual protection as original dramatic works and as films.

A static scene is not capable of being a dramatic work, even if it is artfully arranged.[16] It cannot be said to be 'a work of action'.

The Court of Appeal's definition of 'dramatic work' seems to be wider than the court could ever have intended. It appears to omit a vital component, namely an element of plot or creativity. In the wake of the Court of Appeal decision, some practitioners have sought to argue that recorded sporting sequences, such as goal scoring sequences in a football match, could be dramatic works in the sense that they are works of action which can be shown in public.[17] If this view is correct, any other type of moving sequence which has been filmed is also capable of being a dramatic work. This could have important repercussions for news footage and sports footage.

However, it is likely that the practitioners in question are being a little optimistic about the scope of dramatic work. Dramatic works must be original to qualify for copyright protection. The meaning of originality is considered in more detail below, but it should be noted at this stage that, although the test for originality is not high, it might not be satisfied where action occurs spontaneously without premeditation. Further guidance about limitations on the meaning of 'dramatic work' can be found in the Privy Council decision in *Green v Broadcasting Corpn of New Zealand*,[18] where it was held that a dramatic work must have 'sufficient unity' to be capable of performance. An isolated goal scoring sequence is unlikely to have the required unity.[19]

Clearly, the Court of Appeal formulation of what is meant by dramatic work is generating its own peculiar problems. It must be hoped that the definition is applied in a commonsense way in accordance with general copyright principles or that the court takes the opportunity to clarify the definition further.

A dramatic work is distinct from any script on which it is based. An original script, as we have seen, enjoys protection in its own right as a literary work.

---

16 *Creation Records v News Group Newspapers* [1997] EMLR 444.

17 Eg, 'They think it's all over – it isn't yet' (2000) *The Times*, 8 February.

18 *Green v Broadcasting Corpn of New Zealand* [1989] 2 All ER 1056.

19 Note also that, in relation to performers' rights, the definition of performance in CDPA 1988, s 180(2) would not extend to sporting 'performances' or other types of spontaneous performances. Although performers' rights are not dependent on the existence of copyright, it would make sense to bring the meaning of dramatic work in line with the meaning of performance.

Original musical works

These are defined as original music of all kinds (exclusive of any words or action intended to be sung, spoken or performed with the music). The lyrics to a song will be a *literary* work. The tune will be a separate *musical* work. The music does not have to be an elaborate composition. Advertising jingles can be copyright works. Channel 4 has asserted copyright protection for its signature 'fanfare', even though it consists of only a handful of notes.[20]

The term 'musical work' includes new arrangements of existing music. Separate and distinct copyrights might co-exist in the music (musical work), and the arrangement of the music (a second and separate musical work).

The meaning of 'original' is considered below.

Original artistic works[21]

These are defined to mean a graphic work, photograph, sculpture or collage,[22] *all irrespective of artistic quality*. It also includes a work of architecture (being a building or a model for a building) and works of artistic craftsmanship.

The term 'graphic work'[23] includes paintings, drawings, diagrams, maps, charts, plans, sculptures (including casts or models made for a work of sculpture) and engravings. There are *dicta* in the case of *Creation Records v News Group Newspapers*[24] which suggest that an artistic work cannot be something which is intrinsically ephemeral, such as a posed scene for a photograph. Whilst the photograph recording the posed scene would be an artistic work, the scene itself would not be. ('Photograph' is defined as 'a recording of light or other radiation on any medium or from which an image may by any means be produced and which is not part of a film'.)[25] The result of this seems to be that it would not be an infringement of copyright in a photograph to take a separate photograph of the same scene or to recreate the scene on a different occasion.

The meaning of 'original' is considered below.

Sound recordings

These are defined as a recording of sounds, from which the sounds may be reproduced,[26] or a recording of the whole or any part of a literary, dramatic or

20 (1985) *The Times*, 13 June.

21 CDPA 1988, s 4.

22 A collage involves sticking two or more things together – *Creation Records v News Group Newspapers* [1997] EMLR 444.

23 CDPA 1988, s 4(2).

24 *Creation Records v News Group Newspapers* [1997] EMLR 444.

25 CDPA 1988, s 4(2).

26 *Ibid*, s 5A.

musical work from which sounds reproducing the work or part may be produced. A sound recording is not restricted to the recording of music.

The sounds which are the subject of the recording may be literary works or musical works in their own right. A sound recording of a song can therefore involve a number of separate types of copyright: copyright, for example in the lyrics (literary work), in the tune (musical work) and in the sound recording of the song. The sound recording is a derivative right in the sense that it is derived from the original works which form the subject of the recording. Copyright does not subsist in a sound recording which is, or to the extent that it is, a copy taken from a previous sound recording.[27] It follows that copyright will subsist in a master sound recording – but not in any copies produced from the master tape – even where the subsequent recordings have been authorised by the copyright owner.

Films

Films are defined as a recording on any medium from which a moving image may by any means be reproduced.[28] This will include feature films, newsreels, home and music videos, television programmes and filmed advertisements. Since 1 December 1996, the sound track accompanying a film is treated as being part of the film.[29] Copyright does not subsist in a film which is, or to the extent that it is, a copy taken from a previous film.[30] As with sound recordings, copyright exists in the master tape of the film, but not in copies produced from the master. Infringement requires copying of the physical recording embodied on the film, for example, by video recording the film.[31] It is not, therefore, an infringement of copyright in a film to recreate the subject matter of the film or the filmmaker's overall technique or distinctive editing features.[32]

Broadcasts

Broadcast is defined[33] as a 'transmission by wireless telegraphy of visual images, sounds or other information (for example, Teletext) which is capable of being lawfully received by members of the public or is transmitted for presentation to members of the public'. It includes analogue, terrestrial and

---

27 CDPA 1988, s 5A(2).

28 *Ibid*, s 5B.

29 *Ibid*, s 5B(2).

30 *Ibid*, s 5B(4).

31 *Norowzian v Arks (No 1)* [1998] FSR 394.

32 *Norowzian v Arks (No 2)* [2000] EMLR 1.

33 CDPA 1988, s 6.

satellite broadcasts by television or radio. Broadcasts are protected independently of the material which is the subject of the broadcast. Therefore, if the BBC broadcasts a feature film, copyright subsists in the broadcast *and* in the film itself. Copyright does not subsist in a broadcast which infringes, or to the extent that it infringes, the copyright in another broadcast or in a cable programme.

Special rules apply to determine the place of origin of transnational satellite broadcasts.[34] Where the satellite uplink is located in a State in a European Economic Area (EEA) State, that State is treated as the place where the broadcast is made and the person operating the uplink station is treated as the person making the broadcast. Where the uplink station is not in an EEA State, but a person established in an EEA State has commissioned the broadcast, that person is treated as the person making the broadcast and the place where he has his principal establishment in the EEA is treated as the place from which the broadcast was made.[35]

Cable programmes

These are defined[36] as items included in a cable programme service. A cable programme service is a service consisting: (a) wholly or mainly in sending visual images, sounds or other information; (b) by means of a telecommunication system, otherwise than by wireless telegraphy; (c) for reception at two or more places or for presentation to members of the public. There are a number of exceptions to the definition of cable programmes,[37] most notably where a service or part of a service has as an essential feature the provision for interactivity. Cable telephone networks fall within this exemption, and are not therefore protected as cable programmes. Communications by e-mail are also likely to be excluded on the interactivity grounds, although e-mail could probably be protected by reference to other types of work, for example, literary works (provided that they are original). As with broadcasts, the subject matter of the item transmitted will have its own copyright existing separately from the copyright in the cable programme.

Published editions[38]

Copyright exists in the typographical arrangement of a published edition of the whole or any part of one or more literary, dramatic or musical works. This right exists separately from the material which is the subject matter of the edition. It is a special and narrow type of copyright which protects the image

---

34 CDPA 1988, s 6A.
35 *Ibid.*
36 *Ibid,* s 7.
37 *Ibid,* s 7(2).
38 *Ibid,* s 8.

on the page. Its purpose is to protect the publisher's investment in the typesetting work. Copyright does not subsist in the typographical arrangement of a published edition if, or to the extent that, it reproduces the typographical arrangement of a previous edition. Publication is defined as the issue of copies to the public,[39] which is likely to include making the edition available electronically, for example, over the internet.

New technologies

The development of new technologies is currently outstripping the development of copyright laws. As a result it can be difficult to accommodate new product developments into the existing categories of work.

What types of copyright work are websites?

In *Shetland Times v Wills*,[40] the *Shetland News* reproduced headlines created by its rival publication, *Shetland Times*, and created links on the *Shetland News* home page to the pages of the *Shetland Times*. *Shetland Times* sued *Shetland News* for copyright infringement for the unauthorised reproduction of its headlines and obtained an interim injunction to restrain the further operation of the website link. Lord Hamilton held (on an interim application) that the *Shetland Times* website was a cable programme service. The judge acknowledged that he had little technical information available to him on the application and that the application was made at a preliminary stage of the litigation before pleadings had closed and without the benefit of hearing all of the evidence. The decision has been criticised on the ground that it did not deal adequately with the possibility of interactivity between the website and readers. Readers will recall from the definition of cable programme service set out above that there is an exemption where the service in question involves interactivity as an essential feature. Lord Hamilton found that those possibilities for interactivity which were available to readers (on the facts, a note inviting readers to send in comments or suggestions by email) were not essential to the website as a whole. Alternatively, he found that the interactive parts of the website were easily severable from the rest of the website.

Multimedia works

There is no particular category of multimedia work in copyright law. If a defendant reproduces a particular multimedia work, the claimant would have to bring proceedings in relation to the underlying works out of which the final

---

39 Copyright and Related Rights Regulations 1996, reg 16.
40 *Shetland Times v Wills* [1997] FSR 604.

product has been produced, for example, the musical work, any sound recordings used in such works, artistic works, etc. This situation does not really reflect the fact that the composite multimedia work may be greater than its constituent parts. It might be possible for the multimedia work as a whole to be protected as a film or a dramatic work but this would depend on the multimedia work in question and the position is far from certain.

A lacuna *in copyright law?*

The division of the classes of copyright work into the nine types of work is strict. If a feature does not fall within any one of the categories, copyright will not subsist in that feature. This can lead to injustice for works of originality which cannot be categorised as one of the recognised types of work. An illustration of such injustice was illustrated by the decision of *Norowzian v Arks*.[41]

The claimant was a director of advertising films. In 1992, he directed a short film called *Joy*. The striking feature of the visual impact of the film was the result of the claimant's filming and editing techniques. One of these was the practice of 'jump cutting'. The result of this editing technique was that apparent sudden changes of the actor's position were shown, which could not have been performed as successive movements in reality.

The defendants were Guinness and their advertising agency. The case concerned an advertisement for Guinness, which the claimant alleged was an infringement of his copyright in *Joy*. A similar jump cutting technique was used as in the defendants' film. It was common ground that the advertising agency had instructed the director of the Guinness commercial to produce a commercial with an atmosphere which was broadly similar to that portrayed in *Joy*.

The claimant's claim

The claimant claimed infringement of copyright in the following works:

- copyright in the film 'Joy';
- copyright in the dramatic work .

Copyright in the film (Norowzian (No 1))[42]

Norowzian (No 1) concerned an application to strike out the claim in relation to the film. The application was successful. The court held that infringement of copyright in a film requires copying of the physical recording embodied on

---

41 *Norowzian v Arks (No 2)* [2000] EMLR 1.
42 *Norowzian v Arks (No 1)* [1998] FSR 394.

the film for example, by video recording the film. It is not an infringement in the film to simply reproduce the subject matter of the film as the defendant had done.

Copyright in the dramatic work (Norowzian (No 2))[43]

At first instance the court held that the film was not a dramatic work. This finding was subsequently reversed on appeal (see above). The Court of Appeal held that the *film* was a dramatic work, being a work of action capable of being performed in public. But the subject matter of the two films was different. Copyright did not exist in the filmmaker's style or technique taken in isolation. The categories of work set out in the CDPA do not protect the techniques embodied in the works. Accordingly, there was no infringement on the facts of *Norowzian*. Nourse LJ observed that 'the highest it can be put in favour of the claimant is that there is a striking similarity between the filming and editing styles and techniques used by the respective directors of the two films'.

The judge at first instance (Rattee J) had recognised that 'there is no doubt that the little film [*Joy*] is a striking example of a talented film director's art'. The claimant's counsel argued that this result was a serious *lacuna* in the protection of works of originality. Copyright law offered no protection for the originality of the film as a manifestation of the filmmaker's art. Rattee J appeared to have some sympathy with this view but indicated that his hands were tied. The Court of Appeal agreed. Buxton LJ indicated that 'the general features said to mark out Joy, such as its rhythm, pace and movements; the use of jump cutting and other techniques; and its theme, explained to us of that of a young man releasing his tension by performing a rather bizarre collection of dance movements in a rather surreal setting; could none of them be the subject of copyright'.

Originality

In order for copyright to subsist in a literary, dramatic, musical or artistic work the work must be original. Originality has been interpreted widely by the courts. The threshold is not high. It is not dependent on talent or inventiveness. Nor does it mean that a work has to be ground breaking or unique. The courts generally shy away from any assessment of creative originality.

---

43   *Norowzian v Arks (No 2)* [2000] EMLR 1.

'Original' simply means that the work must have originated from the author; it must not have been copied from something else.[44] The creation of the work must therefore have involved the creator in the exercise of at least a small degree of skill, judgment and labour.

A reworking of an earlier work may still be original provided that the reworked version has involved skill and labour.[45]

A special originality requirement for databases

A database (which the CDPA recognises as a type of literary work for copyright purposes) is original under copyright law if the database constitutes the creator's own intellectual creation by reason of the selection or arrangement of the database contents.[46] This is a more demanding requirement than the test for originality for other types of literary works, artistic works, dramatic works and musical works.

Fixation

Copyright will not subsist in a literary, dramatic or musical work unless the work is recorded in writing or otherwise.[47] In copyright law, recording is often referred to as 'fixation'. It is immaterial whether the work is recorded by or with the permission of the author.[48]

Example

Where a speech is made *ad lib*, for example, without written notes or text, copyright will not exist in the speech as a literary work unless and until it is recorded, for example, by the taking of written notes of the speech or by the making of a sound recording. It does not matter whether the recording was made with the speaker's consent or not. Similarly, an original musical composition must be recorded either by musical notation or by a sound recording.

---

44 *Ladbroke v William Hill* [1964] 1 All ER 465; and *University of London Press v University Tutorial Press* [1916] 2 Ch 601.

45 *Christoffer v Poseidon Films* (1999) unreported. The claimant wrote a script of the Cyclops story from *The Odyssey*. The script was an original work even though the story was the same as that in *The Odyssey*. The script contained many variations of detail, for example, the narrative script had been turned into a script suitable for filming: '... this manifestly involves original work.'

46 CDPA 1988, s 3A(2).

47 *Ibid*, s 3(2).

48 *Ibid*, s 3(3).

In the *Norowzian* litigation, the dance portrayed in the claimant's film was held to have been recorded by filming.[49]

Copyright in ideas

It is often said that copyright does not exist in an *idea*, but only in the form in which the idea is expressed. This is one of the reasons why the law insists on fixation in relation to literary, dramatic and musical works. It is the fixed form which is protected rather than the underlying idea. But taken at face value, the ideas/expression maxim is too glib. It requires qualification. A more accurate reflection of the law is the statement that *copyright will only subsist where the work in question is in a sufficiently developed form*. If the work is too nebulous or imprecise, it will not enjoy copyright protection.

It is useful to keep in mind the fact that one of the objectives of copyright law is to protect the skill and labour of the author of the work from appropriation. A general idea or an undeveloped concept is unlikely to have involved sufficient skill, judgment or labour. Ideas which develop the general concept are more likely to be protected. Anyone can use the basic idea or the underlying concept, but if they copy the detail, they may infringe copyright. By copying the detail, they are likely to be appropriating the skill, judgment and labour which went into the creation. Pritchard J explained this point in eloquent terms in the New Zealand case of *Plix Products v Frank M Winstone*.[50] He said:

> There are in fact two kinds of 'ideas' involved in the making of any work which is susceptible of being the subject of copyright. In the first place, there is the general idea or basic concept of the work. The idea is formed (or implanted) in the mind of the author ... While this 'idea' remains as a thought in the author's mind it is, of course, not copyright.

> Then there is the second phase – a second kind of 'idea'. The author of the work will scarcely be able to transform the basic concept into a concrete form, that is, 'express' the idea – without furnishing it with details of form and shape ... Each author will draw on his skill, his knowledge of the subject, the results of his own researches, his own imagination in forming his idea of how he will express the basic concept. All these modes of expression have their genesis in the author's mind – these too are 'ideas'. When these ideas (which are essentially constructive in character) are reduced to concrete form, the forms which they take are where the copyright resides.

The distinction between the basic idea and its detailed development is often a difficult one to draw. It will always be a question of degree.

49 *Norowzian v Arks* [1999] FSR 79.
50 *Plix Products v Frank M Winstone* [1989] 2 All ER 1056.

Example

In the case of *Green v Broadcasting Corpn of New Zealand*,[51] Hughie Green, the compere of the well known talent show called *Opportunity Knocks*, commenced proceedings for copyright infringement against New Zealand Broadcasting Corporation who, he claimed, had copied the format of his show and were broadcasting a similar show.

Mr Green claimed that he was the owner of copyright in the scripts and dramatic format for *Opportunity Knocks*. However, he did not produce detailed scripts to support his claim, nor a written format. Instead, the court heard only oral evidence that the scripts/format consisted of a number of catch phrases used in each show, the use of a device known as a clapometer and other general, unconnected, ideas.

The court found that in the absence of detailed scripts the claimant was doing no more than seeking to protect the general idea or concept for his talent show and that such a nebulous concept could not be protected by copyright. If the claimant had been able to produce actual scripts and a written summary of the so called format, the result may have been different.

The distinction between expression and ideas is considered further in the infringement section of this chapter.

Copyright in titles, slogans, catchphrases and character names

As a general rule, short phrases, such as titles, advertising slogans and catch phrases are not protected by copyright. In the case of *Francis Day and Hunter v Twentieth Century Fox Film Corpn*,[52] a Privy Council case, Lord Wright observed that:

> In general, a title is not by itself a proper subject matter of copyright. As a rule a title does not involve literary composition, and is not sufficiently substantial to justify a claim to protection. That statement does not mean that in a particular case a title may not be on so extensive a scale, and of so important a character as to be a proper subject of protection against being copied.

The way is therefore left open for a title which is sufficiently substantial, on a sufficiently extensive scale and of an important character to be protectable by copyright law as an original literary work, although a claimant seeking copyright protection for a title or other short phrase would face an uphill struggle in the face of Lord Wright's opinion. The *Francis Day* case concerned the title of the song *The Man Who Broke the Bank at Monte Carlo*. The claimant sought copyright protection in the title against the defendant, who had used

---

51 *Green v Broadcasting Corpn of New Zealand* [1989] RPC 700.
52 *Francis Day and Hunter v Twentieth Century Fox Film Corpn* [1940] AC 112.

the same title for a film. The Privy Council held that the title was not protected by copyright.

The *Francis Day* case should now be read in the context of a later decision of the Court of Appeal which concerned whether copyright subsisted in a single made up word, EXXON, which was part of the claimants' corporate name and which the claimants had invented.[53]

In the *Exxon* case, it was held that, although the invented word was original for copyright law purposes in that it had not been copied from another source *and* it had involved the creators in the exercise of skill, judgment and labour, copyright still did *not* subsist in it as a literary work. This decision was reached on the basis that the word was simply an artificial combination of four letters of the alphabet which served a purpose only when used in conjunction with other English words to identify one or other companies in the claimant group. It did not have any of the 'commonsense qualities' which were required for copyright to subsist. These qualities were defined as the conveyance of information, the provision of instructions or the giving of pleasure (in the form of literary enjoyment). In order to be deserving of copyright protection, the Court of Appeal judgment suggests, a literary work must perform at least one of these functions.

On existing case law, copyright is therefore unlikely to subsist in slogans, titles and catch phrases on the basis that they are too insubstantial to be deserving of such protection and/or that they do not satisfy the criteria laid down in the *Exxon* case.

In the *Shetland Times* case,[54] the Scottish court held (on an application for an interim injunction) that headlines in a newspaper had copyright. This decision has been the subject of criticism on the ground that it represents something of a departure from the *Exxon* decision. However a headline (particularly a headline consisting of a pun) could be said to satisfy at least some of the *Exxon* criteria.

In relation to character names, the general position is that there is no copyright in a name (whether invented or not). The courts have accordingly denied copyright protection to the names 'Kojak',[55] 'James Bond'[56] and 'Burberry'.[57]

Even though copyright is not available to protect material of this type, an action for passing off may be available where damage to the claimant's goodwill can be shown. Where the word, name or phrase has been registered as a trade mark, an action for trade mark infringement may also be available.

---

53 *Exxon v Exxon Insurance Consultants International Ltd* [1981] 3 All ER 241.
54 *Shetland Times v Wills* [1997] FSR 604.
55 *Tavener Rutledge v Trexapalm* [1977] RPC 99.
56 *O'Neill v Paramount Pictures Corpn* [1983] Court of Appeal Transcript 235.
57 *Burberrys v JC Cording* (1909) 26 RPC 693.

The reader is referred to Chapter 14 for further consideration of the protection of character names and likenesses.

Copyright in conversations and interviews

A conversation is theoretically capable of copyright protection as a literary work, provided that it is recorded in a permanent form (whether in writing or otherwise). Copyright in the conversation will belong to the speakers either jointly (as joint authors of the conversation) or separately in relation to each individual's words. The conversation must have involved the expenditure of skill, judgment and labour to satisfy the test of originality. It must also meet the criteria set out in the *Exxon* case by conveying information, providing instruction or giving literary pleasure. A commonplace conversation is unlikely to satisfy these criteria. The author is aware that certain celebrities have asserted copyright in comments they have made during interviews, the objective behind the litigation being the prevention of the unauthorised use of television interview footage. No such case has yet proceeded to trial. Clearly, if copyright does exist in a recorded conversation, its existence could have serious repercussions for freedom of expression.[58]

Copyright in a recording of a literary, dramatic and musical work

We have seen that a literary, dramatic or musical work must be recorded in a permanent form if copyright is to subsist in the work. If the record is a sound recording or a film, the recording or film itself will be a separate copyright work. There is no requirement that sound recordings or films must be original.

However, the situation may be different where the recording takes the form of a written record. Can a verbatim note of a speech be said to be an 'original' literary work in its own right? There is a House of Lords' decision which suggests that a verbatim note of a speech can be a literary work in its own right.[59] However, the case was decided before the requirement for originality was introduced into the law. It is submitted that the case would probably be decided differently under the current law on the ground that

---

58 CDPA 1988, s 58 (discussed below) contains an exception to the general principle in relation to recorded interviews used for reporting current events.

59 *Walter v Lane* [1900] AC 539.

merely reproducing the spoken word does not involve skill, judgment or labour in an authorship context.[60]

Duration of copyright – a guide

Copyright does not subsist in a work for an indefinite period. The provisions relating to the duration of copyright are not without difficulty, but the position can be summarised in relation to works which originate in Member States of the EEA and where the author is a national of an EEA State as follows:

- copyright in *literary works, artistic works, dramatic works and musical works* expires at the end of the period of *70 years* from the end of the calendar year in which the author dies unless the work is computer generated in which case copyright expires at the end of *50 years* from the end of the calendar year in which the work was made. Where artistic works are exploited industrially by or with the licence of the copyright owner, the term of copyright protection will be reduced to *25 years* from the end of the calendar year in which such articles are first marketed in the UK or elsewhere;

- in the case of *films,* copyright expires *70 years* from the end of the calendar year after the death of the last to die of the following persons (or the last of the following persons whose identity is known):
  o the principal director;
  o the author of the screenplay;
  o the dialogue writer;
  o the composer of music specially created for the film and used in the film.

Where there is no person falling under the above descriptions, copyright expires at the end of the period of *50 years* from the end of the calendar year in which the film was made:

---

60 Recent cases on joint ownership of copyright support this view – see, eg, *Robin Ray v Classic FM* [1998] FSR 622 and *Fylde Microsystems v Key Radio* [1998] FSR 449, discussed below. However, the Australian case of *Sands v McDougall* (1917) CLR 49 held that *Walter v Lane* was good law, even after the introduction of a requirement of originality, and this reasoning was upheld by Browne-Wilkinson VC in *Express Newspapers v News (UK) plc* [1991] FSR 36, where it was held that 'if skill, judgment and labour were put into reporting the interviewee's words, copyright will subsist in the report even though the actual words used were the interviewee's'. However, on the facts of the *Express* case, the article containing the interview was not simply a verbatim record of what had been said – it involved the selection of quotations, for example, rather than a complete transcript of the interview. The *Express* case can accordingly be distinguished from *Walter v Lane*.

- copyright in *sound recordings* expires *50 years* from the end of the calendar year in which the recording was first released or *50 years* from the making of the recording if it is not released within 50 years. A sound recording is released when it is first published, played in public, broadcast or included in a cable programme service;

- copyright in *broadcasts and cable programmes* expires *50 years* from the end of the calendar year in which the broadcast was made or the programme was included in a cable programme service. Copyright in a repeat broadcast or cable programme expires at the same time as the copyright in the original broadcast or cable programme. No copyright arises in respect of a repeat made after the expiry of the copyright in the original broadcast or cable programme;

- copyright in typographical arrangements of published editions expires at the end of *25 years* from the end of the calendar year in which the edition was first published;

- where works did not originate in a Member State of the EEA or if the author is not a EEA national, then the general principle is that the duration of copyright will be the same as the work is entitled to in the country of origin, provided that that period does not exceed the periods provided for under the CDPA (as set out above).

The above is only a guide to what are complex provisions. For further detail, the reader is referred to ss 12–15A of the Act, as amended by the Duration of Copyright and Rights in Performances Regulations 1995 and to regs 14–21, 23–25 and 36 of the 1995 Regulations. In particular, there are transitional provisions which apply to works which were in existence before the Regulations came into force on 1 January 1996.

It can be seen from the above that copyright lasts for a generous period of time. If an author writes a book when he is 25, copyright will subsist in the book until the author dies, say aged 95. At that point, copyright will already have subsisted for 70 years. Copyright will then last for a further 70 years following the death of the author. Copyright will therefore have lasted for a total of 140 years from when the book was written.

Who owns copyright?

Copyright exists independently of the physical work in which it subsists. The owner of the work will not necessarily own the copyright in the work, even though he may have the work in his physical possession and vice versa. The first owner of copyright is generally the creator of the work. Copyright will remain with the creator until copyright is transferred, regardless of whether the work itself is transferred.

Example

I buy an original painting in which copyright subsists. The act of buying the painting might transfer physical ownership of the painting to me. However, unless copyright is *assigned* to me (see below for a discussion of the meaning of assignment), my purchase of the painting will not transfer ownership of copyright in the painting. I may own the painting, but I will not own the right to control the exploitation of the painting, that is, the copyright.

Authorship

The basic rule is that the creator (known for copyright purposes as the author) of the work will be the first owner of copyright of literary, dramatic or musical works.[61] Often, the identity of the author will be obvious. If I write a book or paint a picture, I am clearly the author for copyright purposes. In the music industry it is common practice for an author of a musical work to transfer copyright to a music publisher. Therefore, although the author is the first owner of copyright, for most practical purposes it is the author's music publisher who controls the exploitation of the works.

The principal exception to the general rule that the author is the first owner of copyright is where a literary, dramatic, musical or artistic work or a film is created by an employee in the course of his employment. In that case, the employer is the first owner of copyright in the work, unless there is an agreement between employer and employee to the contrary.[62] This agreement does not have to be in writing, although in the interests of certainty it is better if it is.

It will be a question of fact whether the creation of a copyright work was in the course of the employee's employment. If the employee writes a screenplay in his spare time, the writing is clearly unlikely to fall within her employment. However, other situations may not be so clear-cut.[63] Regard should be had to any contract of employment or job description to determine the issue – although these will not in themselves be determinative (as opposed to employees under a contract of employment).

Where freelance staff create copyright works under a contract for services, the freelancer will own copyright unless it is assigned. Whenever there is a doubt about whether someone is an employee or working freelance, written

---

61 CDPA 1988, s 11(1).

62 *Ibid*, s 11(2).

63 For an example of a case where the distinction was not obvious, see *Stephenson Jordan v Harrison* [1952] RPC 10, where copyright in lectures given by an accountant was held to belong to the accountant, rather than his employer. The court held that he was employed to provide accountancy services to clients rather than to give public lectures. The situation might not be the same today, when it is generally acknowledged that it is part of a professional's job to market his practice to potential clients.

assignments should be taken to ensure that copyright ends up where it is intended.

In relation to certain categories of work, the CDPA defines who the author will be in the following terms:

- *computer generated literary, dramatic, musical or artistic works*[64] – the author is the person who undertakes the arrangements for the creation;[65]

- *databases*[66] – the maker of a database is the person who takes the initiative in obtaining, verifying or presenting the contents of the database and assumes the risk of investing in that obtaining, verification or presentation;

- *sound recordings*[67] – the author is the producer. The producer is defined to mean the person by whom the arrangements necessary for the making of the recording were undertaken. In practice, this may be the record company;

- *films*[68] – the authors will be the producer *and* the principal director. As these may not be the same entity, copyright will in some circumstances be owned jointly. The producer is defined to mean the person by whom the arrangements necessary for the making of the film are undertaken. Where the producer and/or director are employees who make the film in the course of their employment, copyright will belong to the producer/director's employer;[69]

- *broadcasts*[70] – the author is the person making the broadcast or, in the case of a broadcast which relays another broadcast by reception and immediate retransmission, the person making that other broadcast;

- *cable programmes*[71] – the author will be the person providing the cable programme service in which the programme is included;

- *typographical arrangements*[72] – the author will be the publisher;

- *photographs*[73] – the author is the person who creates the work – generally the photographer unless the photographer is an employee who takes the photograph in the course of his employment in accordance with the principles set out above.

Ownership of commissioned works is considered below.

---

64 CDPA 1988, s 9(3).
65 Computer generated work is defined in *ibid*, s 178 as a work created by a computer in circumstances where there is no human author.
66 Copyright and Rights in Databases Regulations 1997, reg 14.
67 CDPA 1988, s 9(2)(aa).
68 *Ibid*, s 9(2)(ab).
69 *Ibid*, s 11(2).
70 *Ibid*, s 9(2)(b).
71 *Ibid*, s 9(2)(c).
72 *Ibid*, s 9(2)(d).
73 *Ibid*, s 9(1).

Unknown authorship

Sometimes it is not possible to ascertain the identity of the author of a copyright work. The CDPA provides that a work can be of unknown authorship where the identity of the author is unknown or where, in the case of a work of joint authorship, the identity of none of the authors is known.[74] The identity of the author(s) shall be regarded as unknown if it is not possible for a person to ascertain the identity by reasonable inquiry.[75] In relation to the duration of copyright in original literary, dramatic, musical or artistic works of unknown authorship, copyright expires at the end of 70 years from the end of the calendar year in which the work was made or if, during that period, it is made available to the public, at the end of 70 years from the end of the calendar year in which it was first made available.

Joint authorship

Where a work is produced by the collaboration of two or more authors in which the contribution of one author is not distinct from that of the other author or authors, it will be a work of joint authorship.[76] The joint authors will be the first owners of copyright in the work (provided that they are not employees who have created the work in the course of their employment).

The CDPA provides that a film shall be treated as a work of joint authorship unless the producer and the principal director are the same person.[77]

The courts have considered the circumstances in which someone who contributes to the development of a work can properly be classed a joint author.

In the case of *Fylde Microsystems Ltd v Key Radio Systems Ltd*,[78] Laddie J held that, whilst it was not necessary for the putative joint author to have carried out the act of fixation (for example, the actual putting of pen to paper), he must have contributed the right kind of skill and labour to the finished work before he could be a joint owner of copyright. The right kind of skill and labour must be *authorship* skill and labour. The facts of the *Fylde* case concerned development of software. The defendants asserted that they were joint authors of the software in question because they had outlined to the claimant what the general functions of the software were to be. They had also tested the prototype software which the claimant had designed and in so doing had revealed that certain changes had to be made to it by the claimant.

---

74 CDPA 1988, s 9(4).

75 *Ibid*, s 9(5).

76 *Ibid*, s 10.

77 *Ibid*, s 10(1A).

78 *Fylde Microsystems Ltd v Key Radio Systems Ltd* [1998] FSR 449.

Laddie J held that although the contributions made by the defendant were extensive and technically sophisticated they essentially amounted to testing the program. Such efforts were analogous to the skills of a proofreader, but they were not *authorship* skill. Accordingly they did not give rise to a claim of joint authorship. Similarly, merely outlining the general functions of the program to the claimant did not involve authorship skill.

Lightman J reached a similar decision in *Robin Ray v Classic FM plc*.[79] He held that a joint author must participate in and share responsibility for the way in which the work is expressed. He must accordingly do more than contribute ideas to the author. Whilst there is no need to show actual penmanship, what is required is something approximating to penmanship – a direct responsibility for what appears on the paper. On the facts of the case, the defendant claimed to be a joint author of a catalogue of musical recordings. The court held that the claimant was solely responsible as author for the way that the catalogue had been expressed. Whilst the defendants had discussed the development of the catalogue with the claimant and had initiated and developed a number of ideas which the claimant had then incorporated into the catalogue, that was not sufficient to give rise to a claim of joint authorship. Their input was not sufficient to make them joint authors.

The putative joint author must also have made a significant contribution to the work[80] of an authorship nature. This does not mean that the contribution must be equal to those of the other author(s), but the contribution must be more than slight.

Some interesting cases concern ownership of copyright in musical compositions. In *Stuart v Barrett*,[81] the court was called upon to determine the authorship of a piece of music which had evolved from a jamming session. In his judgment, Sir Thomas Morison QC described the scene as follows:[82]

> Someone started to play and the rest joined in and improvised and improved the original idea. The final piece was indeed the product of the joint compositional skills of the members of the group present at the time.

He went on to observe:

> It would not be sensible to try to lay down any general rules which would apply to all group compositions. One member of a pop group may have an idea which is so nearly perfected that the compositional input of any of the other members of the group would be regarded as insignificant.

This was held to be the case in *Hadley v Kemp*.[83] The case concerned the authorship of the songs of the group Spandau Ballet. The issue before the

---

79   *Robin Ray v Classic FM plc* [1998] FSR 622.
80   *Godfrey v Lees* [1995] EMLR 307.
81   *Stuart v Barrett* [1994] EMLR 448.
82   *Ibid*, p 455.
83   *Hadley v Kemp* [1999] EMLR 539.

court was whether the songs had been written solely by the person acknowledged to be the group's main songwriter, Gary Kemp. Alternatively, could the other members of the group be said to be joint authors by virtue of their interpretation of Gary Kemp's compositions? The court heard evidence that the group's typical songwriting procedure was that Gary Kemp would present a song to the band with the melody and chord structure complete and the structure of the song already laid out. Very few changes would be made leading up to the recording of the song and those that were made would be subject to Gary Kemp's approval.

The court held that Gary Kemp was the sole author of the musical and literary works which made up the Spandau Ballet songs. It held that there was a vital distinction to be drawn between the composition and creation of a musical work on one hand and the performance and interpretation of it on the other. Matters of performance and interpretation did not go to the creation of the musical work. They did not involve the right kind of skill and labour. This would be the case even where there was an element of improvisation in the performances.[84]

Joint authorship example

On the basis of these authorities, if A thinks up the outline plot of a novel and suggests the plot to B who then writes the novel based on A's plot, A will *not* be a joint owner of copyright in the novel. A's input will be insufficient to make him a joint owner. A's skill is not actual authorship skill amounting to responsibility for what appears on the paper. If A wished to protect his idea for the plot, he would have to rely on a claim in breach of confidence against B (assuming that he could meet the criteria for such a claim). The reader is referred to Chapter 5 in this regard and, in particular, to the cases of *Fraser v Thames Television*[85] and *De Maudsley v Palumbo*.[86]

If B subsequently submits the completed novel to her publishers who then spot a number of typographical errors and suggest a number of minor changes, the publisher's input is also unlikely to give rise to a claim of joint authorship, because: (a) the skill which they have exercised is not authorship skill, but more like the skill of a proofreader; and (b) in any event, the input is not extensive enough to give rise to joint authorship.

If, instead of typing the novel herself, B had dictated it to her secretary, then the fact that B had not actually put pen to paper would not deprive her of

---

84 The issue as to whether the group members were joint authors of the musical arrangement (a musical work) does not appear to have been raised in argument and the point is not really considered in the judgment.

85 *Fraser v Thames Television* [1984] 1 QB 44.

86 *De Maudsley v Palumbo* [1996] FSR 447.

her claim to authorship. B's secretary will not be able to claim joint authorship because his skill is not authorship skill.[87]

Indivisible contributions

The CDPA 1988 requires that, in order for a work to be one of joint authorship, it must not be possible to separate the contributions of one author from the contributions of the other.[88] If a book is written by two or more authors, but each author is responsible for distinct parts of a work (say, for separate chapters of a book), they will each be classed as sole authors of their own parts. In the *Hadley v Kemp* case, the judge thought that there was an 'obvious argument' that the contribution of group members who created saxophone solos (known as 'fills') at spaces left for him by the group's main songwriter were separate from the songwriter's contribution to the song. The point does not appear to have been raised in argument and was not developed further in the judgment.

Dealings with copyright works

Assignments

Copyright is property and can be sold or transferred like other forms of property. Transfers can be effected by testamentary disposition or by operation of law (for example, on bankruptcy, copyright will be transferred to the trustee in bankruptcy as part of the bankrupt's estate). It can also be transferred like other personal property.[89]

A transfer of copyright which does not take the form of testamentary disposition or operation of law is called an assignment. Assignments must be in writing and signed by the assignor (the person transferring the copyright) in order to be fully effective.[90] The assignment should be for consideration (usually a payment, however nominal) or by deed. Assignments can transfer copyright in works which are not in existence at the time of assignment. Such an assignment is known as *an assignment of future copyright*.[91]

A mere agreement to assign copyright at a future date does not have to be in writing – it can be in the form of an oral agreement or it can be implied by the conduct of the parties. A binding and enforceable agreement to assign is effective as an equitable assignment and may be carried into effect by an order

---

87 Although refer to *Walter v Lane* [1900] AC 539 and the comments made above, p 229.

88 CDPA 1988, s 10.

89 *Ibid*, s 90(1).

90 *Ibid*, s 90(3).

91 *Ibid*, s 91.

for specific performance or by a vesting order transferring legal title to the equitable owner.[92]

Assignments can be limited in the sense that they can transfer copyright for a limited period or for specified purposes only.[93]

Licences

A licence is a permission by the copyright owner (the licensor) to a third party (the licensee) permitting the licensee to make use of its copyright material in circumstances which would otherwise be an infringement of copyright. A licence does *not* transfer ownership of copyright.

Licences may be exclusive, sole or non-exclusive. It is possible to have licences of future copyright in works which have not yet been created.[94]

An *exclusive licence* is in some ways similar to an assignment in that, whilst it does not transfer ownership of copyright, it gives the licensee the sole and exclusive right to do the acts permitted by the licence to the exclusion of anyone else (including the copyright owner).[95] Exclusive licences must be in writing and signed by or on behalf of the copyright owner.[96] An exclusive licensee can bring proceedings to restrain copyright infringement, although it will generally have to join the copyright owner as a party to the proceedings.

A *sole licence* gives the licensee the right to carry out the acts which are set out in the licence to the exclusion of anyone else apart from the copyright owner, who continues to have the right to carry out the acts alongside the licensee.

A *non-exclusive licensee* will not have exclusive rights to use of the copyright granted in the licence, nor will it be able to sue in its own name for copyright infringement.

Non-exclusive and sole licences can be oral but, as with any agreement, it is advisable to have the terms set down in writing and signed by both parties, in the interests of certainty.

Assignments and licences are considered further in Part 3.

Commissioned works

The rule that the first owner of copyright is the author of the copyright works means that where a work is commissioned, copyright vests in the *creator* of the

92 *Lakeview Computer v Steadman* (1999) unreported, CA.
93 CDPA 1988, s 90(2).
94 *Ibid*, s 91(3).
95 *Ibid*, s 92(1).
96 *Ibid*, s 92(1).

work and not the commissioner[97] in the absence of an express or implied agreement to the contrary.[98]

Example

If a client commissions and pays a design agency to devise a poster, copyright in the artistic and literary works which make up the poster will belong in law to the *agency* and not to the client. The fact that the agency is paid in full for its work will not affect this position. The client may own the physical property such as the original artwork, but the copyright will still belong to the design agency. As we shall see, ownership of copyright means that the agency (and not the client who has paid for the poster) has the right to control the use to which the poster is put.

The commissioner is not, therefore, the automatic owner of copyright in material which it commissions. If copyright is to be acquired in the material, it will have to be transferred to the commissioning party by way of written assignment.

In circumstances where a work is commissioned, the parties should therefore ideally set out in writing, and with as much precision as possible, what the terms of the commission are to be. This provides certainty. Each of the parties will know the extent of their rights. Where it is intended that copyright in the commissioned work will belong to the commissioning party, the agreement should provide for copyright to be assigned to that party. Where copyright is to remain with the author of the work, the agreement should set out what author has agreed that the commissioning party can do with the work (that is, it should set out the terms of the licence (or permission) which the author has granted to the commissioning party).

To take the above example further, the client had commissioned a poster from the design agency. The agency is not prepared to assign its copyright to the client. It is prepared to give the client permission to use the poster in the course of its business for a period of 12 months in the UK. The agreement should set out the extent of this licence granted by the agency to the client.

What happens where there is no written agreement or where the agreement does not deal with the extent of the grant of rights?

Where there is no written agreement between the commissioner and the creator of the work, or where the agreement does not provide for a grant of rights, the courts will imply a term to give effect to the arrangement between the parties. The principles to be applied when doing so were established by

---

97 CDPA 1988, s 9(1).

98 Although, as we have seen, if an employer commissions a work from an employee in the course of his employment, copyright belongs to the employer.

the decision of the House of Lords in *Liverpool CC v Irwin*.[99] A term will only be implied into an agreement where it is *necessary to give business efficacy* to the contract and, even then, it will only be implied *to the extent necessary* in the circumstances.

In the case of *Robin Ray v Classic FM*,[100] the claimant entered into a consultancy agreement with the defendant radio station to advise on the composition of its classical music repertoire. The agreement made no express provision about ownership of copyright in any works which the claimant created. As part of his role, the claimant compiled a number of documents containing proposals for the cataloguing of the defendant's recordings and a database which reproduced the contents of the five documents.

The claimant alleged that he owned copyright in the documents and the database. He claimed that the defendant infringed this copyright by making copies of the database and granting licences to foreign radio stations to use the copies. The defendant asserted that it was entitled to exploit the database by making copies for foreign licensees because the consultancy agreement conferred an implied licence on the defendant to exploit the works. The consultancy agreement was silent on the extent of the grant of rights. The judge applied the general principles relating to implied terms in contracts. The ambit of the grant must not be more than the minimum necessary to secure for the commissioner the entitlement which the parties to the contract must have intended to confer on him. The amount of the purchase price which the commissioner pays for the work could be relevant to help to determine this point. On the facts, the limits of what was contemplated by the parties when the contract was made was that the claimant's work would be used to enable the defendant to carry on its business of broadcasting in the UK only. The term which could properly be implied into the agreement was the grant of a licence to the defendant to use the copyright material for in the UK.

On the facts of our example involving the poster, if there was no written agreement between the design agency and the client, the court would be likely to imply a licence to use the poster in order to give business efficacy to the agreement. The extent of that licence would be no more than what is necessary to secure to the client the entitlement which the design agency and the client must have intended would be conferred. On the facts, this is likely to encompass use of the poster in the client's advertising. However, if the client wanted to use the image on the poster in a different format, say on a T-shirt, the implied grant of rights may not be wide enough to cover such a use. The issue would depend on the particular facts, one of which would be the price paid by the client for the poster. The higher the price, in relation to the normal market, the more likely it is that a wider licence would be implied.

---

99 *Liverpool CC v Irwin* [1977] AC 236; [1976] 2 All ER 39.
100 *Robin Ray v Classic FM* [1998] FSR 622.

Another potential avenue open to the client where there is no agreement about the extent of the grant of rights is the solution that, although the *legal* ownership of copyright rests with the design agency, the client owns the copyright in the work *in equity*. The effect of equitable ownership would be that the client is entitled to call for an assignment of the legal title to the copyright. The court in the *Robin Ray* case considered this approach.

In that case it was held that, in accordance with the general principles relating to the implication of terms in a contract, where it was necessary to imply some form of grant of right (as it was in the *Robin Ray* case) and there was a choice of: (a) implying a licence; or (b) a right for an assignment of the legal title both solutions gave business efficacy to the agreement, then the implied term would be the grant of a licence only. This is in line with the principle that the implied term should go no further than is necessary to give business efficacy to the agreement. The court observed that, although circumstances might exist where it was necessary to imply an assignment, these would be unusual.

The *Robin Ray* decision on the question of an implied right to call for an assignment was not considered in the subsequent case of *Pasterfield v Denham*,[101] a decision of Overend J. In the *Pasterfield* case, the claimant was a designer. He had been commissioned to design two leaflets and a brochure by Portsmouth County Council (the second defendant) to be used to promote a tourist attraction. A few years later the council commissioned the first defendant to update the leaflet. The updated leaflet reproduced much of the claimant's original leaflet with some alterations, for example, a number of figures were omitted from drawings and the colouring was slightly different. The claimant was not asked for permission to update his artwork. He sued for copyright infringement in his original drawings. The judge held that by accepting the commission to design the drawings, the equitable interest in the copyright passed from the claimant to the council. There was therefore an implied term in the agreement between the designer and the council that the council could call for an assignment of the legal ownership of the copyright from the designer to the council. The judge referred to the unreported case of *Warner v Gestetner*[102] (a first instance decision of Whitford J) and an *obiter* comment of Templeman J in *Nichols v Rees*[103] to support his finding. He did not consider *Liverpool v Irwin*[104] or the general principles relating to implied terms in contracts.

The judge in the *Pasterfield* case went onto hold that, even if he was wrong about the implied right to the assignment, there was an implied licence

---

101 *Pasterfield v Denham* [1999] FSR 168.
102 *Warner v Gestetner* (1987) unreported.
103 *Nichols v Rees* [1979] RPC 127.
104 *Liverpool CC v Irwin* [1977] AC 236; [1976] 2 All ER 39.

allowing for the drawings to be used by the council to promote the tourist attraction generally. The judge was satisfied on the facts that the claimant knew that the council might use the drawings in its promotional material generally at the time when the agreement was reached. Accordingly, there was no infringement of copyright. The judge's decision on the grant of rights *was* consistent with Lightman J's judgment in the *Robin Ray* case.

It is submitted that the *Pasterfield* case was wrong on the question of the implied right to an assignment and that the correct approach was that of Lightman J in the *Robin Ray* case. Following that approach, where an implied term is necessary to give business efficacy to an agreement, it should be no more than the minimum necessary. Accordingly, where the *lacuna* in the grant of rights can be addressed by the grant of a licence or an assignment, the term to be implied is the licence – the ambit of which should be ascertained according to the principles set out in the *Robin Ray* case.

These cases illustrate the importance of spelling out the extent of the grant of rights. If the designer in the *Pasterfield* case had not wanted his designs used on any promotional material other than for the specific material he had in mind when he drew them, he should have expressly stated that to be the case in the commissioning agreement – although he might have found that his fee for designing the artwork would have been reduced.

Infringements of copyright

The acts which the copyright owner can prevent others from doing in relation to the copyright work (known as the *restricted acts*) are as follows:[105]

- copying the work;
- issuing copies of the work to the public;
- renting or lending the work to the public;
- performing, playing or showing the work in public;
- broadcasting the work or including it in a cable programme service;
- making an adaptation of the work or doing any of the above acts in relation to an adaptation.

In addition, a person who authorises someone to do any of the above acts also infringes copyright.[106]

These activities are the *primary infringements*. If the above activities are carried out without the copyright owner's permission, copyright in the work will be infringed,[107] unless that particular use of the work is permitted under

105 CDPA 1988, s 16.
106 *Ibid*, s 16(2).
107 *Ibid*.

the provisions of the CDPA 1988 (see below for discussion of the permitted uses). A primary infringement of copyright can be committed unintentionally. There is no requirement that a claimant must be able to show that the infringement was deliberate or that the defendant was reckless or negligent.[108]

Copying

Copying an original literary, dramatic, musical or artistic work means reproducing the work in any material form.[109] This includes storing the work in any medium by electronic means, such as storing the work on computer disks or on any digital media.[110] It also includes making copies which are transient or incidental to another use of the work.[111]

Copying of an artistic work includes making a copy in three dimensions of a two dimensional work or the making of a copy in two dimensions of a three dimensional work.[112] This copying by change of dimensions applies to artistic works *only*. Thus, it would not be an infringement of copyright in a written set of instructions (a literary work) to produce a three dimensional article made to those instructions.

The meaning of a substantial part

It is not necessary for the whole of a literary, artistic, musical or dramatic work to be reproduced in order to give rise to an infringement. The reproduction of a substantial part will suffice. The assessment of substantiality is not a simple question of assessing the quantity of what has been taken. Substantiality is a qualitative test rather than a quantitative test. It depends on the importance of what has been reproduced rather than the physical quantity of the material reproduced. The essential question is whether the defendant has appropriated part of the work on which a substantial part of the author's skill and labour was expended.[113] The part copied can be a relatively small part of the work, but if it is important to the work as a whole it may still infringe copyright. Sometimes people talk of a percentage cut off point, for example, 'we won't infringe copyright if we only copy 10% of the work'. Such an approach is wrong in law and should never be relied on, even as a rule of thumb. Instead, the overall importance of the part that is reproduced must be considered.

---

108 Although the CDPA 1988 provides that damages shall not be awarded against an innocent defendant.

109 *Ibid*, s 17(2).

110 *Ibid*.

111 *Ibid*, s 17(6). But note that transient copies made for the purposes of digital transmission will not be treated as infringements pursuant to the Digital Copyright Directive.

112 *Ibid*, s 17(3).

113 Pumfrey J in *Cantor Fitzgerald v Tradition (UK) Ltd* [2000] RPC 95.

The issue of what is substantial is a question of degree. In the case of *Designers' Guild v Russell Williams*,[114] the Court of Appeal made the point that the antithesis of 'substantial' is 'insignificant'. If only an insignificant part of a work is reproduced, there will be no infringement of copyright.

In relation to films, television broadcasts and cable programmes, the CDPA expressly provides that the making of a photograph of the whole or any substantial part of any image forming part of the work will be an infringement.[115] Only a facsimile copy of a typographical arrangement in a published edition will amount to an infringement of copyright.[116] Mere changes in scale will not prevent the facsimile copy from infringing. The Court of Appeal have held that a defendant did not infringe the copyright in the typographical arrangement of national newspapers by making copy press cuttings. The typographical arrangement related to the whole newspaper. Copying cuttings from the newspaper did not amount to the copying of a substantial part of the arrangement in the whole newspaper.[117]

Has there been a reproduction of the work?

The question whether there has been a reproduction of a literary, dramatic, musical or artistic work involves two questions:

- is there sufficient similarity between the copyright work and the allegedly infringing work?; and
- has there been copying? (This question is often referred to as a 'causal connection' between the copyright work and the allegedly infringing work.)

We shall look at each of these in turn.

Sufficient similarity

In order for a claim for copyright infringement to be successful, there must be a sufficient resemblance between the copyright work and the allegedly infringing work. Similarity is an objective test of fact and degree. It involves asking whether a reasonable person would conclude that the defendant has reproduced a substantial part of the claimant's work. This decision is one for the court, which will compare the two works. In carrying out this exercise, the court will concentrate on the similarities between the two works. It is *not* the correct approach for the court to concentrate on the differences between the

---

114 *Designers' Guild v Russell Williams* [2000] FSR 121.
115 CDPA 1988, s 17(4).
116 *Ibid*, s 17(5).
117 *Newspaper Licensing Agency v Marks & Spencer* (2000) unreported.

two works in order to reach the conclusion that they are not sufficiently similar.[118]

In assessing similarity, the court will generally disregard the reproduction of parts of the work which have no originality on the basis that those parts will not have involved the author in the exercise of skill, judgment or labour. The case of Ladbroke v Hill[119] concerned the copying of fixed odds football betting coupons. The defendant argued that every football coupon had to contain certain features, whoever produced them, and therefore it was entitled to reproduce such information from the claimant's coupon on its own coupon. Lord Pearce observed that the reproduction of a part of a copyright work which itself has no originality will not normally be a substantial part of the copyright and therefore will not be protected. However, on the facts, he held there to be an infringement of copyright, observing:[120]

> There are many things which are common to many coupons. But the respondent's coupon has an individuality. The appellants clearly modelled their coupon on the respondent's coupon and copied many of the things that gave it this originality. I cannot regard those things taken together as other than substantial.

A gloss was added to Lord Pearce's comments by Aldous LJ in *Biotrading and Financing OY v Biohit Ltd*.[121] Aldous LJ indicated that the statement of Lord Pearce must be differentiated from the situation where a person does not just take an unoriginal part of a work in which copyright subsists, but also uses that part in a similar context and way as it was used in the copyright work. In such a case, the defendant takes not only the unoriginal part, but also a part of the work that provided the originality.

To illustrate Aldous LJ's point, take the case of *Warwick Films Production Ltd v Eisinger*.[122] In that case, it was held that the reproduction of part of the transcript of the trial of Oscar Wilde from a book on the trial did not amount to the taking of a substantial amount of the book, because the transcript was not original to the author of the book. According to Aldous LJ, if the defendant had not only taken the transcript, but had also reproduced the way that the transcript was used in the book, there could have been an infringement of copyright.

The remarks of Aldous LJ are of particular relevance to compilations and databases, both of which fall within the definition of literary works contained in s 3 of the CDPA 1988. Even though the works included in the compilation or database may not be original, if a copyist were to reproduce the selection of

---

118 *Biotrading and Financing OY v Biohit Ltd* [1998] FSR 109, CA.
119 *Ladbroke (Football) v William Hill (Football)* [1964] 1 All ER 465.
120 *Ibid*, p 480.
121 *Biotrading and Financing OY v Biohit Ltd* [1998] FSR 109, CA.
122 *Warwick Films Production Ltd v Eisinger* [1967] 3 All ER 367.

material and the ordering of it, that would infringe copyright in the compilation.

Where the copyright work concerns a commonplace subject which is presented in a straightforward manner or a simplistic expression of a basic idea, only an exact reproduction of it, or something that is almost an exact reproduction, is likely to constitute an infringement.

Example

In the case of *Kenrick v Lawrence*,[123] the claimant claimed copyright in the representation of a hand marking a cross on an electoral voting paper. There was nothing artistically significant in the representation. The court held that there was not an exclusive right to represent the act of voting. Nothing more than a literal copy of the claimant's hand would suffice to establish copyright infringement.

On the other hand, where the expression of an idea is detailed, such as a very ornate depiction of the hand marking the cross, the reproduction of some or all of the detailed features of the design would be likely to be an infringement.

Appealing on the issue of copying

The Court of Appeal has reiterated on a number of occasions that it will be slow to reverse the finding of the trial judge on the question whether a substantial part of a copyright work has been reproduced. Parties should not appeal simply in the hope that the impression formed by the appellate judges will be different from that of the trial judge.[124]

Copying an idea

As we have already seen in relation to the subsistence of copyright, copyright will not exist in an undeveloped idea. Copyright exists to protect the skill and labour of the author in expressing his idea, rather than to confer a monopoly in the idea itself. It is not an infringement of copyright in the expression of an idea to take the idea and to apply it in a different way as long as that application does not involve copying the original expression. This will be a question of fact in every case and it is very often a difficult line to draw.

An example of the difficulty of drawing the line is illustrated by the *Designers' Guild* case.[125] The claimant was the designer and manufacturer of fabrics and wallpapers. It launched a new design called 'Ixia'. The design

---

123 *Kenrick v Lawrence* (1890) 25 QBD 93.
124 See, eg, *Pro Sieben v Carlton* [1999] FSR 610 and *Norowzian v Arks (No 2)* [2000] EMLR 1.
125 *Designers' Guild v Russell Williams* [2000] FSR 121.

consisted of a striped pattern with flowers scattered over it in an impressionistic style. The defendant was a wholesaler and retailer of fabrics which had also developed its own design ranges for fabrics. About a year after the claimant had launched the Ixia design, the defendant launched a new design known as 'Marguerite'. This design also featured a striped design with scattered flowers in an impressionistic style. The claimant brought proceedings for infringement of its copyright in the Ixia design (an artistic work). It alleged that the defendant had copied a substantial part of its design and incorporated it into the Margeurite design. The Court of Appeal held that the defendant had copied the *idea* and had used the same design techniques, but the defendant had not copied a substantial part of the way in which the idea was *expressed*. The Marguerite design featured broad stripes of a painted-on effect superimposed with definite images of flowers of four or three petals with different coloured stamens. The Ixia design, on the other hand, featured narrow stripes with a limited amount of leaf shown in the abstract. The size of the leafs in the Ixia design were different, the flowers depicted on the design were less prominent than in the Margeurite design and they were also deliberately faded in effect. The Court of Appeal was of the view that there was no copyright infringement. It observed that there was 'an obvious danger that if the net of copyright protection is cast too wide it will serve to create monopolies of ideas. Its more limited purpose is to protect the skill and labour of the designer in the expression'.

Parodies

To what extent can a parody of a copyright work be an infringement of copyright?

Parodies by their nature involve the exercise of skill, judgment and labour in their creation. They will, however, usually involve a reference to, or incorporation of, at least part of the work which is being parodied.

The question was considered in the case of *Williamson Music v Pearson Partnership*,[126] in which an advertising agency produced an advertisement for a bus company which parodied the lyrics and music of the Rogers and Hammerstein song *There Is Nothing Like A Dame*.

The claimants brought proceedings for copyright infringement.

The court found an arguable case that there was infringement in the music to the song (but not in the lyrics, which had been substantially changed by the defendants).

It was held that the relevant test to apply to the parody was the same as in relation to other instances of copying, namely, whether the author of the parody had reproduced a substantial part of the copyright work. The fact that

---

126 *Williamson Music v Pearson Partnership* [1987] FSR 97.

the defendant may have used mental labour to produce a parody of the work was irrelevant if the resulting parody reproduced without licence a substantial part of the copyright work.

The *Williamson Music* case must now be considered in the context of the judgment of Lightman J in *Clark v Associated Newspapers*.[127] The *Clark* case concerned a series of articles published in the *Evening Standard* which parodied the well known published diaries of the conservative politician and former cabinet minister, Alan Clark. The articles were headed 'Alan Clark's Secret Election Diary' and 'Alan Clark's Secret Political Diary', and featured a photograph of the claimant. The claimant based his claim on passing off and infringement of his moral rights (see below) rather than on copyright infringement. However, the defendant's submissions were also relevant to a copyright infringement claim. The defendant invoked Art 10 of the European Convention on Human Rights, arguing that the claimant's action was an illegitimate limitation on its freedom of expression, namely, its right to parody. Lightman J rejected this argument out of hand on the basis that the passing off and infringement of the moral rights claim were not limitations of the right to parody *per se* because both claims essentially related to the way in which the spoof diaries were presented – leading the reader to suppose (incorrectly) that Ian Clark had actually written the spoof diaries – rather than their content.

The implication of Lightman J's judgment is that an attack on the right to parody might well infringe Art 10. Suppose that the parody had made use of extracts from Alan Clark's own published diary and the claimant had brought proceedings for copyright infringement, it might have been arguable that the action based in copyright *was* an illegitimate restriction on the right to parody the copyright work in breach of Art 10 of the Convention. For if you wish to parody a copyright *work*, it is difficult to envisage how you might do so without incorporating at least part of the work into your parody. If the exercise of copyright were a restriction on the right to freedom of expression, the claimant would then have to show that the enforcement of its copyright was necessary in a democratic society. Where a parody will be recognised as a parody by the general public, the claimant might well have difficulties satisfying that criterion.

Copying plots

In relation to literary works, such as plots for plays or novels, the concept of copying extends to the reproduction of the content of the work even where the actual words or expressions of the author are not copied.[128] The situations

---

127 *Clark v Associated Newspapers* [1998] RPC 261.
128 *Harman v Osborne* [1967] 2 All ER 324; and *Christoffer v Poseidon Films* (1999) unreported.

and incidents in a work, and the mode in which the ideas are worked out and presented, will constitute a substantial part of the claimant's work. On the other hand, the fact that two works share the same idea will not infringe copyright where the works follow independent lines of plotting so that they in fact bear no real resemblance to each other.[129]

Copying films and photographs

Copying a film means copying the actual material recorded on the celluloid or videotape including the reproduction of a single still of such footage.[130] Reproduction of the subject matter of the film will not infringe copyright in the film.[131] Similarly, reproduction of a photograph involves copying the actual image recorded on the negative. It is not an infringement in the photograph to either recreate the image and take a fresh picture or to photograph the same scene as the claimant's photographer so that the defendant's photograph looks the same as the claimant's.[132]

Causal connection – has there been copying?

Copyright protects to restrain the copying of the work in which it subsists. It does not confer a monopoly in the work itself. If the defendant's product is the work of independent research, or the similarity is due to coincidence, copyright will not be infringed. In other words, similarity or substantial similarity will not in itself be sufficient to give rise to copyright infringement unless copying can also be established. In *LB Plastics Ltd v Swish Products Ltd*,[133] Lord Wilberforce said:

> Nor is there infringement if a person arrives by independent work at a substantially similar result to that sought to be protected. The protection given by the law of copyright is against copying, the basis of the protection being that one man must not be permitted to appropriate the result of another's labour. That copying has taken place is for the plaintiff to establish and prove as a matter of fact. The beginning of the necessary proof normally lies in the establishment of similarity combined with proof of access to the plaintiff's productions.

The fact that copying must have taken place can be inferred from the surrounding circumstances (for example, if the defendant's work incorporates errors contained in the claimant's works which the defendant is highly unlikely to have made without having had sight of the claimant's work).

---

129 *Rees v Melville* [1911–16] Mac CC 168.
130 CDPA 1988, s 17(4).
131 *Norowzian v Arks (No 2)* [2000] EMLR 1.
132 *Creation Records v News Group Newspapers* [1997] EMLR 444.
133 *LB Plastics Ltd v Swish Products Ltd* [1979] RPC 551.

Where the claimant and defendant's works are identical, or very similar, the likelihood that copying has taken place will be increased. In practice this means that, where the similarity is clearly established, the onus of proof of establishing that the defendant's work is his/her independent creation will, in practice, be on the defendant (for example, by showing that he/she never had access to the claimant's work or that his/her work pre-dates the claimant's work).

Copying can take place subconsciously, at least in relation to musical works. The copyist may not be aware of having seen heard the claimant's work, but he may still have copied it. Subconscious copying was considered in *Francis, Day and Hunter v Bron*,[134] where the claimant claimed copyright infringement in respect of the copying of a song. The defendant denied that he had never heard the claimant's song, nor had he seen the musical notation. The Court of Appeal held that subconscious copying was a possibility which, if it occurred, could amount to infringement of copyright. In order to establish liability, the claimant must show that the composer of the offending work was exposed to the work which is alleged to have been copied (whether or not he was aware of that exposure). The onus is therefore on the claimant to prove the notoriety of its work in order to show that the defendant must have been familiar with it.

Issuing copies of the work to the public

A further act of primary infringement occurs when copies of the copyright work are issued to the public. Issuing copies to the public means putting copies of the copyright work into circulation in the EEA which have not previously been put into circulation in the EEA by or with the consent of the copyright owner, or putting into circulation outside the EEA copies not previously put into circulation in the EEA or elsewhere.[135]

The CDPA 1988 gives no further guidance about when the act of putting into circulation occurs. For example, where a periodical is sent to a wholesaler and then from there onto a retailer, does the putting into circulation occur on sale to the wholesaler or to the retailer? Clarification of this issue is still awaited, over 12 years after the CDPA was implemented.[136]

Any subsequent distribution, sale, hiring or loan of copies which have previously been put into circulation, will not be primary infringements. Subsequent dealings may be secondary infringements of copyright if it can be

---

134 *Francis, Day and Hunter v Bron* [1963] Ch 587.

135 CDPA 1988, s 18(2).

136 For further discussion of this issue, see Phillips and Bently: 'Copyright issues: the mysteries of s 18' [1999] EIPR 133.

shown that the defendant knew or had reason to believe that he was dealing in infringing copies (see below).

Renting or lending the work to the public

The unauthorised rental or lending of the copyright work to the public is a restricted act giving rise to a primary infringement of copyright in relation to an original literary, dramatic or musical work and an original artistic work other than a work of architecture or a work of applied art. It is also a restricted act in relation to a film or a sound recording.[137]

'Rental' means making a copy of the work available for use, on terms that it will or may be returned, for economic or commercial advantage.[138] An example would be the rental of a film hired from a video shop.

'Lending' means making a copy of a work available for use, on terms that it will or may be returned, otherwise than for economic or commercial advantage through an establishment which is accessible to the public.[139] A public library would fall within this category.

Where the author of a literary, dramatic, artistic or musical work or the principal director of a film has transferred the rental right to the producer of a sound recording or a film, he retains a right to equitable remuneration in relation to the rental right which *cannot* be waived.[140] The remuneration is payable by the person entitled to the rental right.[141] This right to equitable remuneration is an example of the law operating in the interests of the creator of the work rather than in the interests of the party responsible for the commercial exploitation of the work. This represents a shift in emphasis in UK copyright law, and is an initiative flowing from the European Community. There is little statutory guidance about the meaning of equitable remuneration. The amount is to be decided between the parties or by reference to the Copyright Tribunal, which will consider what is reasonable in the circumstances, taking into account the importance of the contribution of the author to the film or sound recording.[142] Remuneration is not inequitable simply because it is paid in the form of a one-off lump sum payment at the time of the transfer of the right.[143] An agreement is of no effect in so far as it purports to exclude or restrict the right to equitable remuneration.[144]

---

137 CDPA 1988, s 18A.
138 *Ibid*, s 18A(2).
139 *Ibid*.
140 *Ibid*, s 93B(1).
141 *Ibid*, s 93B(3).
142 *Ibid*, s 93C.
143 *Ibid*, s 93C(4).
144 *Ibid*, s 93B(5).

Performing, showing or playing the work in public

The unauthorised performance in public of a literary, dramatic or musical work is a primary infringement of copyright.[145] The term 'performance' includes the delivery of lectures, addresses, speeches and sermons and, in general, includes any mode of visual or acoustic presentation, including presentation of the work by means of a sound recording, film, broadcast or cable programme of the work.[146] If I play a sound recording of a song in public without permission, I will infringe copyright in the literary and musical works which make up the song.

The playing or showing in public of a sound recording, film, broadcast or cable programme is also an act of primary infringement.[147] By playing a sound recording in public, I am therefore also infringing copyright in the work.

The meaning of 'public'

The CDPA does not define what is meant by 'public'. It is clear that a performance does not have to be before a paying audience. Case law suggests that, in each case, regard must be had to whether a particular performance is a thing likely to whittle down the value of the copyright owner's monopoly to exploit the copyright work. A purely domestic performance would not be a thing likely to whittle down the value of the monopoly. However, a performance at a public theatre or a public concert hall would have that effect. The key issue is, therefore, the relationship of the audience to the copyright owner and the effect that the performance in question would have on his monopoly. In the case of *Turner v Performing Rights Society*,[148] it was held that companies who broadcast music to their employees in working hours were performing copyright works in public and therefore were infringing copyright if they did so without taking (and paying for) a licence to do so. This was despite the fact that the employees were not a paying audience.

Broadcasting the work or including it in a cable programme service

The broadcasting of the work or its inclusion in a cable programme service is an act restricted by the copyright in an original literary, dramatic, musical or

---

145 CDPA 1988, s 19(1).

146 *Ibid*, s 19(2).

147 *Ibid*, s 9(3).

148 *Turner v Performing Rights Society* [1943] 1 Ch 167.

artistic work, a sound recording or film or a broadcast or cable programme.[149] The topic of incidental inclusion of copyright works is considered later in relation to the permitted acts.

The making of an adaptation of the work

The making of an adaptation of the work is an act restricted by the copyright in an original literary, dramatic or musical work.[150]

An adaptation of a literary or dramatic work (other than a computer program or database) is defined by the CDPA to mean the making of a translation of the work, a version of a dramatic work which is converted into a non-dramatic work or of a non-dramatic work which is converted into a dramatic work or a version of a work in which the story or action is conveyed wholly or mainly by means of pictures in a form suitable for reproduction in a book, or in a newspaper, magazine or similar periodical.[151]

Example

If A adapts B's novel into a screenplay without B's consent, the adaptation will infringe B's copyright in her novel.

In relation to a musical work, an adaptation means an arrangement or transcription of the work.[152]

Example

If A makes a new arrangement of B's new symphony, A will infringe B's copyright in the musical composition unless he first obtains B's permission to do so.

An adaptation of a computer program or database means an arrangement or altered version of the work or a translation of it.[153] Translation is defined to include a version of the program in which it is converted into or out of a computer language or code or into a different computer language or code.

It is not only an infringement to adapt a copyright work. It is also an infringement of the copyright work to do any of the restricted acts set out in s 16 of the CDPA in relation to the adaptation.

---

149 CDPA 1988, s 20.
150 *Ibid*, s 21.
151 *Ibid*, s 21(3).
152 *Ibid*.
153 *Ibid*.

Example

A adapts B's novel into a stage play. C and D perform the play in public. Both the adaptation and the performance would amount to infringement of B's copyright in the novel (literary work). Similarly, a broadcast of the stage play would also infringe B's copyright.

Authorisation of infringing acts

It is a primary infringement of copyright to authorise a third party to commit an infringing act. Authorisation means more than the mere facilitation of the infringement. In order to authorise a copyright infringement, the authoriser must grant or purport to grant the *right* to carry out the act of infringement. The purported grant can only come from someone who purports to have the *authority* to make the grant.

In the case of *CBS Songs v Amstrad*,[154] it was alleged that Amstrad, who were manufacturers of a twin deck tape recorder, had authorised purchasers to infringe copyright in sound recordings by making available to the public the means for cassette tapes to be recorded onto blank cassette tapes. The court held that the mere enabling of the infringement brought about by the supply of the equipment did not amount to authorisation. There was no purported grant of the right to make the illicit recordings.

This case was followed *Keays v Dempster*,[155] which concerned the unauthorised reproduction of a photograph of the claimant in a book written by the first defendant. The claimant, who owned copyright in the photograph, commenced proceedings for copyright infringement against the author of the book and the picture library which had supplied the photograph to the publishers, the second defendant. There was no dispute on the facts that the photograph had been reproduced without the claimant's consent. The second defendant sought to argue that the first defendant had authorised the second defendant's infringement. It was held that there had been no such authorisation. All that the first defendant had done on the facts was to select the pictures that he wanted for his book. He had not purported to give any authority to give the second defendant permission to reproduce the photograph he had selected. Under the terms of the contract between the second defendant and the publishers of the book, the responsibility for ensuring that his wishes had been carried out lay with the publishers.

---

154 *CBS Songs v Amstrad* [1988] RPC 567.
155 *Keays v Dempster* [1994] EMLR 443.

Secondary infringements

We have seen that a defendant can be liable for primary infringement of copyright where the infringement was unintentional – even, potentially, where copying has taken place subconsciously. Secondary infringement is a narrower concept. Unlike primary infringement, acts of secondary infringement depend upon the alleged infringer knowing or having reason to believe that the work with which he is dealing is an infringing copy. 'Infringing copy' is defined by s 27 of the CDPA 1988 as an article whose making constituted an infringement of the copyright in the work in question or an article which has been or is proposed to be imported into the UK and its making in the UK would have constituted an infringement of the copyright in the work in question or a breach of an exclusive licensing agreement relating to that work.

A defendant will be taken to have reason to believe that he is dealing with an infringing copy where it has knowledge of such facts as would lead a reasonable person to suspect that he/she is dealing with infringing copies. This is an objective test involving the question whether a reasonable party in the position of the defendant would have reason to believe that it was dealing with an infringing copy. A defendant will not necessarily have reason to believe that it is dealing with an infringing copy simply because the claimant asserts that he is. The claimant should put the defendant in a position where he can determine whether the claimant's allegation is true.[156] This will not necessarily require the claimant to supply the defendant with the work for which copyright is claimed.[157]

Acts of secondary infringement

The activities set out below are secondary infringements if done without the consent of the copyright owner. It will be seen that the activities which make up the secondary infringement provisions of the CDPA relate mainly to dealings with an infringing work after it has been put into circulation. Other secondary infringements relate to the use of apparatus to make infringing copies and the supply of premises and equipment for the unauthorised public performance of a copyright work:

- importation into the UK (other than for the defendant's private and domestic use) of articles known by the defendant to be an infringing copy of the work or where the defendant has reason to believe that it is an infringement;[158] or

---

156 *LA Gear v Hi Tec* [1992] FSR 121; and *Hutchinson v Hook* [1995] FSR 365.

157 *ZYX Music v King* [1995] FSR 566.

158 CDPA 1988, s 22.

- possession in the course of business;[159]
- selling, hiring, offering or exposing for sale or hire;[160]
- exhibition in public in the course of business;[161]
- distribution in the course of business;[162]
- distribution not in the course of business to an extent as to affect prejudicially the owner of the copyright,[163]

of any article which the defendant knows or has reason to believe is an infringing copy of the work:

- making, importing into the UK, possessing in the course of a business or selling or hiring or offering to do so an article specifically designed or adapted for making copies is a secondary infringement where there is knowledge or reason to believe that the apparatus will be used to make infringing copies.[164]

An act will not be carried out in the course of business under any of the above provisions where it is incidental to the business of the defendant.[165]

Secondary infringements in relation to public performances of copyright works

Where the performance of a literary, dramatic or musical work in public gives rise to an act of primary infringement (see above), the person who gave permission for a place of public entertainment to be used for the performance will be liable for secondary infringement unless, when he gave permission, he believed on reasonable grounds that the performance would not infringe copyright.[166]

Where the performance or the playing or showing of the work in public is carried out by means of equipment for playing sound recordings, showing films or receiving visual images or sounds conveyed by electronic means, the person supplying the apparatus will be liable where he knew or had reason to believe that the apparatus was likely to be used so as to infringe copyright.[167] The same is true for occupiers of premises who gave permission for the apparatus to be brought onto the premises. Where the apparatus is of the kind

---

159 CDPA 1988, s 23.

160 *Ibid.*

161 *Ibid.*

162 *Ibid.*

163 *Ibid.*

164 *Ibid*, s 24.

165 *Pensher v Sunderland DC* (1999) unreported, 21 April, confirming that decisions on other pieces of legislation using the same phrase will apply under CDPA 1988, eg, *Davies v Sumner* [1984] 1 WLR 1301 and *R and B Customs Broker v UDT* [1988] 1 WLR 321.

166 CDPA 1988, s 25.

167 *Ibid*, s 26.

normally used for public performances, the person supplying the apparatus must show that he did not believe on reasonable grounds that it would be used to infringe copyright.[168]

A person who supplies a copy of a sound recording or a film used to infringe copyright, for example, by an unauthorised showing in public, will be liable for infringement if, when he supplied it, he knew or had reason to believe that it (or a copy made from it) was likely to be used to infringe copyright.[169]

Permitted uses of copyright works

Chapter III of the CDPA 1988 sets out a number of uses to which a copyright work, or a substantial part of it, may be legitimately put *without permission from the copyright owner*. These are known as *'the permitted acts'* and they can be found at ss 28–76 of the Act.

The rationale for the permitted acts lies in the fact that the enforcement of copyright necessarily entails a limitation on freedom of expression and of access to the copyright work. As we have seen, the owner of copyright controls the use to which the copyright work can be put. In order to provide a counterbalance to this restriction on freedom of expression, the law provides for certain permitted uses of that work which the copyright owner is not at liberty to restrain. These encroachments on the rights of the copyright owner are directed at achieving a proper balance between protection of the rights of the copyright owner and the wider public interest. The permitted purposes which are of particular relevance to the media are considered below.

The fair dealing provisions

Where the use of a copyright work amounts to a 'fair dealing' for one of the specified purposes set out in the Act, it will *not* infringe copyright. The specified purposes to which the fair dealing provisions apply are:

- fair dealing with a literary (work other than a database), dramatic, musical or artistic work for the purposes of research or private study;[170]
- fair dealing with a work for the purpose of criticism or review of that work or of another work or of a performance of the work, provided that it is accompanied by a sufficient acknowledgment (defined below);[171]

---

168 CDPA 1988, s 26.
169 *Ibid*.
170 *Ibid*, s 29.
171 *Ibid*, s 30(1).

- fair dealing with a work *other than a photograph* for the purpose of reporting current events, provided it is accompanied by a sufficient acknowledgment.[172]

No acknowledgment is required in connection with the reporting of current events by means of a sound recording, film, broadcast or cable programme.[173]

Consideration as to whether the use of the copyright work falls within the fair dealing provisions involves two separate questions:

(a) was the work used for one of the permitted purposes, for example, criticism or review? If the answer to this question is yes, then the second question to consider is;

(b) was the use of the work fair?[174] If the answer to this question is also yes, then the work has been used for a permitted purpose which the copyright owner cannot restrain.

Considering each of these questions in turn.

Was the work used for one of the specified uses?

For the media, the most relevant of the permitted purposes referred to in the fair dealing provisions of the CDPA 1988 are criticism and review and reporting current events.

The general approach

The assessment of whether the use of the copyright work was for one of the permitted purposes should be made *objectively*. The intentions or motives of the user of the copyright work are of little importance to this question (although they will be relevant to the second question, that is, whether the use was a fair dealing). The words 'for the purposes of criticism or review' or 'for the purposes of reporting current events' in s 30 of the CDPA should each be considered as a composite phrase. The words 'in the context of' or 'as part of an exercise in' could be substituted for 'for the purposes of' without any significant alteration of meaning.[175]

It is unnecessary for the court to put itself in the shoes of the defendants in order to decide whether the use was for the purposes of criticism or review or reporting current events. In *Pro Sieben v Carlton*, which is discussed in detail below, Robert Walker LJ observed that:

---

172 CDPA 1988, s 30(2). The meaning of 'sufficient acknowledgment' is considered below.
173 *Ibid*, s 30(3).
174 *Pro Sieben v Carlton* [1999] FSR 610.
175 *Ibid*.

> The court should not in my view give any encouragement of the notion that all
> that is required is for the user to have the sincere belief, however misguided,
> that he or she is criticising a work [or reporting current events].

The meaning of the phrases 'criticism or review' and 'reporting current events' have each been the subject of interpretation by the courts. The courts have resisted defining the phrases in precise terms. In the *Pro Sieben*[176] case, the Court of Appeal stated that, as a general principle, the expressions 'criticism or review' and 'reporting current events' are expressions of wide, unlimited scope and should be interpreted liberally. This approach avoids a rigid interpretation of the fair dealing provisions and allows for flexibility with a view to ensuring that they are interpreted in line with contemporary standards. On the other hand, the approach is not as helpful as it might be to a media law practitioner who may have to make the call about whether a particular use of a work is, or is not, for one of the permitted purposes.

Criticism and review of the copyright work or of another work or a performance of the work

This permitted use of a copyright work is concerned with 'protecting a reviewer or commentator who may want to make quotations from a copyright work in order to illustrate his review, his criticism or his comments'.[177] There must be criticism or review if the fair dealing provisions are to apply. In the case of *Sillitoe v McGraw-Hill Book Co Ltd*,[178] the court held that reproduction of extracts from literary works in examination study aids was not made for the purposes of criticism or review of the literature. The aids were held to have an *explanatory function,* rather than a critical function and could not, therefore, fall within the fair dealing provisions.

The scope of the criticism or review provision appears to be dependent on criticism or review *of a copyright work.* Section 30 of the CDPA 1988 specifies that the criticism or review must concern the work from which the material is taken, or another work or the performance of the work. It is a moot point whether the section extends to criticism and review of material which is extraneous to a copyright work. For example, could use be made of a copyright literary work in order to review the author's character or his lifestyle?

The Court of Appeal considered the scope of criticism or review in *Time Warner Entertainment Co plc v Channel Four Television Corpn plc.*[179] The case concerned the film *A Clockwork Orange,* which was, at that time, not available on general release in the UK. The defendant planned to broadcast a

---

176 *Pro Sieben v Carlton* [1999] FSR 610.
177 *Per* Whitford J in *Independent Television Publications Ltd v Time Out Ltd* [1984] FSR 64.
178 *Sillitoe v McGraw-Hill Book Co Ltd* [1983] FSR 545.
179 *Time Warner Entertainment Co plc v Channel Four Television Corpn plc* [1994] EMLR 1.

documentary about the film during the course of which it intended to use extracts from the film to illustrate the conclusion of the programme makers that the film should be re-released in the UK.

The claimants owned copyright in the film and sought to restrain the broadcast of the programme on the basis that the use of the excerpts from the film infringed copyright in the film. The defendants alleged that the use of the extracts from the film was a fair dealing of the footage for the purposes of criticism or review. The claimant alleged that the real motive and purpose behind the defendant's use of the footage was to campaign for the re-release of *A Clockwork Orange* in the UK and that criticism or review of the *decision to withdraw it from circulation* did not fall within the language of s 30.

The Court of Appeal confirmed that the criticism or review of the copyright work could be: (a) of the work itself; or (b) of another copyright work. In addition, the Court of Appeal held that it could extend to criticism or review *of the thought or philosophy behind the work* (italics for emphasis). Henry LJ observed:

> It seems to me that the fair dealing defence *may* apply equally where the criticism is of the decision to withdraw from circulation a film in the public domain and not just of the film itself. In the present case the two are, in my view, inseparable [emphasis added].

Laddie J put a gloss on this decision in the first instance judgment in the *Pro Sieben* case,[180] where he said:

> The decision to withdraw the film ... was being criticised on the basis of an assessment of the artistic and cultural value of the film itself. The mere fact that criticism or review of a work may be used as a springboard to attack something else does not detract from the fact that the *work* is being criticised or reviewed[181] [emphasis added].

The Court of Appeal in the *Pro Sieben* case[182] endorsed Laddie J's view, holding that the criticism of a work is not restricted to criticism of the *style* of the work. It could also extend to criticism of the ideas found in the work and the social or moral implications of the work.

In the *Pro Sieben* case, television footage was used by the defendant to critique works of chequebook journalism. The Court of Appeal held that the footage had been used for the purposes of criticism or review of a body of work generated by chequebook journalism. The court did not go on to consider whether the criticism or review could extend beyond the body of work to comments about the ethics of chequebook in general. A strict interpretation of the provisions of s 30 would suggest that it could not.

---

180 *Pro Sieben v Carlton* [1998] FSR 43, pp 52–53.

181 *Ibid.*

182 *Pro Sieben v Carlton* [1999] FSR 610.

Use of the work for the purpose of reporting current events

What is a 'current event'?

The term 'current event' was considered in *Newspaper Licensing Agency v Marks & Spencer*[183] by Lightman J. In the that case, the claimant owned the copyright in the typographical arrangements of a large number of national and local newspapers. It sought to establish that the defendant was infringing copyright by making copies of cuttings from newspapers and distributing such copies amongst its employees. The defendant denied copyright infringement on the ground that the reproduction was a fair dealing for the purpose of reporting current events. The judge observed that:

- the threshold to establishing that the use is a report of current events is 'not high or the hurdle difficult to surmount. The value placed on freedom of information and freedom of speech requires the gateway to be wide';[184]

- to be a current event, the event need not be national, political or otherwise an important event. It may be a sporting event (in *BBC v BSB*,[185] a football World Cup match was held to be a current event) and it may be a matter of entirely local interest or of interest to only a few people;

- the term 'current event' is narrower than the term 'news'. Reporting of 'news' can go beyond reporting events which are current and can extend to information relating to past events not previously known. On the other hand, 'current event' does not extend to publishing matters which are merely currently of interest but are not current *events* or to publishing matters not previously known which are of historical interest alone;

- the publication of a report in the press is itself *capable* of constituting a current event. The reproduction of the report may constitute fair dealing even though it contains no analysis or comment or any matter, but this does not mean that whatever is reported in the press will be a current event;

- publication of matters which are not current events can only be justified under the fair dealing provisions if they are reasonably necessary to understand, explain or give meaning to a report of current events;

- the defendant's use of the copyright work for the purpose of reporting current events does not have to be accessible to the general public in order for the defence to be invoked. The fact that the defendant's report only circulated internally within the defendant's employees would not prevent it from falling within the permitted uses.

---

183 *Newspaper Licensing Agency v Marks & Spencer* [1999] RPC 536 and see Court of Appeal decision (2000) *The Times*, 15 June.

184 *Ibid*.

185 *BBC v BSB* [1991] 3 All ER 833.

On the facts, the judge held that the defendant's use of the cuttings went far beyond reporting current events. The use included the reproduction of material such as interviews, comparisons of the products of different retailers, personal interest stories and life stories of entrepreneurs. Such material could not constitute current events.

In the *Pro Sieben* case, the claimant was a German television company. It had purchased exclusive rights to broadcast in Germany an interview with Mandy Allwood, a woman who had achieved temporary celebrity as a result of becoming pregnant with octuplets. The defendant broadcast a current affairs programme, in the course of which they showed an extract which it had recorded from the claimant's exclusive arrangement with Ms Allwood.

The theme of the programme was a critique of chequebook journalism. It was not exclusively about Ms Allwood, although her case was a central part of the programme. The use of the clip in question, which featured the purchase of teddy bears by Ms Allwood for the babies, was used to make the point that, in the defendant's view, Ms Allwood's publicist was tightly controlling the presentation of the image of Ms Allwood and was presenting 'a sanitised version of the truth'.

The claimant alleged infringement of its copyright in the broadcast. In their defence, the defendants claimed that the use of the clip was a fair dealing for the purposes of criticism or review or of reporting current events under the fair dealing provisions of the CDPA.

The Court of Appeal found that the use of the footage was for the purposes of reporting current events.[186] The programme as a whole criticised works of chequebook journalism and in particular the treatment by the media of Ms Allwood's multiple pregnancy. This pregnancy was a current event of real interest to the public. The volume and intensity of the media interest was sufficient to bring the media coverage itself within the ambit of current event.

The meaning of 'current event' was also considered by Jacob J in *Hyde Park Residence v Yelland*.[187] In that case, the claimant provided security services to Mohamed Al Fayed and his family. On 30 August 1997, Diana, Princess of Wales and Dodi Al Fayed visited Mr Al Fayed's house. Still pictures taken from the footage recorded by the claimant's security cameras showed the timing of the arrival and departure of the couple. They demonstrate that the couple were in the house for less than half an hour and that they were unaccompanied. The accident which killed the couple occurred the next day.

Following their deaths, Mohamed Al Fayed led the media to believe that the couple had visited the house in Paris in preparation for their new life together, consistent with their intention to get married and to live in the house.

---

186 *Pro Sieben v Carlton* [1999] FSR 610.
187 *Hyde Park Residence v Yelland* [1999] RPC 655.

The fourth defendant (an employee of the claimant) removed the stills from the video system showing the arrival and departure of the couple and sold them to *The Sun. The Sun* published the stills in order to expose Mr Al Fayed's misrepresentations. The claimants sought summary judgment against *The Sun* for the unauthorised reproduction of the stills. The defendants pleaded that the publication was a fair dealing for the purposes of reporting current events.

On the question of whether the use of the work was for reporting current events, Jacob J held that the a visit of the couple to the villa was a current event, notwithstanding that it had taken place over a year before publication of the photographs by *The Sun*. Only two days before the publication, Mr Al Fayed had again put the matter into the public domain in his interview with *The Mirror*. This was coupled with the fact that at the time of publication Dodi and Diana's relationship was still so much under discussion that it would be pedantic to regard it as anything other than 'still current'.

On appeal,[188] the Court of Appeal did not expressly overturn the finding at first instance that the stills were used for reporting current events, but Aldous LJ observed that submissions by the claimant that the visit to the villa was not a current event had 'force'. Reliance on the *Hyde Park Residence* decision for the meaning of 'current events' should therefore be treated with caution. There are strong grounds for believing that the first instance decision pushed the boundaries too far.

For the purposes of the appeal Aldous LJ seemed to be prepared to accept (albeit rather grudgingly) that the false statements made by Mr Al Fayed – at least some of which had been made a few days prior to the publication of the stills – were current events, and that the use of the stills to rebut the statements was a use for the purpose of reporting the false statements.

Photographs have been expressly excluded from the provision relating to reporting current events. The exclusion preserves the ability of freelance photographers to sell photographs under exclusive deals. In the *Hyde Park Residence* case, stills from a video security system were held not to be photographs.

Is the dealing with the copyright work fair?

We have seen that the courts have held that criticism and review and reporting current events are to be interpreted liberally. The constraints on abuse of this freedom lie in the requirement that the use of the copyright work for the permitted purposes must be *fair*.

---

188 *Hyde Park Residence v Yelland* [2000] RPC 604, CA.

This is a question of fact and degree in every particular case, and will largely be a matter of impression. Lightman J observed in the *Newspaper Licensing*[189] case that 'a common sense judgment is called for'.

In the case of *Hubbard v Vosper*,[190] Lord Denning MR noted that:

> It is impossible to define what is 'fair dealing'. It must be a question of degree ... After all is said and done, it must be a matter of impression. As with fair comment in the law of libel, so with fair dealing in the law of copyright. The tribunal of fact must decide'.

Unlike the decision as to whether the use of the work is for criticism or review or reporting current events (which, as we have seen, requires an objective assessment), the question whether the dealing is fair *is* concerned with the genuineness of the intentions and motives of the user of the copyright material.

In the *Hyde Park Residence* case,[191] Aldous LJ indicated that the standard to apply when considering fair dealing is *whether a fair minded and honest person would have dealt with the copyright work in the manner that the defendant did for the permitted purpose in question.* This is an objective test, although the motives of the subjective alleged infringer will be relevant.

Factors which will help to determine whether the use of the work is fair are as follows:

- the extent of the reproduction of the copyright work should be considered. The essential question is whether the use amounts to an illegitimate exploitation of the copyright holder's work. The number and extent of the reproductions are therefore relevant. Are they too many and too long to be fair?;[192]

- the issue of proportion of original comment or criticism as compared to the copyright work should be considered. To take long extracts and attach short comments may be unfair. Short extracts and long comments may be fair. It may be a fair dealing to reproduce the whole of the copyright work (especially if the work is very short) provided that sufficient original comment or criticism accompanies the use of the work;[193]

- has the copyright work been published to the world at large? Publication of a previously unpublished work is more likely to be unfair. Note the judgment of Ungoed-Thomas in *Beloff v Pressdram*:[194] '... the law by bestowing a right of copyright on an unpublished work bestows a right to

189 *Newspaper Licensing Agency v Marks & Spencer* [1999] RPC 536.
190 *Hubbard v Vosper* [1972] 2 QB 84; [1972] 1 All ER 1023.
191 *Hyde Park Residence v Yelland* [2000] RPC 604, CA.
192 *Hubbard v Vosper* [1972] 2 QB 84; [1972] 1 All ER 1023.
193 *Ibid.*
194 *Beloff v Pressdram* [1973] 1 All ER 241.

prevent its being published at all: and even though an unpublished work is not automatically excluded from the defence of fair dealing, it is yet a much more substantial breach of copyright than publication of a published work.';[195]

- where the copyright work is unpublished to the world at large, the extent to which the copyright work has been circulated will be a relevant consideration. Even if the work is unpublished, the fair dealing provisions may still operate where the work has been widely circulated, albeit to a limited class of persons. In *Hubbard v Vosper*,[196] Lord Denning observed that 'although a literary work may not be published to the world at large, it may, however be circulated to such a wide circle that it is 'fair dealing' to criticise it publicly in a newspaper or elsewhere';

- the genuineness of the intentions and motives of the user are relevant to fair dealing. Lightman J observed in the *Newspaper Licensing* case[197] that, if it appears that the reporter has dealt with the copyright work not in order to report current events or for the purposes of criticism or review, but for some extraneous purpose, for example, in order to exploit the copyright work under the guise of reporting current events, the use will not be fair. This was echoed in the *Time Warner* case,[198] where the judge at first instance noted that, if the intention behind use of the extracts from *A Clockwork Orange* was to profit from the infringement of copyright under the pretence of criticism, then no matter how balanced or representative the infringing excerpts might be, the purpose would not be for criticism or review;

- where the copyright owner and the user are competitors in relation to the same material, the reproduction of the copyright work is more likely to be unfair. Lord Denning observed in *Hubbard v Vosper*:[199] '... it is not fair dealing for a rival in the trade to take copyright material and use it for his own benefit.' However, trade rivalry in itself will not automatically render a dealing in a copyright work unfair;

- the Court of Appeal in the *Hyde Park Residence*[200] case drew attention to the fact that *The Sun's* reproduction of the stills was not *necessary* to expose Mr Al Fayed's falsehoods as militating against fair dealing;

- in the *Newspaper Licensing* case,[201] Lightman J noted that one of the factors relevant to the question of fair dealing is whether the report could

---

195 *Beloff v Pressdram* [1973] 1 All ER 241, p 263.
196 *Hubbard v Vosper* [1972] 2 QB 84; [1972] 1 All ER 1023.
197 *Newspaper Licensing Agency v Marks & Spencer* [1999] RPC 536.
198 *Time Warner Entertainment Co plc v Channel Four Television Corpn plc* [1994] EMLR 1.
199 *Hubbard v Vosper* [1972] 2 QB 84; [1972] 1 All ER 1023.
200 *Hyde Park Residence v Yelland* [2000] RPC 604, CA.
201 *Newspaper Licensing Agency v Marks & Spencer* [1999] RPC 536.

reasonably have been made in a manner which was less intrusive upon the copyright owner's rights;

- in the case of a previously unpublished work, the method by which the copyright work was obtained may be relevant to fair dealing.

Where a work is already in the public domain, it seems that the way in which the work was obtained will *not* have a bearing on the fairness of the dealing. In the *Time Warner* case,[202] the claimant argued that the fair dealing provisions did not apply because of the underhand manner in which the defendants had obtained their copy of the film. Neill LJ indicated that criticism and review of a work already in the public domain which would otherwise be a fair dealing would seldom, if ever, be rendered unfair because of the method by which the copyright material had been obtained.

However, in the *Hyde Park Residence* case,[203] Aldous LJ thought that the fact that the defendants knew that the stills had been dishonestly removed from the claimant's possession militated against fair dealing. The *Hyde Park* decision can be distinguished from the *Time Warner* case on the ground that *Hyde Park* concerned previously unpublished material, whereas *Time Warner* concerned material which was already in the public domain. *It would seem to follow that where previously unpublished work is improperly obtained, there is a strong likelihood that any dealing with it will be unfair. This is likely to have important repercussions for the media;*

- the fact that the user has paid for the copyright material and is publishing it in order to make profits did not prevent the use of the material being a fair dealing at first instance in the *Hyde Park Residence* case.[204] Jacob J indicated: 'The reality is that the press often have to pay for information of public importance. And when they publish they will always expect to make money. They are not philanthropists. I do not think that the fact that [the fourth defendant] was paid and that *The Sun* expected to make money derogates in any way from the fair dealing ... justification.'

This point was not expressly overturned in the Court of Appeal,[205] but one of its grounds for rejecting the fair dealing defence was that a fair and reasonable person would not have paid for the stills in the circumstances;

- in the case of use of a work for criticism or review, the fact that the criticism is restricted to only one aspect of a copyright work is unlikely to make the use unfair. In the *Time Warner* case,[206] Neill LJ observed that the court should be very slow before it rejects a defence of fair dealing on this

---

202 *Time Warner Entertainment Co plc v Channel Four Television Corpn plc* [1994] EMLR 1.
203 *Hyde Park Residence v Yelland* [2000] RPC 604, CA.
204 *Ibid.*
205 *Ibid.*
206 *Time Warner Entertainment Co plc v Channel Four Television Corpn plc* [1994] EMLR 1.

ground. It is therefore not the case that the criticism or review has to be of the work as a whole in order for the dealing to be fair. Neill LJ indicated that 'one can envisage many cases where it would be legitimate to select and criticise, for example, a single scene of violence even though the rest of the work was free of objectionable material';

- where the claimant has paid for exclusive rights to the copyright work, the use of the work by the user is more likely to be unfair;

- trade practice may be relevant to the fairness of the dealing. In the *Time Warner* case,[207] the court considered evidence from the claimant that it was film industry practice that clips of films released for review would normally not exceed one minute's duration per clip and four minutes in length in the aggregate.

Decisions on whether use is unfair

Pro Sieben v Carlton[208]

The total item which had been broadcast by the claimant in Germany was nine minutes long. The defendants had used 30 seconds of that footage.

The dealing was held to be 'fair'. The extract in question was short. It contained no words spoken by Ms Allwood. It did not, therefore, amount to unfair competition with Pro Sieben's use of the exclusive interview rights it had acquired. The use of the footage was not an attempt to dress up infringement of copyright in the footage in the guise of criticism or reporting current events.

Newspaper Licensing Agency v Marks & Spencer[209]

The reproduction of the articles was not for the purposes of reporting current events, nor was it a fair dealing, as it involved the wholesale copying of material which went far beyond what is necessary to report current events.

Hyde Park Residence v Yelland[210]

The use of the video stills was not a fair dealing for the purpose of reporting current events. Aldous LJ observed that 'to describe what *The Sun* did as fair dealing is to give honour to dishonour'. The extent of use of the stills was excessive. The only part of the stills relevant to the alleged purpose was the information as to the timing of arrival and departure and that information

---

207 *Time Warner Entertainment Co plc v Channel Four Television Corpn plc* [1994] EMLR 1.
208 *Pro Sieben v Carlton* [1999] FSR 610.
209 *Newspaper Licensing Agency v Marks & Spencer* [1999] RPC 536.
210 *Hyde Park Residence v Yelland* [2000] RPC 604, CA.

could have been given without reproducing the stills. The information about the timing of the arrival and departure did not conclusively establish that Mr Al Fayed's statements were false. The court held that *a fair minded and honest person would not have paid for the dishonestly taken stills and publish them, knowing that they had not previously been published or circulated when all they did was to establish the time of arrival and departure at the villa.*

From the media's point of view, the Court of Appeal decision contains a number of troubling features:

- first, the emphasis on the fact that the use of the video stills was not necessary to report a current event carries the clear implication that use must be shown to be necessary if it is to constitute a fair dealing.

  But it will usually be difficult to demonstrate that it was absolutely necessary to make use of the copyright work to report a current event or to criticise or review. Often, the copyright work does not *need* to be reproduced. But the use of the work adds force and realism to reports. Would it be a fair dealing if the journalist makes use of a copyright work for the purpose of improving his report? The Court of Appeal judgment suggests that it might not;[211]

- secondly, the emphasis in the Court of Appeal judgment on the published status of the copyright work will make it more difficult for the media to establish fair dealing in relation to a previously unpublished work, especially where there is a question mark over the way in which the copyright work was obtained.[212]

Time Warner v Channel Four[213]

The film clips used by the defendant totalled 12 minutes of a 30 minute documentary. They made up 8% of the *A Clockwork Orange* film. On the facts, this was held by the Court of Appeal not to go beyond the bounds of fair dealing. However, Neill LJ indicated that he found this issue to be the most troublesome part of the case. Aspects which he thought relevant to the decision were the fact the clips were accompanied by voiceover commentary containing comments and criticisms and the 'great force' which he found in a comment made by the defendant that serious criticism of the film required the defendant to spend sufficient time showing the film itself.

---

211 Note, also, that the provisions of the current draft of the Digital Copyright Directive considered on pp 282–85 provide for a more limited fair dealing exception together with a direction that the exceptions be interpreted with a bias towards the copyright owner.

212 The Court of Appeal judgment also concerned the availability of a public interest defence for copyright works. This is considered below.

213 *Time Warner Entertainment Co plc v Channel Four Television Corpn plc* [1994] EMLR 1.

BBC v British Satellite Broadcasting Ltd[214]

The BBC sued BSB for copyright infringement arising out of BSB's use of BBC broadcast footage of 1990 World Cup football matches as part of BSB's contemporaneous news coverage. Each excerpt used by BSB was between 14 and 37 seconds in length and was shown by BSB up to four times in its sports news programmes during the 24 hour period following each match. The source of the film was acknowledged to be the BBC in each excerpt. BSB claimed that its use of the footage was a fair dealing for the purpose of reporting current events.

The court held that a World Cup football match was a current event for the purposes of the fair dealing provisions. The issue was whether the use of the footage was a fair dealing. It held that both the quantity and the quality of what was taken were important. As regards duration, the clips used were very short in relation to the length of the match (30 seconds or thereabouts of a broadcast lasting, say, 90 minutes). Also relevant was the number of times that each excerpt was shown by the defendant. The fact that the clips were repeated in successive news reports over a 24 hour period was not a matter of justifiable criticism, nor was the fact that each clip was repeated up to three times in each news report. The court's overall impression was that the use of the material was short and pertinent to the news reporting character of BSB's programme.

On the issue of quality, the excerpts tended to be the highlights of the matches. The court held to show the best bits (that is, the goal scoring sequences) when reporting on the results of a football match 'is such a normal and obvious means of illustrating the news report as, in my opinion, to deprive [the claimant's] criticism of weight'.

The court held that BSB's dealing with the broadcast footage was fair.

In the *BSB* case, the judge was impressed by guidelines on the fair dealing rules which BSB had given to its staff. The judge saw them as evidence of good faith on the part of BSB. They helped to show that BSB was not simply exploiting the BBC's copyright under the guise of reporting current events, but that there was a genuine intention to report the football matches.

Sufficient acknowledgment

The fair dealing provisions of the CDPA refer to the requirement that use of a copyright work for the purposes of criticism or review must be accompanied by a sufficient acknowledgment.[215] Use of a copyright work for the purpose of reporting a current event must also be accompanied by a sufficient

---

214 *BBC v British Satellite Broadcasting Ltd* [1991] 3 WLR 174.
215 CDPA 1988, s 30(3).

acknowledgment, except where the current event is reported by means of a sound recording, film, broadcast or cable programme.

Sufficient acknowledgment is defined in s 178 of the CDPA as meaning an acknowledgment identifying the work in question by its title or other description and identifying the author, unless in the case of a published work it is published anonymously and, in the case of an unpublished work, it is not possible for a person to ascertain the identity of the author by reasonable inquiry.

In the *Pro Sieben* case,[216] the Court of Appeal held that the requirement of a sufficient acknowledgment of the identification of the author does not extend to requiring that the author be identified by name. Another form of identification may be adopted, such as a corporate logo by which the author is accustomed to identify itself. In the *Newspaper Licensing Agency* case,[217] Lightman J observed that, in principle, newspaper publishers should be sufficiently identified by the name of the newspaper which they publish and with which they are identified in the public mind. It would not therefore be necessary to identify the publisher of the newspaper.

Other permitted uses

Incidental inclusion of a copyright work

Copyright in a work is not infringed by its incidental inclusion in an artistic work (for example, a photograph), a sound recording, a film, a broadcast or cable programme.[218]

The term 'incidental' is not defined in the CDPA. In the case of *IPC Magazines Ltd v MGN Ltd*,[219] the term was held to bear its ordinary everyday meaning, namely 'casual, not essential, subordinate or merely background'. The *IPC* case illustrates the approach which should be used when considering whether a use is incidental.

The claimant, IPC Magazines, published *Woman* magazine. The defendant published a woman's magazine supplement to *The Sunday Mirror*. The cover of *Woman* was featured in a television advertisement for the *Sunday Mirror* supplement with a black band superimposed across the middle of it indicating that the cost of *Woman* was 57 p, whereas the defendant's supplement was provided 'free' with *The Sunday Mirror*. The claimant sought summary judgment on the issue of whether the advertisement infringed its artistic copyright in the following elements of the magazine cover: (a) the

---

216 *Pro Sieben v Carlton* [1999] FSR 610.

217 *Newspaper Licensing Agency v Marks & Spencer* [1999] RPC 536.

218 CDPA 1988, s 31.

219 *IPC Magazines Ltd v MGN Ltd* [1998] FSR 431.

logo/masthead; (b) the layout; and (c) the photographs featured on the cover. The defendant claimed that the inclusion of the magazine cover was 'incidental' to the broadcast, because the purpose of the advertisement had been to advertise *The Sunday Mirror*, not *Woman*.

The court held that the inclusion of the claimant's magazine cover was not incidental. It was, in fact, an essential and important feature of the advertisement. The impact of the advertisement would have been lost altogether if the cover had not been used.

It follows that the correct approach when assessing whether a particular use is incidental is to assess the *impact* of the use of the copyright work rather than the *purpose* for which the copyright work was used.

The CDPA provides that a musical work, words spoken or sung with music or so much of a sound recording, broadcast or cable programme as includes such works shall not be regarded as incidentally included in another work if it is deliberately included.[220] An example cited in Parliament during the passage of the Bill was the filming and broadcast of a football match. If, at half time, a band began to play a piece of music which is still in copyright to the crowd and that performance was broadcast, the music would not be regarded as incidental if it were deliberately included. So, if the camera crew were to zoom in deliberately on the band that might be regarded as deliberate inclusion of the music and therefore an infringement of copyright in the musical work. On the other hand, if the cameras were filming interviews with pundits who were commenting on the first half of the match, and happened also to pick up the music on the microphone, that would not be a deliberate inclusion of the music.

Inclusion of material consisting of the spoken word

Copyright may subsist in spoken words as a literary work once the words are recorded in writing or otherwise.[221] Filming or tape recording the speaker will be 'recording' for the purposes of the CDPA. Copyright in the words spoken will belong to the speaker, not to the recorder (although the recorder may own copyright in his record).[222] The speaker could theoretically use his copyright to restrain the broadcast of his words.

It would clearly be draconian restriction on their freedom of expression if the media were to need permission before they could make use of recorded interview footage. In order to minimise the potential restriction, s 58 of the CDPA provides that, where a record of spoken words is made in writing or otherwise for the purpose of reporting current events or of broadcasting or

---

220 CDPA 1988, s 31(3).

221 *Ibid*, s 3(3).

222 See p 229 for further discussion of this issue.

including in a cable programme service the whole or part of the work, it is not an infringement of any copyright in the words to use the record or material taken from it (or to copy the record, or any such material, and use the copy) for the purpose of reporting current events, provided that the following conditions are met:

- the record is a direct record of the spoken words and is not taken from a previous record or from a broadcast or cable programme;

- the making of the record was not prohibited by the speaker and, where copyright already subsisted in the work, did not infringe copyright;

- the use made of the record or material taken from it is not of a kind prohibited by or on behalf of the speaker or copyright owner before the record was made; and

- the use is by or with the authority of a person who is lawfully in possession of the record.

Works on public display

Copyright in buildings and models of buildings, sculptures and other works of artistic craftsmanship is not infringed by photographing then when they are permanently situated in a public place or premises open to the public.[223]

Copyright and the public interest

Section 171(3) of the CDPA provides that 'nothing in this Part affects any rule of law preventing or restricting the enforcement of copyright on grounds of public interest or otherwise'.

The extent to which use of a work in the public interest might provide a defence to an infringement claim was recently considered by the Court of Appeal in *Hyde Park Residence v Yelland*.[224]

Prior to that decision, there was a school of thought that the public interest defence would provide a defence against enforcement of copyright where the copyright work contained information which it would be in the public interest to publish. It was thought that the copyright public interest defence was analogous to the public interest defence in breach of confidence cases.[225] The first instance decision in the *Hyde Park Residence* case endorsed this view.[226] But this view appears now to have been authoritatively refuted by the Court of Appeal, whose decision has severely restricted the defence of public interest in copyright infringement cases.

---

223 CDPA 1988, s 62.
224 *Hyde Park Residence v Yelland* [2000] RPC 604, CA.
225 Discussed in Chapter 5.
226 *Hyde Park Residence v Yelland* [1999] RPC 655.

The Court of Appeal held that the courts have the inherent jurisdiction to refuse to enforce an action for copyright infringement on the grounds of public interest only where the enforcement of copyright *offends against the policy of the law*. Aldous LJ gave a non-exhaustive list of circumstances where this might be the case as follows:

- the copyright work is immoral, scandalous or contrary to family life; or
- the copyright work is injurious to public life, public health and safety or the administration of justice; or
- the copyright work incites or encourages others to act in a way referred to above.

All the above criteria relate to the *nature of the work itself*. Aldous LJ indicated that the circumstances leading to the conclusion that enforcement would be against the policy of the law must derive from the copyright work, not from the identity of the owner of the copyright. The result is that where the nature of the work offends against policy, the copyright owner loses his right to control the exploitation of the work.

Mance LJ was not so restrictive. He indicated that it might be possible to conceive of situations where a copyright document appeared innocuous on its face, but its publication would be justified in the public interest in the context of other facts, which might include the identity of the owner of the copyright. In such circumstances, he opined, it might be in the public interest to restrain the enforcement of copyright. Mance LJ did not expand on this observation. Its scope is, for the moment, unclear.

It is interesting to consider the decision of the House of Lords in the *Spycatcher* litigation[227] in the light of this judgment. The consensus of the law lords in *Spycatcher* was that Peter Wright would not be able to enforce any copyright which he owned in his memoirs. Lord Keith noted that the courts would not:

> ... enforce a claim ... to the copyright in a work the publication of which [was] brought about contrary to the public interest.

And Lord Jauncey felt that:

> ... the publication of *Spycatcher* was against the public interest and was in breach of the duty which Peter Wright held to the Crown. His action reeked of turpitude. It is in these circumstances inconceivable that a UK court would afford to him or his publishers any protection in relation to any copyright which either of them may possess in the book.

On Aldous LJ's reasoning, this finding would not have been so easily available to the Law Lords. The decision not to enforce copyright would have to be based on the *work itself* rather than on the identity and wrongdoing of

---

227 *AG v Guardian Newspapers (No 2)* [1990] 1 AC 109.

the copyright owner. Unless the *Spycatcher* book could be said to be immoral or damaging to public health (or, by analogy, national security), the enforcement of copyright could not have been restrained on public interest grounds.

Mance LJ's judgment permits a broader approach – the work itself may be innocuous but enforcement of copyright might be against public policy because of other factors, such as the identity and the discreditable actions of the copyright owner.

This uncertainty of the scope of what is, on any reading, a much reduced public interest defence, is unsatisfactory.

Example

Consider a borderline case. In the 12 March 2000 edition of *The Independent on Sunday*, the newspaper reported that it had received a letter from the convicted murderer, Ian Brady, in which he claimed to have in his possession a number of letters which had been written to him by his accomplice, Myra Hindley. Brady claimed that the letter refuted Hindley's on the record comments that Brady had coerced her into carrying out the moors murders.

Now suppose that a newspaper obtained the Brady/Hindley letters. Would Myra Hindley (the author of the letters) be able to enforce copyright in the letters to restrain publication?

Could it be argued that it is against the policy of the law to permit her to enforce her copyright and restrain publication? On Aldous LJ's analysis, probably not, unless the contents of the letters were, for example, immoral or injurious to public safety. Unless Aldous LJ's criteria were satisfied, Hindley could restrain publication of the letters. On Mance LJ's analysis the background facts – for example, the fact that the information might shed light on the sequences of events surrounding the Moors murders – might give rise to public interest considerations which justify restraining Hindley from stopping the publication of the letters.

The rationale for the Yelland decision

The reasoning behind the Court of Appeal's decisions was explained by Aldous LJ. He observed that the CDPA already provides for certain permitted uses which override the right to enforce copyright. Examples are the fair dealing provisions. The only ground on which the court can refuse to enforce copyright are those provided for in the CDPA and the limited circumstances in which enforcement would offend against the policy of the law. It would be wrong for a court that has rejected a fair dealing defence to uphold a common law defence on the ground that publication was in the public interest.

Aldous LJ went on to observe that copyright is concerned with the form of the work in which copyright subsists, rather than in the underlying information itself. Its objective is to protect the product of the skill and labour of the author of the copyright work from appropriation. Copyright does not afford protection to information *per se*. An injunction to retrain infringement of copyright would not prohibit the publication of the information contained in the copyright work if it were expressed in a different form so as not to amount to an appropriation of the skill and labour involved in the creation of the copyright work. On the facts of the *Hyde Park Residence* case,[228] *The Sun* could have given the information about the timings at the villa without reproducing the stills.

The practical effect of the Yelland *decision*

It is submitted that the practical effect of Aldous LJ's words on investigative journalism is wider than he suggested. The impact of media reporting is likely to be significantly weakened if a copyright work cannot be reproduced or quoted from.

The sensationalism of the *Hyde Park Residence* case makes it a poor model on which to judge the issue. Take, instead, similar facts to those which arose in *Lion Laboratories v Evans*.[229] The case is primarily a breach of confidence case, although it does contain some observations on copyright infringement (which seem now to have been overturned in the wake of the *Hyde Park Residence* decision). It concerned a confidential memorandum which came into the possession of a journalist. The memorandum revealed that a device used for breathalysing motorists had a number of defects, leading to doubts about its accuracy. The journalist wrote an article referring to and quoting from the memorandum.

In the wake of the *Hyde Park Residence* case, the journalist could no longer quote from the memorandum unless the malfunction of the device could be called a 'current event' and the use of the memorandum a fair dealing. Assume that the fair dealing provisions do not apply and the journalist must fall back on a public interest defence, unless the memo itself offends against policy (which is unlikely), the fair dealing defence will not succeed on Aldous LJ's analysis. If an action for copyright infringement is to be avoided, the information contained in the document may be utilised (provided that publication is not in breach of confidence) but the memo may not be reproduced. But the force and the impact of the article will be lessened. Readers/viewers are less likely to sit up and take notice of an article expressed along the lines of 'we have obtained evidence which shows that ...' than they are to 'the memorandum states that ...'.

---

228 Set out above, pp 262–63.
229 *Lion Laboratories v Evans* [1984] 2 All ER 417.

There is also a significant danger for the media that, in paraphrasing or summarising the memorandum, inaccuracies may slip into the report, which, in a worst case scenario, might expose the media to defamation actions. Quotations from the underlying work would be one of the surest ways of guaranteeing the accuracy of what is reported.

A further effect is that the ability of journalists to carry out investigations will be impeded. If a journalist makes a photocopy or a verbatim note of the memorandum or of a substantial part of it for his professional use, he will have infringed copyright. The ability to amass information during the course of investigations has therefore been significantly restricted.

Whilst Aldous LJ's judgment is in line with the traditional role and functions of copyright law, it has, to a large extent, placed the law in a straight jacket so far as the media are concerned. The fair dealing provisions on which it must now rely are fairly rigid, despite judgments which emphasise the flexibility of the terms 'reporting current events' and 'criticism or review'. Aldous LJ's emphasis in the *Yelland* decision on fair dealing, on necessity for the use of the copyright work, protection of the status of previously unpublished works and the way in which a previously unpublished work was obtained by the defendant give the media little room for manoeuvre on the issue of the fairness of any dealing. At the same time, the prospect of a public interest defence appears to have all but disappeared.

The public interest and the Human Rights Act 1998

The Human Rights Act 1998 is considered in Chapter 1. In essence, the Act places public authorities, including courts, under an obligation to give further effect to the Convention rights contained in the European Convention of Human Rights, one of which is freedom of expression (Art 10). Under the case law of the European Court of Human Rights, a limitation on the right to freedom of expression is only permitted, *inter alia*, where it is necessary in a democratic society. One wonders whether the Court of Appeal's limitation of the public interest defence will be vulnerable on the ground that it goes further than is necessary to protect the rights of the copyright owner.

Protecting your copyright

A creator of a copyright work should take steps to deter potential infringers from reproducing the work and to ensure that he is in a position to show that an original literary, dramatic, musical or artistic work is original. The following procedures should therefore be considered:

- mark copyright works with the © symbol. The symbol is not a formal requirement in order to bring copyright into being under UK law (although it is a requirement under the Universal Copyright Convention in relation to international copyright protection). The symbol will, however, serve to alert potential users to the fact that copyright is claimed in the work. The following formula should be used:

© [name of copyright owner] [year of creation of the work];

- ensure that you *do* own copyright. Often, businesses who commission material believe that they own copyright once they pay for the work. But, as we have seen, that is not the case. Remember that unless the copyright work has been created by an employee in the course of their employment, you will need to take an assignment of copyright. Do not let yourself be caught out by this common misconception;

- ensure that you can prove that the work is original. Retain all material which will help you to show how the work was developed, such as drafts, briefings, samples. Keep a record of the identity of people who worked on the project;

- keep a record of the dates when the work was developed. You may need to prove that your work predates that of the alleged infringer. A useful device for establishing originality and timing is to post a copy of the work to yourself using registered post. The post office stamp will show the date of delivery. You should ensure that it is placed across the flap of the envelope to demonstrate that the envelope has not been tampered with since you posted it.

Avoiding copyright infringement: a case study

Blueboy Ltd is a designer of children's clothes. It wishes to mount a poster advertising campaign in the UK for its latest range of designs using a particular photograph for the poster. The photograph which Blueboy want to use is now 15 years old (and so is still in copyright). The copyright belongs to the photographer, Bill. Blueboy will clearly be reproducing a substantial part of the photograph in its poster. This use of the photograph does not fall within the permitted uses discussed above.

How can Blueboy use the photograph without infringing copyright?

Assignments

The most complete way of avoiding copyright infringement would be for Blueboy to take an assignment of copyright in the photograph from Bill so that ownership of the copyright is transferred to Blueboy. The assignment could transfer copyright for all purposes or for certain limited purposes. The assignment would give Blueboy the right to use the copyright work (the photograph) in the finished advertisement. Blueboy would also have the right to exploit the photograph in the future (unless the assignment was a transfer of copyright for certain purposes only). If Blueboy wishes to take assignments, it should ensure that Bill *is* the owner of the copyright. It should also ensure that the assignment is otherwise adequate for its purposes. The reader is referred to Part 3 for more detail. The assignment must be in writing.

Blueboy should bear in mind that Bill is likely to want to be paid for assigning copyright in the photograph. The grant of an assignment of copyright is usually relatively expensive. Bill may not even be willing to assign copyright. By doing so, he will lose the right to control the exploitation of his work in the future. An assignment may not therefore be the most practical way forward for Blueboy.

Licences

As an alternative to taking an assignment, Blueboy could obtain an exclusive or non-exclusive licence to use the photograph. The licence would not operate as a transfer of copyright. Instead it would be a permission to use the photograph for the purposes that the licence covers. Blueboy should take care to ensure that Bill is the owner of copyright and has the authority to grant the licence. The licence must also be wide enough to cover the uses that Blueboy intends to make of the photograph. The reader is referred to Part 3 for further detail about licences.

Music and collecting societies

For reasons of convenience many songwriters, composers and music publishers allow collecting societies to administer and enforce copyright on their behalf and to collect royalties. Record companies also make use of collecting societies to administer their copyright in sound recordings. Collecting societies administer hundreds of similar copyrights for different authors. Often it is the relevant collecting society which is authorised to grant a licence for the use of, for example, a piece of music, rather than the author of the work. The potential user of a copyright work should accordingly approach the collecting society for permission to use the copyright work.

Examples of collecting societies are:

- *the Performing Rights Society* (PRS), which administers the rights to perform works in public or to broadcast such works or include them in a cable programme service on behalf of its member songwriters, composers and music publishers. The PRS licenses the right to carry out these acts in return for a fee payable by the user which it distributes amongst its members in accordance with its regulations;

- *the Mechanical Copyright Protection Society* (MCPS) administers the right to record music in any format, such as on to CD, video, multimedia products and broadcast programmes. It does so on behalf of its member songwriters, composers and music publishers;

- *Phonographic Performance Ltd* (PPL) administers phonographic rights. Phonographic rights are the rights to broadcast or perform *sound recordings* in public. PPL (sound recordings) is the equivalent body to PRS (musical works). PPL has a sister organisation, *Video Performance Ltd* (VPL), which administers the right to its members' music videos.

The roles of the collecting societies are considered further in Chapter 18.

CRIMINAL OFFENCES

The CDPA provides for a number of criminal offences of copyright infringement which make it a criminal offence to make for sale or hire, to import into the UK (other than for private use), to possess with a view to committing an infringing act, to sell, hire or offer or expose for sale or hire, to exhibit or to distribute an article which is, *and which the defendant knows or has reason to believe is*, an infringement of copyright.

It is also an offence to make or possess an article designed to copy a particular copyright work knowing or having reason to believe that it will be used in relation to infringing works.

The criminal offences are aimed principally at counterfeiters and pirates of branded goods, films and sound recordings, although they can also have a wider application.

There are also related offences involving public performance of literary, dramatic and musical works and films.

The offences are punishable by fines or imprisonment.

COPYRIGHT IN DATABASES AND DATABASE RIGHT

Copyright and Rights in Databases Regulations 1997 SI 1997/3032 ('the Regulations')

An overview of the Regulations

The Regulations came into force in the UK on 1 January 1998 by way of amendment to the CDPA. They implement the provisions of Council Directive (96/9/EC) on the legal protection of databases which was intended both to *harmonise* the laws of Member States relating to protection of copyright in databases and to *introduce a new database right* to prevent the extraction and re-utilisation of the contents of a database.

Database is defined as a collection of independent works, data or other materials which are arranged in a systematic or methodical way and which are capable of being individually accessed by electronic or other means. This is a wide definition, which does not just relate to information stored on computer. Material such as directories of restaurants or entertainment venues fall within the definition, as do encyclopedias (in any format, for example, on CD-ROM or in book form).

The Regulations amend the law relating to copyright in databases and create a new database right which can exist alongside copyright.

The maker of a database is the first owner of both the database right and the copyright in it. Where the maker is an employee who makes the database in the course of his employment, his employer shall be regarded as the maker of the database, subject to any agreement to the contrary.

Changes to copyright law in relation to databases

Prior to the Regulations, the CDPA made no specific provision for databases. Databases were generally viewed as being literary work in the form of compilations provided that they met the originality requirements in s 3 of the CDPA. The Regulations made certain changes to the Act. The CDPA now provides that:

- 'literary work' is defined to specifically include databases. The CDPA provides that a database is *not* to be classed as a compilation for copyright purposes. Databases are a type of literary work in their own right;
- the originality requirements which apply to databases are stricter than the requirements for other types of copyright works. A database is original, and therefore has the status of a copyright work if, *and only if*, by reason of the selection or arrangement of the contents of the database the database constitutes the author's own intellectual creation. Certain databases will not meet the originality criteria; however, they may still qualify for database right (considered below);
- the duration of copyright in a database is the same as for other types of literary work;
- it is not an infringement of copyright for a person with a right to use the database or any part of it to do, in the exercise of that right, anything which is necessary for the purposes of access to and use of the contents of the database or that part of the database.

Introduction of a new database right for databases

The database right subsists in a database where there has been a substantial investment in obtaining, verifying or presenting the contents of the database. The database right can exist even though the database may not satisfy the originality requirements for a copyright work which are referred to above.

A person infringes database right in a database if, without the consent of the owner of the right, he extracts or re-utilises all or a substantial part of the contents of the database. The *repeated and systematic* extraction or re-utilisation of insubstantial parts of the contents of the database may amount to the extraction or re-utilisation of a substantial part of those contents (and therefore infringe the database right). 'Extraction' means the transfer (permanent or temporary) of the contents of the database to another medium. 'Re-utilisation' means making the contents of the database available to the public by any means. It is not an infringement for a lawful user of the database to extract or re-utilise insubstantial parts of the database. Any term or condition in an agreement which seeks to prohibit or restrict such extraction or re-utilisation is rendered void.

Database right expires at the end of 15 years from the end of the calendar year in which the making of the database was completed or if it is made available to the public before the end of that period, 15 years after the end of the calendar year in which the database was first made available to the public. Substantial changes to the database give a further period for protection. There are transitional provisions for databases completed on or after 1 January 1983 (database right for 15 years from 1 January 1998).

There is a fair dealing exception for database right where a substantial part of the database is extracted for teaching or research purposes (but not for any commercial purpose) and the source of the extract is acknowledged and the user is someone with a right to use the database.

Copyright and database rights are not alternatives. Where a database qualifies for both copyright and database right protection, the owner can choose to enforce both rights.

PUBLICATION RIGHT

Publication right came into force in the UK on 1 December 1996. It applies to literary, dramatic, musical, artistic works and to films. The right applies to any person who, after the expiry of copyright in the work, lawfully publishes or lawfully communicates to the public a previously unpublished work *for the first time*. It confers on the owner of the right a right akin to copyright which lasts for 25 years from the time when the work was first lawfully published or communicated to the public.

In order to acquire the right, the publisher must be able to show that:

- the work once enjoyed copyright protection;
- the copyright period has now expired;

- the work has not been published. Publication means that the work must not previously have been communicated to the public, including by exhibition or public showing;
- the publication must be authorised by the owner of the physical work; and
- the work must be published first within the EEA and undertaken by a national of an EEA State.

THE FUTURE: COPYRIGHT AND DIGITAL MEDIA

Amended proposal on copyright and related rights in the information society (COM (99) 250 final)

The Directive seeks to harmonise copyright and related rights in certain key areas, primarily to deal with digital technology (but the amendments are *not* restricted to digital media). The Directive provides for the following rights:

- *reproduction right* – States are required to provide for the exclusive right to authorise or prohibit direct, indirect, temporary or permanent reproduction of a copyright work by any means and in any form in whole or in part (Art 2). The right applies to authors, performers in respect of fixations of their performances, phonogram producers, film producers and broadcasting organisations. The reproduction right confirms the existing situation under the CDPA which provides that copying a copyright work includes reproduction in any material form.

  Exempted from this right are temporary acts of reproduction which are an integral and essential part of a technological process whose sole purpose is to enable use to be made of a work or other subject matter and which have no independent economic significance (Art 5);

- *communication right* – States are required to provide for the exclusive right to authorise or prohibit any communication to the public of originals or copies of their work by wire or wireless means, including the making available to the public of their works in such a way that members of the public may access them from a place and at a time individually chosen by them. This right shall not be exhausted by any act of communication to the public of a work, including their being made available to the public. The mere provision of physical facilities for enabling or making a communication does not, itself, amount to an act of communication to the public (Art 3). Online services will be covered by the new communication right, as will digital transmissions allowing for the identification and recording of specific items, such as musical tracks. The communication right covers transmission by wireless means (for example, mobile telephone networks) and wire means (for example, by cable service or the internet).

The right applies to authors, performers in respect of fixations of their performances, phonogram producers, film producers and broadcasting organisations;

- *distribution right* – States shall provide authors in respect of the originals of their works or copies of them with the exclusive right to any form of distribution to the public by sale or otherwise (Art 4). This right is only exhausted within the EC where the first sale or other transfer of ownership in the EC is made by the rights owner or with his consent.

The draft Directive provides for certain exceptions to the above exclusive rights.

Member States have the *option* to introduce certain limitations to the right of reproduction and, in some cases, the right of communication. Where the Member State wishes to provide for such exceptions, the Directive gives an exhaustive list of the exceptions which are permitted. They include:

- use for the sole purpose of illustration for teaching or scientific research, as long as the source is indicated and to the extent justified by the non-commercial purpose to be achieved, on condition that the rights owners receive fair compensation;

- uses for the benefit of people with a disability which are directly related to the disability and of a non-commercial nature and to the extent required by the specific disability;

- use of excerpts in connection with the reporting of current events, as long as the source and, if possible, the author's name is indicated, and to the extent justified by the informatory purpose and the objective of illustrating the event concerned;

- quotations for purposes such as criticism or review, provided that they relate to a work or other subject matter which has already been lawfully made available to the public, that the source and, if possible, the author's name is indicated, and that their use is in accordance with fair practice, and to the extent required for the specific purpose;

- use for the purposes of public security or to ensure the proper performance or reporting of an administrative, parliamentary or judicial procedure.

But any such exceptions shall:

(a) only be applied to certain specific cases;

(b) not be interpreted in such a way as to:

- allow their application to be used in a manner which unfairly prejudices the right holders' legitimate interests; or

- conflict with the normal exploitation of their works or other subject matter.[230]

This provision is not at all clear. For example, what might 'legitimate interests' be? What constitutes unfair prejudice of those interests? What is meant by 'normal exploitation'?

Both the criticism or review exemption and the reporting current events exemption appear to be more restrictive that the current fair dealing provisions of the CDPA. Even more alarming for the user of copyright works, the Directive states that Art 5(4) must be interpreted with a copyright owner bias. The text of the Directive imposes a worrying threat to the media industries. The author understands that it is the subject of vigorous lobbying by media interests at the time of writing. It must be hoped that the effect of the lobbying will be to produce a piece of legislation which offers a more workable alternative for the media.

Obligations as to technical measures (Art 6)

'Technical measures' is defined as any technology, device or component that in the normal course of its operation is designed to prevent or inhibit the infringement of copyright or related rights.

Member States are obliged to provide adequate legal protection against the circumvention without authority of any effective technological measures designed to protect any copyright or related right which the person concerned carries out in the knowledge or with reasonable grounds to know that he or she pursues that objective.

Obligations concerning rights management distribution (Art 6)

Rights management information means any information provided by rights holders which identifies the work or other subject matter, the author or information about the terms and conditions for use of the work or other subject matter and any numbers or codes that represents such information.

Member States shall provide for adequate legal protection against any person performing without authority any of the following acts:

- the removal or alteration of any electronic rights management information;
- the distribution, importation for distribution, broadcasting, communication or making available to the public of copies of works or other subject matter from which electronic rights management information has been removed or altered without authority,

---

230 Legal Protection of Databases Directive, Art 5(4).

if such a person knows or has reasonable grounds to know that by so doing he is inducing, enabling or facilitating an infringement of any copyright or any rights related to copyright.

Sanctions and remedies (Art 8)

States shall provide for appropriate sanctions and remedies for infringement and take all measures to ensure that those sanctions and remedies are applied. The sanctions provided shall be effective, proportionate and dissuasive and act as a deterrent to further infringement.

Each State shall take the measures necessary to ensure that rights owners whose interests are affected by an infringing activity carried out in its territory can bring an action for damages and/or apply for an injunction and seizure.

(b) Moral rights

Moral rights exist alongside copyright. They are, however, a different concept from copyright. The owner of copyright in a work may not own the moral rights in the work and vice versa. Moral rights belong to the *author* of a copyright work and they cannot be assigned. They are concerned with protecting the name and reputation of that person as the creator of the work. Upon the death of the owner they pass to his/her estate. So, irrespective of who owns copyright in a work at any particular time, the author still owns the moral rights in the work.

Unlike copyright, which gives the owner the right to exploit the copyright, moral rights control the way in which the work is *treated*. Moral rights stem from the notion that the author's reputation is bound up with the work that he has created. It follows that the author is entitled to protect his reputation by controlling certain aspects of the way in which the work is treated. English law has traditionally concentrated on the economic rights protected by copyright. The concept of 'moral rights' did not exist in English national law until the CDPA, although the Berne Convention for the Protection of Literary and Artistic Works 1886, to which the UK is a signatory, recognises such rights. Art 6 *bis*, para 1 of the Berne Convention states as follows:

> Independently of the author's economic rights, and even after the transfer of the said rights, the author shall have the right to claim authorship of the work and to object to any distortion, mutilation or other modification of, or other derogatory action in relation to, the said work, which would be prejudicial to his honour or reputation.

The CDPA, which came into force on 1 August 1989, expressly recognises the following rights:

- *the right of paternity* – this is the right to be identified as author or director of a copyright literary, dramatic, musical or artistic work or a film;
- *the right of integrity* – this is the right of the author or director to object to derogatory treatment of a copyright literary, dramatic, musical or artistic work or a film;
- *the right against false attribution* – this right entitles a person not to have a literary, dramatic, musical or artistic work or a film falsely attributed to him/her;
- *the right of privacy in photographs/films/videos taken for private or domestic purposes.*[231]

The first three of these rights will now be examined in more detail.

The right of paternity[232]

The right to be identified as author or director cannot be infringed unless it is first *asserted* by the author/director in writing.[233] The right may be asserted generally, or in relation to any specified act or acts. If the right is not asserted, there is no claim against a person who makes use of the work without giving the author credit.

The right of paternity exists only in relation to works in which copyright subsists. If a literary work is not original, and copyright does not subsist in it, there will be no right of paternity in relation to it.

The right entitles the author of a literary work (other than words intended to be sung or spoken with music) or a dramatic work to be identified whenever the work is published commercially, performed in public, broadcast or included in a cable programme service or whenever copies of a film or sound recording including the work are issued to the public. The right also includes the right to be identified as the author of the work from which an adaptation is made whenever any of those events occurs in relation to an adaptation of the work.[234]

The right entitles the author of a musical work or of a literary work consisting of words intended to be sung or spoken with music to be identified whenever the work is published commercially, or copies of a sound recording of the work are issued to the public or a film whose sound track includes the work is shown in public or copies of such a film are issued to the public. As

---

231 The right of privacy is considered in Chapter 8.
232 CDPA 1988, s 77.
233 *Ibid*, s 78.
234 *Ibid*, s 77.

with a literary or dramatic work, the right also applies to adaptations of a musical work.[235]

The author of an artistic work has the right to be identified whenever the work is published commercially or exhibited in public or where a visual image of the work is broadcast or included in a cable programme service. It also applies where a film which includes a visual image of the work is shown in public, or copies of such a film are issued to the public. In the case of a work of architecture in the form of a building or a model of a building, a sculpture or a work of artistic craftsmanship, the right applies where copies of a graphic work which represents it or of a photograph of it are issued to the public.[236]

The director of a film has the right to be identified whenever the film is shown in public, broadcast or included in a cable programme service or copies of the film are issued to the public.[237]

In every case, the identification must be clear and reasonably prominent so that it is likely to bring the author/director's identity to the notice of the audience/user.[238]

There are a number of exceptions to the right of paternity.[239] The right does not apply to works made for the purpose of reporting current events, for example, a newspaper article or a photograph taken for that purpose.[240] Similarly, it does not apply to the publication in a newspaper, magazine or similar periodical or an encyclopedia, dictionary, yearbook or other collective work of reference of a literary, dramatic, musical or artistic work made for the purpose of such publication or made available by the author for any such purpose.[241]

Other exceptions to the rights are the following descriptions of work: a computer program, the design of a typeface or any computer generated work. The right also does not apply to anything done by or with the authority of the copyright owner where copyright in the work in question was originally vested in the author's employer (that is, where the work was created in the course of the author's employment and there is no agreement that copyright will belong to the employee).[242]

---

235 CDPA 1988, s 77.
236 *Ibid*.
237 *Ibid*.
238 *Ibid*.
239 Set out at *ibid*, s 79.
240 *Ibid*, s 79(5).
241 *Ibid*, s 79(6).
242 *Ibid*, s 79(3).

Other exceptions to the right are where the use of the work would not infringe copyright under the fair dealing provisions (see above), or because the work is included incidentally.[243]

The right of integrity

The right of integrity entitles the author of a copyright literary, dramatic, musical or artistic work and the director of a copyright film to restrain and/or object to the subjection of the whole or any part of his work to derogatory treatment.[244] Note that, like copyright, it does not protect the integrity of the author's idea, only the way in which the idea has been expressed. The right is dependent on the existence of the copyright work. Unlike the right of paternity, the right of integrity does not have to be asserted before it can be exercised. The right of integrity is only exercisable if copyright subsists in the work for which the moral right is claimed.

Treatment means any addition to, deletion from or alteration to or adaptation of the work other than a translation of a literary work or an arrangement or transcription of a musical work involving no more than a change of key or register.[245] Treatment is *derogatory* if it amounts to distortion or mutilation of the work or is otherwise prejudicial to the honour or reputation of the author or director.[246] The treatment can relate to the whole or any part of the work.[247]

The test of whether treatment of a work is derogatory is an objective one and it is a question which will fall to be decided by the court. In *Pasterfield v Denham*,[248] the claimant was a designer who produced some artwork for a promotional brochure for Plymouth City Council. Some years later, the council used the artwork for an amended brochure. A number of minor changes were made to the claimant's drawings, for example, certain shades of colour were changed and a number of peripheral features were removed. The claimant alleged that the alteration of drawings in the updated brochure amounted to derogatory treatment of his artwork and was therefore an infringement of his moral right of integrity. The court held that it is not sufficient to give rise to an infringement that the author is aggrieved by the treatment of his work. It is the opinion of the court which determines whether in any particular case the work has been subjected to derogatory treatment. On the facts, the differences in the drawings were so trivial as to be only detectable on close inspection. The judge observed that 'the differences may be such that the two versions could well be the subject of a "Spot the

---

243 CDPA 1988, s 79(4).
244 *Ibid*, s 80.
245 *Ibid*, s 80(2).
246 *Ibid*.
247 *Ibid*, s 89.
248 *Pasterfield v Denham* [1999] FSR 168.

Difference" competition in a child's comic'. He said that it would be wrong to elevate that to the status of derogatory treatment. It would therefore seem that the extent of the treatment to which the work is subjected is a relevant factor in determining whether the treatment is, in fact, derogatory.

The right of integrity is infringed in the case of a literary, dramatic or musical work by a person who publishes commercially, performs in public, broadcasts or includes in a cable programme service a derogatory treatment of the work or issues to the public copies of a film or sound recording of, or including, a derogatory treatment of the work. In the case of an artistic work, the right is infringed by a person who publishes commercially or exhibits in public a derogatory treatment of the work, or broadcasts or includes in a cable programme services a visual image of a derogatory treatment of a work or issues to the public copies of such a film or in the case of a work of architecture in the form of a model of a building, a sculpture or a work of artistic craftsmanship, issues to the public copies of a graphic work representing, or of a photograph of, a derogatory treatment of the work. In the case of a film, the right is infringed by a person who shows in public, broadcasts or includes in a cable programme services a derogatory treatment of a film or issues to the public copies of a derogatory treatment of a film.[249]

The right is also infringed by a person who possesses in the course of a business, or sells or lets for hire or offers or exposes for sale or hire or in the course of a business exhibits in public or distributes or distributes other than in the course of a business so as to affect prejudicially the honour or reputation of the author or director an article which he knows or has reason to believe is an infringing article, that is, a work or copy of a work which has been subjected to derogatory treatment and has been or is likely to be the subject of any of the acts mentioned above which would infringe the right.[250]

There are a number of exceptions to the right of integrity.[251] The right does not apply to works made for the purpose of reporting current events, for example, a newspaper article or a photograph taken for that purpose.[252] Similarly, it does not apply to the publication in a newspaper, magazine or similar periodical or an encyclopedia, dictionary, yearbook or other collective work of reference of a literary, dramatic, musical or artistic work made for the purpose of such publication or made available by the author for any such purpose.[253]

---

249 CDPA 1988, s 80.
250 *Ibid*, s 83.
251 Set out at *ibid*, s 81.
252 *Ibid*, s 81(3).
253 *Ibid*, s 81(4).

The right of integrity does not apply to a computer program or any computer generated work.[254]

Further, the right is not infringed by anything done for the purpose of avoiding the commission of an offence, complying with a duty imposed by or under any enactment.[255] In the case of the BBC (but not, apparently, other broadcasters), the right is not infringed by anything done for the purpose of avoiding the inclusion in a programme broadcast by them of anything which offends against good taste or decency or which is likely to encourage or incite to crime or to lead to disorder or to be offensive to public feeling.[256]

Where copyright in the work which has been subjected to derogatory treatment originally vested in the author's employer (because it was a work created by the author in the course of his employment), the right of integrity shall not apply to anything done to the work by or with the authority of the copyright owner unless the author or director is identified at the time of the relevant act or has previously been identified in or on published copies of the work.[257]

The right against false attribution

A person has the right not to have the whole or any part of a literary, dramatic, musical or artistic work falsely attributed to him as author or a film falsely attributed to him as director.[258] In the case of *Clark v Associated Newspapers*,[259] the claimant was Alan Clark, a well known politician who had previously published his political diaries with much success. The defendant published the *Evening Standard*, which published a series of articles entitled 'Alan Clark's Secret Election Diary' and 'Alan Clark's Secret Political Diary'. The articles featured a photograph of the claimant. Alan Clark had nothing to do with the articles and had not given any consent to the use of his name and identity in connection with the articles. They were 'spoof' items. The claimant alleged passing off and infringement of his moral right against false attribution.

The court held that for the purposes of s 84 of the CDPA attribution meant a claim (express or implied) about the identity of the author of a particular item. In deciding whether there is a false attribution, the court has to determine the single meaning which the work would convey to reasonable readers (an approach akin to defamation cases). The claimant does *not* have to show that a substantial number of readers would believe there to be a false

254 CDPA 1988, s 81(1).
255 *Ibid.*
256 *Ibid.*
257 *Ibid*, s 82(2).
258 *Ibid*, s 84(1).
259 *Clark v Associated Newspapers* [1998] RPC 261.

attribution. On the facts, there was a clear unequivocal false statement that the claimant was the author of the articles and therefore a false attribution had taken place. The court also observed that, in order to exercise the moral right against false attribution, the claimant must be a professional author (as Mr Clark was). Once a finding of false attribution had been made, the right is infringed without proof of damage.

The right is infringed by a person who issues to the public copies of a work in or on which there is a false attribution or exhibits in public an artistic work or a copy of an artistic work in or on which there is a false attribution. The right is also infringed by a person who, in the case of a literary, dramatic or musical work, performs the work in public, broadcasts it or includes it in a cable programme service as being the work of a person or, in the case of a film, shows it in public, broadcasts it or includes it in a cable programme service as being directed by a person knowing or having reason to believe that the attribution is false. The right is also infringed by a person who possesses or deals with a copy of a work in or on which there is a false attribution or, in the case of an artistic work, possesses or deals with the work when there is a false attribution in or on it knowing or having reason to believe that there is such an attribution and that it is false.[260]

Duration of moral rights

Moral rights generally continue as long as copyright subsists in the work in question.[261] The only exception to this rule is in relation to the right against false attribution, which only lasts until 20 years after a person's death.[262]

Consent and waiver

Moral rights cannot be transferred. They are personal to the author. Moral rights can be waived (or relinquished).[263] A waiver must be in writing.[264] The waiver can relate to a specific work, to works of a specified description or to works generally, including future works which are not yet in existence.[265] The waiver may be conditional or unconditional, and may also be expressed to be revocable or irrevocable.[266] It is common practice for a party who is commissioning a copyright work or purchasing the rights to such a work to

---

260 CDPA 1988, s 84.
261 *Ibid*, s 86.
262 *Ibid*, s 86(2).
263 *Ibid*, s 87.
264 *Ibid*, s 87(2).
265 *Ibid*, s 87(3).
266 *Ibid*.

require the author of the work to waive his moral rights unconditionally and irrevocably (see Part 3 of this book for further details).

In *Pasterfield v Denham*,[267] the passing of equitable title to copyright or the grant of an implied licence was held not to mean that an author has waived his moral rights, even on an informal basis. Something more definite was required.

Performance rights

Performers do not own copyright in their performances. If an actor stars in a one-woman play, the play is a dramatic work in which copyright subsists. There is no copyright in the actor's performance itself. Instead, the performer may have performance rights in the performance which can be used to control its commercial exploitation. Performance rights have some similarity with copyright. The consent of a performer is generally required to the exploitation of their performance. Section 180(4) of the CDPA provides that performance rights may exist independently of both copyright and moral rights.

'Performance' means a dramatic (including a dance or mime) or musical performance, a reading or recitation of a literary work or a performance of a variety act or any similar presentation, all of which consist of (or so far as they consist of) a live performance given by one or more individuals.[268] Dancers, musicians and actors may therefore all own rights in their performances. A performance must be a 'qualifying performance'.[269] A qualifying performance must take place in the UK or another Member State of the EEA or it must be given by a citizen who is a subject of or resident in the UK or another Member State.[270]

The performer has the following rights:

- the *reproduction right* is the right of a performer to prevent any person making a copy of a recording or a substantial part of his performance (other than for their own private or domestic use) without the performer's consent;[271]

- 'recording' means a sound or film recording either made directly from the live performance or made from a broadcast of or a cable programme including the performance or made directly or indirectly from another recording of the performance;[272]

---

267 *Pasterfield v Denham* [1999] FSR 168.
268 CDPA 1988, s 180(2).
269 *Ibid*, s 181.
270 *Ibid*, s 206.
271 *Ibid*, s 182.
272 *Ibid*, s 180(2).

- the *distribution right* is the right of the performer to prevent any person issuing to the public copies of his performance or a substantial part of his performance without the performer's consent. Issuing copies to the public means the act of putting into circulation in the EEA copies of the performance not previously put into circulation in the EEA by or with the consent of the performer, or the act of putting into circulation outside the EEA copies not previously put into circulation in the EEA or elsewhere. It does not include any subsequent distribution, sale, hiring or loan of copies previously put into circulation;[273]

- the *rental and lending right* gives performers the right to authorise or prohibit the rental and lending to the public of copies of a recording of their performance or a substantial part of their performance. 'Rental' means making a copy of the recording available for use, on terms that it will or may be returned, for direct or indirect economic or commercial advantage (such as videos available for hire). 'Lending' means making a copy of a recording available for use, on terms that it will or may be returned, otherwise than for direct or indirect economic or commercial advantage, through an establishment that it is accessible to the public (such as a public library).[274]

Where a musician has an exclusive recording contract with a record company, the record company may be able to grant permission to use the musician's performance.

The above rights are rights of property which may be assigned in the same way as copyright. They may also be transferred as testamentary dispositions or by operation of law.[275] The rights may be assigned in writing, signed by or on behalf of the assignor. The assignment can be partial, that is, limited to apply to one or more (but not all) of the things requiring the consent of the rights owner or to part, but not the whole, of the period for which the rights are to subsist.[276]

Where a film production agreement is concluded between a performer and a film producer, the performer shall be presumed, unless the agreement provides to the contrary, to have transferred to the film producer his rental rights arising from the inclusion of a recording of his performance in the film.[277] The performer retains a right to equitable remuneration for the rental which cannot be assigned.[278] Equitable remuneration is payable by the person entitled to the rental right. An agreement is of no effect in so far as it purports

---

273 CDPA 1988, s 182B.
274 *Ibid*, s 182C.
275 *Ibid*, s 191B.
276 *Ibid*.
277 *Ibid*, s 191F.
278 *Ibid*, s 191G.

to exclude or restrict the right to equitable remuneration. Even where a performer expressly assigns the rental right to the producer of the film, rather than relying on the presumed transfer, he retains the right to equitable remuneration for the rental.[279]

The performer also has a number of non-property rights which are infringed where the following activities take place without the performers' consent:

- showing or playing the whole or a substantial part of a qualifying performance in public;[280]

- broadcasting or including in a cable programme service the whole or a substantial part of a qualifying performance;[281]

- importing into the UK other than for private or domestic use a recording of a qualifying performance which is, and which that person knows or has reason to believe is, an illicit recording;[282]

- possessing, selling or letting for hire, offering or exposing for sale or hire or distributing a recording of a qualifying performance which is, and which that person knows or has reason to believe is, an illicit recording.[283]

Illicit recording is defined to mean a recording of the whole or a substantial part of a performance which was made otherwise than for private purposes without the performers' consent.[284]

These non-property rights cannot be assigned. They can only be transferred on death, when they will pass to the performer's estate.[285]

The performer's rights each expire at the end of 50 years from the end of the calendar year in which the performance took place, or if, during that period, a recording of a performance is released, 50 years from the end of the calendar year in which it was released.

Where a commercially published sound recording of the whole or any substantial part of a performance is played in public, or is included in a broadcast or cable programme service, the performer is entitled to equitable remuneration. The performer cannot transfer this right. An agreement between the performer and the copyright owner is void in so far as it purports to exclude or restrict the right to equitable remuneration.[286] A new collecting society, the Performing Artists' Media Rights Association (PAMRA) collects

---

279 CDPA 1988, s 191G.
280 *Ibid*, s 183(a).
281 *Ibid*, s 183(b).
282 *Ibid*, s 183(c).
283 *Ibid*, s 184(1)(b).
284 *Ibid*, s 197.
285 *Ibid*, s 192.
286 *Ibid*, s 182D

income from record companies on behalf of the performers for the public broadcast of their performances.

Similarly, where a performer transfers his rental right in a sound recording to the producer of the sound recording, he retains the right to equitable remuneration for the rental.

The CDPA also contains provisions relating to delivery up and seizure of illicit recordings which are outside the scope of this book.

The UK Patent Office has issued a consultation paper on the possible implementation of moral rights for performers, namely the right to be identified as the performer when a performance is used and the right to object to distortion, mutilation or other modification of a performance which is prejudicial to the honour of the performer. The results of this consultation process are yet to be published at the time of writing.[287]

---

287 Implementation of performers' moral rights would bring the law into line with the World Intellectual Property Organisation Performances and Phonograms Treaty.

CHAPTER 7

THE PROTECTION OF TELEVISION FORMATS

The 'format' of a television show means the underlying features of the show. These could include distinctive themes or characters, the use of music or a catchphrase. Formats are valuable to the broadcast media. They define the distinctive character of popular programmes. The media guard them closely and will often take legal action to restrain a rival from copying popular formats.[1]

It is not uncommon for unsolicited formats to be submitted to a media entity for consideration – for example, if I think of a great idea for a game show, I might send it to the BBC or to another television station or production company in the hope that they will commission it. If the recipient does not commission my idea, but subsequently makes its own programme on a similar theme, what redress will be available to me for the unauthorised use?

This chapter examines the extent to which the law provides protection against the copying of formats. Many of the issues considered have already been analysed in Chapters 5 and 6. The reader should refer to those chapters for detail on the points set out below. The aim of this chapter is to draw together the various strands in order to provide an overall picture in a practical context.

COPYRIGHT PROTECTION

Copyright works

Copyright subsists in the types of work which are set out in the Copyright, Designs and Patents Act 1988 (CDPA). The types of work put in place by the CDPA do not include formats as such. But formats usually consist of various features. Some of these features taken individually may be copyright works. The following are examples of this.

---

1   An example of this type of action occurred in *Green v Broadcasting Corpn of New Zealand* [1989] 2 All ER 1056, which is considered below.

Written material and music

Copyright will exist in original written proposals and scripts (literary works), artistic material (for example, storyboards) (artistic works) and music (for example, theme tunes and jingles) (musical works). The more detailed the material, the easier it will be to establish that copyright subsists in it. Titles, catch phrases and slogans are unlikely to attract copyright protection (see Chapter 6 for further detail). They can, however, often be protected by trade mark registrations (the trade mark registration system is described in Chapter 14) or in some cases by way of an action in passing off (this is also considered in Chapter 14).

Dramatic format

Copyright may subsist in the dramatic format of television shows as an original dramatic work. A dramatic work is a work of action which is capable of being performed in public.[2]

In *Green v Broadcasting Corpn of New Zealand*,[3] the claimant sought to restrain the defendant from broadcasting a television programme which was similar to the claimant's *Opportunity Knocks* show. Opportunity Knocks was essentially a talent show which was presented in a particular manner incorporating certain original features. The claimant relied on copyright in the 'dramatic format' of the show. The dramatic format on which he based his case was not the overall show, but the distinctive features which were repeated in each programme. These consisted of the programme title, the use of certain catch phrases and the use of a device known as a clapometer which measured audience reaction to competitors' performances.

In essence, what the claimant sought to do was to isolate these constant features of the series from the material which changed in each show (for example, the performers' acts). The court found that the features selected by the claimant were too nebulous to be protected by copyright. The court stated that 'a dramatic work must have sufficient unity to be capable of performance and that the features claimed as constituting the 'format' of a television show being unrelated to each other except as accessories to be used in the presentation of some other dramatic or musical performance, lack the essential characteristic'.

Opportunity Knocks was essentially a talent show, the general formula of which is not in itself original. Where the format for a show is original, or where the new features are more substantial and unified than they were in the

---

2   *Norowzian v Arks (No 2)* [2000] EMLR 1.
3   *Green v Broadcasting Corpn of New Zealand* [1989] 2 All ER 1056.

Opportunity Knocks case, it might be possible for a claimant to establish that copyright subsists in a dramatic format as a dramatic work.

Copyright infringement

Copyright will be infringed where a substantial part of the work has been reproduced without consent. 'Substantial' is a test of the quality of what has been reproduced rather than the quantity. If a small, but key, part of the material/format is taken, that might infringe copyright in the material.

The claimant must demonstrate the fact that copying has taken place, but if it can adduce evidence to show that the alleged copyist had access to the material which has been reproduced, and if it can also be shown that there is sufficient similarity between the copyright work and the alleged copy, the two factors taken together will create an inference that copying has taken place which the defendant must displace, for example, by showing that its material pre-dates the claimant's material.

Hints and tips under copyright law

In order to support a claim under copyright law, evidence which shows that the material which makes up the format is original should be retained. These might include scripts, drafts, briefings, artwork and other relevant documents. Details of the identity of the creator(s) and the relevant dates should also be kept.

The retention of this type of information will also assist those faced with a copyright claim against them to prove that their work has not been copied from the claimant's material.

It is advisable that the symbol which denotes the existence of copyright (©) followed by the copyright owner's name and the year when the work was first created, is used on all works. It should be shown prominently, for example, on any title page or at the foot of artwork. Whilst the symbol does not in itself confer rights on the copyright owner, it informs third parties that copyright is claimed in the material. It can therefore operate as a deterrent to potential copyists.

Protection for formats: the future for copyright law

In 1996, the patent office produced a consultation paper on a proposal for copyright protection for programme formats as copyright works in their own right. So far as the author is aware, there are no firm proposals for the law to be amended in line with the proposals. However, developments in this area may well take place in the near future.

Further details about copyright infringement claims are contained in Chapter 6.

BREACH OF CONFIDENCE

An action for breach of confidence can prevent the unauthorised use of formats even where copyright protection cannot be claimed. It will, however, apply only where the format has not been made public.

There is a broad principle recognised in law that a party who receives information in confidence, either directly or indirectly, should not profit from the unauthorised use of that information. The principle applies not only to the original recipient of the information, but also, as a general rule, to any subsequent recipient of the information, provided that the subsequent recipients are on notice of the obligation in confidence.

The principle requires that the following criteria should be satisfied:

* the information must not be known to the general public;
* it must have been imparted in circumstances importing an obligation of confidentiality, whether express or implied;
* there must be unauthorised use of the information to the detriment of the person who originally supplied it.[4]

The confidential information or idea can be in writing or oral. To be capable of protection, the idea must be sufficiently developed in the sense that it is an identifiable idea which is capable of being realised as an actuality.[5] It should be at a development stage where it has some attractiveness as an advertisement or promotion. This does not necessarily mean that it has to be in the form of a full synopsis or script. It does not necessarily have to be developed to the same extent as would be required under copyright law.

The information must be original in the sense that it is not yet in the public domain. It must also be new. Originality can either mean a significant new twist or slant to a well known concept or a completely new idea.

The obligation of confidence

The obligation of confidence does not have to be provided for expressly. But in the interests of certainty it is always preferable to have a written agreement signed by all relevant parties confirming the existence and the terms of the duty of confidence.

4   *Coco v AN Clark (Engineers) Ltd* (1969) 86 RPC 41; [1968] FSR 415.
5   *Fraser v Thames Television* [1983] 2 All ER 101; *De Maudsley v Palumbo* [1996] FSR 447.

For the sake of clarity, it will help if confidential material submitted to third parties is clearly labelled as such (although merely labelling material as confidential will not guarantee that it will be found to have that status. The question whether material is confidential focuses on substance rather than form). An express statement that material is confidential which is accepted on that basis will create a presumption that the information has been imparted in confidence.

Case law indicates that where information or ideas of a commercial or industrial value are given on a businesslike basis with some avowed common object in mind, for example, a joint venture, there is a presumption that an obligation of confidence exists even where there is no express obligation in place.[6] Any person seeking to show that there was, in fact, no implied obligation of confidence, will have a heavy burden to discharge.

In industries where there is generally perceived to be an ethical or moral obligation to treat ideas or information as being submitted in confidence, that perception will give rise to a presumption that an obligation of confidence exists.

How to protect confidential information

The information should be in writing for reasons of certainty. Where disclosures are made orally, they should be confirmed in writing. Confidential information should be clearly labelled as such.

The fact that the information has been submitted in confidence should be stated clearly and in writing. Ideally, a confidentiality agreement should be drawn up and signed by all relevant parties. Such an agreement need not be complex. They may take the form of a one page letter.[7]

Confidential information should be kept secure.

Recipients of confidential information

Recipients of information which may be confidential, for example, unsolicited ideas for programmes, should safeguard their position against claims for breach of confidence. To help them to rebut any such claim, they should make a note of exactly what has been disclosed to them, on what basis, by whom and to whom. Often, claims for breach of confidence are difficult to defend because the defendant has no record of the above details.

All relevant development material should be recorded in writing and retained with a view to demonstrating that the complainant's idea has not been copied or otherwise made use of.

---

6   *Fairie v Reed* (1994) unreported.
7   The contents of a typical confidentiality agreement are considered in Chapter 17.

Where recipients do not intend to make use of a proposal which is contained in unsolicited material, the material should be returned to the recipient with a note indicating that the recipient is not interested in the material. The note should state that copies of the material have not been retained. Such a step will help to avoid future proceedings for breach of confidence.

The law relating to breach of confidence was considered in more detail in Chapter 5.

CHAPTER 8

PRIVACY AND THE MEDIA

Newspapers are there to expose: that is their function. At their best, the media expose crooks, spies and fraudsters, although at their worst they intrude into private lives when no public interest is served. The difficulty is obviously in drawing a line.[1]

The judges are pen-poised, regardless of incorporation of the Convention, to develop a right to privacy to be protected by common law. This is not me saying so: they have said so. It must be emphasised that the judges are free to develop the common law in their own judicial sphere.[2]

THE CONCEPT OF PRIVACY: WHAT IS PROTECTED?

At the present time, there is no satisfactory definition in law of the concept of 'privacy'. Attempts to introduce a statutory tort of infringement of privacy have tended to fall at the preliminary hurdle of securing a definition of the concept for which protection is sought.

In its 1972 Report, the Younger Committee[3] expressed the view that privacy was not capable of being satisfactorily defined – of the available definitions, the committee thought 'either they go very wide, equating the right to privacy with the right to be let alone, or they boil down to a catalogue of assorted values to which the adjective 'private' or 'personal' can reasonably, but not exclusively, be attached'. There is an obvious danger that a wide privacy law will make it difficult for the media to perform the watchdog function to which the European Court of Human Rights attaches great importance.[4]

The 1990 Calcutt Committee on privacy and related matters agreed with the Younger Committee that there was little possibility of producing a precise definition of privacy.[5] It adopted a working definition with reference to the media in the following terms:

> The right of the individual to be protected against intrusion into his personal life or affairs, or those of his family, by direct physical means or by publication of information.

---

1   Sir Norman Fowler, *Hansard*, 17.6.1998, col 404.
2   The Lord Chancellor, *Hansard*, 3.11.1997, col 1229.
3   *Report of the Committee on Privacy*, Cmnd 5012, 1972.
4   See, eg, *Observer v UK* (1991) 14 EHRR 153.
5   *Report of the Committee on Privacy and Related Matters*, Cmnd 1102, 1990.

The Calcutt Committee was of the view that a right to privacy in this form could include protection from physical intrusion, publication of hurtful or embarrassing personal material (whether true or false), publication of inaccurate or misleading personal material, or publication of photographs or recordings of an individual taken without consent.

The Committee also observed that it was not possible to lay down a definitive benchmark against which to judge whether material does or does not infringe privacy. The decision of what constitutes an unwarranted infringement of privacy could only be made in a particular case in terms relative: (a) to that subject's status and conduct; and (b) in the context of what is socially acceptable at the time.

In the view of the Calcutt Committee, the application of any test for violation of privacy involves a value judgment based on the attitudes and perceptions of society generally at the time of publication. The British public as a whole likes to see human interest stories – especially where they involve well known figures. In the review of press self-regulation which followed on from the 1990 Calcutt Report, Sir David Calcutt observed that many of the highly publicised cases involving alleged violations of privacy of well known figures by the press had led to significant increases in the circulation of the newspapers concerned.[6] Yet the public mood can be subject to swift changes. In the wake of the death of Diana, Princess of Wales, there was a public backlash against the methods of the paparazzi employed in taking the very photographs which the public had so loved to see. The editor of *The Sun* misjudged the public mood in 1999 when he published, on the eve of her marriage, photographs of Sophie Rhys Jones 'cavorting' with a well known media personality. The public uproar generated by the photographs led to a stern reprimand from the PCC and a public apology from the newspaper's editor in the following terms:

> Publication of the photograph has caused an outcry and *The Sun* now realises its mistake.[7]

The Sun misjudged the mood, but perhaps it was an understandable error in this shady area of the public-private divide if one of the determining factors is something as changeable as the public's taste.

The precise ambit of a person's privacy becomes crucial when we begin to talk of a protectable right enforceable at law. If an issue which essentially involves a value judgment becomes subject to legal control, any error in the exercise of the value judgment will sound in legal remedies. On that basis, defining the extent of any legally enforceable right of 'privacy' becomes of crucial importance to ensure that the media are aware of the standards with which they must comply.

6   Sir David Calcutt QC, *Review of Press Self-Regulation*, Cmnd 2135, 1990.
7   (1999) *The Sun*, 27 May.

The importance of setting down the nature and ambit of the right to privacy is reflected in the jurisprudence of the European Convention on Human Rights. A right to privacy operates as a limitation on freedom of expression (the freedom enshrined in Art 10 of the Convention). If privacy is to be a justifiable restriction to freedom of expression, it must be prescribed by law. This requirement is considered in some detail in Chapter 1. The gist of the requirement is that the restriction must have a basis in law *and the law must be sufficiently precise to enable a citizen to regulate his conduct*.[8] A privacy law which is dependent on arbitrary considerations, such as personal taste, is unlikely to satisfy this requirement.

In *R v Broadcasting Standards Commission ex p BBC*,[9] Lord Mustill gave his opinion on the nature of privacy in the following terms:

> To my mind, the privacy of a human being denotes the personal 'space' in which the individual is free to be itself, and also the carapace, or shell, or umbrella, or whatever other metaphor is preferred, which protects that space from intrusion. An infringement of privacy is an affront to personality, which is damaged both by the violation and by the demonstration that the personal space is not inviolate ...

This analysis of privacy is centred not so much on the sensibilities of the general public in determining what is or is not acceptable, but on the psychological damage to the individual whose rights have been violated. The right flows from the feeling of violation rather than the social *mores* of the time. This offers a more certain basis from which the law may develop.

Whose privacy may be violated?

Another reason why it is so important to pinpoint the nature and extent of the right to privacy is in order to determine who will be able to maintain an action for violation of the right. In particular, is the right limited to individuals (as the Calcutt report envisaged) or may companies and other bodies corporate bring proceedings too? In the *BBC* case referred to above,[10] Lord Mustill expressed the view that, because a company is an impersonal entity without personal sensitivities which might be wounded or a 'selfhood' to protect, he found it difficult to square his concept of privacy with a body corporate.[11] His

---

8   *Sunday Times v UK* (1979) 2 EHRR 242, para 49.

9   *R v Broadcasting Standards Commission ex p BBC* (2000) unreported, 6 April, CA.

10   *Ibid*.

11   The first instance decision of Forbes J in *R v BSC ex p BBC* (1999) unreported, 6 July, (which was overruled by the Court of Appeal) contained an analysis of the jurisprudence of the European Court of Human Rights in relation to Art 8 (respect for private and family life) and Art 9 (freedom of thought, conscience and religion). This analysis was conspicuously lacking in the Court of Appeal judgment. On his analysis, Forbes J agreed with Lord Mustill's opinion that a company could not entertain an action for violation of its right to privacy.

views are *obiter*, but the speech is likely to operate as a strong persuasive authority.

The law in England pre-Human Rights Act

To date, English common law has not recognised an enforceable right to privacy as a cause of action *per se*. The Court of Appeal decision in *Kaye v Robertson* graphically illustrated the judiciary's reluctance to affirm an enforceable right to privacy.[12]

In that case, the Court of Appeal granted a limited injunction restraining the defendants from publishing anything which could be reasonably understood to covey to a reader that Mr Kaye had voluntarily permitted the photographs to be taken or the interview to take place. The court held that on the application for an interim injunction Mr Kaye could make out a sufficiently strong case that any such representation would amount to a malicious falsehood.[13]

The court did not restrain publication of the material altogether. It professed its hands to be tied. Glidewell LJ observed: 'It is well known that in English law there is no right to privacy, and accordingly there is no right of action for breach of a person's privacy. The facts of the present case are a graphic illustration of the desirability of Parliament considering whether and in what circumstances statutory provision can be made to protect the privacy of individuals.'

All of the Appeal Court judges expressed regret that the common law did not grant Mr Kaye an enforceable right of privacy which would enable him to restrain any publication of the interview or photographs. However, all three Appeal Court judges thought that any such right could only be recognised by the Parliament.[14]

Although English law does not presently enforce a general right to privacy, it does afford protection to various interests which may be categorised as aspects of 'privacy'.

The protection it offers is patchy – relying not on one discrete cause of action, but rather from a hotchpotch of law drawn from various sources.

The prime sources are as follows:

---

12 *Kaye v Robertson* [1991] FSR 62.

13 This aspect of the decision was considered further in Chapter 4.

14 Eg, Bingham LJ: '... the right has so long been disregarded here that it can be reconciled now only by the legislature.' For criticism of the conservative nature of this decision, see Sherman and Kaganas. 'The protection of personality and image – an opportunity lost' [1991] 9 EIPR 340 and, more generally, Lester, A, 'English judges as law makers' [1993] PL 269.

RIGHT TO PRIVACY OF CERTAIN
PHOTOGRAPHS AND FILMS

Section 85 of the Copyright, Designs and Patents Act (CDPA) 1988 sets out a narrow right of privacy in the following terms:

> A person who for *private and domestic purposes* commissions the taking of a photograph or the making of a film has, where copyright subsists in the resulting work, the right not to have:
>
> (a) copies of the work issued to the public;
>
> (b) the work exhibited or shown in public; or
>
> (c) the work broadcast or included in a cable programme service,
>
> and ... a person who does or authorises the doing of any of those acts infringes the right.

There are a few exceptions to the right which are set out in s 85(2) of the CDPA, most notably for the incidental inclusion of the work in an artistic work, film, broadcast or cable programme.[15]

The following points should be noted about this right:

- the right belongs to the person who commissions the photograph or film. That person may not be the subject of the material. There is, therefore, no guarantee that the subject will be able to prevent the exploitation of the material where they did not commission it;

- the photograph or film must have been commissioned for a private and domestic purpose. Commissions for commercial purposes will not give rise to a right of privacy under this section;

- if a photographer takes a photograph on a private occasion, the right of privacy under this section will not apply. The photograph must have actually been commissioned for a private and domestic purpose. The CDPA does not define 'commission'. It is not therefore clear whether a mere request that the photograph be taken can amount to commission or whether something more formal would be required;

- copyright must subsist in the photograph or film before the right of privacy can arise. The right of privacy will continue to subsist only so long as copyright subsists in the work.[16]

---

15 CDPA 1988, s 31.
16 *Ibid*, s 86.

HARASSMENT

Where the infringement of privacy takes the form of harassment by the media, the subject of the intrusive conduct can seek redress under the causes of action set out below.

The Protection from Harassment Act 1997

The Act introduces two criminal offences[17] and a statutory tort.[18]

Section 1 of the Act is a general prohibition on conduct which amounts to harassment or which the defendant knew or ought to know amounts to harassment (an objective test). Unhelpfully, the Act does not define what is meant by harassment. It goes some way to confining the concept within limits, in that it provides that a course of conduct will not amount to harassment if the defendant shows that it was pursued for the purpose of preventing or detecting crime or if it was carried out under any enactment or rule of law or that in the particular circumstances the pursuit of the course of conduct was reasonable.

The lack of a definition of harassment makes the Act unacceptably wide. In *DPP v Selvanayagam*,[19] Collins J indicated that 'whatever may have been the purpose behind the Act, its words are clear and it can cover harassment of any sort'. The definition could easily extend to harassment by the media, including conduct such as persistent telephone calls, 'doorstepping' or prolonging contact with a subject when he/she has made it clear they wish to terminate it. There is no defence that the harassment was for the purposes of reporting material which is in the public interest.

The criminal offences

Section 2 provides for an offence of harassment triable on summary conviction and carrying a maximum penalty of imprisonment for a term not exceeding six months and/or a fine not exceeding level 5 on the standard scale.

Section 4 creates a more serious offence where the accused is guilty of a course of conduct which causes another to fear, on at least two occasions, that violence will be used against him where the accused knows or ought to know (an objective test) that his course of conduct will cause the other to fear on each of those occasions.

---

17 Protection from Harassment Act 1997, ss 2 and 4.
18 *Ibid*, s 3.
19 *DPP v Selvanayagam* (1999) *The Times*, 23 June.

It is a defence to the s 4 offence for the accused to show that the course of conduct was pursued for the purpose of preventing or detecting crime, or was pursued under any enactment or rule of law or that it was reasonable for the protection of himself or another or for the protection of his or another's property.

A person guilty of the s 4 offence is liable on conviction on indictment to imprisonment for a term not exceeding five years or a fine or both or on summary conviction to imprisonment for a term not exceeding six months or a fine not exceeding the statutory maximum or both.

Where a defendant is charged under s 4, the court may find him not guilty under s 4, but guilty under of the lesser offence provided for in s 2.

In addition to the above penalties, the court is also empowered to make a restraining order under s 5 of the Act for the purpose of protecting the victim or any other person mentioned in the order from further conduct which amounts to harassment or which will cause a fear of violence. Breach of the restraining order is itself a criminal offence carrying the same sanctions as the s 4 offence.

The civil cause of action

Section 3 provides that an actual or apprehended breach of the s 1 prohibition may be the subject of a claim in civil proceedings by the person who is or may be the victim of the course of conduct in question. The Act provides that amongst the available remedies are damages to compensate for anxiety caused by the harassment and any financial loss caused by the harassment. The remedies also include an injunction.

The breach by the defendant of an injunction made under s 3 is not punishable as a contempt of court in the usual way.[20] Instead, a specific criminal offence is committed where the breach was without reasonable excuse.[21] The offence carries a maximum penalty of indictment of imprisonment for a term not exceeding five years or a fine or both and on summary conviction a term of imprisonment not exceeding six months or a fine not exceeding the statutory maximum or both.

Harassment and the common law

The Protection from Harassment Act provides the most likely avenue for redress at law for an individual who feels harassed by the media. The common law offers a more speculative cause of action which could also be

---

20 Protection from Harassment Act 1997, s 3(7).

21 *Ibid*, s 3(6).

employed against the media. The case of *Wilkinson v Downton*[22] established that an intentional act of a defendant which is calculated to cause harm to the claimant (calculated is used in the sense of meaning 'likely to') is a tort actionable at common law. Physical harm includes psychiatric illness, but would not, as the law currently stands, include simple emotional distress. The *Wilkinson* case concerned a practical joke played by the defendant, who told the claimant that her husband had been involved in an accident and was badly injured. As a result of this news, the claimant suffered nervous shock which made her physically ill.

In the more recent case of *Khorasandijian v Bush*,[23] the Court of Appeal seemed to favour an extension of the scope of the *Wilkinson v Downton* tort to cover harassment. The court recognised that there was an obvious risk that the cumulative effect of persistent unwanted telephone calls to the claimant would cause her physical illness or psychiatric harm if they were not restrained by interim injunction. In *Hunter v Canary Wharf*,[24] Lord Hoffman went further and expressed the view (on an *obiter* basis) that distress, inconvenience or discomfort caused by harassment may be sufficient in themselves to give rise to liability without the need to show actual damage to physical or mental health or the likelihood of such damage.

DATA PROTECTION

Data protection laws impose an important restraint on the uses to which information about individuals may be put. They offer vital protection for privacy. The Data Protection Act 1998 is considered in Chapter 9.

INDIRECT PROTECTION FOR PRIVACY VIA THE ENFORCEMENT OF INTERESTS IN LAND

Protection for privacy may be indirectly secured where the claimant has an interest in land which is the subject of interference by the defendant. The two principal ways in which the protection may be secured are as follows:

Trespass to land

A defendant may be liable for trespass to land if he enters or remains on land which belongs to the claimant without permission. The claimant must own an

---

22   *Wilkinson v Downton* [1897] 2 QB 57.
23   *Khorasandijian v Bush* [1993] 3 All ER 669.
24   *Hunter v Canary Wharf* [1997] 2 All ER 426, p 451.

interest in the land (freehold or leasehold) or have a right to exclusive occupation in order to have a cause of action.[25] A tenant in possession or a licensee with exclusive possession can also sue. However, a mere licensee or occupier cannot. In the *Kaye* case referred to above, Mr Kaye was unable to bring a claim in trespass against *The Sport* in respect of their unauthorised entry into his hospital room because he did not have the necessary proprietary interest.[26]

In order to give rise to a claim of trespass to land, there must be an entry onto the claimant's land. If photographs of the claimant are taken from a public highway or from land on which the claimant has no interest, an action in trespass will be available to the claimant.[27]

In *Baron Bernstein v Skyviews*,[28] an aerial photograph of the claimant's property was taken without his consent. The claimant sued for trespass. The court held that a landowner's rights in the air space above his land extended only to such height as is necessary for the ordinary use and enjoyment of his land. Above that height, he has no greater rights in the air space than any other member of the public.

If a defendant has a right of action, he does not have to prove actual damage in order to bring a claim. Where a claim for trespass is brought in circumstances where the action essentially concerns an infringement of privacy, the measure of damages is likely to be small, unless an award for aggravated or exemplary damages is also made. An injunction may be awarded to restrain any further trespass.

Nuisance

The tort of nuisance will lie for any activity causing a substantial and unreasonable interference with a claimant's land or his use or enjoyment of his land. The tort is directed at protecting the claimant's enjoyment of his rights over his land. As with trespass, the cause of action will only lie at the suit of a person who has a right to the land affected. The primary remedy is compensation for the diminution of the value of the land and/or to the amenity of the land and an injunction. Compensation will not be awarded for personal injury or interference with personal enjoyment.[29]

To be an actionable nuisance, the activity must cause substantial interference with the above interests. In the *Bernstein* case,[30] the court held

---

25   *Hickman v Maisey* [1900] 1 QB 752.

26   *Kaye v Robertson* [1991] FSR 62.

27   *Hickman v Maisey* [1900] 1 QB 752.

28   *Baron Bernstein v Skyviews* [1978] QB 479.

29   *Hunter v Canary Wharf* [1997] 2 All ER 426.

30   *Baron Bernstein v Skyviews* [1978] QB 479.

that the taking of a single photograph of the claimant's property was not an actionable nuisance. However, the judge opined on an *obiter* basis that, had the circumstances been such that the claimant had been subjected to the harassment of constant surveillance of his house from the air, accompanied by the photographing of his every activity, then that might amount to an actionable nuisance for which the court would grant relief. But in reality the remedy would not have been for infringement of privacy *per se*, but rather for the impairment of the claimant's use of and enjoyment of his property.

THE REGULATION OF THE INTERCEPTION OF COMMUNICATIONS

Where telephone conversations or postal communications are the subject of unauthorised interception, a criminal offence is committed.

The Wireless Telegraphy Act 1949 prohibits the unauthorised use of wireless apparatus with intent to obtain information about the contents of any message being sent through the postal or telecommunications system.

The Interception of Communications Act 1985 creates a criminal offence of unlawful (that is, unauthorised) interception of communications by post or by a public telecommunications system (it does not apply to cordless telephones).[31] The Act also does not apply to the use of bugs or other types of listening apparatus planted in a room (even if the effect of the apparatus is to pick up the contents of telephone conversations). Nor does the Act apply to the interception of telephone conversations on internal telephone systems.

New interception of telecommunications legislation is due to come into force in the near future (the Regulation of Investigatory Powers Act 2000). The Act will amend the law to take into account technological developments and the rights of individuals.[32] The Act will place the interception of telephone conversations on internal telephone systems on a statutory footing for the first time. The Government's proposals will extend the law to all telecommunications networks, to communications carried by wireless telegraphy and mail delivery systems. The new legislation is intended to cover communications sent by e-mail and fax and pager communications.[33]

---

31 *R v Effick* [1994] 3 WLR 583.

32 The European Court of Human Rights has found that the absence of any basis in law for the regulation of the interception of telephone conversations on internal systems is a violation of Art 8 of the Convention: *Halford v UK* (1997) 24 EHRR 523.

33 The Act received Royal Assent on 28 July 2000. The majority of the Act's provisions are not yet in force.

REPORTING RESTRICTIONS AND THE COURTS

The privacy of individuals is sometimes safeguarded by reporting restrictions imposed on the media by the courts during trials. The overriding aim of such restrictions is generally the administration of justice rather than the protection of privacy.

These restrictions are considered in detail in Chapter 10.

PRIVACY BY ANY OTHER NAME

If the defendant's activities are not covered by the above specific actions set out above, a claimant seeking redress for infringement of his right to privacy must rely on other areas of the law, just as Gorden Kaye had to. A typical claimant might bring a claim for copyright infringement, defamation, malicious falsehood, passing off and/or breach of confidence provided he can satisfy the requirements of the various causes of action. But the substance of the complaint essentially concerns a violation of his privacy. Of these existing causes of action, the most significant is breach of confidence. The flexible nature of this cause of action has offered the courts a method of fashioning a *de facto* remedy for privacy where the breach of confidence involves personal information. The development of the law in this area, and the limitations of breach of confidence as a way of protecting privacy, were examined in Chapter 5.

In view of the difficulties in fashioning a satisfactory definition of privacy *per se*, this piecemeal protection might be considered to be the most satisfactory solution to an insoluble problem. But is it really? At the very least, the protection of privacy is dependent upon the claimant coincidentally being able to satisfy the requirements of what are often quite unconnected causes of action. A reading of the *Kaye* decision vividly reveals how deserving complaints can slip through the cracks.

Reliance on these disparate causes of action in order to protect privacy often results in claimants having to assert contrived claims in order to meet the criteria giving rise to any of the causes of action. For example, in the *Kaye* case, the claimant was forced to extract the implied falsehood that he had consented to publication in order to obtain what was, in any event, only partial relief. The real claim was the fact that the newspaper had intruded upon his privacy in the most blatant way, for which he was unable to obtain any redress.

Example

Consider a case involving the publication of a photograph of a public figure walking along a public street arm in arm with a new lover. The public figure wishes to keep this relationship secret in order to protect his partner from media scrutiny. The publication has not involved any conduct which amounts to harassment, nor has it involved the interception of communications or the interference with the claimant's land. What action might a claimant take?

There is at present no cause of action for infringement of privacy.

If the photograph has not been doctored in any way, it will depict a factually correct situation. An action for defamation will not succeed if the publication is true (the defendant could rely on the defence of justification). A claim for malicious falsehood will also not be available if the information is true.

A claim for copyright infringement will only be available if the publication involves the reproduction of a copyright work in which the claimant owns copyright. Under copyright law, copyright belongs to the photographer, rather than the subject.

Passing off is unlikely to be available unless the publication takes the form of a misrepresentation by the defendant which causes or is likely to cause damage to the claimant's trading reputation. This is unlikely on these facts.

The most likely cause of action is breach of confidence, provided that the personal material is confidential and the information is the subject of an express or implied obligation of confidence on the part of the defendant. But if the client was walking quite openly along a street and the photographer did not have to engage in surreptitious activity to take the picture, it may be difficult to satisfy these requirements.

The claimant may be without any form of relief.

The detailed requirements of the above causes of action are considered in more detail in the relevant subject chapters.

PRIVACY AND THE HUMAN RIGHTS ACT 1998

The question whether the Human Rights Act 1998 will give rise to the development of a privacy law was considered in Chapter 1. The Lord Chancellor has made clear that, in his view, the courts will not be empowered to create a common law right to privacy unless there is sufficient in the existing common law to enable them to fashion such a remedy. In his opinion, the courts will be able to fashion such a remedy by continuing to apply the existing law of trespass, nuisance, copyright and confidentiality. The shortcomings of such development are considered above.

In 1997, the then Lord Chief Justice, Lord Bingham, also indicated that, in his view, Parliament would not need to introduce a statutory law of privacy. Instead, he predicted that a privacy law would develop through individual cases before the courts as an 'inevitable' consequence of the incorporation of the European Convention on Human Rights into British law.[34] What remains to be seen is whether the courts will continue to try to fit a law to protect privacy into the confines of the existing causes of action as the Lord Chancellor envisages or whether, given time, the courts will enforce a right of privacy *per se*.

In the remainder of this chapter we examine the privacy provisions of the media industry Codes of Practice. We also examine the relationship between the law and the Codes and whether that relationship could over time lead to the development of a *de facto* legal standard for the protection of privacy.

PRIVACY AND THE REGULATORY CODES

Whilst the law does not generally recognise a right of privacy *per se*, the various Codes of Practice which regulate the activities of the media all contain provisions relating to privacy. The fact that the media has complied with the relevant Code – or has not – is a factor that the court should consider when deciding whether to grant relief, although it is not determinative. Section 12 was considered in more detail in Chapter 1.

The Codes share a common feature that compliance with their provisions is not an obligation as a matter of law. A breach of the Codes does not necessarily mean that the defendant has behaved unlawfully. However, the scheme of s 12 of the Human Rights Act will mean that the provisions of the Codes are likely to come under close scrutiny by the courts in cases involving assertions of infringement of privacy.

The press

The Press Complaints Commission Code of Practice as a whole, and the system of self-regulation generally, is considered in Chapter 16. The provisions of the Code which are relevant to privacy are as follows.

---

34   (1997) *The Times*, 9 October.

Privacy

(a) Everyone is entitled to respect for his or her private and family life, home, health and correspondence. A publication will be expected to justify intrusions into any individual's private life without consent.

(b) The use of long lens photography to take pictures of people in private places without their consent is unacceptable.

Private places are public or private property where there is a reasonable expectation of privacy.

The Code provides that there may be exceptions to the above where includes they can be demonstrated to be in the public interest.[35] The public interest *includes* (but is not limited to):

(a) detecting or exposing crime or serious misdemeanour;

(b) protecting public health and safety;

(c) preventing the public being misled by some statement or action of an individual or organisation.

In any case where the public interest is invoked, the PCC will require a full explanation by the editor demonstrating how the public interest was served. The Code recognises that there is a public interest in freedom of expression itself. It provides that the Commission will therefore have regard to the extent to which material has, or is about to, become available to the public. In cases involving children, editors must demonstrate an exceptional public interest to override the normally paramount interests of the child.

The Code also contains provisions relating to *harassment* in the following terms at cl 4:

(a) journalists and photographers must neither obtain nor seek to obtain information or pictures through intimidation, harassment or persistent pursuit;

(b) they must not photograph individuals in private places (as defined above) without their consent; must not persist in telephoning questioning, pursuing or photographing individuals after being asked to desist; must not remain on their property after being asked to leave and must not follow them;

(c) editors must ensure that those working for them comply with these requirements and must not publish material from other sources which does not meet these requirements.

Clause 8 of the Code prohibits the obtaining and publication of material obtained by the use of *clandestine listening devices* or the *interception of private telephone conversations*.

---

35 Public interest is defined in cl 1.

The provisions on harassment and the use of listening devices can be overridden in the public interest as defined above.

Special rules apply to *children*. The Code states as follows (cl 6):

(a) young people should be free to complete their time at school without unnecessary intrusion;

(b) journalists must not interview or photograph a child under the age of 16 on subjects involving the welfare of the child or any other child in the absence of or without the consent of a parent or other adult who is responsible for the children;

(c) pupils must not be approached or photographed while at school without the permission of the school authorities;

(d) there must be no payment to minors for material involving the welfare of children nor payments to parents or guardians for material about their children or wards unless it is demonstrably in the child's interest;

(e) where material about the private life of a child is published there must be justification for publication other than the fame, notoriety or position of his or her parents or guardian.

Although the provisions relating to children can be overridden in the public interest, the Code makes clear that the publication concerned should be able to demonstrate an exceptional public interest, the privacy of the child normally taking precedence.

In Lord Wakeham's view, it is the third of these provisions prohibiting approaches to children on school premises without consent, which has been highly effective in protecting Princes William and Harry from press intrusions during their time at Eton – in effect, denying the photographers a market in the UK for any pictures which they take.[36]

Clause 5 of the Code provides that in cases involving *personal grief or shock*, inquiries should be carried out and approaches made with sympathy and discretion. Publication must be handled sensitively at such times (but this should not be interpreted as restricting the right to report judicial proceedings). This clause cannot be overridden in the public interest. Clause 9 of the Code refers to inquiries at *hospitals*. It provides that the restrictions on intruding into privacy are particularly relevant to inquiries about individuals in hospitals or similar institutions, again subject to public interest considerations.

Most of these provisions of the Code of Practice came into force in January 1998 and in part reflected public and media concern over press activity in the wake of the death of Diana, Princess of Wales. In the view of the PCC chairman, Lord Wakeham, they represent a 'substantial toughening' of the Code. By way of example, the specific reference to material obtained through

36   Speech to the Independent Schools Association, 8 May 1998.

persistent pursuit in the harassment provisions of the Code coupled with the onus on publications to ensure that the sources of their material have complied with the Code, is intended to stamp out the market in the UK for photographs of celebrities obtained from photographers who stalk, pursue or hound their subjects.

History of the Code

The first version of the PCC Code of Practice was promulgated in 1991 following the Report of the Committee on Privacy and Related Matters (the Calcutt report). The Calcutt report had proposed the terms of a Code to be implemented by the PCC, but the Code of Practice which was actually produced and implemented in the wake of the Calcutt report was one drafted by the *newspaper industry*. It differed in a number of significant respects from the Code put forward in the Calcutt report. The differences tended to shift the balance of the Code away from the public and in favour of the press. The January 1998 amendments to the Code which are referred to above have brought the Code more in line with the original recommendations in the Calcutt report, but there remain significant differences between the Code put forward by Calcutt and the Code of Practice which is currently in force.

The most significant of these remaining differences are as follows:

- the Code of Practice refers to an entitlement to respect for privacy and states that publications must be able to justify intrusions. The Calcutt wording had a different emphasis, stating that making inquiries about the personal lives of individuals and the publication of such material was not generally acceptable without consent. The starting point under Calcutt was prohibitive. Under the Code, the prohibitive approach has not been adopted, there is a reference to the need for respect unless an intrusion is justified, but this more permissive approach reads as more favourable to the press;

- Calcutt stated that an intrusion into an individual's private life could only be justified on certain grounds – namely, for detecting or exposing crime or seriously antisocial conduct, protecting public health or safety or preventing the public being misled by some public statement or action of the individual. The Calcutt Committee deliberately rejected a generalised 'public interest' exception to the basic prohibition observing that the term was not helpful in giving meaningful guidance as to whether an intrusion was justified or not – leaving the press to their own assessment as to what is or is not justifiable when probing into people's private lives. However, the industry Code of Practice refers to the 'public interest' generally. It gives a number of non-exhaustive instances of what might amount to publication in the public interest, but the concept of 'public interest' might extend much further than was envisaged by the Calcutt Committee. The danger here is that the press is prone to confuse the public interest with their own commercial interests in increasing their circulation figures;

- the Calcutt Code stated that journalists should not obtain their pictures through trespass. This was not reflected in the industry Code of Practice, which prohibits pictures taken through intimidation, harassment or persistent pursuit. The omission of trespass was justified by the press on the ground that it might be necessary for a journalist to trespass on private property to obtain information which would ultimately be in the public interest.

In his review of press self-regulation,[37] Sir David Calcutt was highly critical of the industry Code. In particular, he observed that the different treatment of 'public interest' significantly reduced the protection from that envisaged by the Calcutt Committee.

In order to get a flavour of the way in which the Code operates in practice, set out below are a number of random examples of PCC adjudications under the privacy provisions of the Code.

Paul Burrell v The Express on Sunday[38]

Paul Burrell is the fundraising manager of the Diana, Princess of Wales Memorial Fund. The newspaper published an article which asserted that he was paying the price of fame making intrusive references to his home and family life. He complained that the article was in breach of cl 3 of the Code (privacy).

The complaint was upheld. The PCC accepted that the claimant had always sought to maintain a division between his public role (in which he expected media scrutiny) and his private life. The article ignored that dividing line, eliding legitimate comment on his fundraising role with comment on his family life. The PCC did not accept that it was axiomatic that the family life of those involved in soliciting public donations to charities was a legitimate subject of media scrutiny and intrusion.

Private places

Begum Aga Khan and His Highness the Aga Khan v Daily Mail[39]

The complaint concerned a photograph showing the complainants on the deck of their yacht. The complainants alleged that the photograph had been published in breach of cl 3 (privacy) of the Code. They claimed that it must

---

37 Calcutt, D (Sir), QC, *Review of Press Self-Regulation*, Cmnd 2135, 1990.

38 (1998) PCC adjudication, 3 May.

39 (1998) PCC adjudication, 16 July.

have been taken from a private island near to where the yacht was moored to preserve privacy. The newspaper argued that the decks of the yacht was in full sight of casual observers, it was moored on the Mediterranean in the height of summer and was not therefore a place where the complainants could expect privacy. If they wanted privacy they should have gone below deck.

The PCC upheld the complaint. When the photograph had been taken, the complainants had been on board their private yacht, moored near a private island on which the general public was not allowed. This was a place where there was a reasonable expectation of privacy.

Sir Elton John v The Sport[40]

Sir Elton John complained that a photograph of guests relaxing in the privacy of his home in the South of France was a breach of cl 3 of the Code (privacy). He alleged that the photographs had been taken secretly, possibly from the top of a ladder placed against the wall of Sir Elton's property. The complaint was upheld. An individual had the right to respect for his home life. The taking of the photographs and the subsequent publication intruded into that home life and the privacy to which he and his guests were entitled. There was no public interest justification.

The newspaper argued that it obtained the pictures from a picture agency, which said that they had been taken from a public footpath adjacent to the property. This did not affect the Commission's decision against the newspaper.

Sir Paul McCartney v Hello![41]

Sir Paul McCartney complained about the publication of photographs of him with his family in Paris shortly after the death of his wife were in breach of cl 3 (privacy) and cl 5 (intrusion into grief and shock). The photographs showed him and his children walking through Paris and eating lunch outside a café. One picture showed the family inside Notre Dame cathedral. The editor of *Hello!* said that the pictures had been obtained from news agencies rather than being specially commissioned, and in addition that the picture in the cathedral had been added without her consent. She also made the point that the photographs depicted the family's very close relationship.

The PCC upheld the complaint. It stressed that the editor was responsible for the content of her publication. The fact that the pictures had been obtained from news agencies was irrelevant, as was the fact that a picture had been

---

40 (1998) PCC adjudication, 4 June.
41 (1998) PCC adjudication, 30 May.

added without her knowledge. The argument that the public interest was served by depicting the close relationship of the family was rejected.

The PCC 'deplored' the photograph in the cathedral. Journalists should respect the sanctity of acts of worship. The cathedral was a clear example of a place where there was a reasonable expectation of privacy.

Children

Blair v Mail on Sunday[42]

The Prime Minister, Tony Blair, and his wife complained that a story in the *Mail on Sunday* was in breach of cl 6 of the Code (children) and cl 1 (inaccuracy). The story concerned the decision of a certain secondary school to admit the Prime Minister's daughter, while rejecting local children. The article referred to suspicion that the school was operating an 'under the counter' selection policy.

The complaint was upheld. In relation to the cl 6 claim, the PCC observed that, while an article itself could be in the public interest, it was wrong to make an individual the focus of the story which could have been written without mentioning him or her. The reference to Tony Blair's daughter appeared to arise solely from the position of her father.

The Commission went on to consider whether there was an exceptional public interest which justified the reference to Miss Blair in the circumstances. It said that it believed it would be permissible to name the children of public figures in newspaper articles in a manner proportionate to the issues and facts involved in circumstances where:

- there is reasonable substance to a charge or allegation that provides the exceptional public interest required by the Code; and
- it is necessary to report the story and to identify the child because that child, and that child alone, had to be the centre of the story.

The Commission could find no justification for naming Miss Blair alone in connection with the admissions policy of the school nor, on the facts, was there reasonable substance to the allegations in question.

The Broadcasting Standards Commission

The BSC is the statutory body that monitors and sets standards and fairness in broadcasting. The Broadcasting Act 1996 places the BSC under a duty to draw up and review Codes of Practice on certain areas which include the unwarranted infringement of privacy in or in connection with the obtaining of

---

42 (1999) PCC adjudication, 20 July.

material to be included in programmes.[43] It is also the duty of the BSC to consider and adjudicate on complaints made to them under the Codes of Practice.[44] The BSC Codes of Practice are in part based on those of the former Broadcasting Standards Council, which the BSC replaced. The Codes apply to all broadcasters of radio and television programmes.

The Code on fairness and privacy provides that any invasion of privacy must be justified by an overriding public interest in the disclosure of the information. This, the Code provides, would include revealing or detecting crime or disreputable behaviour, protecting public health or safety, exposing misleading claims made by individuals or organisations or disclosing significant incompetence in public office.[45] Privacy may be infringed during the obtaining of material for a programme, even if none of the material is broadcast, as well as in the way in which material is used within a programme.[46]

The Code distinguishes people who are in the public eye through the position that they hold or the publicity they attract from non-public figures. However, it stresses that not all matters which are interesting to the public are in the public interest: 'Even where personal matters become the proper subject of inquiry, people in the public eye or their immediate family and friends do not forfeit the right to privacy, though there may be occasions when private behaviour raises wide public issues either through the nature of the behaviour itself or by the consequences of its becoming widely known. But any information broadcast should be significant as well as true.'[47]

In relation to non-public figures, the Code cautions that the private lives of most people are of no legitimate public interest and consent must generally be obtained in relation to the broadcast of information which is not in the public domain.[48]

The means of obtaining the information must also be proportionate to the matter under investigation.[49] The Code covers such issues as the use of hidden microphones and cameras,[50] the conduct and recording of telephone calls[51] and 'doorstepping'.[52] There are special provisions relating to dealings with individuals who are suffering and distressed,[53] and children.[54]

---

43 Broadcasting Act 1996, s 107.
44 *Ibid*, s 110.
45 Clause 14.
46 Clause 15.
47 Clause 17.
48 Clause 16.
49 Clause 14.
50 Clauses 18–21.
51 Clauses 22–24.
52 Clauses 25–27.
53 Clauses 28–31.
54 Clause 32.

The ITC Code

The ITC sets the standards for the programme content of commercial broadcasters. Its functions are not limited to adjudications on complaints. It has the power to require compliance with a range of effective sanctions which are considered in Chapter 16.

Section 2 of the ITC Programme Code regulates privacy and the gathering of information. The Code refers to the individual's right to privacy, but makes the point that there are occasions where the individual's right to privacy must be balanced against the public interest. 'Public interest' is not defined but, by way of example, the Code refers to the detection or exposure of crime or serious misdemeanour, the protection of public health and safety, preventing the public being misled by some statement or action of an individual or organisation or exposing significant incompetence in public office. The Code provides, that even where there is a public interest in the broadcast, the act in question must be proportional to the interest served.

Where members of the public are filmed or recorded in public places, the broadcaster must satisfy itself that the words spoken or actions taken by the individuals are sufficiently in the public domain to justify their broadcast without express permission being sought from the individuals concerned. Where they are not sufficiently in the public domain, consent should be sought.

Interviews or conversations conducted on the telephone should not normally be recorded for inclusion in a programme unless the interviewer has identified himself as speaking on behalf of the broadcaster, has described the general purpose of the programme and the interviewee gives consent to the use of the conversation in the programme. The Code provides that, in exceptional cases, these requirements may not be observed, for example, in relation to matters involving the investigation of allegedly criminal or disreputable behaviour. In such cases, the consent of the broadcaster's most senior programme executive should be sought before the material is broadcast and a record of such consents should be maintained and made available to the ITC on request.

The use of hidden microphones and cameras to record individuals who are aware that they are being recorded is acceptable only when it is clear that the material so acquired is essential to establish the credibility and authority of a story and where the story is equally clearly of important public interest. The Code provides that the consent of the broadcaster's most senior programme executive be obtained before the recording (where practicable) and the transmission of the material in question and that records of this consultation process should be kept and made available to the ITC on its request.

Interviews sought on private property without the subject's prior agreement should not be included in a programme unless they serve a public interest purpose. The same consideration applies to other places where the individual would reasonably expect personal privacy, such as restaurants and churches. Reporters and crews should leave 'media scrums' (involving large numbers of representatives from different organisations typically gathered outside the subject's home, the combined effect of which can be intimidating or unreasonably intrusive) unless there is a continuing public interest in their presence.

There are relatively few ITC adjudications or statements which concern violations of the right to privacy. In early 1998, the ITC issued a formal warning to Live TV for what it termed a serious breach of the Programme Code requirements on privacy. The violation concerned secretly filmed footage of Piers Merchant (a former MP) and a young woman in bed together, clearly indicating sexual activity between them. Mr Merchant had resigned as an MP a few days previously, following a storm of media activity about his alleged relationship with the woman in question.

As seen above, the Programme Code specifies that secretly filmed footage is acceptable only where it is acceptable to establish the credibility and authority of a story and where the story itself is clearly in the public interest. Live TV argued that the footage provided the first conclusive footage that Mr Merchant had consistently lied about his relationship with the woman, making the story one of important public interest. Only selected scenes had been shown – the more explicit material had been excluded.

The ITC did not accept these arguments. It concluded that the showing of such intimate and private material required a much stronger public interest justification. Further, the amount of footage shown exceeded that necessary to establish the credibility of the story.

Live TV had not itself shot the footage, but had acquired it from an independent source. It questioned whether such material should be treated in the same way under the Code. The ITC thought that the extent of the invasion of privacy was in no sense lessened by the material being supplied by an external source.

The Radio Authority also operates a Code of Practice which is in similar terms to the ITC Code.

The BBC producers' guidelines

The producers' guidelines contain comprehensive guidance about privacy and newsgathering. In general terms, they provide as follows:

They state that it is essential that the BBC operates within a framework which respect people's right to privacy, treats them fairly, yet allows the investigation of matters which it is the public interest to know about. Intrusions into privacy must accordingly be justified by the greater good.

Hidden recording and filming must only be used where appropriate, and records must be kept of consultations involving such techniques.

The guidelines make specific references to the privacy of public figures. They recognise that public figures are in a special position, but that they retain rights to a private life. The public should be given facts which bear upon the suitability and ability of the individual to perform their duties, but there is no general entitlement to know about their private behaviour unless broader public issues are raised either by the behaviour itself or by the consequences of it becoming widely known.

The Committee of Advertising Practice Code of Practice

The Committee of Advertising Practice Code of Practice is considered in relation to merchandising rights in Chapter 14.

Judicial review, the Codes and privacy

The ITC and the BSC have both been held to be susceptible to judicial review. By analogy, it is probable that the PCC would also be amenable, although the point is yet to be determined by the courts.[55] As we have seen in Chapter 1, it also probable that where a body is amenable to judicial review, it will also be a public authority for the purposes of the Human Rights Act 1998.

Decisions under the Codes of Practice might therefore be subject to review by the courts in the circumstances outlined in Chapter 2. Most applications to date have been based on a complaint that the body has acted unreasonably in reaching its decision or that it acted outside its authority. The courts have been able to resolve the application on the basis that the authority has acted within the scope of its authority (or not) and that the decision is one which a reasonable authority could have reached.

However, under the Human Rights Act there will be a new ground for judicial review where the body in question is claimed to have acted incompatibly with the Convention rights referred to in the Human Rights Act 1998[56] (which include the right to respect for home and family life under Art 8). A consideration of this type of claim will involve the courts answering either yes – the decision is compatible with Art 8, or no – it is not. Over time, a body of law on the scope and ambit of Art 8 is likely to emerge.

---

55 During the passage of the Human Rights Bill through Parliament, the Government indicated that the PCC would be a public authority for the purposes of ss 6 and 7 of the Act.

56 HRA 1998, ss 6 and 7.

Applications which concern the body's application and interpretation of the privacy provisions of the Codes have come before the courts on judicial review applications.

Examples

R v PCC ex p Stewart-Brady[57]

The applicant in that case was Ian Brady, one of the infamous 'moors murderers'. He was a patient at Ashworth Hospital. He sought judicial review of a PCC decision concerning an article which had appeared in *The Sun* accompanied by a photograph of Mr Brady in the hospital. The photograph had been taken with a long lens camera. Mr Brady complained that the photograph was a breach of clause of the privacy provisions of the Code of Practice together with provisions of the Code relating to hospitals and harassment. The PCC rejected the complaint. Mr Brady sought leave to apply for judicial review of the PCC's decision.

The Court of Appeal felt that the article was justified in the public interest; it concerned the treatment in hospitals of persons who had committed crimes. It then went on to consider whether the appearance of the photograph of Mr Brady alongside the article changed the public interest position. It observed that the photograph was indistinct and appeared to show Mr Brady in profile through the hospital window. Millett LJ observed that from looking at the photograph, it was not obvious that Mr Brady was in private or on private property.

Lord Woolf did not think that there had been a breach of the Code. His judgment is not as clear as it might have been on this point, but he appeared to be of the view that, given that the photographer had not intruded on private property, 'any privacy of the individual is completely removed'. Even if there was a breach, he did not think that it was a serious one. The PCC was entitled to come to the conclusion that the breach did not warrant censure.

Millett LJ observed that, whilst one could object to how the photograph had been obtained, one could not object to what was actually depicted in the photograph. It was an indistinct picture and not in itself objectionable. It had been taken without intrusion or harassment and without any 'exploitation of the vulnerability of the subject'. In the light of the above, and given that the picture was used to illustrate a story in the public interest, it was not, he said, necessary for the courts to interfere with the PCC's decision.

This decision serves to give pause to those parties who believe that nothing short of a judicially administered right to privacy will serve to protect

---

57 (1996) 18 November. On an application for leave to apply for judicial review against a decision of the PCC, the PCC reserved its position as to whether it was amenable to judicial review until the full hearing. As it happens, the court declined leave.

the interests of the public against the prying eyes of the media. The judicial reasoning reflects a limited interpretation of what is meant by 'privacy'. It seems to be out of step with current PCC adjudications, as set out above. It is submitted that the court erred in using the nature of what was depicted in the photograph as its starting point. The key point ought to have been whether Mr Brady was photographed in a public or private place where he had a reasonable expectation of privacy (cl 3 of the Code). A hospital would seem to meet this test without much difficulty – this is supported by clause 9 of the Code (privacy and hospitals). Assuming that Mr Brady had a reasonable expectation of privacy, the next question was whether there was justification for its violation – such as the relationship between the article and the photograph. The fact that the photograph was indistinct or that the photographer was not on private property when he took the picture ought to be irrelevant. In any event, Millett LJ's view that there was no exploitation of the vulnerability of Mr Brady is naïve. The taking of, and publication of, the picture was exploitation of Mr Brady's status and position in itself.

R v Broadcasting Standards Commission ex p BBC[58]

The BBC applied for judicial review of a decision of the BSC whereby it upheld a complaint by Dixons Retail Ltd against the BBC of an unwarranted infringement of privacy in the making of a 'Watchdog' programme. The complaint concerned secret filming by the BBC of 12 sales transactions at various branches of Dixons. The filming was carried out with a view to demonstrating that Dixons were in the habit of misrepresenting second hand goods as new (the secret filming did not produce evidence to this effect and the material obtained by the filming was not ultimately used in the programme, although reference was made to the transactions which had been filmed).

In its adjudication, the BSC found that the secret filming was an infringement of Dixon's privacy. The BBC sought review of this decision on three grounds as follows:

- a company or body corporate cannot enjoy a right to privacy;
- privacy cannot apply to the filming of events to which the public has access; and
- the decision of the BSC was unreasonable or failed to have regard to relevant factors.

The Court of Appeal adopted a narrow focus and confined its decision to the functions of the BSC as laid down in the Broadcasting Act 1996 and the application of the BSC Code of Practice. The appeal judges went out of their

---

58   *R v Broadcasting Standards Commission ex p BBC* (2000) unreported, 6 April, CA.

way to stress that they were not laying down principles of privacy *law*, or even principles which might apply in a wider context.[59] The appeal court held that

- for the purposes of the Broadcasting Act 1996 and the BSC Code of Practice, a body corporate could claim to the BSC of an unwarranted intrusion of its privacy;
- on the question of filming in a public place, the Court of Appeal held that the BSC acted reasonably in reaching its decision that secret filming could violate rights of privacy even where it took place in a public place. The court did not attempt to give an indication of whether this decision was correct as a matter of law;[60]
- accordingly, the decision of the BSC that there had been a violation of Dixons' privacy stood under the BSC Code of Practice.

The court stressed that the Code of Practice did not have legal status. Lord Mustill opined 'the task of the Commission is not to declare and enforce sharp-edged legal rights, but rather to establish and by admonition uphold general standards of decent behaviour. This regime leads itself to an expanded reading of privacy'.

All three judges indicated that if they had been considering the ambit of the legal right, the right would have been less extensive than the right which prevailed under the Codes.

THE ROLE OF THE CODES OF PRACTICE IN THE FUTURE

Some commentators have observed that the Human Rights Act 1998 has permitted the introduction of a right to privacy through the back door so far as the media are concerned.[61] The Act could have this effect in the following ways:

- the availability of judicial review against public authorities is likely to continue to involve the courts in a review of the decisions of the PCC, the ITC and Radio Authority and the BSC on the privacy provisions of the Codes. However, if the court's judgments follow the Court of Appeal's approach in the *BBC* case, a distinction will emerge between the Codes, which do not have the force of law, and the law. The Codes are likely to be interpreted more widely than any law of privacy would be;

---

59 With the exception of the speech of Lord Mustill, which contained a detailed opinion of the nature of the right to privacy in general.

60 At first instance, Forbes J had held this finding to be irrational.

61 See, eg, Lord Wakeham in (1997) *Mail on Sunday*, 2 November.

- significantly, under s 7 of the Human Rights Act, a judicial review application might be on the ground that the body has failed to have adequate regard for the Convention right to respect for home and family life in reaching its decision. Over time, a body of law is likely to emerge on the relationship between the decisions under the Codes and the Convention right to respect for private and family life, especially where the regulatory bodies do not give adequate protection to privacy (a complaint often levelled at the PCC). The Lord Chancellor told Parliament that 'it is strong and effective self-regulation if it – and I emphasise the if – provides adequate remedies which will keep these cases away from the courts';[62]

- in cases where the court is considering granting relief which could affect freedom of expression, one of the matters which the court must consider is whether any relevant privacy Code has been complied with by the defendant. The Codes will accordingly become subject to consideration by the court in private law actions involving considerations of privacy. But compliance with the Codes will not automatically mean that a remedy ought not to be granted against the defendant. For example, if the courts do not think that the Codes are sufficiently stringent to deal with a particular case, relief may be granted notwithstanding that the Codes may have been complied with.

This scrutiny and consideration by the judiciary in private law actions is likely to lead to a body of judicial comment about the Codes which may result in the establishment of a *de facto* right to privacy – albeit one which principally arises through the system of self-regulation.

One wonders whether the government has had this Machiavellian intention all along – fighting shy of blatantly legislating for a right of privacy, but adopting a course which may gradually, and indirectly, achieve the same result.

All of this is, of course, speculative. One thing is sure: there are interesting times ahead.

---

62   *Hansard*, HL, 3.11.1997, col 1229.

CHAPTER 9

DATA PROTECTION AND THE MEDIA

THE DATA PROTECTION ACT 1998

The Data Protection Act 1998 ('the Act') implements the EU Data Protection Directive,[1] which had the twin objectives of: (a) harmonising data protection laws throughout the EC; and (b) protecting the privacy of individuals in relation to the processing of personal data. The preamble to the Act describes it as a measure to provide for 'the regulation of the processing of information relating to individuals, including the obtaining, holding, use or disclosure of such information'. The Act came into force on 1 March 2000, replacing the Data Protection Act 1984. It contains transitional provisions for data processing which was under way prior to 24 October 1998. Processing which postdates 24 October 1998 will be subject to the Act's provisions.

The media makes considerable use of information about individuals. Under the scheme of the Act, this information may be classed as data if it is held on computer or in a structured paper filing system. The Act provides that any use which is made of personal data must be in accordance with the provisions of the Act. The Act contains eight data protection principles with which data controllers must comply.

In addition to the data protection principles, the Act confers legal rights on individuals in respect of personal data held about them. In summary, the individual has the right to control the use to which the data is put and to know the source of the information.

From the above, it is clear that the provisions of the Act are incompatible with the majority of media reporting. In recognition of this fact, the Act contains an important exemption for the media which will apply in the circumstances set out in the Act. The exemption is considered towards the end of the chapter.

Terminology

In order to understand the provisions of the Act, it is necessary to familiarise oneself with its terminology. The Act contains basic interpretative provisions in s 1(1). The key concepts are defined as follows.

---

1   Directive (95/45/EC) on the protection of individuals, with regard to the processing of personal data and the free movement of such data.

Data – it is important to realise that the Act operates by reference to the way that the information is processed rather than by reference to the content of the information itself.

The Act defines 'data' as information which:

(a) is being processed by means of equipment operating automatically in response to instructions given for that purpose;

(b) is recorded with the intention that it should be processed by means of such equipment;

(c) is recorded as part of a relevant filing system or with the intention that it should form part of a relevant filing system; or

(d) does not fall within the above provisions but forms part of an accessible record (the meaning of this phrase is considered below).

Relevant filing system – includes paper-based material. It means any set of information relating to individuals to the extent that the set is structured, either by reference to individuals or by reference to criteria relating to individuals, in such a way that specific information relating to a particular individual is readily accessible.

The information may be stored in a variety of ways, such as in paper files, on microfiche or card index systems.

The mere fact that data is stored in a file will not automatically make it part of a relevant filing system. The definition of relevant filing system does *not* cover unstructured files. The Commissioner (see below for an explanation of the role of the Commissioner) has given general guidance as to what might fall to be classed as a relevant filing system, although she has emphasised that the final decision in a particular case would lie with the courts. The guidance indicates the following:

• there must be a set of information about individuals. This suggests a grouping of things together by reference to a distinct identifier, for example, a set of information about customers;

• the set of information need not be physically grouped together in files. It may be grouped together in other ways, for example, by prefix codes;

• the set of information does not need to be maintained centrally by the data controller. It may, for example, be dispersed over different branch offices;

• the set must be structured, for example, by reference to the individuals themselves or by reference to criteria relating to the individuals, such as their credit history or their membership of particular organisations;

• the structuring has to enable specific information about a particular individual to be readily accessible. What amounts to specific information will be a question of fact in every case;

- the act does not define 'readily accessible'. The Commissioner points out that, in its ordinary meaning, the phrase means 'information capable of being reached easily by virtue of the structure'. The Commissioner suggests that information referenced to individuals or criteria relating to individuals will be caught by the Act if it is generally accessible at any time to one or more people within the data controller's organisation in connection with the day to day operation of that organisation.

Information which forms part of a health record, an educational record recorded by a local education authority school or a special school, a local authority housing record or a local authority social services record will also be classed as 'data' for the purposes of the Act, whether or not it meets the above requirements. These types of record are known as 'accessible records'.

Personal data are particular types of data in respect of which the subject has private rights under the Act.[2] These rights are discussed below.

Personal data are data about a living individual who can be identified:

(a) from those data; or

(b) from those data and other information which is in the possession of, or is likely to come into the possession of, the data controller.

Personal data is not confined to factual information. Significantly, it includes any expression of opinion about an individual and any indication of the intentions of the data controller (or any other person) in respect of the individual.

Data controller means a person who determines the purposes for which and the manner in which any personal data are, or are to be, processed.

Data processor means a person who processes the data on behalf of the data controller (other than an employee of the data controller).

Data subject means an individual who is the subject of personal data.

Processing means obtaining, recording or holding information or data or carrying out any operation or set of operations on the information or data including:

(a) organisation, adaptation or alteration of the information or data;

(b) retrieval, consultation or use of the information or data;

(c) disclosure of the information or data by transmission, dissemination or otherwise making available; or

(d) alignment, combination, blocking, erasure or destruction of the information or data.

---

2 Remember that in order to be classed as data, the information must satisfy the requirements of the Data Protection Act 1998, s 1(1).

This is clearly a wide definition. It extends to pretty much everything which can be carried out in relation to data. So far as the media are concerned, it could extend to journalistic enquiries which lead to the obtaining of information which is then stored on computer or in a relevant filing system. It could also extend to publication or amendment of that data or any other kind of use.

The processing of data will not be lawful unless the data protection principles contained in the Act are complied with. The principles are considered below.

The Data Protection Commissioner

The Data Protection Commissioner has powers to enforce the provisions of the Act. Her detailed powers are outside the scope of this book. Her duties include the promotion of good practice by data controllers and, in particular, the promotion of the observance of the Act's requirements. Reference is made below to a number of guidance documents which the Commissioner has issued in relation to the Act.

The data protection principles

The data protection principles apply to all personal data processed by data controllers.

The principles are set out in Pt 1 of Sched 1 to the Act – Pt 2 of Sched 1 contains interpretation provisions which clarify and supplement the principles.

The principles are as follows.

The first data protection principle

1   Personal data shall be processed fairly and lawfully and, in particular, shall not be processed unless at least one of the conditions set out in Sched 2 is met.

Processed fairly and lawfully

The first principle requires that the data must be processed fairly and lawfully.

The Act gives guidance in Part 2 of Sched 1 ('the fair processing code') about the meaning of fair processing.[3] Compliance with the fair processing code will not, in itself, ensure that processing is fair, but if the code is complied with there will be a presumption that the processing was done fairly unless there is evidence to the contrary.

The fair processing code

- The Act indicates that in determining whether data is processed fairly, regard should be had to the method by which data are obtained, including in particular whether any person from whom they are obtained is deceived or misled as to the purpose or purposes for which they are to be processed.
- Data are generally to be treated as being obtained fairly if they consist of information obtained from a person who is *authorised* by or under any enactment to supply it, or is *required* to supply it by or under any enactment.

Providing information to the data subject

Personal data are not to be treated as processed fairly, unless:

(a) in the case of data obtained direct from the data subject, the data controller ensures so far as practicable that the data subject has, is provided with, or has made readily available to him the information set out below;

(b) in any other case, the data controller ensures so far as is practicable that before the relevant time (relevant time is defined below) or as soon as practicable after that time the data subject has or is provided with or has made readily available to him the information set out below.

The information which must be supplied to the data subject

The information required is as follows:

- the identity of the data controller;
- if the data controller has nominated a representative, the identity of that representative;
- the purpose or purposes for which the data are intended to be processed; and
- any further information which is necessary, having regard to the specific circumstances in which the data are or are to be processed, to enable processing in respect of the data subject to be fair.

---

3   The fair processing code – see below.

The relevant time

Where the data controller has obtained data from someone other than the data subject, the fair processing information must be given or made readily available to the data subject at the 'relevant time'. The relevant time means the time when the data controller first processes the data, or in a case where disclosure of the data by the data controller to a third party within a reasonable period is envisaged:

- if the data are in fact disclosed to such a person within that period, the time when the data are first disclosed;

- if, within that period, the data controller becomes, or ought to become, aware that the data are unlikely to be disclosed to such a person within that period, the time when the data controller does become, or ought to become, so aware; or

- in any other case, the end of the reasonable period.

Exceptions to the duty to inform under the fair processing code

The fair processing code provides that the duty to provide the data subject with the information set out above will not apply where it would involve a disproportionate effort on the part of the data controller. This term is not defined in the code. The Commissioner has indicated that she will take into account the following factors in deciding whether informing the data subject would involve a disproportionate effort:[4]

- the cost to the data controller in providing the information, for example, postage, employee time;

- the length of time it would take to provide the information;

- how easy or difficult it would be for the data controller to provide the information.

All these considerations should be weighed against the benefit to the data controller of processing the information *and* the extent to which the withholding of the information may be prejudicial to the data subject.

A second exemption from the duty to inform applies where the recording of the information contained in the data or the disclosure of the information by the data controller is necessary for compliance with any legal obligation to which the data controller is subject (other than an obligation imposed by contract).

---

4   *Data Protection Act 1998 – An Introduction*, October 1988, available from the Data Protection Registrar.

In addition to providing that data must be processed fairly and lawfully, the first data protection principle provides that at least one of the conditions set out in Sched 2 to the Act must be met.

Failure to meet at least one of the conditions will mean that the processing will be in breach of the first data protection principle.

The Sched 2 conditions

At least one of these conditions has to be met:

1   The data subject has given consent to the processing.

   The Act does not define what is meant by 'consent'. However, the directive which the Act is intended to implement defined 'the data subject's consent' as 'any freely given specific and informed indication of his wishes by which the data subject signifies his agreement to personal data relating to him being processed'.

   The Commissioner has indicated[5] that 'signifies' entails active communication between the relevant parties and that consent cannot be inferred. The Commissioner takes the view that a blanket consent to the processing of personal data is unlikely to be sufficient (particularly in the case of 'sensitive personal data' – see below). The more ambiguous the consent, the more likely that there will be questions about its validity or existence. The data subject may withdraw consent.

2   The processing is necessary:

   (a) for the performance of a contract to which the data subject is a party; or

   (b) for the taking of steps at the request of the data subject with a view to entering into a contract.

3   The processing is necessary in order to protect the vital interests of the data subject.

   The Commissioner considers that reliance on this condition may only be claimed where the processing is necessary for matters of life and death, for example, the disclosure of a data subject's medical records to a hospital casualty department which is treating the data subject after a serious road accident.

4   The processing is necessary:

   (a) for the administration of justice;

   (b) for the exercise of any functions conferred by or under any enactment;

   (c) for the exercise of any functions of the Crown, a minister of the Crown or a government department; or

---

5   *Data Protection Act 1998 – An Introduction*, October 1988, available from the Data Protection Registrar.

(d) for the exercise of any other functions of a public nature exercised in the public interest.

5 The processing is necessary for the purposes of the legitimate interest pursued by the data controller or by the third party or parties to whom the data is disclosed, except where the processing is unwarranted in any particular case because of prejudice to the rights, freedoms or legitimate interest of the data subject.

The Sched 2 grounds and sensitive personal data

The Act introduces a category of 'sensitive personal data'.[6] The Act contains additional conditions which must be satisfied before sensitive data can be processed. Sensitive personal data consists of information about:

- the racial or ethnic origin of the data subject;
- their political opinions;
- their religious beliefs or other beliefs of a similar nature;
- their physical or mental health or condition;
- whether they are a member of a trade union;
- their sexual life;
- the commission or alleged commission by them of any offence; or
- any proceedings for any offence committed or alleged to have been committed by them, the disposal of such proceedings or the sentence of any court in such proceedings.

Where the data is sensitive personal data, at least one of the additional conditions listed below must be satisfied *in addition to* at least one of the general Sched 2 conditions listed above. The special conditions are as follows:

1 The data subject has given their explicit consent to the processing of the personal data.

'Explicit' is not defined. The Commissioner has indicated that the word suggests that the consent of the data subject must be absolutely clear, covering the specific detail of the processing, the purposes of the processing and any specific aspects of the processing which may affect the individual.

2 The processing is necessary for the purposes of exercising or performing any right or obligation which is conferred or imposed by law on the data controller in connection with employment.

---

6 Defined in the Data Protection Act 1998, s 2.

The Secretary of State may by order specify cases where this condition is either excluded altogether or only satisfied upon the satisfaction of further conditions.

3   The processing is necessary:

(a) in order to protect the vital interests of the data subject or another person in a case where:

- consent cannot be given by or on behalf of the data subject; or
- the data controller cannot reasonably be expected to obtain the consent of the data subject; or

(b) in order to protect the vital interests of another person, in a case where consent by or on behalf of the data subject has been unreasonably withheld.

4   The processing:

(a) is carried out in the course of the legitimate activities by any body or association which is not established or conducted for profit and which exists for political, philosophical, religious or trade union purposes;

(b) is carried out with appropriate safeguards for the rights and freedoms of data subjects;

(c) relates only to individuals who either are members of the body or association or have regular contact with it in connection with its purposes; and

(d) does not involve disclosure of the personal data to a third party without the consent of the data subject.

5   The information contained in the personal data has been made public as a result of steps deliberately taken by the data subject.

6   The processing:

(a) is necessary for the purpose of or in connection with, any legal proceedings (including prospective legal advice);

(b) is necessary for the purpose of obtaining legal advice; or

(c) is otherwise necessary for the purposes of establishing, exercising or defending legal rights.

7   (1) The processing is necessary:

(a) for the administration of justice;

(b) for the exercise of any functions conferred on any person by or under an enactment; or

(c) for the exercise of any functions of the Crown, a minister of the Crown or a Government department.

(2) The Secretary of State may by order specify cases where this condition is either excluded altogether or only satisfied upon the satisfaction of further conditions.

8 The processing is necessary for medical purposes and is undertaken by:

(a) a health professional; or

(b) a person who in the circumstances owes a duty of confidentiality which is equivalent to that which would arise if that person were a health professional.

9 The processing:

(a) is of sensitive personal data consisting of information as to racial or ethnic origin;

(b) is necessary for the purpose of identifying or keeping under review the existence or absence of equality of opportunity or treatment between persons of different racial or ethnic origins with a view to enabling such equality to be promoted or maintained; and

(c) is carried out with appropriate safeguards for the rights and freedoms of data subjects.

The Secretary of State may by order specify circumstances in which such processing is or is not to be taken to be carried out with appropriate safeguards for the rights and freedoms of data subjects.

10 The personal data are processed in circumstances specified in an order made by the Secretary of State.

So far, we have considered the first data protection principle with which the data controller must comply when processing personal data. The other seven principles which also must be complied with will now be considered.

The second data protection principle

Personal data shall be obtained only for one or more specified and lawful purposes, and shall not be further processed in any manner incompatible with that purpose or those purposes.

The purpose or purposes for which personal data are obtained may, in particular, be specified:

(a) in a notice given by the data controller to the data subject; or

(b) in a notification given to the Commissioner.

The third principle

Personal data shall be adequate, relevant and not excessive in relation to the purpose or purposes for which they are processed.

The fourth principle

Personal data shall be accurate and, where necessary, kept up to date.

The fifth principle

Personal data processed for any purpose or purposes shall not be kept for longer than is necessary for that purpose or for those purposes.

The sixth principle

Personal data shall be processed in accordance with the rights of data subjects under the Act.

The seventh principle

Appropriate technical and organisational measures shall be taken against unauthorised or unlawful processing of personal data and against accidental loss or destruction of, or damage to, personal data.

The measures taken must ensure a level of security appropriate to:

(a) the harm that might result from any unauthorised or unlawful processing or accidental loss, destruction or damage; and

(b) the nature of the data to be protected having regard to the state of technological development and the cost of implementing any measures.

The data controller must take reasonable steps to ensure the reliability of any employees who have access to the personal data.

Where the processing is carried out by a data processor on behalf of the data controller, the data controller must choose a data processor providing sufficient guarantees in respect of the technical and organisational security measures governing the process and the controller must take reasonable steps to ensure compliance with those measures. The data controller will not be regarded as complying with the seventh principle unless the processing is carried out under contract made or evidenced in writing under which the data processor is to act only on instructions from the data controller. The contract must also require the data processor to comply with obligations equivalent to those imposed on the data controller under the seventh principle.

The eighth principle

Personal data shall not be transferred to a country or territory outside the European Economic Area unless that country or territory ensures an adequate level of protection for the rights and freedoms of data subjects in relation to the processing of personal data.

An adequate level of protection is one which is adequate in all the circumstances of the case, having regard to:

- the nature of the personal data;
- the country or territory of origin of the information contained in the data;
- the country or territory of final destination of that information;
- the purposes for which and period during which the data are intended to be processed;
- the law in force in the country or territory in question;
- the international obligations of that country or territory;
- any relevant codes of conduct or other rules which are enforceable in that country or territory (whether generally or by arrangement in particular cases; and
- any security measures taken in respect of the data in that country or territory.

The rights of the data subject in relation to the processing of personal data

The Act gives rights to individuals in respect of personal data held about them by others. The rights are as follows:

- right of subject access (s 7).

  The individual is entitled, upon making a request in writing and paying a fee to the relevant data controller, to be told by that data controller whether they or someone on their behalf is processing the individual's data and, if so, to be given a description of the personal data, the purposes for which they are being processed and the persons to whom the data are or may be disclosed.

  The individual is also entitled to be told in an intelligible manner all the information which forms any such data *and any information as to the source of the data*. The disclosure of the identity of their sources is something which journalists are at great pains to prevent. Indeed, journalists are placed under an obligation not to make such disclosures by the code of practice produced by the National Union of Journalists and by the terms of the code which is enforced by the Press Complaints Commission.[7]

Where a decision significantly affecting a data subject is or is likely to be made about them by fully automated means for the purpose of evaluating matters such as their performance at work or their creditworthiness, the data subject is entitled to know the logic involved in the decision making process (except where the information in question constitutes a trade secret).

The data controller must not make any amendment or deletion to the data which would not otherwise have been made before it is supplied to the data subject. In particular, the data controller may not alter data to make it more acceptable to the data subject.

The data controller must generally supply the above information within 40 days of receipt of the request and fee.

Special rules apply to the provision of data in circumstances where the information contained in the data will enable another individual to be identified.

If the data subject believes that the data controller has failed to comply it may apply to the court for an order requiring compliance;

• the right to prevent processing likely to cause damage or distress (s 10).

A data subject is entitled to serve on a data controller a written notice (a 'data subject notice') requiring the data controller to cease or not to begin processing personal data concerning the data subject where such processing is likely to cause unwarranted substantial damage or substantial distress to the data subject or to another.

Where the data subject believes that a data controller has not complied with a data subject notice, it may apply to the court for an order ensuring compliance;

• the right to prevent processing for purposes of direct marketing (s 11).

'Direct marketing' means the communication by whatever means of any advertising or marketing material which is directed to particular individuals;

• rights in relation to automated decision making (s 12).

These rights are beyond the scope of this book. Automated decision making includes matters such as evaluating matters relating to the data subject such as their creditworthiness;

---

7   This is considered further in Chapter 11.

- the right to compensation (s 13).

  An individual who suffers damage or damage and distress (but not simply distress) as a result of any contravention of the provisions of the Act is entitled to compensation where the data controller cannot prove that they have taken such care as was reasonable in the circumstances to comply with the relevant requirement.

  Where the processing of the data is for a 'special purpose',[8] damages can be awarded for distress caused to the data subject, without the need to establish any other type of damage. The special purposes are considered below. *They include the use of data for journalistic purposes;*

- rectification, blocking, erasure and destruction (s 14).

  A data subject may apply to the court for an order requiring the data controller to rectify, block, erase or destroy data relating to them which is incorrect or misleading. This right extends to an expression of opinion which is based on factually inaccurate data. The court may also direct that the data controller notify third parties to whom the data has been disclosed of any rectification, etc, where it is reasonably practicable to do so;

- requests for assessment.[9]

Any person may ask the Commissioner to assess whether it is likely that any processing of personal data has been or is being carried out in compliance with the Act. The Commissioner has information gathering powers in relation to this exercise. Any person who is, or believes themselves to be, directly affected by any processing of personal data can make the request.

Exemptions under the Act

The Act provides for a number of exemptions to the above principles. The *key exemption* for the media is the special purposes exemption.[10]

Special purposes are defined to include any one or more of the following:

- journalism;
- artistic purposes;
- literary purposes.[11]

None of these purposes is defined in the Act. Will the mere fact that the data is for publication by the media mean that it will be deemed to have been

---

8   Defined in the Data Protection Act 1998, s 4 and discussed further below.
9   *Ibid*, s 42.
10   *Ibid*, s 32.
11   *Ibid*, s 4.

processed for journalistic purposes, or will the media have also to establish that the data is newsworthy or is to be used for reporting current events? This point has to be clarified. It is likely that over time, a body of case law will emerge to define the special purposes with greater precision. The European Court of Human Rights has emphasised the media's role as public watchdogs – media activities which fall within this watchdog role will almost certainly fall within the definition of journalism.

The phrase 'journalistic, literary or artistic works' also appears in s 12 of the Human Rights Act 1998[12] in relation to the grant of relief which might affect freedom of expression. Case law under s 12 might throw help to clarify the material covered by the special purposes exemption.

There are four conditions which must *all* be present before the processing of personal data for any of the above special purposes can qualify for the exemption.[13] They are:

- the personal data must be processed *only* for journalistic, artistic or literary purposes; and

- the processing must be undertaken with a view to the publication by any person of any journalistic, literary or artistic material; and

- the data controller must reasonably believe that publication would be in the public interest taking into account in particular the special importance of the public interest in freedom of expression; and

- the data controller must reasonably believe that, in all the circumstances, compliance with the provision in respect of which the exemption is claimed is incompatible with the special purposes.

In relation to the third of the above criteria (the data controller's reasonable belief that publication would be in the public interest), regard may be had to the data controller's compliance with any relevant industry code designated for these purposes by the Secretary of State. During the passage of the Data Protection Bill through Parliament, reference was expressly made to the PCC Code (the press), the ITC Code (independent television) and the Code of the Broadcasting Standards Commission (all broadcasters). The most relevant provisions of these codes are the privacy provisions, which were set out and considered in Chapter 8. Compliance with the privacy provisions of the codes make it likely that the data controller will be able to demonstrate a reasonable belief that publication of the data is in the public interest (although it will not necessarily be determinative of this question. The Act does not equate reasonable relief to the provisions of the codes. Similarly, non-compliance with the codes ought not to mean that the data controller will be deemed not to be able to show a reasonable belief).

---

12 Considered in Chapter 1.
13 Data Protection Act 1998, s 32(1).

It is significant that the language used in the Act draws attention to the wider public interest in imparting and receiving information as well as to the public interest in the receipt of the particular information in question.

If the above criteria are not met, the special purposes exemption will not apply and the Act's provisions will apply to regulate the processing of the data.

If *all* the above conditions are met, the exemption will apply to the following provisions of the Act:

- the data protection principles *except* the seventh principle (security measures) which *will continue* to apply;
- the right of subject access and disclosure of sources in s 7;
- the right to prevent processing likely to cause unwarranted damage or distress in s 10;
- rights in relation to automated decision taking in s 12;
- the provisions relating to the right to rectification, blocking, erasure and destruction of inaccurate data in s 14.

Section 32(4) provides that proceedings against a data controller who falls within the special purposes exemption will be stayed if the personal data is being processed only for the special purposes with a view to publication and it has previously been published by the data controller (excluding the 24 hour period prior to the publication of the data). This protection covers proceedings brought before publication of the material and in the immediate 24 hour period following publication. It is intended to provide a safeguard against the provisions of the Act being used as a prior restraint measure to restrain the publication of personal data covered by the special purposes exemption by the media.

Example

X applies to the court for an order under s 10 of the Act to restrain the publication of personal data by the *Daily Tabloid*. X claims that the information is likely to cause him distress.

The publication of the data by the newspaper will be 'processing' for the purpose of the Act, if the information about X falls within the definition of personal data. For example, if it is held in a structured filing system and it would enable X to be identified, X might be able to obtain an order to prevent the publication of the data.

The *Daily Tabloid* can resist the application by demonstrating that the processing of the data falls within the special purposes exemption. It must show that:

- the data is being processed (published) for journalistic purposes only. The more newsworthy the article, the more likely it is that the newspaper will be able to establish this fact – pending judicial guidance on the meaning of 'journalistic';

- the processing is undertaken with a view to publication of the journalistic material;

- in the reasonable belief of the *Daily Tabloid* the publication would be in the public interest. The newspaper can rely on the nature of the story which it proposes to publish – is it in the public interest? It can also rely on the wider public interest in allowing freedom of expression generally. Any limitation on this freedom must be compatible with the European Convention on Human Rights if it is to be acceptable;[14]

- if the *Daily Tabloid* has complied with the Code of Practice in relation to the data which is enforced by the Press Complaints Commission, that will help the newspaper to establish its reasonable belief;

- in the reasonable belief of the *Daily Tabloid* compliance with the processing requirements Act would be incompatible with the journalistic purpose – for example, agreeing not to publish the data would not be compatible with the news reporting role of the media.

Provided that the *Daily Tabloid* can demonstrate these factors to the satisfaction of the court, X's application under s 10 will be stayed.

The length of the stay

The stay remains in force until the claim is withdrawn or until the Commissioner makes a determination in writing stating either that it appears to her that the data are not being processed for special purposes, or confirming that they are not being processed with a view to the publication by any person of any journalistic, literary or artistic material which has not previously been published by the data controller.[15]

Where the Commissioner makes a determination, she is required to give the data controller notice. There is a right of appeal against her decision to the Data Protection Tribunal and thereafter to the High Court.[16]

---

14 More detail about this is contained in Chapter 1.
15 Data Protection Act 1998, s 45.
16 *Ibid*, s 48.

A summary of the Commissioner's powers under the provisions of the Act

Assessment

As we have seen, individuals have the right to request the Commissioner for an assessment as to whether the processing of personal data has been or is being or is not being carried out in compliance with the Act.[17]

In addition to her powers of assessment, the Commissioner can issue the following notices under the Act:

- special information notices.[18]

  Where, during an assessment, the data controller claims a special purposes exemption, the Commissioner can serve a special information notice where she has reasonable grounds for suspecting that the personal data to which the proceedings relate are not being processed only for the special purposes or are not being processed with a view to publication by any person of any journalistic, literary or artistic material which has not previously been published by the data controller.

  The special information notice can require the controller to provide information to enable her to ascertain whether the special purposes exemption applies.

  There is a right of appeal against a special information notice to the Data Protection Tribunal.

  Material covered by legal professional privilege does not have to be disclosed.

  It is an offence to fail to comply with a special information notice. The offence carries a maximum fine of £5,000 on summary conviction and an unlimited fine on indictment. The controller has a defence if it can show that it exercised all due diligence to comply with the notice;

- information notices.[19]

  If, during the course of an assessment which does not involve the special purposes exemption, the Commissioner requires information from the data controller, the Commissioner may serve an information notice requiring the data controller to provide that information. The consequences of non-compliance with an information notice are the same as not complying with a special information notice;

---

17 Data Protection Act 1998, s 42.

18 *Ibid*, s 44.

19 *Ibid*, s 43.

- enforcement notices.[20]

  Enforcement notices may be served on a data controller where the Commissioner is satisfied that the controller has contravened or is contravening the Act's provisions. There is a right of appeal against an enforcement notice to the Data Protection Tribunal.

  An enforcement notice may not be served on a data controller with respect to the processing of data for the special purposes without permission from the court.[21] Permission will only be granted where the court is satisfied that the Commissioner has reason to suspect a contravention of the Act which is of substantial public importance. The media should be given notice of the Commissioner's application for permission unless the urgency of the application does not allow notice to be given.

  Failure to comply with an enforcement notice is a criminal offence carrying a maximum fine of £5,000 on summary conviction or an unlimited fine on indictment. The data controller has a defence where it can show that it has exercised all due diligence to comply with the notice.

Powers of entry and inspection[22]

If there are reasonable grounds for suspecting that the data protection principles have or are not being complied with, the Commissioner may apply to the court for a warrant to enter and search premises on which it is suspected that evidence of contravention of the principles is to be found.

No warrant should be issued unless the court is satisfied that there are reasonable grounds for the Commissioner's suspicion and that:

- the Commissioner has already demanded access by giving seven days' notice to the occupier;
- access was demanded at a reasonable hour and was unreasonably refused, or entry was granted but the occupier unreasonably refused to comply with a request of the Commissioner relating to the execution of the warrant; and
- the Commissioner has notified the occupier of the application for the warrant and the occupier has had an opportunity of being heard by the judge as to whether or not the warrant should be issued.

Where the court is satisfied that the case is urgent, or that giving notice would defeat the object of entry (for example, it would lead to destruction of the evidence), the court may issue the warrant without notice to the occupier.

---

20 Data Protection Act 1998, s 40.

21 *Ibid*, s 46.

22 *Ibid*, Sched 9.

It is an offence intentionally to obstruct a person in execution of a warrant or to fail without reasonable excuse to give anyone executing a warrant such help as may reasonably be required to execute the warrant. An offender is liable to a fine not exceeding £5,000.

Other criminal offences[23]

It is a criminal offence for a person knowingly or recklessly to obtain or disclose personal data or the information contained in the data or procure the disclosure to another person of the information contained in the personal data without the consent of the data controller. It is also an offence to sell or offer to sell personal data obtained in contravention of this provision.

Notification[24]

Data controllers are required to notify the Commissioner of certain information relating to their data processing.

The notification requirements do not apply to information recorded in a relevant processing system (that is, structured paper-based filing systems). But where the information is kept on computer, notification must take place.

The following information must be notified:

- the name and address of the data controller;
- the name and address of any nominated representative;
- a description of the personal data being processed and the categories of data to which they relate;
- a description of the purposes for which the data are being processed;
- a description of the recipients to whom the controller intends to disclose the data;
- the name or description of any countries or territories outside the EEA to which the data controller transfers or intends to transfer the data.

The notifications are kept on a public register which is maintained by the Commissioner. The data controller must also provide a general description of the security measures taken to protect the he personal data. These will not appear on the register.

Where the requirement to notify applies, it is an offence to process data without notification.

It is also a criminal offence to fail to notify the Commissioner of changes to the register entry.

---

23 Data Protection Act 1998, s 55.
24 *Ibid*, Pt 3, ss 16–26.

CHAPTER 10

THE MEDIA AND OPEN JUSTICE

REPORTING COURT PROCEEDINGS

This chapter sets out the law which regulates the reporting of legal proceedings. The first section explains the law of contempt of court. The second section sets out the more commonly encountered methods in which the court can order the postponement or restriction of media reports of legal proceedings.

CONTEMPT OF COURT – PREJUDICING A FAIR TRIAL

There is an obvious danger that reports of, or relating to, civil or criminal proceedings might affect the administration of justice and, in particular, that it might prejudice the right to a fair trial.

Consider the following example: a well known celebrity has been charged with possession of Class A drugs. His trial is due to take place in six months' time. Today, a national newspaper with a large circulation has published exclusive revelations about the celebrity's lifestyle, including detailed allegations about his regular drug abuse.

Could the article prejudice the trial of the celebrity? Might members of the public who are empanelled on the trial jury be swayed by what they have read rather than the evidence presented at trial? If so, the trial would normally be stayed, and the publishers of the article in question might be found to be in contempt of court, an offence punishable by fines and, potentially, by imprisonment.

The law which determines whether the article is a contempt of court is set out below. There are two forms of contempt – strict liability contempt and intentional contempt.

(a) Strict liability contempt – the Contempt of Court Act 1981

> Make no mistake, this is a liberalising bill and it is intended to be a liberalising Bill.[1]

The Contempt of Court Act 1981 ('the Act') establishes parameters to regulate how far the media can legitimately go in reporting or commenting on ongoing

---

1   Lord Hailsham, HL Deb, Vol 419, col 659.

or anticipated civil and criminal proceedings. The Act provides for a criminal offence of contempt of court for the publication of statements which carry a substantial risk of serious prejudice to the proceedings. Under the provisions of the Act, publication can take place in a wide variety of ways. 'Publication' is defined to include any speech, writing, programme included in a programme service[2] or other communication in whatever form.[3] This is a broad definition. The offence carries maximum penalties of an unlimited fine and/or two years' imprisonment.

The offence is committed whether or not the publisher had any intention of interfering with the administration of justice. This is known as 'the *strict liability rule*'.[4] There is a real possibility that a publisher may accidentally or negligently publish a statement in contempt of court even though he had no intention of prejudicing legal proceedings.[5] Any person responsible for publication may be prosecuted under the strict liability rule. Liability can therefore extend not only to publishers in the strict sense of the word, but also to editors or to distributors of the material in question.

As a safeguard against capricious private prosecutions, proceedings for contempt under the strict liability rule may only be brought by or with the consent of the Attorney General or on the motion of the court having jurisdiction to deal with the issue.[6] The burden of establishing contempt lies on the party who brings the proceedings (typically, the Attorney General) who must establish contempt to the criminal standard.[7]

Limitations to liability

There are three major limitations to the operation of the strict liability offence, which are set out in s 2 of the Act.

First, the offence only applies to publications which are addressed to the public at large or to any section of the public.[8] Private communications do not fall within the strict liability rule. Second, for the strict liability rule to apply, the proceedings about which comment is made must be 'active'. The meaning of 'active' is set out in Sched 1 of the Act. The question whether proceedings are active varies according to the type of proceedings in question as follows:

---

2   Inserted by the Broadcasting Act 1990, s 203(1).
3   Contempt of Court Act 1981, s 2(1).
4   *Ibid*, s 1.
5   The Act provides for limited defences of innocent publication which are considered below.
6   Contempt of Court Act 1981, s 7.
7   *AG v Independent Television News Ltd* [1995] 2 All ER 370, p 375; *AG v English* [1982] 2 All ER 903.
8   Contempt of Court Act 1981, s 2(1).

Criminal proceedings become active with: (a) an arrest; or (b) the issue of a warrant for arrest or summons; or (c) the service of an indictment or other document specifying the charge; or (d) an oral charge.

It follows that comments made during a police investigation will not fall within the strict liability rule until a suspect has been apprehended in one of the ways set out in the Act. Where a suspect voluntarily attends the police station to help with inquiries, proceedings will not yet be active.

Civil proceedings become active when arrangements are made for the hearing of the action – typically, when the case is set down for trial or a trial date is fixed. In the case of emergency applications, such as injunctions, the case becomes active when the hearing commences.

Appellate proceedings (civil or criminal) become active when permission to appeal is applied for or when a notice of appeal is lodged.

Sched 1 of the Act also sets out when proceedings cease to be active.

In relation to *criminal proceedings*, the usual way in which proceedings cease to be active is where the defendant is acquitted or sentenced or where any other verdict, finding, order or decision is made which puts an end to the proceedings, for example, where a defendant is found unfit to plead. Where the arrested person is released without charge, the proceedings will cease to be active (unless the suspect is released on bail). If no arrest is made within 12 months of the issue of a warrant, the proceedings will cease to be active (although they become active again if an arrest is subsequently made).

Both civil and criminal proceedings cease to be active where the case is discontinued. Civil proceedings also cease to be active where the proceedings are otherwise disposed of without being formally discontinued.

Appellate proceedings cease to be active when the hearing of the appeal is over or when a new trial is ordered or the case is remitted to a lower court.

The third restriction on the strict liability rule under the Act is that the rule only applies:

> ... to a publication which creates a *substantial risk* that the course of justice in the proceedings in question will be *seriously impeded or prejudiced*.[9] This is a double limbed test and both limbs must be satisfied.

Substantial risk and serious prejudice – the law in practice

Substantial risk

The prosecution must prove that the publication gave rise to a substantial risk of prejudice. The assessment of the risk must be considered at the date of

---

9   Contempt of Court Act 1981, s 2(2).

publication,[10] not the date of trial. It is unnecessary to show actual impediment or prejudice. It is the potential effect of a publication that is relevant.

A substantial risk has been defined as a risk which is more than remote or minimal.[11]

Serious impediment or prejudice

There must be a substantial risk that the legal proceedings will be *seriously prejudiced or impeded* before the strict liability offence is made out. In *AG v Hat Trick*,[12] the court stressed that, before serious prejudice could be found, the course of justice must be put at risk, for example, something affecting the outcome of a trial or necessitating the discharge of a jury. In *AG v Unger*,[13] Simon Brown LJ observed that if serious prejudice is to be held to exist, the publication must:

- materially affect the course of a trial; or
- require directions from the court 'well beyond more ordinarily required and routinely given to juries'; or
- create at least a 'seriously arguable' ground for appeal on the basis of prejudice.

Substantial risk of serious prejudice – applying the test

Pre-trial publicity

In *AG v Mirror Group Newspapers and Others*,[14] the Court of Appeal gave guidance about the application of the two limbs of the strict liability rule. This decision has been categorised as a high point for the media – because it provided an interpretation of the rule which comes down strongly in favour of freedom of expression.

The facts

Between May 1989 and March 1995, the relationship between Geoff Knights and his girlfriend (the 'EastEnders' star Gillian Taylforth) was given

---

10 *AG v English* [1982] 2 All ER 903, p 918.
11 *Ibid*, p 919; *AG v News Group Newspapers* [1986] 2 All ER 833.
12 *AG v Hat Trick* [1997] EMLR 76.
13 *AG v Unger* [1998] Cr App R 308, p 318.
14 *AG v Mirror Group Newspapers and Others* [1997] 1 All ER 456.

saturation media coverage. During that time, disclosures had appeared in the media about Knights' violent behaviour and previous convictions.

In April 1995, Knights was arrested and charged with wounding with intent. Various newspapers published articles about the incident in the days following his arrest. Some of the contents of the articles were inaccurate, exaggerating the nature of the victim's injuries. References were also made in the articles to Knights' previous convictions, although this latter information had already been publicised by the media on separate occasions before the offence in question had been committed.

Knights was committed for trial and a provisional date for trial was set for October 1995. He successfully applied for the proceedings to be stayed on the ground that the pre-trial publicity made it impossible for him to have a fair trial. The Attorney General subsequently commenced proceedings for contempt against the newspapers involved. He claimed that the pre-trial publicity had created a substantial risk of serious prejudice. The court held that the newspapers were not in contempt.

The guidance

The court laid down the following guidelines for applying the strict liability rule:

(a) each case must be considered on its own facts. Schiemann LJ cited with approval the following comment from the earlier case of *AG v News Group Newspapers*:[15]

> The degree of risk of impact of a publication on a trial and the extent of that impact may both be affected, in differing degrees according to the circumstances, by the nature and form of the publication and how long it occurred before trial. Much depends on the combination of circumstances in the case in question and the court's own assessment of their likely effect at the time of publication. This is essentially a value judgment for the court, albeit that it must be sure of its judgment before it can find that there has been contempt. There is little value in making detailed comparisons with the facts of other cases;

(b) the court will look at each individual publication separately and apply the test at the time of each publication. This individual publication rule works in the media's favour. In *AG v Mirror Group Newspapers*, the effect of the press coverage taken together was quite devastating. However once the coverage of each newspaper had been isolated, the effect was less dramatic. The court held that the isolation of each paper's coverage was the appropriate approach. This position may change. In an address to University College, Dublin, the English Lord Chancellor observed that 'an

---

15 *AG v News Group Newspapers* [1986] 2 All ER 833, p 843.

outstanding question is whether the law should nevertheless become that cumulative prejudice counts as contempt for which all may be held liable'.[16] It is probable that any such change will be effected by statutory amendment;

(c) if several newspapers publish prejudicial material (as in the *Knights* case) they cannot necessarily escape from liability by contending that the damage has already been done.[17] The fact that, at the time of publication, there is already some risk of prejudice to proceedings as a result of earlier articles will not automatically prevent a finding that a publication has created a further risk of prejudice.

On the facts of the *Knights* case, the judges, having emphasised the above principle, then proceeded to make no further reference to it in reaching their decision. In particular, the court made no attempt to reconcile it with its finding that in the light of the previous publicity there was no contempt on the facts of the *Knights* case. It is not therefore clear whether and how this principle will be applied in subsequent cases;

(d) the publication must create some risk that the course of justice and the proceedings in question will be impeded or prejudiced by that publication;

(e) the risk must be substantial;

(f) the substantial risk must be that the course of justice in the proceedings in question will not only be impeded or prejudiced, but *seriously* so;

(g) the court will not convict of contempt unless it is *sure* that the publication has created a substantial risk of serious prejudice on the course of justice. This standard is the same as the criminal standard of proof (beyond reasonable doubt);

(h) in making an assessment of whether the publication creates this substantial risk of that serious effect on the course of justice, the following matters (amongst others) arise for consideration:

- the likelihood of the publication coming to the attention of a potential juror. This will involve consideration of whether the publication circulates in the area from which the jurors are likely to be drawn and the circulation figures for the publication in question. To declare in a speech at a public meeting in Cornwall that a man about to be tried in Durham is guilty of the offence charged and has many previous convictions for the same offence may well not carry a substantial risk of affecting his trial.[18] The same declaration at a meeting in Durham is more likely to carry such a risk;

16 14 April 1999, available at http://www.open.gov.uk/lcd/speeches.
17 See, also, *AG v ITN* [1995] 2 All ER 370, p 381.
18 Sir John Donaldson MR in *AG v News Group Newspapers* [1986] 2 All ER 833, p 840.

- the likely impact of the publication on an ordinary reader at the time of publication. This will involve consideration of (amongst other matters) the prominence of the article in the publication and the novelty of its content judged through the eyes of the likely readers of that publication. It may be the case that comments concerning a figure in the public eye are more likely to be remembered;[19]

- the residual impact of the publication on a notional juror at the time of trial. Schiemann emphasised that 'it is this last matter which is crucial'. It will involve consideration of the length of time which has, or will have, elapsed between publication and the likely trial date. As a general rule, the greater the length of time, the more likely that the impact of the publication will have become blunted by the time of the trial date, although this will depend on the particular publication. Sensational, emotive reporting may be more likely to be remembered than straightforward factual reporting.

In *AG v News Group Newspapers*,[20] Parker LJ had explained that:

> The imminence or remoteness of the proceedings will vitally affect both the existence of a substantial risk of prejudice and the question whether, if there is such a risk, it is a risk that the course of justice will be seriously impeded or prejudiced. Both the risk and the degree of prejudice will, as it seems to me, increase with the proximity of the trial but it is not possible, and indeed would be contrary to the Act, to say that no publication earlier than a certain number of months before trial could be subject to the application of the strict liability rule. Each case must be decided on its own facts and a publication relatively close to trial may escape whereas another much further from trial will not do so by reason of the impact of its content on the reader, listener or viewer, as the case may be.

This consideration of the residual impact of a publication has been dubbed the 'fade factor'.

Another important factor identified in the *Knights* case is the focusing effect on the jury of listening over a prolonged period to evidence in a case and the likely effect of the judge's directions. The court in the *Knights* case cited the decision in *Ex p Telegraph plc*,[21] when Lord Taylor had observed that:

> ... a court should credit the jury with the will and ability to abide by the judge's discretion to decide the case only on the evidence before them. The court should also bear in mind that the staying power and detail of publicity, even in case of notoriety, are limited and the nature of a trial is to focus the jury's

---

19 This was one of the factors leading to a finding of contempt in *AG v Hat Trick* [1997] EMLR 76, although the Court of Appeal did not appear to find it relevant to the question of residual impact in the *Knights* case.

20 *AG v News Group Newspapers* [1986] 2 All ER 833.

21 *Ex p Telegraph plc* [1993] 1 WLR 980, p 987.

minds on the evidence put before them rather than on matters outside the courtroom.

Or, in the words of Lawton J, 'the drama ... of a trial almost always has the effect of excluding from recollection that which went before'.[22]

On the facts on the *Knights* case, the court found that, despite the fact that the articles were written in 'typical graphic tabloid style', there was no contempt. The application of the residual impact test involved multiplying 'the long odds' against a potential juror reading the publication by 'the long odds' of any reader remembering it.

References to previous convictions and bad general character

The *Knights* case provides a touchstone for a liberal interpretation of the strict liability rule. However, the Divisional Court has subsequently appeared to favour a more restrictive interpretation of the application of the substantial risk of serious prejudice test, at least in relation to reports which reveal the accused's previous convictions and/or general bad character. The publication of information of this kind (particularly information relating to previous convictions) is problematic, because it is particularly likely to lead juries to the belief that the accused has a propensity to commit the offence with which he has been charged.

In *AG v Piers Morgan and News Group Newspapers*,[23] the court considered an article published by the *News of the World* concerning an investigation carried out by the newspaper in relation to a counterfeit currency operation. Two men were identified by name in the article as being involved in the operation. One of these men was described as having 'a long criminal record for fraud, deception, car crime, drugs offences and burglary'. The article was also found to create the impression that both men were guilty of a criminal offence.

Prior to publication, the newspaper had notified the police of the results of its investigation. There was no argument on the facts that proceedings had became active and that this occurred before publication of the newspaper's article. The trial of the criminal proceedings against the men whom the newspaper had identified was subsequently stayed by the trial judge on the ground that the article presented a substantial risk that the accused men would not receive a fair trial.

The divisional court agreed with the trial judge and held that the article was 'beyond doubt' a contempt under the strict liability rule. The court bore the following considerations in mind in reaching its decision:

---

22 *R v Kray* (1969) 53 Cr App R 412, p 415.

23 *AG v Piers Morgan and News Group Newspapers* (1997) Independent Legal Reports.

- the wide circulation of the article, which made it likely to have come to the attention of potential jurors;
- the skilful manner of presentation of the article, such as the banner headline 'We smash £100 million fake cash ring', was well designed to have a big impact on the reader;
- the reference to the bad character of the accused (including the criminal background) was seen by the court as being a striking feature which was likely to be remembered by readers because of its non-standard nature;
- in relation to the residual impact of the article, the court found that the newspaper reporter would have been a key witness for the prosecution. His appearance as a witness would have the effect of increasing the chance that jurors who had read the article at the time of publication would recall it;
- the court attached weight to the lapse of time between trial and the publication of the article (about eight months) as being a time period which might have blunted the effect of the article, but felt that it was not a persuasive enough factor to deflect the substantial risk that the course of justice would be seriously impaired. Neither the conscientiousness of the jurors nor the directions of the judge, the court thought, could prevent this substantial risk.

The *Piers Morgan* case also concerned a second, unconnected, article which had also appeared in the *News of the World* concerning the presence in the UK of a gang of 'vicious Vietnamese thugs'. Two alleged members of the gang had been identified by name and by photographs in the newspaper, but the article did not contain the assumptions of guilt which had permeated the fake cash ring story, nor did it refer to any previous convictions of the gang members. Unlike the fake cash article, this second article was not found to be in contempt.

The features which distinguished the articles were the reference to previous convictions/bad character which appeared in the first article but not the second, and the general assumption of guilt which permeated the first article but not the second. The court held that the first article would lead readers to the conclusion that the men identified in the article were guilty of a criminal offence whilst the second was less likely to have that effect.

The danger of publishing reports which are predicated on an assumption of guilt was also emphasised by Simon Brown J,[24] when he said that articles of that kind:

> ... undoubtedly expose the publishers to a real risk of being found in breach of the strict liability rule. To publish as fact, the guilt of a named person after his arrest and before his trial, is not a step to be taken lightly. The risk is,

---

24   Simon Brown J in *AG v Unger* [1998] Cr App R 308.

moreover, heightened the more vulnerable the accused, the more high profile the case and the less accurate the reporting ... All those, therefore, in the business of crime reporting should recognise that articles such as these are published at great peril. They should exercise great caution.

Television – an ephemeral medium?

The cases on the strict liability rule provide support for the view that the residual impact of a publication on a juror at the time of trial may be less strong in the case of television or radio than it would be if the publication is made in writing.

In *AG v ITN*,[25] an item in a television news bulletin concerning the arrest of two men for murder referred to a previous murder conviction of one of the men. The reference to the previous conviction was only made in one bulletin – it was removed from later bulletins. The reference was made some nine months before the trial. The court held that the broadcast had not created a substantial risk of serious prejudice. The court observed that television is 'in its nature ephemeral' and was not persuaded that there was a substantial risk that anyone who had seen or heard the broadcast would have remembered it nine months later. Different considerations might apply, said the court, if the broadcast had been repeated. Publications in newspapers might be more likely to be remembered, since even a casual reader had the opportunity of reading a particular passage twice.

Despite this ephemeral nature, television broadcasts can still be a contempt of court even when they are made months before trial. In *AG v Hat Trick*,[26] the BBC and the makers of the popular show *Have I Got News For You* were found to be in contempt of court for remarks made about the sons of Robert Maxwell, who were due to stand trial for fraud some six months after the programme. The brothers were described by the programme makers as 'heartless, scheming bastards'.

The court held that those words were 'strikingly prejudicial', in that they went to the heart of the forthcoming trial of the brothers and carried the clear implication that the Maxwells were guilty. The court balanced the fact the programme in question was humorous and irreverent and that the remarks were brief and made in the impermanent medium of television against the prejudicial nature of the words, the fact that they were addressed to a large national audience (of about 6.14 million) and the fact that the Maxwells were figures already in the public eye. On the facts, it held that a substantial risk of serious prejudice had been made out.

---

25 *AG v ITN* [1995] 2 All ER 370.

26 *AG v Hat Trick* [1997] EMLR 76.

Publicity during the trial

Where reports are made during the trial, the strict liability rule continues to apply. In the light of the fact that coverage will not benefit from the application of the 'fade factor' and is therefore particularly likely to be recalled by jurors, particular care must be taken over reports during this period.

The fact that the trial judge decides to stay proceedings in the light of media coverage during the trial will not of itself be determinative of contempt. However, it will operate as a 'telling pointer' if an application for contempt is subsequently made.[27]

Media coverage during a trial which does no more than accurately relate what has taken place in open court is unlikely to be a contempt, as it will be doing no more than report what took place in the presence of the jury.[28] However, if the coverage strays beyond a simple report, the chances of being in contempt are high. A recent example occurred in *Taylor and Taylor*,[29] where the Court of Appeal quashed a murder conviction and refused to order a retrial on the ground that the reporting of the trial was 'unremitting, extensive, sensational, inaccurate and misleading' to such an extent that even the trial judge's directions to the jury that they should disregard what had been reported in the media could not have prevailed against it. The court observed that:

> The press is no more entitled to assume guilt in what it writes during the course of a trial than a police officer is entitled to convince himself that a defendant is guilty and suppress evidence.[30]

Proceedings which do not take place before a jury

The most common ground on which a publication may be a contempt is where it involves the risk of prejudicing members of the jury. As a general rule, judges and other legally qualified persons, such as stipendiary magistrates, are presumed to be able to put aside what is reported in the media and to judge cases on the evidence before them.[31] But non-jury cases may also be impeded or prejudiced if the effect of publicity on the parties to

---

27 *AG v Birmingham Post and Mail* [1998] 4 All ER 49.
28 Contempt of Court Act 1981, s 4.
29 *Taylor and Taylor* [1993] 98 Cr App R 983.
30 For further detail, see Naylor, B, 'Fair trial or free press' [1994] CLJ 492.
31 *Re Lonrho* [1989] 2 All ER 1100.

the litigation or on witnesses[32] is such as to create a substantial risk of serious prejudice. An example where this might arise is where media coverage intimidates witnesses from coming forward or from giving evidence.

Defences to the strict liability rule

The Act provides for a number of defences to the strict liability offence as follows.

Innocence

Section 3(1) of the Contempt of Court Act 1981 provides for a limited defence of innocent publication if the publisher can show that, having taken all reasonable care, he did not know *or had no reason to suspect* that proceedings were active at the time of publication. Note that the mistake must concern the active status of the proceedings. It is no defence under s 3(1) for the publisher to show that it did not know that the publication contained material which was a contempt (although, in some circumstances, this defence is available to a distributor, as set out immediately below).

A defence is available to *distributors* under s 3(2) of the Act (rather than to publishers in the strict sense of the word) where the distributor can show that it did not know and had no reason to suspect having taken all reasonable care that, at the time of distribution, it contained such material.

The burden of proof in relation to both the s 3 defences lies upon the person who seeks to rely on the defence,[33] who must show that he took reasonable care in establishing whether proceedings were active (s 3(1) defence) or in relation to the content of the material he is distributing (s 3(2) defence).

Contemporary reports of proceedings

Under s 4 of the Act, a person is not guilty of contempt under the strict liability rule in respect of a 'fair and accurate report of legal proceedings held in public, published contemporaneously and in good faith'.[34] The defence

---

32 And see *AG v Channel Four* (1987) *The Times* 18 December, where the broadcast of a re-enactment of an appeal hearing was ordered to be delayed until after judgment had been given by the Court of Appeal on the ground that the enactment might give a misleading impression about the credibility of witnesses and might influence the public view of the rightness of the court's judgment. This decision has not been followed, and in the light of Schiemann LJ's guidelines in *AG v MGN*, the chances of it being followed are even more remote.

33 Contempt of Court Act 1981, s 3(3).

34 *Ibid*, s 4(1).

relates to *reports* of proceedings. If the media exceed this boundary and begin to comment in their reports of the proceedings, or to seek out and report extraneous events, s 4 will not provide a defence. Trial by newspaper will not be permitted.[35] The court has power to postpone the reporting of certain matters which take place during a trial until the end of the trial. If a report is made in contravention of a s 4 postponement order, the offending publisher might be in contempt of court for disobedience of the terms of a court order. Section 4 orders are considered further below.

Incidental discussion in good faith

Section 5 of the Act provides for a defence to prosecutions brought under the Act where the report is made in the context of a general discussion of public affairs. It provides as follows:

> A publication made as part of a discussion in good faith of public affairs or other matters of general public interest is not to be treated as a contempt of court under the strict liability rule if the risk of impediment or prejudice to particular legal proceedings is merely incidental to the discussion.

Section 5 purports to implement a recommendation of the Phillimore Committee[36] to provide against the gagging of *bona fide* discussion on the ground that legal proceedings in which some particular instance of the issue is being considered just happen to be ongoing.

The Act does not define what is meant by 'public interest'. Case law on public interest was considered in Chapter 5 in the context of breach of confidence. Establishing public interest generally means showing that the material in question is of legitimate concern to the public.

It is important to note that s 5 involves more than simply showing that the report is on a matter of public interest. If the defence is to be made out, it must also be shown that the risk of prejudice to particular legal proceedings is only incidental to the more general discussion.

The requirement that the discussion must be in good faith raises difficulties. The Act gives no indication as to whether good faith is to be assessed subjectively or objectively. The onus is on the Attorney General to show that the publication was not in good faith. This is likely to involve showing some kind of improper motive in publishing the material in question[37] – although this issue is yet to be definitively resolved.

---

35 *AG v News Group Newspapers* [1988] 2 All ER 906, *per* Watkins LJ, p 915.
36 *Report of the Committee on Contempt of Court*, Cmnd 5794, 1974.
37 *AG v English* [1982] 2 WLR 959.

The operation of the defence is illustrated by the case of *AG v English*,[38] which concerned a doctor who was on trial for the murder of a baby which had been born with Down's Syndrome. During his trial, the *Daily Mail* published an article about the candidature for Parliament of a woman who had been born without arms. In the course of the article, the writer stated that 'today, the chances of such a baby [as the candidate] surviving would be very small indeed. Someone would surely recommend letting her die of starvation or otherwise disposing of her'. The article made no express reference to the trial of the doctor.

The Attorney General brought proceedings against the publishers of the article for contempt of court, alleging that the article created a substantial risk that the course of justice in the criminal proceedings against the doctor would be seriously impeded or prejudiced. The House of Lords agreed with the Attorney General that a substantial risk and serious prejudice had been made out, but it went on to uphold the newspaper's defence under s 5 of the Act.

The Law Lords adopted the following reasoning:

- the article was found to constitute a discussion in good faith of public affairs of general public interest – the moral justification of mercy killing;
- under s 5, it was necessary to determine whether the risk of prejudice to the proceedings against the doctor was merely incidental to the general discussion.

The House of Lords held that the onus was on the prosecution to show that the risk of prejudice to the doctor's trial was *not* 'merely incidental' to this discussion, rather than for the defence to show that it was.

The test to determine whether the risk was incidental was not whether an article could have been written as effectively without the passages but whether the risk created by the words chosen by the author was no more than an incidental consequence of expounding the main theme.

On the facts, the prosecution was not able to show that the risk of prejudice to the proceedings was not incidental to the discussion. The decision would probably have been different if the article had made express reference to the prosecution or had involved reports of or scenarios involving the same or similar facts to those at issue in the criminal proceedings.

Guidance on the application of the s 5 'incidental' test was also considered by Lloyd J in *AG v TVS Television*,[39] who thought that the following was a relevant consideration:

---

38 *AG v English* [1982] 2 WLR 959, although it would seem that the usual practice would be to refer the matter to the Attorney General: *AG v Times Newspapers* [1974] AC 273; and Hodgson J in *AG v Sports Newspapers* [1992] 1 All ER 503.

39 *AG v TVS Television* (1989) *The Times*, 7 July.

... look at the subject matter of the discussion and see how closely it relates to the particular legal proceedings. The more closely it relates, the easier it will be for the Attorney General to show that the risk of prejudice is not merely incidental to the discussion. The application of the test is largely a matter of first impression.

(b) Common law contempt

As we have seen, the Contempt of Court Act provides for an offence of strict liability contempt in relation to media reports which can only be invoked when proceedings are active. But the Act is not a complete codification of the law of contempt. Section 6(c) of the Contempt of Court Act 1981 provides that nothing in the Act 'restricts liability for contempt in respect of conduct intended to impede or prejudice the administration of justice'.

An offence of intentional contempt of court continues to exist at common law and, as we shall see, many of the safeguards built into the Act to protect the media against capricious prosecutions do not apply to the common law offence.

The requirements of intentional contempt at common law

In order to give rise to a contempt at common law, the publication in question must give rise to a risk of prejudice to a fair trial which must be shown by the prosecution to be a real possibility.[40]

The prosecution must also prove a *specific intent* on the part of the publisher to impede or prejudice a particular trial. A general intent to interfere with the administration of justice will not be sufficient. The intent need not be the sole motivation for publishing the article. The intent of the publisher may be inferred from the surrounding circumstances, including the foreseeability of the consequences of the publication – although the probability of such consequences occurring must be 'little short of overwhelming' before intention is inferred on the grounds of foreseeability alone.[41]

Unlike strict liability contempt, the common law does *not* require that proceedings must be 'active' in order for a prosecution to be brought. The common law offence is most likely to be invoked in relation to proceedings which are not active – for example, before an arrest in criminal proceedings or between the trial and the filing of an application for permission to appeal. As we have seen, once proceedings have become active, the strict liability rule applies and proceedings for contempt may be brought without any need to prove the publisher's intent to cause prejudice.

---

40   *R v Duffy* [1960] 2 All ER 891.
41   *AG v News Group Newspapers* [1988] 2 All ER 906.

The lack of a requirement that proceedings must be active at common law means that a publication may be a contempt even where proceedings have not yet been commenced. The orthodox view is that proceedings must at least be imminent before a prosecution for intentional contempt may be brought.[42] The term 'imminent' is vague, and this uncertainty was one of the defects in the common law of contempt which the Phillimore Committee identified in its 1974 Report, where it observed that:[43]

> A particular cause for anxiety on the part of the press is the uncertainty as to the time when the law of contempt applies ... The view was pressed on us that these uncertainties have an unfortunately inhibiting effect upon the press and that it is of great importance to those who are concerned with public communication to be given more definite guidance.

The Committee recommended the introduction of demarcation lines governing the time at which publications may be held to be in contempt (this recommendation was taken up in an amended form in the definition of 'active' in the Contempt of Court Act 1981). The Committee also recommended that contempt proceedings should only be brought where proceedings have been commenced or in criminal cases where a suspect has been charged or a summons served.

These recommendations have not been incorporated into the common law. It remains possible for the media to commit an intentional contempt at common law by reporting the commission of a crime before anyone has been arrested or charged.

The question of whether proceedings are imminent should be judged through the eyes of the publisher, and it is a test of apparent imminence judged at the time of publication. The court should ask itself: 'What appeared to the publisher at the time of publication to be likely to happen?'[44] The issue should not be judged with the benefit of hindsight in the light of what actually happened.

In *AG v Sport Newspapers*, *The Sport* newspaper published an article about a man that the police wished to question concerning the abduction of a young girl. The article identified the man and described him as 'a vicious evil rapist' with 'a horrific history of sex attacks'. At the time that the article was published, all that was known about the suspect was that he had disappeared. There was nothing to indicate that he would be apprehended shortly after publication. In fact, a warrant was issued shortly after publication, and the suspect was arrested shortly after that. The court held that proceedings were not apparently imminent at the time of publication judged through the eyes of the publisher at that time – although, on the facts, they turned out to be so.

---

42   *AG v Sport Newspapers* [1992] 1 All ER 503.

43   *Phillimore Committee on Contempt of Court*, Cmnd 5794, 1974.

44   *AG v News Group Newspapers* [1988] 2 All ER 906.

Imminence – an unacceptable extension?

We have seen that the vague test of imminence is an unsuitable yardstick against which the media should have to regulate their actions. Yet, worryingly, the courts have sought to extend the circumstances in which a prosecution for contempt at common law may be brought by seeking to do away with the need for proceedings to be imminent at all.

In *AG v News Group Newspapers*,[45] *The Sun* was found to have committed intentional contempt by publishing an article which the court found was intended to prejudice the trial of a doctor against whom the newspaper were *considering* funding a private prosecution. The publication was in contempt, even though proceedings were only contemplated or envisaged. The court observed that:

> The circumstances in which a criminal contempt at common law can be committed are not necessarily, in my judgment, confined to those in which proceedings are either pending or imminent ... The common law surely does not tolerate conduct which involves the giving of encouragement and practical assistance to a person to bring about a private prosecution accompanied by an intention to interfere with the course of justice by publishing material about the person to be prosecuted which could only serve to and was so intended to prejudice the fair trial of that person.[46]

In the later case of *AG v Sport Newspapers*,[47] Bingham LJ expressed himself technically unable to depart from *The Sun* decision, although he had reservations about it. He observed that *The Sun* decision had the effect of 'enlarging a quasi-criminal liability in a field very recently considered by Parliament [in the Contempt of Court Act 1981].[48] In the same case, Hodgson J described *The Sun* decision as 'wrong' and indicated that he would refuse to follow it. He drew attention to the fact that *The Sun* decision concerned unusual facts. The newspaper had not only published the offending report about X, but was also giving active support for the commencement of a private prosecution against X over the matters which were the subject of its report. It is possible that, in the light of the *Sport* decision, *The Sun* case will be confined to its own facts in the future.

The common law offence militates against freedom of expression

The retention of common law contempt presents a real difficulty for the media.

---

45 *AG v News Group Newspapers* [1988] 2 All ER 906.

46 Watkins LJ in *ibid*, p 920.

47 *AG v Sport Newspapers* [1992] 1 All ER 503.

48 *Ibid*, p 514.

The wider the interpretation of the term 'imminent' (or the removal of that requirement altogether, à la *The Sun* decision), the more serious are the potential implications for freedom of expression. There was no consideration in *The Sun* case of the implications that the removal of the need for imminence might have on the media's freedom of expression.

Example

A newspaper wishes to highlight an alleged crime and to stimulate a demand for prosecution against the alleged perpetrator. This is part of the media's role as watchdogs which the European Court of Human Rights has highlighted on numerous occasions (provided that the reporting is carried out in a responsible fashion).[49] Yet, the possibility of prosecution at common law for contempt of court may deter the media from reporting such stories on the ground that they will cause prejudice to any trial which might eventually take place. As Hodgson J observed in the *Sport* case, 'many of the "targets" of investigative journalism are rich and powerful, and who is to say that they, when attacked, will not respond by seeking leave to move for contempt [at common law]'.[50]

It is therefore important that common law contempt is applied in a similar way to strict liability contempt – to ensure that an application for contempt will only be made out where there is a realistic possibility that a report will influence the outcome of legal proceedings.

There have, in fact, been few prosecutions for common law contempt since the 1981 Act came into force. In the light of the importance of the 'fade factor' which the courts have emphasised in relation to the strict liability rule, the residual impact of publications made before proceedings were even commenced is especially unlikely to be found to be sufficiently sharp in the minds of jurors by the time of any eventual trial to give rise to a finding of contempt. But each case must be judged on its merits. The possibility remains that a successful prosecution for contempt at common law may be brought in appropriate circumstances where proceedings were not active at the time of publication.

Contempt of court and the Human Rights Act 1998

The incorporation of the Human Rights Act 1998 is likely to be beneficial to the media in the field of contempt of court. A successful prosecution for contempt of court is a restriction on freedom of expression, and in order to be

---

49 Eg, *Observer v UK* (1991) EHRR 153.
50 Hodgson J in *AG v Sport Newspapers* [1992] 1 All ER 503, p 535.

compatible with European Convention jurisprudence it must be prescribed by law and necessary in a democratic society. The risk of prejudice caused by a publication to the proceedings in question must accordingly be realistically evaluated in every case. The *Knights* judgment focuses on the importance of assessing whether prejudice is *really* likely to have been caused from a realistic standpoint. To that extent, the judgment is in line with the requirements of the Convention. It serves to underline the fact that freedom of expression ought only to give way to other interests where there is a real, rather than a fanciful or remote, need for them to do so.

Penalties for strict liability and intentional contempt

In the *Piers Morgan* case, a fine of £50,000 was imposed. The court accepted that there was no intention to interfere with the course of justice. However, the public interest required that the penalty reflected the very serious effect which the article had had on the administration of justice. The article had resulted in the counterfeiting prosecution being permanently stayed. Factors taken into account in imposing the penalty were deterrence and the means of the defendant on the one hand, and in mitigation on the other hand the fact that the *News of the World* had a laudable record of co-operating with the police in the investigation of crime.

The *Piers Morgan* case was used as a benchmark in the case of *AG v Associated Newspapers*,[51] where a fine of £40,000 was imposed in respect of the publication in the *Evening Standard* of information which the court had ordered not to be disclosed. Kennedy LJ observed that the publication was a serious contempt which had resulted in a criminal trial being aborted and a significant penalty was required. Relevant to the amount of the fine was the culpability of the offender and the offender's means. It was accepted that there had been no intention to interfere with the administration of justice. The publication had been a negligent mistake. Also relevant in mitigation was the fact that the newspaper had never previously been found to be in contempt, that an apology had been given to the court and that steps had now been put in place by the newspaper to prevent a recurrence. These factors justified a lesser fine than had been imposed in the *News of the World* case.

In the *Birmingham Post and Mail* case,[52] a fine of £20,000 was imposed. The court weighed aggravating factors against mitigating factors as follows.

---

51   *AG v Associated Newspapers* (1997) unreported.
52   *AG v Birmingham Post and Mail* [1998] 4 All ER 49.

Aggravating

- The fact that the jury had had to be discharged and the proceedings started afresh involving additional expense of £87,000.

Mitigating

- This was the first finding of contempt against the respondents.
- The publication took place in a regional rather than a national newspaper with a circulation of approximately 26,000.
- The publication resulted from a mistake. There was no intention to prejudice the administration of justice, nor a conscious and deliberate taking of risk with a view to selling papers. The mistake had been taken seriously and proper procedures had been put in place to guard against any recurrence.
- An apology was given to the court. However, in the light of the fact that the contempt allegation had been contested by the respondent, the court observed that it was difficult to place much weight on the plea.

In *AG v Hat Trick*, fines of £10,000 were imposed on each respondent. Auld LJ described the case as involving 'a most serious contempt' following a decision to publish of 'a risk taking variety'.

The culpability of the offender is relevant to the amount of the fine both under the strict liability rule (although, as we have seen, liability itself is not dependent on the guilt or otherwise of the offender) and at common law (where it *is* necessary to prove intent in order to establish liability). Where an intention to interfere with the administration of justice is proved, the penalties are likely to reflect that fact. In *AG v News Group Newspapers*, where intention contempt was established against *The Sun*, a fine of £75,000 was imposed.

REPORTING RESTRICTIONS[53]

Open justice

The courts have long recognised the principle of open justice – the right of public access to the workings of the courts. In *AG v Leveller Magazine*,[54] Lord Diplock opined on why open justice is important. He said:

---

53 The Newspaper Society has produced a useful fact sheet on Guidelines on court reporting restrictions available on www.newspapersoc.org.uk.

54 *AG v Leveller Magazine* [1979] AC 440, pp 449–50.

As a general rule, the English system of administering justice does require that it be done in public. If the way that courts behave cannot be hidden from the public ear and eye, this provides a safeguard against judicial arbitrariness or idiosyncrasy and maintains the public confidence in the administration of justice. The application of this principle of open justice has two aspects: as respects proceedings in the court itself, it requires that they should be held in open court to which the Press and public are admitted and that, in criminal cases at any rate, all evidence communicated to the court is communicated publicly. As respects the publication to a wider public of fair and accurate reports of proceedings that have taken place in court, the principle requires that nothing should be done to discourage this.

In other words, justice must not just be done; it must be seen to be done.

Art 6(1) of the European Convention on Human Rights requires that, in general, court hearings are to be held in public. The press and public may be excluded only for the reasons specified in the article, namely 'in the interests of morals, public order or national security, where the interest of juveniles or the protection of the private life of the parties so require, or to the extent strictly necessary in the opinion of the court in special circumstances where publicity would prejudice the interests of justice'.

Where a court – whether criminal or civil – does not sit in public, the hearing is known as a hearing held *in camera*.

Hearings in private – civil proceedings

This principle of open justice is incorporated into the Civil Procedure Rules, which regulate the conduct of civil (that is, non-criminal) proceedings in England and Wales.

Rule 39.2 of the CPR provides that:

(1) The general rule is that a hearing is to be in public.

...

(3) A hearing, or any part of it, may be in private if:

    (a) publicity would defeat the object of the hearing;

    (b) it involves matters relating to national security;

    (c) it involves confidential information (including information relating to personal financial matters) and publicity would damage that confidentiality;

    (d) a private hearing is necessary to protect the interest of any child or patient;

    (e) it is a hearing of an application made without notice and it would be unjust to any respondent for there to be a public hearing;

    (f) it involves uncontentious matters arising in the administration of trusts or in the administration of a dead person's estate;

    (g) the court considers this to be necessary in the interests of justice.

The practice direction to this rule provides that the decision as to whether to hold a hearing in public or private must be made by the judge conducting the proceedings having regard to any representations which may have been made to him and to Art 6 of the European Convention on Human Rights. The direction provides that the judge may need to consider whether the case is within any of the exceptions permitted by Art 6(1).

The principles embodied in the criminal law cases regarding private hearings should also be considered.

Civil hearings in chambers

Some court hearings are held in chambers. Such hearings generally relate to procedural matters and they usually take place before trial. As a matter of administrative convenience, hearings in chambers invariably take place in the judge's rooms rather than in open court. But hearings in chambers are not private in the same sense as hearings held *in camera*.

In the recent case of *Hodgson v Imperial Tobacco*,[55] the Court of Appeal clarified the following principles about hearings in chambers:

- the public (and the press) have no right to attend hearings in chambers because of the nature of the business transacted in chambers and because of the physical restrictions on the room available, but, if requested, permission should be granted to the public attend the hearing when and to the extent that this is practical;

- what happens during proceedings in chambers is not confidential – information about what occurs and the judgment or order of the court can, and in the case of a judgment or order should, be made available to the public when requested;

- if members of the public who seek to attend proceedings in chambers cannot be accommodated in the judge's room, the judge should consider adjourning the proceedings in whole or in part into open court to the extent that this is practical or allowing one or more representatives of the media to attend the hearing in chambers;

- the disclosure of what occurs in chambers does not constitute a breach of confidence, nor does it amount to contempt so long as any comment which is made does not substantially prejudice the administration of justice;

- the above general principles do not apply in exceptional circumstances where a court with authority to do so orders otherwise. It is likely that CPR 39.3 will apply to determine the exceptional circumstances in which a court is justified in departing from the general rules.

---

55 *Hodgson v Imperial Tobacco* [1998] 1 WLR 1056.

Hearings in private – criminal proceedings

There is no equivalent of the Civil Procedure Rules in relation to criminal trials. The general principles about hearings held *in camera* are drawn from case law, which has consistently emphasised that the decision to sit *in camera* should only be made in exceptional circumstances where the administration of justice requires it. There must be compelling reasons for the decision to exclude the public. In *AG v Leveller*,[56] Lord Diplock emphasised that the departure from the norm of open justice must be justified to the extent and to no more than the extent that the court reasonably believes to be necessary in order to serve the ends of justice.

In *R v Lewes Prison (Governor) ex p Doyle*,[57] the Divisional Court observed that it was impossible to enumerate all the contingencies, but that where the administration of justice would be rendered impracticable by the presence of the public, whether because the case could not effectively be tried or the parties entitled to justice would be reasonably deterred from seeking it at the hands of the court, the court has power to exclude the public.[58]

Later cases have emphasised that sitting in private is an exceptional step to take and should be avoided if there is any other way of serving the interests of justice.[59] Alternatives to sitting in private are contained in ss 4 and 11 of the Contempt of Court Act 1981, which are considered below.

Postponing media reports

Section 4(2) of the Contempt of Court Act 1981

This section provides as follows:

> The court may, where it appears necessary for avoiding a substantial risk of prejudice to the administration of justice in those proceedings or any other proceedings, pending or imminent, order that the publication of any report of the proceedings or any part of the proceedings be postponed for such period as the court thinks necessary for that purpose.

Note the following about the section:

- the court must *order* postponement. A judicial request will not suffice;[60]
- the risk of prejudice must be to the proceedings in question or to other proceedings which are imminent or pending. The same uncertainty as to

---

56 *AG v Leveller Magazine* [1979] AC 440, p 450.

57 *R v Lewes Prison (Governor) ex p Doyle* [1917] 2 KB 254, DC, p 271 (Viscount Reading CJ).

58 This has been put on a statutory footing in relation to vulnerable or intimidated witnesses by the Youth Justice and Criminal Evidence Act 1999 – see below.

59 See, eg, *R v Reigate Justices ex p Argus Newspapers* (1983) 5 Cr App R(S) 181, DC.

60 *AG v Leveller Magazine* [1979] AC 440, p 473.

the meaning of 'imminent' bedevils the application of this section as it does the application of the common law of intentional contempt (considered above). What is clear is that the risk must be to some specific proceedings rather than in the interest of the administration of justice generally;

• the risk of prejudice must be substantial. As we have seen in relation to s 2, this means that the risk must be more than remote;[61]

• the order is for postponement of a report of the whole or any part of the proceedings. It is not an open-ended postponement. The period of delay must be as long as the court thinks necessary for avoiding the substantial risk of prejudice;

• the order must be necessary. In the context of interpreting s 10 of the same Act, the House of Lords have held that 'necessary' means more than desirable, convenient, expedient or useful.[62]

The courts have interpreted s 4(2) restrictively. In *R v Horsham Justices ex p Farquharson*,[63] Lord Denning remarked of the section:

> I cannot think that Parliament in s 4(2) ever intended to cut down or abridge the freedom of the press as hitherto established by law. All it does is to make clear to editors what is permissible and what is not. In considering whether to make an order under s 4(2), the sole consideration is the risk of prejudice to the administration of justice. Whoever has to consider it should remember that at a trial judges are not influenced by what they may have read in the newspapers. Nor are the ordinary folk who sit on juries. They are good, sensible people. They go by the evidence that is adduced before them and not by what they may have read in the newspapers. The risk of their being influenced is so slight that it can usually be disregarded as insubstantial and therefore not the subject of an order under s 4(2).

This *dictum* was cited by Lord Lane CJ in a case involving a misuse of the powers under s 4(2), *Ex p Central Television*.[64] In that case, the jury retired to a hotel overnight to consider its verdict. The trial judge made an order that no report of the case should be broadcast that night. He did so with the express purpose of ensuring that the jury was able to relax that night. On appeal, the order was overturned. Nothing in the broadcast reports during the trial gave rise to the fear that the reports would be anything other than fair and accurate. There were no grounds on which the judge could have concluded that there was a substantial risk of prejudice. Lord Lane CJ indicated that, even where

---

61 *AG v English* [1982] 2 All ER 903.
62 *Re an Inquiry under Company Securities (Insider Dealing) Act 1985* [1988] AC 660, *per* Lord Griffiths, p 704.
63 *R v Horsham Justices ex p Farquharson* [1982] 2 QB 800.
64 *Ex p Central Television* [1991] 1 WLR 4.

there was a slight risk of prejudice, a judge should bear in minds the extract from Lord Denning's judgment in *R v Horsham Justices* when deciding whether to make a s 4(2) order.

An example of circumstances where a s 4(2) order might be appropriate was given by the House of Lords in *AG v Leveller*,[65] who remarked that a *voire dire* (or a trial within a trial), which is held in the absence of a jury on matters such as the admissibility of evidence, might be an appropriate subject of an order postponing a report of those proceedings until the jury has given its verdict. A fair and accurate report of that procedure might prejudice the position of the defendant if published prior to the jury's verdict.

Section 11 of the Contempt of Court Act 1981

Section 11 of the Contempt of Court Act 1981 provides as follows:

> In any case where a court (having power to do so) allows a name or other matter to be withheld from the public in proceedings before the court, the court may give such directions prohibiting the publication of the name or matter in connection with the proceedings as appear to the court to be necessary for the purpose for which it was so withheld.

The section is recognition of the court's ability to withhold publication of certain types of information, such as the identity of a witness, from the public in the course of civil or criminal proceedings. Where the court has such power, s 11 provides that the court may prohibit publication of the material in question, *but only where it appears necessary to do so for the purpose for which the material has been withheld during the proceedings.*

The section does not permit a court to prohibit publication of material which has not been withheld from the public during the trial.[66]

The form of s 4(2) and s 11 orders

Where the court makes an order under s 4(2) or s 11 of the Contempt of Court Act, it must keep a permanent record of the order. The order must be formulated in precise terms, setting out its precise scope and, where appropriate, the time at which the order will cease to have effect and the specific purpose for making the order.

The courts should normally give notice to the press that an order has been made, and court staff should be prepared to answer any inquiry about a particular case, but it is the responsibility of the media to ensure that no

---

65 *AG v Leveller Magazine* [1979] AC 440, p 473.

66 *R v Arundel Justices ex p Westminster Press* [1985] 2 All ER 390, where it was held that the court could not prohibit publication of the name of a defendant where the name had been freely used during the course of the trial.

breach of the order occurs and the onus rests with them to make any inquiry in cases of doubt.[67]

Other reporting restrictions

There are a ragbag of statutes which contain restrictions on the reporting of certain court proceedings. As a result, it can be difficult to get a complete overview of the law. A selection of the most important restrictions which apply to particular types of proceedings are set out below.

Anonymity for victims of sex offences

Victims of the following types of sex offence may not be identified in reports of both civil and criminal proceedings:[68] rape (including male rape),[69] attempted rape, aiding, abetting, counselling or procuring rape or attempted rape, incitement to rape, conspiracy to rape and burglary with intent to rape. Similar restrictions apply to various other sexual offences, including buggery and indecent assault.[70] The restrictions apply not only to the victim's identity, but also to material which could lead the victim to be identified. This prohibition on identification is mandatory. No court order is required to implement it.

The restrictions apply from the time of an allegation of the above offences by the victim or by some other person. They continue to apply throughout the victim's lifetime, even where the allegation is withdrawn or the accused is ultimately tried for a lesser offence. The restrictions apply throughout the UK.[71]

A judge can remove the victim's anonymity where he is satisfied that it imposes a substantial and unreasonable restriction on the reporting of the trial and that it is in the public interest to lift it.[72] The anonymity may also be lifted on the application of the defence to bring witnesses forward where the judge is satisfied that the defence would otherwise be substantially prejudiced or the accused would suffer substantial injustice.

The victim may also waive his/her right to anonymity provided that the consent is given freely.

---

67   *Practice Direction* [1983] 1 All ER 64.
68   Sexual Offences (Amendment) Act 1976, as amended by the Criminal Justice Act 1988 and set out in the Sexual Offences (Amendment) Act 1992.
69   Criminal Justice and Public Order Act 1994.
70   Sexual Offences (Amendment) Act 1992.
71   Youth Justice and Criminal Evidence Act 1999.
72   Sexual Offences (Amendment) Act 1976, s 4(3).

The restrictions do not apply to the identity of the *accused*[73] (unless naming the accused is likely to reveal the identity of the victim), but the trial judge might place restrictions on the identification of the accused by virtue of his powers under s 11 of the Contempt of Court Act 1981.

The reader is also referred to s 25 of the Youth Justice and Criminal Evidence Act 1999 for details of the court's ability in criminal proceedings to make orders for the exclusion of persons from the court when vulnerable witnesses are giving evidence. Section 25(4) provides that such orders (known as 'special measures directions' under the Act) may be made where the proceedings relate to a sexual offence.[74]

In addition to the above statutory provisions, the Code of Practice which is enforced by the Press Complaints Commission provides that newspapers should not publish material which is likely to contribute to the identification of victims of sexual assault, unless there is adequate justification for it and by law they are free to do so.[75]

Committal hearings

Section 8 of the Magistrates' Court Act 1980 places restrictions on the contents of reports of preliminary hearings of indictable offences which take place in magistrates courts, for example, committal proceedings. Such reports are limited to the provision of general information – typically the names of the parties (if not prevented by other reporting restrictions), the charges and the decision of the bench to commit. The accused can apply to have the restrictions lifted.[76] Even where they are lifted, the general law of contempt will apply, in particular the strict liability rule set out in the Contempt of Court Act 1981 and the common law of intentional contempt.

---

73   Criminal Justice Act 1988.
74   Section 62 defines 'sexual offences' for the purposes of the 1999 Act.
75   PCC Code, cl 12.
76   Magistrates' Court Act 1980, s 8(2).

CHILDREN AND YOUNG PERSONS

Civil proceedings

Section 39 of the Children and Young Persons Act 1933 (as amended by s 49 of the Criminal Justice and Public Order Act 1994)

Section 39 of the Children and Young Persons Act 1933 provides as follows:

(1) In relation to any proceedings in any court ... the court may direct that:

(a) no newspaper report of the proceedings shall reveal the name, address, or school, or include any particulars calculated to lead to the identification of any child or young person concerned in the proceedings, either as being the person [by or against] or in respect of whom the proceedings are taken, or as being a witness therein;

(b) no picture shall be published in any newspaper as being or including a picture of any child or young person so concerned in the proceedings as aforesaid,

except in so far (if at all) as may be permitted by the direction of the court.

The section applies to any person under the age of 18.[77] It applies to civil proceedings. Criminal proceedings are now covered by the Youth Justice and Criminal Evidence Act 1999 (considered below).

The section applies to broadcasts as well as to press reports.

Criminal proceedings

Youth Justice and Criminal Evidence Act 1999

This Act contains a bundle of reporting restrictions which apply to *criminal proceedings*. The restrictions have their origins in a Government document entitled *Speaking Up For Justice* (June 1998). The document made a number of recommendations about the treatment of vulnerable and intimidated witnesses in criminal proceedings. The objective of the recommendations, and of the Act's provisions, is to assist such witnesses to give evidence where they would otherwise have difficulty doing so or would be reluctant to do so. The restrictions contained in the Act on media reports have the potential to be extremely significant unless they are implemented with caution.

The Act contains the following restrictions on media reports:

---

77 Criminal Justice Act 1991, s 68.

Reports concerning persons under the age of 18

Section 44

The section applies where a *criminal* investigation has begun in respect of an alleged offence against the law of England and Wales or Northern Ireland. The term 'criminal investigation' is defined as an investigation conducted by police officers or other persons charged with the duty of investigating offences with a view to it being ascertained whether a person should be charged with the offence.[78]

The restrictions in the section accordingly apply at an early stage – before criminal proceedings could be said to be imminent or pending.

The section provides that no matter relating to any person involved in a criminal offence as defined above shall, while the person is under the age of 18, be included in any publication if it is likely to lead members of the public to identify the person as a person involved in the offence.[79] If the person reaches the age of 18 whilst the proceedings are ongoing, it appears that the restrictions cease to apply.

The Act provides a non-exhaustive list of the type of information which will fall foul of the restrictions. These include the person's name, address, school or place of work or a still or moving picture.[80]

The court may dispense with the restrictions where it is satisfied that it is necessary in the interests of justice to do so,[81] but the court must have regard to the welfare of the person concerned when deciding whether to lift the restrictions.[82] Note that a court order is not required to implement the provisions in s 44.

Most controversial is the definition of 'person involved in an offence'.[83] It includes the person by whom the offence is alleged to have been committed. But it also includes the following persons:

(a) a person against or in respect of whom the offence is alleged to have been committed; and

(b) a witness to the alleged offence.

The inclusion of the latter two categories of persons to whom the restrictions will apply caused great consternation amongst the media. A restriction on reporting any matter which would be likely to lead members of the public to identify the victim of a crime or a witness to it would effectively prevent the

---

78   Youth Justice and Criminal Evidence Act 1999, s 44(13).
79   *Ibid*, s 44(2).
80   *Ibid*, s 44(6).
81   *Ibid*, s 44(7).
82   *Ibid*, s 44(8).
83   *Ibid*, s 44(4).

media from reporting many incidents. The media supplied the Government with bundles of articles which, it was claimed, would have been impossible to write if the s 44 restrictions had been in force at the time when they were published. These included reports of the stabbing of the headmaster, Philip Lawrence and the attack on the Wolverhampton nursery school teacher, Lisa Potts. As a result of this lobbying, something of a fudge was arrived at.

The restrictions set out in s 44 will apply to the extent that they could lead to identification of the alleged perpetrator of the offence. But the Government agreed to keep the s 44 restrictions in reserve in so far as they relate to persons against or in respect of whom the offence is alleged to have been committed and witnesses to the offence. The restrictions will only be brought into force in respect of such persons when the Home Secretary lays a draft order before Parliament which is to be approved only after separate debates in both the House of Commons and the House of Lords.[84] Speaking on behalf of the Government, Paul Boateng MP stated:

> We are persuaded of the need to provide protection for children who might be harmed by publicity in relation to a crime. It is only sensible, when crimes and criminal investigations are reported, to ensure that attention is paid to the welfare of children and the possible consequences of their being identified in the media. Children should not be identified if this would put them at risk or do them harm.
>
> But we are also clear that there is a proper balance in the public interest to be struck and that Parliament should not without good reason bring into effect restrictions on responsible and legitimate reporting of news.

This speech can be interpreted as a guarded warning to the media – be responsible in your reporting of criminal offences involving persons under the age of 18, or the provisions of s 44 may be implemented in full.

The restrictions contained in s 44 cease to apply once the offence becomes the subject of criminal proceedings. At that stage, s 45 of the Act enables the court to separate restrictions on reporting criminal proceedings involving persons under the age of 18.

Section 45

Section 45 of the Act applies to reports concerning persons under the age of 18 after criminal proceedings have begun (the Act does not contain a definition of the starting point for such proceedings). The restrictions apply to criminal proceedings for an alleged offence against the laws of England and Wales or Northern Ireland.[85]

---

84 Government press release, 16.6.1999.
85 Youth Justice and Criminal Evidence Act 1999, s 45(1).

During the course of such proceedings, *the court may direct* that nothing relating to any person concerned in the proceedings shall, while that person is under the age of 18, be included in any publication if it is likely to lead members of the public to identify that person as a person concerned in the proceedings.[86] Note that a court order is required – the provisions of s 45 are not mandatory.

The Act provides that, for the purposes of s 45, a reference to a person concerned in the proceedings is a reference to a person against or in respect of whom proceedings are taken or to a person who is a witness in the proceedings.[87]

The Act contains a non-exhaustive list of the type of matters which is likely to lead to identification.[88] It is in identical terms to the list contained in s 44 above.

A court may dispense with any restrictions imposed by an order referred made under s 45 where:

(a) it is satisfied it is necessary to do so in the interests of justice;[89] or

(b) it is satisfied that their effect is to impose a substantial and unreasonable restriction on the reporting of the proceedings *and* it is in the public interest to remove or relax the restriction.[90]

When considering whether to make an order restricting publication or a direction dispensing with such restriction, the court shall have regard to the welfare of the person concerned.[91]

REPORTING RESTRICTIONS AND INTIMIDATED AND VULNERABLE PERSONS

The Youth Justice and Criminal Evidence Act 1999 also provides for reporting restrictions to be imposed when vulnerable or intimidated persons are giving evidence, irrespective of the age of the persons concerned.

The Act provides that a court can apply 'special measures' to assist or encourage such persons to give evidence. The special measures include screening a witness from the accused while he/she is giving evidence, provision for evidence to be given by way of a live link and provision for video recorded evidence. One of the special measures relates to the exclusion

---

86 Youth Justice and Criminal Evidence Act 1999, s 45(3).

87 *Ibid*, s 45(7).

88 *Ibid*, s 45(8).

89 *Ibid*, s 45(4).

90 *Ibid*, s 45(5).

91 *Ibid*, s 45(6).

of the public from the court while the witness is giving evidence.[92] Representatives of news gathering or reporting organisations may be amongst the excluded persons.

In recognition of the principle of open justice, the Act does make provision[93] that, where a direction is made to exclude members of the public, one named representative of a news gathering or news reporting organisation may remain in court. The representative should be nominated for the purpose by one or more news gathering/reporting organisations.

A special measures direction (or order) may be made on the application of the prosecution or the defence, or the court may make such a direction of its own motion.

The Act provides that a special measures direction may only provide for exclusion of members of the public where:

(a) the proceedings relate to a sexual offence as defined in s 62 of the Act; or

(b) it appears to the court that there are reasonable grounds for believing that any person other than the accused has sought or will seek to intimidate the witness in connection with testifying in the proceedings.

Where the public is excluded from part of a hearing under the above provisions, the Act provides that proceedings shall nevertheless be taken to be held in public for purposes of any privilege or exemption from liability for contempt of court in respect of fair, accurate and contemporaneous reports of legal proceedings in public.[94]

In making a special measures direction (including an exclusion direction), the court must consider all the circumstances of the case including, in particular, any views expressed by the witness and whether the measure might tend to inhibit such evidence being effectively tested by a party to the proceedings.[95]

Special measures may only be directed where the witness in question meets criteria set out in ss 16 and 17 of the Act.

Section 16 applies to witnesses suffering from mental or physical impairment and witnesses under the age of 17 at the time of the hearing.

Section 17 has a wider scope. A complainant in a sexual offences case who is a witness in proceedings relating to that offence is automatically classed as eligible unless she/he has informed the court of their wish not to be so eligible.[96] Also eligible under s 17 are witnesses in respect of whom the court

---

92 Youth Justice and Criminal Evidence Act 1999, s 25.

93 *Ibid*, s 25(3).

94 *Ibid*, s 25(5).

95 *Ibid*, s 19(3).

96 *Ibid*, s 17(4).

is satisfied that the quality of their evidence is likely to be diminished by reason of fear or distress in connection with testifying on the part of the witness.[97]

Other reporting restrictions under the Act

Section 46 of the Youth Justice and Criminal Evidence Act 1999 provides for further reporting restrictions where the court makes a 'reporting direction' in relation to any witness, regardless of his age. A reporting direction will provide that no matter relating to the witness shall, during the witness's lifetime, be included in any publication if it is likely to lead members of the public to identify him as a witness to the proceedings.[98] The Act gives a non-exhaustive list of the type of matter which might be likely to lead to identification. It includes the following matters:

- the name of the witness;
- the address of the witness;
- identification of his place of work or educational establishment;
- a still or moving picture of the witness.[99]

A reporting direction may be made in relation to criminal proceedings against the laws of England and Wales or Northern Ireland and it may concern a witness in such proceedings (other than the accused) who is 18 or over.[100]

A court may give a reporting direction if it determines:

- a witness is eligible for protection; and
- the reporting direction is likely to improve the quality of the witness's evidence, and the level of co-operation given by the witness to any party to the proceedings in connection with that party's case.[101] The Act states that this will include co-operation with the prosecution.[102]

A witness is eligible if the court is satisfied that:

(a) the quality of the evidence given by the witness; or

(b) the level of co-operation,

is likely to be diminished by reason of fear or distress on the part of the witness in connection with being identified by the public as a witness in the proceedings.[103]

---

97 Youth Justice and Criminal Evidence Act 1999, s 17(1).
98 *Ibid*, s 46(6).
99 *Ibid*, s 46(7).
100 *Ibid*, s 46(1).
101 *Ibid*, s 46(2).
102 *Ibid*, s 46(12).
103 *Ibid*, s 46(3).

The court must also take into account the following matters when determining eligibility:

- nature and alleged circumstances of the offence;
- the age of the witness;
- social and cultural background and ethnic origins of the witness;
- the witness's domestic and employment circumstances;
- the witness's religious or political opinions;
- any behaviour towards the witness on the part of the accused, members of the accused's family or his associates, or any other person who is likely to be accused or a witness to the proceedings.[104]

The court should also take into account the views expressed by the witness.[105]

The court should also consider:

(a) whether the direction would be in the interests of justice; and

(b) the public interest in avoiding the imposition of a substantial and unreasonable restriction on the reporting of the proceedings.[106]

Challenging reporting restrictions

The media can challenge orders restricting the reporting of proceedings in court.

Orders made by magistrates' courts may be challenged by way of an application to the Divisional Court for judicial review.

Other orders relating to criminal proceedings may be challenged under the procedure set out in s 159 of the Criminal Justice Act 1988, which provides for appeal to the Court of Appeal against orders made under s 4 or 11 of the Contempt of Court Act 1981:

(a) restricting admission of the public to the proceedings or any part of the proceedings;

(b) restricting the reporting of proceedings or part of the proceedings (for example, a reporting direction under the Youth Justice and Criminal Evidence Act 1999).

It is likely that s 4 or 11 orders made during the course of civil proceedings may be challenged by way of application for judicial review or on appeal to the Court of Appeal.

---

104 Youth Justice and Criminal Evidence Act 1999, s 46(4).
105 *Ibid*, s 46(5).
106 *Ibid*, s 46(8).

CHAPTER 11

DISCLOSURE OF JOURNALISTS' SOURCES

> So that journalists can effectively discharge their right, indeed their duty, to
> expose wrongdoing, abuse, corruption and incompetence in all aspects of
> central and local government, of business, industry, the professions and all
> aspects of society, they have to receive information, including confidential
> information, from a variety of sources including seedy and disloyal sources.[1]

It is a long standing journalistic tenet that the identity of sources of
information provided to the media for possible publication should not be
revealed. The Press Complaints Commission Code of Practice places print
journalists under an obligation not to reveal their sources,[2] by providing that
journalists have a moral obligation to protect confidential sources. The
National Union of Journalists code of conduct contains a similar provision.
The rationale for this principle was described by Morland J in *John v Express*[3]
in the following terms: '... it is vitally important, if the press is to perform its
public function in our democracy, that a person possessed of information on
matters of public interest should not be deterred from coming forward by fear
of exposure. To encourage such disclosure, it is necessary to offer a thorough
protection to confidential sources generally.'

It follows that the empowerment of the courts to order a journalist to
disclose his sources of information can act as an impediment to freedom of
expression. Potential informants will be deterred from coming forward by the
prospect that their identity might be made known. These are sentiments
expressed in the judgment of the European Court of Human Rights in
Goodwin v UK.[4] We shall see in this chapter that, whilst the English courts
have paid lip service to these principles, some of their judgments have done
little to guarantee the anonymity of sources, although a recent decision of the
Court of Appeal offers the prospect of a more promising future.[5]

The English *law* on disclosure of sources is governed by statute – the
Contempt of Court Act 1981. Section 10 of that Act provides as follows:

> No court may require a person to disclose, nor is any person guilty of
> contempt of court for refusing to disclose, the source of information contained
> in a publication for which he is responsible, unless it is established to the

---

1   Morland J in *John v Express* [2000] 1 All ER 280.
2   PCC Code of Practice, cl 15.
3   Morland J in *John v Express* [2000] 1 All ER 280.
4   *Goodwin v UK* (1996) 22 EHRR 123.
5   *John v Express* [2000] 3 All ER 267, CA.

satisfaction of the court that disclosure is necessary in the interests of justice or national security or for the prevention of disorder or crime.

The starting point in construing the section is that it is intended to protect the source from identification. At the time that s 10 came into force, it was heralded as 'a change in the law of profound significance'.[6] It established a specific right of immunity from disclosure which was enjoyed by the media. In doing so, it reversed the majority of the House of Lords in *British Steel Corpn v Granada*,[7] who had expressed the view that the media enjoyed no special privileges in this area.

When does s 10 apply?

The courts have given a wide interpretation to the circumstances where s 10 will apply. The immunity from disclosure applies both before and after publication of the information provided by the source. Even where the information never actually results in publication, the immunity provisions will still apply.[8]

The section grants immunity not only from disclosure of the identity of the source, but also from disclosure of material from which the source may be identified.[9] This immunity will apply notwithstanding that it may operate to defeat rights of ownership in the material (for example, under the law of confidence or copyright).

The immunity from disclosure is not absolute

Whilst recognising the importance of preserving the anonymity of a source, s 10 makes it clear that the media's immunity from disclosure is not absolute. In the instances set out in the Act, namely, where disclosure is necessary in the interests of justice or national security or for the prevention of disorder or crime, the court may require the journalist to disclose his source. But if the exceptions are not relevant to the case in question, the statutory immunity from disclosure will be absolute.[10]

The onus is on the party seeking disclosure to show that disclosure is necessary for one or more of the reasons set out in s 10.[11] This is a question of

---

6   Lord Scarman in *Secretary of State for Defence v Guardian Newspapers* [1985] AC 339.

7   *British Steel Corpn v Granada* [1981] AC 1096.

8   *O'Mara Books v Express* [1999] FSR 49.

9   *Trinity Mirror v Punch Ltd* [2000] unreported, 17 July. Where a party seeks delivery up of documents to try to determine how they were leaked, s 10 of the Act is a bar to such an application if there is a reasonable chance that the source of the information would be disclosed.

10 *Secretary of State for Defence v Guardian Newspapers* [1985] AC 339; [1984] 3 All ER 601; [1984] 3 WLR 986.

11 *Per* Lord Diplock in *Secretary of State for Defence v Guardian Newspapers* [1985] AC 339.

fact in each particular case. The claimant's evidence must be as specific as possible about the reasons why disclosure is sought. A bare assertion of necessity will not suffice. If clear and specific evidence is not adduced, disclosure ought not to be ordered.[12]

Let us examine how the courts have interpreted the exceptions.

The interests of justice

The phrase 'in the interests of justice' did not appear in the original Contempt of Court Bill, which confined itself to removing immunity from disclosure where it was necessary in the interests of national security or the prevention of disorder or crime. The introduction of the interests of justice exception can be traced back to the committee stage of the Bill, when the then Lord Chancellor, Lord Hailsham, recommended that an exception be introduced where disclosure was vital 'for the administration of justice'. His exception was intended to apply to legal proceedings where it was necessary for the claimant to know the source of information in order to make out its case – for example, a defamation case where the claimant is seeking to show the defendant published a statement maliciously. However, the text of the Act does not reflect Lord Hailsham's amendment. Instead of limiting the exception to immunity where it was necessary for the *administration of justice*, the drafter used the words 'the interests of justice' – a vague and undefined term which lends itself to a number of interpretations. As Lord Hailsham observed, 'What are the interests of justice? I suggest that they are as long as the judge's foot'.[13]

In *Secretary of State for Defence v Guardian Newspapers Ltd*,[14] Lord Diplock sought to limit the interests of justice exception. He expressed the view that s 10 used the word 'justice' in the technical sense of the administration of justice in the course of legal proceedings already in existence. Lord Diplock went on to say that, where the only or predominant purpose of a legal action was to obtain possession of a document in order to identify the source of a leak, he found it impossible to envisage any case where it would be *necessary* in the interests of justice to order disclosure. The *Guardian* case concerned an application for disclosure in the interests of *national security*. Lord Diplock's narrow interpretation of s 10 was therefore *obiter*. It was, however, followed by the Court of Appeal in *Maxwell v Pressdram*,[15] a defamation case in which the claimant wished to know the identity of the defendant publication's source of information. The court refused to order disclosure, finding that as a question of fact it was not *necessary* to make such an order in the context of the

---

12 *Per* Lord Fraser in *Secretary of State for Defence v Guardian Newspapers* [1985] AC 339. The court requires evidence and not assumption.

13 *Hansard*, HL, 10.2.1982, Vol 416, col 2.

14 *Secretary of State for Defence v Guardian Newspapers* [1985] AC 339, p 350.

15 *Maxwell v Pressdram* [1987] 1 WLR 298.

proceedings. The judge was of the view that the claimant's interests could be protected by a statement in his summing up to the jury without any need for the source to be identified.

However, in the later case of *X v Morgan-Grampian*,[16] the House of Lords rejected Lord Diplock's interpretation of the meaning of the interests of justice as too narrow. The Law Lords referred to 'the interests of justice' as extending to enabling a person to: (a) exercise important legal rights; and (b) protect himself from serious legal wrongs, regardless of whether the person resorts to legal proceedings to attain those objectives. On this wider definition, enabling an employer to know which of its employees has leaked confidential information could be said to be in the interests of justice because it would put the employer in a position where it could terminate the employment of the disloyal employee in order to protect itself from further disclosures. This would be the case even though the employer may not have to commence legal proceedings in order to be in a position where it could dismiss the employee. In the words of Lord Oliver, 'the interest of the public in the administration of justice must, in my opinion, embrace its interest in the maintenance of a system of law within the framework of which every citizen has the ability and the freedom to exercise his legal right to remedy a wrong done to him ... whether or not through the medium of legal proceedings'.

The breadth of concept of the interests of justice has, as we shall see below, substantially reduced the media's immunity from disclosure.

National security

The case of *Secretary of State for Defence v Guardian*[17] concerned the leak of confidential information by a government employee. The Crown sought disclosure of the name of the employee on the ground that the disclosure was necessary in the interests of national security. The House of Lords favoured a narrow interpretation of 'national security'. It stressed that, in deciding whether disclosure of the identity of the source was necessary in the interests of national security, it is the circumstances and subject matter of the material which has been disclosed that matters, and not just the category of persons who were lawfully entitled to see the material. It will not always follow that, because a document is restricted to a limited high level circulation, its 'leak' will constitute a risk to national security. If a Crown employee were in breach of trust by disclosing material to the media, it would not necessarily follow that national security has been endangered. The court observed that there must be many documents dealing with parliamentary, political and other matters unconnected with national security which a government will wish to

---

16 *X v Morgan-Grampian* [1990] 2 WLR 1000; [1990] 2 All ER 1; [1991] 1 AC 1.
17 *Secretary of State for Defence v Guardian Newspapers* [1985] AC 339; [1984] 3 All ER 601; [1984] 3 WLR 986.

be confined to the eyes of a few in high places. However, that will not mean that any leak of their contents will be damaging to national security.

The prevention of disorder or crime

In *Re An Inquiry*,[18] the House of Lords were called on to consider the phrase 'the prevention of ... crime'. In their Lordships' view, the phrase referred to the prevention of crime generally. The detection of and punishment for a crime would be an example of something which serves to prevent crime generally because it would have an overall deterrent value. Accordingly, disclosure of the identity of a source could be ordered where it was necessary for the detection or punishment of a particular crime.

The courts have not been called upon to consider the necessity of disclosure for the prevention of disorder. Most instances of disorder will involve crimes – for example, public order offences. It would not be surprising if the courts were to adopt a similar approach to the interpretation of 'disorder'.

The meaning of 'necessary'

National law

If disclosure of a source is to be ordered, it must be necessary in at least one of the interests specified in s 10. In *Re An Inquiry*,[19] Lord Griffiths observed that the word 'necessary' has a meaning lying somewhere between 'indispensable' on the one hand and 'useful' or 'expedient' on the other. It was, he said, a question for the judge to decide which end of the scale of meaning he would place it on the facts of any particular case. The nearest paraphrase he could suggest was 'really needed'.

It has been generally accepted at all levels of the judiciary that the word 'necessary' has a higher meaning than 'expedient'. It would not, therefore, be sufficient for a claimant to show that disclosure by the media offers the easiest way of identifying the leak. Similarly, an order for disclosure will not be necessary where there are other means of establishing the identity of the source, unless the case has a special urgency.[20] In the *Special Hospital Service* case, the judge observed:

> What weighs in my mind in considering whether it is necessary to make an order are:
>
> (1) the failure of ... members of the management to make any attempt to discover the source other than making an application to the court, and

---

18 *Re An Inquiry* [1988] 2 WLR 33; [1988] 1 All ER 203.
19 *Ibid.*
20 *Special Hospital Service Authority v Hyde* [1994] BMLR 75.

(2) the absence of any evidence to show that inquiries, if made, would not have been fruitful.

In *John v Express*,[21] Lord Woolf agreed with this observation, noting:

... before the courts require journalists to break what a journalist regards as a most important professional obligation to protect a source, the minimum requirement is that other avenues should be explored ... It cannot be assumed that it will not be possible to either find the culprit or, at least, to narrow down the number of persons who could have been responsible.

In the *John* case, a draft written opinion from counsel found its way to a journalist. The Court of Appeal placed great weight in deciding that disclosure was not necessary on the fact that no internal inquiry had been held before the application for disclosure was made.

A party who seeks disclosure of the identity of a source should try to adduce evidence to deal with these points where relevant.

The European Court of Human Rights

The European Court of Human Rights has considered the word 'necessary' in the context of whether an order that the identity of a source be disclosed is in contravention of Art 10 of the European Convention on Human Rights.[22] An order to disclose a source is, the Court held, a restriction on freedom of expression. Pursuant to the provisions of Art 10(2) any such restriction must be necessary in a democratic society. The restrictions must be narrowly interpreted and the necessity for them convincingly established. The restriction must also be proportionate to the aim pursued. The right to freedom of expression as enshrined in Art 10 of the Convention required that any order to reveal a source's identity must be limited to exceptional circumstances where vital public or individual interests are at stake. In each instance where the Court has to decide whether disclosure was to be ordered, the Court should consider whether exceptional circumstances existed in that particular case.

The Strasbourg Court's interpretation of 'necessary' is clearly more rigorous than the 'sliding scale' approach identified by English national courts. National courts are obliged to take Strasbourg jurisprudence into account when deciding cases which involve a question concerning Convention rights.[23] This requirement may lead to the national courts following the approach of the Strasbourg Court more closely. The Court of Appeal decision in *John v Express*[24] may herald the beginning of this approach.

---

21 *John v Express* [2000] 3 All ER 267, CA.
22 *Goodwin v UK* (1996) 22 EHRR 123.
23 HRA 1998, s 2.
24 *John v Express* [2000] 3 All ER 267, CA.

The application of s 10 – the interests of national security and the prevention of disorder or crime

In those cases where the courts have been called on to consider whether disclosure of a source is necessary in the interests of national security or the prevention of crime or disorder, the courts have treated the question as a straightforward question of fact. In *Re An Inquiry*, the House of Lords expressly rejected the need to balance competing interests. Lord Reid said:

> The judge in deciding whether or not a journalist has 'reasonable excuse' for refusing to reveal his sources is not carrying out a balancing exercise between two competing areas of public interest. The court starts with the presumption that the journalist's refusal to reveal his sources does provide a reasonable excuse for refusing to answer the inspector's questions and the burden is upon the inspectors to satisfy the judge *as a question of fact* that the identification of his source is necessary for the prevention of crime.

The interests of justice

We saw in the earlier part of this chapter that the phrase 'interests of justice' has been interpreted widely by the courts. This wide definition has meant that the courts have generally not applied s 10 in relation to the interests of justice in the same way that they have in relation to the national security and prevention of crime.

In *John v Express*,[25] the Court of Appeal observed that s 10 imposes a two stage process of reasoning on the court in relation to the interests of justice. First, the judge has to decide whether disclosure is necessary for one of the reasons set out in the Act. If so, the judge is left with the task of deciding whether, as a matter of discretion, he should order disclosure. This involves a second stage of reasoning – and it is this second stage which is not generally required in relation to the national security/prevention of crime exceptions.

The second stage involves weighing the conflicting interest involved – the need for disclosure on the one hand and the need for the protection of the source on the other. Lord Woolf observed that 'it is important that when orders are made requiring journalists to depart from their normal professional standards, the merits of their doing so in the public interest are clearly demonstrated'.

The first instance decision in the *John* case[26] had found that the disclosure of the identity of the source who supplied the draft opinion was necessary in the interests of justice in order to safeguard the integrity of legal professional privilege without which the trust and confidence in the legal system would collapse.

---

25   *John v Express* [2000] 3 All ER 267, CA.
26   *Ibid.*

The Court of Appeal disagreed, holding that even if it were necessary in the interests of justice to order disclosure, the first instance order should not be allowed to stand. It would be wrongly interpreted by the public as an example of lawyers attaching a disproportionate significance to the danger to their professional privilege while undervaluing the interests of journalists (and therefore the public).

Earlier case law

The Court of Appeal's decision in the *John* case is something of a departure from the way in which the courts had previously applied the balancing exercise inherent in the second stage of the interests of justice test.

In the *Morgan-Grampian* case,[27] the House of Lords had held that the question whether disclosure is necessary in the interests of justice is a balancing exercise which would turn on the facts of each particular case. Lord Bridge observed as follows:

> It will not be sufficient, *per se*, for a party seeking disclosure of a source protected by s 10 to show merely that he will be unable without disclosure to exercise his legal right or to avert the threatened legal wrong on which he bases his claim in order to establish the necessity of disclosure. The judge's task will always be to weigh in the scales the importance of enabling the ends of justice to be attained in the circumstances of the particular case on the one hand against the importance of protecting the source on the other hand ...

He went on to say:

> It would be foolish to attempt to give comprehensive guidance as to how the balancing exercise should be carried out. But it may not be out of place to indicate the kind of factors which will require consideration ... One important factor will be the nature of the information obtained from the source. The greater the legitimate public interest in the information which the source has given to the publisher or the intended publisher, the greater will be the importance of protecting the source. But another and perhaps more significant factor which will very much affect the importance of protecting the source will be the manner in which the information was itself obtained by the source. If it appears to the court that the information was obtained legitimately, this will enhance the importance of protecting the source. If it appears to the court that the information was obtained illegally, this will diminish the importance of protecting the source unless, of course, this factor is counterbalanced by a clear public interest in publication of the information, as in the classic case where the source has acted for the purpose of exposing iniquity.

The *Morgan-Grampian* case concerned a confidential document about the financial affairs of the claimant company (Tetra). The document was removed from the claimant's premises and its contents were revealed to a journalist, Mr

---

27   X v Morgan-Grampian [1990] 2 WLR 1000; [1990] 2 All ER 1; [1991] 1 AC 1.

Goodwin, who promised not to reveal the identity of the informant. The claimant sought, and obtained, an interim injunction to restrain the disclosure of the information which the source had disclosed and sought an order to require the delivery up of the journalist's notes in the hope that they would reveal the identity of the informant and enable them to recover the missing document.

Applying the balancing exercise to determine whether disclosure of the notes were necessary, Lord Bridge, who gave the leading speech, held that the notes should be delivered up. The importance to the claimants of obtaining disclosure lay in the threat of severe damage to their business and consequentially to the livelihood of their employees which would arise from disclosure of what was contained in the document. The threat could, according to the House of Lords, only be diffused if Mr Goodwin's source could be identified. On the other hand, the importance of protecting the source was much diminished by the source's complicity in the breach of confidentiality. This was not counterbalanced by any legitimate interest which publication of the information was calculated to service. According to Lord Bridge, 'disclosure in the interests of justice is, on this view of the balance, clearly of preponderating importance so as to override the policy underlying the statutory protection of sources'.

The application of the balancing exercise

The House of Lords

The problem with the interest of justice balancing exercise as implemented by the House of Lords in the *Morgan-Grampian* case is that it is likely to lead to disclosure of the identity of the source. The court is, in essence, weighing unquantifiable and non-specific arguments in favour of freedom of expression and the so called chilling effect on the one hand against, on the other hand, specific and quantifiable claims about the potential for further harm if the leak is not identified. Look how Donaldson LJ expressed the balance in the *Morgan-Grampian* case when he purported to weigh 'the *general* public interest in maintaining the confidentiality of journalistic sources against the necessity for disclosure in a *particular* case'. The balance is the tangible against the hypothetical. The tangible will be accorded priority in the vast majority of cases. The presence of a chilling effect on sources coming forward has thus effectively been consigned to the back burner.

The European Court of Human Rights

When the European Court of Human Rights came to consider the *Morgan-Grampian* case,[28] its application of the balance came down in favour of non-disclosure of the notes.

---

28 *Goodwin v UK* (1996) 22 EHRR 123.

It held that the order for disclosure of the source was an interference with freedom of expression.

In order to be a legitimate interference it must be necessary in a democratic society. The necessity must be convincingly established. The order to disclose the source had to be viewed in the light of the fact that publication of the information had already been successfully restrained by way of interim injunction. The Court conceded that Tetra did have further legitimate reasons for wanting disclosure (namely, the prevention of any further disclosures and the termination of the errant employee's contract), but the interest of a democratic society in a free press outweighed Tetra's residual interests. The disclosure order had a potential chilling effect on the readiness of people to give information to journalists. The Court observed that the protection of the sources from which journalists derive information is an essential means of enabling the press to perform its important function of 'public watchdog' in a democratic society. The Court also took into account the fact that, although about six years had passed since the case was before the House of Lords, Tetra had no further harm arising from unauthorised disclosures despite the continuing anonymity of the leak. This latter information had not, of course, been available to the House of Lords.

The application of the balance by the House of Lords and the European Court of Human Rights shows a difference in emphasis between the rights of the parties (in particular Tetra) and the wider interest of the general public. The House of Lords paid lip service to the wider public interest, but clearly felt that it was outweighed by the importance of reducing the potential for serious damage to Tetra if the source was not identified. The European Court of Human Rights accorded priority to the wider public interest, envisaging that disclosure should only be ordered in exceptional cases. The Court of Appeal decision in the *John* case[29] was in line with the decision of the Strasbourg Court because it also accorded real weight to the general public interest of the general public in imparting and receiving information rather then consigning it to the background.

In *Camelot Group v Centaur Ltd*,[30] the Court of Appeal sought to reconcile the judgments of the European Court of Human Rights and the House of Lords in the *Morgan-Grampian* case in a case involving very similar facts to *Morgan-Grampian*. The claimant sought disclosure of a leaked document to assist it in identifying the source of the leak. The Court of Appeal considered the judgment of the House of Lords and the European Court. It concluded that the tests applied by the two courts were substantially the same, albeit that the courts reached different conclusions. The Court of Appeal drew the following principles from the cases:

---

29 *John v Express* [2000] 3 All ER 267, CA.

30 *Camelot Group v Centaur Ltd* [1998] 2 WLR 379; [1999] QB 124; [1998] 1 All ER 251.

(a) there is an important public interest in the press being able to protect the anonymity of its sources;

(b) the law does not enable the press to protect that anonymity in all circumstances. Hence, the exceptions set out in s 10;

(c) when assessing whether an order forcing disclosure of the source should be made, a relevant but not conclusive factor is that an employer may wish to identify an employee so as to exclude him from future employment;

(d) whether sufficiently strong reasons are shown in any case to outweigh the important public interest in the protection of sources will depend on the facts of each case. The mere fact that there is a disloyal employee present will not invariably lead to an order for disclosure;

(e) great weight should be attached to judgments, particularly recent judgments on the disclosure of sources, in order to achieve consistency in decision making when applying s 10.

In the *Camelot* case, the court heard evidence that the continued anonymity of the informant posed a future threat of further disclosure (as in the *Morgan-Grampian* case) and that the continued unidentified presence of the disloyal employee on Camelot's staff would be damaging to staff relations and morale. On the other side of the balance, the court examined the publication at issue in the case and inquired whether it was itself in the public interest. The leaked document had contained the claimant's unpublished annual accounts. The accounts were due to be published in the press a few days later, but at the time of disclosure they were the subject of an embargo. The court did not consider that it would further the public interest to secure publication of the accounts a week earlier than planned. On the other hand they felt that the early publication had enabled the defendant and the informant to further their private interests.

The Court of Appeal were following the approach of the House of Lords in *Morgan-Grampian*, placing the emphasis on private rights and the individual nature of the source, and barely giving credence to the wider public interest in securing confidence amongst potential informants. Indeed, Schiemann LJ dismissed the chilling effect in the following terms:[31]

> To some extent, the effect of disclosing the identity of one source who has leaked important material can have a chilling effect on the willingness of other sources to disclose material which is important. If the other sources are put in the position of having to guess whether or not the court will order disclosure of their names then they may well not be prepared to take the risk that the court's decision will go against them. That is a consideration, however, which will only be met if there is a blanket rule against any disclosure. That is, however, not part of out domestic law or of the Convention. So the well

---

31 *Camelot Group v Centaur Ltd* [1998] 1 All ER 251, p 261.

informed source is always going to have to take a view as to what is going to be the court's reaction to his disclosure in the circumstances of his case.

The Court of Appeal accordingly ordered disclosure. There was the risk of future leaks if the source was not uncovered (this will almost always be present in such cases), and the continued presence of a disloyal employee was damaging to morale and staff relations (again, something which will almost always be present). The actual publication in question could not be said to be in the public interest given that the contents were due to be made public a few days later in any event. Therefore, the balance came down in favour of disclosure. Although the court was at pains to point out that the presence of a disloyal employee will not automatically lead to disclosure, its approach suggests that it usually will unless the material which is disclosed happens to be on a matter which is in the public interest (for example, if it exposes wrongdoing).

The future

The apparent change of approach demonstrated by *John v Express* has been emphasised above. The *John* case postdates both the *Morgan-Grampian* case and the *Camelot* case. The media must hope that future cases follow the spirit of the *John* decision and afford real weight to the wider public interest in freedom of expression if the anonymity of sources is to be truly protected.

The Human Rights Act 1998

The coming into force of the Human Rights Act may have a profound change in the way that s 10 is applied – indeed, it is one of the major reasons for the 'media friendly' Court of Appeal decision in the *John* case. As explained in Chapter 1, the emphasis in the jurisprudence of the European Court of Human Rights is on the preservation of the right to receive and impart information and ensuring a free media. As the *Goodwin* case shows, any exceptions to this right must be narrowly interpreted, both in the sense of what is 'necessary' and in the interpretation of 'the interests of justice'. The specific interest of an applicant in a particular case ought not to be accorded precedence over the protection of the source unless the interests of justice really do demand it. The fact that the information is, or is about to be made public in any event is a factor which ought to be taken into account.[32] It is to be hoped that the future offers the media a rosier picture than they have been presented with to date.

---

32 HRA 1998, s 12.

Hints and tips for the media

(a) The media should avoid making unqualified promises that they will not disclose the identity of their source. The court may order disclosure pursuant to s 10 of the Contempt of Court Act 1981. The fact that a journalist has promised anonymity to the source will not provide a defence. The media entity in question and the individual journalist may be in contempt of court if it refuses to comply with a court order.

(b) If the media receive documents from a source from which the source may be identified, serious consideration should be given to the destruction of the documents by the media *before* any legal action is taken to recover the documents or to seek the identity of the source. However, where the documents are original documents of or belonging to any government department, it will be a criminal offence dishonestly to destroy or deface such documents.[33] Once legal proceedings have been begun, or where the media entity is aware that they are contemplated, documents must *not* be destroyed or defaced. Any such action is likely to be a contempt of court.

(c) The media may be able to resist disclosure of information where it would incriminate them in a crime, for example, receiving stolen goods.[34] This is known as the privilege against self-incrimination. The privilege will not apply in civil proceedings involving intellectual property claims or 'commercial information'. It will not, therefore, apply in cases where proceedings are brought for breach of confidence or copyright infringement.

---

33 Theft Act 1968, s 20.
34 Supreme Court Act 1981, s 72.

CHAPTER 12

MORALITY AND THE MEDIA: OBSCENITY, INDECENCY, BLASPHEMY AND SEDITION

Even if accepted public standards may to some extent vary from generation to generation, current standards are in the keeping of juries, who can be trusted to maintain the corporate good sense of the community and to discern attacks upon values that must be preserved.[1]

OBSCENITY

The law relating to obscenity is governed by the Obscene Publications Act 1959.[2] The long title of the Act describes itself as:

> An Act to amend the law relating to the publication of obscene matter; to provide for the protection of literature; and to strengthen the law concerning pornography.

The Act was intended to provide safeguards for the publication of serious literary, artistic, scientific or scholarly work, whilst at the same time facilitating the suppression of hard pornography.

The Act provides for a number of *criminal offences*. The relevant sections of the Act are in the following terms:

Section 2

2 Prohibition of publication of obscene matter.

(1) Subject as hereinafter provided, any person who, whether for gain or not, publishes an obscene article [or who has an obscene publication for publication for gain (whether gain to himself or gain to another)][3] shall be liable:

(a) on summary conviction to a fine not exceeding £5,000 or to imprisonment for a term not exceeding six months;

(b) on conviction on indictment to a fine or to imprisonment for a term not exceeding three years or both.

---

1   Lord Morris in *Shaw v DPP* [1962] AC 220, p 292.
2   Plays are governed by the Theatres Act 1968. The same test for obscenity (see below) will apply as under the Obscene Publications Act 1959.
3   Added by the Obscene Publications Act 1964, s 1(1).

'Publication' is defined broadly by s 1(3) of the Act as distribution, circulation, selling, letting on hire, giving, lending, offering for sale or offering for letting on hire.

Where the article contains material to be looked at, or a record, publication means showing, playing or projecting it. Where the material is stored electronically, it means transmitting the data. Making images or text available over the internet constitutes 'publication'. Under s 162 of the Broadcasting Act 1990, the broadcasting industries (television and radio) were made subject to the provisions of the Act (having both previously been excluded).

'Article' does not simply encompass the written word. It covers any description of article containing or embodying matter to be read or looked at or both, any sound record and any film or other record of a picture or pictures.[4] By way of example, in *AG's Reference (No 5 of 1980)*,[5] a video cassette was held to be an 'article' and a cinema showing video films was held to be 'publishing' the cassette by playing or projecting the images. In 1991, proceedings were commenced against Island Records in respect of a recording by the rap artists Niggaz With Attitude.

Publication also extends to anything which is intended to be used, either alone or as one of a set, for the reproduction or manufacture of articles, for example photographic negatives.[6]

The consent of the Director of Public Prosecutions is required before proceedings may be instituted in respect of moving picture films of a width of not more than 16 mm where the publication takes place in the course of a film exhibition[7] and in respect of articles included in a cable programme service.[8]

Section 3

Section 3 of the Act imposes summary liability on articles which are kept for publication for gain. The section is in the following terms:

3   Powers of search and seizure.

(1) If a justice of the peace is satisfied on oath that there is reasonable ground for suspecting that, in any premises in the petty sessions area for which he acts, or on any stall or vehicle in that area ... obscene articles are, or are from time to time, kept for publication for gain, the justice may issue a warrant empowering any constable to enter (if need be, by force) and search the premises, or to search the stall or vehicle, and to seize and remove any articles found therein or thereon which

---

4   Obscene Publications Act 1959, s 1(2).
5   *AG's Reference (No 5 of 1980)* [1980] 3 All ER 816.
6   Obscene Publications Act 1964, s 2(1).
7   Obscene Publications Act 1959, s 2(3A), as amended by the Cinemas Act 1985.
8   Cable and Broadcasting Act 1984, Sched 5.

the constable has reason to believe to be obscene articles and to be kept for publication for gain ...

(2) Any articles seized under sub-s (1) of this section shall be brought before a justice of the peace acting for the same petty sessions area as the justice who issued the warrant, and the justice before whom the articles are brought may thereupon issue a summons to the occupier of the premises or, as the case may be, the user of the stall or vehicle to appear on a day specified in the summons before a magistrates' court for that petty sessions area to show cause why the articles or any of them should not be forfeited [the owner, author or maker of the articles or any person through whose hands they have passed before being seized shall also be entitled to appear on the day specified in the summons to make such representations];[9] and if the court is satisfied, as respects any of the articles, that at the time when they were seized they were obscene articles kept for publication for gain, the court shall order those articles to be forfeited.

The onus is on the defendant to show good cause why the article(s) should not be forfeited. A justice of the peace may not issue a warrant except on information laid by or on behalf of the Director of Public Prosecutions or by a constable.[10]

This section is not restricted to articles intended for publication in England. The court is entitled to seize an obscene article kept for publication for gain even where the article is kept in England for publication outside the jurisdiction of the English courts.[11]

The meaning of 'obscene'

Section 1(1) of the Act sets out the test for obscenity. It is in the following terms:

For the purposes of this Act an article shall be deemed to be obscene if its effects or (where the article comprises two or more distinct items) the effect of any one of its items is, if taken as a whole, such as to tend to deprave and corrupt persons who are likely, having regard to all relevant circumstances, to read, see or hear the matter contained or embodied in it.

The following points should be noted in relation to the test:

(a) the article must have *a tendency* to deprave and corrupt. No actual depravity or corruption need be proved to bring a successful prosecution;

(b) the intention of the publisher will not be relevant to the issue of whether the article is obscene;

---

9   Obscene Publications Act 1959, s 3(4).
10   Criminal Justice Act 1967, s 25.
11   *Gold Star Publications Ltd v DPP* [1981] 2 All ER 257, HL.

(c) 'depravity' and 'corruption' are not defined by the Act. In *R v Calder and Boyars Ltd*,[12] the judge at first instance directed the jury to consider the words in their ordinary everyday meaning – an approach endorsed by the Court of Appeal. On that basis, the essence of the test for obscenity is a tendency to cause moral corruption: 'to make morally bad; to pervert or corrupt morally'.[13]

In *Knuller v DPP*,[14] Lord Reid observed that the Act 'appears to use the words 'deprave' and 'corrupt' as synonymous as I think they are'. He also observed that 'to deprave and corrupt does not merely mean to lead astray morally'. A distinction must therefore be drawn between leading someone astray morally (not obscene) and making them morally bad (obscene). This is a fine line to draw, and one which is difficult to apply in practice. In the *Knuller* case, Lord Reid observed: 'We may regret that we live in a permissive society, but I doubt whether even the most staunch defender of a better age would maintain that all or even most of those who have at one time or in one way or another been led astray morally have thereby become depraved or corrupt.';[15]

(d) depravity and corruption are not to be confused with shock, repulsion or disgust. A shocking or a repulsive image or description will not necessarily corrupt a person. In fact, it is likely to have the opposite effect by deterring the reader or viewer from the activity in question. This point is considered below in relation to the aversion defence;

(e) depravity and corruption do not necessarily involve the encouragement of depraved *conduct*. The effect on the *minds* or *emotions* of the likely audience for the article may in itself render an article obscene. In a case involving the publication of hard pornography, it was not necessary to prove that physical sexual activity resulted from exposure to the material. The fact that the material would suggest 'thoughts of a most impure and libidinous character' was sufficient;[16]

(f) where the article in question consists of a number of distinct items (such as a magazine), s 1 of the Act provides that each item must be considered on an individual basis. If the test shows that any one of the distinct items is obscene, then that will render the whole article (for example, the whole magazine) obscene.[17]

---

12 *R v Calder and Boyars Ltd* [1968] 3 All ER 644.
13 *Ibid*, p 646.
14 *Knuller v DPP* [1973] AC 435, p 456.
15 *Ibid*.
16 *Whyte v DPP* [1972] 3 All ER 12, *per* Lord Pearson, p 22.
17 *R v Anderson* [1971] 3 All ER 1152.

Subject to that point, each article or individual item must be looked at *as a whole*. It is not permissible to isolate one particular part of an article and to take it out of its context;

(g) despite the reference in the long title of the Act to pornography, there is nothing in the Act to confine depravity and corruption to sexual matters. In *Calder Ltd v Powell*,[18] a book which described the imaginary life of a drug addict in New York was held to be obscene on the ground that it had a tendency to encourage its readers to experiment with drugs. Articles which encourage brutal violence might also have a tendency to deprave and corrupt. The width and vagueness of the definition could at least in theory encompass the fostering of attitudes which the court or members of the jury might find to be morally distasteful – perhaps misogynistic or homophobic attitudes;

(h) whether an article is obscene is a question of *fact* (for the jury where the case is tried on indictment). Expert evidence (for example, psychological or sociological evidence) will only be allowed to assist the court on this question in very exceptional circumstances;

(i) it is the potential effect of the article that matters. An article is not inherently obscene in isolation from its likely audience. The 'deprave and corrupt' test should be directed towards those people who are likely to read, see or hear the material in question.[19] It does not have to be judged against society as a whole or against particularly vulnerable or sensitive people, unless they are part of the likely readers, viewers or listeners. It is, therefore, incorrect to invoke the standards of the average man or woman when applying the test for obscenity. When applying the test of obscenity, the first step is to identify the likely audience. They are the standard against which the test for obscenity will be judged. Where cases are tried on indictment, the jury must put themselves in the shoes of that audience.

This means that the question whether an article is obscene depends also on what is being or is going to be done with it.

Example

A medical treatise which depicts sexual acts would not be obscene if its readership were restricted to doctors or scientists in their professional capacity. If the same material were published to the general public, it might be classed as obscene;

(j) the article must have a tendency to deprave and corrupt *a significant proportion* of those people who would be likely to read, see or hear the material.[20] What amounts to a significant proportion is a matter for the

---

18 *Calder Ltd v Powell* [1965] 1 OB 509.
19 *DPP v Whyte* [1972] AC 849.
20 *R v Calder and Boyars Ltd* [1968] 3 All ER 644.

jury.[21] It is not necessarily synonymous with a substantial proportion. In *DPP v Whyte*, Lord Cross described 'significant proportion' as being a proportion which is 'not numerically negligible, but which may be much less than half';[22]

(k) members of the audience who are already depraved or corrupted may become more so. The test does not necessarily revolve around the corruption of the wholly innocent. In *DPP v Whyte*,[23] the defendant's bookshop sold pornographic books. The court found as a matter of fact that the majority of customers were men of middle age and upwards. Having identified the likely readership, the court had to decide whether the pornography had a tendency to deprave and corrupt a significant proportion of that readership. The justices had taken the view at the trial that there was no such tendency. A significant proportion of the readership were 'inadequate, pathetic, dirty-minded men, seeking cheap thrills – addicts to this type of material, whose morals were already in a state of depravity and corruption'. The readers being already depraved, the magistrates reasoned, the articles could have no tendency to cause further corruption. The House of Lords rejected this approach. The majority of the Law Lords expressed the view that the Act was not merely concerned with the once for all corruption of the wholly innocent. In Lord Wilberforce's view, '[the Act] equally protects the less innocent from further corruption, the addict from feeding or increasing his corruption'.[24] The articles were therefore capable of tending to deprave and corrupt a significant proportion of the likely readership.

Defences

Defences to the s 2 offence

Section 2(5) of the Act provides a defence to a distributor of obscene material who can prove that he had not examined the article in question and had no reasonable cause to suspect that it was obscene. A similar defence is provided for in Sched 15 of the Broadcasting Act 1990 in relation to cable or broadcast or radio material which the defendant did not know and had no reason to suspect would include material rendering him liable to be convicted of an offence.

---

21 *R v Calder and Boyars Ltd* [1968] 3 All ER 644.
22 *DPP v Whyte* [1972] 3 All ER 12, p 24.
23 *Ibid.*
24 *DPP v Whyte* [1972] AC 849.

The aversion defence – ss 2 and 3

Defendants often argue that an article does not have a tendency to deprave and corrupt because the effect of the article, rather than encouraging depraved thoughts or behaviour, would be to repel the reader, viewer or listener. Such a defence was summarised by Salmon LJ in *R v Calder and Boyars*, an appeal from prosecution for obscenity in respect of the novel *Last Exit to Brooklyn*. He said:[25]

> The defence was, however, that the book had no such tendency [to deprave and corrupt]; it gave a graphic description of the depths of depravity and degradation in which life was lived in Brooklyn ... The only effect that it would produce in any but a minute lunatic fringe of readers would be horror, revulsion and pity; it was admittedly and intentionally disgusting, shocking and outrageous; it made the reader share in the horror it described and thereby so disgusted, shocked and outraged him that, being aware of the truth, he would do what he could to eradicate those evils and the conditions of modern society which so callously allowed them to exist. In short, according to the defence, instead of tending to encourage anyone to homosexuality, drug taking or senseless, brutal violence, it would have precisely the reverse effect.

The appeal court held that the trial judge had neglected to deal adequately with the aversion defence in his summing up. The conviction was accordingly quashed on the ground that, had the jury been properly directed, they might not have convicted.[26]

The public interest defence – ss 2 and 3

The Act provides a defence for offences under ss 2 and 3 of the Act where, despite the fact that an article has a tendency to deprave and corrupt, its publication may be said to be justified as being for the public good. The defence is contained in s 4 of the Act, which states as follows:

> A person shall not be convicted of an offence ... if it is proved that publication of the article in question is justified as being for the public good on the ground that it is in the interests of science, literature, art or learning, or of other objects of general concern.

The public good defence was extended to broadcasting by the Broadcasting Act 1990. The broadcasting defence is in the same terms as for non-broadcast media save that instead of the word 'art' the broadcasting defence refers to 'drama, opera, ballet or any other art'.

The onus is on the defendants to make out such a defence on the balance of probabilities.[27]

---

25 *R v Calder and Boyars Ltd* [1968] 3 All ER 644, p 647.
26 The conviction for indecency was similarly overturned on appeal in *R v Anderson*.
27 *R v Calder and Boyars Ltd* [1968] 3 All ER 644, p 648.

Sub-section 2 of s 4 provides that expert evidence may be adduced on the literary, artistic, scientific or other merits of an article. However, the evidence must be confined to the inherent merits of the article.[28] As we have seen, expert evidence is not generally permitted on the question whether the article is obscene.

Section 4 has been interpreted restrictively to apply only to material which can be said to be of a 'high order'. For example, 'learning' has been held to mean 'a product of scholarship'. It does not extend to teaching or any form of education (such as sex education).[29] It is unlikely that 'literary' or 'artistic' is synonymous with mere entertainment value.

The words 'or other objects of public concern' which appear in s 4 do not include material which just happens to confer some benefit on the public. The objects must be conducive to the public good *and* of concern to members of the public in general before the section can be brought into play.[30] In *R v Staniforth*,[31] the defendant argued that pornographic material fell within the scope of the s 4 defence because it had a beneficial effect on those who are sexually repressed or 'deviant'. The Court of Appeal held that such material did not fall within s 4 because whatever beneficial effects the material had, they could not be said to be of general public concern. They were felt only by a minority of the public.

The interplay between ss 2 and 3 of the Act and s 4

In *R v Calder and Boyars*, the court considered the way in which the jury should approach the public good defence. Salmon LJ observed:[32]

> The proper direction on a defence under s 4 in a case such as the present is that the jury must consider on the one hand the number of readers they believe would tend to be depraved and corrupted by the book, the strength of the tendency to deprave and corrupt and the nature of the depravity and corruption; on the other hand they should assess the strength of the literary, sociological or ethical merit which they consider the book to possess. They should then weigh up all these factors and decide whether on balance the publication is proved to be justified as being for the public good ... the jury must set the standards of what is acceptable, of what is for the public good in the age in which we live.

---

28 *R v Staniforth* [1976] 2 All ER 714.
29 *AG's Reference (No 3 of 1977)* [1978] 3 All ER 1166.
30 *R v Staniforth* [1976] 2 All ER 714.
31 *Ibid.*
32 *R v Calder and Boyars Ltd* [1968] 3 All ER 644, p 649.

INDECENCY OFFENCES

Common law

Conspiracy to corrupt public morals

Conspiracy to corrupt public morals is a criminal offence at common law. The offence was 'rediscovered' by the majority of a House of Lords in the case of *Shaw v DPP*,[33] which concerned the publication of a directory containing details and pictures of prostitutes (some of whom were shown as engaged in what were described as 'perverse practices'). Controversially, the majority of the House of Lords were of the view that the courts had residual powers to superintend offences which were prejudicial to the welfare of the public where Parliament had not expressly legislated for them. This residual power took the form of a revival of the common law defence of conspiracy to corrupt public morals.

A conspiracy consists of agreeing or acting in concert to do an unlawful act or a lawful act by unlawful means. The essence of the offence is the *agreement* to corrupt rather than the question whether corruption actually occurred.

The decision as to what type of publication might corrupt public morals is broad and subjective. The majority of the House of Lords in the *Shaw* case felt that the jury should be the final arbiter on the issue. In his dissenting speech in the *Shaw* case, Lord Reid disagreed with this approach and observed that 'the law will be whatever any jury happen to think it ought to be, and this branch of the law will have lost all the certainty which we rightly prize in other branches of our law'. In recognition of the uncertain scope of the offence[34] the House of Lords subsequently confined the offence to activities 'reasonably analogous' to conduct which have been successfully prosecuted as corrupting public morals in the past. The Solicitor General also assured Parliament that charges for corrupting public morals would not be brought in simply to circumvent the defences in the Obscene Publications Act 1959.[35] Where a prosecution essentially involves a consideration of whether an article is obscene, the prosecution ought to be brought under the Obscene Publications Act and not the common law.

The meaning of corruption

The House of Lords has emphasised that 'corrupt' has a strong meaning. In considering whether corruption has taken place, the jury should keep in mind both the current standards of ordinary decent people and also that 'corrupt'

---

33 *Shaw v DPP* [1961] 2 All ER 446.

34 *Knuller v DPP* [1973] AC 435.

35 *Hansard*, Vol 695, col 1212.

means more than simply leading someone morally astray.[36] Lord Simon referred to conduct which corrupts public morals as being suggestive of conduct which a jury might find destructive of the very fabric of society.[37]

In the *Knuller* case (which was decided in the early 1970s), a conviction for conspiracy to corrupt public morals was upheld in respect of advertisements in a magazine which invited readers to meet with the advertisers for the purpose of homosexual sex. It is a moot point whether a jury in the 21st century who are asked to consider a similar publication would come to the same conclusion. However, given that there are no universally accepted standards in today's society, this result cannot be predicted with any degree of certainty.

The conspiracy offence is clearly unsatisfactory. Its vagueness makes it difficult for the media to regulate their conduct. The yardstick will be the collective opinion of the jury, who must set the standards of what is acceptable. There is a real possibility that a law of such uncertain scope is incompatible with the European Convention on Human Rights, in that it cannot be said to be prescribed by law.[38] The validity of the offence may therefore be subject to challenge once the Human Rights Act comes into force.

Outraging public decency/conspiracy to outrage public decency

It is a criminal offence at common law to commit an act in public which amounts to an outrage of public decency (or to conspire to commit such an act). The rationale for the offence is that members of the public ought not to be exposed to material which will outrage them or leave them disgusted by what they read or see.[39] It is not necessary to show that the act causes actual disgust or outrage, simply that it is calculated (in the sense of likely to) to have that effect.

In the *Knuller* case, Lord Simon emphasised that 'outrage' is a strong word and observed that outraging public decency 'goes considerably beyond offending the susceptibilities of, or even shocking, reasonable people'.[40] The standards of decency which the jury should apply in deciding whether the offence has been committed will be those which are prevalent in contemporary society.

The material which is complained of must be exposed to the public in the sense that it is possible that it could have been seen by more than one person (even if, as a matter of fact, only one person did see it). The offence may be

---

36 [1973] AC 435, p 457.
37 *Knuller v DPP* [1973] AC 435, p 491.
38 The meaning of 'prescribed by law' is considered in Chapter 1.
39 Lord Reid in *Knuller v DPP* [1973] AC 435, p 457.
40 *Ibid*, p 495.

committed even where the outrageous material is hidden from public view (for example, in the inside pages of a magazine) if the public is expressly or impliedly invited to see it (for example, to open up the magazine).[41]

There is no requirement that the prosecution must show an intention to cause outrage on the part of the accused. All that needs to be proved in order to establish the offence is that the accused has deliberately made the material public.[42]

Like the offence of corrupting public morals, the generalised nature of the outraging public decency offence gives the court a residual ability to widen the scope of the offence to fit the circumstances of the case before it. The notion of outrage is equated with the opinion of the jury, leading to a lack of clarity.

The outraging public decency offence may be vulnerable to challenges once the Human Rights Act comes into force on the ground that it cannot really be said that its scope is prescribed by law.

Circumventing the safeguards in the Obscene Publications Act

Section 2(4) of the Obscene Publications Act provides that, where an offence essentially involves the question whether material is obscene, prosecutions ought to be brought under the Act.[43] The objective of s 2(4) was to ensure that a person who is accused of publishing an obscene article should be able to avail himself of the protections from arbitrary prosecution contained in the Act – most significantly the public good defence contained in s 4 and the rule that an article must be construed as a whole when deciding whether it has a tendency to deprave and corrupt.[44] Prosecutions should not be brought under the common law offences of corrupting public morals or outraging public decency simply as a way of circumventing the Act's provisions.

Section 2(4) was interpreted restrictively in R v Gibson,[45] where the defendants were convicted under the common law for outraging public decency by exhibiting in a public gallery a pair of earrings consisting of freeze dried human foetuses. The Court of Appeal expressed the view that the Obscene Publications Act is only relevant to prosecutions where the prosecution concerns the question whether an article was obscene in the sense that the word is used in the Act, that is, whether the article tends to deprave and corrupt a significant proportion of its likely audience. There was no suggestion in the Gibson case that the earrings had any such tendency.

---

41   Knuller v DPP [1973] AC 435, p 495.
42   R v Gibson [1990] 2 QB 619.
43   Obscene Publications Act 1959, s 2(4).
44   Knuller v DPP [1973] AC 435, p 456.
45   R v Gibson [1990] 2 QB 619.

It was not, therefore, contrary to s 2(4) of the Act's provisions to prosecute the accused under the common law offence of outraging public decency rather than under the Obscene Publications Act.

In any event, the Court of Appeal said, it was unlikely that the s 4 defence of public good could ever arise in respect of material which caused outrage to public decency. In other words, even if the public good defence had been available to the defendants in the *Gibson* case, it would not have assisted them, according to the court. This last point was *obiter*. The actual decision as to whether the public good defence would have availed the defendant had it been available to them would have been a question of fact for the jury.

In the wake of the *Gibson* decision, it would seem that prosecutions might be brought against material which causes public outrage provided that no tendency to deprave or corrupt is alleged. The accused will not then be able to avail himself of the equivalent of the public good defence, nor will the jury have to consider the article as a whole in deciding whether the material is likely to cause public outrage.

Statutory indecency offences

Section 11 of the Post Office Act 1953 – indecent material sent by post

It is a criminal offence to send, attempt to send or procure to be sent a postal package which encloses any indecent or obscene print, painting, photograph, lithograph, engraving, cinematograph film, book, card or written communication or any other indecent or obscene article. It is also an offence to carry out the above activities where the package has, on its cover, any words, marks or design which are grossly offensive or of an indecent or obscene character.

A defendant found guilty of the above offences is liable on conviction on indictment to imprisonment for a term not exceeding 12 months or on summary conviction to a fine not exceeding the prescribed sum.

The Act does not define what is meant by the terms 'obscene' or 'indecent'. For the purposes of the Act, both terms bear their everyday meaning (so that 'obscene' does not bear the technical meaning provided for in the Obscene Publications Act – there is no requirement that the material must have a tendency to deprave and corrupt). The test of indecency (and by analogy obscenity) is an objective one.[46] The character of the addressee is immaterial. It is for the jury to determine the current standards against which to judge whether the article is indecent or obscene.[47] This is a question of fact. No expert evidence will be permitted to help the jury with their task.

---

46 *R v Straker* [1965] Crim LR 239.
47 *R v Stamford* [1972] 2 QB 391.

There is no equivalent to the s 4 public good offence under the Obscene Publications Act.

Unsolicited material

It is an offence under the Unsolicited Goods and Services Act 1971 to send or cause to be sent to another person any book, magazine or leaflet or advertising material for any such article (whether or not the advertising material depicts or describes human sexual techniques),[48] which he knows or ought reasonably to know is unsolicited and which describes or illustrates human sexual techniques. The offence carries a maximum penalty on summary conviction of a fine not exceeding level 5 on the standard scale.

Proceedings for such an offence can only be instigated with the consent of the Director of Public Prosecutions.

Section 49 of the British Telecommunications Act 1981 – sending indecent, obscene or false messages by telephone

It is a criminal offence to send a message or other material which is grossly offensive or of an indecent, obscene or menacing character by means of a public telecommunications system (presumably including fax transmissions and e-mail). This section does not apply to anything done in the course of providing a programme service within the meaning of part 1 of the Broadcasting Act 1990. 'Obscene' and 'indecent' are to be interpreted in the same way as would apply under the Post Office Act. A person found guilty under this Act is liable on summary conviction to a fine not exceeding level 3 on the standard scale.

Section 1 of the Protection of Children Act 1978

It is an offence for a person to:

- take or to permit to be taken any indecent photograph of a child; or
- distribute or to show such indecent photographs; or
- have in his possession such indecent photographs with a view to their being distributed or shown by the defendant or others; or
- publish or cause to be published any advertisement likely to be understood as conveying that the advertiser distributes or shows such indecent photographs or intends to do so.

---

48   *DPP v Beate Uhse (UK) Ltd* [1974] 1 All ER 753.

'Child' means a person under the age of 16.[49] The term 'photograph' includes the negative of the picture. It also includes an indecent film and copies of an indecent photograph or film.[50]

'Indecent' is not defined by the Act. The Court of Appeal has adopted the standard of 'recognised standards of propriety'.[51] It is for the jury to determine whether the photograph is indecent on the basis of the photographs themselves – evidence as to the photographer's intentions in taking the photograph will not be relevant to the question whether the photograph was indecent.[52]

In order to be guilty of taking an indecent photograph, the defendant must deliberately and intentionally have taken the photograph and to have deliberately included the indecent subject matter.[53] The Court of Appeal indicated in *R v Graham-Kerr* that the correct approach for the jury to follow is first to satisfy themselves that the picture was taken deliberately and intentionally and that the offending material had not been inadvertently included, and secondly to determine whether the photograph is indecent, by reference to the recognised standards of propriety.

There is a defence to the charge of distribution or showing of an indecent photograph where the defendant can prove that he had a legitimate reason for distributing or showing the photographs or having them in his possession with a view to distributing them or showing them or that he had not himself seen the photographs and did not know or have cause to suspect that they are indecent.[54]

Proceedings for the above offences can only be instituted with the consent of the Director of Public Prosecutions.[55]

Section 160 of the Criminal Justice Act 1988 – possession of indecent photographs of children

It is a criminal offence for a person to have any indecent photographs of a child in his possession. A person charged with this offence has a defence if he can prove:

- that he had a legitimate reason for having the photograph in his possession;

---

49 Protection of Children Act 1978, s 1(1)(a).
50 *Ibid*, s 7(1).
51 *R v Graham-Kerr* [1988] 1 WLR 1098. The formula was originally put forward in *R v Stamford* [1972] 2 QB 391.
52 *R v Graham-Kerr* [1988] 1 WLR 1098.
53 *Ibid*.
54 Protection of Children Act 1978, s 1(4).
55 *Ibid*, s 1(3).

- that he had not himself seen the photograph and did not know nor had any cause to suspect it to be indecent; or
- that the photograph was sent to him without any prior request made by him or on his behalf and that he did not keep it for an unreasonable time.

No proceedings for this offence may be instituted without the consent of the Director of Public Prosecutions.[56]

The terms 'child' and 'photograph' bear the same meanings under the Criminal Justice Act as they do under the Protection of Children Act 1978.

A person shall be liable on summary conviction under this section to imprisonment for a term not exceeding six months or a fine not exceeding £5,000.

Indecent Displays (Control) Act 1981

It is an offence to display indecent matter in public or to cause or permit such a display. The Act is intended to restrict the 'public nuisance' element of indecent displays. It regulates the public display of indecent material rather than the nature of such material. The offence is punishable on indictment to imprisonment for a term not exceeding two years or a fine or to both or on summary conviction to a fine not exceeding the statutory maximum.

'Matter' includes anything capable of being displayed, excluding a human body or any part of a human body.[57] It extends to the written word as well as to pictures or other visual material. 'Public place' means any place to which the public have access (whether on payment or otherwise),[58] subject to certain exceptions, largely relating to sex shops where persons under the age of 18 are not permitted entry. Any matter which is displayed in or which is visible from a public place is deemed to be publicly displayed.[59] Magazine covers which can be seen in newsagents' shops could constitute an indecent display for the purposes of the Act.

The term 'indecent' is undefined.

Whilst the Act does not provide the equivalent of the Obscene Publications Act 'public good defence', there are a number of exceptions to this offence, most notably:

- matter included in a television programme service within the meaning of Pt 1 of the Broadcasting Act 1990;
- matter included in the display of an art gallery or museum and visible only from the gallery or museum;

---

56 Protection of Children Act, s 1(3), applied by Criminal Justice Act 1988, s 160(4).
57 Indecent Displays (Control) Act 1981, s 1(5).
58 *Ibid*, s 1(3).
59 *Ibid*, s 1(2).

- matter included in a performance of a play;
- matter included in certain types of film exhibition.

Video recordings

The distribution of video recordings is regulated by the Video Recordings Act 1984. The Act was intended to curb the distribution of 'video nasties' – home videos depicting violence and sexual activity which it was feared were being watched by children in their homes.

The Act provides for a system of classification of videos and prohibits the supply of unclassified videos. The classification is carried out by the British Board of Film Classification (BBFC) which certifies videos as being suitable for home viewing. Where a classification certificate is issued, it must state that the work is suitable for general viewing and unrestricted supply or that it is suitable for viewing only by persons above a specified age and that no recording should be supplied to a person under that age. There is a third type of classification under which works may only be supplied by licensed sex shops. In deciding whether to grant or refuse a certificate, the BBFC is required to have 'special regard to the likelihood of video works ... being viewed in the home'.[60] In the wake of the James Bulger murder, where the trial judge referred to a potential connection between the murder by the two young accused and the fact that they had been exposed to videos of an adult nature, the criteria which the BBFC must have regard to were widened. Special regard must now also be had to 'any harm that may be caused to potential viewers or, through their behaviour, to society by the manner in which the work deals with: (a) criminal behaviour; (b) illegal drugs; (c) violent behaviour or incidents; (d) horrific behaviour or incidents; or (e) human sexual activity.[61]

Certain types of video work are exempt from the classification requirements (see below).

The Act defines a video recording as any disc, magnetic tape or other device capable of storing data electronically containing information by the use of which the whole or part of a video work may be produced.[62] A video work is defined as any series of visual images (with or without sound) produced electronically by the use of information contained on any disc, magnetic tape or any other device capable of storing data electronically and shown as a moving picture.[63]

---

60 Video Recordings Act 1984, s 4(1)(a).
61 Criminal Justice and Public Order Act 1994, s 90.
62 Video Recordings Act 1984, s 1(3).
63 *Ibid*, s 1(2).

A person who supplies or offers to supply a video recording containing a video work in respect of which there is no classification certificate issued is guilty of an offence and liable on summary conviction to a fine not exceeding £20,000, unless the supply is, or would if it took place be, an exempted supply or the video work is an exempted work. A video work is an exempted work if, taken as a whole, it is designed to inform, educate or instruct, is concerned with music, sport, religion or is a video game. However, such a work will not be exempt if to any significant extent it depicts the following:

- human sexual activity or acts of force or restraint associated with such activity (or is likely to any significant extent to stimulate or encourage such activity);
- mutilation or torture or other acts of gross violence towards humans or animals (or is likely to stimulate or encourage such activity);
- human genital organs or human urinary or excretory functions;
- techniques likely to be useful in the commission of offence; or
- criminal activity which is likely to any significant extent to stimulate or encourage the commission of offences.

It is a defence if the accused believed on reasonable grounds that the video work concerned or if the video recording contained more than one work to which the charge relates, was either an exempted work or a work in respect of which a classification certificate had been issued or that the supply was or would be an exempted supply.

Where a video recording contains a video work in respect of which no classification certificate has been issued, a person who has the recording in his possession for the purposes of supplying it is guilty of an offence and liable on summary conviction to a fine not exceeding £20,000 and imprisonment not exceeding six months, unless he has it in his possession for the purpose of a supply which, if it took place, would be an exempted supply or the video work is an exempted work. The offence is also triable on indictment carrying a maximum sentence of imprisonment of two years.

It is a defence to a charge of committing such an offence if the accused proves:

- that the accused believed on reasonable grounds that the video work concerned or if the video recording contained more than one work to which the charge relates each of those works was either an exempted work or a work in respect of which a classification certificate had been issued; or
- that the accused had the video recording in his possession for the purpose only of a supply which he believed on reasonable grounds would, if it took place, be an exempted supply; or

- that the accused did not intend to supply the video recording until a classification certificate had been issued in respect of the video work concerned.

BLASPHEMY (OR BLASPHEMOUS LIBEL)

Despite recommendations for its abolition, the common law of blasphemy (known in its permanent form as blasphemous libel) remains in being. Prosecutions have been rare in modern times. Nevertheless, the offence carries criminal liability and is something which the media lawyer cannot afford to regard as obsolete or archaic. The European Court of Human Rights has expressed itself to be willing to uphold restrictions on freedom of expression which have the objective of protecting religious feelings provided that they are prescribed by law and proportionate to the objective pursued.[64]

The offence was originally 'designed to safeguard the internal tranquillity of the kingdom'.[65] It fell within the jurisdiction of the ecclesiastical courts, but over time the secular courts came to share jurisdiction. Historically, the interests of the established Church and the State were so entwined that an attack on the former would of necessity sound in an attack on the latter. This historical association of the interests of Church and State has led to the anomalous position where the blasphemy law protects the established Church in England, but it will not extend the same protection to other religions or denominations.

The criteria for blasphemy

The attack

There is no comprehensive definition of blasphemy. The type of material held to be blasphemous has evolved over time. Under modern law, the mere denial of the truth of the Christian religion will not amount to blasphemy, nor will a temperate attack on Christianity. But there is a dividing line between moderate and reasoned criticism (which will not be blasphemous) and offensive treatment (which may be blasphemous). The test is whether the words at issue are likely to outrage and insult a Christian's religious feelings. In *R v Lemon*,[66] Lord Scarman quoted with approval the following passage from *Stephen's Digest of the Criminal Law*:[67]

---

64 *Wingrove v UK* (1996) 24 EHRR 1.
65 Lord Scarman in *R v Lemon* [1979] 1 All ER 898.
66 *R v Lemon* [1979] 1 All ER 898.
67 *Stephen's Digest of the Criminal Law*, 9th edn, 1950.

Every publication is said to be blasphemous which contains any contemptuous, reviling, scurrilous or ludicrous matter relating to God, Jesus Christ or the Bible, of the formularies of the Church of England as by law established. It is not blasphemous to speak or publish opinions hostile to the Christian religion, or to deny the existence of God, if the publication is couched in decent and temperate language. The test to be applied is as to the manner in which the doctrines are advocated and not as to the substance of the doctrines themselves.

R v Lemon concerned a poem and drawing which appeared in an edition of *Gay News*. The poem and drawing purported to describe in detail certain sexual acts with the body of Christ immediately after his death and to ascribe homosexual practices to him during his lifetime. The publication was found to be blasphemous, on the basis that they were likely to outrage and insult a Christian's religious feelings.

The Law Commission has recommended the abolition of the blasphemy laws.[68] One of their reasons for doing so is the inherent uncertainty of the test for blasphemy. What might the tests of 'scurrilous', 'abusive' or 'insulting' cited with approval by the House of Lords extend to?

But in *Wingrove v UK*,[69] the European Court of Human Rights did not share the Law Commission's concerns. It was of the view that English blasphemy law was sufficiently prescribed by law to be a legitimate restriction on freedom of speech.

Mens rea

Blasphemy is a strict liability offence. This means that the defendant can be guilty of the offence even where it had no intention to vilify the Christian religion.

In order to secure a conviction for the offence of blasphemous libel, the prosecution must show the following:

(a) an intention on the part of the defendant to publish the material about which complaint is made; and

(b) that the material is in fact blasphemous.[70] This is *not* a subjective test – it is *not* dependent on the intention and motivation of the author.

In *R v Lemon*, the author of the poem in question was not permitted to give evidence about his intention in publishing the poem or the drawings. This evidence was held to be irrelevant to liability.

The Law Commission has criticised this aspect of the offence. It observed that someone holding profound religious beliefs who publishes material with

---

68 Law Commission, Working Paper No 79.

69 *Wingrove v UK* (1996) 24 EHRR 1.

70 *R v Lemon* [1979] 1 All ER 898.

sincere motives could still be guilty of the offence if the language in which he expresses himself is deemed to be sufficiently shocking and insulting. Indeed, this would appear to have been the situation in *R v Lemon*.[71]

It should also be noted that the artistic or other merits of the material in question will not provide a defence. Under blasphemy law, there is no equivalent to the public good defence in s 4 of the Obscene Publications Act. The author of the poem in the *Lemon* case was an established poet and a member of the Royal Society of Literature. Despite the aesthetic merit of his poem, he was still convicted.

Breach of the peace

It is no longer necessary for the prosecution to prove that the article has a tendency to cause a breach of the peace.[72] Although, historically, the offence of blasphemy was rooted in the historical need to protect the State from destabilising influences, Lord Scarman described this factor as a reminder of the historical character of the offence rather than an essential element of the offence in modern times.

Protection for the Christian religion only

The law of blasphemy applies only to the Christian religion and, strictly speaking, only to the Anglican religion – it being the established Church within England.[73] Under the present law, it may be accurately said that:

> A person may without being liable for prosecution for it, attack Judaism or Mahomedanism or even any sect of the Christian religion (save the established religion of the country).[74]

In *R v Chief Metropolitan Stipendiary Magistrate ex p Choudhury*,[75] the Court of Appeal confirmed that the offence did not extend to the vilification of the Islamic religion. In its judgment, the Court of Appeal relied on *dicta* of Lord Scarman in *R v Lemon*, in which, having reviewed the existing case law, the Law Lord regretted that it was not open to the House of Lords in a modern multicultural society to extend the limits of the law to cover non-Christian religions. He observed that the offence was 'shackled by the chains of history' and said that Parliament, rather than the House of Lords, must restate the existing law 'in a form conducive to the social conditions of the late 20th century rather than to those of the 17th, 18th or even the 19th century'.

---

71 See Robertson, G, *The Justice Game*, 1999, Vintage, for more detail.
72 Lord Scarman in *R v Lemon* [1979] 1 All ER 898.
73 *R v Gathercole* (1838) 2 Lewin 237.
74 *Ibid*.
75 *R v Chief Metropolitan Stipendiary Magistrate ex p Choudhury* [1991] 1 All ER 306.

Parliament not having taken up Lord Scarman's suggestion at the time of the *Choudhury* case, it was not open to the court in that case to rule that the law extended to Islam. But the court observed that, even if it were open for them to do so, it would still refrain from ruling in favour of the prosecution on the ground that it would be virtually impossible by judicial decision to set sufficiently clear limits to the offence if it were extended to religions other than the Christian religion. The courts would be called upon to grapple with such metaphysical inquiries as 'what amounts to a religion?'[76] – issues about which the appeal court expressed itself unsuited to judge.

There is at the very least a strong possibility that the current state of English blasphemy law is irreconcilable with the European Convention on Human Rights. Blasphemy laws operate as a restriction on the right to freedom of expression (enshrined in Art 10 of the Convention). Article 14 of the Convention provides that the Convention rights should be applied in a non-discriminatory way. If non-Christian religions are not treated on an equal footing with other religions, there is a real risk that the UK is not complying with its Convention obligations. This point was raised before the court in *Wingrove v UK*, but the European Court declined to reach a view on the question, it not being directly relevant to the facts at issue in the *Wingrove* case.

Reform/abolition?

The Law Commission recommended the abolition of the offence as long ago as 1985,[77] but there has been no indication that this will occur. Since the early 1990s, prosecutions have been almost non-existent, the most recent of which the author is aware of being the private prosecution launched against the author and publisher of the novel *The Satanic Verses*[78] (the *Choudhury* case).

In the wake of the *Choudhury/Satanic Verses* decision, the then Home Secretary, John Patten, issued a statement addressed to a number of influential British Muslims, indicating that 'the Christian faith no longer relies on [the law of blasphemy], preferring to recognise that the strength of their own belief is the best armour against mockers and blasphemers'.[79]

Public prosecutions for blasphemy are likely to remain rare. Yet, despite this lack of activity, it would be foolhardy to regard the law as a dead letter. The offence had lain dormant for 50 or so years before the prosecution in *R v Lemon*. It is interesting to note that both the recent cases – *Lemon* and

---

76 This would not be the first time that the courts have had to grapple with such questions – see, eg, *Re South Place Ethical Society* [1980] 3 All ER 918, a decision in the context of revenue law.

77 Law Commission, Working Paper No 79.

78 *R v Chief Metropolitan Stipendiary Magistrate ex p Choudhury* [1991] 1 All ER 306.

79 4 July 1989.

Choudhury – were private prosecutions. It is probable that any future prosecutions will follow the same route.

A measure of protection against vexatious private prosecutions has been granted to newspapers under s 8 of the Law of Libel Amendment Act 1888 (but not to other forms of media). The consent of a judge in chambers must be obtained before any such prosecution can be instituted. Such consent will only be forthcoming if the criteria set down in the Act are met. These criteria were set out in Chapter 3 in relation to criminal libel.

The sanctions for blasphemy

Blasphemy is triable on indictment. It carries penalties of an unlimited fine and/or imprisonment. In *R v Lemon* (a case heard in the late 1970s), fines of £1,000 and £500 were imposed on the editor of, and the periodical in which, the offending poem appeared. At trial, a suspended sentence of nine months' imprisonment was imposed on the editor, but this sentence was later quashed by the Court of Appeal.

SEDITIOUS LIBEL

The common law offence of seditious libel carries criminal liability. Like the law of blasphemy, it is an offence rooted in history. The last prosecution for seditious libel was a private prosecution in 1991.[80] It concerned the novel *The Satanic Verses*, in which it was alleged that the author and publishers of the novel were guilty of seditious libel in that the novel had raised widespread discontent and dissatisfaction amongst the Muslim population of England and Wales. The court cited with approval the Canadian case of *Boucher v R*,[81] which held that in order for there to be a seditious libel, there must be a *seditious intention* on the part of the publisher or author. Mere proof of an intention to promote feelings of ill will and hostility between different classes of subject will not alone establish a seditious intention. *The intention must be founded on an intention to incite violence or to create public disturbance or disorder against the Crown or institutions of government.*[82]

The prosecution in the *Choudhury* case was dismissed, because the prosecution could not prove that the author had intended to attack, obstruct or undermine public authority.

---

80 *R v Chief Metropolitan Stipendiary Magistrate ex p Choudhury* [1991] 1 All ER 306.
81 *Boucher v R* (1951) 2 DLR 369.
82 Persons holding public office or discharging a public function of the State would fall within this definition of the institutions of government.

The Law Commission has recommended the abolition of the offence of seditious libel.[83] In practice, prosecutions for seditious activity are more likely to be commenced by the State under public order legislation rather than under this offence. The danger for the media lies in the commencement of private prosecutions, although such prosecutions are likely to be dismissed on the same grounds as defeated Mr Choudhury's attempted prosecution, namely, an inability to show an intention to attack a public authority.

Where prosecutions are brought against the press, it is likely that the requirements of s 8 of the Law of Libel Amendment Act 1888 will have to be met. These were discussed in Chapter 3 in relation to criminal libel.

BROADCASTERS AND TASTE AND MORALITY

The Independent Television Commission (ITC) programme code and the Broadcasting Standards Commission (BSC) code contain provisions regulating the taste and decency of material broadcast on television. The parties to whom the codes apply and the sanctions for breach are considered in Chapter 16. There are no equivalent provisions in the Code of Practice which is enforced by the Press Complaints Commission.

Viewers may complain to the ITC or the BSC about material which they find offensive (including the use of bad language and sexual portrayal). The ITC may also consider of its own initiative whether material broadcast by its licensees is in breach of its code. It should be remembered that the codes are not law. A broadcaster might be in breach of the Codes of Practice, but that does not mean that it has committed an unlawful act. Conversely, it is possible that a broadcaster might behave unlawfully, yet not be in breach of the Codes.

---

83 Law Commission, *Treason, Sedition and Allied Offences*, Working Paper No 72.

CHAPTER 13

GOVERNMENT SECRECY AND FREEDOM OF INFORMATION

OFFICIAL SECRETS

Statutory restraints

Official secrets legislation imposes wide ranging restrictions on freedom of expression which apply to the communication of what might be termed government or 'official' information. The law which applies to the communication of official secrets is to be found in a number of statutes which provide for various criminal offences.

The Official Secrets Act 1911

Section 1

The section creates a criminal offence, punishable by up to *14 years'* imprisonment for the following activities:

(1) If any person *for any purpose prejudicial* to the safety or interests of the State:

    (a) approaches, inspects, passes over or is in the neighbourhood of, or enters any prohibited space[1] within the meaning of the Act; or

    (b) makes any sketch, plan, model or note which is calculated to be or might be or is intended to be directly or indirectly useful to an enemy; or

    (c) obtains, collects, records or publishes or communicates to any other person any secret official code word or pass word or any sketch, plan, model, article or note or other document or information which is calculated to be or might be or is intended to be directly or indirectly useful to any enemy,

he shall be guilty of a felony [emphasis added].

Section 1(2) provides that where the charge concerns the making, obtaining, collection, recording, publication or communication of any sketch, plan, model, article, note, document or information relating to or used in a prohibited place it will be deemed to be for a purpose prejudicial to the safety or interests of the State, unless the contrary is shown by the defendant.

---

1   See SI 1994/968 for the definition of 'prohibited place'. It is a wide definition, in large part dependent on declarations by the Government as to whether the place is prohibited on the ground that information about the place or its destruction or obstruction would be useful to the enemy.

In other words, the burden of proof of showing that the s 1(2) activities were *not* for a purpose prejudicial to the safety or interests of the State lies on the *defence*. And, as any lawyer knows, trying to prove a negative is a very difficult thing indeed.[2]

The Act provides that no prosecution under s 1 may be brought without the consent of the Attorney General.[3]

Section 1 has been described as 'the most draconian law on the British statute book'.[4] The section is headed: 'Penalties for spying'. But the actual wording of the section does not confine itself to spying. It uses the phrase 'prejudicial to the safety or interest of the State'. The width of the offence is therefore dependent on the way in which that phrase is interpreted.

The House of Lords had to consider the ambit of the s 1 in *Chandler v DPP*.[5] In the *Chandler* case, the accused persons, who were pacifists, organised a demonstration at a military airfield. The airfield fell within the definition of 'prohibited place' under the Act. The demonstration was to involve the unauthorised entry onto a number of aircraft in order to prevent them taking off. The accused were charged with conspiracy to commit a breach of s 1 of the Act. The issue was whether their actions fell within s 1 – were they for purposes prejudicial to the safety or interest of the State? The House of Lords were of the view that they were, expressly confirming that s 1 was *not* confined to espionage. The following points are of relevance to the media:

(a) the Act refers to purposes prejudicial to the State. But who determines what the interests of State are? The House of Lords held that this was a decision for the government rather than for the court, at least in relation to matters relating to defence and national security. It was not for the court to determine what the government's policy should have been. This view was confirmed by Lord Diplock in *Council of Civil Service Unions v Minister for the Civil Service*,[6] who said:

> National security is the responsibility of the executive government, what action is needed to protect its interests is ... a matter for which those on whom the responsibility rests, and not the courts of justice, must have the last word. It is par excellence a non-justiciable question. The judicial process is totally inept to deal with the sort of problems which it involves;

(b) having identified what the State regards as the interests of the State, the question whether the accused's act was prejudicial to those interests *is* a question for the jury. Lord Reid stressed that a trial judge was entitled to

---

2   This switch in the conventional burden of proof may fall foul of Art 6 of the European Convention on Human Rights (right to a fair trial).

3   Official Secrets Act 1911, s 8.

4   Robertson, G, *The Justice Game*, 1999, Vintage.

5   *Chandler v DPP* [1962] 3 All ER 142.

6   *Council of Civil Service Unions v Minister for the Civil Service* [1984] 3 All ER 935, p 952.

direct the jury that if they find that the accused acted with the purpose of interfering with the interests of the State as identified by the government they must hold that the purpose was prejudicial;

(c) on the facts of the *Chandler* case, did the intended sabotage amount to a prejudicial purpose? The House of Lords were unanimous in upholding the convictions under s 1. The majority held that the word 'purpose' in s 1 did not involve an examination of the subjective motives of the accused (which might have been, in the *Chandler* case, the avoidance of the threat of war). Instead, the relevant factor in deciding what the purpose of the demonstration had been was the direct and immediate *effect* of the defendant's acts which, on the facts, was the immobilisation of the airfield. This purpose was prejudicial to the interests of the State.

Under s 1(b) and (c) of the 1911 Act, the mere possession of any document or article which *might* be useful directly or indirectly to an enemy constitutes an offence provided that it is obtained or collected for a purpose prejudicial to the safety or interest of the State. Investigative journalism may fall within the ambit of the section. A journalist who collects or publishes articles which relate to defence matters, for example, might be guilty of an offence under the section unless she can prove that the material is not held or published for a purpose prejudicial to the State.

The only real protection against prosecution lies with the Attorney General. It is to be hoped that he will exercise a sense of proportion in deciding whether to permit a prosecution under s 1. Case law indicates that s 1 charges should only be brought in the clearest and most serious of cases.[7]

The danger for the media of having s 1 lurking on the statute book was highlighted in the 1970s with the prosecution of two journalists under s 1 of the Act.[8] The prosecution is known as the *ABC* case – from the initials of the surnames of the defendants. The charges centred on an interview conducted by the journalists with a former soldier who, during the course of the interview, disclosed details about the interception of communications by the military and security services. One of the journalists also faced charges because he had been found to have an extensive private library of information relating to communication interception activities – even though he information contained in his library was already in the public domain.

The s 1 charges against the journalists were eventually dropped at the trial at the insistence of the trial judge rather than as a result of a decision by the prosecution.

---

7   *R v Audrey, Berry and Campbell*, unreported, but see Aubrey, C, *Who's Watching You?*, 1980, Penguin, for more detail.

8   *Ibid.*

The Human Rights Act 1998 will hopefully provide a safeguard against disproportionate prosecutions under s 1. The provisions of that Act were considered in Chapter 1.

Under s 5 of the Official Secrets Act 1989, a person is guilty of an offence under the 1989 Act if without lawful authority he discloses any information, document or other article which he knows, or has reasonable cause to believe, to have come into his possession as a result of a contravention of s 1 of the Official Secrets Act 1911.

Section 1 of the Official Secrets Act 1920

The 1920 Act provides for the following offences which may be of relevance to the media:

1(2) If any person:

> (a) retains for any purpose prejudicial to the safety or interests of the State any official document, whether or not completed or issued for use, when he has no right to retain it, or when it is contrary to his duty to retain it, or fails to comply with any directions issued by a government department or any person authorised by such department with regard to the return or disposal thereof; or
>
> (b) allows any other person to have possession of any official document issued for his use alone, or communicates any secret official code word or pass word so issued, or, without lawful authority or excuse, has in his possession any official document or secret official code word or pass word issued for the use of some person other than himself, or on obtaining possession of any official document by finding or otherwise, neglects or fails to restore it to the person or authority by whom or for whose use it was issued, or to a police constable; or
>
> (c) without lawful authority or excuse, manufactures or sells, or has in his possession for sale any such die, seal or stamp as aforesaid,

he shall be guilty of a misdemeanour.

The Official Secrets Act 1989

The 1989 Act identifies specific areas in relation to which the disclosure and/or publication of official information by the media may give rise to criminal liability.

The Home Secretary who had responsibility for introducing the legislation professed that the intention was to prise the criminal law away from the great bulk of official information[9] by:

(a) limiting the categories of official information for which a prosecution may be brought under the 1989 Act; and

(b) providing that the disclosure must cause damage before a prosecution may be brought.

The consent of the Attorney General is required before a prosecution may be brought under the 1989 Act (unless the prosecution relates to crime and special investigation powers, where the consent of the DPP is required).[10]

The categories of information to which the 1989 Act applies are as follows:

(a) security and intelligence matters (s 1);

(b) defence (s 2);

(c) international relations (s 3); and

(d) crime and special investigation powers (s 4).

Each of the above sections makes it an offence for Crown servants, government contractors[11] or, in the case of s 1 (security and intelligence matters), past and present members of the security and intelligence services, to disclose information, documents or articles relating to the type of information covered by the section in question.

The Act contains a definition of each of the above categories of information, as follows:

- *'Security and intelligence'* means the work of, or in support of, the security and intelligence services or any part of them.[12]

- *'Defence'* means:

    (a) the size, shape, organisation, logistics, order of battle, deployment, operations, state of readiness and training of the armed forces of the Crown;

    (b) the weapons, stores or other equipment of those forces and the invention, development, production and operation of such equipment and research relating to it;

    (c) defence policy and strategy and military planning and intelligence;

---

9 Douglas Hurd, *Hansard*, 21.12.88, Vol 144, col 460.

10 Official Secrets Act 1989, s 9.

11 Which includes any person who is not a Crown servant, but who provides or is employed in the provision of goods and services to the Government.

12 Official Secrets Act 1989, s 1(9).

(d) plans and measures for the maintenance of essential supplies and services that are or would be needed in time of war.[13]

- *'International relations'* means the relations between States, between international organisations or between one or more States and one or more international organisations and includes any matter relating to a State other than the UK or to an international organisation which is capable of affecting the relations of the UK with another State or with an international organisation.[14]

- In relation to *crime and special investigation powers,* s 4 applies to information, documents or other articles the disclosure of which would or would be likely to:

    (a) result in the commission of an offence; or

    (b) facilitate an escape from legal custody or the doing of any act prejudicial to the safekeeping of persons in legal custody; or

    (c) impede the prevention or detection of offences or the apprehension or prosecution of suspected offenders.

Section 4 also applies to information obtained through a lawful interception of communications or as a result of an unauthorised warrant issued under s 3 of the Security Services Act 1994.

The activities of the media in relation to official information are regulated by s 5 of the Act.

Section 5 applies where:

(a) any information, document or other article protected against disclosure by the earlier sections of the Act [that is, relating to security and intelligence, defence, international relations or crime and special investigation powers] has come into a person's possession as a result of having been:

    (i) disclosed (whether to him or another) by a Crown servant or government contractor without lawful authority; or

    (ii) entrusted to him by a Crown servant or government contractor on terms requiring it to be held in confidence or in circumstances in which the Crown servant or government contractor could reasonably expect that it would be so held; or

    (iii) disclosed (whether to him or another) without lawful authority by a person to whom it was entrusted or mentioned in sub-paragraph (ii) above; and

(b) the disclosure without lawful authority of the information, document or article *by the person into whose possession it has come* is not an offence under

---

13   Official Secrets Act 1989, s 2(4).

14   *Ibid,* s 3(5).

ss 1, 2, 3 or 4 [that is, the person to whom the information, etc, has been given is not himself a member of the security and intelligence service or a Crown employee or government contractor. If the person did fall within these categories, any disclosure would be an offence under whichever of ss 1, 2, 3 or 4 is relevant to the category of information in question].[15]

Example

X is a journalist who is not a Crown servant or a government contractor. He is given an official memo from the Secretary of State for Defence's office to the Treasury. The memo states that that a significant number of machine guns used by the British Army have defective firing mechanisms. The information is disclosed to him by a civil servant. The disclosure is not authorised.

Section 5 will apply to this scenario. The memo concerns defence matters and so falls within one of the categories of information protected under the Act (in this case, by s 2).

The provisions of s 5

(2) Subject to sub-ss (3) and (4) below, the person into whose possession the information, document or article has come is guilty of an offence if he discloses it without lawful authority *knowing, or having reasonable cause to believe*, that it is protected against disclosure by ss 1, 2, 3 and 4 and that it has come into his possession as mentioned in sub-s (1) above.

Example

In our scenario, X will commit an offence if he discloses the contents of the memo provided that he knew or had reasonable cause to believe:

(a) that the information is protected against disclosure under s 2 of the Act; and

(b) that it has come into his possession in one of the ways set out above in relation to s 5(1).

This is for the prosecution to prove.

Section 5 contains other requirements. They are as follows:

(3) In the case of information or a document or article protected against disclosure under ss 1 to 3 above [relating to security and intelligence, defence and international relations respectively], a person does not commit an offence under s 5 unless:

(a) the disclosure by him is damaging; and

---

15 Official Secrets Act 1989, s 5(1).

(b) he makes it knowing, or having reasonable cause to believe, that it would be damaging.

The burden of proof in relation to these matters rests with the prosecution.

The test for damage is drawn widely in relation to each type of disclosure. In relation to *security and intelligence,* a disclosure is damaging if it causes damage to the work of, or any part of, the security and intelligence services or it is information or a document or other article which is such that its unauthorised disclosure would be *likely* to cause such damage or which falls within a class or description of information, documents or other articles, the unauthorised disclosure of which would be *likely* to have that effect.

In relation to *defence,* a disclosure is damaging if it damages the capability of, or any part of, the armed forces of the Crown to carry out their tasks or leads to loss of life or injury to members of those forces or serious damage to the equipment or installations of those forces or otherwise endangers the interests of the UK abroad, seriously obstructs the promotion or protection by the UK of those interests or endangers the safety of British citizens abroad. A disclosure is also damaging if it is of information, documents or other articles which is *likely* to have any of the above effects.

In relation to *international relations,* a disclosure is damaging if it endangers the interests of the UK abroad, seriously obstructs the promotion or protection by the UK of those interests or endangers the safety of British citizens abroad or it is of information or of a document or article which is such that its unauthorised disclosure would be likely to have those effects.

There is no requirement for the prosecution to show damage in relation to disclosures relating to crime and special investigation powers.

Example

In our example scenario, the prosecution must prove that the disclosure by X of the contents of the memo caused damage of the type set out above in relation to defence matters, or was likely to do so, and that X made the disclosure knowing or having reasonable cause to believe that it would be damaging.

If, at the time of the disclosure, British troops were engaged in hostile military activity, the disclosure of failings in its artillery could be said to be likely to be damaging according to the above criteria. The enemy might be encouraged to take advantage of the deficiencies which X has revealed. X would probably be found to have reasonable cause to believe that damage would be caused.

Continuing with the requirements of s 5:

(4) A person does not commit an offence under sub-s (2) above in respect of information or a document or other article which has come to his possession as a result of having been disclosed:

(a) as mentioned in sub-s (1)(a)(i) above by a government contractor; or

(b) as mentioned in sub-s (1)(a)(iii) above,

unless that disclosure was by a British citizen or took place in the UK, in any of the Channel Islands or in the Isle of Man or a colony.

In our example, the memo must have been disclosed to X by a person who satisfies these requirements.

Disclosures in the public interest

There is no public interest defence under the 1989 Act.

Example

X's disclosures about the defective guns which have been supplied to the Army might raise matters which are of genuine public concern. However, under the 1989 Act that will not provide X with a defence to the charge.

An attempt to insert into the Freedom of Information Bill[16] a public interest defence which would apply to the 1989 Act has been unsuccessful. One of the grounds which the new Labour Government has given for rejecting the insertion of such a defence is that a person to whom the 1989 Act applies would feel able to decide for himself whether the disclosure of sensitive information is justified on public interest grounds.

This argument is disingenuous. The decision whether a public interest defence had been made out would be for the jury, not for the party making the disclosure.

The omission of a public interest defence has been criticised on the basis that Crown servants and government contractors who fall within the Act's provisions are discouraged from disclosing official information of the type covered by the Act because of a fear that the disclosure will be found likely to cause the damage specified in the Act. Crimes, abuses and scandals may accordingly go undetected. If a public interest defence were in place, officials would be encouraged to come forward to disclose wrongdoing. The court could weigh the damage which has been caused by the disclosure, or the likelihood of such damage, against the fact that the publication of the information is in the public interest when deciding whether an offence had been committed.

The lack of a public interest test may also render the official secrets legislation incompatible with the European Convention on Human Rights. The reader is referred to Chapter 1 for an analysis of the jurisprudence of the European Court of Human Rights on the Convention right to freedom of

---

16 Which is going through Parliament at the time of writing.

expression. The court has emphasised that limitations on the publication of material which is in the public interest must be shown to be necessary. Under the Convention, the acceptable limitations on freedom of expression include national security, territorial integrity and public safety. However, the danger is that broad restrictions on disclosure of information concerning these matters may go further than is strictly necessary to safeguard the permitted derogations from the right to freedom of expression. A public interest defence would go a long way to ensuring that limitations on disclosure are compatible with the Convention.

Supporters of the 1989 Act point out that there is no need for a public interest defence, because the scheme of the Act provides that information should not be communicated, only where it is damaging to the interests identified in the Act. However, the definition of damage in relation to each of the categories identified above is both broad and vague. Almost any disclosure about the armed forces might be said to be likely to damage their capability to carry out their tasks and therefore satisfy the requirements of damage. This is the case even though the disclosure might be made with the objective of alerting the public to serious deficiencies in, for example, the provision of equipment. The same is true of the other categories of information.

As matters currently stand, the media's ability to report on security and intelligence services, defence matters, international relations and crime and investigation powers are curtailed more restrictively than is necessary to safeguard the public interest. It is to be hoped that the coming into force of the Human Rights Act will help to confine official secrets restrictions to ensure that they operate only where they are both necessary and proportionate.

Disclosure of information in the public domain

Equally significant is the omission of a defence under the Act that the information which has been disclosed by the media is already in the public domain. The government responsible for the introduction of the 1989 Act justified this omission by pointing out that prior publication is taken into account in the Act because it is a relevant consideration in assessing whether damage has been caused by the disclosure. A defendant can argue that the fact that the material in question is already in the public domain makes it unlikely that damage will be caused by the publication. But that will not automatically be the case. The then Home Secretary observed that:

It is perfectly possible to have partial, incomplete publication in a distant publication with no particular circulation and then to argue that to pick up that information, put it in a different form, and splash it across the news, so ensuring major circulation, would provide a further harm. We cannot assume in advance that it would not, and it would be foolish to admit an overarching defence of prior publication. That is why we propose to leave the matter to the jury.[17]

The first prosecution of a writer/journalist under s 5 of the Act was recently dropped before it came to trial. The prosecution was against the writer Tony Geraghty and concerned his book about the military history of 'the Troubles' in Northern Ireland, *The Irish War*. A military internal inquiry found that the book did not threaten lives or the conduct of present operations in Northern Ireland.[18] Nevertheless, a prosecution was commenced against Mr Geraghty on the ground that he had been given access to confidential information. It would appear that the contents of the book were in the public domain before the publication of Mr Geraghty's book. However, as we have seen, that in itself is not a defence (although it is likely to make it more difficult to show that the disclosure was damaging). Mr Geraghty pleaded not guilty, relying on the fact that the book did not cause damage to Irish security or defence. In December 1999, the charge was dropped against him. It is interesting to note that no action was taken against the book, which remained on sale whilst the prosecution was proceeding.[19] It would be difficult for the prosecution to show that the book was damaging when it had made no attempt to obtain an order removing the book from sale.

Other provisions under the 1989 Act

Section 6 of the Act applies to information, documents or other articles entrusted in confidence to other States or international organisations. It is an offence to make an unauthorised disclosure of such information when it relates to security and intelligence, defence or international relations where it is known or where there is reasonable cause to believe that the information was disclosed to the State or international organisation in accordance with s 6 and that its disclosure would be damaging (see above for the definition of 'damaging'). Where the information is disclosed without the authority of the State or organisation, the prosecution must prove that this fact is known and that there is reason to believe that it has been disclosed in such circumstances.

Section 8(4) of the Act provides that, where a person has in his possession or control any document or other article which it would be an offence for him to disclose under s 5, he commits an offence if he fails to comply with an official direction for its return or disposal. Similarly, where he obtained the document or article from a Crown servant or government contractor on terms requiring it to be held in confidence or in circumstances where there is a reasonable expectation that it will be so held, he fails to take such care to

---

17 *Hansard*, 21.12.1998, Vol 144, col 464.

18 Geraghty, T (2000) *The Times*, 8 February.

19 See, also, (1999) *The Guardian*, 12 May and (1999) *The Guardian*, 23 June.

prevent its unauthorised disclosure as a person in his position may reasonably be expected to take.

Non-statutory restraints

The DA notice system

The DA (or defence advisory) notice system is a method of providing guidance to the media as to what information relevant to national security may or may not be made public. The guidance is provided by the Defence Press and Broadcasting Advisory Committee, which is a body made up of civil servants, and representatives of the media.

The system is voluntary and non-binding.

The committee has issued a number of DA notices which are written in broad terms and which are intended to provide general guidance to the media. They have no legal standing. Compliance with a DA notice will not necessarily mean that the publication of material will not give rise to criminal liability under the official secrets legislation or, indeed, any other type of liability.

The DA notices currently in force cover the following matters:

(a) operations, plans and capabilities;

(b) non-nuclear weapons and operational equipment;

(c) nuclear weapons and equipment;

(d) cyphers and secure communications;

(e) identification of specific installations;

(f) security and intelligence services.

The key figures in the system are the committee's secretary and deputy secretary who can be contacted by the media for advice. A request for advice usually concerns the application of the broad wording of the notices to a specific set of circumstances. The secretary's advice is not binding. The media may therefore choose not to follow it.

CHAPTER 14

CHARACTER MERCHANDISING AND ENDORSEMENTS

CONTROLLING THE USE TO WHICH AN IMAGE IS PUT

Character merchandising means the use of the name or likeness of a well known celebrity or fictional character in order to increase the sales potential of goods or services. It is well accepted that the name and image of public figures and fictional characters can be used to promote, advertise and market products and services. Sponsorship and product endorsement agreements are a normal feature of the business activities of celebrities and sports personalities. The net result is that the fictional or living character in question often becomes a commodity in its own right and can demand large fees in return for product endorsement. The usual way in which a manufacturer of a product goes about using the name or likeness of a celebrity or fictional character is by obtaining a licence (or, in other words, permission) in return for payment. This is especially the case in relation to fictional characters such as The Simpsons or Disney characters. Commercial businesses invest large amounts of money to secure rights to use these names and likenesses for their products or services.

But not all advertisers or merchandisers are willing to pay large fees for a licence to use the personality or character. In 1997, a company produced a sticker album featuring images of the Spice Girls. No permission was sought for the use of their likenesses. In 1999, a radio station advertised itself using a poster part of which featured a photograph of the football player Jamie Redknapp. No licence was taken for the use of his image. These instances, and many others like them, raise the issue of whether a personality or the creator or owner of the rights to a fictional character can control the use to which the name, likeness and image are put and what steps (if any) can be taken to secure effective exclusivity for use of the image.

We shall see that it is generally more straightforward to restrain the unauthorised use of an fictional character (such as Bart Simpson) than it is for a living person.

No personality right for living persons

Under English law, there is no free standing *personality right* which a living person can exercise to control the commercial exploitation of his name, likeness or image. Personalities do not, therefore, have a directly enforceable legal right to exercise to restrain the use of their name and likeness. Their likeness or name may be used for commercial purposes *except to the extent* that the use gives rise to a claim in intellectual property, defamation or trade description law.

On the other hand, the media industry codes – most notably, the Committee of Advertising Practice Code – (which are examined in more detail in Chapter 16) contain restrictions on the unauthorised use of people. For most practical purposes, it is the codes which govern the effective position on the use of famous personalities.

THE LEGAL RESTRICTIONS

(a) Defamation[1]

The law of defamation protects the *reputation* of a living person or of a corporation. Statements will be defamatory if they tend to make ordinary people think less of the subject. In order to bring a successful action for defamation, a personality has to show that the use or reference to his name or likeness has caused damage to his reputation. A defamation claim of this type will generally involve an allegation that the use of the name or likeness carries the implication of bad faith on the part of the personality or exposes the personality to ridicule. *The estates of dead people* cannot bring proceedings for defamation.

An example of a defamation claim arising from an unauthorised reference to a personality is the case of *Tolley v Fry*.[2] The claimant was a well known amateur golfer. He was caricatured in an advertisement for Fry's chocolate in such a way as suggested that he was endorsing the product. Mr Tolley had not given permission for his likeness to be used in the advertisement. He commenced proceedings on the basis that the advertisement was defamatory, in that it suggested that, despite his amateur status, he had agreed to advertise the product in return for payment. He alleged that this suggestion was damaging to his credit and reputation as an amateur golfer. The court upheld the claim, finding that the advertisement inferred that Mr Tolley was a hypocrite when he presented himself as an amateur golfer. The court made clear in its judgment that the unauthorised use of the likeness of Mr Tolley would not have been actionable in the absence of this defamatory inference.

Most of the defamatory meanings likely to arise in connection with the unauthorised use of a personality involve meanings that are not apparent from the face of the publication. The advertisement in *Tolley v Fry* would not

---

1   Defamation was considered in detail in Chapter 3.
2   *Tolley v Fry* [1931] AC 333.

have had a defamatory meaning unless the audience was already aware of Mr Tolley's amateur status. That status was not apparent from the face of the advertisement.

This type of 'hidden' meaning is known as an *innuendo*. Care should be taken to assess material which refers to a personality for innuendo meanings. This exercise will involve knowledge the public stance of the personality on relevant issues so as to ensure that a committed animal rights activist is not shown wearing animal fur or a known teetotaller is not used to promote alcohol. Both of these scenarios would involve an inference that the personality in question is a hypocrite by suggesting they would disregard their publicly expressed opinions for the sake of personal gain. The fact that the publisher of the defamatory material did not intend to make a defamatory statement is irrelevant to liability.

Care should be taken where the personality is known to have an exclusive merchandising contract or an employment contract which forbids them to participate in promotional activities or product endorsements. The unauthorised use of the name and/or likeness could be defamatory if the personality is able to prove that *some* of the audience would have believed that he had agreed to appear in the advertisement in breach of contract.

(b) Malicious falsehood[3]

Where a party makes a false representation about a personality knowing it to be false or reckless as to whether it is or is not true, it could be liable for malicious falsehood provided that the falsehood causes (or in some cases is likely to cause) the personality financial loss. In the case of *Kaye v Robertson*,[4] a newspaper which sought to portray as an exclusive an interview obtained without consent with the then gravely injured Gorden Kaye was held liable in malicious falsehood. The false portrayal of the interview as something which Mr Kaye had willingly consented to was held to be a falsehood, causing him a likelihood of pecuniary loss, because he might otherwise have been able to sell his story to the media.

---

3   Malicious falsehood was considered in detail in Chapter 4.
4   *Kaye v Robertson* [1991] FSR 62.

(c) Copyright and moral rights[5]

*The use of photographs or film footage of the
personality for commercial purposes*

A limited right of privacy

A person who commissions photographs (or videotapes and films or stills taken from them) for private or domestic purposes has the right to prevent the unauthorised publication of the material.[6] The right applies only to material which is *commissioned* for private or domestic purposes. It will not apply to uncommissioned material which happens to be taken on a private occasion, for example, photographs taken by the paparazzi. The right is owned by the *commissioner* of the material, who may not necessarily be the subject of the photograph or film, and it cannot be transferred. This right was considered further in Chapter 8.

Copyright in photographs

Copyright subsists in photographs as artistic works. The unauthorised publication of a photograph will infringe copyright in the photograph, unless it falls within one of the permitted uses discussed in Chapter 6. In order to avoid infringement, the copyright owner should be approached for permission to use the photograph. Alternatively, the user might acquire copyright in the photograph by way of an assignment.

Copyright in photographs, whether commissioned or not, will belong to the *photographer*, unless copyright has been assigned to a third party. Unless the subject of the photograph has acquired the copyright by way of assignment, he will have no right to restrain the publication of the photograph on the ground that it is an infringement of copyright. A person can prevent reproduction of drawings and photographs of him in which he owns copyright, but has no right to prevent the reproduction or exploitation of any photographs and drawings in which he does not own copyright simply by reason of the fact that they contain or depict his likeness.

Copyright and photographs comprising of stills of films

The unauthorised use of a still from a film, television broadcast or cable programme is an infringement of copyright of the work from which it was taken.[7] A licence should therefore be obtained from the copyright owners (who will usually be the *production company and the principal director* in the case

---

5   Copyright and moral rights were considered in detail in Chapter 6.
6   CDPA 1988, s 85(1).
7   *Ibid*, s 17(4).

of a film and the *broadcaster* in the case of a broadcast or cable programme). The copyright owner will probably *not* be the individual(s) who appear in the still.

The film may also be a dramatic work for copyright purposes.[8] This was discussed further in Chapter 6. Where a substantial part of a dramatic work is reproduced without consent, it will infringe copyright in the dramatic work. It is arguable that the reproduction of a single still in the film might represent a substantial part of the *dramatic work* – especially as the Copyright, Designs and Patents Act (CDPA) 1988 expressly provides that a reproduction of a still infringes copyright in the film as a copyright work.[9]

Where the still is taken from a cartoon or other type of work of animation, the drawings will be artistic works for copyright purposes and the reproduction is likely to infringe copyright in the artistic work as well as the film or broadcast.

Will photographs which are taken from stills infringe performance rights?

A performer has the right to prevent the unauthorised exploitation of the recording of their performance. This right is a relatively recent introduction to English law. So far as the author is aware, an English court has not been called on to consider whether the use of a single still featuring a performer could be said to constitute an infringement of the performer's rights. In the author's opinion, a still is *capable* of infringing a performer's rights. In order to err on the side of caution, consent should be sought from the owner of the performance right. This may not be the performer. The rights can be, and often are, assigned: usually, in the case of a film, to the film production company.

Copyright and the use of film footage

The above observations apply equally to the use of footage as to the use of stills. A licence to use the footage will be required from the copyright owner. Performance rights should also be cleared.[10]

Copyright in signatures

An individual's signature may be protected under copyright law as an artistic work. If so, the unauthorised reproduction of the signature will infringe copyright. The name itself will *not* be protected by copyright; it is the *appearance* of the signature which is protected.

---

8   *Norowzian v Arks (No 2)* [2000] EMLR 1. This case is considered in detail in Chapter 6.
9   CDPA 1988, s 17(4).
10 Clearance procedures are described in Chapter 18.

It should be remembered that copyright only subsists in works which are the product of skill, judgment and labour. An everyday signature of a rudimentary nature is unlikely to satisfy these requirements. Similarly, if the name were written in a simple form, say, in block capitals, the reproduction would not infringe copyright. The more elaborate the signature, the more likely that it will be protected by copyright.

Copyright in a name

It is well established under copyright law that copyright does not exist in a name. For example, in the 1869 Privy Council case of *Du Boulay v Du Boulay*,[11] the court observed that:

> ... in this country we do not recognise the absolute right of a person to a particular name to the extent of entitling him to prevent the assumption of that name by a stranger.

This is so whether the name in question is the name of a living individual or an invented word for a fictional character. The name of the fictional character 'Kojak'[12] has been refused copyright protection under English copyright law, as has the real life surname of Burberry.[13]

Copyright in appearance

There is no copyright in a living person's appearance, even if that person has a carefully crafted image. This was illustrated by the case of *Corpn of America v Harpbond*.[14] The case concerned the unauthorised reproduction of the pop star Adam Ant's distinctively made-up face. The court found that no copyright existed in the pop star's appearance.

Copyright and the appearance of fictional characters

Where the merchandising concerns cartoon or animated characters, copyright can exist in the drawings of the characters as artistic works (although design right may replace copyright where the character is an article, such as a puppet. This is discussed below).

It is a copyright infringement of a two dimensional artistic work to reproduce it in three dimensions and vice versa.[15] Hence, it will be an infringement of copyright in a drawing to produce a model of a cartoon character.[16]

---

11 *Du Boulay v Du Boulay* (1869) LR 2, PC.
12 *Tavener Rutledge v Trexapalm* [1977] RPC 275.
13 *Burberrys v Cording* (1909) 26 RPC 693.
14 *Corpn of America v Harpbond* [1983] FSR 32.
15 CDPA 1988, s 17(3).
16 Eg, *King Features Syndicate v Kleeman* [1941] AC 417, where the manufacturer of 'Popeye' dolls was held to have infringed copyright in the drawings of the Popeye figure.

(d) Design rights and merchandising

The CDPA removed copyright protection from design drawings for functional articles created after 1 August 1989 and replaced it with design right. At first sight this may not seem to have implications for character merchandising. But the removal of copyright has been held to apply to the copying of three dimensional puppets and models. Design right might therefore have a wider scope than the protection of purely functional articles.

Section 51 of the CDPA provides that:

(1) It is not an infringement of any copyright in a design document or model recording or embodying a design for anything other than an artistic work or a typeface to make an article to the design or to copy an article made to the design.

(2) Nor is it an infringement of the copyright to issue to the public, or include in a film, broadcast or cable programme service, anything the making of which was, by virtue of sub-s (1) not an infringement of that copyright.

(3) In this section:

'design' means the design of any aspect of the shape or configuration (whether internal or external) of the whole or part of an article, other than surface decoration; and

'design document' means any record of a design, whether in the form of a drawing, a written description, a photograph, data stored in a computer or otherwise;

the effect of the section is to remove copyright protection from what is potentially a wide category of articles and to replace it with a new right, design right.

The approach which should be adopted when determining whether a design is protected by copyright or design right is as follows:

- is the drawing/model for an article? If no, copyright applies;
- if yes, is the article an artistic work, for example, a work of sculpture, or a typeface? If yes, copyright will apply. 'Artistic work' includes a work of artistic craftsmanship;
- if the design is not for an artistic work, design right may apply. The definition of 'design' should be considered to ensure that the article falls within it.

Key differences between copyright and design right

The distinction between copyright and design right is important because design right affords a more limited protection than copyright law. Copyright subsists in an artistic work for the life of the author plus 70 years (unless the work has been exploited by an industrial process, in which case the period of protection is reduced to 25 years from the end of the calendar year in which the goods are first marketed).[17] Design right, on the other hand, expires:

(a) 15 years from the end of the calendar year in which the design was first recorded in a design document or an article was first made to the design, whichever first occurred; or

(b) if articles made to the design are made available for sale or hire within five years from the end of that calendar year, 10 years from the end of the calendar year in which that first occurred.[18]

Any person is entitled as of right to a licence to do anything which would otherwise infringe the design right in the last five years of the design right term.[19]

Under design right law, a designer can therefore have effectively only five years' protection for a commercially exploited design.

Another important difference between copyright and design right is that copyright subsists in original artistic works. As we have seen in Chapter 6, the test for 'originality' requires only that the design must not have been copied from something else.

Design right has a higher threshold than copyright. It will only apply if a design is original (in the copyright sense) *and if it was not commonplace in the design field in question at the time that the design was created.* The meaning of commonplace is considered below. It is a more stringent test than originality.

Recent cases have demonstrated the width of design right and, in particular, its application to character merchandising.

BBC Worldwide Ltd v Pally Screen Printing Ltd[20]

The claimant alleged that it owned the intellectual property rights and associated merchandising rights in the TV programme 'Teletubbies'. The first and second defendants were respectively a printing company and its sole director. They printed pictures of the Teletubbies on items of clothing. This activity was not authorised by the claimant, which sought summary judgment for infringement of its copyright in the drawings of the Teletubby characters.

The defendants argued that the drawings of the Teletubbies which the claimant relied on to show infringement in its artistic works had been created for the purpose of creating the three dimensional puppets used in the programme. These puppets were articles for the purposes of the CDPA. It

---

17 CDPA 1988, s 52.

18 *Ibid*, s 216.

19 *Ibid*, s 237(1).

20 *BBC Worldwide Ltd v Pally Screen Printing Ltd* [1998] FSR 665.

followed that, under s 51, it was not an infringement of copyright in the design documents to copy the puppets made to the design.

The judge found that the defendants had made out a clearly arguable case that design right law rather than copyright law was applicable in respect of the alleged copying of the puppets.[21] The case does not appear to have proceeded any further than this application. However, in a subsequent case concerning design right in circuit diagrams, Pumfrey J cited the judgment in the *Teletubbies* case, observing that 'it seems to me that [the judge] came to a clear construction for reasons which I find compelling'.[22]

It is therefore quite possible in the wake of the *Teletubbies* decision that protection for three dimensional characters such as puppets or models will fall under design right protection rather than copyright, unless the claimant can demonstrate that the puppets or models are artistic works for copyright law purposes.

Jo-Y-Jo Ltd v Matalan Retail Ltd[23]

The shape of an item of clothing (a knitted vest) was held to be an article for the purpose of s 51 and was accordingly protected by design right, rather than copyright. This judgment has important repercussions for the fashion industry,[24] which may no longer be able to rely on copyright in relation to the shape of their designs.

What is design right?

The definition of design right is set out in the CDPA. The relevant provisions are as follows:

Section 213(1)

Design right is a property right which subsists in an original design.

Design: the design of any aspect of the shape or configuration (whether internal or external) of the whole or part of an article.

---

21 It might have been possible for the claimants to argue that the puppets were works of artistic craftsmanship and so were copyright works under s 51. The point does not appear to have been considered.

22 *Mackie Designs Inc v Behringer Specialised Studio Equipment (UK) Ltd* [1999] RPC 717.

23 *Jo-Y-Jo Ltd v Matalan Retail Ltd* (1999) unreported.

24 See, eg, '*Jo-Y-Jo v Matalan*: threadbare protection for clothing designs?' [1999] EIPR 627.

Section 213(2)

Design right does not subsist in:

(a) a method or principle of construction;

(b) features of shape or configuration of an article which:

(i) enable the article to be connected to, or placed in, around or against, another article so that either article may perform its function ('must fit' exemption); or

(ii) are dependent upon the appearance of another article of which the article is intended by the designer to form an integral part ('must match' exemption); or

(c) surface decoration.

Section 213(4)

A design is not original if it is commonplace in the design field in question at the time of its creation.

Section 226(1)

Primary infringement of design right.

The owner of the design right in a design has the exclusive right to reproduce the design for commercial purposes:

(a) by making articles to that design; or

(b) by making a design document recording the design for the purpose of enabling such articles to be made.

Section 226(2)

Reproduction of a design by making articles to the design means copying the design so as to produce articles exactly or substantially to that design ...

Section 226(3)

Design right is infringed by a person who authorises another to do anything which is the exclusive right of the design owner.

Section 226(4)

Reproduction may be direct or indirect.

Note that s 227 defines acts of secondary infringement equivalent to those affecting copyright under ss 22 and 23(a)–(c).

Guidance on the above provisions

As design right is a relatively new innovation, there have been a limited number of cases concerning the above statutory provisions. Such guidance that has emerged has established the following:

'Original' and commonplace design – s 213

Section 213 provides that a design is not original if it is commonplace in the design field in question at the time of its creation. The *Farmers' Build*[25] case laid down important guidance about the meaning of 'original' and 'commonplace' as follows:

(a) 'original' has the same meaning as in Pt 1 of the CDPA relating to copyright in literary, dramatic, musical and artistic works;

(b) designs which are original in the 'copyright sense' can cease to be 'original' for design right purposes where they are commonplace (s 213(4));

(c) 'the approach of the court should be as follows:

- compare the design of the article in which design right is claimed with the design of other articles in the same field at the time of its creation and with the alleged infringing article;

- the court must be satisfied that the design for which design right is claimed has not simply been copied from the design of an earlier article. The court must bear in mind that, in the case of functional articles, one design may be very similar to or even identical to another design and yet not be a copy. If the court is satisfied that it has been slavishly copied from an earlier design, it is not 'original' in the 'copyright sense' and the commonplace issue does not arise;

- if the court is satisfied that the design has not been copied from another design, the design is original in the 'copyright sense'. The court must then decide if it is 'commonplace'. For that purpose, it is necessary to ascertain how similar the design is to the design of similar articles by persons other than the parties to the litigation in the same field of design at the time when the design was created;

- this is a comparative exercise to be conducted objectively in the light of the evidence (including expert evidence) pointing out the similarities and differences and explaining their significance. It is for the court to decide whether the design is commonplace. This is a question of fact and degree. The closer the similarity of the various designs, the more likely that the designs are commonplace (especially if there is no causal link – such as copying – to account for the similarity);

---

25 *Farmers' Build v Carier Bulk Material* [1998] All ER (D) 681.

- if there are aspects of the claimant's design of the article not to be found in any other design in the field in question and those aspects are in the defendant's design, the court is entitled to conclude that the design in question was not commonplace. A commonplace article may have a shape and configuration which is not commonplace – it is the shape and configuration which is protected by design right, not the article itself;

- the burden is on the claimant to identify the relevant aspects of the shape and configuration of the article and what is original about the design. The burden is then on the defendant to allege and adduce evidence showing that, although the design is original in the 'copyright sense', it is commonplace in the field in question;

- there can be design right in the overall shape and configuration of an article, even if all the individual parts are commonplace provided the overall shape and configuration is different to other designs in the field in question.

In the *Jo-Y-Jo v Matalan* case,[26] the shape of a vest was held to be a commonplace design, which did not qualify for copyright protection.

The meaning of 'design'

The definition of 'design' is wide enough to include the shape or configuration of the individual parts of an item and of the item as a whole. The individual parts, combinations of those parts and the parts made up into the whole item are all 'articles' with a shape and a configuration for the purposes of s 213,[27] meaning that 'the proprietor can choose to assert design right in the whole or any part of his product. If the right is said to reside in the design of a teapot, it can mean it can reside in the whole pot design or the design of the spout or the handle or the lid – or part of the lid. So, design right can be trimmed to closely match what has been taken.'[28]

Meaning of 'surface decoration' – s 213 of the CDPA (excluded from design right protection)

Surface decoration includes decoration lying on the surface of the article and decorative features of the surface itself. It is not confined to features which are two dimensional.[29] In *Mark Wilkinson Furniture*, it included the painted finish, beading and 'v-grooves' in a fitted kitchen. These features were accordingly excluded from design right protection. The rounded cornice on kitchen

---

26 *Jo-Y-Jo Ltd v Matalan Retail Ltd* (1999) unreported.
27 *Farmers' Build v Carier Bulk Material* [1998] All ER (D) 681.
28 Laddie J in *Ocular Sciences v Aspect Visioncare* [1997] RPC 289.
29 *Mark Wilkinson Furniture Ltd v Woodcraft Designs (Radcliffe) Ltd* [1998] FSR 63.

cupboards, on the other hand, was not surface decoration. It was part of the shape of the cupboard.

Surface decoration includes those decorative features which also serve a functional purpose.[30]

In the case of a knitted vest, design right would exist in the shape of the article (provided it is original and not commonplace), but not in the surface decoration. It was held that *the essence of surface decoration is the application of a decorative process to a pre-existing surface*, for example, embroidery applied to the knitted vest.[31] Seam lines and piping on a mobile phone case have been held to be surface decoration.[32]

The 'must match' exclusion – s 213 of the CDPA (excluded from design right protection)

The 'must match' exclusion did not apply to a fitted kitchen as a whole because the complete fitted kitchen was not an article itself, but instead was a series of matching articles, that is, separate cupboards, none of which formed an integral part of another article.[33] Each individual unit was therefore to be regarded as a separate entity. The same reasoning will probably apply to other constituent elements of a set: for example, the cups, sugar bowl, teapot, etc, making up a tea set, will each be an article in their own right.

The 'must fit' exclusion – s 213 of the CDPA (excluded from design right protection)

The fact that a breast prosthesis was flexible and compliant such that it could fit a number of different styles of bras was sufficient to take it outside the 'must fit' exemption. The exemption is concerned with a much more precise correspondence between the two articles, such as with a rigid plug and socket, where the functional requirement that one article should fit in or against the other displaces the original design work.[34]

In relation to the mobile telephone case, it was held that a basic function for a case is to enclose the telephone. Those aspects of the case which enabled it to be placed around the telephone so that either the telephone or the case could perform its function were excluded from design right protection.[35]

---

30   *Mark Wilkinson Furniture Ltd v Woodcraft Designs (Radcliffe) Ltd* [1998] FSR 63.

31   *Jo-Y-Jo Ltd v Matalan Retail Ltd* (1999) unreported.

32   *Philip Parker v Steven Tidball* [1997] FSR 680.

33   *Mark Wilkinson Furniture Ltd v Woodcraft Designs (Radcliffe) Ltd* [1998] FSR 63.

34   *Amoena v Trulife* (1995) unreported.

35   *Philip Parker v Steven Tidball* [1997] FSR 680.

Any feature of shape and configuration which met the 'must fit' exemption is excluded from design right protection, even if it performed some other purpose.[36]

'Article' applies equally to animate and inanimate things for the purpose of this exception. Therefore, those features allowing a contact lens to fit against the eyeball to enable the lens to perform its function were excluded.[37]

Infringement of design – making articles to the design

The same general principles apply to infringement of design right as to copyright infringement.[38] First, there has to be objective similarity (excluding features of surface decoration) between the infringing article and the design, or a substantial part thereof. Secondly, there has to be causal connection between the design and the infringing article, that is, copying. Where copying is not established, there is no design right infringement.[39]

Similarity is to be assessed in the eyes of the person to whom the design was directed, that is, the potential user or acquirer of the claimant's products.[40] It is *not* necessary to show a deliberate intention to copy on the part of the defendant in order to give rise to a primary infringement,[41] nor is it necessary that the defendant must actually have the claimant's design in front of them when making the item complained of.[42] Mere changes in scale do not produce different designs.[43]

Ownership of design right

Section 215

The person who creates the design ('the designer') is the first owner of design right unless it is created in the course of a commission or the course of employment. Where the design is computer generated, the designer is the person who made the arrangements which were necessary for the creation of the design.[44]

---

36 *Ocular Sciences v Aspect Visioncare* [1997] RPC 289.
37 *Ibid.*
38 *Mark Wilkinson Furniture Ltd v Woodcraft Designs (Radcliffe) Ltd* [1998] FSR 63.
39 *Amoena v Trulife* (1995) unreported.
40 *Mark Wilkinson Furniture Ltd v Woodcraft Designs (Radcliffe) Ltd* [1998] FSR 63.
41 *Ibid.*
42 *Philip Parker v Steven Tidball* [1997] FSR 680.
43 *Ocular Sciences v Aspect Visioncare* [1997] RPC 289.
44 CDPA 1988, s 214(2).

Section 215(2)

Where the design is created in the course of a commission, the person commissioning the design is the first owner of design right in it. *This is the opposite to the position under copyright law.*

Section 215(3)

Where the design is created by an employee in the course of his employment, his employer is the first owner of design right in the design (unless the design is commissioned, in which case it is the commissioner pursuant to s 215(2)).

(e) Passing off

Although there is no copyright or other property right in a name, it can in theory be the subject of a passing off claim. As Parker J observed in *Burberrys v JC Cording and Co Ltd*:[45]

> On the one hand, apart from the law as to trade marks, no one can claim monopoly rights in the use of a word or name. On the other hand, no one is entitled by the use of any word or name, or indeed in any other way, to represent his goods as being the goods of another to that other's injury. If an injunction be granted restraining the use of a word or name, it is no doubt granted to protect property, but the property, to protect which it is granted, is not property in the word or name, but property in the trade or goodwill which will be injured by its use.

The basis of a passing off action is the protection of in the claimant's goodwill (or trading reputation). Goodwill is usually generated by the claimant's use of a distinguishing feature, such as a name or logo. The English courts have resisted extending the law of passing off to include the unauthorised exploitation of a person or a character's identity, likeness or image. The reluctance has been justified on the ground that the individuals who have commenced proceedings in passing off have been unable to establish that they have used name and likeness to generate goodwill, which is likely to be damaged by the defendant's activities.

The elements of the passing off action were formulated in a useful way in the case of *Reckitt and Colman Products Ltd v Borden Inc* (the *Jif Lemon Juice* case)[46] as follows:

- the claimant must establish a *goodwill or reputation* attached to the goods or services in question. The goodwill should be present in the mind of the public to an extent that the identifying feature (such as the personality's name or image) under which particular goods or services are offered to the

---

45   *Burberrys v JC Cording and Co Ltd* (1909) 26 RPC 693.
46   *Reckitt and Colman Products Ltd v Borden Inc* [1990] 1 WLR 491.

public is recognised by the public as distinctive of goods or services associated with the claimant;

- there must be a *misrepresentation* by the defendant to the public which leads, or is likely to lead, the public to believe that goods or services offered by him are the goods or services of the claimant or are associated with the claimant;

- there must be *damage* suffered, or likely to be suffered, to the claimant's goodwill by reason of the erroneous belief engendered by the defendant's misrepresentation. The damage is likely to be evidenced by confusion on the part of the public. The confusion should be shown to affect a substantial number of members of the public.

Goodwill or reputation

As a prerequisite to a claim in passing off, a claimant has to establish its goodwill.

What is goodwill?

Goodwill is a nebulous concept. A useful definition was formulated in *IRC v Muller*,[47] in which goodwill was characterised as 'the attractive force which brings in custom'. It is essentially the commercial benefit that a good name and reputation brings with it. It is important to grasp that goodwill is *not* synonymous with 'fame' or public recognition.

Three decisions from the 1970s illustrate the court's approach to passing off in the context of merchandising rights.

In the case of *Lyngstad v Anabas Products*,[48] the court refused relief to members of the pop group ABBA who sought to restrain the reproduction of their name on items of clothing. There was little evidence of substantial exploitation by ABBA of any merchandising rights in the UK. ABBA's case was based on the argument that, by producing the item bearing the ABBA name, the defendants were giving the public the erroneous impression that the goods were in some way associated with the group, in the sense that the group must have in some way endorsed them.

Oliver J observed as follows:

Essentially, what the plaintiff complains of here is not that there is a possibility of confusion between the defendants' business activities and their activities as singers, but that their activities as singers have generated a public interest which has enabled the defendants to exploit for their own purposes the use of the plaintiff's photographs and names.

---

47 *IRC v Muller* [1901] AC 217.

48 *Lyngstad v Anabas Products* [1977] FSR 62.

But this public interest or recognition is not the same as 'goodwill'.

A similar decision concerned The Wombles, the well known fictitious characters who appeared in a television series popular with children.[49] The defendant called his company Womble Skips Ltd. Its business was the provision of rubbish skips. The word 'Wombles' was printed on the sides of the defendant's rubbish skips. The claimant's business was the commercial exploitation of the Womble characters. Unlike the ABBA case, there was therefore evidence of merchandising activity on the part of the claimant. But Walton J held that the claimant did not even have an arguable case in passing off against the claimant. There was no common field of business activity between the claimant and the defendant. No one seeing a Womble skip would think that there was really any connection between the skip and the merchandising business carried on by the claimant. There was accordingly no likelihood of confusion and therefore no likelihood of damage to the goodwill.

The *Wombles* case was decided prior to the decision in *Lego Systems v Lego M Lemelstrich*.[50] The *Lego* case departed from the then orthodox view that, in order to establish a passing off, there had to be a common field of business activity between the claimant and defendant. In the *Lego* case, there was no common field of activity between the parties (the claimant made construction kit toys and building bricks and the defendant produced garden irrigation equipment). Nevertheless, the court held that the defendant's use of the LEGO brand was a passing off, because confusion or a real possibility of confusion existed, despite the fact that the parties operated in different spheres of business. The court held that the claimant's LEGO mark was so well known that the goodwill attached to it extended beyond the field in which the claimant had been engaged.

In the light of the *Lego* case, it may well be that the *Wombles* case would be decided differently. It might now be accepted that the goodwill of a claimant such as Wombles, whose business was the licensing of merchandising rights, could be damaged by the unauthorised use of the characters. The damage to the goodwill might typically take the form of the loss of licensing royalties, the depreciation of the value of the royalties due to the loss of exclusivity in the image or the tarnishing of the goodwill if the claimant is associated with goods of an inferior quality.

But the recognition that passing off can occur where there is no common field of activity does not remove the need for the claimant to establish goodwill generated by the use of the name or likeness and damage and the likelihood of damage to the goodwill as a result of the defendant's misrepresentations. The courts tend to be slow to find that these exist in character merchandising cases.

---

49   *Wombles v Wombles Skips* [1977] RPC 99.
50   *Lego Systems v Lego M Lemelstrich* [1983] FSR 155.

The 1990s initially promised encouragement to claimants. An apparent shift in the court's attitude towards a recognition of the goodwill generated by merchandising activities occurred in a case concerning the unauthorised reproduction of pictures of the cartoon characters 'Teenage Mutant Ninja Turtles' on items of clothing.[51] The owners of the rights to the image of the Turtles alleged that the unauthorised clothing was a passing off. They produced evidence to show that they had carried out substantial merchandising activity in relation to the Turtles and that they had exploited the name and likeness of the Turtles on a wide variety of products.

The court found that an arguable case of passing off was made out in the light of evidence which was produced on the following matters:

- there was active licensing of the merchandising rights to the name and likeness of the Turtles. The judge accepted evidence that a substantial number of the buying public now expect and know that where a famous character is reproduced on goods, the reproduction is the result of a licence granted by the owner of copyright or other rights in the character;
- there was a connection in the public mind between the Turtles and the products bearing their likeness;
- a substantial number of people knew of and wished to acquire the product bearing the likeness of the Turtles.

The court appeared to recognise that character merchandising was a common and recognised activity and that the claimants had the necessary goodwill to support a passing off action. The judge noted that a major part of the claimant's business included the licensing of reproductions of the Turtles on goods sold by third parties. If others were to reproduce the characters without paying licence royalties, the value of the Turtle images would depreciate.

At the time of the judgment it was generally thought that whenever the factors set out above could be demonstrated in relation to unauthorised character merchandising, a case might succeed in passing off. But in more recent cases the courts have shown a tendency to limit the effect of the *Turtles* case. In *Re Elvis Presley Trade Marks*,[52] Laddie J said of the *Turtles* judgment: 'I do not read it as laying down a finding of fact of universal application that the products of the plaintiffs in similar circumstances are viewed by the public as "genuine" and that traders in competing goods are therefore making a misrepresentation.'

He noted that it was not the general public perception that goods bearing the image or name of a well known figure are 'genuine'. He said 'my own experience suggests that ... when people buy a toy of a well known character because it depicts that character, I have no reason to believe that they care

---

51   *Mirage Studios v Counter-Feat Clothing Co Ltd* [1991] FSR 145.
52   *Re Elvis Presley Trade Marks* [1997] RPC 543.

who made, sold or licensed it. When a fan buys a poster or a cup bearing an image of his star, he is buying a likeness, not a product from a particular source'. The finding in the *Ninja Turtles* case that the public associated the Turtle images with the claimants cannot, therefore, according to Laddie J, be taken as read in every case. Specific evidence will be needed to show the public's awareness that products bearing a person's likeness come from a particular source which is associated with the celebrity.

This was confirmed in a 1997 case involving unauthorised pop merchandise featuring the likeness of members of the pop group, the Spice Girls.[53] The court said that the group was unable to demonstrate even an arguable case in passing off against Panini SpA, which was supplying an unauthorised sticker collection featuring the group. Using much the same type of arguments which had been successful in the *Ninja Turtles* case, the group argued that the reproduction of their images on Panini's product amounted to a misrepresentation that the Spice Girls had authorised the sticker collection. This argument did not find favour with the court, which held that, in the absence of special circumstances, the public would not be misled into buying Panini's product on the assumption that it was authorised by the group. The judge also queried whether the source of the product would be of concern to the public who would be more interested in buying a product which featured the image of their heroes (or heroines) than in where the product originated.

The judgment in the *Ninja Turtles* case was recently re-assessed by the Court of Appeal in *Re Elvis Presley Trade Marks*.[54] Robert Walker LJ stressed that the *Turtles* judgment 'does not give a green light to extravagant claims based on any unauthorised use of a celebrity's name, but makes clear the relatively limited scope of the principle on which it proceeds'. He drew attention to the fact that the finding of an arguable case in passing off in the *Turtles* judgment was closely linked to the judge's additional finding of copyright infringement in the drawings of the Turtle characters. In the light of his assessment of the *Turtles* decision, the following guidance can be extracted:

(a) a claimant who owns copyright in drawings and which is in business licensing the use of the copyright in those drawings in the UK on a sufficiently large scale to generate a goodwill in the drawings might have an arguable case in passing off against someone who misrepresents that his drawings are the drawings of the claimant or are licensed by the claimant;

(b) evidence should be produced to establish the points demonstrated in the *Turtles* case if the claim is to succeed, namely:

---

53 *Halliwell and Others v Panini* (1997) unreported.
54 *Re Elvis Presley Trade Marks* [1999] RPC 567.

- there was active licensing of the merchandising rights to the name and likeness of the Turtles;

- there was a connection in the public mind between the Turtles and the products bearing their likeness;

- a substantial number of people knew of and wished to acquire the product bearing the likeness of the Turtles;

(c) the position in relation to living celebrities who wish to make a claim in passing off is less optimistic.

A claim in passing off in relation to a living celebrity is unlikely to be successful unless it can be shown on the special facts of any case that the public are likely to be confused by the use of the claimant's name or likeness into believing that there is a connection between the claimant and the goods. Specific evidence will be required to support such a claim. Reliance on the fact that the use of merchandising agreements is now commonplace is unlikely in itself to be sufficient.

The court has not defined what type of 'special facts' will give rise to a connection in the mind of the public between the celebrity and the defendant/defendant's products. Marking products as 'official' may lead the public to an inference of association with the owner of the name or likeness – but it does not necessarily mean that if the word 'official' does not appear, members of the public would draw the inference that the product is not 'genuine'. In *Re Elvis Presley Trade Marks*,[55] Morritt LJ indicated that the celebrity must ensure 'by whatever means may be open to him' that the public associate his name with the source of the goods. The court will be very slow to infer such evidence. Simon Brown LJ stressed that there should be no assumption that only a celebrity or his successors may ever market (or license the marketing of) his own character. Monopolies should not be so readily created without compelling evidence to justify the position.

Passing off – the Australian position

Australian passing off law is more favourable to celebrities who wish to restrain the unauthorised use of their image. In the field of character merchandising, the Australian courts do not regard goodwill (in the sense of a trading reputation) as a prerequisite to an action in passing off. The establishment of a general reputation or fame will be sufficient to give rise to a cause of action. It is sufficient that the claimant can show that the public would be confused into believing that a form of commercial arrangement exists between claimant and defendant under which the claimant has allowed

---

55 *Re Elvis Presley Trade Marks* [1999] RPC 567.

his name or image to be used. There is no additional requirement that damage to goodwill must also be demonstrated.

The difference in approach between English and Australian law is illustrated by the Australian case of *Henderson v Radio Corp Pty Ltd*.[56] The Hendersons were well known professional ballroom dancers. The defendant made and distributed records one of which was entitled 'Strictly for dancing' and consisted of music which was suitable for ballroom dancing. The front cover of the record featured a ballroom scene in which the Hendersons were prominently featured. The Hendersons commenced proceedings in passing off. In the course of his judgment Manning J observed:

> The plaintiffs in this case had acquired a reputation which doubtless placed them in a position to earn a fee for any recommendation which they might be disposed to give to aid the sale of recorded dance music of the type in question ... The result of the defendant's action was to give the defendant the benefit of the plaintiff's recommendation and the value of such recommendation and to deprive the plaintiffs of the fee or remuneration they would have earned if they had been asked for their authority to do what was done. The publication of the cover amounted to a misrepresentation of the type which will give rise to the tort of passing off, as there was implied in the acts of the defendant an assertion that the plaintiffs had 'sponsored' the record.

The judge said that he was satisfied that the unauthorised use by the defendant of the commercially valuable reputation of the claimants justified the intervention of the court.

The case of *Hogan v Koala Dundee Pty Ltd*[57] concerned a business selling 'Australian souvenirs', some of which were strongly reminiscent of the title character in the film *Crocodile Dundee*. The claimants, who respectively co-wrote and owned the merchandising rights in the film, brought proceedings for passing off in relation to the souvenirs. The Federal Court of Australia held that a person may bring a passing off action in respect of an image, including a name, which is not connected with any business carried on by that person.

Pincus J observed as follows:

> I think the law now is, at least in Australia, that the inventor of a sufficiently famous fictional character having certain visual or other traits may prevent others using his character to sell their goods and may assign the right so to use the character. Furthermore, the inventor may do these things even where he has never carried on any business at all, other than the writing or making of the work in which the character appears.

If English law were to develop along the same lines, it would clearly provide an effective redress to well known personalities – whether fictional or not – whose image is associated with goods and services. But as matters currently

---

56 *Henderson v Radio Corp Pty Ltd* [1969] RPC 218.

57 *Hogan v Koala Dundee Pty Ltd* (1989) 14 IPR 398.

stand, there seems little chance that the English judiciary will choose to follow the example set by the Australian courts.

(f) Registered trade mark registration

For a lawyer, the primary function of a registered trade mark is to indicate the origin of a product or service (the so called badge of origin function). Trade marks can be thought of as identification symbols. As part of this function, trade marks serve to distinguish the goods or services of one business from those of other businesses. There is no reason in principle why a name or likeness of a personality cannot operate to distinguish goods and services from one source from those of others – provided that the use of the name and image is carefully policed from the outset of its commercial use to ensure that the public associate the name and likeness with the source of the goods for which registration is sought and with no other source.

The main reasons why marks fail to be distinctive are: (a) if they are too descriptive of a type of product as opposed to distinctive of a product from a particular source; or (b) if they become too commonplace or 'generic'.

Applying for a registration

Any sign that is capable of graphic representation can be registered as a trade mark, *provided that* it is capable of distinguishing the goods or services of the applicant from those of other undertakings. The mark must, therefore, earmark the goods and services in question as being distinct from those of other producers of such goods.

The name and likeness of an individual can, in theory, be registered as a trade mark, provided it operates as a badge of origin. By way of example, Alan Shearer, Paul Gascoigne and Damon Hill have all registered their names as trade marks. Eric Cantona and Alan Shearer have also registered their likeness.

In order to register a name, likeness, etc, as a trade mark it is not sufficient to show that a name, likeness or signature is well known and that it is associated with a personality. What must also be shown is that the public associates the name, etc, as *a badge of origin* for the goods or services for which registration is sought. If the mark is seen by the public as no more than a depiction of the personality, it will *not* be sufficient to secure a trade mark registration. The mark must be distinctive in that it enables the public to distinguish the trade mark owner's goods or services from identical or similar goods marketed by other parties. The difficulty is that, as we have seen in relation to the law of passing off, the name and likeness of a personality are often not distinctive of any particular source of goods.

Example

Elvis Presley Enterprises, the official merchandising company for Elvis Presley memorabilia, applied to register three trade marks as follows: ELVIS, ELVIS PRESLEY and ELVIS A PRESLEY (the latter as a signature). The principal object of Elvis Presley Enterprises was the exploitation of the name and likeness of the late Elvis Presley. The application to register was unsuccessful, because the applicant was unable to provide evidence that the public saw the Elvis marks as anything other than a depiction of the Elvis character. Members of the public would purchase merchandise because it carried the name and likeness of Elvis, rather than because it came from a particular source. In particular, no evidence was adduced to show that the marks served to delineate the applicant's goods from goods that came from another source. The judge rejected the applicant's argument that the public are now familiar with merchandising rights and would infer that an article bearing the name or likeness of Elvis Presley was authorised. He observed that the public would be indifferent to the source of the item in question, caring only that the article bears the name or likeness of their hero. The name and likeness was not therefore sufficiently distinctive to merit registration as a trade mark.[58] The Court of Appeal confirmed this judgment.[59] The Elvis marks did not denote a connection between the applicant and the products for which the application was sought (toiletries) so as to show that the marks served to distinguish its products from others.

A similar issue arose on an application to register the name TARZAN as a trade mark in respect of films and tape recordings.[60] It was held by the Court of Appeal that by the time the application to register the trade mark was made (1965), the word TARZAN had passed into the language and become a household word. It was no longer distinctive of any particular source. There was no longer anything in the word which suggested that goods bearing the TARZAN name necessarily had anything to do with the applicant for the trade mark. Those interested in exploiting the Tarzan character had waited until it was too well known by the public as a generic term before they sought the benefits of registered trade mark rights.

It is therefore important to apply to register a mark as soon as possible in order to avoid the loss of distinctiveness which will occur if the mark is used generally. It is distinctiveness at the date of application for registration which is relevant. The Trade Marks Registry has also rejected an application by the Princess of Wales Memorial Fund to register images of the face of Diana, Princess of Wales as trade marks. The fund sought trade mark registrations in order to try to control the memorabilia industry which has developed since

---

58   *Re Elvis Presley Trade Marks* [1997] RPC 543.

59   *Re Elvis Presley Trade Marks* [1999] RPC 567.

60   *TARZAN*^{TM} [1970] RPC 450.

Diana's death. The Trade Mark Registry's Workbook (which provides guidance on the registrability of trade mark applications) indicates that pictures of famous people on articles of memorabilia commemorating their life and work are *unlikely* to be understood as indications of the origin of the articles. This will be particularly so if the likeness has been widely used by a variety of manufacturers of memorabilia before the date of the trade mark application. The image would not, in such circumstances, serve to distinguish the source of such articles.

It remains to be seen how safe the existing registrations of names and likenesses will prove to be following the Elvis Presley and Diana, Princess of Wales decisions. The registrations could be challenged on the ground that they lack the necessary distinctiveness to remain on the register.

Signatures

Signatures may be registrable as trade marks provided that they are sufficiently distinctive. If a distinctive signature is registered, it will usually be accompanied by a disclaimer stating that nothing in the registration will give exclusive rights in the actual words making up the name except if they are in substantially the script shown.

The rights that a trade mark owner has

The owner of a trade mark has exclusive rights in the trade mark, which are infringed by the use of the trade mark without his consent.

What amounts to use for the purposes of infringement?

The Trade Marks Act 1994 Act refers to use as being, in particular:
- affixing the sign to goods or packaging;
- offering goods for sale or offering or supplying services under the sign;
- importing or exporting goods under the sign;
- using the sign in business papers or advertising.

Those involved in the *preparation of* infringing material will be treated as infringers if they know or have reason to believe that the use of the mark is not authorised by the mark's owner. Use has to be in the course of trade to constitute an infringement.

What amounts to infringement?

The following unauthorised acts amount to infringement:

- use of a sign which is *identical* to the trade mark in relation to goods and services which are *identical* with those for which it is registered (s 10(1) of the Act);
- use of a sign which is *identical* to the trade mark in relation to goods and services which are *similar* to those for which it is registered so that there is a likelihood of confusion or association on the part of the public (s 10(2) of the Act);
- use of a sign which is *similar* to the trade mark in relation to goods and services which are *identical* to those for which it is registered so that there is a likelihood of confusion or association on the part of the public (s 10(2) of the Act);
- use of a sign which is *identical or similar to* the trade mark in relation to goods or services which are *not similar* to the goods and services for which it is registered where the mark has a reputation in the UK and the use of the sign being without due cause takes unfair advantage of or is detrimental to the distinctive character or the repute of the trade mark (s 10(3) of the Act).

Section 11(2) of the Act provides that a registered trade mark is not infringed by:

... the use by a person of his own name or address provided the use is in accordance with honest practice in industrial or commercial matters.

So, even if a name is registered as a trade mark, anyone else sharing that name would not infringe the registered mark if they used their name in the course of trade, provided that they did so in an honest manner.

(g) The Trade Descriptions Act 1968

It is a *criminal* offence under the Trade Descriptions Act 1968 to give a false indication, direct or indirect, that goods and services are of a kind supplied to any person, for example, a well known personality (s 13).

It is also an offence to make false representations as to royal approval or award in relation to goods or services (s 12).

(h) The advertising codes of practice

The various industry codes of practice offer the most effective avenue of complaint for celebrities to restrain the unauthorised use of their name or likeness in advertising or sales promotions. However, the codes are not a substitute for legal action. For example, none of the codes gives celebrities the right to compensation for unauthorised use and there are only very limited grounds for appeal if a celebrity is unhappy with the decision of the regulatory authority.[61]

The Committee of Advertising Practice Codes

Protection of privacy – the portrayal of or referral to individuals

The CAP Codes govern the use of individuals in advertisements and sales promotions to which the codes apply. The reader is referred to Chapter 16 for details of advertising/promotions to which the Codes apply.

Advertisers are *urged* to obtain permission in advance if they wish to portray or refer to individuals in advertisements. The requirement applies to any individual whether or not he/she is a public figure.

'Urged' is not defined in the code. In essence, it means that there must be a good reason for a failure to obtain permission. A permissible exception to the general rule has been held to be where a photograph depicted a crowd scene and the participants were not so well known that the advertiser could be expected to try to contact them before publication.[62]

Prior permission may not be needed under the codes when the advertisement does not contain anything that is inconsistent with the position or views of the person featured.

It is also unnecessary to obtain permission where the product being advertised is a book or a film and the individual who is referred to in the advertisement is the subject of the book or film.

Care should be taken when portraying, or referring to, people who are dead, to avoid causing offence or distress.

Where the individual who is portrayed or referred to without prior permission has a high public profile and specifically where he or she is an entertainer, a politician or a sports person, a further restriction applies. Advertisers should ensure that such persons are not portrayed in an offensive or adverse way.

Example of an adverse and offensive portrayal

An example of an adverse and offensive portrayal occurred when, as part of the 1997 election campaign, the Conservative Party used a national press advertisement that featured a photograph of the leader of the Labour party, Tony Blair. In place of Mr Blair's eyes, the poster featured demonic looking eyes. The advertisement featured the caption 'NEW LABOUR, NEW DANGER'.

---

61 Judicial review of the decision might be available in some circumstances (see Chapters 2 and 16 of this book for more detail), but this is not necessarily a right of appeal. The courts will not substitute its decision for that of the decision maker.

62 *Halifax Building Society ASA Monthly Report*, No 77, October 1997.

Complaints were received, alleging that the advertisement portrayed Tony Blair, who had not given his permission for the use of his photograph, in an offensive way. The ASA upheld the complaints. It considered that the advertisement depicted Tony Blair as a sinister and dishonest figure and that this amounted to an adverse or offensive portrayal of Mr Blair.

Endorsements

The code states that advertisers must not imply an endorsement of a product or service by people with a high public profile where none exists.

What constitutes an endorsement?

The mere appearance of a public figure in relation to a product will not necessarily be an endorsement. Each advertisement must be considered on its own merits.

An instance where endorsement was found related to an advertisement by Key 103 and Magic 1152 radio stations. Jamie Redknapp complained to the Advertising Standards Authority about a poster for a radio station headlined 'Who should get their kit off?' It showed the heads of David Beckham and Jamie Redknapp superimposed on very muscular bodies. The poster gave a telephone number for people to ring to place their vote. Jamie Redknapp objected to the poster, claiming that it implied that he endorsed the radio station, an implication that he believed would diminish his reputation and affect his future income from genuine endorsements. The complaint was upheld. The advertisers claimed that the poster was intended to be seen as good humoured and light hearted. They pointed out that it was one of a campaign that featured a host of celebrities who were used as the subject of phone polls. They said that Jamie Redknapp was chosen because he was a famous Liverpool footballer. The ASA considered that the poster could be seen to imply that Jamie Redknapp endorsed the radio station. The ASA concluded that the poster could diminish the reputation of Jamie Redknapp or affect his future income from genuine endorsements. The ASA asked the advertisers not to repeat the advertisement.[63] As we have seen, if Jamie Redknapp had brought proceedings in passing off over the use of his likeness, he would probably not have been successful. The CAP codes were therefore his only effective means of redress.

References to the royal family

References to members of the royal family or to the royal arms and emblems are not permitted under the code without consent from the Lord

---

63 *ASA Adjudication*, June 1999.

Chamberlain's office. The use of royal warrants should be cleared with the Royal Warrant Holders' Association.

The Independent Television Commission Code

The ITC Code provides that individual living persons must neither be portrayed nor *referred to* in advertisements without their permission having first been obtained except where the ITC approves the advertisement. Portrayal extends to impersonations (including impersonations of well known voices), parodies and caricatures.

Permission is required even where an individual is referred to indirectly, provided the reference enables the viewer to identify him/her clearly.

There is an exception to the rule for prior permission in relation to advertisements for books, films, particular editions of TV or radio programmes, newspapers, magazines, etc, which feature the person referred to in the advertisement, provided that the reference or portrayal is neither offensive nor defamatory.

In the case of generic advertising for news media, ITC licensees may waive the requirement for prior permission if it seems reasonable to expect that the individual concerned would not have reason to object. However, such generic advertising should be immediately withdrawn if individuals who are portrayed without their permission do object.

The Radio Authority Code

The Radio Authority Code states that individual living persons must not normally be portrayed or referred to in advertisements without their prior permission.

Similar exceptions to those contained in the ITC Code exist in relation to advertisements for books, films, radio and television programmes, newspapers, magazines, etc, and generic news media advertising.

The code advises that advance permission be obtained where impersonations or soundalikes of well known characters are to be used.

References to, and portrayals of, people who are active in politics should be carefully worded to avoid falling foul of the rules which require that political matters should be treated impartially and that advertisements must not be directed towards any political end.

CHAPTER 15

COMPETITIONS

The media sometimes try to increase viewing/circulation figures by running competitions. But competitions involve serious legal risks. Care must be taken to ensure that a competition does not take the form of a lottery. This is because, subject to very limited exceptions (for example, the National Lottery), lotteries are *illegal* under the Lotteries and Amusements Act 1976 ('the Act'). The Act makes it a *criminal offence* to conduct an illegal lottery.

WHAT IS A LOTTERY?

The Act uses the word 'lottery' in a broader sense than most people would expect. A lottery has been defined as the distribution of prizes by chance where the participants, or a substantial number of them, make a payment or other consideration in return for obtaining the chance to win a prize.[1] It is the substance of the competition that is important, and not the label that is applied to it.

The definition of a lottery breaks down into three elements as follows:

(a) the distribution of *prizes*;

(b) which must be *by chance*;

(c) in circumstances where a *contribution* is made by participants in return for the chance of winning a prize.

If one of these elements was removed, a competition would *not* be a lottery and consequentially would not be illegal under the Act. Whenever a competition is devised, care should therefore be taken to ensure that it does not satisfy all three of the above criteria.

Example of an illegal lottery

Packets of tea were produced containing a coupon which informed purchasers that he/she had won a named prize. It was only after opening the packet that the purchaser knew what the prize was.

This promotion was illegal for the following reasons:

(a) it involved a distribution of prizes;

(b) which depended on chance; and

---

1   *Reader's Digest Association Ltd v Williams* [1976] 3 All ER 737.

(c) by purchasing the tea, the consumer was making a payment for the chance of winning a particular prize.[2]

How to ensure that a promotion is not an illegal lottery

The creation of an illegal lottery will be avoided if *any one* of the three elements set out above is removed.

Ensuring that prizes are not distributed by chance

To ensure that prizes are not distributed by chance, the promotion must involve participants in the exercise of skill or judgment. The degree and type of skill or judgment which is required must meet certain requirements.

Type of skill

The Act contains restrictions on certain types of skill as follows:

- where prizes are offered for the forecast of a future event, the competition will be unlawful;
- where prizes are offered for the forecast of a past event where the result is not yet ascertained or is not widely known, the competition will be unlawful.

What is 'skill'?

The Act does not define what is meant by skill. Each competition must be judged on its own merits.

Competitions which involve *questions* will generally involve the necessary skill and judgment. However if a *very* obvious question is asked (for example, 'what is the name of the day that follows Monday?'), the competition will risk falling foul of the legal requirements on the ground that the degree of skill required to answer the question is insufficient.

Competitions which involve puzzles, multiple choice type questions or the exercise of judgment (for example, 'arrange the following criteria in the order of importance ...') will generally involve sufficient skill, as will competitions which involve originality (for example, 'devise a slogan in x words' type promotions).

---

2   *Taylor v Smeton* (1883) 11 QBD 207.

Two stage promotions

Competitions sometimes have two stages. It is important that neither stage is determined by chance. Success must depend on the exercise of skill at each stage of the promotion. If any part of a promotion involves a lottery, the whole promotion will become unlawful.

Example of an illegal two stage promotion

Tins of cat food were sold bearing labels on the inside of which were a bingo card and a line of numbers. If the numbers matched the numbers on the bingo card, the consumer was entitled to a prize. In order to claim the prize, the contestant had to solve an accompanying puzzle, involving an element of skill.

It was held that the scheme was in two stages. The first was the chance of finding a label with numbers that matched the numbers on the card. This stage was determined entirely by chance. The second stage was the puzzle and involved skill. No skill was required by the first stage. The inclusion of an element of skill in stage two was not sufficient to prevent the scheme being an illegal lottery.[3]

The selection of prize winners

The selection of prize winners must not be dependent on chance. If a tiebreaker decides the winner, it will probably be legal. But if the prize winner is chosen at random, for example, where the winning answer is pulled out of a hat, it is likely to be illegal, because the selection is dependent on chance.

Removal of the requirement for contribution

In order to remove the requirement for contribution, a competition has to be free of *any charge whatsoever* to at least a substantial number of participants. It is not sufficient that the entry into the promotion does not involve an *extra* charge over and above what the contestant would usually pay, for example, the cover price of a newspaper or magazine.

In the case of *Imperial Tobacco v HM AG*,[4] packets of cigarettes were sold containing scratch cards which featured cash prizes The packets containing the cards were distinguishable from packets which did not have cards. The packs with cards retailed at the same price as the packs without the cards.

---

3   *DPP v Bradfute Associates Ltd* [1967] 2 QB 291.
4   *Imperial Tobacco v HM AG* [1981] AC 718.

It was held that the promotion was an illegal lottery. It involved a payment for the chance to win a prize; namely, the price of the cigarettes. It was immaterial that no part of the purchase price could be allocated to the chance to win a prize.

A good working test to adopt in determining whether a competition is free is whether entry into the competition is conditional on any type of cost to the participant. Is there a hidden entry fee, such as the cost of a premium rate telephone call? If so, warning bells should start to ring alerting all concerned to the possibility that the promotion may be an illegal lottery.

Alternative methods of entry

The creation of an illegal lottery can be avoided by offering participants an alternative way of taking part which does not involve any cost.

In the case of *Express Newspapers v Liverpool Daily Post*,[5] a newspaper bingo game was held not to be dependent on payment. Copies of the newspaper, and therefore of the bingo numbers, were available free of charge from a number of sources, such as public libraries or from contestants' friends. The numbers could also be obtained by telephoning the newspaper.

The Crown Prosecution Service has issued a policy statement concerning alternative methods of entry. The statement indicates that:

- it is not in itself sufficient to make a scheme lawful that some participants do not have to purchase a chance in the draw;
- however, the competition may be lawful where there is a *genuine, realistic and unlimited* alternative method of entry which is free of charge.

How to ensure that the alternative entry method is genuine, realistic and unlimited

Information about the existence of the alternative method of entry should be available to potential participants *before* they make a decision to purchase. Ideally, the information should appear on all promotional or advertising material relating to the competition, in the rules of the competition itself and on all packs of any products to which the promotion relates. The statement should be sufficiently prominent to come to the attention of purchasers without them having to scrutinise small print.

Where prizes are awarded by means of something that is found within the product packaging, for example, in coupons enclosed in goods or within the pages of a magazine, the alternative entry procedure should give contestants the opportunity to send away for the means of entry free of charge, without the need to make a purchase.

---

5   *Express Newspapers v Liverpool Daily Post* [1985] 1 WLR 1089.

Only one of the elements which make up a lottery has to be removed in order to avoid the creation of an illegal lottery. A competition which depends on chance, such as a prize draw or a scratch card promotion, will not be illegal if entry to the competition is free. On the other hand, an entry charge can be levied for competitions involving skill. The introduction of the requirement for skill will avoid the creation of an illegal lottery.

The criminal offences relating to lotteries

If the *promoter of an illegal lottery* or *any party which is directly involved in running an illegal lottery* does any of the activities set out below, it will have committed a criminal offence. The offences are punishable by imprisonment and/or fines. The activities giving rise to criminal liability are as follows:

- printing tickets for use in the lottery. *Tickets* include any documents which are evidence of participation in a lottery and will include entry forms or scratch cards, for example;

- selling or distributing or offering or advertising for sale or distributing any tickets or chances in the lottery;

- possessing tickets or chances in the lottery for the purpose of publication or distribution;

- bringing or inviting any person to send into Great Britain any ticket in or advertisement of the lottery for the purpose of sale or distribution;

- sending out of Great Britain, or attempting to do so, the proceeds of sale of any ticket or chance in the lottery or any document recording such sale or distribution or the identities of the holders of the tickets/chances;

- printing, publishing or distributing or possessing for the purpose of doing so:
  - ○ an advertisement for the lottery;
  - ○ a list of prize winners or of winning tickets in the lottery;
  - ○ any document descriptive of the drawing of the lottery which is calculated to induce people to enter;

- using any premises or causing or knowingly permitting any premises to be used for purposes connected with the promotion or conduct of the lottery;

- causing, procuring or attempting to procure any person to do any of the above acts.

Liability does not depend on the intention of the promoter. Lotteries can be created inadvertently.

Who can be liable?

The company whose goods are the subject of the promotion will usually be liable as the *publisher* of the promotion. A *third party handling house* may also be liable if it is engaged in activities which are caught by the above provisions.

In theory, *printers* and *retailers* will also be guilty of a criminal offence if they engage in the above activities. In practice, the authorities will be more likely to direct their attention to the publisher of the promotion.

PART 2

CHAPTER 16

EXTRA-JUDICIAL REGULATION OF MEDIA CONTENT

In addition to the legal causes of action considered in the previous chapters, the content of media publications is regulated by a number of industry Codes of Practice, some of which are part of an industry self-regulatory system and others are provided for by statute. In this chapter, we look at the work of the following regulatory bodies in relation to publication content:

(a) the Press Complaints Commission (PCC);

(b) the Independent Television Commission (ITC);

(c) the Radio Authority;

(d) the BBC Producers' Guidelines;

(e) the Broadcasting Standards Commission (BSC);

(f) the Advertising Standards Authority (ASA).

It is important to appreciate that the legal issues, which were considered in the first part of this book, run parallel with the Codes. Compliance with the Codes will not automatically provide a defence to a legal action. On the other hand, non-compliance will not necessarily mean that the broadcaster or the publication have acted unlawfully.[1]

THE PRESS COMPLAINTS COMMISSION AND THE EDITORS' CODE OF PRACTICE

The PCC enforces a Code of Practice which was drawn up by representatives of the press. The PCC itself refers to the Code as 'the editors' Code of Practice'. It is, therefore, not strictly correct to refer to the PCC Code of Practice. The fact that the Code was drawn up by the very parties whose activities the Code seeks to regulate has given rise to the perception that the Code is a self-serving piece of regulation. In his 1993 review of press self-regulation,[2] Sir David Calcutt observed that the Code in its original form did not hold the balance fairly between press and public. In Chapter 8, a number of Sir David's concerns about the apparent weighting of the Code's provisions towards the press were examined in the context of the provisions on privacy. Since that

---

1   Although compliance with the privacy provisions of the codes is relevant under the Human Rights Act 1998, s 12 and the Data Protection Act 1998. These statutes are considered below and in Chapters 1 and 9 respectively.

2   Sir David Calcutt QC, *Review of Press Self-Regulation*, Cmnd 2135, 1993.

review, there have been a number of revisions to the Code. Revisions to the Code are made by the Code of Practice Committee, which consists of representatives from the newspaper and magazine publishing industry. But in order to displace the perception of self-interest, any changes to the Code must be ratified by the PCC.

The Code applies to all newspapers and magazines across the country, whether regional, local or national.

The Press Complaints Commission

The PCC was established on the recommendation of the Calcutt Committee in its 1990 Report on privacy and related matters.[3] It is a non-statutory body. The PCC, and the Code which it enforces, are examples of *voluntary self-regulation*. The term 'voluntary' is used in the sense that there are no direct legal sanctions which may be imposed for a breach of the provisions of the Code. The PCC's literature explains that 'the main role of the Press Complaints Commission is to serve members of the public who have complaints about newspapers or magazines'.[4]

The Commission currently has 16 members, a minority of whom are connected to the press.

The PCC's remit

The PCC adjudicates upon complaints alleging that the Code of Practice has been breached. The PCC does not 'clear' material for publication in advance of publication.

Complaints

The PCC is a reactive body rather than a proactive one. It can only act on complaints. It cannot consider alleged breaches of the Code of its own initiative. This means that the way in which the Commission and the Code of Practice are perceived becomes very important. If the self-regulatory system is perceived to be weak, then the victims of conduct which breaches the Code will be deterred or discouraged from complaining. This then gives rise to something of a self-fulfilling prophecy in that, if no complaints are made, the PCC is unable to take action to restrain or criticise the offensive conduct. The credibility of the Code is further damaged, and so on. The current perception of the PCC Code tends to be that it has few teeth. This perception might be improved if the Commission had the authority to investigate and impose

---

3   *Report of the Committee on Privacy and Related Matters*, Cmnd 1102, 1990.
4   PCC document entitled 'Key benefits of the system of self-regulation'.

sanctions of its own initiative, thereby assuming the mantle of a proactive standard bearer for the industry. No such developments appear to be imminent at the time of writing.

Complaints may be made by individuals or organisations which are *directly affected* by the matters about which they are complaining. The PCC guidelines indicate that occasionally, complaints may be considered by people who are not directly affected by the alleged breach, but only where the complaint raises a significant issue which has not already been resolved.

When making a complaint on behalf of a person who has been directly affected (for example, as a solicitor acting on behalf of a client), the complaint should include a signed statement from the person or organisation affected stating that they wish the third party to make the complaint on their behalf. Where it is not possible to obtain a statement, the reason should be explained to the PCC. The relationship between the person/organisation affected and the party acting on its behalf should also be explained.

The PCC generally only accepts complaints which are made within one month of publication or the cessation of correspondence between the complainant and the editor of the publication in question. It may extend this deadline in exceptional circumstances.

The PCC does *not* adjudicate on the following types of complaint:

(a) legal or contractual matters or matters which are the subject of legal proceedings. Therefore, if legal action has been commenced in respect of a publication, the PCC will not entertain a complaint involving the same subject matter and issues. A complainant may take legal action or complain to the PCC, but it cannot do both;

(b) matters of taste, decency and the choice of what has been published in a newspaper or magazine;

(c) advertisements, promotions and competitions appearing in newspapers or competitions (these are subject to the Committee of Advertising Practice Codes of Practice, which is enforced by the ASA (see below));

(d) other material which does not form part of the editorial content of the magazine or newspaper in question;

(e) broadcast material – this is regulated by the ITC or Radio Authority Codes of Practice and the Broadcasting Standards Commission Codes, considered below.

How to make a complaint to the PCC

Before complaint is made to the PCC, the complainant should contact the editor of the newspaper or magazine in question. The editor should be given between seven days to one month to deal with the complaint in a satisfactory manner.

If the editor's response is unsatisfactory, then a letter of complaint may be written to the PCC together with:

(a) a cutting of the article or a clear dated photocopy of the article;

(b) a summary of the complaint giving details of why the complainant believes that the item is in breach of the Codes of Practice, where possible indicating which provisions(s) of the Code are alleged to have been breached;

(c) copies of any relevant correspondence which the complainant believes may help the PCC to understand and assess the complaint.

A copy of the letter of complaint will usually be sent by the PCC to the editor of the relevant publication.

The PCC operates a helpline to assist complainants to formulate their complaint. It can be contacted on 020 7353 3732.

The complaint should be sent to:

PCC
1 Salisbury Square
London
EC4Y 8JB
<www.pcc.org.uk>

The complaints procedure

On receipt of the complaint, the PCC will decide if it falls within its powers and that it does not fall within the excluded matters set out above. If the complaint falls outside the remit of the PCC, the complainant will be notified promptly.

If the complaint falls within the authority of the PCC, the PCC will examine the complaint to check that it raises a possible breach of the Code. If the PCC are of the view that the complaint raises a possible breach of the Code, it will send the editor of the publication a copy of the complaint and will try to mediate an amicable resolution of the complaint. The emphasis at this stage is on conflict resolution. Lord Wakeham, the chairman of the PCC, has described the primary role of the PCC as conciliation.[5] This might be by means of the publication of an apology or a letter from the editor to the complainant. In 1998, nine in 10 complaints to the PCC were resolved amicably, without the need for adjudication. Eighty-six complaints proceeded to adjudication, 45 of which were upheld by the PCC.[6]

---

5   Wynne Baxter Godfree Lecture, 15 May 1998.
6   1998 Annual PCC Report.

If it is not possible to resolve the mater amicably, the PCC will investigate the complaint further. It may ask for further information from the complainant.

The PCC will then make its decision. Oral hearings are not generally held. Copies of the adjudication will be sent to the complainant and to the offending publication. A copy of the adjudication is also published in the regular PCC adjudication reports. This exposes an offending publication to bad publicity.

Sanctions for breach

The PCC has no power to award monetary compensation to a complainant. Nor does it have power to prevent the publication of offending material. The only direct sanction is the requirement of publication of the adjudication. Where a publication breaches the provisions of the Code, it is obliged to publish the adjudication in full with due prominence.

Adjudications are published on the PCC website and in the PCC quarterly bulletins. Publications which have adverse adjudications against them may accordingly suffer adverse publicity.

Some publications impose a term in journalists' contracts of employment that employees will comply with the Code of Practice. Most editors are subject to such contractual provisions. Any employee who breaches the Codes of Practice will then also be in breach of his or her contract of employment – something which might be punishable by dismissal.[7] However, there is no requirement that the employee must be dismissed.

A lack of credibility?

As mentioned above, there is a general perception that the PCC lacks credibility as an adjudicatory body. It is widely viewed as a self-serving industry body whose decisions carry little weight and whose sanctions lack meaningful bite.[8]

The fact that most complaints are resolved amicably means that most of the PCC's work is carried out in private. Only those cases which are dealt with by adjudication are referred to in detail in the PCC reports. This fosters the impression that much of the work of the Commission takes place behind closed doors on an *ad hoc* basis. The opportunity for a detailed corpus of guidance to emerge from PCC decisions is much reduced.

---

7   Subject to any claim which the employee might have for wrongful or unfair dismissal.

8   See, eg, Sir David Calcutt QC, *Review of Press Self-Regulation*, Cmnd 2135; 'Straw chains for paper tigers' (1999) *The Observer*, 30 May; 'Power and the people' (1999) *The Guardian*, 5 April; and 'Bring me your woes' (1999) *The Guardian*, 7 June.

Periodically, there are calls for the PCC to be replaced by a statutory body whose functions and powers would be codified by legislation, akin to the ITC or the Radio Authority. The statutory body would be accountable to Parliament. So far, the press have successfully beaten off such innovations. Whether this position will continue is largely in the hands of the press themselves. If their worst excesses are curbed and they are seen to be acting responsibly, self-regulation may still be a viable prospect. If not, the prospect of a statutory regulator accountable to Parliament may prove to be more than just a speculative suggestion. The Government's position at the time of writing is that effective self-regulation presents the best way of ensuring high editorial standards. It has no plans to introduce specific legislation to regulate the press. It is, however, keeping the situation under review.

The Independent Television Commission

The ITC is a statutory body established under the Broadcasting Act 1990. Broadly, it has the following functions:

(a) issuing licences which allow commercial television companies (that is, not the BBC) to broadcast in and from the UK;

(b) regulation of the services broadcast by its licensees, including setting standards for programme content.

Regulation by the ITC

The ITC has drawn up and enforces a programme code. The code applies to all terrestrial, cable and satellite services licensed by the ITC under the Broadcasting Acts 1990 and 1996. All licensees are required to ensure that any programmes they transmit comply with the code and to satisfy the ITC that they have adequate procedures to fulfil this requirement – including procedures for ensuring that programme makers can seek guidance on the code within the organisation at a senior level.

The ITC monitors compliance with the code and investigates complaints. Unlike the PCC, the ITC's powers are not limited to adjudicating upon complaints received. The ITC may take action on its own initiative. The code contains guidelines covering:

- taste and decency, including strong language and sexual portrayal;
- violence;
- privacy;
- impartiality;
- charitable appeals;
- religious programmes;
- undue prominence for commercial products.

The ITC does not preview or 'clear' programmes in advance of broadcast.

Sanctions

In the event of non-compliance with the programme code, the ITC has a range of sanctions at its disposal against its licensees ranging from formal warnings, an order for the publication of on-screen corrections, or the imposition of a fine. In extreme cases, the ITC may shorten a broadcasting licence or revoke it. Adjudications are published in the ITC complaints and interventions reports, which are usually brought out monthly, and on the ITC website. The reports are circulated widely, meaning that a broadcaster who has a complaint upheld against it is likely to receive bad publicity.

Complaining to the ITC

Complaints under the ITC Codes are made to the ITC using an ITC official complaint form. Before making a complaint, consideration should be given to complaining directly to the broadcaster concerned. Television companies are under an obligation to reply to complaints about their programmes.

The ITC can be contacted at:
33 Foley Street
London
W1P 7LW
Tel: 0207 255 3000
<www.itc.org.uk>

Complaints received by the ITC are generally dealt with within four to six weeks of receipt.

Complaints should be made promptly, especially in light of the facts that television companies are only obliged to keep copies of their programmes for a limited time – three months in the case of major networks and two months for other services.

The Radio Authority

The Radio Authority is the sister organisation to the ITC. It is the body which licenses and regulates the independent (that is, non-BBC) radio industry in the UK. Its authority is derived from the Broadcasting Act 1990. One of its roles is to regulate programmes and advertising on independent radio. In this regard, it has published codes on programme content and advertising. The Radio Authority adjudicates upon complaints received under the codes and enforces standards of its own initiative. It may award the same range of sanctions which we saw in relation to the ITC for non-compliance.

The Radio Authority may be contacted at:
Holbrook House
14 Great Queen Street
London
WC2B 5DG

The BBC

The BBC is not regulated by the ITC or the Radio Authority in relation to those domestic services which are funded by the television licence fee. Instead, the BBC is self-regulated by means of producers' guidelines, which are publicly available documents. They set out the BBC's editorial standards. In summary, they provide that programmes will be accurate, fair and impartial, they will avoid reinforcing prejudice and will be sensitive to the tastes and beliefs of audiences.

Complaints about breaches of the producers' guidelines may be made to the BBC's Programme Complaints Unit. The complaint must be in writing and must:

(a) suggest a specific and serious breach of the programme standard set out in the guidelines; and

(b) relate to the BBC's domestic licence-funded public broadcasting and online services.

An appeal from an adverse decision lies to the Governors' Programme Complaints Commission. The results of the complaints are published in the quarterly programme complaints bulletins which are produced by the BBC.

Complaints about standards, unfair treatments and violation of privacy may be made to the Broadcasting Standards Commission, which is independent of the BBC. Complaints about the BBC's commercial (that is, non-licence funded) activities may be made to the ITC or the Radio Authority as appropriate.

THE BROADCASTING STANDARDS COMMISSION

The BSC is a statutory authority established under Pt 5 of the 1996 Broadcasting Act. It is accountable to Parliament. It has the remit of drawing up codes giving guidance about the principles to be observed in connection with the avoidance of:

(a) unjust or unfair treatment in broadcast programmes; and

(b) unwarranted infringement of privacy in or in connection with the obtaining of material in broadcast programmes.[9]

The provisions which relate to unwarranted infringement of privacy also extend to activities carried out in connection with obtaining material included in programmes – not just to the material actually transmitted.

9　Broadcasting Act 1996, s 107.

The BSC have produced Codes of Guidance on the following topics:

(a) Code on Fairness and Privacy;

(b) Code on Standards. This Code contains provisions on scheduling, taste and decency, portrayal of violence and portrayal of sexual conduct.

The Codes apply to all UK broadcasters, including the BBC. They apply to television and to radio, including text, cable and digital services and to broadcast advertisements. The provisions of the Codes must be reflected by the broadcasters and by their regulators in their own Codes (for example, the ITC or Radio Authority Codes) or producer guidelines (in the case of the BBC).

The BSC is also required under the terms of the 1996 Broadcasting Act to consider and adjudicate on complaints on standards and fairness. It may not intervene of its own initiative. Complaints are decided by the BSC Commissioners, who are independent people appointed by the Secretary of State for Culture, Media and Sport.

The BSC may be contacted at:
7 The Sanctuary
London
SW1P 3JS
Tel: 020 7233 0544
<www.bsc.org.uk>

The BSC Code on Standards

The Code on Standards contains provisions on scheduling, taste and decency and the portrayal of sex and violence.

The BSC Code on fairness and privacy

The fairness provisions of the Code begin as follows:

> Broadcasters have a responsibility to avoid unfairness to individuals or organisations featured in programmes, in particular through the use of inaccurate information or distortion, for example, by the unfair selection or juxtaposition of material taken out of context, whether specially recorded for a programme, or taken from library or other sources. Broadcasters should avoid creating doubts on the audience's part as to what they are being shown if it could mislead the audience in a way which would be unfair to those featured in the programme.

The Code goes on to contain more detailed provisions about dealing fairly with contributors, accuracy of programme content and the obtaining of material for factual programmes through deception or misrepresentation.

It provides that, where a broadcaster recognises that a programme has been unfair, the inaccuracy should be corrected promptly with due prominence if the person affected so wishes unless there are compelling legal reasons for not doing so. An apology should also be broadcast whenever appropriate.

The provisions relating to privacy were considered in Chapter 8.

Complaints about broadcasting standards

Any viewer or listener can complain about a broadcast programme or advertisement. Typical complaints may concern the portrayal of sex or violence or the use of bad language. Complaints must be in writing and must be made within two months of a television broadcast and within three weeks of a radio broadcast.

Complaints about fairness and privacy

The category of persons who may complain about unfair treatment and violation of privacy is narrower than it is in relation to standards. Only those people with a direct interest in a broadcast can complain of unfair treatment or unwarranted infringement of privacy. The complaint may be made by an individual, an association or a corporate body. Complaints may be made on behalf of someone with a direct interest, but it must be made clear that the agent has been authorised to make the complaint. If the affected person has died within five years preceding the broadcast a personal representative, family member or someone closely connected to the deceased may bring a complaint, although the BSC reserves the right to decide that the connection between the deceased and the complainant is not sufficiently strong.

Complaints under the unfairness and privacy Code must be made with a reasonable time which, according to BSC guidance, is normally within three months of broadcast or six weeks in the case of radio programmes. If a complaint is made after this period, the application should explain the reason for the delay. The BSC will then consider whether, in the particular circumstances, the application was made within a reasonable period.

Whatever BSC Code the complaint is brought under, the procedure is as follows:

(a) there is a complaints form which must be used for the complaint. It may be contained from BSC;

(b) on receipt of the form, the BSC will decide whether the complaint is one it can consider. It will not consider a complaint in the following circumstances:

- the complainant is not eligible to complain (see above);
- the complaint is not made within the above time limits;

- the complainant has started legal proceedings in respect of the subject of the complaint. In these circumstances the BSC will not hear the complaint. Where legal proceedings have not been commenced, but the complaint relates to an issue on which the complainant could take legal action if it chose to do so (for example, defamation), then the BSC may not be able to consider the complaint. Where a complaint is made and litigation is then started, the BSC will discontinue consideration of the complaint.

If the BSC cannot entertain the complaint, the complainant is notified by letter of this fact.

If the complaint is one which the BSC is able to pursue, the procedure is as follows:

(a) the complaint is copied to the broadcaster for a written response;

(b) the broadcaster's response is sent to the complainant and the complainant is given an opportunity to respond in writing;

(c) the broadcaster is sent a copy of that response and is given a final opportunity to respond in writing if it wishes to.

The complaint will then be considered at a hearing, or at its discretion it may decide that a hearing is not appropriate. If a hearing is held, it will be in private at the BSC's offices. Reasonable travelling expenses may be claimed for the costs of attending the hearing.

The adjudication

The adjudication and a summary of it are sent by the BSC to the complainant and to the broadcaster. Where the complaint is upheld against a commercial broadcaster, a copy is also sent to the ITC. If the complaint is upheld or partially upheld, the BSC may direct the broadcaster to publish on television or radio and in the press a summary of the complaint and the BSC's findings or a summary of them.

There are no other sanctions open to the BSC. It has no power to award monetary compensation or to order an apology.

Advertising

The British Codes of Advertising and Sales Promotion

The British Codes of Advertising and Sales Promotion (the Codes) are drawn up and administered by the Committee of Advertising Practice (CAP). The Advertising Standards Authority (ASA) considers complaints which are made under the Codes.

The CAP is made up of representatives from the advertising, direct marketing, sales promotion and media industries. The Codes are therefore drawn up by members of the industries to which they apply.

Copy advice service

The CAP offers a free copy advice service to advertisers and agencies to help them comply with the Codes. The fact that advice has been taken from the CAP will not prevent complaints being upheld by the ASA.

The ASA

The ASA is independent of the CAP. It is charged with ensuring that the Codes work in the public interest. It is most associated with its role in considering, and adjudicating on, complaints made under the Codes. The ASA is the final arbiter on the interpretation of the Codes.

Complaints under the Codes

The ASA Council considers complaints made under the Codes. It can also consider advertisements or promotions on its own initiative.

Complaints can be made by any entity. They are often made by trade competitors. It is often cheaper and quicker for a competitor to complain about an advertisement through the ASA, rather than to litigate through the courts. There is a requirement that industry complainants should, wherever possible, endeavour to resolve their differences between themselves or through any relevant trade or professional organisations before complaining to the ASA. Trading Standards Departments or other interested organisations often make complaints to the ASA. Many complaints are made by members of the public and the ASA promotes the complaints system to members of the public to encourage them to make use of it.

Sanctions for breach of the Codes

The following sanctions apply to advertisers who are in breach of the Codes:

(a) advertisers are requested by the ASA to withdraw any advertisement or promotion which breaches the Codes or to amend it to ensure that it does comply. Copy advice is available from the CAP to advise advertisers how to make adequate amendments;

(b) an adverse finding by the ASA will generate publicity. Adjudications are published monthly. The monthly reports give details of the advertisers or promoters and their agencies. The reports are widely available and are circulated as a matter of course to the media, the advertising industry, consumer bodies and government agencies. Adverse adjudications often receive extensive media coverage. Details of ASA adjudications are also published on the ASA's website;

(c) if advertisers refuse to amend or withdraw offending advertisements, then there are a number of measures which can be taken against them including:

- *the enforcement of contractual requirements for compliance with the Codes.* The ASA will ask CAP to inform its members about the advertiser's non-compliance with its decision. Most media organisations have a term in their standard conditions of business that advertisers or promoters must comply with the Codes. If advertisements have been found not to comply, advertisers may find that they are in breach of this provision and that their advertisements are denied advertising space. The Royal Mail may also withdraw mail sort contracts where advertisers or promoters are in breach;

- *removal of trade incentives.* For example, membership of trade or professional associations may be jeopardised;

- *legal proceedings.* The ASA can refer a *misleading* advertisement (but not a promotion) to the Office of Fair Trading (OFT) under the Control of Misleading Advertisements Regulations 1988.[10] It regularly does so in relation to persistent or deliberate offenders. The OFT can obtain an injunction under the regulations to prevent the advertiser using the offending advertisement in the future.

There is no provision for a direct financial penalty for non-compliance with the Codes, although the sanctions may cause an indirect financial loss.

The application of the Codes

The Codes apply to advertisements and promotions appearing in the following media in the UK:

- newspapers, periodicals and magazines including specialist and trade publications (subject to certain exceptions relating to the advertisement of medicines to the medical professions);

- inserts in printed publications;

- posters;

- cinema;

- video;

- the internet;

- mail shots;

- direct marketing;

---

10 The Control of Misleading Advertisements Regulations 1988 (SI 1988/915), as amended by the Control of Misleading Advertisements (amendment) Regulations 2000 (SI 2000/914).

- brochures, leaflets and circulars;
- aerial announcements;
- catalogues including individual entries in catalogues;
- viewdata services;
- all other types of printed publications including printed directories;
- literature sent out as a follow up to an advertisement.

The Codes *do not* apply to the following:

- commercials on television or the radio;
- the contents of premium rate telephone services;
- advertisements in foreign media;
- private classified advertisements – this does not include advertisements placed by commercial dating agencies, which *are* covered by the Codes;
- flyposting;
- press releases and public relations material;
- packaging, *unless* it advertises a sales promotion or is visible as an advertisement;
- point of sale displays, *unless* it is otherwise covered by the sales promotion Code or the cigarette Code (see below);
- oral communications, for example, telemarketing;
- private correspondence;
- official notices;
- health related claims in advertisements and promotions addressed only to the medical or allied professions;
- the editorial content of books and newspapers.

The Codes' basic principles

The Codes set out a number of basic principles as follows:

- advertisements/promotions must be legal, decent, honest and truthful;
- they must be prepared with a sense of responsibility to consumers and to society;
- they should respect the principles of fair competition generally accepted in business;
- they should not bring advertising or sales promotion into disrepute;
- they must conform to the Codes.

Primary responsibility for ensuring compliance with the Advertising Code rests with the advertiser. Responsibility for compliance with the Code cannot be abrogated by the engagement of outside professionals, for example, advertising agencies or even outside legal advisers.

Advertisers must be able to demonstrate to the ASA that they have complied with the Code. If the ASA requires evidence of compliance, it should be furnished without delay:

- conformity with the Codes is assessed by looking at the advertisement or promotion as a whole;
- conformity is assessed by looking at advertisements and promotions in the context in which they appear;
- the Codes are designed to be interpreted flexibly. It follows that the *spirit* of the Codes must be complied with, as well as the letter;
- the intention of the advertiser is irrelevant. Breaches can be committed accidentally.

The ASA may be contacted at:
2 Torrington Place
London
WC1E 7HW
<www.asa.org.uk>

THE INDEPENDENT TELEVISION COMMISSION CODES OF ADVERTISING STANDARDS AND PRACTICE AND PROGRAMME SPONSORSHIP

One of the duties imposed on the ITC by ss 8 and 9 of the Broadcasting Act 1990 is the drawing up and enforcement of Codes governing standards and practice in television advertising and programme sponsorship. The ITC has promulgated two Codes, respectively:

- the Code of Advertising Standards and Practice, which sets the standards for the content of television advertising; and
- the Code of Programme Sponsorship.

In addition, there is a Code of Practice on the Amount and Scheduling of Advertising, setting out the rules which the ITC requires its licensees to observe on the amount, distribution, separation and scheduling of advertising.

The above Codes apply to all the television companies that are licensed by the ITC.

Complaints about advertisements are considered by the ITC, which publishes regular television advertising complaints reports setting out details of all complaints of substance which have been considered. Unfavourable decisions are likely to attract adverse publicity for the advertiser.

The authority of the ITC

The ITC has authority over its licensees rather than over the advertisers themselves. All holders of ITC licences are required to ensure that the advertising which they broadcast complies with the Codes. Broadcasters are directly responsible for the advertisements which they transmit and the ITC can require broadcasters to withdraw advertising which does not comply with the Codes. Such a requirement will have immediate effect. The end result is harmful to the advertiser, who will find that its advertising is denied a broadcast outlet.

As we have seen in relation to programme content, television companies can be subject to heavy sanctions for non-compliance with ITC decisions, including large fines and ultimately, revocation of their licences.

The way that the advertising Codes work in practice

In practice, the advertisers liaise with broadcasters about the content of advertisements which it wishes to have broadcast. The broadcasters are required by the ITC to have procedures in place to ensure compliance with the Codes. The ITC provides advice to broadcasters about the Codes. Advertisers who require advice about the Codes in relation to specific advertisements should contact the broadcasters or their representatives rather than the ITC.

Most television companies require the advertising which they carry on a national basis to be cleared by the Broadcast Advertising Clearance Centre (BACC). This is an organisation set up and funded by the participating broadcasters. It provides pre-transmission clearance services for ITV, GMTV, Channel 4, Channel 5, BSkyB and UK Gold amongst others. Not all television companies use the BACC for advertising clearance. Some will clear advertisements themselves.

Pre-clearance by or behalf of television companies is, in practice, a mandatory requirement.

Clearance procedures

The clearance requirements and procedures of individual television companies will differ. The BACC's procedure is described below. Whatever the procedure, it is advisable to submit material for clearance at an early stage, ideally at pre-production script stage before filming begins. This will avoid unnecessary expense on filming if the basic concept of the advertisement is flawed. The BACC ask for submission of scripts for proposed advertisements prior to filming.

The BACC clearance practices

Agencies should ideally send pre-production scripts for advertisements to the BACC for its initial examination. Where amendments are required by the BACC to ensure compliance with the Codes, the BACC will discuss them with the agency so that a revised script can be agreed. Where appropriate, the BACC will offer guidance about the visual content of the advertisements at this preliminary stage. Where matters of taste are involved, advertisers may find that it is cost effective to submit a storyboard or other visual device to the BACC at an early stage.

The BACC will view video tapes of the filmed commercial to check that it is in line with the approved script (where there is an approved script) and the Codes.

Where an advertisement contains factual claims, advertisers *must* submit supporting evidence with the script or videotape of the advertisement. Technical or scientific claims will be sent to BACC appointed experts for evaluation.

Sometimes, the BACC will recommend scheduling restrictions for advertisements, for example, that they should not be broadcast in breaks in or around children's programming.

All material submitted to the BACC is submitted in the strictest confidence.

The BACC has produced guidance notes on the precise requirements for material submitted to it for clearance. They are available from the BACC.

Limitations of BACC clearance

The BACC advises under the Codes. Its staff are not legal advisers. Advertisers or television companies seeking advice on the law should seek legal advice. Clearance by the BACC will not mean that the advertisement is not an infringement of a third party's rights. Nor will clearance by the BACC guarantee that the advertisement complies with the Codes. That decision is for the ITC alone.

The above points also apply to television companies who elect to clear advertisements themselves without the BACC.

THE ITC CODE OF ADVERTISING STANDARDS AND PRACTICE

General principles

The Code sets out four general principles which should be read in conjunction with the Code's more detailed provisions. They are as follows:

- television advertising should be legal, decent, honest and truthful;
- advertisements must comply in every respect with the law, common or statute, and licensees must make it a condition of acceptance that advertisements do so comply;
- the detailed rules set out in the Code are intended to apply in their spirit, as well as their letter;
- the standards in the Code apply to any item of publicity inserted in breaks or between programmes, whether in return for payment or not, including publicity by licensees themselves.

Products/services which cannot be advertised on television

Advertisements for the following products/services or for other products or services which would indirectly publicise the following products/services are currently unacceptable:

- all tobacco products;
- pornography;
- breath testing devices and products that purport to mask the effect of alcohol;
- the occult;
- betting tips;
- betting and gaming (except football pools and certain lotteries);
- private investigation services;
- guns and gun clubs;
- commercial services offering advice on personal or consumer problems.

Rules for particular situations

In addition to the general rules discussed above, the Code contains detailed rules applicable to the following:

- advertising and children;
- alcoholic drink;
- lotteries and pools;

- financial advertising;
- medicines, treatments, health claims, nutrition and dietary supplements;
- the use of animals in advertisements;
- homework schemes;
- matrimonial and introduction agencies;
- charity advertising;
- religious advertising.

The above rules are outside the remit of this book.

THE RADIO AUTHORITY ADVERTISING AND SPONSORSHIP CODE

The Radio Authority Code is in many respects similar to the ITC Codes. Readers should therefore cross-refer to the section of this chapter about the ITC.

Licensees (that is, commercial radio stations) are charged with complying with the Code. This means that they must ensure that the advertising and sponsorship which they broadcast meets the requirements of the Code. The Radio Authority will give advice to its licensees about the Code's provisions. Advertisers should liaise with the radio stations about specific advertisements rather than approach the Radio Authority direct. The Radio Authority investigates complaints made under the Codes and publishes details of its decisions in regular reports. An adverse decision is likely to generate adverse publicity for the advertiser. It will also mean that the advertisement must be withdrawn unless it is amended to ensure compliance with the Code. The advertiser will, therefore, find that its advertising will be denied an outlet on independent radio.

The Radio Authority can impose sanctions against those radio stations which breach the Code including fines and, in severe cases, the withdrawal of the station's licence.

The Codes and the courts

Challenging adjudications

Each of the above regulatory authorities with the exception of the PCC is subject to judicial review of their actions. The PCC is probably also subject to judicial review, although the point has not been authoritatively determined by the courts at the time of writing.

Essentially, this has meant that their decisions under the above Codes are open to challenge by way of judicial review where they can be shown to be irrational or beyond the scope of the regulator's authority. The topic of judicial review was considered further in Chapter 2. It should be remembered that the court will not substitute its own judgment for that of the regulatory body on a judicial review application. If the court agrees that an adjudication is irrational or there are otherwise grounds for review, it will remit the decision back to the regulatory body for further review. The end result may be that the body makes the same decision that led to the review application, but that it applies different grounds or reasoning in reaching that decision.

The regulatory bodies and the Human Rights Act 1998

When the Human Rights Act comes into force in October 2000, each regulatory authority is almost certainly a public authority for the purposes of the Act,[11] (although the decision will ultimately be for the courts). As such, any decision made by the bodies or any procedure which they follow must be compatible with the Convention rights.[12] Where a decision is incompatible with the Convention rights, it will be open to challenge under the provisions of the Act. The likely effect of the Human Rights Act on the various Codes was analysed in Chapter 1 (and Chapter 8 in relation to privacy).

The approach of the courts to the Codes

Essentially, it would appear on the very limited authorities available at the time of writing that the courts will maintain the distinction between the law and the Codes when an application is made under s 7 of the Human Rights Act 1998.[13] They will not try to blur the Codes into the law (or vice versa). The indications are that the courts recognise that the Codes do not have the force of law and are not concerned with establishing legal rights. As such, they may be interpreted more flexibly than legal rules and obligations. In the *R v BSC ex p BBC* case,[14] the court upheld a finding of violation of privacy against the BBC whilst recognising that under black letter law, such a claim would be unlikely to succeed.

More prominence for the Codes?

In two respects, the Codes have been elevated into a more prominent position than they have had previously. First, under the Data Protection Act 1998

---

11 Refer to Chapter 1 for further detail.

12 HRA 1998, s 6.

13 *R v BSC ex p BBC* (2000) unreported, CA.

14 *Ibid.*

material is exempt from certain of the Act's provisions where it is created for the purposes of journalism, literature or art in order to qualify for the exemption.[15] The publisher must, however, reasonably believe that publication of the material is in the public interest. In deciding whether this requirement is met, the court may have regard to 'any relevant Code of Practice' which will include the PCC Code, the ITC Code, the Radio Authority Code and the BSC Code. The importance of complying with the Codes then assumes an importance that it does not otherwise have. There is at least a possibility that the court's interpretation of the Codes will begin to build up a body of guidance on the Codes which may supplement the decisions of the regulatory authority.

A similar position exists in relation to s 12 of the Human Rights Act 1998. The section was considered in detail in Chapter 1. Essentially, it requires the court to have regard to any relevant privacy Code when considering whether to grant relief which may affect the exercise of the right to freedom of expression in relation to journalistic, literary or artistic material. As with the Data Protection Act, the relevant provisions of the Codes will assume an importance which they did not otherwise have and the media will have a greater incentive to comply with the provisions of the Code.

Benefits of the regulatory system

The regulatory systems which are considered in this chapter have the following beneficial effects:

- the complaints systems examined above are more accessible to the majority of the general public than legal proceedings would be. They involve no cost to the public and involve little in the way of technicalities. The writing of a letter or completion of a complaint form is all that is required in order to start a complaint. Legal proceedings, on the other hand, generally involve substantial costs and, even after the introduction of the new Civil Procedure Rules in April 1999, they involve technical procedural rules which have to be followed. Complainants under the above Codes have no need to instruct a lawyer if they do not wish to or cannot afford to. The complaints bodies themselves offer free assistance to those complainants who require it;

- the systems put in place by the Codes offer the opportunity for redress to be obtained more quickly than it could under the litigation process;

- the Codes are more flexible than the law considered in the first part of this book. Accordingly, it is often easier for the provisions to be interpreted in line with contemporary standards than it is in relation to the law. They can

---

15   Data Protection Act 1998, s 32.

also be amended relatively easily to deal with new issues as and when they arise. On the whole, the law is a slower moving animal;

- the spirit of the Codes is to be interpreted as well as the letter. They generally cannot be circumvented because of a mere technicality;

- many of the regulatory bodies such as the ASA and the BSC carry out research activities to assess public views on various matters, for example, the use of swear words in advertisements or on television. The results of such surveys are taken into account when adjudicating on complaints. It might, therefore, be said that the regulatory bodies are more in touch with public opinion than the judiciary;

- many of the provisions of the various Codes are fundamentally unsuited for legal regulation. For example, take the topic of bad taste. This is an inherently subjective issue. What appears to you or I to be in bad taste might well be admired or accepted by others, and vice versa. It is inappropriate that the application of the law should be focused on individual sensibilities which might be arbitrarily determined. There is a risk that such an arbitrary legal regulation would not be sufficiently precise to be 'prescribed by law' and therefore that it would be incompatible with the Convention on Human Rights. Many of these considerations were discussed in Chapter 12 in relation to indecency offences. The defects identified in the indecency laws would be amplified in relation to a law which seeks to regulate taste.

The ITC Programme Code makes the following provision in relation to language in the section of the Code dealing with offence to good taste:

1.4 There is no absolute ban on the use of bad language. But many people are offended, some of them deeply, by the use of bad language, including expletives with a religious (and not only Christian) association. If, therefore, the freedom of expression of writers, producers and performers is not to be jeopardised, gratuitous use of bad language must be avoided. It must be defensible in terms of context and authenticity and should not be a frequent feature of the schedule.

If the Codes had the force of law, the court would have to grapple with what amounts to 'gratuitous', what uses might be defensible and what is authentic. These concepts defy analysis other than by reference to the individual susceptibilities of the viewer or listener and the particular circumstances of the case.

The various Codes, on the other hand, do not seek to set out legal rights and obligations. The industry bodies do not adjudicate in such terms. Indeed, the BSC literature expressly states that where a legal remedy is available to a complainant, it may be inappropriate for the BSC to consider the matter. The Codes are concerned with setting standards of best practice for the appropriate industry to follow. It is right that such standards may vary according to public sensibilities in order that the media reflect the society in which we live. But it does not necessarily follow that a failure to meet the standards should be rendered unlawful.

It is to be hoped that the courts maintain this distinction when issues involving the Codes come before them.

PART 3

CHAPTER 17

TYPICAL CONTRACTUAL PROVISIONS

This chapter examines typical contractual provisions which are likely to be found in contracts relating to the media. The objective is to provide examples of the way in which certain of the principles considered in Part 1 have relevance in practice.

The chapter examines typical provisions contained in assignments and licences of intellectual property. It also looks at a special type of licence: namely, a book publishing agreement. It then goes onto consider confidentiality agreements and agreements between advertising agencies and their clients.

BOILERPLATE CLAUSES

Boilerplate clauses are provisions contained in most types of commercial agreements. They are reasonably standard in form and are generally uncontroversial. Examples of boilerplate provisions are as follows.

Entire agreement clause

Parties to a contract will normally wish to ensure that all their obligations are recorded in one agreement. They will also want to avoid evidential difficulties which may arise when one party to a contract alleges that the written agreement was amended or supplemented by oral representations and discussions. It is a common law principle that extraneous evidence cannot be used to vary a written contract. This rule is subject to a number of exceptions, in particular where the court is persuaded that the document does not reflect the entire agreement between the parties.

A simple entire agreement clause would state that:

> This agreement shall constitute the entire agreement and understanding between the parties.

This type of clause will not exclude liability for pre-contractual misrepresentations. A separate clause will be required to achieve that effect. This might take the following form:

> Each of the parties acknowledges and agrees that in entering into this Agreement it does not rely on and shall have no remedy in respect of any representation other than as expressly set out in this Agreement save that nothing in this clause shall operate to limit or exclude any liability for fraud.

Choice of governing law clause

Where the contract has an international element, it should expressly provide which national laws will govern the contract, for example, the laws of England and Wales.

Choice of jurisdiction clause

Where the contract has an international element, the clause should identify the country whose courts will have jurisdiction to hear disputes which arise under the contract.

Arbitration clause

Contracts often contain arbitration clauses or alternative dispute resolution clauses if the parties wish to avoid court proceedings in relation to any disputes which arise under the contracts.

Service of notices

A provision on how the notices under the agreement (for example, notices of termination) are to be served – this clause is designed to ensure that notices come to the attention of the appropriate party.

Severance

Parties who have agreed to enter into an agreement may subsequently find that part of it is unenforceable (for example, wide exclusions of liability may be void under the provisions of the Unfair Contract Terms Act 1977). The purpose of a severance clause is to make it clear that, in such a case, the parties intend the rest of the agreement to survive by means of the severance of the offending provisions from the rest of the agreement. The court also has a residual power to sever, irrespective of whether a severance provision is included. An example of a severance clause is:

> The invalidity or enforceability for any reason of any part of this Agreement shall not prejudice the continuance in force of the remainder.

LICENCE AGREEMENTS

Licence agreements enable the exploitation of intellectual property rights, such as copyright or registered trade marks. A licence is essentially permission by the *licensor* to the *licensee* to make use of the right in question in the ways specified in the licence. A licence does not transfer ownership of the right which is the subject of the licence. It is simply a permission.

Licences may be exclusive, sole or non-exclusive.

An *exclusive licence* means that the grant of rights is exclusive to the licensee. No other party, including the licensor, may exercise the rights granted by the licence in the territory covered by the licence. Exclusive licences of copyright must be in writing and signed by or on behalf of the copyright owner.[1]

A *sole licence* means that the licensee is the only party to whom the licensor grants rights *but the licensor retains the right to exploit the rights himself*. A sole licence of copyright may be in writing, or it may be an oral agreement. For reasons of certainty, it is better if the terms are recorded in writing.

A *non-exclusive* licence means that licensee may have to share the exploitation of the rights with other parties, including the licensor. The licensee has no exclusivity. A non-exclusive licence of copyright may be oral or written.

Where the right which is the subject of the licence is a registered trade mark, s 28 of the Trade Marks Act 1994 provides that the licence must be in writing signed for or on behalf of the licensor whether it is an exclusive licence, a non-exclusive licence or a sole licence.

A licensee will generally have to pay more for exclusive rights.

Scenario

X is the creator of a number of animated characters who appear in a weekly cartoon which is broadcast on national television. X owns the copyright in the drawings of the characters (artistic works). He wishes to grant a licence to Beinz, who are manufacturers of tinned foods. The licence will give Beinz permission to reproduce the drawings of the characters on the labels of their tinned products. What provisions should the licence contain?

---

1   CDPA 1988, s 92(1).

The parties

Care should be taken to ensure that the licensor and licensee are correctly identified in the agreement. For example, negotiations for the licence may take place with a director of the company, but the company should be named as licensor and not the individual director. Where a company has a separate trading name to its corporate name, the corporate name should be inserted into the agreement.

The territory covered by the licence

The licence should set out the territory in respect of which the permission applies. For example, X may grant rights in the drawings to Beinz for the UK only, or the grant of rights might extend further, perhaps across the European Community.

We saw in Chapter 6 that if the licence is silent on the extent of the grant of rights, the courts will imply the minimum term necessary to give business efficacy to the licence.[2] It is in both parties' interests to set out the terms of the licence as precisely as possible to avoid disputes arising in the future.

The licence term

Licences may be for a fixed term, an indefinite term or a fixed term with an option to extend a fixed term licence for a further period, which itself might be a fixed period or an indefinite period. Where renewal of a fixed term licence is envisaged, the licence should make clear whether the renewed licence will be on the same terms as the previous licence.

Termination provisions

The licence should state how it could be brought to an end.

Typical termination provisions are:

- provision for termination on breach of the terms of the licence at the option of the parties (sometimes the right to terminate will be restricted to material or serious breaches of the licence);
- provision for termination if a party becomes insolvent.

---

2   See, eg, *Robin Ray v Classic FM* [1998] FSR 622, where the defendant claimed that it had the right to deal with the subject matter of the licence across the world. In the absence of any provision about the territory covered by the licence, the court implied the minimum term necessary to give efficacy – namely, that the licence applied to the UK only.

Licensees in the position of Beinz should seek to ensure that the termination provisions which can be applied against them are as narrow as possible.

The termination provisions should put a procedure in place for the termination to be effected. Typical contents of termination clauses deal with the following: is the party who is bringing the agreement to an end required to serve a notice of termination? How long should the notice be? What is to happen to stocks of the licensee's products which have made use of the right before the licence came to an end? Should there be a 'sell off' period to dispose of such stock?

The licensor generally seeks to reserve the right to terminate the licence if there is a change in control of the licensee. The licensee may also want the same right in relation to the licensor.

The rights which are being licensed

The scope of the licence should be clearly set out and the rights which are the subject of the licence should be precisely identified. In our scenario, the exact drawings to which Beinz is being granted rights should be identified and, ideally, they should be attached to the licence in the form of a schedule to the agreement.

As we have seen in Chapter 6, copyright gives the right to restrict reproduction of the work to the copyright owner. A well drafted licence will give Beinz the right to reproduce the works, but this need not be a once and for all grant of rights. The licensor may permit reproduction of the work in certain ways only.

In our scenario, Beinz may be granted the right to reproduce and publish the drawings on its tinned products or perhaps only on certain types of its tinned products. The licence might also extend to Beinz's promotional literature and advertisements for tinned products. If Beinz exceeds the limit of its authority, it will infringe copyright in the drawings. It is therefore very important for a party such as Beinz that it ensures that the licence is sufficiently wide for its purposes. If Beinz were to overlook obtaining a licence for use of the drawings in its promotional material, it could not use the drawings for advertising purposes without infringing copyright.

The consideration for the grant of the licence

Consideration for the licence usually takes one of two forms. The form of the consideration and the amount will be a matter for negotiation between the parties. The usual forms of consideration are:

Royalties

Royalties are generally expressed to be a percentage of sales revenue of the product which is the subject of the licence. In our scenario, the royalties would be paid by Beinz to X, based on the sale of the tinned products bearing the drawings of X's characters. Sometimes, a licence will impose minimum royalty obligations on the licensee.

Where the consideration is payable by way of royalties, the licence should provide the licensor with a right to inspect the licensee's financial records in order to verify the sales figures and the amount of royalties which should have been paid. The right is usually expressed to be exercisable on notice to the licensee and restricted to inspection in normal office hours.

Fees

Instead of or in addition to royalties, the consideration may take the form of a licence fee. This can be a one off payment or a recurring fee – for example, a fee payable annually.

Sometimes an initial (or upfront) fee will be payable as well as royalties or an annual licence fee. Such a payment is known as an advance, and may be recoupable against royalties. It is essentially a payment on account of future earnings.

Whether consideration is paid by way of royalties or fees, the licence should state when payment becomes due and payable.

Obligations on the licensee

A well drafted licence should allow the licensor to control the manner in which the licensee is able to use the rights granted by the licence. A licensor such as X will want these rights to prevent the use of the drawings by Beinz in a manner which is damaging to the integrity of the works.

This is done by imposing 'quality control' restrictions on the licensee. In our scenario, typical control measures include the right of X to inspect samples of the labels on Beinz's tins, and any promotional literature used by Beinz which bear the drawings, in advance of distribution to the public.

The licence may provide quite detailed restrictions on the way that the drawings are used, for example, by providing that the drawings can only be reproduced in the manner and the colours specified by the licensor.

Often, the licence will contain indemnity provisions under which the licensee will agree to indemnify the licensor against loss or damage caused by a breach of its obligations.

Warranties from the licensor

The licensor usually has to give warranties (which are essentially contractual promises) about the rights which are the subject of the licence. Typical warranties which would be given by X in our scenario are:

- X has the authority to enter into the licence;
- X owns the copyright which is the subject of the licence;
- the use of the drawings by Beinz in accordance with the terms of the licence of the rights granted will not infringe the rights of any third party.

The licence will usually contain indemnity provisions under which the licensor will indemnify the licensee for any loss or damage which it incurs as a result of a breach of its warranties. So, if Beinz is sued successfully for copyright infringement by a third party who claims to own copyright in the cartoon drawings which are the subject of the licence granted by X, Beinz could seek an indemnity against X for compensation for the legal costs and damages which it has to pay as a result of the action.

Moral rights

Moral rights were considered in Chapter 6. In summary, the creator of a copyright work has a right to be identified as the author of the work (provided that this right has been asserted) (*right of paternity*), the right not to have a work falsely attributed to him (*right against false attribution*), and a right to object to derogatory treatment of the work (*right of integrity*).

Where a licence grants a permission to use a work (for example, a cartoon drawing), the parties should not neglect to address the question of moral rights.

The rights may be waived by the owner of the moral rights. The waiver must be in writing[3] and signed by the owner of the moral right. The waiver may be conditional or unconditional, and it may be expressed to be revocable. From the licensee's point of view, it should, ideally, be expressed to be both unconditional and irrevocable.

Remember that the owner of copyright in a work will not necessarily be the owner of the moral right. Moral rights will always reside in the author or creator of the work. They cannot be assigned. Copyright, on the other hand, may be assigned.

The above comments are made about a typical licence of intellectual property rights. We will now consider a more specific agreement involving the grant of a licence, namely, a typical book publishing contract.

---

3   CDPA 1988, s 87.

PROVISIONS IN A TYPICAL BOOK PUBLISHING CONTRACT

A typical publishing contract will deal with the following matters.

The rights granted to the publisher by the author

The rights granted under the book publishing agreement would generally be a grant of the right to produce and publish the author's book. The grant of rights is a licence of the copyright in the book (the book is a literary work for copyright purposes, provided that it is original). If the licence were not granted, the production and distribution of the book would be an infringement of the author's copyright.

The publisher will generally want to have an exclusive licence for the territory covered by the book.

The date for delivery of the book to the publishers

The conditions for acceptance and approval of the book by the publisher

Where a book has been commissioned, the agreement will generally oblige the publisher to accept a book which is in conformity with the terms of the commission.

The agreement will usually have the right to decline to publish a book which does not conform to the commission, for example, if it not to an acceptable standard, or if it is on a different subject matter from that originally agreed by the parties. If the publisher declines to publish a book on this ground, the agreement will generally provide that it will terminate.

It is usual for the agreement to provide that if it is terminated on the above grounds, the author may not offer the book for publication elsewhere (for example, if the author carries out improvements to the text) without first offering it to the publisher.

Competing works

The agreement will generally prohibit the author from involvement in any separate publication which might reasonably be considered to compete with or prejudice sales of the book which is the subject of the agreement without first obtaining consent from the publisher.

Warranties and indemnities

Warranties

The author will generally be required to make the following warranties to the publisher:

- that he has the authority to enter into the agreement;
- that he is the sole author of the book (if the author is a joint author, both authors must license the right to publish the work to the publisher);
- that he is the owner of the rights which are the subject of the licence (that is, that he has not previously assigned his copyright to anyone else);
- that the book is original to the author (if the book is not original, no copyright will subsist in it);
- that the book has not previously been published;
- that the book does not infringe copyright in any other copyright work (that is, that the author has not reproduced a substantial part of another work in which copyright subsists without consent from the copyright owner);
- that the book does not breach a duty of confidentiality (owed by the author to a third party. The duty of confidentiality may be express or implied.);
- that the book does not breach a duty to respect privacy owed to any party;
- that the book does not infringe any other rights of any party (this is designed to be a 'catch all' provision);
- that the book contains nothing libellous;
- that all factual statements contained in the book are true;
- that any instruction contained in the book will, if followed accurately, not cause any injury, illness or damage to the user;
- that the book contains no obscene or blasphemous material;
- that the book is not in breach of Official Secrets legislation;
- that the book is not in any other way unlawful (this is designed to be a 'catch all' provision).

The effect of these warranties is to place responsibility for compliance on the author. If the author were in breach of the warranty, for example, if the book were to contain libellous material, the author would be in breach of the publishing contract.

Indemnities

A book publishing agreement invariably provides that the author will indemnify the publisher against any legal expenses and damages which the publisher incurs as a result of the author's breach of the warranties provided for in the agreement.

If the publisher were to be successfully sued for defamation in respect of the book, it could, therefore, seek an indemnity from the author in respect of costs and damages.

Sometimes the indemnity also extends to claims made against the publisher which *allege* that the book constitutes a breach of warranty, even if the claims are not ultimately successful.

In those circumstances, the author will be obliged to indemnify the publisher for its legal costs and expenses – to the extent that these cannot be claimed from the unsuccessful claimant – even though the claim had no real merit.

Warranties and indemnities are normally expressed to survive the termination of the publishing agreement.

Reservation of the right to alter the book

The publisher generally reserves the right to alter the book in ways which appear to the publisher to be appropriate to modify or remove passages considered actionable. From the author's point of view, the agreement should provide for prior notification to the author before any change is made.

Rights clearance

The agreement will make provision for the clearance of rights in copyright works which are reproduced in the book. It is not unusual for this obligation to be put on the author.

Responsibility for publicity and promotion of the book

It is not unusual for matters relating to the production and promotion of the book to be at the discretion of the publishers.

A procedure for correction of proof copies of the book

Consideration payable to the author

The consideration payable to the author will generally be in the form of royalties. The royalties will be expressed to be a percentage of the sales revenue generated by sales of the book. The percentage amount may vary according to the form in which the book is published, for example, hardback, paperback or electronically.

Sometimes, an author may receive an advance payment from the publishers which is essentially a payment on account of future royalties.

The agreement should contain provisions about when the royalties will be paid to the author. Typically, this may be at three or six-monthly intervals with provisions for royalties which fall below a specified minimum figure to be rolled over into the next period. The agreement should also *contain* provisions about the procedure for overpayment of royalties, for example, will the amount of overpayment be deducted from future payments, or should the author have to account for it immediately?

Provision of a statement of sales to the author

The agreement will generally entitle the author to a statement of account providing details of its book sales over the accounting period in respect of which royalties are payable. This statement allows the author to identify how the royalty payment is made up.

Grant of right to inspect publisher's records of account

The author may be granted the right to inspect the financial records of the publisher in order to verify the amount of royalties payable to him.

Infringement of copyright in the book

The book will be a literary work in which copyright subsists. If, having been published, the copyright in the book is subsequently infringed by a third party, the commercial interests of the publisher may be jeopardised. Because its own interest is being jeopardised by the infringement, the publisher is unlikely to want to leave the decision whether or not to sue for copyright infringement to the author.

The basic rule is that infringement of copyright is actionable by the copyright owner.[4] Where the publisher is an *exclusive* licensee, it has the right to bring proceedings for infringement of copyright against anyone except the copyright owner.[5] This position applies to exclusive licensees only. Sole or non-exclusive licensees do not have the same rights. The exclusive licensee's

---

4   CDPA 1988, s 96.
5   *Ibid*, s 101.

rights are concurrent with the rights of the copyright owner. Where the exclusive licensee brings proceedings, the defendant can rely on any defence which would have been available had the action been brought by the copyright owner.[6]

Where the copyright owner and exclusive licensee have concurrent rights of action, the copyright owner or exclusive licensee may not, without the consent of the court, proceed with an action for copyright infringement unless the other is joined as a claimant or a defendant.[7] The other party will be joined as a defendant where it does not willingly consent to being a party to the action. Where it is joined as a defendant in such circumstances, it is not liable for any costs in the proceedings unless it plays an active part in the proceedings.[8]

The above provisions do not apply where the application is for an interim injunction where the copyright owner or exclusive licensee may make the application alone.[9]

A well drafted exclusive agency agreement will put the above provisions into effect.

If the agreement is a sole or non-exclusive agreement where the copyright owner is the only party with the right to take action for an infringement of copyright, the agreement will place the author under an obligation to take such steps as the publisher deems necessary to protect its rights – which may include the commencement of proceedings. The agreement may provide that the publisher will indemnify the author for its costs and expenses incurred in taking the action. Note that, in some circumstances, an agreement to finance legal action can be unlawful under the law relating to champerty. A detailed treatment of champerty is beyond the scope of this book.

Grounds for termination of the agreement

An assertion of the moral right of paternity by the author

Boilerplate clauses

The licence should contain such boilerplate clauses as are relevant.

Relevant boilerplate clauses

Set out below is an example book publishing agreement which may be considered against the above commentary.

---

6   CDPA 1988, s 101(3).
7   *Ibid*, s 102(1).
8   *Ibid*, s 102(2).
9   *Ibid*, s 102(3).

Memorandum of Agreement

made this   **day of**   **200**

between

of

(hereinafter called 'the Author', which expression shall include the plural and, where the context admits, include the Author's executors and assigns) of the one part and   (hereinafter called 'the Publishers', which expression shall where the context admits include any publishing imprint whether under its present or any future style subsidiary to or associated with the Publishers, and the Publishers' assigns or successors in business as the case may be) of the other part.

Whereby it is mutually agreed as follows concerning a work original to the Author and provisionally entitled:

(hereinafter called 'the Work').

1   Rights granted

In consideration of the payments hereinafter mentioned and subject to the terms and conditions herein contained, the Author hereby grants to the Publishers throughout the world, for the legal term of copyright, the exclusive publishing rights, meaning the right to publish and exploit the Work in all media whether now known or as developed in the future or to license such publication and exploitation including but not limited to publication in volume form in hardback or paperback or other binding and/or publication in electronic form, that is, the production of any system or program derived from or utilising the Work in whole or in part and designed for use in electronic information storage or retrieval systems now in existence or hereafter invented, and the licensing of all subsidiary rights in the Work.

2   Delivery of the Work

The Author has delivered/shall deliver material for the complete Work conforming to the specifications set out in Appendix A to this Agreement not later than

The Author agrees to retain an additional copy of all material.

Should the Author fail to deliver acceptable material and such other material as may be specified in Appendix A on the due date(s) or by such other date(s) as may be agreed by the Publishers in writing, the Publishers shall be at liberty to decline to publish the Work. If the Publishers so decline in writing, this Agreement shall terminate subject to the proviso that the Author shall not be at liberty to publish the Work elsewhere without having first offered the completed typescript to the Publishers on the terms of this Agreement.

3   Acceptance and conditions of acceptance and approval

The Publishers shall accept the Work provided that the material as delivered by the Author shall be technically competent and shall conform to a reasonable extent to the specifications set out in Appendix A hereto; and they shall have the right as a condition of acceptance of the Work to require amendments to ensure that the Work does so conform. If the Author is unable or unwilling to undertake such amendments or arrange for them to be made within such reasonable period of time as shall have been agreed by the Publishers, then the Publishers shall have the right to employ a competent person or persons to make the amendments and any fees payable shall be deducted from any sums due to the Author under the terms of this Agreement. The Work, as finally amended and marked for press, shall be subject to the Author's approval and such approval shall not be unreasonably withheld or delayed.

4   Competing work

While the Work is in course of preparation or in current publication:

(a)   the Author shall be entitled to use material written or compiled by him/her for the purposes of the Work in articles submitted to learned or professional journals and in papers presented at professional conferences PROVIDED THAT the Author shall make appropriate acknowledgment to the Work and the Publishers BUT

(b)   the Author shall not without the written consent of the Publishers write, edit or contribute jointly or severally to any work which may be reasonably considered by the Publishers to compete with or prejudice sales of the Work or the exploitation of any rights in the Work granted to the Publishers under this Agreement.

5   Warranties and indemnities

The Author hereby warrants to the Publishers and their assignees and licensees that he/she has full power to make this Agreement, that he/she is the sole Author of the Work and is the owner of the rights herein granted, that the Work is original to him/her, and that it has not previously been published in any form covered by this Agreement and is in no way whatever a violation or infringement of any existing copyright or licence, or duty of confidentiality, or duty to respect privacy, or any other right of any person or party whatsoever, that it contains nothing libellous, that all statements contained therein purporting to be facts are true and that any recipe formula or instruction contained therein will not, if followed accurately, cause any injury, illness or damage to the user.

The Author further warrants that the Work contains no obscene, or improper or blasphemous material nor is in breach of Official Secrets Acts nor is in any other way unlawful.

Where others contribute ('the Contributor') to the Work, the Author shall secure similar warranties under this Clause from the Contributor.

The Author shall indemnify and keep the Publishers indemnified against all actions, suits, proceedings, claims, demands and costs (including any legal costs or expenses properly incurred and any compensation costs and disbursements paid by the Publishers on the advice of their legal advisers to compromise or settle any claim) occasioned to the Publishers in consequence of any breach of this warranty, or arising out of any claim alleging that the Work constitutes in any way a breach of this warranty.

The Publishers reserve the right having first notified the Author to alter, or to insist that the Author alter, the text of the Work as may appear to them appropriate for the purpose of modifying or removing any passage which in their absolute discretion or on the advice of their lawyers may be considered objectionable or actionable at law, but any such alteration or removal shall be without prejudice and shall not affect the Author's liability under this warranty and indemnity.

All warranties and indemnities herein contained shall survive the termination of this Agreement.

6 Publishers' responsibility to publish

The Publishers shall, unless otherwise mutually agreed or unless prevented by circumstances beyond their control, at their own expense produce and publish the Work within three months of approval by the Author of the Work as ready for press in accordance with Clause 3 and Clause 11 of this Agreement.

7 Textual copyright material

Should the text of the Work contain extracts from other copyright works, the Author shall at his/her own expense obtain from the owners of the respective copyrights written permission (which shall be forwarded to the Publishers no later than on delivery of the material) to reproduce such extracts in the Work in all territories and editions and in all forms which are the subject of this Agreement.

8 Illustrations

The Author shall, on delivery of the Work, supply to the Publishers any photographs, pictures, maps, diagrams and other material which have been mutually agreed to be necessary for the proper illustration of the Work as set out in Appendix A.

In respect of any copyright material, the Author shall obtain from the owners of the respective copyrights written permission (which shall be forwarded to the publishers no later than on delivery of the material) to reproduce such material in the Work and in all territories and editions and in all forms which are the subject of this Agreement.

All illustrations supplied by the Author shall be in a form acceptable to the Publishers, but the Publishers shall have the right to reject such material or to require of the Author such substitutions or amendments as may in the reasonable view of the Publishers be required on the grounds of poor quality, excessive cost or otherwise.

The cost of supplying illustrative material, including copyright fees, shall be borne equally between the Author and the Publishers, such costs having been agreed in advance of such supply.

9 Index

If in the opinion of the Publishers it is desirable that an index be included in the Work, the Publishers shall prepare such an index at their own expense unless the Author notifies the Publishers in writing at the time of delivery of the material that he/she wishes to prepare his/her own index.

10 Production and promotion responsibility

All matters relating to the publication of the Work, including the paper, printing, design, binding and jacket or cover, the manner and extent of promotion and advertising, the number and distribution of free copies for the press or otherwise, the print number and the price and terms of sale of the first or any subsequent edition or impression of the Work shall be under the entire control of the Publishers.

The Publishers undertake to set the name of the Author in its customary form with due prominence on the title page and on the binding, jacket and/or cover of every copy of the Work published by them and shall use their best endeavours to ensure that a similar undertaking is made in respect of any editions/forms of the Work licensed by them.

11 Author's corrections

(a) The Author undertakes to read, check and correct the proofs of the Work (and finished artwork) and return them to the Publishers within TEN days of their receipt.

(b) If the Author fails to return the proofs duly read and corrected within the period provided, the Publishers shall be entitled to arrange for the proofs to be read and corrected and the cost of such reading and correcting shall be borne by the Author and shall be deducted from any sum which may become payable to the Author under this Agreement. The cost of all alterations and corrections made by the Author in the finished artwork and in the proofs (other than the correction of artist's, copy-editor's or printer's errors) in excess of 10 per cent of the cost of origination and/or origination of artwork shall be borne by the Author.

Should any charge arise under this Clause, the amount may be deducted from any sums due to the Author under the terms of this Agreement PROVIDED THAT the Publishers shall not invoke this sub-clause by reference only to alterations and corrections reasonably justified at proof stage by changes in the subject matter after completion and delivery of the Work.

(c)   All parts of the Work supplied by the Author shall, when done with, be returned to the Author if he/she so requests in writing. The Publishers shall take due care of material while it is in their possession but they shall not be responsible for any loss or damage to any part of the Work while it is in their possession or in the course of production or in transit or otherwise.

12   Royalties and fees payable on own editions

Subject to the terms and conditions set out in this Agreement, the Publishers shall make the following payments to the Author (either to the Author direct or to the Author's Agent under Clause 26 if appropriate) in respect of sales of the Work on all Home and Export Sales: a royalty of TEN per cent of the sum received by the Publishers on all copies of the Work sold by the Publishers wherever sold, less:

(a)   sums agreed by the Author and the Contributor as payable to the Contributor;

(b)   sums agreed by the Author and Publishers and paid in advance by the Publishers including but not limited to fees under Clauses 7 and 8 above.

The term 'sum received by the Publishers' in this Clause shall mean the amount received by the Publishers after deducting any discounts or commissions granted by the Publishers and any sales or similar taxes, duties or costs incurred by the Publishers in respect of sales of copies of the Work.

Where there is more than one Author of the Work, any payments under this Agreement shall be split equally between them unless the Publishers are notified otherwise in writing.

13   Subsidiary rights

In consideration of the payment by the Publishers to the Author of the following percentages of all moneys received by them in respect of the undermentioned rights, the Author hereby grants exclusively to the

Publishers such rights in so far as they are not granted by Clause 1 above to the Publishers during the term of this Agreement. The negotiation of and final agreement to terms of exploitation of rights granted under this Agreement shall be in the control of the Publishers who shall wherever practicable consult the Author concerning the sale of the undermentioned rights.

RIGHTS	PAYMENT DUE TO THE AUTHOR
(a) **Quotation, extract and translation rights**	40 per cent
(b) **Sub-licensed paperback and hardback editions**	40 per cent
(c)(i) **Mechanical reproduction rights** (that is, the right to license the reproduction of the Work or any part thereof by film micrography, gramophone record, compact disc, tape cassette, or by means of any other contrivance whether by sight or sound or combination of both, whether now in existence or hereafter invented for purposes of mechanical reproduction except in so far as reproduction is for use as part of or in conjunction with a commercial cinematograph film or videogram of such film)	40 per cent
(ii) **Electronic publishing rights** (that is, the right to license the production of any system or program derived from or utilising the Work in whole or in part and designed for use in electronic information storage or retrieval systems now in existence or hereafter invented)	40 per cent
(iii) **Reprographic reproduction rights** The Author and the Publishers shall license the Work non-exclusively to the Author's Licensing and Collecting Society and/or to the Publishers Licensing Society for the collective reprographic licences or licensing schemes operated by the Copyright Licensing Agency as agents for such Societies and the Author shall receive the Author's share of any proceeds from use of the Work under such licences or licensing schemes through the	

Author's Licensing and Collecting Society in
accordance with such Society's standard
terms and conditions   50 per cent

(d)   *Non-commercial rights for the print-handicapped*
(that is, the right to convert the Work to Braille or
to record it for the sole use of the blind and
print-handicapped)   free of charge

General proviso

The Author on written request from the Publishers undertakes to waive
his/her right to object to derogatory treatment of his/her work as
provided for in section 80 of the Copyright, Designs and Patents Act 1988
when such a partial waiver is an essential condition of the exercise of any
of the subsidiary rights set out in this Clause.

14   Statement of sales

(a)   The Publishers shall prepare accounts for the Work twice yearly
to 30 June and 31 December following publication and the said
accounts shall be delivered to the Author and settled within
three months thereafter, provided however that no payment
need be made in respect of any period in which the sum due is
less than £50, in which case the amounts shall be carried forward
to the next accounting date.

(b)   Upon reasonable written notice and during the Publishers'
normal business hours, the Author or the Author's appointed
representative shall have the right to examine the Publishers'
records of account at the place at which they are normally kept,
in so far as such records relate to sales and receipts in respect of
the Work. Such examination shall be at the cost of the Author
unless errors shall be found, to the disadvantage of the Author,
in excess of 2.5 per cent of the amount due to the Author in
respect of the last preceding accounting period, in which case the
cost of such examination shall be borne by the Publishers. Any
amount thereby shown to be due to the Author shall be paid to
the Author on receipt by the Publishers of the Author's account
relating thereto. No more than one such inspection shall be made
in any 12 month period.

(c)   Any overpayment (which shall include any debit royalties caused by returns of copies of the Work for which the Author shall previously have received royalty payments from the Publishers) made by the Publishers to the Author in respect of the Work may be deducted from any sums due subsequently to the Author from the Publishers in respect of the Work.

15   Review copies

Any sums which may be received in respect of single specimen or review copies distributed to individuals, press or journals for review for the purposes of publicity shall be regarded as a contribution to the expenses of such publicity and shall not be accounted for as sales.

16   VAT

All moneys due under the terms of this Agreement are exclusive of any VAT due thereupon. The Publishers operate a self-billing system for the payment of royalties and to account for Value Added Tax. The Publishers therefore require details of the Author's VAT registration number where applicable which shall be supplied upon signature of this Agreement. Should the Author fail to supply a VAT registration number, the Publishers shall not pay VAT on any sums due under the terms of this Agreement.

17   Death of the author

In the event of the death of the Author, the following provisions shall apply:

(a)   All sums payable under the terms of this Agreement shall be paid to the deceased Author's estate on any edition in print at the time of his/her death and on any reprints of such an edition.

(b)   On the next edition subsequent to the Author's death including any reprints thereof, the entire copyright in the deceased Author's Work shall be assigned to the Publishers or as the Publishers direct and all sums payable under the terms of this Agreement shall be paid to the deceased Author's estate less any fees and/or royalties payable to an editor or reviser in the course of preparing such new edition for press.

(c)   The deceased Author's estate shall then cease to participate financially in any further editions but the Publishers reserve to themselves the right of continuing the use of the Author's name on any or all editions subsequent to the Author's death.

18   Copyright

The copyright in the Work shall remain the property of the Author EXCEPT THAT the copyright of the typographical and design of the Work shall remain the property of the Publishers and the copyright notice to be printed in every copy of the Work shall be in the Author's name, with the year of first publication.

Where others contribute to the Work, the Author shall arrange to acquire copyright in the contributions from the Contributors.

19   Infringement of copyright

It is agreed that if the Publishers consider that the copyright in the Work has been or is likely to be infringed, they shall on giving notice to the Author of such infringement be at liberty to take such steps as they may consider necessary for dealing with the matter and, if they desire to take proceedings, they shall, on giving the Author an undertaking in writing to pay all costs and expenses and to indemnify the Author against all liability for costs, be entitled to use the Author's name as a party to such proceedings, but at the same time to control, settle or compromise as they see fit. The Publishers shall further be entitled to take urgent proceedings in their own sole name for interlocutory relief without prior notice to the Author. Any profits or damages which may be received in respect of any infringement of the copyright shall after deduction of all costs and expenses be divided 30 per cent to the Author and 70 per cent to the Publishers. The provisions of this Clause are intended to apply only in the case of an infringement of the copyright in the Work affecting the interest in the same granted to the Publishers under this Agreement. The Author agrees to execute any documents and do any acts reasonably appropriate to give effect to the rights of the Publishers granted by this Clause.

20   Author's copies

The Author shall be entitled to receive on publication   copies of any printed edition and shall be entitled to purchase further copies at trade terms for personal use but not for resale and shall pay for such copies within 30 days of invoice. The Author shall receive one copy of any sub-licensed edition on receipt by the Publishers from the sub-licensed publishers.

21   Revision of the Work

Should the Publishers consider that a new edition of the Work is necessary, the Author shall, without charge to the Publishers, edit and revise the Work during the currency of this Agreement and shall supply any new matter that may be needed to keep the Work up to date within a reasonable period. In the event of the Author neglecting or being unable for any reason to finish, revise or edit the work or supply new matter where needed within a reasonable period, the Publishers may procure some other person to finish or revise the Work, or supply new matter, and may deduct the expense thereof from royalties or other sums payable to the Author under this Agreement.

22   Termination of contract

(a)   The Author may terminate this agreement by summary notice in writing to the Publishers if the Publishers are in material breach of any of the provisions of this Agreement and have failed to remedy such breach within one month of notice to them from the Author of such breach.

(b)   Upon termination of this Agreement under (a) above, but subject to the terms of Clause 24, all rights granted herein shall revert to the Author without further notice, without prejudice to any rights of the Publishers or of third parties in respect of contracts or negotiations properly entered into by them with any such third party prior to the date of such reversion, and without prejudice to any moneys already paid or then due to the Author from the Publishers.

23   Reversion of rights

If the Work shall become out of print and unavailable in any English-language edition issued or licensed by the Publishers and if there is no agreement in existence between the Publishers and a third party for the publication within a reasonable period of a sub-licensed edition in the English language, then the Author may give notice in writing to the

Publishers to reprint or reissue the Work within 12 months. In the event of the Publishers' failure to do so, all the Publishers' rights in the Work (subject to Clause 24 hereof) shall terminate upon the expiration of the said notice, without prejudice to all rights of the Publishers and any third party in respect of any agreement previously entered into by the Publishers hereunder with any such party. Except nevertheless that no rights shall revert if it is not possible to reprint or reissue the Work for reasons connected with any war, strikes, lock-outs or other circumstances beyond the Publishers' control.

24   Moneys owing

Notwithstanding the foregoing provisions of this Agreement, the rights hereby granted to the Publishers shall not revert unless any moneys owing by the Author to the Publishers shall have been paid.

25   Moral rights

The Author hereby asserts his/her right to be identified as the Author of the Work and the Publishers undertake to use all reasonable endeavours to include the Author's assertion in any contract for volume rights with any licensee concerning any edition of the Work to be published in the United Kingdom EXCEPT THAT the Author acknowledges that the Publisher may in developing electronic or other editions of the Work, whether for sale or for publicity purposes, need to carry out some or all of the activities listed below provided that the Publishers shall wherever practicable consult the Author:

(a)   adaptation of form or structure of the Work to enhance its use;

(b)   publication of whole or part in combination with other works;

(c)   maintenance of the Work's accuracy by producing supplements and new editions;

(d)   preparation of abridgements and other adaptations of the Work.

26 Agency

The Author hereby authorises and empowers his/her Agent,

, to collect
and receive all sums of money payable to the Author under the terms of
this Agreement and declares that such receipt shall be a good and valid
discharge to all persons paying such moneys to them and that the Agent
shall be empowered to act in all matters arising out of this Agreement
unless the Publishers are notified in writing otherwise by the Author.

27 Arbitration

If any difference shall arise between the Author and the Publishers
touching the meaning of this Agreement or the rights and liabilities of
the parties thereto, the same shall in the first instance be referred to the
Informal Disputes Settlement Scheme of the Publishers Association of
Great Britain and, failing agreed submission by both parties to such
Scheme, shall be referred to the arbitration of two persons (one to be
named by each party) or to a mutually agreed umpire in accordance with
the provisions of the Arbitration Act 1996, or any amending or substitute
statute for the time being in force.

28 Interpretation

The headings in this Agreement are for convenience only and shall not
affect its interpretation.

29 Governing law

This Agreement shall be deemed to be a contract made in England and
shall be construed and applied in all respects in accordance with English
law and the parties hereto submit and agree to the jurisdiction of the
English courts.

AS WITNESS THE HANDS OF THE PARTIES

For and on behalf of the Author:
(where there is more than one author, each author needs to sign)

Author

VAT registration number (if applicable)

Witnessed by:

Witness   Name and address

For and on behalf of the Publishers:

Managing Editor

Appendix A

Author

Title (provisional)

Series title (provisional)

Nature of the Work

> As set out in the
> Author's proposal to the
> Publishers
> dated/received
>
>
> or
>
> As attached to this
> Memorandum of
> Agreement

TEXT

Length

Medium for delivery

> Computer disk and one
> hard copy printed from
> such disk with
> no alterations

Date by which to be
delivered to the Publishers

ILLUSTRATIVE MATERIAL

Type

Extent

Date by which to be
delivered to the Publishers

Otherwise in accordance with Clause 8

ASSIGNMENTS OF INTELLECTUAL PROPERTY RIGHTS

Copyright and registered trade marks may be transferred by way of assignment. The assignment must be in writing and signed by the assignor before it is effective in law.[10] Assignments need not be a once and for all transfer. They can operate to transfer the right for a limited period or for limited territories. It is possible to assign copyright for, say, 10 years, and at the end of that period the copyright will revert back to the original owner. An assignment may only transfer some of the rights which constitute copyright – for example, if a copyright owner assigns the broadcast rights in a musical work, it will retain the other rights which make up copyright.

Set out below is an example copyright assignment in relation to commissioned artwork. Readers will recall from Chapter 6 that, where work is commissioned, copyright belongs to the artist rather than to the commissioner unless an assignment is taken. When considering the terms of an assignment, it is important that the party to whom the rights are transferred (the *assignee*) ensures that it acquires the rights it needs. The person who assigns its rights is known as the *assignor*.

ASSIGNMENT

This ASSIGNMENT is made the [   ] day of [   ] 200[ ]

BETWEEN

('The Publisher') to include the Publisher's assigns or successors in business

And

('The Artist') to include the Artist's executors and assigns

(A) The Artist has created (an) original artistic work(s) at present entitled [   ] ('the Artwork') and wishes to assign his/her copyright in the Artwork to the Publisher in accordance with the provisions of this Agreement

(B) The Publisher agrees to take an assignment of the copyright in the Artwork from the Artist

---

10   CDPA 1988, s 90(3) and the Trade Marks Act 1994, s 24.

IT IS AGREED AS FOLLOWS:

1 The Artist assigns to the Publisher entire copyright whether vested contingent or future in the original artistic work at present entitled [ ] ('the Artwork') in any and all forms and media throughout the world and all rights of action and all other rights of whatever nature whether now known or in future created to which the Artist is now or may at anytime after the date of this Assignment be entitled by virtue of or pursuant to any of the laws in force in any part of the world TO HOLD the same to the Publisher its successors assignees and licensees absolutely for the whole period of such rights for the time being capable of being assigned by the Artist together with any and all renewals reversions and extensions throughout the world.

[*Note the right transferred in this Assignment is copyright for all forms and media. Copyright is transferred throughout the world. The rights transferred relate to rights which are now known and which may become known in the future. This is intended to cover copyright in new forms of media which may emerge in the future. For example, 30 years ago, few people would have predicted the explosion in internet publishing. Assignments dating back to the 1970s may not be drafted in sufficiently wide terms to have transferred the electronic publishing or digital transmission rights. If the assignment were silent about future rights, it would be a question of construction as to whether the parties intended to confer such rights at the time of their agreement.*[11]]

[*The assignment also states that it is for the whole period of the right plus any extensions of the copyright term which may be implemented in the future, for example, under new copyright legislation.*]

2 PUBLISHER'S UNDERTAKINGS

2.1 The Publisher shall pay to the Artist the sum of £[   ] by [   ] subject to the delivery by the Artist of the Artwork by the delivery date such sum to be payable within (30) days of the receipt by the Publisher of the Artwork.

[*As an assignment operates as a transfer of ownership of the rights in the work, the consideration takes the form of an initial lump sum payment rather than the royalty provisions which we saw above in relation to the licence.*]

2.2 The Fee shall be inclusive of all expenses incurred by the Artist to produce and deliver the Artwork.

---

11   *Hospital for Sick Children v Walt Disney* [1967] 2 WLR 1250.

3 THE ARTIST'S UNDERTAKINGS

The Artist warrants and undertakes and agrees with the Publisher that:

3.1 The Artist is the sole creator of the Artwork and the sole owner of all rights of copyright and all other rights of copyright and all other rights whatever in the Artwork throughout the world.

3.2 The Artist has not assigned or licensed or otherwise disposed of any rights of copyright or any other rights in or to the Artwork and has not entered into any agreement which might conflict with the Publisher's rights under this Agreement.

3.3 The Artwork is original to the Artist and does not infringe any existing copyright or breach any existing licence.

3.4 There is no present or prospective claim or litigation anywhere in the world in respect of the Artwork which may in any way impair inhibit diminish or infringe upon the rights granted to the Publisher in this agreement.

3.5 To the best of the Artist's knowledge the Artwork is not defamatory of any third party.

3.6 That the Artist has full power to make this Agreement and to grant the Publisher the rights granted in it.

[The reader is referred to comments about warranties made in relation to the specimen book publishing agreement.]

4 INDEMNITIES

4.1 The Artist will indemnify and keep the Publisher indemnified against all proceedings, claims, demands, damages and costs (including legal costs or expenses incurred by the Publisher and any compensation, costs and disbursements paid by the Publisher to compromise or settle any claim) made against the Publisher in consequence of a breach of any of the provisions of clause 3 of this Agreement or arising out of any claim alleging that the Artwork is in any way a breach of the provisions of clause 3.

[The reader is referred to comments about indemnities made in relation to the specimen book publishing agreement.]

5 THE PUBLISHER'S RIGHTS AND OBLIGATIONS

5.1 All copies of the Artwork published by the Publisher shall contain the following notice:

© (name of artist) (year of first publication)

5.2 The Publisher its assignees and licensees shall have the right to adapt, add to, delete from and/or alter in any way the Artwork.

5.3 The Publisher shall not be under any obligation to use or exploit the Artwork and if the Publisher in its sole discretion decides not to do so the Artist shall not have any claim against the Publisher for loss of opportunity to enhance the Artist's reputation or for any other reason whatsoever and shall not be entitled to payment on any sum other than the Fee to the extent the same falls to be paid.

5.4 The Fee shall be Full and Final consideration in respect of all rights granted to the Publisher and no Further sums shall be payable in connection with the use of the Artwork by the Publisher or anyone on its behalf.

6 OPTION ON FUTURE WORK

The Publisher shall have the first option to consider for publication subsequent artwork created by the Artist. Such artwork shall be the subject of a fresh agreement between the Publisher and the Artist. The Publisher shall exercise this option within six weeks of receipt of the Artwork. If the Publisher and the Artist are unable to agree terms the Artist shall be at liberty to enter into an agreement with another publisher provided that the Artist shall not accept terms less favourable than are offered by the Publisher.

7 OBLIGATION NOT TO COMPETE

The Artist shall not during the continuance of this Agreement prepare or publish (or collaborate in the production of) any Artwork similar to the Artwork or dealing with the same subject matter as the Artwork which is of a nature considered by the Publisher to be likely to compete with or affect prejudicially the sales of the Publisher's products or the exploitation of the rights granted to the Publisher by this Agreement

8 MORAL RIGHTS

The Artist unconditionally and irrevocably waives the benefit of its moral rights to which he is or may become entitled under the law in force in any part of the world.

[Remember that an assignment of copyright will not assign moral rights. These remain with the artist and, from the publisher's point of view, they should be waived.]

9 RELEVANT BOILERPLATE CLAUSES

SIGNED

....

For and on behalf of the Publisher

....

For and on behalf of the Artist

CONFIDENTIALITY AGREEMENTS

Scenario

The law relating to breach of confidence was considered in Chapter 5.

One of the matters examined in that chapter was the extent to which the law of confidence will protect confidential ideas or proposals submitted to publishers or film or television production companies. One of the difficulties which claimants are likely to encounter in this area is the need for them to show that the recipient of the information is under an express or implied obligation of confidence in relation to the information. In the interests of certainty, it is better to have an express obligation of confidence in place in the form of a confidentiality agreement. Note that the agreement need not be particularly formal. Often, a simple letter will suffice.

The agreement should deal with the following matters:

(a) identify the information or material for which confidentiality is alleged. Do not forget that the information must be defined with sufficient precision. In Chapter 5, we looked at the case of *CMI v Phytopharm*,[12] where it was held that, where the claimant cannot identify with sufficient precision the information for which protection is sought, a claim in breach of confidence will not succeed;

---

12 *CMI-Centers for Medical Innovation GmbH v Phytopharm plc* [1999] FSR 235.

(b) expressly state the purpose for which the confidential information is being disclosed;

(c) place the recipient under an obligation to use the information only for the purposes set out in the agreement and, in particular, state that it must not be disclosed to a third party or otherwise used for any other purpose;

(d) where appropriate, the obligation to keep the information confidential should be expressly extended to cover employees of the recipient by placing the recipient under a duty to extract confidentiality undertakings from those of its employees who come into contact with the material;

(e) the agreement might also place the recipient under an obligation to return the confidential information to the sender upon demand;

(f) for the avoidance of doubt, a well drafted confidentiality agreement will make clear that in disclosing the confidential information, the owner of the information is not granting any rights in the information, such as a licence to make use of any copyright which might subsist in the copyright work.

ADVERTISING AGENCY AGREEMENTS

In this last section of the chapter we consider the typical contents of an agreement between client and advertising agency.

Imagine that our notional food producer Beinz has engaged Image Advertising Agency (Image) to devise a marketing campaign for Beinz's tinned food products. What provisions would the agreement with the agency usually contain?

Most agencies will have their own standard terms and conditions which will form the basis of negotiation between client and agency.

The standard agreement will generally contain the following type of provisions.

The agency's duties towards the client

These will include:

- a description of the activities which the agent is undertaking on behalf of the client. This will typically set out the media in respect of which the agency is engaged to produce material – billboards, television campaigns, cinema advertising, etc, and the nature of the material which is to be produced;

- details of the approval process will be set out. Is it envisaged that Beinz will have the right of prior approval of the advertising material as it develops? Will there be regular meetings between Beinz and Image? If so, at what intervals will the meetings be held?;

- a schedule setting out relevant deadlines will generally be incorporated into the agreement.

Clearing materials

Who will be responsible for finding out whether third party consent is required for the use of material which is not created by the agency for the purposes of the Beinz campaign? If the obligation is to be placed on the agency (and, as a matter of practice, it generally will be, unless Beinz itself actually provides the material for the agency's use), the agreement should make the obligation clear. Image will then be under a duty to obtain permission for the use of the material before it is used. The agreement should specify that the approval should be in writing. The contract should also contain an *indemnity* from Image in favour of Beinz, under which Image will agree to reimburse Beinz for loss and damage suffered as a result of any claims which are commenced against it. The procedure for obtaining third party approval is set out in Chapter 18.

The ownership of material created for the campaign

The agreement should deal with the physical ownership of material created for the campaign – for example, who will own the original artwork for a poster? If Beinz wishes to acquire the artwork, the contract should contain an express provision to that effect.

The contract should also deal with ownership of intellectual property rights in the advertising material, for example, who will own copyright in the artwork? Remember that ownership of the physical art will not of itself mean that Beinz will own copyright in the art. If Beinz is to acquire copyright, it should take an assignment from the copyright owner. It is usual for an agreement between client and advertising agency to contain a provision that the agency will assign such copyright as it owns in material that it produces on the client's behalf. But this clause will not oblige the agency to obtain copyright from third parties which it commissions to do work on its behalf. Where Beinz wishes to acquire copyright in all material, including work which Image subcontracts to third parties, the agreement between Beinz and Image should oblige the agency to undertake to acquire copyright from third parties.

Material created for pitches

Ownership of copyright can be of particular relevance in relation to materials created by an agency for advertising pitches or beauty parades. The case of *Hutchinson Personal Communications Ltd v Hook Advertising Ltd*[13] offers a warning of the difficulties that can arise if ownership of copyright in materials created for the pitch is not determined at the time of the pitch. Hook Advertising Ltd created a logo for Hutchinson as part of a pitch for Hutchinson's business. Hook's pitch was successful, and a contract between the parties was drawn up which stipulated that copyright in all material 'produced or created' by Hook for Hutchinson's advertising would vest in Hutchinson.

A dispute subsequently arose between the agency and the client about ownership of the logo. Hook argued that Hutchinson did not own copyright in the logo under the contract terms referred to above. The court found that the words 'produced and created for their advertising' which were contained in the contract did *not* cover material produced for the pitch. The words only covered material which originated during the term of Hook's appointment.

Special provision should therefore be made for material which originates outside an agency's term of appointment.

Agency fees

The agreement should provide for fees. The basis on which Image charge for their services should be set out. If a flat fee has been agreed, that should be made clear. If Beinz is to be charged out on a time basis, the agreement should clearly specify how the arrangement works.

If Beinz wish to place a ceiling on the fees which Image can run up without prior approval, the contract should set out this arrangement.

The contract should also state whether payment is to be made to Image if Beinz decides not to make use of the material which Image produces.

---

13   *Hutchinson Personal Communications Ltd v Hook Advertising Ltd* [1995] FSR 365.

CHAPTER 18

CLEARING RIGHTS

This chapter explains the considerations which are relevant to the clearance of rights in the context of television programmes and films. The same principles apply equally to clearance of rights for inclusion in other types of material, for example, books. The chapter considers clearance of copyright, moral rights and performance rights. It should be read in conjunction with Chapters 6 and 17.

'Clearing rights' means the process of ensuring that the use of a work is not an infringement of copyright, moral rights or performance rights.

Note that the chapter considers rights clearance in the context of the UK. Different considerations may apply for other territories. Rights clearance is a complex process, and this chapter gives only an overview of the clearance process. For more detail, regard should be had to specialist texts.[1]

GENERAL POINTS

Copyright

Where copyright in a work has not expired, unauthorised use of a substantial part of the work will infringe copyright unless the use of the work falls within one of the permitted uses considered in Chapter 6.

Authorisation for the use of the work must therefore be obtained. You should always seek to have the consent confirmed in writing. Never assume that you have obtained consent – for example, because of the circumstances which surround your use of the work. In particular, do not use the device of asking for permission and relying on a lack of response by the rights owner as giving rise to consent. Positive consent should be sought.

Consent should ideally be obtained before the copyright work is used. Although consent may be obtained retrospectively, a party who has already made use of a work and subsequently applies for consent will usually find it difficult to negotiate from a position of strength the terms on which the right is used.

---

1   Eg, Edwards, S, *Rights Clearances for Film and Television Productions*, in association with the Producers' Alliance for Cinema and Television (PACT), available from PACT.

Consent for the use of copyright will generally take one of two forms:

(a) an assignment; or

(b) a licence.

These terms are described in the preceding chapter.

Remember that the consent must come from the owner of copyright. Sometimes, it can be difficult to establish who the owner is. You may encounter a long chain of title to copyright, where the right has been assigned a number of times. You should also remember that the owner of copyright will not necessarily be the physical owner of the work in question, so if you want to copy film footage the fact that it is in the possession of, say, a film library does not mean that permission to borrow the film from the library equates to a copyright licence to make use of the material.

Different owners for different rights

Do not forget that, where it seems that copyright has been assigned, it may be the case that only some of the rights which make up copyright have been transferred. An assignment can transfer certain rights only and leave the rest in the hands of the copyright owner. This means that it is possible that one party may own the rights to record a musical work, whilst another party may own the rights to perform it in public or to broadcast it. We shall see that this is the position which governs the use of most musical works.

Different owners for different territories

Remember, also, that rights may be assigned to a party for a particular territory only – for example, A may own the reproduction rights in a work for the UK, but B may own them for the US. If you wish to make copies of the work in both territories, you may need to obtain consents from A and B.

The terms of the licence/assignment

When permission is obtained for use of a copyright work, take care to ensure that you obtain the rights that you need. Consider the following points:

(a) does the licence/assignment cover the uses to which I want to put the copyright work?;

(b) is the grant of rights specific enough?;

(c) is the consent subject to conditions, and if it is, can you fulfil those conditions? For example, sometimes the copyright owner may want prior approval of the finished work before he will confirm consent to use the copyright work. Is that feasible? If not, can you renegotiate?;

(d) is the term/duration of the licence (and where the assignment is to take effect for a certain period only, the assignment) sufficient for your needs?;

(e) is the territory covered by the licence/assignment sufficient?;

(f) if you are taking a licence, consider whether it gives you sufficient exclusivity to make use of the work.

Moral rights

As we have seen, moral rights cannot be transferred, but they may be waived. The contents of the waiver are considered in the preceding chapter. If you wish to make use of a copyright work, you should check whether the moral rights have been waived and whether any waiver is wide enough for your purposes. If this is not the case, consider whether to take a waiver from the moral rights owner. Remember that the right of paternity (the right to be identified as the author) must be asserted before it may be enforced by the author.

Where you do take a waiver, or where there is a waiver in place, check that it is wide enough for your purposes. Is it revocable or irrevocable? Is it conditional or unconditional? Does the waiver cover the use which you wish to make of the work? Remember that the waiver may be for certain purposes only and expressed to be in respect of only some of the moral rights, for example, it may waive the right to object to derogatory treatment of the work, but assert the right to be identified as the author. If you do not wish to identify the author, you would need to negotiate a separate waiver for that moral right. Consider also whether the waiver will be effective in the territories in which you wish to make use of the work.

Example

You wish to commission A to write a screenplay which is to be based on B's novel. The novel is a literary work for copyright law purposes. Assume that the term of copyright has not expired.

The making of a screenplay based on the book is an adaptation of the book for the purposes of s 21 of the Copyright, Designs and Patents act (CDPA) 1988. This is one of the acts of primary infringement identified in the CDPA.

As an initial step, you would need to identify the copyright owner. It may be B, or B may have assigned his copyright to a third party – perhaps to his publisher (although, in the book publishing industry, an assignment of copyright would be unusual). If B has died, the copyright will form part of his estate and may have been bequeathed to a relative or to an unconnected party. Having carried out the necessary checks, you establish that B is the copyright owner.

You must therefore obtain permission from B to adapt his novel. If you fail to do so, you will infringe copyright.

On these facts, a licence is generally the most appropriate method of obtaining permission. As you are unlikely to want your screenplay to be in competition with another screenplay from the same source, you will probably seek an exclusive licence to adapt the screenplay. The effect of such a licence would be that no one else (including B himself) could adapt the novel into a screenplay during the licence period in question in the territory covered by the licence. You would need to satisfy yourself that the licence period and its territory are sufficient for your purposes.

B will also own moral rights in the book. Have these been waived? If they have not, consider how appropriate they are for your purposes.

If B has asserted his right to be identified as author of the novel, are you happy to identify him as such in the film credits? Under s 77 of the CDPA, the right of paternity extends to identifying the author of the work from which an adaptation is made. If you are not happy to do this, then you should seek an unconditional irrevocable waiver of this right from B.

Consider also the right of integrity. This is the right to object to derogatory treatment of a copyright work. In this case, B has a right to object to derogatory treatment of his novel. Treatment includes an adaptation of a work. If it could be said that the adaptation which you commission is prejudicial to B's honour or reputation, then the screenplay will infringe B's right of integrity. In order to protect your position as fully as possible, you should check whether B has waived his right of integrity. If not, persuade him to do so and ensure that the waiver is sufficient to meet your needs. The waiver should be unconditional and irrevocable.

Clearance of music and sound recordings

Music

The profitability of the music industry is largely dependent on effective exploitation of copyright. Unsurprisingly, the music industry has evolved a very systematic procedure for the exploitation of copyright.

In Chapter 6, reference was made to a number of collecting societies which administer rights on behalf of their members. The term 'administer' means that they grant licences and collect royalties for distribution amongst their members. The existence of the societies simplifies the clearance procedures. A potential user of a piece of music will not need to identify and locate a composer of a piece of music to obtain permission to record the music. Instead, the collecting society can be contacted and arrangements made for use of the music in accordance with the rates which prevail throughout the industry.

Remember that a new arrangement of music will be a copyright work in its own right. Therefore, permission may be needed on behalf of the original composer and a separate permission from the arranger. Similarly, take care where a musical work is out of copyright (that is, copyright has expired in the work). A new arrangement of an out of copyright work attracts a separate copyright. You may therefore have to clear rights in music which was composed hundreds of years ago.

The two relevant collecting societies which operate in relation to music are the Performing Right Society (PRS), and the Mechanical Copyright Protection Society (MCPS).

The PRS

The Members of the PRS assign part of their copyright to the society, namely, the right to control the *broadcast, public performance and inclusion in cable programme services* of a work. These rights are often referred to as the 'performing rights'. The term 'performing rights' is not to be confused with *performers'* rights, which belong to the musicians who actually perform a piece of music. Performers' rights are described at the end of Chapter 6.

The PRS licenses the rights and collects and distributes licence fees on behalf of its members. Licensees prepare and submit information to the PRS about the music which has been broadcast, transmitted or performed. The PRS uses that information to carry out the distribution of royalties.

A broadcaster who wishes to broadcast a piece of music which is in copyright, should contact the PRS for permission to do so. Note that it is the *broadcaster* who contacts the PRS, rather than the maker of the programme. Similarly in the case of a film, the cinema where a film which contains music is to be exhibited, rather than the filmmaker, should obtain a PRS licence.

Where the owner of copyright is not a member of the PRS, it must be approached direct for permission to broadcast, transmit or perform the music. Where the broadcaster wishes to broadcast a song, the owner of copyright in both the music and lyrics should be contacted, one or both of whom might be a member of the PRS.

In Chapter 6, we saw that, in the music industry, copyright in music and lyrics is usually assigned by the author to a music publisher. It is generally the publisher who gives permission to make use of the work where the relevant rights are not administered by a collecting society. The publisher's role is to promote the work of the composer and to generate revenue from the exploitation of the work.

The PRS has reciprocal agreements in place with its equivalent overseas collecting societies, which enable the PRS to collect revenue from overseas use of its members' music for distribution amongst its members.

The MCPS

The MCPS administers the right to *record* music and to *issue copies of the record* to the public. Unlike the PRS, members of the MCPS do not assign their rights to the MCPS. Instead, the MCPS acts as agent for its members.

The right to record encompasses what are referred to as *'synchronisation rights'*. Synchronisation rights are the rights to copy music and synchronise it with pictures – for example, the montages which broadcasters often show at the end of sporting events consisting of highlights of the event set to appropriate music. Synchronisation is essentially a specialised form of copying. The recording of the music by the broadcaster would infringe the copyright owner's rights if permission were not obtained.[2]

Where the copyright owner is not member of the MCPS, it should be approached directly for permission to record and issue copies of the record to the public. This will involve inquiries about the identity of the copyright owner. In Chapter 6, we saw that, in the music industry, copyright in music and lyrics are usually assigned by the author to a music publisher. It is generally the publisher who gives permission to make use of the work where the relevant rights are not administered by a collecting society.

MCPS has reciprocal agreements in place with its equivalent overseas collecting societies which enable MCPS to collect revenue from overseas recording of its members' music for distribution amongst its members.

Blanket agreements

Most national broadcasters have 'blanket agreements' in place with the PRS and MCPS. The terms of each broadcaster's blanket agreement varies, but in each case the blanket agreement is intended to eliminate the need for the broadcaster to seek specific permission in advance of broadcast for each particular piece of music used. The broadcaster completes 'music cue sheets' setting out details of the music which is broadcast, and submits the sheets to the collecting society. The music cue sheets generally set out the title of the music, the name of the composer (or arranger), the performers, details of any sound recording used, the timing of the music used and details of how it was used.

---

2   But note that, where music is commissioned for recording onto a soundtrack of a film or television programme, the synchronisation rights will be administered by the PRS rather than the MCPS.

Sound recordings

Readers will recall from Chapter 6 that the sound recording of a piece of music is a separate copyright work from the music. Care must therefore be taken to ensure that permission is sought not just for the use of the music, but also for the use of the sound recording of the music. As a general rule, copyright in a sound recording belongs to the record company which released the recording.

Because a sound recording is a different copyright work to the musical work itself, copyright may subsist in a recording of a work which is itself out of copyright, for example, because copyright has expired. Similarly a sound recording whose copyright has expired may attract a new copyright where the recording is re-mastered (digital re-mastering is much in vogue today).

There is a collecting society which administers copyright in sound recordings: Phonographic Performance Ltd (PPL).

PPL administers the rights in the *broadcast, public performance and inclusion in a cable programme service* of sound recordings. It is essentially the equivalent body to PRS – but for sound recordings rather than music. PPL also administers the right to record the recording for inclusion in a television programme or film – the so called 'dubbing right'. (The synchronisation rights and the dubbing rights are essentially the same thing, except synchronisation relates to *music* whereas dubbing relates to the *sound recording*.)

Most broadcasters have blanket agreements in place with PPL. If the owner of rights in a sound recording is not a member of PPL, it should be approached directly for permission to make use of the sound recording.

Moral rights

The author of music and lyrics own moral rights in their work. As these cannot be assigned, any waivers or permissions relating to the moral rights should be obtained directly from the authors. There is no collecting society administering moral rights on behalf of authors. The reader is referred to the earlier part of this chapter for comments about clearing moral rights.

Performers and music and sound recordings

Performance rights subsist in both the musical work itself and the sound recording of that work. Some of the performance rights may have been assigned (namely, the reproduction right, the distribution right and the rental and lending right), usually to the relevant record company. The owner of the performance rights – whether musician or record company – should be contacted for permission to make use of the performance.

Some performance rights may not be assigned, although they may be waived. Details of these rights were set out in Chapter 6. As with moral rights, checks should be made as to whether an adequate waiver has been given. If not, a waiver or permission should be sought from the musician in question.

Where a musician is a member of the Musicians' Union, the union may grant consent on behalf of their member to the exploitation of their performance rights under the terms of the relevant MU agreement. If the musician is not a union member, he/she must be contacted directly.

At the time of writing, performers do not own moral rights in their performances, although there are proposals to introduce such rights into UK law, as indicated at the end of Chapter 6.

Music promotional videos

There is a collecting society in place to administer copyright in music videos. The collecting society is a sister organisation of PPL, called Video Performance Ltd (VPL). Most of the members of VPL are record companies. Note that VPL licenses the use of music promotional *videos* (that is, the 'film' and 'sound recording' to use the terminology of the CDPA), but it does not license the music or the lyrics used in the video. These are separate copyright works, and must be cleared in accordance with the procedures described above.

The musicians' rights in music videos are usually dealt with the in the musicians' contract with the record company, meaning that it is generally not necessary to obtain a separate consent to the broadcast, transmission or performance of the video.

Clearing film clips

Where a film or programme maker wishes to make use of a film clip in which copyright has not expired, he must obtain permission from the owner of the various copyrights which make up the clip.

As a preliminary step to clearing rights, he should identify the various copyrights which make up the film. This will involve consideration, not just of the film, but of the underlying rights within the film. These are likely to be:

(a) the film itself. Copyright in a film may be infringed by the reproduction of a single image from the film;[3]

(b) the film may be a dramatic work if it is a work of action capable of being performed in public.[4] The reader is referred to Chapter 6 for more information about films as dramatic works. Copyright in the dramatic

---

3   CDPA 1988, s 17(4).

4   *Norowzian v Arks (No 2)* [2000] EMLR 1.

work will be infringed where a substantial part of the work is reproduced. From a clearance point of view, copyright in both the film and dramatic work may be wise. The owner of the copyright in the film may not be the owner of copyright in the dramatic work, especially as the confirmation that a film can be a dramatic work was made in a very recent case with the result that it is possible that copyright in the dramatic work may have been overlooked in any assignment of rights in the film;

(c) if the clip contains music, the music must be cleared in accordance with the procedures set out above;

(d) copyright in the screenplay must be considered – has a substantial part of the screenplay been reproduced? Remember that substantiality is a qualitative test. A very small part of the screenplay may have been reproduced in terms of quantity, but if it formed a substantial part of the film in terms of its quality, the unauthorised use may infringe copyright.

In addition, the performance right of the actors should be cleared. There is a standard form agreement in place between the Producers Alliance for Cinema and Television (PACT) and Equity governing consents in relation to the exploitation of performers' rights in footage.

The same principles will apply in relation to the clearance of clips which make up television footage. Remember that broadcasts and cable service transmissions are copyright works in their own right, and so consents will be required for the use of those works.

Clearance issues and insurance cover

A producer of a television programme or film may insure against the risk of legal liability for content of the programme or film by way of an *errors and omissions policy* (an E&O policy). Not all broadcasters have E&O cover, and relatively newspaper publishers carry such cover. This is partly because the amount of premium payable for such cover can be prohibitively expensive, especially where the insured has a bad track record of being sued, but also because insurance cover can compromise the editorial independence of the media. The insurers are likely to want to reserve the right to demand changes to a production where it perceives a danger of liability. If the insured refuses to make such changes, it will face the risk of being placed off cover.

The cover provided for an E&O policy extends beyond copyright, moral rights and performers' rights infringement. The policy will cover matters such as liability for defamation or malicious falsehood, other forms of intellectual property infringement and many of the other issues considered in Part 1 of this book.

The policy generally insures for payment of legal costs and damages arising from a claim which relates to content (subject to an excess figure). In order for the cover provided by the policy to be effective, the producer generally has to comply with clearance procedures put in place by the insurer. Common examples of such procedures are:

(a) insurer/insurer's legal adviser reads script or screenplay before production to eliminate at an early stage material which infringes legal rights, for example, defamatory material;

(b) a copyright report must usually be obtained to check whether the film or television programme will infringe copyright in any relevant territories. There are a number of specialist copyright research agencies that compile such reports. The costs of the reports are generally included in the insurance premium payable by the insured;

(c) similarly, a title report must normally be obtained confirming that the chosen title does not infringe any rights in any relevant territory;

(d) where music is used, all relevant licences should be obtained in writing in advance of production;

(e) written agreements must be in place between the producers and all authors, performers and persons who are providing material for the production, for example, set designers. Written permission for the exploitation of their work must be obtained. Where extracts from copyright works are to be used, for example, quotations from literary works, written licences for the use of the work should be in place in advance of production;

(f) the insured generally reserves the right to check both the actual shooting script and rough cuts as the production develops for possible areas carrying the risk of legal liability and to demand changes which it feels are necessary to avoid the risk. There is an obvious risk that this can lead to tension between insurer and insured during the production process.

INDEX